1 Samuel

REFORMED EXPOSITORY COMMENTARY

A Series

Series Editors

Richard D. Phillips
Philip Graham Ryken

Testament Editors

Iain M. Duguid, Old Testament
Daniel M. Doriani, New Testament

1 Samuel

RICHARD D. PHILLIPS

P&R PUBLISHING

P.O. BOX 817 • PHILLIPSBURG • NEW JERSEY 08865-0817

Page design by Lakeside Design Plus

Printed in the United States of America

Library of Congress Cataloging-in-Publication Data

Phillips, Richard D. (Richard Davis), 1960-
  1 Samuel / Richard D. Phillips. -- 1st ed.
      pages cm -- (Reformed expository commentary)
  Includes bibliographical references and index.
  ISBN 978-1-59638-197-1 (cloth)
  1. Bible. O.T. Samuel, 1st--Commentaries. I. Title. II. Title: First Samuel.
  BS1325.53.P49 2012
  222'.43077--dc23
                              2012000717

To

The Reverend Eric Alexander, in whose life and ministry I have been
privileged to observe both Christ the Lion and Christ the Lamb

and

The God of grace, who "sees not as man sees . . . but . . . looks on the
heart" (1 Sam. 16:7)

CONTENTS

Contents

SERIES INTRODUCTION

In every generation there is a fresh need for the faithful exposition of God's Word in the church. At the same time, the church must constantly do the work of theology: reflecting on the teaching of Scripture, confessing its doctrines of the Christian faith, and applying them to contemporary culture. We believe that these two tasks—the expositional and the theological—are interdependent. Our doctrine must derive from the biblical text, and our understanding of any particular passage of Scripture must arise from the doctrine taught in Scripture as a whole.

We further believe that these interdependent tasks of biblical exposition and theological reflection are best undertaken in the church, and most specifically in the pulpits of the church. This is all the more true since the study of Scripture properly results in doxology and praxis—that is, in praise to God and practical application in the lives of believers. In pursuit of these ends, we are pleased to present the Reformed Expository Commentary as a fresh exposition of Scripture for our generation in the church. We hope and pray that pastors, teachers, Bible study leaders, and many others will find this series to be a faithful, inspiring, and useful resource for the study of God's infallible, inerrant Word.

The Reformed Expository Commentary has four fundamental commitments. First, these commentaries aim to be *biblical*, presenting a comprehensive exposition characterized by careful attention to the details of the text. They are not exegetical commentaries—commenting word by word or even verse by verse—but integrated expositions of whole passages of Scripture. Each commentary will thus present a sequential, systematic treatment of an entire book of the Bible, passage by passage. Second, these commentaries are unashamedly *doctrinal*. We are committed to the Westminster Confession of Faith and Catechisms as containing the system of doctrine taught in the Scriptures of the Old and New Testaments. Each volume will teach, promote, and defend the doctrines of the Reformed faith as they are found in the Bible. Third, these commentaries are *redemptive-historical* in their orientation. We believe in the unity of the Bible and its central message of salvation in Christ. We are thus committed to a Christ-centered view of the Old Testament, in which its characters, events, regulations, and institutions are properly understood as pointing us to Christ and his gospel, as well as giving us examples to follow in living by faith. Fourth, these commentaries are *practical*, applying the text of Scripture to contemporary challenges of life—both public and private—with appropriate illustrations.

The contributors to the Reformed Expository Commentary are all pastor-scholars. As pastor, each author will first present his expositions in the pulpit ministry of his church. This means that these commentaries are rooted in the teaching of Scripture to real people in the church. While aiming to be scholarly, these expositions are not academic. Our intent is to be faithful, clear, and helpful to Christians who possess various levels of biblical and theological training—as should be true in any effective pulpit ministry. Inevitably this means that some issues of academic interest will not be covered. Nevertheless, we aim to achieve a responsible level of scholarship, seeking to promote and model this for pastors and other teachers in the church. Significant exegetical and theological difficulties, along with such historical and cultural background as is relevant to the text, will be treated with care.

We strive for a high standard of enduring excellence. This begins with the selection of the authors, all of whom have proved to be outstanding communicators of God's Word. But this pursuit of excellence is also reflected in a disciplined editorial process. Each volume is edited by both a series editor and a testament editor. The testament editors, Iain Duguid for the Old Testament and Daniel Doriani for the New Testament, are accomplished pastors and respected scholars who have taught at the seminary level. Their job is to ensure that each volume is sufficiently conversant with up-to-date scholarship and is faithful and accurate in its exposition of the text. As series editors, we oversee each volume to ensure its overall quality—including excellence of writing, soundness of teaching, and usefulness in application. Working together as an editorial team, along with the publisher, we are devoted to ensuring that these are the best commentaries our gifted authors can provide, so that the church will be served with trustworthy and exemplary expositions of God's Word.

It is our goal and prayer that the Reformed Expository Commentary will serve the church by renewing confidence in the clarity and power of Scripture and by upholding the great doctrinal heritage of the Reformed faith. We hope that pastors who read these commentaries will be encouraged in their own expository preaching ministry, which we believe to be the best and most biblical pattern for teaching God's Word in the church. We hope that lay teachers will find these commentaries among the most useful resources they rely on for understanding and presenting the text of the Bible. And we hope that the devotional quality of these studies of Scripture will instruct and inspire each Christian who reads them in joyful, obedient discipleship to Jesus Christ.

May the Lord bless all who read the Reformed Expository Commentary. We commit these volumes to the Lord Jesus Christ, praying that the Holy Spirit will use them for the instruction and edification of the church, with thanksgiving to God the Father for his unceasing faithfulness in building his church through the ministry of his Word.

Richard D. Phillips
Philip Graham Ryken
Series Editors

PREFACE

Most people think of David as one of the Bible's great romantic heroes. Believers of Scripture will not doubt his historical significance, but it is David the man who captures the imagination. Accordingly, most sermons on the hero of 1 Samuel will focus on ways in which David's example is deemed relevant to us today. For many, David is the model young believer as he stands before the giant Goliath, armed with only his shepherd's sling and his faith in God. We also witness David living out the struggles of young adulthood in an unfair world. David provides a model of Christian leadership: not only does he face the obstacles of his own life and calling, but his leader behavior also plays a decisive role in forging the kingdom he will lead. With all these points of contact with readers, to which we would add David the poet and singer of the Psalms, it is no wonder that believers in every generation feel such a strong bond with David.

For all the fascination of the romantic David, however, the discerning Christian will realize an even stronger interest in David as one of the Old Testament's principal types or models of Jesus Christ. It is as *an anointed one*, one called and provided by God to lead Israel, that David plays his chief role in redemptive history and makes his distinctive contribution in preparing God's people for *the Anointed One*, the Messiah who comes to rule and to save. Scholars agree that the theological center of the Samuel corpus rests in 2 Samuel 7, which records God's covenant promise of an eternal throne from the line of David. This being the case, the center of 1 Samuel occurs in chapter 16, where the prophet-judge Samuel anoints David to that royal office. Everything beforehand is prologue to David's anointing, and all the fascinating plot tension that follows results from David's having been set apart as the king "after [God's] own heart" (1 Sam. 13:14).

The theme of David as Israel's anointed one is especially highlighted in his epic battle with the giant Goliath, when the youthful shepherd arrives unexpectedly to grant victory over foes too strong for God's people. To be sure, in this and other great passages David remains a fascinating subject of interest as an example for our faith. The traditional perspective on David the man of faith remains a valid approach in expositing 1 Samuel. Yet above merely serving as an *example*, David more importantly directs us to the promised Savior who is the *object* of our faith. Not everything David does in 1 Samuel is Christlike—far from it!—but as the anointed one in his own time, he begins to show God's people how the true Messiah will bring salvation to his needy people for all time.

Despite all the attention on David, 1 Samuel also presents two other significant figures. In the book's namesake, Samuel, we meet an epochal figure in Scripture whose significance equals that of Joshua, Moses' successor. Samuel's place in redemptive history is greatly underestimated by most students of Scripture; his life and ministry play an important role in the Bible's story and provide an inspiration that rivals that associated with David. It was Samuel whom God used to guide Israel out of the chaos of the period of the judges and to serve the coming of the kingdom in the arrival of David. Standing next to Samuel is Saul, who serves as alter ego first to Samuel and then to David, and who embodies the idolatry and unbelief that will plague Israel throughout the rest of the Old Testament. By means of the contrasts between Saul and Samuel/David, the narrative of 1 Samuel will present numerous valuable lessons for us to consider. Together with these main figures, the lesser characters in 1 Samuel are hardly incidental, including Eli the corrupted priest, Hannah the tearful believer, and Jonathan the faithful friend, to name just a few.

These expositions on 1 Samuel were first preached in the evening worship services of Second Presbyterian Church in Greenville, South Carolina. I thank this dearly beloved congregation, with special thanks for the encouragement I have received from the session and congregation for my commitment to study and writing. I am also grateful to Drs. Philip Ryken and Iain Duguid, whose editorial labors have measurably improved the quality of this book, to Mrs. Shirley Duncan for her invaluable aid in proofreading the manuscript, as well as to Marvin Padgett and my many friends at P&R Publishing. This commentary is dedicated to the Reverend Eric Alexander, with thanks to God for the sweetness of his friendship to me and my wife and for his extraordinary example as a preacher of God's mighty Word.

Additionally, I give praise to God for the loving companionship and ministry of my dear wife, Sharon, apart from whose faithful help I could accomplish very little for the Lord, as well as to our five beloved children. Finally, I give thanks to the God and Father of the Son of David: to him be glory forever.

Richard D. Phillips
Greenville, South Carolina, April 2011

1 Samuel

A KING AFTER GOD'S OWN HEART

PART 1

Last of the Judges

1

THE BARREN WIFE

1 Samuel 1:1—8

*Elkanah, her husband, said to her, "Hannah, why do you weep?
And why do you not eat? And why is your heart sad? Am I not
more to you than ten sons?" (1 Sam. 1:8)*

mong the treasures of our world are the great stories that
shape the identity of whole peoples. Homer's *Iliad* provided
the ancient Greeks with a literary foundation on which centuries of great culture were erected. Out of the chaos of the Dark Ages, the
Britons found a noble ideal in the story of King Arthur and Camelot. More
ancient than either of these is the Old Testament book of Samuel, with its
story of the rise of King David and the establishment of Israel's kingdom.

As literature, Samuel is unsurpassed in the richness of its plot, the complexity and depth of its characters, the intensity of its action, and the profundity of its lessons. This is all the more the case when we realize that
Samuel is not a fictional tale, but a true historical narrative. These people
lived on our earth, and these events happened in our world. Homer and
King Arthur inspire us through their fantasy world of heroes, maidens,
and monsters. Samuel refuses to yield the palm when it comes to these. But
Samuel's importance lies not only in that its story is true, but also in that

it forms a part of the unfolding story of God's salvation that is the greatest truth of all.

LAST OF THE JUDGES, FIRST OF THE PROPHETS

Samuel was born sometime around the year 1050 B.C. "In those days there was no king in Israel," says the book of Judges. "Everyone did what was right in his own eyes" (Judg. 21:25). This summarizes the condition of the nation at the time of Samuel's birth. Israel faced a leadership crisis that was accompanied by a spiritual crisis. Having entered the Promised Land in victory and strength, the people of God had lost their way spiritually, politically, and militarily. Judges 2:10 explains why: after Joshua and his generation, "there arose another generation after them who did not know the LORD."

Forgetting the Lord is the greatest evil that can befall any generation. Absent God's help, Israel failed to drive out the remnants of the Canaanites, but instead began to follow in their pagan ways and to worship their unholy idols. In punishment, God gave the Israelites over into the hands of their enemies, periodically showing mercy by raising up judges to deliver them (see Judg. 2:10–23). The book of Judges concludes with a series of stories that depict the decadent setting in which Samuel was born and raised, including the spiritual corruption of the Levites, the idolatry of the people, and the moral squalor of Israelite society.

The birth of Samuel portended a new age. Just as God would later prepare Israel for her Messiah by sending John the Baptist, God prepared the way for a king after God's own heart (1 Sam. 13:14) by sending Samuel, who was at once the last of Israel's judges and the first of the great line of the prophets who served during Israel's kingdom. David Tsumura observes: "Samuel takes the decisive role in the period of transition from the days of the judges to the monarchical era, leading to the establishment of the House of David and the beginning of the worship of Yahweh in Jerusalem."[1]

The historical significance of Samuel is evidenced by the birth narrative that begins the two books of the Bible that bear his name. The Scriptures always take care to inform us of the birth and upbringing of its most important figures, and so it is here. Just as Moses, Samson, John the Baptist, and

---

1. David Toshio Tsumura, *The First Book of Samuel*, New International Commentary on the Old Testament (Grand Rapids: Eerdmans, 2007), 104.

Jesus Christ were all born in times of distress to humble, godly parents, Samuel enters history as the child of Elkanah and Hannah. The book begins: "There was a certain man of Ramathaim-zophim of the hill country of Ephraim whose name was Elkanah the son of Jeroham, son of Elihu, son of Tohu, son of Zuph, an Ephrathite" (1 Sam. 1:1).

Samuel's father was a "certain man," hardly a description for someone of prominence. We are told two things about Elkanah, starting with the place where he lived. Ramathaim-zophim was a small town in the very heart of Israel, belonging to the territory allotted to Ephraim, not far from its border with Judah, about five miles north of what would later be the city of Jerusalem. Samuel would put Ramah, as it was later called, "on the map," making it Israel's virtual capital during his judgeship (1 Sam. 8:4) and founding there the school of the prophets (1 Sam. 19:18–20). Neither Elkanah nor Samuel was an Ephraimite, however. They traced their lineage through Tohu to Zuph, who was an Ephrathite, a denizen of the region of Bethlehem in the land of Judah. Moreover, theirs was a priestly family, of the tribe of Levi and the clan of Kohath, as we learn in 1 Chronicles 6:33–38; the Kohathites were originally charged with guarding the ark of the covenant and serving as the tabernacle's gatekeepers (Num. 3:31). Under David, the "sons of Kohath" were dedicated to the ministry of song in the tabernacle. Samuel's grandson Heman is denoted as "the singer" and seems to have enjoyed the enormous privilege of serving as music director for Israel's worship under David (1 Chron. 6:31–33). Samuel's descendants were probably among "the sons of Korah," to whom authorship of eleven psalms is ascribed.

God's Barren Wife

The primary focus in Samuel's birth is not on his father, however, but on his mother, Hannah. We can often trace the faith of remarkable children to their remarkable mothers. So it is with this woman, who presents one of the most striking feminine characters in the Bible. Robert Bergen observes that "the spiritual powerhouse in this narrative was a socially impotent woman ... [who] alone understood the true power of undivided faith in the Lord."[2]

---

2. Robert D. Bergen, *1, 2 Samuel*, New American Commentary (Nashville: Broadman & Holman, 1996), 63.

There is much to say about this extraordinary woman, but at the time there was one fact that dominated her existence. Hannah's womb was closed, so she was unable to bear Elkanah any children. After telling us that Hannah is Elkanah's wife, the Bible simply reports, "Hannah had no children" (1 Sam. 1:2).

Hannah's barrenness seems to correspond to Israel's spiritual state. Women who suffer this condition often wonder how God is involved, but in Hannah's case we know, since the text informs us that "the LORD had closed her womb" (1 Sam. 1:5). There are many reasons why God brings trials into the lives of his people, often to stimulate our faith, but in the case of the mother of so important a figure as Samuel, the point has to do not with Hannah but with Israel. The Lord closed Hannah's womb to remind Israel that he had also caused the people to be spiritually barren because of their idolatry and unbelief. Israel was God's barren wife, having failed to give him the children of faith he desired. As a nation, Israel particularly manifested her barrenness in the resultant lack of the strong leadership of a true king. Bruce Birch explains: "The situation in Elkanah's family is intended as a parable of Israel's situation at this moment in history. Hannah's anxiety over having no children, even though Elkanah loves her, parallels Israel's anxiety over having no king in spite of the care and love of God."[3]

What God shows us through Hannah is relevant for every Christian whose faith seems barren. It is true for barren churches, as the church in the West, including America, can largely be considered today, bearing very little of the harvest of holiness and zeal for truth that God desires. As we continue in Hannah's story, she will model for us the grace-seeking prayer that we need to offer to God. But in these opening verses we see another essential point. For in a time when Israel as a whole had forgotten the Lord, "this man used to go up year by year from his city to worship and to sacrifice to the LORD of hosts at Shiloh, where the two sons of Eli, Hophni and Phinehas, were priests of the LORD" (1 Sam. 1:3).

Shiloh was the location of the tabernacle and the ark of the covenant in Elkanah's time. Eli was hardly an impressive spiritual leader, and his wicked sons, Hophni and Phinehas, made a mockery of ministry, as we will see (1 Sam. 2:22–25). Elkanah did not go up to Shiloh to see Eli or his sons,

3. Bruce C. Birch, *1 & 2 Samuel*, New Interpreter's Bible, vol. 2 (Nashville: Abingdon, 1998), 973.

but to come before the Lord and renew his covenant fidelity. Elkanah did what we must also do: he prioritized the place of God in his life and gave his attention to the Lord. However little Elkanah knew of true religion at a time like this, he knew enough to come as a sinner, seeking grace from God by means of the shed blood of a sacrifice.

This is how salvation begins for any barren soul. It begins with realizing that we must get right with God. Sinners come to the cross of Jesus Christ, the Lamb of God to whom the old sacrifices pointed, seeking forgiveness through his atoning blood and renewal through his redeeming grace. Spiritually barren Christians come back to the cross, confessing to God their sin and spiritual neglect and finding cleansing and acceptance through Christ's once-for-all sacrifice. This is what God desired from Israel: a sincere and repentant seeking after him and his grace, for which purpose he had afflicted them with the barrenness of the time of the judges, and which he reflected in the childless condition of godly Hannah. When we see Hannah's tears, shed not for her own but for Israel's failings, we should grieve for our own sins and the barren lives they cause. Her deliverance will likewise remind us of God's redeeming love and transforming power that is available to us.

TEARS IN THE TABERNACLE

The theology of Hannah's barren condition would have been little on her heart, however, as she returned to the tabernacle with her family. It was a dysfunctional family, primarily because Hannah was not Elkanah's only wife: "He had two wives. The name of the one was Hannah, and the name of the other, Peninnah. And Peninnah had children, but Hannah had no children" (1 Sam. 1:2).

The practice of polygamy is frequently seen in the Old Testament, though it was probably not the norm. The book of Genesis makes it clear that God designed marriage to be between one man and one woman (Gen. 2:24), a definition that is confirmed by Jesus Christ (Matt. 19:5). Elkanah's polygamy was probably provoked by Hannah's inability to bear children, which threatened both economic hardship and the cutting off of his name and lineage. Therefore, like the patriarchs Abraham and Jacob, Elkanah took a second wife to bear him children while his affections remained fixed on Hannah.

The emotional divide in this marriage that necessarily followed corresponds to the names of the two wives: Hannah, whose name means "gracious," and Peninnah, whose name means "prolific." Polygamy always causes family conflict, but much more certainly when one wife receives affection and the other receives children. The discord in Elkanah's house mirrors the intertribal dissension within Israel and reminds us all of the importance of family and church unity.

Hannah's emotional distress over her barren womb would have been grief enough without Peninnah to goad her. Her trial is familiar to women today who suffer an inability to bear children. She had never had the thrill of bringing the news of a pregnancy to her husband, but had instead known the monthly frustration of infertility. Whenever she went to the marketplace or socialized with other families, the sound of infant voices—the very sound she most desired—plunged into her heart like a knife. William Blaikie adds that "the trial which Hannah had to bear was particularly heavy . . . to a Hebrew woman. To have no child was not only a disappointment, but seemed to make one out as dishonoured by God, as unworthy of any part or lot in the means that were to bring about the fulfillment of the promise, 'In thee and in thy seed shall all the families of the earth be blessed'"[4] (Gen. 12:3). It is always cruel, and almost always unwarranted, to assume another's affliction as a sign of God's disfavor, especially a trial so painful to a woman's heart. But since children were considered a sign of God's favor (Deut. 7:14; 28:4), and since the Mosaic law listed barren wombs as one sign of God's curse for covenant-breaking (28:18), childless women were often scorned in female society, depriving them of the emotional support they needed. All this was Hannah's bitter portion, month by month and year by year.

Then there was Peninnah. While Hannah had Elkanah's heart, Peninnah had his children, and she missed no opportunity to inflict misery on this account: "[Hannah's] rival used to provoke her grievously to irritate her, because the LORD had closed her womb. So it went on year by year" (1 Sam. 1:6–7).

A typical example is what took place during this visit to Shiloh: "On the day when Elkanah sacrificed, he would give portions to Peninnah his wife and to all her sons and daughters. But to Hannah he gave a double portion,

---

4. William G. Blaikie, *Expository Lectures on the Book of First Samuel* (1887; repr., Birmingham, AL: Solid Ground, 2005), 5.

because he loved her, though the Lord had closed her womb" (1 Sam. 1:4–5). We can imagine Elkanah's quandary: should he distribute all the portions for Peninnah and her many children, but only one to Hannah? In order to express his sympathy and love, he gave Hannah a double portion. This sign of special favor enraged Peninnah, inciting her to savage mockery. Perhaps this was delivered backhandedly, as imagined by Dale Ralph Davis:

"Now do all you children have your food? Dear me, there are so *many* of you, it's hard to keep track."

"Mommy, Miss Hannah doesn't have any children."

"What did you say, dear?"

"I said, Miss Hannah doesn't have any children."

"Miss Hannah? Oh, yes, that's right—she doesn't have any children."

"Doesn't she *want* children?"

"Oh, yes, she wants children very, very much! Wouldn't you say so, Hannah? [In a low aside] Don't you wish you had children too?"

"Doesn't Daddy want Miss Hannah to have kids?"

"Oh, certainly he does—but Miss Hannah keeps disappointing him; she just can't have kids."

"Why not?"

"Why, because God won't let her."

"Does God not like Miss Hannah?"

"Well, I don't know—what do you think?"[5]

This imagined conversation may or may not reflect Peninnah's actual strategy for afflicting Hannah's heart, though it fits the Bible's description that Peninnah would "provoke her grievously to irritate her" to the point of tears (1 Sam. 1:6–7). A loathsome heart like Peninnah's calls for our reflection, especially since it bears such a resemblance to our own hearts. Blaikie writes, "To suffer in the tenderest part of one's nature is no doubt a heavy affliction. But to have a heart eager to inflict such suffering on another is far more awful." Blaikie warns all who play the part of Hannah's fellow-wife, who mock those who suffer and lord over those who are cast down: "You may succeed for the moment, and you may experience whatever of

5. Dale Ralph Davis, *1 Samuel: Looking on the Heart* (Fearn, Ross-shire, UK: Christian Focus, 2000), 13–14.

satisfaction can be found in gloated revenge. But know this, that you have been cherishing a viper in your bosom that will not content itself with fulfilling your desire. It will make itself a habitual resident in your heart, and distil its poison over it."[6] That Elkanah's second wife would conduct herself in such a way during a visit to the tabernacle reminds us that the outward show of religion, without an inward correspondence, will often be a mask for the most spiteful hearts.

At the time, however, Peninnah must have felt quite the sensation of triumph. The truth is that our tongues can drive others into despair. We read simply that "Hannah wept and would not eat" (1 Sam. 1:7). In the very place where hope should reign—the house of God—Hannah experienced only distress. The church sanctuary is sometimes the most depressing place for those who feel singled out by their trials, though it is also the place they most need to be. Realizing this, Christians are reminded to be thoughtful of the afflictions of others, to be sensitive in our conduct and speech, and while rejoicing in our own blessings to go out of our way to provide heartfelt sympathy and support to those who grieve. Pastors should likewise aim to be sensitive to broken hearts like Hannah's when they lead in pastoral prayers. In general, worship in the church should not assume a lighthearted happiness in all the worshipers but should reflect and embrace the full range of human emotions as the covenant community meets with God.

A Greater Love than This

Even here at the beginning of her story, however, there are signs of hope for Hannah. The first sign of hope is the very statement about God's involvement that many dread about their afflictions: "the Lord had closed her womb" (1 Sam. 1:5). Instead of resenting God's sovereignty in our trials, we Christians should lift up our hearts. Our God has proved his faithfulness and love by sending his own Son to die for our sins. In Hannah's day, he was known as the God who was faithful to deliver Israel from bondage in Egypt and who was mighty in securing for them the Promised Land. Rather than assuming some unholy, spiteful, or condemning purpose in God's afflictions, believers need to remember that God is holy, so all his

6. Blaikie, *First Samuel*, 7–8.

deeds are holy; God is good, so he intends our sorrows for good; and God is filled with mercy for the brokenhearted. God does not seek to destroy us through our trials but to save us through our trials. As Hannah herself would later testify: "He raises up the poor from the dust; he lifts the needy from the ash heap" (1 Sam. 2:8). So if God is the One who closed the womb, we should take heart, since he can surely also open it.

In Hannah's case, God was using her plight to orchestrate Israel's deliverance from the dark era of the judges. This was a cause dear to Hannah's heart, as we know from the song she later lifted up to God's praise (1 Sam. 2:10). We may never know how God has worked through our most bitter trials to bring others to salvation, to equip us with sensitivity in ministry to others, or even to launch a significant gospel advance. But we do know God, and we know from his Word that "for those who love God all things work together for good" (Rom. 8:28), so we can have confidence in God's purpose in our lives.

A famous example from church history is the tearful experience of Monica, the mother of the early church's greatest theologian, Augustine of Hippo. As a devoted Christian, Monica was grieved by her brilliant son's disdain for the gospel, and even more so for the sexually dissolute life that she witnessed him leading. Night after night she pleaded with the Lord for Augustine. One night was especially trying, for in the morning her son planned to board a ship bound for Rome, where a young man could be expected to plunge deeply into sin. All night she prayed, and when Monica arose in the morning to find her son gone, she wept bitterly before the Lord. Little did she know that in Italy her son would come under the influence of the noted preacher Ambrose of Milan, and that during his stay there he would be converted to faith in Jesus. Moreover, the very wickedness over which this faithful mother grieved provided Augustine with a keen appreciation for God's grace in salvation. His teaching of salvation by grace alone would have a profound influence on generations of later Christians, including a direct influence on the men used by God to lead the Protestant Reformation.

Take heart, then, if you grieve under afflictions, to know that God has willed them for you. John Chrysostom, the great preacher of the early church, wrote of sorrows like Hannah's:

Even if we are suffering grief and pain, even if the trouble seems insupportable to us, let us not be anxious or beside ourselves but wait on God's providence. He is well aware, after all, when is the time for what is causing us depression to be removed . . . It was not out of hatred, in fact, or of revulsion that [God] closed [Hannah's] womb, but to open to us the doors on the values the woman possessed and for us to espy the riches of her faith and realize that he rendered her more [fruitful] on that account.[7]

The second cause for Hannah's hope was the tender love displayed by her husband, Elkanah: "Elkanah, her husband, said to her, 'Hannah, why do you weep? And why do you not eat? And why is your heart sad? Am I not more to you than ten sons?'" (1 Sam. 1:8). Before we turn to his words, we should not overlook the simple fact that Elkanah went to his wife. How comforting it is simply to be present with those who suffer! Our mere presence with the sick, the troubled, and the grieving is often more powerful than any words. And when he did speak, Elkanah made to Hannah the essential point that he loved her very much and that her inability did not sour him toward her. If others scorned her, she could draw strength from her husband's solidarity, and though she might easily fear losing everything because of her barren womb, Elkanah reminded her that she would not lose his love.

As is typical of men (who are sometimes inept concerning women's hearts), Elkanah's words are not above criticism, and might even be considered self-centered. Notice that he asks her, "Am I not more to you than ten sons?" rather than telling her, "You are worth more to me than ten sons." So it will often be that the most well-meaning friends may not know what to say, and they may say it imperfectly (or worse). But there is One whose comfort does not fail and whose remedy does not err. The final cause for Hannah's hope lay in the Lord and in the reality that she had not, in fact, given up her faith in him. Great as Elkanah's love for Hannah was, there was a greater love than his and a Comforter who could do what her husband never could, One who could answer Hannah's plea and grant the desire of her heart.

7. John R. Franke, ed., *Joshua, Judges, Ruth, 1–2 Samuel*, Ancient Christian Commentary on Scripture, Old Testament vol. 4 (Downers Grove, IL: InterVarsity Press, 2005), 195.

We sometimes suspect that a broken heart like Hannah's would have little concern for theology, yet it is at times like these that we most need the truths we have learned about God. Just as the people of Israel had descended into idolatry because they had forgotten the Lord, so Hannah most needed to remember the Lord. She needed theology—that is, the knowledge of God's character and ways. There is good reason to suspect that while Hannah's heart wept, her mind was reflecting on the Bible. Perhaps she remembered how God had so often granted special sons through the barren wombs of believing women. She would certainly have known about how God gave the covenant heir Isaac through Abraham's wife, Sarah, though she was not only barren but well beyond childbearing age. She would also have known about how Isaac prayed for his barren wife, Rebekah, and she gave birth to twin boys, including Jacob, the father of Israel. Jacob's wife, too, suffered childlessness. In fact, Rachel suffered in a situation similar to Hannah's, because of the malice of her sister and co-wife, Leah, who though little loved was prolific in childbearing. But God remembered Rachel and answered her prayer by giving her Joseph, the greatest of Jacob's sons, along with Benjamin, the most beloved.

The prevalence of barren wombs among women most blessed by God may have caught Hannah's attention, and if so, she may have realized that a son whom she should bear could be of special importance to God. This idea is suggested by the prayer that Hannah goes on to offer (1 Sam. 2:1–10). The biblical theme of God's blessing on the barren womb makes the important point that God saves not by human capability, human achievement, or human working. God saves by grace. God causes the barren womb to bear children, just as he causes the lifeless heart to believe. God thus calls his people not to trust human wisdom and human effort, and not to despair in the face of human failure, but to trust God, who gives life to the dead and salvation through the barren womb. Hannah's affliction, like ours, was therefore a call to faith in God. Her weakness was a call to reliance on God's power. Her failure was a call to believe in God's faithfulness. And her grief was a call to seek for God's grace.

Grateful though Hannah might be for her husband's love, her true hope lay in a greater love than this. Her hope lay in the Lord, whose whole record of dealing with Israel was one of faithfulness, power, and grace. Our true hope, in all our trials, and especially in the burden of

15

our guilt for sin, is that same God, the God who has revealed his love forever by sending his own Son to redeem us by his blood. Indeed, when the time came for our Savior to be born, he was conceived by the Holy Spirit not in a barren womb like Hannah's but in the virgin womb of Mary, proving that nothing is impossible for our God. Davis applies the lesson to us: "When his people are without strength, without resources, without hope, without human gimmicks—then [God] loves to stretch forth his hand from heaven. Once we see where God often begins we will understand how we may be encouraged."[8]

King David once asked himself, "Why are you cast down, O my soul, and why are you in turmoil within me?" His answer? It is the answer that we will see revealed through the faith of Hannah, an answer that all who know the Lord can come to embrace in every trial: "Hope in God; for I shall again praise him, my salvation and my God" (Ps. 43:5).

8. Davis, *1 Samuel*, 13.

2

THE GOD WHO HEARS

1 Samuel 1:9—20

And she vowed a vow and said, "O LORD of hosts, if you will
indeed look on the affliction of your servant and remember me
and not forget your servant, but will give to your servant a son,
then I will give him to the LORD all the days of his life, and no
razor shall touch his head." (1 Sam. 1:11)

One of the ways in which the Bible teaches about God is through the various names given to him in the Old Testament. The most basic name for God is *Elohim*, or *El* in its shortened form, which refers to God as the great Creator. Another name frequently used is *Yahweh*, the name God gave to Moses at the burning bush, meaning "I AM WHO I AM" (Ex. 3:14). These names are then used in combination with other words to reveal specific things about God. When God looked with pity on Hagar, Sarah's slave girl and the mother of Abraham's son Ishmael, she named him *El-Roi*, "a God of seeing" (Gen. 16:13). After God provided a ram as an offering in the place of Isaac, Abraham named the place *Yahweh-Yireh*, meaning "the LORD will provide" (Gen. 22:14).

One of the most majestic names for God makes its first appearance in the story of Hannah and the birth of Samuel. We read in 1 Samuel 1:3 that

Elkanah sacrificed to "the LORD of hosts." The Hebrew is *Yahweh Sabaoth*, often translated as "the LORD Almighty." This expression is used in 230 different Old Testament verses. "LORD of hosts" refers to God's command of armies, most especially the legions of heaven, and describes his omnipotent power. Hannah worshiped with the same faith as her husband, and given her dire predicament, the Lord of hosts was precisely the God she needed. When Hannah turned to God in prayer, her very first words were, "O LORD of hosts" (1 Sam. 1:11).

HANNAH'S PRAYER

When we left Hannah in the previous chapter, she was weeping in bitterness at the tabernacle because of her inability to bear a child and because of the vicious mocking of her rival co-wife, Peninnah. Her caring husband, Elkanah, came to comfort her, using words that conveyed his sympathy and affection (1 Sam. 1:8). It seems that this ministry helped her enough that she could rejoin the family meal, because verse 9 tells us, "After they had eaten and drunk in Shiloh, Hannah rose."

Hannah rose and went toward the tabernacle, where Eli was sitting on his high-priestly chair. But Hannah was not seeking Eli; she was seeking the Lord in prayer. Her prayer is a model for us, starting with the simple fact that *she turned to the Lord in her need.* This may seem surprising, given that it was the Lord who had closed her womb, as Hannah knew. Many people will turn away from God when feeling his hand of affliction, or else simply resign themselves to their fate. Christians sometimes advise friends in such a situation simply to move on and give thanks to God for the trial. We should be thankful to God for everything, even trials, but that does not mean we should be resigned to our situation! The apostle James gives better advice: "Is anyone among you suffering? Let him pray" (James 5:13). Of all the things Hannah might have done—becoming angry or bitter, fretting in tears, or reviling the Lord—she did the very best thing. She simply went to the Lord in prayer for her need.

The second thing we should note is that, having turned to God in prayer, Hannah prayed *knowing who God is.* "O LORD of hosts," she began (1 Sam. 1:11). Hannah honored God by ascribing to him all the power she needed, the might of the Lord of the hosts of heaven. She then asked God to "look on the affliction of your servant and remember me and not forget your servant, but . . . give to your servant a son" (1 Sam. 1:11). This is not a random request, but rather one that mirrors what she had learned of God through the greatest of his saving deeds up to that time: the exodus. Whether or not Hannah had access to the writings of Moses, she knew the story well enough. The Lord told Moses, "I have surely seen the affliction of my people who are in Egypt and have heard their cry because of their taskmasters. I know their sufferings" (Ex. 3:7; cf. Ex. 4:31; Deut. 26:7). God's statement to Moses shows that his deliverance in the exodus was in answer to prayer. Now, in a new day of Israel's need and of her own, Hannah calls on the Lord in a prayer of faith. "Hannah begged God to do for her what he had done for Israel in the days of Moses. She was asking God to do what God had shown to be his characteristic behavior toward his people."[1]

Third, Hannah prayed *knowing who she was*. She referred to herself as God's humble servant (1 Sam. 1:11). She did not demand of the Lord, nor is there any evidence that she complained about her particularly intense sorrows. She came not with her rights but with her humble request. Moreover, she knew what kind of world she lived in. Gordon Keddie writes, "She knew that this world is not heaven, but a fallen sin-sick place in which all of its inhabitants have a personal share in its imperfections and afflictions."[2] Notice, too, that Hannah did not ask for God to take vengeance on Peninnah. Hannah knew that she was coming to God for mercy, and it is poor practice to ask for God's justice toward others while seeking mercy for ourselves. Hannah identified herself as a servant of the Lord and brought her requests in humble faith.

This leads to a fourth item of note in Hannah's prayer: *she knew what she wanted* and was not afraid to ask it of the Lord. It is true that our prayers should consist of more than a list of things we desire to receive from God. We need to worship God in prayer, to give thanks for our blessings, and to confess to him our sins, seeking cleansing. But we must also realize that God invites us to make requests of him, and that it honors the Lord when we do so. Therefore, we should come to God knowing what we are asking and then asking for it humbly and clearly. James states a rule that, sadly,

---

1. John Woodhouse, *1 Samuel: Looking for a Leader* (Wheaton, IL: Crossway, 2008), 30.
2. Gordon J. Keddie, *Dawn of a Kingdom: The Message of 1 Samuel* (Darlington, UK: Evangelical Press, 1988), 21.

explains so much of our spiritual poverty: "You do not have, because you do not ask" (James 4:2).

Notice that Hannah's prayer did not rely on any ritual formula of words or any other technique of prayer. She simply knew the Lord, believed his promise to care for his people, and prayed to him for what she needed. This is the benefit of knowing God, including his attributes, his promises, and his saving deeds. Hannah was able to pray confidently because she knew the God to whom she prayed.

Another reason why Hannah prayed with such confidence was that she knew that her motives in prayer were right. James chides us not only for not asking in prayer, but also for having wrong motives when we do ask: "You ask and do not receive, because you ask wrongly, to spend it on your passions" (James 4:3). With this in mind, *Hannah prayed with an eye to God's will.*

We see this especially in the vow that plays such an important part in Hannah's prayer: "O LORD of hosts, if you will indeed look on the affliction of your servant and remember me and not forget your servant, but will give to your servant a son, then I will give him to the LORD all the days of his life, and no razor shall touch his head" (1 Sam. 1:11). Hannah refers to the rites of a Nazirite, as described in Numbers 6—someone who has vowed total separation to the service of the Lord. Normally, Nazirite status was limited to a defined period of time, during which the person separated to God's work would abstain from alcohol, avoid touching a dead body, and allow his hair to go uncut, which was the visible sign of a Nazirite (see Num. 6:2–8). The most famous Nazirite was Samson, the mighty warrior who slew so many Philistines and was the last judge of Israel before Samuel. Samson was born to the barren wife of Manoah, and according to an angel's instructions, he was to be separated as a Nazirite all the days of his life (Judg. 13:5). Hannah was likely born and raised during the time of Samson's judgeship, so the Nazirite status would have prominently shaped her idea of consecration to the Lord. She may also have identified with Manoah's childless wife. Now she vows that the first son God gives her will be similarly devoted to Israel's cause in this desperate time of need.

Was this an attempt to bargain with God? Was Hannah saying, "God, you give me this and I will give you that"? If so, then Hannah prayed wrongly; it is the pagans who approach their gods, seeking to appease them with offers and bribes. But Hannah's vow was nothing of the sort. William Blaikie writes: "No doubt she wished the child, and asked the child in fulfillment of her own vehement desire. But beyond and above that desire there arose in her soul the sense of God's claim and God's glory, and to these high considerations she desired to subordinate every feeling of her own. If God should give her the child, he would not be hers, but God's."[3] Keddie says, "The whole climate is one of holy motives, hallowed desires, and humble submission."[4]

We should consider the sacrifice involved in Hannah's vow: she was offering to forgo the joys of parenting the child she longed to bear. She was also forfeiting the status that a child would bring in her society. So her prayer was not a bargain in which she offered something to God to get what she wanted. Rather, what she wanted was a child to offer to the Lord. She wanted to play her role in God's plan of salvation, and she was zealous to play a most meaningful role: to bear a lifelong Nazirite who would wholeheartedly serve the Lord. John Chrysostom comments: "She had not yet received the child and was already forming a prophet."[5] In this, Hannah sets an example for Christian parents in that our chief desire for our children should be that they would be fully committed to the Lord and useful to his kingdom.

A sixth and last thing to note about Hannah's prayer is that *she fervently opened her heart to the Lord.* As she explained to Eli, "I have been pouring out my soul before the LORD" (1 Sam. 1:15). If we ever think that Old Testament believers were denied the privilege of personal communion with the Lord, we should remember Hannah's prayer. She did not come with a formula to manipulate God or an offer to bribe God, but she prayed with a mind that knew God and a heart that poured out in pain and godly desire. Matthew Henry writes, "The prayer came from her heart, as the tears from her eyes."[6]

On the one hand, we need to realize that emotional passion does not make our prayers any better or more effective, as if we have to push our hearts onto the Lord. Jesus taught, "When you pray, do not heap up empty

3. William G. Blaikie, *Expository Lectures on the Book of First Samuel* (1887; repr., Birmingham, AL: Solid Ground, 2005), 10.

4. Keddie, *Dawn of a Kingdom*, 22.

5. John R. Franke, ed., *Joshua, Judges, Ruth, 1–2 Samuel*, Ancient Christian Commentary on Scripture, Old Testament vol. 4 (Downers Grove, IL: InterVarsity Press, 2005), 197.

6. Matthew Henry, *Commentary on the Whole Bible*, 6 vols. (Peabody, MA: Hendrickson, 1992), 2:218.

phrases as the Gentiles do, for they think that they will be heard for their many words" (Matt. 6:7). On the other hand, the passions that are in our hearts—our frustration, our grief, even our anger and doubt—can and should be brought to God in prayer. Dale Ralph Davis advises: "Many Christians need to realize that Yahweh our God allows us to do this—to pour our griefs and sobs and perplexities at his feet. Our Lord can handle our tears; it won't make him nervous or ill at ease if you unload your distress at his feet."[7] With such anguish in her heart, Hannah prayed long and hard for God's help. As David said of his prayers, "I pour out my complaint before him; I tell my trouble before him" (Ps. 142:2).

The High Priest's Blessing

All the while that Hannah prayed, the high priest of Israel sat in his chair, watching. Eli presents a sharp contrast to Hannah, a contrast that will be all the more telling when revealed in their respective sons. Here is the kind of ironic role-reversal so common in Scripture. We would expect Eli, a man in the highest spiritual position of God's holy nation, to be the upholder of true spirituality and the one who would break through to God's grace. Yet he is virtually the one furthest from these things. Meanwhile, the humble wife of a country Levite—one who is treated by others as accursed of God because of her barren womb, a woman as socially and religiously disempowered as could be imagined in that day—is the one whose heart is closest to God. Hannah, not the high priest, is the spiritual figure who really matters in that hour of distress. This is in keeping with the great scriptural principle: "God opposes the proud but gives grace to the humble" (1 Peter 5:5).

Eli displayed his lack of spiritual discernment in his rebuke to praying Hannah. He saw her lips moving but heard no sound coming forth, for "Hannah was speaking in her heart" (1 Sam. 1:13). "Therefore Eli took her to be a drunken woman. And Eli said to her, 'How long will you go on being drunk? Put your wine away from you'" (1 Sam. 1:13–14). Eli's reaction was perhaps conditioned by past sordid experiences at the tabernacle. But John Woodhouse is surely right to complain: "If Israel had a leader who could not

---

7. Dale Ralph Davis, *1 Samuel: Looking on the Heart* (Fearn, Ross-shire, UK: Christian Focus, 2000), 16.

tell the difference between a godly woman's heartfelt prayer and drunken rambling, no wonder Israel had a leadership crisis!"[8]

Hannah defended herself: "No, my lord, I am a woman troubled in spirit. I have drunk neither wine nor strong drink, but I have been pouring out my soul before the Lord. Do not regard your servant as a worthless woman, for all along I have been speaking out of my great anxiety and vexation" (1 Sam. 1:15–16). In addition to explaining Hannah's intense, emotional behavior, her words make it clear that there were other women who deserved the high priest's rebuke. Her statement that she is not "a worthless woman" is literally referring to "a daughter of Belial," that is, a woman of destructiveness. Instead, her apparent murmuring was a prayer of great intensity born of a provoked soul. The other kind of woman may foolishly drown her sorrows with strong drink, but Hannah had bathed hers in prayerful tears. At this, Eli spoke to her a priestly benediction: "Go in peace, and the God of Israel grant your petition that you have made to him" (1 Sam. 1:17). Hannah was content with this answer, humbly replying, "Let your servant find favor in your eyes." With this, "the woman went her way and ate, and her face was no longer sad" (1 Sam. 1:18).

Hannah "Remembered"

It is evident that Hannah took Eli's words as a response from the Lord, which is understandable, since Eli was Israel's high priest. We will be seeing more of Eli, and it will be clear that he was no spiritual giant; in fact, the child born to Hannah would be sent by the Lord to replace the corrupt priesthood of Eli's family.

Nevertheless, Eli was the high priest, and thus one who spoke on God's behalf, so Hannah was right to take his words in this way. "[May] the God of Israel grant your petition" was more than well-wishes when spoken by a man in this divinely ordained office. We might go even a step further and say that Hannah believed Eli as she was trusting in Jesus Christ to represent her before God. Eli occupied one of three anointed offices in the Old Testament—prophet, priest, and king—and since there were neither prophets nor kings at that time, Eli the priest was the sole anointed mediator with

8. Woodhouse, *1 Samuel*, 32.

God. The Hebrew word for "anointed one" is *Messiah*, which translated into Greek is *Christ*. We might say that Eli was temporarily holding the place in God's economy that would ultimately be filled by Jesus. It was not the personal character of Eli that Hannah trusted, therefore, but his representation of the mediation that God would provide in the person of his own Son.

What Eli represented, however poorly, was the reality that came with Christ. When Christians pray "in Christ's name," we are saying that we come to God through the priestly ministry of Jesus Christ. And when Jesus speaks words of comfort and assurance to us through the Scriptures, we should follow Hannah's example by taking them to heart. Jesus speaks wonderful words of peace and hope as he mediates for us with the Lord of hosts. "Do not be anxious about your life," he tells us, for your heavenly Father knows what you need and cares for you (Matt. 6:25–32). To those who are burdened and weary, he promises, "I will give you rest" (11:28). Jesus restores us to God, saying, "My peace I give to you" (John 14:27). He promises to lead us through this world and to lay down his own life to free us from the penalty of our sins: "I am the good shepherd," he says; "I lay down my life for the sheep" (10:14–15). Jesus promises never to leave or forsake us, but to lead us safely through this life to the glory of heaven. If we listen with the faith of Hannah, we will respond with the words of Hebrews 13:5–6: "For he has said, 'I will never leave you nor forsake you.' So we can confidently say, 'The Lord is my helper; I will not fear'" (quoting Josh. 1:5; Ps. 118:6).

Hannah's experience shows us two things that happen when God's people pray to him in faith. The first is that *prayer changes us*. We see this in her dramatic change of demeanor. Hannah entered into prayer shattered and depressed. But as she rose from prayer, she "went her way and ate, and her face was no longer sad" (1 Sam. 1:18). She experienced the blessing of renewed faith, which the writer of Hebrews says is "the assurance of things hoped for, the conviction of things not seen" (Heb. 11:1). However God would answer Hannah's prayer, the time spent with him was rewarding, as it always is. To focus our hearts on God is to remember that the Lord who reigns is also the God of grace who invites us into his presence. He blesses those who trust him according to his wise, holy, good, and sovereign will. It is for this reason that those who neglect prayer, or who pray without faith, deprive themselves of this world's chief resource for peace and joy. Peter's counsel is essential for a strong spiritual life: "[Cast] all your anxieties on [God], because he cares for you" (1 Peter 5:7).

If prayer only changed us, it would be worthwhile. But the second thing that happened was that God answered Hannah's prayer. Not only does prayer change us, but *prayer changes things*. God is pleased to act in response to our prayers. Some people react to the knowledge of God's sovereignty by thinking that prayer therefore does not matter, since God has decided everything in advance. Hannah did not reason this way, but understood that God's sovereign will is achieved through the acts of men and women, especially our prayers. John Woodhouse comments that her turning to the Lord "will turn out to change not only her life but the life of the nation, and, indeed . . . , the history of the world." He adds, "Faith in God, therefore, leads us in our troubles to pray to the God who is sovereign over all things."[9]

The language of verse 19 is noteworthy: "They rose early in the morning and worshiped before the LORD; then they went back to their house at Ramah. And Elkanah knew Hannah his wife, and the LORD remembered her." Hannah not only believed God's answer to her prayer, but acted on the belief, going about her spiritual duties in worship and her conjugal duties in married life. And in the course of time, we find that "the LORD remembered her." This does not suggest that God had previously forgotten Hannah or that he was too busy running the universe to pay attention to her needs before she pointed them out. It means, rather, that God was mindful of her prayer and ordered events to work in blessing for Hannah. The same verb is used in Genesis 8:1, when after the great flood "God remembered Noah," that is, God kept his covenant promise and made sure to save Noah. This language speaks of God's faithfulness in hearing the prayers and meeting the needs of his people.

Some will wonder what it means when God does not seem to answer our prayers as he did for Hannah. Many a woman will pray in equally earnest tears for a dying child, an unbelieving husband, or an unfulfilled desire to bear a child. Yet the child does not live, the husband does not believe, or the child is not born. So she looks at Hannah and agonizes that her prayer was just as fervent and believing, yet the prayer was not answered. Does

9. Ibid., 29–30.

this mean that God did not remember such a woman or that God was less faithful to her?

Blaikie responds: "In spite of all such objections and difficulties, we maintain that God is the hearer of prayer. Every sincere prayer offered in the name of Christ is heard, and dealt with by God in such way as seems good to Him."[10] It is true that some prayers are not answered because they are offered in a wrong spirit or with selfish motives. Others are not answered because God knows that to do so would be harmful. Many of those taken from us by death early in life are being spared by God from agonizing sorrows. Yet there is no way for us to know this at the time when the prayer seems to have failed. In other cases, prayer is denied or delayed because God knows that we need the discipline of learning to wait on him trustingly, walking by faith and not by sight (2 Cor. 5:7). Blaikie therefore urges us:

> Whatever be the reasons for the apparent silence of God, we may rest assured that hearing prayer is the law of His kingdom. Old Testament and New alike bear witness to this. Every verse of the Psalms proclaims it. Alike by precept and example our Lord constantly enforced it. Every Apostle takes up the theme, and urges the duty and the privilege. . . . And what true Christian is there who cannot add testimonies from his own history to the same effect? If the answer to some of your prayers be delayed, has it not come to many of them? . . . And if there be prayers that have not yet been answered, or in reference to which you have no knowledge of an answer, can you not afford to wait till God gives the explanation? And when the explanation comes, have you not much cause to believe that it will redound to the praise of God, and that many things, in reference to which you could at the time see nothing but what was dark and terrible, may turn out when fully explained to furnish new and overwhelming testimony that "God is love?"[11]

ASKED FROM GOD

We know that Hannah reasoned in a believing manner, because she did not wait until her prayer was answered to regain a joyful attitude. Her example urges us similarly to find our peace in waiting on the Lord, knowing his mercy and grace.

10. Blaikie, *First Samuel*, 16.
11. Ibid., 17–18.

The key to Hannah's prayer is that she knew the Lord. She began her prayer by naming him the "LORD of hosts," the Almighty God who is able to overcome every difficulty in answering prayer. But her experience in casting her burden on God in prayer and then trusting God caused her to know God even better. For just as Hagar called the name *El-Roi* when she realized that God saw her, and as Abraham named the place *Yahweh-Yireh* when he saw that God would provide the ram as the sacrifice, Hannah also commemorated God's grace to her with a name: "In due time Hannah conceived and bore a son, and she called his name Samuel, for she said, 'I have asked for him from the LORD'" (1 Sam. 1:20).

Scholars debate the precise meaning of the name *Samuel*. Since the form of the name employs letters that could be taken a number of ways, different solutions are provided. One solution is that *Samuel* means "name of God," the idea being that as God's gift the child bears God's name. Most naturally, however, the name is taken to mean "God hears." This is reflected in Hannah's explanation. She named her son *Samuel*, "God hears," because "I have asked for him from the LORD" (1 Sam. 1:20). Hannah asked for the son, and she knew that God had heard her as soon as she prayed because she knew God. Now that the child was born, she wanted to bring praise to God's faithfulness in answering her prayer.

Wherever Samuel went and whatever he did, Samuel's name testified to a great and important truth about God. He would be a living example that when God's people humbly ask, the Lord hears and answers with mercy and grace. God calls us to know this, to know him, and therefore to cast our burdens on him, believing that he hears. If we believe this, however God chooses to remember us, we can be sure not only that our prayers will change our own hearts, but also that in God's faithful hands they will make a vital difference in the world. Hannah's prayer brought the coming of Jesus Christ one step closer in history. Our prayers, offered with the same faith as Hannah's, will bring the blessings of Christ's kingdom in ways small and large, and all in ways that will touch God's heart and bring him praise.

3

OFFERED TO THE LORD

1 Samuel 1:21–28

*For this child I prayed, and the LORD has granted me my
petition that I made to him. Therefore I have lent him
to the LORD. As long as he lives, he is lent to the LORD.*
(1 Sam. 1:27–28)

n its promotional materials, the United States Marine Corps
communicates its desire for quality over quantity. All the
Marines are looking for is "a few good men." There are times
in the Bible when it seems that a few good men and women is all God has
at his disposal. But what a difference even a few committed believers can
make, by his power, in a dark time. So it was with the birth of the child
Samuel, who would grow up to be one of Israel's greatest leaders. A story
that began with a humble priestly family who appeared before the Lord
to worship leads to much greater events as God answers Hannah's prayer
and so meets Israel's need.

HANNAH'S VOW FULFILLED

So far, so good, we might say regarding Hannah. Arriving at the tabernacle with the grief of childlessness on her heart, Hannah turned to the Lord

for help. Afflicted by the mean-spirited barbs of her rival co-wife, Hannah prayed not for vengeance but for a son whom she might offer to God. Instead of stuffing her heart with bitterness and resentment, Hannah poured out her soul before the Lord. And when Eli, speaking *ex cathedra* in his office as high priest, gave words of benediction over her prayer, Hannah received it as God's answer and went home with peace and joy. Since God responded by providing Hannah with her cherished son, we might say that her approach "worked." Indeed, Hannah does provide a model of effective prayer, however God may have chosen to respond. Most importantly, humble and prayerful Hannah possessed just the kind of believing heart that God always looks for and is pleased to bless for the sake of many others.

But now, at the end of this opening chapter, these critical questions remain: Will Hannah make good on her promise to the Lord? Will she fulfill her vow to consecrate her little son in lifelong service to God? Or will she see things differently once the baby boy is rocking in her arms? Were Hannah to hedge on her vow—a promise made under duress but forgotten once the trouble passed—she would not be the first and certainly not the last to do so. Perhaps God would understand if she adjusted her promise to allow little Samuel to serve the Lord at home in Ramah. Perhaps she would now think it best to devote more time to spiritually nurture the child and allow him to make his own decision.

As we wonder about Hannah's response to her son's birth, we should inquire about God's attitude toward solemn vows made to him. The Bible answers: "When you vow a vow to God, do not delay paying it, for he has no pleasure in fools. Pay what you vow. . . . Why should God be angry at your voice and destroy the work of your hands?" (Eccl. 5:4, 6). It turns out that God takes our vows most seriously. Vows made to God—including marriage vows, ordination vows, church membership vows, and oaths of office—should be made soberly and with mature judgment. Ecclesiastes continues, "It is better that you should not vow than that you should vow and not pay" (Eccl. 5:5). For this reason, vows "should not be entered into by those who are immature and do not have the means to carry out the intents of their hearts."[1] Hannah's actions suggest that she was mature and that she made her vow to God in sober judgment and honest intent. Because of this, what she began well in

---

1. Cyril J. Barber, *The Books of Samuel*, 2 vols. (Neptune, NJ: Loizeaux, 1994), 1:49.

prayer she now concludes well in action, as she follows through in offering her son to the Lord.

Several characteristics evident in Hannah's response explain why she was willing to keep so demanding a vow. First, it is clear that Hannah's godly behavior is animated by *gratitude to the Lord*. We see this in her explanation in presenting Samuel to Eli: "For this child I prayed, and the LORD has granted me my petition that I made to him. Therefore I have lent him to the LORD" (1 Sam. 1:27–28). Notice the sequence: "I am giving him to God because God gave him to me." In just this way, all true Christian service and offerings are presented to God in thanks for his gracious provision to us.

Hannah's example shows that God's grace rightly demands that we respond by giving back to the Lord. All that God gives us belongs to him and is intended for our good and for God's glory. To receive God's gifts merely for our own pleasure is to misuse them and despise the Giver, little appreciating God's generosity and little realizing our dependence on his grace. J. C. Ryle puts this principle in the context of the gospel: "Grateful love is the true spring of real obedience to Christ. Men will never take up the cross and confess Jesus before the world and live for him until they feel that they are indebted to him for pardon, peace, and hope. . . . The godly are what they are because they love him who first loved them and washed them from sin in his own blood."[2] It is for this reason that the gospel of Jesus Christ is the greatest force for transforming greedy, proud, and self-loving people so that instead they seek after holiness and love. Ryle states, "The secret of being holy ourselves, is to know and feel that Christ has pardoned our sins."[3] With thanksgiving for God's grace, Hannah's "allowing Samuel to be brought up in the temple was seen by her not as a necessary but terrible sacrifice but rather as a deep joy,"[4] in spite of the loss she suffered.

Hannah was not only grateful, but also *faithful* in fulfilling her vow. It is noteworthy that she refused to go up again to the tabernacle until she was prepared to leave her young son: "The man Elkanah and all his house went up to offer to the LORD the yearly sacrifice and to pay his vow. But Hannah did not go up, for she said to her husband, 'As soon as the child is weaned,

---

2. J. C. Ryle, *Luke*, 2 vols. (1858; repr., Edinburgh: Banner of Truth, 1986), 2:287.
3. Ibid., 1:238.
4. Mary J. Evans, *The Message of Samuel* (Downers Grove, IL: InterVarsity Press, 2004), 29.

I will bring him, so that he may appear in the presence of the Lord and dwell there forever'" (1 Sam. 1:21–22). Foremost in Hannah's mind was her promise to the Lord and her obligation to see it through. William Blaikie explains: "Had she gone before her son was weaned she must have taken him with her, and brought him away with her, and that would have broken the solemnity of the transaction when at last she should take him for good and all. . . . The very first time that she should present herself at that holy place where God had heard her prayer and her vow would be the time when she should fulfil her vow."[5] As people who rely on God's promises, Christians should be careful to keep our own. Regardless of difficulties, our chief desire should be to remain faithful to our duties and obligations before the Lord.

Third, Hannah showed great *generosity* in her manner of offering up her son. Instead of doing the minimal amount to justify keeping her vow, she offered the most that she could manage: "When she had weaned him, she took him up with her, along with a three-year-old bull, an ephah of flour, and a skin of wine, and she brought him to the house of the Lord at Shiloh" (1 Sam. 1:24).

A translation issue with this verse sheds some light on Hannah's generosity. Most English versions say that Hannah brought "a three-year-old bull" (ESV, NIV, NASB), but the original Hebrew text states that Hannah brought three young bulls (KJV). Scholars consider the original reading to be problematic, amending it to a single three-year-old bull, in part because verse 25 says that they "slaughtered the bull" (singular). But the main objection to the original text is the extreme economic sacrifice involved in such an offering. To such a primitive agricultural people, three bulls represented a staggering amount of wealth. Unable to imagine such generosity in giving to God, scholars have needlessly changed the text, following the example of influential ancient translations.[6] But Hannah's additional gift of an ephah of flour (an ephah amounted to about three-fifths of a bushel, or twenty-two liters) seems to fit the offering of three bulls, since the law prescribed that three-tenths of an ephah of flour should be offered along with each bull, so that Hannah's offering of a whole ephah was slightly more than

5. William G. Blaikie, *Expository Lectures on the Book of First Samuel* (1887; repr., Birmingham, AL: Solid Ground, 2005), 20.

6. In conflict with the Masoretic Text's "three bulls," the Septuagint, Dead Sea Scrolls, and Peshitta all render this "a three-year old bull."

required for three bulls (Num. 15:8–10). In addition, Hannah brought "a skin of wine," which is better understood to be a large vessel containing as many as twenty liters.[7]

Of course, Hannah's greatest generosity was in offering her young son to the Lord. Thus, after the bulls and the flour and wine are mentioned, we read: "And the child was young" (1 Sam. 1:24). Here was Hannah's truly generous gift: "I have lent him to the LORD. As long as he lives, he is lent to the LORD" (1 Sam. 1:28).

It turns out that the same Hebrew word (*sa'al*) means either "to ask" or "to lend," depending on the mode of the verb.[8] Hannah makes use of this wordplay to acknowledge that the proper response to her answered prayer is the dedication of the child to the Lord's service. The faith that receives God's gifts also returns God's gifts, using them to serve God's cause and advance his kingdom. Samuel would always be Hannah's child, but as she had received the boy in stewardship to God, she was happy to make him God's child and God's servant forever. Those who use God's gifts in this way are never losers but always gainers in the end. Kenneth Chafin notes that Hannah had gained "the blessing of God and the respect of both her husband and of Eli. Later she was to be given three sons and two daughters, but they were not necessary to her joy. In the gift of her son, God had given her a larger reason for living and much happiness."[9]

When Hannah says that "he is lent to the LORD" (1 Sam. 1:28), the word for "lent" happens to be the name *Saul*. Israel's King Saul has yet to appear in the narrative of 1 Samuel, but the original readers of this account could not have failed to notice the connection. One of the main transitions in 1 Samuel, as well as in Israel's history, would take place when the elders demanded that aged Samuel be replaced by a king, who would make Israel "like all the nations" (1 Sam. 8:20). That king would be named *Saul*. In advance of that ominous moment, Hannah points out that God has already given a *Sa'al* to Israel in the form of the son whom Hannah would offer back to the Lord in faith. In this way, Hannah proves that there was never a need for Israel to rebel against the Lord by calling for a worldly leader such as King Saul, since God had proved

---

7. See David Toshio Tsumura, *The First Book of Samuel*, New International Commentary on the Old Testament (Grand Rapids: Eerdmans, 2007), 129–31, for an extended discussion.

8. *Qal* = "ask"; *Hiphil* = "lend."

9. Kenneth L. Chafin, *1 & 2 Samuel*, Preacher's Commentary, vol. 8 (Nashville: Thomas Nelson, 1989), 28.

his willingness to provide a true Saul who had been asked for in faith and lent back to the Lord in fervent devotion. Like Hannah, believers today can trust the Lord by offering all that he has given us to his service, with no need to hold back or desire more worldly gifts for our own enjoyment and security.

REFLECTIONS ON THE HOME

A proper understanding of Hannah's account will recognize the uniqueness of her situation. If it seems extreme for a mother to bring her young son to church and leave him to be raised by the minister, the reason is that Hannah was bound up in a singular work of God for the sake of his people. Nonetheless, the account of Hannah's offering gives a good deal of insight into her marriage and home from which we should seek to profit. Hannah was an extraordinary woman of faith, and the godly home out of which young Samuel sprang provides a model for Christian homes today.

The first thing that stands out about the members of Elkanah's household is their commitment to worship. Theirs was a churchgoing family, present at the house of God for stated times of worship, regardless of the difficulty or expense. The law of Moses dictated that Israelites were to make pilgrimages to worship before the Lord:

> You shall seek the place that the LORD your God will choose out of all your tribes to put his name and make his habitation there. There you shall go, and there you shall bring your burnt offerings and your sacrifices, your tithes and the contribution that you present, your vow offerings, your freewill offerings, and the firstborn of your herd and of your flock. And there you shall eat before the LORD your God, and you shall rejoice, you and your households, in all that you undertake, in which the LORD your God has blessed you. (Deut. 12:5-7)

The failure to observe this command contributed to the widespread idolatry in that generation and all through the centuries that followed. But despite the difficulty of travel in that ancient day, and the great expense involved in making sacrifices to the Lord, Elkanah faithfully brought his family to Shiloh each year: "The man Elkanah and all his house went up to offer to the LORD the yearly sacrifice and to pay his vow" (1 Sam. 1:21). Elkanah's example reminds us that above all other motives for attendance in worship is the simple fact that God is worthy to receive our praise. Moreover, the making of costly sacrifices underscored the Lord's greatness and his incomparable blessings to his people.

Second, we can perceive the spiritual unity that joined the hearts of Elkanah and Hannah as husband and wife. This was revealed when Elkanah prepared to depart for Shiloh but Hannah declined to join him: "Hannah did not go up, for she said to her husband, 'As soon as the child is weaned, I will bring him, so that he may appear in the presence of the LORD and dwell there forever'" (1 Sam. 1:22). Elkanah understood Hannah's motives and supported her understanding of what was required to fulfill her vow. Under the law, a vow made by a wife needed to be confirmed by her husband (Num. 30:10–15). Elkanah was glad to do this: "Do what seems best to you; wait until you have weaned him; only, may the LORD establish his word" (1 Sam. 1:23). It is unclear what he meant by asking the Lord to "establish his word." Most likely, Elkanah joined Hannah in taking the high priest's benediction as divine confirmation of Hannah's prayer (1 Sam. 1:17), and he generally agreed with her in seeing God's sovereign purpose in Hannah's circumstances.

In like manner, any home is blessed when the husband and wife live in spiritual companionship. Couples should seek a shared sense of purpose in their worship and Christian service. As either is led to undertake special giving or ministry, the two should collaborate in their family's service to God. This is possible only when husband and wife join together in the Word of God and in prayer, being evenly yoked in their spiritual walk and providing mutual support for the sanctification and service of each.

Husbands, having received spiritual headship in the family, should be especially keen to perceive the gifts and ministry callings of their wives. The Bible's mandate for male leadership in the church and home does not limit the full partnership of women in the work of both (1 Cor. 11:3; Eph. 5:22–24; 1 Tim. 2:11). The Bible is filled with Spirit-filled and gifted women who make vital contributions to God's work, Hannah herself providing an eminent example. Elkanah seems to have understood the extraordinary role Hannah was playing, and rather than being defensive or resentful, he accommodated himself to support her fully. Let us not forget that Samuel was Elkanah's son as well as Hannah's; so highly did he value the spiritual contributions of his wife that he did not oppose the gift of his son to the Lord. Christian men today should likewise be keen to foster important

Christian service from women, in accordance with the gender pattern given in God's Word, and to look upon our daughters and wives as vital partners in the work of the Lord.

Finally, Hannah and Elkanah provide a valuable model in the attitude that Christian parents should have toward their children. Too many believing parents are driven by worldly motivations concerning their boys and girls. One of the reasons that some young people raised in the church go on to abandon their faith is that their Christian parents directed them onto worldly paths. They grew up being taught to dream of making a great success in the world: attaining great wealth, becoming famous, or being adored for beauty and talent. Meanwhile, the sad reality is that when young people feel God's calling to ministry or missionary service, their believing parents sometimes present the greatest obstacle, urging them to callings of greater ease, prestige, or proximity rather than rejoicing in the consecration of a child to serve the Lord.

The duty of Christian parents is to fit their children for service to God, whether in formal ministry or as productive members of the church. Hannah could "lend" her young son to the Lord because she was aware that Samuel belonged to the Lord before he belonged to her. Parents are stewards of children's upbringing on behalf of the Lord, and godly parents will make it their chief ambition and prayer that their children will serve the Lord to the greatest extent possible and with the utmost faithfulness. Believing parents who truly love their children will raise them with Jesus' promise firmly in view: "There is no one who has left house or brothers or sisters or mother or father or children or lands, for my sake and for the gospel, who will not receive a hundredfold now in this time, houses and brothers and sisters and mothers and children and lands, with persecutions, and in the age to come eternal life" (Mark 10:29–30).

How to Make an Offering to God

Hannah provides an outstanding example in her attitude of gratitude, faithfulness, and generosity, in her spiritual partnership with her husband, and in her zeal to offer her son to God's service. Recognizing the unique features of her calling and service, we also realize that every believer is called to give to the Lord and serve in the cause of his gospel. So how do we go about offering our gifts and service to God? Hannah models three principles: she acknowledged that what she offered came from the Lord and rightly belonged to him; her offering involved considerable preparation and effort; and she presented herself and her offering not in light of her own merits but on the basis of God's mercy and grace.

First, what Hannah offered to God had come from him in the first place. When Hannah brought young Samuel to Eli, the high priest, she told him: "Oh, my lord! As you live, my lord, I am the woman who was standing here in your presence, praying to the LORD. For this child I prayed, and the LORD has granted me my petition that I made to him" (1 Sam. 1:26–27). The only reason Hannah had something valuable to offer the Lord was that God had given her the treasure in the first place. Paul rightly asks, "Who has given a gift to [God] that he might be repaid?" (Rom. 11:35). Anything we might give to God is something that he made and enabled us to possess, including our talents, our wealth, and even our lives. This was the logic in the firstfruits offerings of Israel's worship, just as it provides the logic of tithes offered today: the first portion is brought to the Lord to show that the whole of what we are and have comes from and belongs to him.

Understanding that everything belongs to God in the first place will greatly restrain our pride, which is always a temptation to those making gifts to the Lord. Do you devote your intellect to studying God's Word? This is only appropriate, since your intelligence was given to you by God. Do you offer your tithe to God? It was God who gave you the ability and the opportunity to earn your money, so it is only fitting that you acknowledge his right to it. We are not performing some extraordinary and praiseworthy service when we obey God's Word and live as God calls us to do, offering our talents, time, and money to the Lord. As Paul reminded the boastful Corinthians: "What do you have that you did not receive? If then you received it, why do you boast as if you did not receive it?" (1 Cor. 4:7). Not one of us can claim to be rendering to God a true profit on his investment in us; the truth is that all that God may gain through our work is merely the fruit of his own gifting and labor, coupled with many failures and sins for him to forgive.

Second, a truly significant offering to God usually requires much preparation and effort. When Hannah brought Samuel to live in Shiloh, she had invested a great deal of effort in the boy. She did not bring him until he would be able to stay without being a burden to the high priest: "She said to her husband, 'As soon as the child is weaned, I will bring him, so that he may appear in the presence of the LORD and dwell there forever'" (1 Sam. 1:22). According to extrabiblical sources, Jewish children were breast-fed for as long as three years, and perhaps even longer.[10] It is hard to imagine how Hannah could have safely left Samuel until he was departing his toddler years, which means that she carefully prepared him during the vital first few years for the calling she had vowed for his life.

This need for preparation extends to all kinds of offerings we make to God. If a man believes himself called into the ministry, the years devoted to seminary training are not a pointless hindrance but a vital time of study for rightly handling God's Word (see 2 Tim. 2:15). Those devoting themselves to long-term missionary service will need to gain proper skills, learn languages, and raise financial support. The preparation is an essential part of the service they offer. Likewise, Christians desiring to be faithful in tithing to the church will often need to prepare by removing debts and simplifying their lifestyle. This only makes the offering to God more valuable and precious to him. In fact, a good deal of any meaningful offering to God will consist of preparing to give: undertaking evangelism training so as to be able to communicate the gospel effectively; biblical training to be effective as Christian parents; even the organization and forethought that is essential to any fruitful ministry of intercessory prayer. Mature and serious Christians, like Hannah, realize that few things of real value can be offered to God without extensive preparation and effort.

Third, it is absolutely essential that Christians realize that any offering we make to God can be brought only on the basis of his mercy and grace. This was the purpose for at least one of the bulls Hannah brought, to offer a blood sacrifice for her and Samuel's sins. First "they slaughtered the bull," and then "they brought the child to Eli" (1 Sam. 1:25). They remembered that even to approach the Lord required a cleansing of their sins; how much more for whatever they offered for his service. However we may praise Hannah's offering of Samuel, she knew that even her best motives required cleansing through atoning blood, as did the son she offered to the Lord.

10. See 2 Macc. 7:27. As Robert Bergen points out, "no Israelite homes had running water, and most villages did not have access to a reliable supply of safe drinking water," which likely extended breast-feeding beyond what is normal today. Robert D. Bergen, *1, 2 Samuel*, New American Commentary (Nashville: Broadman & Holman, 1996), 72.

Blaikie advises all who come with offerings to God: "Remember how unworthy you are to stand before Him. Remember how stained your garments are with sin and worldliness, how distracted your heart is with other thoughts and feelings, how poor the service is you are capable of rendering." How, then, can we ever give to the Lord? The answer is found in the cleansing blood of Christ. Blaikie says, "When you give yourselves to Him, or ask to be allowed to take your place among His servants, seek as you do so to be sprinkled with the blood of cleansing, own your personal unworthiness, and pray to be accepted through the merit of His sacrifice."[11]

The good news is that not only must we come to God through the atoning blood of Christ, but however bad we are or have been, we *are always accepted* by God through the sprinkled blood. While it is necessary that we come to God by Christ's blood, it is also certain that we will be received in God's grace. The apostle John stated that "the blood of Jesus his Son cleanses us from all sin" (1 John 1:7). So when we come to God, presenting our gifts for his service, we come only through the merit and blood of the Savior, Jesus Christ, and we come certain of God's acceptance, favor, and spiritual enabling. As Paul put it, Christ has "qualified" even sinners like us to enter God's beloved family, to participate in the work of his glorious kingdom, and "to share in the inheritance of the saints in light" (Col. 1:12).

LIVING WORSHIP

The final words of the chapter provide a fitting conclusion: "And [Samuel] worshiped the LORD there" (1 Sam. 1:28). This was the great purpose in all that Hannah had desired and performed: that her son might worship and serve the Lord in his house. The purpose for our lives is no different. Paul writes, "I appeal to you therefore, brothers, by the mercies of God, to present your bodies as a living sacrifice, holy and acceptable to God, which is your spiritual worship" (Rom. 12:1). Paul's "therefore" refers to the whole gospel teaching that precedes his exhortation. Just as Hannah responded to God's gift of a son by bringing little Samuel to serve all his days in the tabernacle, so we are to respond to God's grace in Jesus Christ by offering ourselves as living sacrifices for the sake of his praise.

11. Blaikie, *First Samuel*, 22.

Realizing our calling to serve the Lord, we see that while Samuel would fulfill a unique and vital role in Israel's history, there is just as much value in one who serves God faithfully in the home as in one called to serve God in the church. Christian ministry is not the sole purview of a small number of prominent religious professionals; it is the calling and privilege of every Christian regardless of vocational setting. Many believers will be called to offer to God their full-time labors in ministry. But many more will serve God in secular vocations, while still offering their time, effort, money, prayers, and spiritual gifts to the service of the Lord. Really, what God wants from us is our whole lives, which he gave to us in the first place, and which he has purchased with the precious blood of his Son, Jesus (1 Cor. 6:19–20). Jesus said, "Whoever would save his life will lose it, but whoever loses his life for my sake will find it" (Matt. 16:25).

So whatever plans our parents had for our lives, we should present ourselves to God in the manner that Hannah presented young Samuel. Hannah acknowledged that God had given Samuel to her, so now it was right for her to give him to God in return. Likewise, let each of us say to God: "Lord, you made me, and you have redeemed me from my sin through the death of your own Son. I now belong to you, so I offer my whole life for your praise and for service to your glorious kingdom." As Hannah offered Samuel, offer yourself to God gratefully, faithfully, and generously. And when you make your offering to the Lord, hand it over completely and unreservedly, as John Wesley prayed when he offered himself to the service of Christ and the gospel:

> I am no longer my own but yours. Put me to what you will. Put me to doing, put me to suffering. Let me be employed for you or laid aside for you. Let me be full, let me be empty. Let me have all things, let me have nothing. I freely and wholeheartedly yield all things to your pleasure and disposal.[12]

---

12. John and Charles Wesley, *Selected Writings and Hymns*, ed. Frank Whaling (New York: Paulist Press, 1981), 140.

4

HANNAH'S SONG

1 Samuel 2:1—10

*Hannah prayed and said, "My heart exults in the LORD; my
strength is exalted in the LORD. My mouth derides my enemies,
because I rejoice in your salvation." (1 Sam. 2:1)*

On October 31, 2008, a crowd estimated to be as large as 3 million
people lined a parade route in downtown Philadelphia. The city,
known for its tough and sometimes surly attitude, was for once
able to live up to its name: City of Brotherly Love. What caused so many
people to join in this delirious celebration? The answer is that after a long
generation of athletic futility, Philadelphia finally had a champion, as the
Phillies captured baseball's World Series. On this occasion, everyone in the
city, it seemed, came to cheer and rejoice.

Like sports fans, Christians have times of triumph when we just have to
rejoice and sing. This attitude is fully endorsed by the Bible: "Sing praises
to the LORD, O you his saints, and give thanks to his holy name" (Ps. 30:4);
"Sing and rejoice, O daughter of Zion" (Zech. 2:10). One of Israel's singing
daughters was Hannah, the once-barren wife of Elkanah. God's gift to her
of a son made Hannah break forth into song. Strictly speaking, the Bible
says that Hannah prayed, not that she sang, but so beautiful is the poetry
of Hannah's prayer and so strong is its connection to other victory songs

in the Bible that it is commonly referred to as *Hannah's Song*. "My heart exults in the LORD; my strength is exalted in the LORD," Hannah's spirit sang (1 Sam. 2:1). Bill Arnold comments: "Hannah had to sing! God had turned her barrenness into joy . . . And her song reveals that she understood full well the significance of God's sovereign, gift-giving love."[1]

The importance of Hannah's Song extends far beyond its personal and sentimental value. To Hannah was given "the privilege of providing the main theological introduction to the whole account of the history of the Israelite monarchy."[2] Hannah offered intelligent, theological, and biblically informed praise to God at this great moment in her life. But just as would happen a thousand years later when the virgin Mary gave praise to God for the birth of her Son—a prayer strikingly similar to Hannah's—the Holy Spirit made use of Hannah's tongue so that, in the marvelous process of the inspiration of Holy Scripture, Hannah's Song provides a forward-looking summary of what God was about to do in her period of history.

We become especially aware of the importance of Hannah's Song when we see how perfectly it corresponds to David's song of praise in 2 Samuel 23:1–7. These two praise songs serve as a pair of bookends to encase the whole Samuel corpus that lies between them. The themes that Hannah saw anticipated in the birth of Samuel find their reprise as David looks back to see Hannah's hope marvelously fulfilled through his own reign. For both Hannah and David, the God of Israel is their "Rock." What Hannah foresees that God will do, David celebrates as accomplished in the faithfulness of God's will. Augustine therefore said of Hannah: "Through this woman . . . there speaks, by the spirit of prophecy, the Christian religion itself, . . . with which the humble are filled so that they rise up, which was in fact the chief theme that rang out in her hymn of praise."[3]

EXALTED IN THE LORD

If baseball fans can be moved to tearful joy by a World Series victory, then it is no wonder that Hannah's triumph filled her with thanksgiving

1. Bill T. Arnold, *1 & 2 Samuel*, NIV Application Commentary (Grand Rapids: Zondervan, 2003), 76.
2. Mary J. Evans, *The Message of Samuel* (Downers Grove, IL: InterVarsity Press, 2004), 30.
3. Augustine, *City of God*, in *Joshua, Judges, Ruth, 1–2 Samuel*, ed. John R. Franke, Ancient Christian Commentary on Scripture, Old Testament vol. 4 (Downers Grove, IL: InterVarsity Press, 2005), 202.

and praise. For years she had traveled to the tabernacle, facing the bitterness of her barren womb while suffering the cruel mocking of her rival co-wife, Peninnah, who had succeeded in bearing children for Hannah's husband. Turning in faith to the Lord, Hannah had offered her son for lifelong service if only God would open her womb. Chapter 1 ends with this son, Samuel, delivered into the care of the high priest: "And he worshiped the LORD there" (1 Sam. 1:28). Hannah, too, worshiped the Lord, and her praise was filled with jubilation: "Hannah prayed and said, 'My heart exults in the LORD; my strength is exalted in the LORD'" (1 Sam. 2:1).

Hannah shows us what a difference it makes when we turn to God in time of need. The last time we saw her praying, her situation was very different. Hannah catalogues her transformation in terms of her heart, her horn, and her mouth. Earlier, her husband Elkanah had asked her, "Why is your heart sad?" (1 Sam. 1:8). Hannah described herself as "a woman troubled in spirit" (1 Sam. 1:15). But now her heart "exults in the LORD."

Some English translations obscure Hannah's second point of reference, substituting the word "strength" for the original word, "horn." "My horn is exalted in the LORD," she exults (NKJV). Those who lived in Hannah's agricultural world knew that a beast holds its head and horns high as a symbol of victory and power. In this way, Hannah refers to the removal of her disgrace: now she can hold her head high because of what the Lord has done for her.

Third, Hannah speaks of her mouth: "My mouth derides my enemies" (1 Sam. 2:1). The Hebrew literally states, "My mouth is opened wide." The idea seems to combine a devouring of one's foes, along with a gloating over defeated enemies. Given Hannah's refusal to complain about Peninnah or seek God's vengeance, it is unlikely that Hannah has suddenly turned bitter and hateful. Rather, thinking theologically, as she does all through this prayer, Hannah sees Peninnah as an example of the enemies of God and his people. Hannah now gloats to see the voice of unbelieving mockery silenced because of God's saving grace.

A question is raised by some commentators as to whether Hannah overstated the significance of her own deliverance. The answer is that Hannah represented Israel in those barren and forlorn days; her salvation was designed to encourage all Israel to hope for a greater deliverance. William Blaikie says: "Looking on herself as representing the nation of Israel, she seems to have felt that what had happened to her on a small scale was to happen to the nation on a large; for God would draw nigh to Israel as He had to her, make him His friend and confidential servant, humble the proud and malignant nations around him, and exalt him."[4]

It is of great importance that the source of Hannah's joy and strength is the covenant God himself. She states: "I rejoice in your salvation." Hannah rejoices not merely that she received something she had wanted. More significant in her eyes than the gift is the Giver: the Lord is her song and her salvation. Robert Bergen comments: "The object of Hannah's delight is neither herself—that she has overcome the disgrace of barrenness—nor her son; instead it is the Lord, who is the source of both her son and her happy circumstance."[5] Much as Hannah loved her son Samuel, he was not her Savior, and he could not provide the salvation for God's people that she sought. Salvation is always of the Lord, and our praise should be focused on the Lord himself rather than merely on the blessings he has provided. Hannah had not simply received a son—as if a baby would solve all her problems—but had received gracious help from the Lord, and the Lord is the solution for everything that Hannah and Israel needed.

None like Our God

Some years ago, Philip Yancey wrote a book titled *Disappointment with God*.[6] The book relates the sentiments of numerous Christians who had written to Yancey to complain. They had trusted the Lord, but God seemed to have let them down. One had suffered by seeing his parents divorce despite praying a thousand times for their reconciliation. Another had lost a child. Yet another just wasn't able to be happy, and God didn't seem to care or be willing to help. In contrast to Hannah, who received the thing she prayed for and praised God, these people doubted God and were disappointed by the results of their faith.

Yancey's response to these complaints was insightful. For instance, he pointed out that many of these people were disappointed in God because

---

4. William G. Blaikie, *Expository Lectures on the Book of First Samuel* (1887; repr., Birmingham, AL: Solid Ground, 2005), 26.

5. Robert D. Bergen, *1, 2 Samuel*, New American Commentary (Nashville: Broadman & Holman, 1996), 75.

6. Philip Yancey, *Disappointment with God* (Grand Rapids: Zondervan, 1988).

they were demanding things that God had never promised to provide: most especially, God had never promised to spare his people from the pain and sorrow of this present life. Furthermore, Yancey pointed out that even when people receive what they have sought from the Lord, they usually do not praise or thank him. At the heart of this disappointment with God, Yancey concluded, was the problem that so many Christians valued God only for what he could do for them. God himself, in the glory of his person, was lightly considered, so it is no wonder that people were disappointed in God when he did not do what they thought he should do.

No such problem can be seen in the prayer life of Hannah. During the long years of bitter frustration, she had not lost hope in the Lord. Therefore, in the jubilation of her celebration, it is the Lord himself that she first considers. Just as Hannah earlier was a model of heartfelt prayer, so now she models godly praise, glorifying God first for who he is and then marveling at the salvation God has given.

Hannah makes four statements about God in verses 2–3, all of which cause her to rejoice. Her thought first turns to the Lord's holiness: "There is none holy like the LORD" (1 Sam. 2:2). This is entirely appropriate, because it is God's holiness that comforts and encourages us in every situation. The holiness of God implies his separation from all his creatures, but it carries especially the notion of God's moral perfection. Since God is holy, all his intentions for his people are holy. It is not possible for God's motives to be perverse or callous or mean—even in judgment and especially toward his beloved people—for he is "of purer eyes than to see evil and cannot look at wrong" (Hab. 1:13). Blaikie observes, "To the wicked this attribute is no comfort, but only a terror. . . . Yet to those who can appreciate it, how blessed a thing is the holiness of God! No darkness in Him, no corruption, no infirmity; absolutely pure, He governs all on the principles of absolute purity."[7] Since God is perfectly holy, what truly matters is not what circumstances befall us in life but our relationship with the Holy One.

God's holiness encourages those who are presently afflicted. It would be easy to complain that Hannah is spiritually cheerful because her desire has been granted. But this fails to account for the long years of her bitter disappointment. It is only now, when her prayer has been answered, that

7. Blaikie, *First Samuel*, 28.

Hannah can discern God's holy purpose in her trials. But long before the prayer was answered, she could still know that God was holy and patiently await his holy resolution of her need. Knowing that God's purpose in your afflictions must be holy, pure, and good, you can be comforted by Hannah's example that the day of God's deliverance will come for you in the manner and timing of his choosing; when it does, you will have every reason to praise him as the holy God that he is.

Having praised God for his holiness, Hannah adds that "there is none besides you" (1 Sam. 2:2). Hebrew poetry often employs a parallelism in which one statement is followed by another that develops and expands the initial idea. Not only is the Lord holy, but God is so incomparable that no one else is even in his class. The Lord of Israel is the only true God; alone among all those worshiped as divine, Hannah's Lord is truly God. Therefore, there is none to thwart God's marvelous plans; the Lord's will is always established, since there is "none besides you."

To this, Hannah adds a third statement that carries her prayer to its culmination. Not only is God the holy and only true God, but "there is no rock like our God" (1 Sam. 2:2). The image of God as a rock conveys his faithfulness to protect and establish his people. The Lord is the immovable rock on whom all our hopes are safe and secure. Gordon Keddie writes, "He is the Rock in which his people can always trust, because he cannot be overthrown."[8]

Hannah's God-centered prayer sets a vital example for us. If we place a higher glory on the blessings that God gives than on God himself, we commit idolatry, esteeming the creature above the Creator, and we engage in a folly that will ultimately spoil everything. Hannah is right: there is none holy like the Lord, none besides him, no rock like our God. Therefore, like Hannah, we should always have as our chief glory and hope that we know God and have been accepted into his loving care through the atoning ministry of his Savior-Son, Jesus Christ.

Hannah adds a fourth statement about God, couched as a rebuke to scornful mockers: "Talk no more so very proudly, let not arrogance come from your mouth; for the LORD is a God of knowledge, and by him actions are weighed" (1 Sam. 2:3). The wicked and arrogant should realize that God

8. Gordon J. Keddie, *Dawn of a Kingdom: The Message of 1 Samuel* (Darlington, UK: Evangelical Press, 1988), 32.

45

sees and knows all things, and knows how to respond to them all. Blaikie comments: "His eye is on every plot hatched in the darkness. He knows His faithful servants, what they aim at, what they suffer, what a strain is often put on their fidelity."[9] God has a response, calculated by infinite wisdom, for every situation; God acts and permits actions in accordance with his perfect knowledge of past, present, and future, always achieving his sovereign will for his own glory and the highest good of his people.

When we read these two verses, suddenly we can understand this remarkable woman, Hannah. What was the source of her humble steadfastness under a great trial? What enabled her to offer her treasured son for lifelong service to the Lord? And what caused her to praise God with such beauty and power? The answer is that Hannah was absorbed with the Lord. Her heart was filled with the knowledge of God, her faith anchored on the glorious perfections of his character and attributes. This was the source not only of Hannah's hope and joy, but also of her greatness; as the prophet Jeremiah would later put it: "Let him who boasts boast in this, that he understands and knows me, that I am the LORD who practices steadfast love, justice, and righteousness in the earth. For in these things I delight, declares the LORD" (Jer. 9:24).

Hannah's relationship with her Lord is a reproof to those who are little interested in God. Do you come to church primarily to meet with God among his people? Is your primary concern in a sermon its teaching about God, rather than its supposed practical value for yourself? If not, if you are little interested in God himself but only in what you can get from God, then your spiritual condition must be weak at best and perilous at worst. If we desire a faith that burns even in dark places and a character that honors God at all times, then let our faith be focused on the Lord himself, seeking first the kingdom of God, whom to know is eternal life (John 17:3).

THE LORD'S SALVATION

This is not to say that Hannah did not rejoice in God's wonderful actions on her behalf. We, too, should know and understand God's saving works in order to love and praise him as we should. Hannah praises God for what

9. Blaikie, *First Samuel*, 28.

he has done in two groups of statements. In the first section, verses 4–5, Hannah reflects on what God has done for her, seeing a general pattern in God's salvation. Then, in verses 6–8, she praises God for his actions toward the godly and the ungodly, respectively.

The key to Hannah's first string of praises comes at the end of verse 5: "The barren has borne seven, but she who has many children is forlorn." This relates, of course, directly to Hannah's personal situation. She who was barren is exalted, while her haughty opponent is cast down by Hannah's blessing.

Some scholars puzzle over the statement that "the barren has borne seven," since this was Hannah's first child and the total number of children she would go on to bear is six (see 1 Sam. 2:21). The point, poetically expressed, is that God has thoroughly blessed the one who was barren, seven being a symbolic number for fullness of blessing (cf. Ruth 4:15). God is to be praised because he lifts up the lowly and casts down the arrogant and ungodly. Seeing this point typified in her answered prayer, Hannah joins it with other typical examples: "The bows of the mighty are broken, but the feeble bind on strength. Those who were full have hired themselves out for bread, but those who were hungry have ceased to hunger" (1 Sam. 2:4–5).

According to Hannah, God's salvation involves a reversal of fortune in which the proud and violent are humbled and the poor and meek are exalted. This was the very message taught by Jesus: "Blessed are the poor in spirit, for theirs is the kingdom of heaven. . . . Blessed are the meek, for they shall inherit the earth" (Matt. 5:3, 5). God is to be praised because in a world where it seems that the rich get richer and the poor get poorer, the Lord takes up the cause of the downcast and gives salvation to the weak.

In verses 6–8, Hannah expands her thought to God's salvation as it pertains to the ultimate issues of life and death: "The LORD kills and brings to life; he brings down to Sheol and raises up. The LORD makes poor and makes rich; he brings low and he exalts. He raises up the poor from the dust; he lifts the needy from the ash heap to make them sit with princes and inherit a seat of honor." In a world such as ours, in which everyone is finally brought to death—a world where any one of us can suddenly become poor, sick, needy, and lowly—God wonderfully lifts his people from death and destruction.

This was the God Hannah needed in her barren desperation: the Savior of the broken, crushed, condemned, and weak, who humble themselves in faith. John Calvin wrote to his friend William Farel with a similar idea of

God, when suffering grief over the death of his wife, Idelette: "May the Lord Jesus . . . support me . . . under this heavy affliction, which would certainly have overcome me, had not He, who raises up the prostrate, strengthens the weak, and refreshes the weary, stretched forth His hand from heaven to me."[10] Likewise, when Hannah was downcast, God lifted her head; when she was barren, he brought life to her womb; when she was disgraced, he gave her an honored place. The Lord will do likewise, in ways and at times of his sovereign choosing, for all who humble themselves in faith and look to him to be their God and Savior.

These reflections led Hannah to a grand object lesson: "For the pillars of the earth are the Lord's, and on them he has set the world. He will guard the feet of his faithful ones, but the wicked shall be cut off in darkness, for not by might shall a man prevail. The adversaries of the Lord shall be broken to pieces; against them he will thunder in heaven. The Lord will judge the ends of the earth" (1 Sam. 2:8–10). God is sovereign over all things, having created all that is and ruling over all with divine power. Those who walk before him in faithfulness find that God "will guard their feet." The same point is made by Psalm 121: "My help comes from the Lord, who made heaven and earth. He will not let your foot be moved . . . The Lord will keep you from all evil; he will keep your life" (Ps. 121:2–3, 7). But on the other hand, "the wicked shall be cut off in darkness," and the Lord's adversaries "shall be broken to pieces" as the Lord judges "the ends of the earth" (1 Sam. 2:9–10).

With this in mind, Hannah comes to the moral of her prayer, which is also the grand lesson of 1 and 2 Samuel as a whole: "for not by might shall a man prevail," but by the Lord. This was the lesson enshrined in Moses' and Miriam's song at the Red Sea crossing: "Sing to the Lord, for he has triumphed gloriously; the horse and his rider he has thrown into the sea" (Ex. 15:21). Young David would later teach the same lesson to the giant Goliath: "You come to me with a sword and with a spear and with a javelin, but I come to you in the name of the Lord of hosts, the God of the armies of Israel" (1 Sam. 17:45).

"Not by might shall a man prevail," but by the Lord! Have you learned this lesson? Have you learned that God is the One who ultimately matters,

---

10. Quoted in Dale Ralph Davis, *1 Samuel: Looking on the Heart* (Fearn, Ross-shire, UK: Christian Focus, 2000), 19.

to whom you must ultimately give account, and by whose grace alone you can hope to be saved? Have you realized that even if you succeed in climbing to the top of life's ladder, unless you are righteous before God all must ultimately be lost, if not sooner, then in the final judgment? Have you learned that all who humble themselves and come to the Lord in faith receive from him the saving care they need, so that they may prevail in the end "not by might" but by the Lord, who shows mercy and gives grace?

God's King and Messiah

Perhaps it is because Hannah's thought had turned to God's judgment, in which every one of us is rightly condemned as a sinner, that she concluded her prayer with a remarkable reference to God's king and his promised Messiah: "he will give strength to his king and exalt the power of his anointed" (1 Sam. 2:10).

This concluding mention of a king provided by God, along with God's *Messiah*, which is the Hebrew word for "anointed," highlights the importance of Hannah's Song as an introduction to the books of Samuel. Whether through some insight from the Scriptures or through the prophetic inspiration of the Holy Spirit, Hannah foresaw that God intended to meet Israel's need by providing "his king." God would provide a king to rule on God's behalf in true faith. The chapters that follow tell the story of how Hannah's prophecy was fulfilled: King David would be strengthened by God as he humbly led God's people in faith.

But the story of God's king does not stop with 1 and 2 Samuel, for God did not intend merely to provide a godly king to rule over Israel. He further intended to "exalt the power of his anointed," that is, the Messiah. For even David, in all his glory and might, was but a picture of the true King, the true Anointed One, the Messiah Jesus, who would come to save God's people and rule forever in righteousness and peace.

Hannah's Song is the first direct reference in the Old Testament to God's promised *Messiah*, which in New Testament Greek is rendered as *Christ*. How appropriate that this promise should come from Hannah's lips! Who better to foretell God's gift of his own Son to be the Savior of sinful mankind than the woman who freely gave her firstborn son to serve the Lord and minister in God's name? Blaikie comments that here at the end of her prayer, Hannah's "son seems to give place to a higher Son, through whom the land would be blessed as no one else could have blessed it, and all hungry and thirsty souls would be guided to that living bread and living water of which whosoever ate and drank should never hunger or thirst again."[11]

How appropriate, as well, that Hannah's Song would find its New Testament counterpart in the song of a godly young woman so much like her, the maiden Mary, when the angel came to foretell the birth of the promised Savior through her virgin womb. Moved by the Holy Spirit, Mary picked up Hannah's themes to glorify God in her own exaltation: "My soul magnifies the Lord, and my spirit rejoices in God my Savior, . . . for he who is mighty has done great things for me, and holy is his name. . . . He has shown strength with his arm; he has scattered the proud in the thoughts of their hearts . . . and exalted those of humble estate" (Luke 1:46–52). Hannah believed that the birth of her son portended a new day of hope for God's people. Mary realized that through her Son would come the hope of all the world. While Samuel would be great as a prophet and judge for Israel, Jesus Christ would be exalted in power by God through his death on the cross for the forgiveness of our sins.

How else, after all, can God lift up the poor and save the condemned, except that his own Son became poor for us, and the One who knew no sin was made sin "so that in him we might become the righteousness of God" (2 Cor. 5:21)? What Hannah saw from far away has come near to us all through the coming of Jesus, the promised Messiah. It is now in his name alone that "the feeble bind on strength" (1 Sam. 2:4) through the spiritual power that Jesus gives. It is now through Jesus that "those who were hungry have ceased to hunger" (2:5), since as Jesus said, "The bread of God is he who comes down from heaven and gives life to the world. . . . I am the bread of life" (John 6:33, 35). Therefore, whoever believes on Jesus Christ as God's King and Messiah, our Savior through his blood of the cross, will be made, as Hannah foresaw, to "sit with princes and inherit a seat of honor" (1 Sam. 2:8). For as Jesus taught, "whoever hears my word and believes him who sent me has eternal life" (John 5:24).

11. Blaikie, *First Samuel*, 35.

5

THE WICKED SONS OF ELI

1 Samuel 2:11—36

Therefore the LORD, the God of Israel, declares: "I promised that your house and the house of your father should go in and out before me forever," but now the LORD declares: "Far be it from me, for those who honor me I will honor, and those who despise me shall be lightly esteemed." (1 Sam. 2:30)

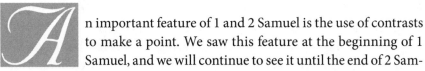n important feature of 1 and 2 Samuel is the use of contrasts to make a point. We saw this feature at the beginning of 1 Samuel, and we will continue to see it until the end of 2 Samuel. First, there was the contrast between humble, believing Hannah and the arrogant hostility of Peninnah, her rival co-wife. At the end of chapter 1 Hannah brings her young son, Samuel, to serve in God's house, initiating a contrast between Samuel and the wicked sons of Eli. This chapter thus "artfully alternates between the sinful practices of Eli's wicked sons and the innocent purity and righteousness of Samuel and his family."[1]

The reason for these contrasts is the grace of God at work in a dark world. Early in 1740, an American pastor named Samuel Blair complained that

---

1. Bill T. Arnold, *1 & 2 Samuel*, NIV Application Commentary (Grand Rapids: Zondervan, 2003), 70.

"religion lay as it were a-dying and ready to expire its last breath of life in this part of the visible church." In fact, however, God was on the brink of launching one of the great revivals in history, the Great Awakening, which dates from that very year.[2] God had been quietly working behind the scenes, preparing what would soon be broadcast on the front pages of history. A similar situation is seen in the early chapters of 1 Samuel. The contrast between Samuel and Eli's sons does more than warn us against the way of the wicked. It also reminds us that God is at work behind the scenes, so that even amid wickedness and unbelief there is always hope for grace.

THE SINS OF ELI'S SONS

Israel's hope for grace is represented by little Samuel, whom his parents left behind in the tabernacle to serve the Lord: "Then Elkanah went home to Ramah. And the boy ministered to the LORD in the presence of Eli the priest" (1 Sam. 2:11). Meanwhile, Israel's desperate need for grace is displayed in the lives of Eli's sons, whose wicked conduct debauched the priesthood.

The introduction of Eli's sons leaves little to the imagination: "Now the sons of Eli were worthless men. They did not know the LORD" (2:12). This is about as condemning an introduction as anyone could receive, especially if one is a minister. To say that they were "worthless men" is to say that they were agents of destruction. To then say that they "did not know the LORD" is to say that for all their access to divine religion and their knowledge of theology and the rituals of worship, these were unconverted men, spiritually ignorant of God's saving grace, and caring nothing for the demands of his holiness. What a crisis it was for Israel that such men were its spiritual leaders. No wonder Israel's spiritual life had been represented by Hannah's barren womb!

The wickedness of Eli's sons is seen in their contemptuous treatment of the offerings brought to the Lord at the tabernacle. The law of Moses provided that the priests serving at God's house would receive their food from the sacrifices that were offered. But whereas the law specified certain portions for the priests, depending on the animal (cf. Lev. 7:34; Deut. 18:3),

---

2. Quoted in Dale Ralph Davis, *1 Samuel: Looking on the Heart* (Fearn, Ross-shire, UK: Christian Focus, 2000), 23.

Eli's sons demanded their own form of potluck, sending their servant to randomly skewer meat from the family pots:

> The custom of the priests with the people was that when any man offered sacrifice, the priest's servant would come, while the meat was boiling, with a three-pronged fork in his hand, and he would thrust it into the pan or kettle or cauldron or pot. All that the fork brought up the priest would take for himself. This is what they did at Shiloh to all the Israelites who came there. (1 Sam. 2:13–14)

Emboldened by their success at stabbing for juicy meat, the young priests went further and demanded even the fat portions, which were reserved for the Lord:

> Moreover, before the fat was burned, the priest's servant would come and say to the man who was sacrificing, "Give meat for the priest to roast, for he will not accept boiled meat from you but only raw." And if the man said to him, "Let them burn the fat first, and then take as much as you wish," he would say, "No, you must give it now, and if not, I will take it by force." (1 Sam. 2:15–16)

Devout Israelites who came to sacrifice before the Lord not only witnessed the priests' sacrilegious attitude toward the offerings but also suffered the theft of what the Lord had allotted for themselves and their families. Verse 17 gives a withering indictment: "Thus the sin of the young men was very great in the sight of the Lord, for the men treated the offering of the Lord with contempt."

Worst of all was the contempt these young ministers showed toward God's holiness. Their desecration went so far that "they lay with the women who were serving at the entrance to the tent of meeting" (1 Sam. 2:22). This tent—the tabernacle—was the place where Israelites entered God's holy presence. How great was the sacrilege of the priests' sexual sins in this sacred place! These Israelite women, probably serving to clean and otherwise address the needs of the tabernacle, ought to have been treated with the utmost chastity, but they were instead treated like the temple prostitutes of pagan shrines.

This conduct by the high priest's sons could have only the worst effect on both the spiritual and moral character of the nation, just as sins of greed and sexual infidelity among ministers do today. After all, if the leaders of religion think so little of the Lord, why would anyone else revere him? Furthermore, given the tendency of our sinful nature to commit these kinds of sins, the sordid example of the priests would inevitably provide an incentive for a widespread tolerance of similar debaucheries. William Blaikie thus summarizes: "Men of corrupt lives at the head of religion, who are shameless of their profligacy, have a lowering effect on the moral life of the whole community."[3]

The gross failure of Eli's sons reminds those who exercise authority in the church that their holy calling carries a holy obligation, for which they should be held to account. How easy it is, and how often seen today, for preachers to use their ministry primarily for personal gain—employing worldly approaches that bring large crowds and sizable offerings—rather than seeking the glory of God and the spiritual health of his people. And how often ministers who begin seeking personal gain end up disgracing themselves in sensual sins.

By contrast, we are told of the growing spirituality of little Samuel. After his parents left him at Shiloh, "the boy ministered to the LORD in the presence of Eli the priest" (1 Sam. 2:11). And while Eli's sons were busy exploiting their sacred positions, "Samuel was ministering before the LORD, a boy clothed with a linen ephod" (2:18). This "linen ephod" was probably a white apron, signifying Samuel's status as a priest-in-training. Dressed in this fashion, Samuel not only played the part but also looked the part given to him. His faithful example encouraged sincere faith and godliness in others. He reminds us that individual Christians may serve the Lord faithfully and with holy lives regardless of the general spiritual environment. Christian managers in a harsh work environment may treat their workers with respect. Where others gain success through dishonest manipulation, Christians can serve God by honest ministry. In churches in which most members are prayerless and uninterested in gospel mission, believers may daily call out to God to help shine his light into the darkness of the world. How important such believers are who rise above their surroundings, and how often God uses them to bring revival to his seemingly lifeless church.

3. William G. Blaikie, *Expository Lectures on the Book of First Samuel* (1887; repr., Birmingham, AL: Solid Ground, 2005), 41.

ELI'S INEFFECTIVE REBUKE

Samuel is contrasted not merely with Eli's wicked sons but also with the high priest himself. Verse 21 tells us that "the young man Samuel grew in the presence of the LORD," and immediately adds, "Now Eli was very old" (1 Sam. 2:22). Eli comes across as a well-meaning and personally godly man, but as an ineffective spiritual leader and a failure in governing his sons.

Naturally, Eli knew about his sons' exploits, so "he said to them, 'Why do you do such things? For I hear of your evil dealings from all the people. No, my sons; it is no good report that I hear the people of the LORD spreading abroad'" (2:23–24). Eli's failure is seen in that although he heard about his sons' sins and he talked to them about their behavior, he did nothing to curb these wicked actions.

We can easily imagine that this pattern had characterized Eli's parenting all through his sons' upbringing. His first error was in failing to supervise their priestly service. The result was that instead of intervening and correcting his sons on the spot, Eli merely came to them later to discuss what he had heard. His second and greater error was that his rebuke did not lead to immediate punishment. According to the Bible, the failure to discipline our children is the surest way of ruining their souls (cf. Prov. 13:24). It will later be said of David that he never "displeased" his sons by holding them to account (1 Kings 1:6); the treachery, murder, rape, and treason committed by his progeny bear testimony to David's parental failure.

In dealing with his grown sons, Eli had an obligation at least to remove them from their office and install other qualified and godly priests. In the original days of the Israelite priesthood, even Aaron's sons Nadab and Abihu had been struck dead by God for bringing "unauthorized fire" into the tabernacle (Num. 3:4). How much more atrocious were the sins of Hophni and Phinehas! But though Eli rebuked his sons, he took no action. Blaikie writes that Eli "could not bring himself to be harsh to his own sons. He could not bear that they should be disgraced and degraded. He would satisfy himself with a mild remonstrance, notwithstanding that every day new disgrace was heaped on the sanctuary, and new encouragement given to others to practice wickedness."[4]

4. Ibid., 43.

For their part, Eli's sons would have been wise to receive their father's rebuke, "but they would not listen to the voice of their father" (1 Sam. 2:25). Few things are more vital to children than humility in receiving parental correction. When the fifth commandment says to "honor your father and your mother, that your days may be long in the land" (Ex. 20:12), it teaches that receiving correction from parents and succeeding in life go hand in hand. This is true as well for adults, who are no longer under their parents' authority but should still be humble in accepting godly counsel. The Bible says, "Whoever loves discipline loves knowledge, but he who hates reproof is stupid" (Prov. 12:1).

Verse 25 tells us that Hophni and Phinehas would not accept their father's reproof because "it was the will of the LORD to put them to death." This statement does not remove responsibility from Eli's sons. The point, rather, is to show that God was so outraged by the young men's sins that he resolved to punish them with death, and to this end he hardened their hearts to their father's reproof.

The apostasy of these two bad sons went hand in hand with the Lord's giving them over for destruction. Eli got to the heart of the matter in his warning: "If someone sins against a man, God will mediate for him, but if someone sins against the LORD, who can intercede for him?" (1 Sam. 2:25). His point was that sins against other people can be forgiven through the atoning blood of the Lord's sacrifices. But what can be done for sins that show contempt for the sacrifices themselves? Their sins against God's way of salvation—much like those of people who despise the gospel today—left Eli's sons with no means of forgiveness. So great were their sins against God's means of grace that the Lord gave them over to the lethal condition of hardened hearts. Dale Ralph Davis applies this as a warning to us all: "Someone can remain so firm in his rebellion that God will confirm him in it, so much so that he will remain utterly deaf to and unmoved by any warnings of judgment or pleas for repentance."[5]

Behind the scenes, and in contrast to Eli's corrupt family, is the family of Samuel. If God works powerfully in faithful individuals, how much more powerful is the behind-the-scenes presence of whole godly families. In Elkanah and Hannah we see the value of loving, godly involvement with

---

5. Davis, *1 Samuel*, 27.

one's children. We read that "his mother used to make for him a little robe and take it to him each year when she went up with her husband to offer the yearly sacrifice" (1 Sam. 2:19). Gordon Keddie writes: "The family is to be an arena in which personal godliness is promoted and the glory of God is manifested in personal relationships that are rooted in commitment to the Lord."[6]

Hannah and her husband were imperfect sinners like us all, but their sincere commitment to God made an impact on their son. We can imagine the prayers that Hannah wove into every strand of her growing son's annual robe, along with the exhortations and encouragements that came with its delivery. F. B. Meyer applies this lesson to our own parenting: "Mothers still make garments for their children—not on the loom or with their busy needles merely, but by their holy and ennobling characters displayed from day to day before young and quickly-observant eyes, by their words and conversation, and by the habits of their daily devotion."[7]

Hannah's spiritual fruitfulness was mirrored in the increase of her family's size. Every year, Eli would bless her, and before long "she conceived and bore three sons and two daughters" (1 Sam. 2:21). Hannah gave to the Lord and received an abundance from him in return. Verse 26 describes Samuel's increasing spiritual maturity in words that indicate the highest commendation, especially since the Gospel of Luke will echo them to describe the growing maturity of the boy Jesus: "Now the young man Samuel continued to grow both in stature and in favor with the LORD and also with man" (cf. Luke 2:52).

Eli must have spent many sleepless nights wondering how things had gone so wrong with his children. We can imagine that his thoughts of what he would have done differently, given the chance to raise his sons again, would make for interesting reading. When our own children are grown, what will we wish we had done differently? Will we wish we had been more diligent in teaching and discussing God's Word? Will we regret that we were not more determined and consistent in correcting sin? Will we wonder why we did not make the effort to set a better example of faith and godliness? Will we question the priorities we demonstrated by our lifestyle choices, or

6. Gordon J. Keddie, *Dawn of a Kingdom: The Message of 1 Samuel* (Darlington, UK: Evangelical Press, 1988), 42.

7. F. B. Meyer, *Great Men of the Bible*, 2 vols. (Grand Rapids: Zondervan, 1981), 1:275.

wish that we had made the time to be more involved in our children's lives? The problem is that once our children are grown, it will be too late to act on any such resolutions. For Eli, all that remained was the downfall of his house, while God worked behind the scenes to make new provision for the leadership of his people. Parents today who may feel that they have failed in raising their children should redeem the remaining time by praying for God's intervening grace and seeking all godly means to do good to their offspring.

GOD'S REJECTION OF ELI'S HOUSE

News of God's judgment, along with a stinging rebuke, was not long delayed:

> There came a man of God to Eli and said to him, "Thus the LORD has said, 'Did I indeed reveal myself to the house of your father when they were in Egypt subject to the house of Pharaoh? Did I choose him out of all the tribes of Israel to be my priest, to go up to my altar, to burn incense, to wear an ephod before me? I gave to the house of your father all my offerings by fire from the people of Israel. Why then do you scorn my sacrifices and my offerings that I commanded, and honor your sons above me by fattening yourselves on the choicest parts of every offering of my people Israel?'" (1 Sam. 2:27–29)

This rebuke was based on a history lesson. During the time of the exodus, Aaron and his sons were ordained as a perpetual priesthood (Ex. 29:9), consisting of three tasks: "to go up to my altar," that is, to bring the people's sacrifices before the Lord for the forgiveness of their sins; "to burn incense," which speaks of the priest's ministry of intercessory prayer; and "to wear an ephod before me," referring to the vestment on which the twelve stones represented Israel before the Lord. These were the very ministries so desecrated by Eli's sons. Yet here God's complaint is with Eli: "Why then do you scorn my sacrifices and my offerings that I commanded, and honor your sons above me by fattening yourselves on the choicest parts of every offering of my people Israel?" (1 Sam. 2:29).

By allowing his sons to violate the priesthood, Eli had regarded their honor above the Lord's. This happens today when men reveal themselves to be morally or spiritually unfit for ministry but are retained in pastoral office. Whether for sentimental reasons, because of political pull, or from a misplaced sense of showing "grace" to fallen leaders, today's heirs of Hophni and Phinehas can be permitted only when there is little thought for the reputation of the Lord or the good of his people. Eli was not responsible for everything his sons did, but he was responsible for their committing sins while remaining priests. Therefore, his house was rejected by the Lord because he treated the privileges of his Aaronic birthright so lightly:

> Therefore the Lord, the God of Israel, declares: "I promised that your house and the house of your father should go in and out before me forever," but now the Lord declares: "Far be it from me, for those who honor me I will honor, and those who despise me shall be lightly esteemed. Behold, the days are coming when I will cut off your strength and the strength of your father's house, so that there will not be an old man in your house. Then in distress you will look with envious eye on all the prosperity that shall be bestowed on Israel, and there shall not be an old man in your house forever. The only one of you whom I shall not cut off from my altar shall be spared to weep his eyes out to grieve his heart, and all the descendants of your house shall die by the sword of men." (1 Sam. 2:30–33)

God had promised Aaron's house the privilege of serving as priests, but there was a clear obligation involved: "for those who honor me I will honor, and those who despise me shall be lightly esteemed" (1 Sam. 2:30). Because Eli despised the Lord, his house would be cut off from the priesthood. Only one would be left, being "spared to weep his eyes out to grieve his heart," while all of Eli's other descendants "shall die by the sword of men" (1 Sam. 2:33). This promise was fulfilled in the days of David, when Doeg the Edomite slaughtered all of Eli's descendants at the tabernacle, with the sole exception of Abiathar (1 Sam. 22:6–23). Abiathar served David as priest until he supported the usurpation of Adonijah against David's heir, Solomon. When Solomon expelled Abiathar from the priesthood, the Scripture notes that this fulfilled "the word of the Lord that he had spoken concerning the house of Eli in Shiloh" (1 Kings 2:27). Abiathar was replaced by Zadok, who was from a more preeminent family of the line of Aaron, thus restoring an earlier promise that this family would hold the priesthood (cf. Num. 25:6–13). In this way, Eli's descendant was forced to the sidelines during the glories of Solomon's reign, looking with envy on those permitted to the priesthood and surviving off the generosity of the man who supplanted him, as

1 Samuel 2:36 predicted. Zadok would be the faithful priest mentioned in verse 35, "who shall do according to what is in my heart and in my mind."

All this would take place in generations to come, but Eli would see its proof, for God said, "This that shall come upon your two sons, Hophni and Phinehas, shall be the sign to you: both of them shall die on the same day" (1 Sam. 2:34). It would not be long until Eli's wicked sons would be slain on a single day, certifying to Eli the further judgment yet to come.

The principle behind God's rejection of Eli's house is one we should note: "Those who honor me I will honor, and those who despise me shall be lightly esteemed" (1 Sam. 2:30). This is a fixed principle of God's kingdom. For while the world will generally honor those who serve its cause, the Lord promises to honor those who treasure his glory. History bears this out. Those who despise the Lord may often rise in great power and fame. But the day of God's retribution comes, and for every despot, corrupt politician, and cheating executive there comes a day of reckoning when his or her name is cast down. Meanwhile, as Blaikie comments:

> The men that have honoured God, the men that have made their own interests of no account, but have set themselves resolutely to obey God's will and do God's work; . . . and have laboured in private life and in public service to carry out the great rules of His kingdom—justice, mercy, love of God and the love of man—these are the men that God has honoured; these are the men whose work abides; these are the men whose names shine with undying honour, and from whose example and achievements young hearts in every following age draw their inspiration and encouragement.[8]

A famous example of God's honoring the honorable is that of Eric Liddell, the Scottish Olympian who won a gold medal at the 1924 Olympics in Paris. Liddell was born and raised in China as the son of Christian missionaries. Returning to Scotland in his adolescence, he emerged as one of the finest runners Britain ever produced, at a time when British national pride greatly coveted Olympic glory. Liddell was a favorite to win the 100-meter race. But a problem emerged as he learned that the championship race would be held on a Sunday. Liddell was convinced by Scripture that he should not compete in a race on the Lord's Day, so he refused to

8. Blaikie, *First Samuel*, 47–48.

participate. Denounced by newspapers as a traitor, and personally pressured by the Prince of Wales to compromise his principles, Liddell held firm, determined to honor the Lord above his personal well-being and even before his country.

A compromise was reached in which Liddell would bypass the 100 meters and compete instead in the 400 meters, one of the few races with no heats on a Sunday. Liddell had not trained for this event, yet he would run it as his sole opportunity to win at the Olympics. As he prepared that morning, a member of the British training staff approached Liddell and handed him a note. Eric opened the piece of paper on the track before the race. On it were written these words from 1 Samuel 2:30: "He who honors Me, I will honor." With the piece of paper balled in his hand, Liddell ran the race, not only winning the gold medal but shattering the world record.

Britain went wild with adulation for Liddell, but instead of cashing in on his fame, he fulfilled a commitment to return to China as a missionary. When he departed from Scotland, the crowd seeing him off was so large that more than a thousand people were unable to be admitted to his farewell. Twenty years later, Liddell was still honoring the Lord in China when he died valiantly in a Japanese internment camp shortly before the end of World War II. At the end of the movie made in Liddell's honor, *Chariots of Fire*, the screen bore these words: "Eric Liddell, missionary, died in occupied China at the end of World War II. All of Scotland mourned." Liddell had honored God behind the scenes and on the international stage, and God honored his name before angels and men.[9]

A PRIEST TO SERVE

Just as Eric Liddell stood out in his generation, young Samuel made quite a contrast to the condemned house of Eli. As God was preparing to tear down, God was also preparing to raise up, providing a godly leader for his forlorn people. God's last word on this sad situation is thus a word of hope: "I will raise up for myself a faithful priest, who shall do according to what is in my heart and in my mind. And I will build him a sure house, and he shall go in and out before my anointed forever" (1 Sam. 2:35).

9. For a good biography detailing not just Liddell's Olympic heroism but his entire life of faith, see David McCasland, *Eric Liddell: Pure Gold* (Grand Rapids: Discovery House, 2004).

We can see the beginnings of this purpose taking shape in young Samuel's life. He would indeed serve faithfully as a priest to the Lord, and as Israel's prophet and judge he would do God's will. These words also refer to faithful Zadok and the priestly line of his house that would serve in the days of King Solomon. But this divine resolution could be fulfilled only in the coming of Jesus, God's true High Priest. Whenever we consider the roles given to Israel's priests, we should realize that Jesus is the One who truly performs and fulfills this sacred office.

A priest was ordained first, God said, "to go up to my altar" (1 Sam. 2:28), presenting the sacrifices to atone for the people's sin. Only Jesus makes the true sacrifice for our sin, having been made "a merciful and faithful high priest in the service of God, to make propitiation for the sins of the people" (Heb. 2:17). Jesus is the Priest who offers the effectual atoning blood—the blood of his cross—to cover our sins forever in the presence of God.

The priests were also called "to burn incense" (1 Sam. 2:28), representing the intercessory ministry of prayer before the heavenly Father. Though he was the Son of God, Jesus became man in order "to sympathize with our weaknesses" (Heb. 4:15) and pray to God the Father on our behalf. God promised that his Priest would serve in his house, going in and going out "forever." Indeed, the heavenly temple would be the true Priest's own house—the house, God says, of "my anointed" (1 Sam. 2:35). Jesus thus ministers forever as Priest in the house where he is both Savior and King. Hebrews 7:25 says that "he is able to save to the uttermost those who draw near to God through him, since he always lives to make intercession for them."

Just as the high priest was to wear the ephod, bearing the stones of the twelve tribes into God's presence, so also Jesus is the true and eternal Priest who bears all his redeemed on his heart and secures their place in glory, having engraved their names on the palms of his hands (Isa. 49:16).

WHERE GOD IS HONORED

What lesson do we learn from seeing little Samuel serve in the failing priestly house of Eli? Samuel's obedience reminds us to look behind the scenes to where God is working with grace. Regardless of fleshly appearances, the real action is always taking place wherever God is honored, where his Word is revered, and where humble commitment to the Lord is sincerely lived out. The message of godly little Samuel and the wicked sons of Eli is that nothing is ever more important than individual godliness, in godly and gracious families, with a simple commitment to God's Word and to prayer. If we want to make a real difference with our lives, we will not seek out arenas of worldly influence, especially when they require us to compromise biblical principles. It is better for God's people humbly to serve the Lord, often behind the scenes, remembering his promise that "those who honor me I will honor" (1 Sam. 2:30).

6

HERE I AM!

1 Samuel 3:1—4:1

And the LORD came and stood, calling as at other times, "Samuel! Samuel!" And Samuel said, "Speak, for your servant hears."
(1 Sam. 3:10)

We would be wrong to think that the dark period in which Samuel grew up was devoid of religion. There was a great deal of religious activity in Israel. There were priests serving and rituals observed. All of this religion went on side by side with widespread idolatry and nationwide debauchery. How can religion and immorality so comfortably coexist? The answer is given in the first verse of 1 Samuel 3: "The word of the LORD was rare in those days; there was no frequent vision." For all the religious activity, there was no revelation from God; and without God's Word, there can never be true spiritual life.

First Samuel 3 tells of God's remedy in calling young Samuel to serve as his prophetic mouthpiece to Israel. "Now the young man Samuel was ministering to the LORD under Eli" (1 Sam. 3:1), the chapter begins. It concludes: "The LORD revealed himself to Samuel at Shiloh by the word of the LORD. And the word of Samuel came to all Israel" (3:21–4:1). Thus began a new era for God's people and for the Bible's unfolding story of God's redemption in

64

the world. The imagery of this chapter tells its story: at a time when Israel's light was burning dimly, God summoned a youth whose heart was close to him, and by restoring God's Word Samuel opened wide again the doors to God's presence and power.

HEARING GOD'S WORD

Many of the great figures of the Bible began their careers with a dramatic call from the Lord, including Abraham, Moses, the prophet Isaiah, and the apostle Paul. Samuel's importance in Bible history is seen by his inclusion on this list of chosen and specially called servants of the Lord.

Popular literature likes to picture Samuel as answering God's summons as a little boy, but it is more likely that enough years had passed for Samuel to have at least entered his adolescence. In chapter 2 we read that "the young man Samuel continued to grow" (v. 26), and in 3:2 we read that Eli was now so old that his "eyesight had begun to grow dim." Whereas chapter 2 compared little Samuel to the wicked sons of Eli, chapter 3 describes him in contrast to aged Eli. While Eli was growing blind, young Samuel received a vision of the Lord. While Eli was "lying down in his own place," suggesting a room or chamber off the temple, "Samuel was lying down in the temple of the LORD, where the ark of God was" (1 Sam. 3:3). In effect, Samuel was filling Eli's shoes, and now he would be formally installed by God in Eli's place. Just as Israel's spiritual decrepitude followed Eli's blind infirmity, now the Word of the Lord will come to Israel through the spiritual vigor of young Samuel.

The setting for Samuel's calling is provocatively stated: "The lamp of God had not yet gone out" (1 Sam. 3:3). This indicates that it was in the early hours before dawn that God called to Samuel, since the lamps were kept lit until morning. But this was also symbolically true: the lamp of God's presence in Israel was dim but not completely out. In such a setting, the voice of the Lord was once more heard within his house: "Then the LORD called Samuel" (3:4). What grace there is in these words! At a time when God's Word had been violated and trampled on by even the high priest's sons, when God's injured law provided every reason for a judgment of eternally divine silence, yet still the voice of the Lord was heard calling to a child of his covenant.

And yet, in the most tragic irony, even the most devoted and worthy of God's servants did not know his voice! "Here I am!" cried Samuel, and then ran to Eli's chamber. "Here I am," Samuel reported, "for you called me." But Eli replied, "I did not call; lie down again" (1 Sam. 3:4–5). The Lord called to Samuel again, and the same thing happened. Verse 7 explains why: "Now Samuel did not yet know the LORD, and the word of the LORD had not yet been revealed to him." This makes the simple point that Samuel had never heard God's voice before, so he did not recognize it. But it also implies that since Samuel, Israel's brightest and best, did not know the voice of the Lord, he also did not really know God. While we would not say that Samuel was an unbeliever, "Samuel did not yet have the intimate knowledge of personal relationship with the Lord."[1] This was about to change, and as always, salvation would come by the gracious call of God's Word.

The third time that God called Samuel and the youth appeared in Eli's chamber, the high priest suspected what was happening. "Go, lie down," he said, "and if he calls you, you shall say, 'Speak, LORD, for your servant hears'" (1 Sam. 3:9). Finally, on the fourth summons, one given the urgency of repetition—"Samuel! Samuel!"—the young minister was ready: "Speak, for your servant hears" (3:10).

THE INSPIRATION OF GOD'S WORD

The calling of Samuel not only reveals God's grace, both in simply returning to Israel with his Word and also in his patience with Samuel's lack of understanding, but also provides a remarkable instance of prophetic inspiration. For here we see not merely the calling of *a* prophet, but *the first* in the long line of prophets who will serve under Israel's kings. Thus, the manner in which the Word of the Lord comes to Samuel sets a precedent for God's revelation through the prophets.

The apostle Peter gave the classic formula of divine inspiration: "No prophecy was ever produced by the will of man, but men spoke from God as they were carried along by the Holy Spirit" (2 Peter 1:21). In other words, prophecy and inspiration do not begin with the thoughts of the human author but by the hearing of God's Word. The men who wrote the Bible "spoke from God"; that is, they delivered to us the message that God gave

1. David Toshio Tsumura, *The First Book of Samuel*, New International Commentary on the Old Testament (Grand Rapids: Eerdmans, 2007), 177.

to them. Moreover, the entire process was supervised (or "carried along") "by the Holy Spirit."

Another classic definition of inspiration was given by Paul in 2 Timothy 3:16: "All Scripture is breathed out by God." When we say that the Bible was inspired by God, we should really be saying that God's revelation was "breathed out" or "expired" from God's own mouth. In the Bible we read God's Word to man, communicated through his Spirit-inspired and Spirit-supervised messengers, so that the writer of Hebrews can simply declare, "God spoke . . . by the prophets" (Heb. 1:1). Just as God spoke to Samuel so as to provide his Word to Eli, and later to reveal his Word to all Israel, so also God spoke to all the prophets and apostles in order that his revealed Word might be provided to us in the Bible.

The Bible shows considerable variation in the manner by which God's messengers experienced inspiration. Much of the Bible consists of historical narratives that were written by known or unknown human authors. The Psalms are poems and songs written by David and others to express their spiritual experience and devotion to God. The New Testament Epistles are actual letters written by the apostles to the early churches. All these kinds of Scripture are the Word of God as inspired and superintended by the Holy Spirit.

But here at the beginning of the prophetic era, in the calling of Samuel, we see the most basic form of divine revelation. God appears to young Samuel and speaks a message for him to record and pass on. This "dictation" approach is often denigrated in academic scholarship, as if it were somehow unworthy of God to speak to his creatures in this way. But in fact, much of the prophetic material is presented as having been dictated orally by God and written down more or less verbatim by the prophets. The Lord said, "I will put my words in his mouth, and he shall speak to them all that I command him" (Deut. 18:18). The prophets do not tell us that they have been wrestling with ideas that they now want to share with us. Instead, they uniformly tell us, "The word of the Lord came to me" (Jer. 1:4; cf. Isa. 2:1; Ezek. 1:3; Hos. 1:1; Jonah 1:1; Mic. 1:1; etc.) and "Thus says the Lord" (Amos 1:3; Obad. 1:1; Nah. 1:12; etc.).

Here God appears to Samuel in person, in a divine visitation (most of the prophets likewise received visions, which is why they are called *seers*), and presents an oral message for him to pass on. This is the basic model for all Scripture, the theme on which numerous variations are played, so that in whatever form the Bible presents itself we can know that we are reading what God has committed to his servants to be communicated to us. Therefore, we are duty-bound to receive all that the Bible teaches as God's own Word, carrying God's divine authority, and thus demanding our trusting belief and obedient response.

NEW LIFE THROUGH GOD'S WORD

The beginning of new life in Israel came with Samuel's hearing God's Word. The same pattern holds true today: God's people are revived when they give ear to God's Word. Our own generation bears much similarity to that of Eli: we have a great deal of religious activity, with legions of preachers, and large amounts of time and money devoted to the church and its activities. But where is the Word of the Lord? Gordon Keddie writes: "Now, as then, there is no shortage of 'religion' and certainly no shortage of clergymen! It is the revealed truth of God that is conspicuous by its absence from the theology, the preaching, and, not least, the lives of clergy and people alike."[2]

Today, we have what Eli and his sons did not have: the completed revelation of God's Word in the Bible. With the coming of Jesus Christ, God's revelation is complete, and the church possesses God's final written Word as we await the return of our Lord. Yet the famine of the Word of God can be just as severe for us who possess the Bible as for those who do not, because of our lack of interest. Revival and reformation in the church, and in our individual lives, can come only in the same manner as it came to the Israel of Samuel's day: by the restoring of the divine Word in the hearts and minds of God's people.

An example of this truth is seen in the experience of a Chinese man named Xiao-Hu Huang, who was living in Germany with his wife, Kirstin. Xiao was a Buddhist and his wife an unbeliever. Wanting a special birthday gift for her husband, Kirstin sought a book written in Chinese, but the only such book she could find was a Chinese translation of the Bible. Displeased by her options, she nonetheless bought the Bible, hoping that her husband would appreciate the gesture. Xiao was not pleased to receive a Bible, but longing for his native tongue, he began reading it anyway. As he did so, he was struck by the truth revealed in the Bible's pages; before long he was

2. Gordon J. Keddie, *Dawn of a Kingdom: The Message of 1 Samuel* (Darlington, UK: Evangelical Press, 1988), 51.

persuaded and began believing God's Word. This, in turn, displeased his wife, since Kirstin was a Westerner who had rejected Christianity. As they came into conflict over the book she had bought him, Kirstin began to read it, too, simply to argue more effectively against her husband. But in the process, she also was persuaded and became a believer in Jesus. Before long, they began studying their Chinese Bible together and grew in their faith. Soon they realized that they needed the fellowship and support of other believers, so they attended a faithful church where God's Word was preached. There they were baptized as followers of Christ and continued to grow as his disciples.[3]

This has been God's way throughout history. It was by his Word that God brought the universe into being (Gen. 1:1–26). It was by his Word that God called Abraham, Moses, and Samuel into his service, and through them that he called and gathered his people. Peter wrote that Christians "have been born again, not of perishable seed but of imperishable, through the living and abiding word of God" (1 Peter 1:23). David rejoiced that God's Word is "perfect, reviving the soul"; "sure, making wise the simple"; "right, rejoicing the heart"; "pure, enlightening the eyes"; and "true, and righteous altogether" (Ps. 19:7–9). This is what we have written for us to read in our Bibles: God's Word, which brings life for salvation into our souls. Realizing this made John Wesley cry out: "O give me that book! At any price give me the Book of God!"[4]

SPEAKING GOD'S WORD

Essential as it is for God's people to hear God's Word, this is not enough. It is also necessary for us to *speak* God's Word. So it was for young Samuel, having received a message from God for Eli.

Receiving God's Word created a problem for Samuel because of the content of the message, which was a confirmation of the judgment that Eli had earlier received from the visiting man of God. "Behold, I am about to do a thing in Israel at which the two ears of everyone who hears it will tingle," God told Samuel (1 Sam. 3:11). What was about to happen would strike fear into God's people:

3. Bill T. Arnold, *1 & 2 Samuel*, NIV Application Commentary (Grand Rapids: Zondervan, 2003), 89–90.
4. Quoted in ibid., 90.

> On that day I will fulfill against Eli all that I have spoken concerning his house, from beginning to end. And I declare to him that I am about to punish his house forever, for the iniquity that he knew, because his sons were blaspheming God, and he did not restrain them. Therefore I swear to the house of Eli that the iniquity of Eli's house shall not be atoned for by sacrifice or offering forever. (3:12–14)

This statement of judgment makes some important points. The first is that God judges sin with the severity it deserves. The sins of Eli's sons were a gross offense to the Lord, and his justice demanded a reckoning. It is noteworthy, however, that God's ire is directed not merely at Eli's sons, but especially against Eli himself. What had Eli done? Literally, nothing. He had not committed the sins of his sons, but he had done nothing to halt them, either: "He knew . . . his sons were blaspheming God, and he did not restrain them" (1 Sam. 3:13). This also tells us that God expects the officers of his church to oversee its affairs and ensure reverent worship that is acceptable to him.

Second, the Lord states that "the iniquity of Eli's house shall not be atoned for by sacrifice or offering forever" (1 Sam. 3:14). The apparent reason for God to forbid forgiveness was that Eli's sons had blasphemed against the very sacrifices that God had ordained for the cleansing of sin. How could they be forgiven then when they had despised God's means of grace? The same is true today for those who deny the atoning work of Christ or despise God's Word, since they are "crucifying once again the Son of God to their own harm and holding him up to contempt" (Heb. 6:6).

Like Samuel, we have been given a message from God that is difficult both to deliver and to receive. Keddie writes: "The gospel message is essentially a very hard message both to preach and to hear, because it is a call to sinners to confess their helplessness to save themselves and turn in repentance and faith to the Lord Jesus Christ for salvation through his substitutionary atonement for sin."[5] God's message to the world includes his condemnation of sin, his threat of severe and eternal judgment, and his call for sinners to repent. Coupled with this hard message is God's mercy for sinners through the blood of his Son. Jesus died to save us from our sin. To be saved, we must therefore confess our sin and also our complete need of the mercy of God through the cross of Christ.

5. Keddie, *Dawn of a Kingdom*, 56–57.

Some Christians misguidedly believe that if they downplay the Bible's denunciation of sin, they are being more humble and winsome and are making it easier for people to embrace Christ as their Savior. To the contrary: to remove the Bible's message of God's wrath on sin is arrogantly to tamper with the message that God has entrusted to us and coldheartedly to withhold from sinners a truth that they must embrace in order to be saved. Withholding the Bible's message of sin and judgment renders meaningless the message of the cross. Paul said that "Jews demand signs and Greeks seek wisdom" (1 Cor. 1:22); that is, the Jews wanted God to approve them for their works-righteousness, and the Greeks wanted to be saved by philosophy. "But," Paul added, "we preach Christ crucified, a stumbling block to Jews and folly to Gentiles, but to those who are called, both Jews and Greeks, Christ the power of God and the wisdom of God" (1:23–24). The gospel desired by both Jews and Greeks was one that omitted God's condemnation of their sins, yet Paul insisted on preaching the gospel of Christ, in which Jesus died to save us from God's wrath.

True ministers of God's Word will possess the same tender heart that made Samuel reluctant to bring bad news to his mentor. The Bible states that "Samuel lay until morning; then he opened the doors of the house of the LORD. And Samuel was afraid to tell the vision to Eli" (1 Sam. 3:15). Samuel did not eagerly or gleefully speak wrath to Eli. But if Samuel was truly to open the doors to God's presence and grace, then he must learn not to withhold God's Word. Eli, knowing how vital it was for Samuel not to withhold God's Word, called the youth and demanded, "What was it that he told you? Do not hide it from me" (3:17). Eli added a warning about holding back the truth of God's Word that everyone should heed: "May God do so to you and more also if you hide anything from me of all that he told you" (3:17). "So Samuel told him everything and hid nothing from him" (3:18). Every servant of Christ should do the same, and should thus be able to echo Paul's words to the elders of Ephesus: "I did not shrink from declaring to you the whole counsel of God" (Acts 20:27).

Eli, an unhappy and unfaithful man, but still a believer, however weak, was submissively resigned to God's will: "He said, 'It is the LORD. Let him do what seems good to him'" (1 Sam. 3:18). Eli is surely a complex figure! For all his faults, he had some virtues, although they seem to have been passive ones. William Blaikie comments: "He could bear much, though he could dare little. He could submit, but he could not fight."[6]

EXPERIENCING GOD'S WORD

Spiritual revival always involves hearing and speaking God's Word. When the Word is heard and spoken, the result is power for growth and godliness and witness to others. So it was for Samuel. A new day had begun in his life and ministry as he began hearing and speaking God's Word to the people. The result was that "Samuel grew, and the LORD was with him" (1 Sam. 3:19). To serve Jesus Christ, hearing and speaking his Word, is to grow continually. The apostle Paul experienced the thrill of never-ending sanctification, writing late in his life, "Not that I have already obtained this or am already perfect, but I press on to make it my own" (Phil. 3:12). Those were not words of cynical resignation, but rather of excitement and eager anticipation. There is growth in the Lord through his Word!

If we study passages describing a Christlike character—such as the Beatitudes in Matthew 5 or the fruit of the Spirit in Galatians 5:22–23—the truth is that not one of us perfectly reflects the biblical ideal. But the exciting news is that as we walk with the Lord, abiding in his Word, we continually grow in spiritual power, purity, peace, and joy.

In addition to his spiritual growth, Samuel found that God authenticated his ministry: "The LORD was with him and let none of his words fall to the ground. And all Israel from Dan to Beersheba knew that Samuel was established as a prophet of the LORD" (1 Sam. 3:19–20). The statement that none of Samuel's words fell to the ground means that God caused his prophetic messages to come true. Samuel as a prophet was able to speak truth to the people in a way that was valid and credible. As we grow in the Lord, hearing God's Word from the Bible and faithfully speaking it to others, our speech will also mark us as true servants of the Lord.

Finally, Samuel discovered what great things God could do through him. The chapter concludes by saying: "The LORD appeared again at Shiloh, for the LORD revealed himself to Samuel at Shiloh by the word of the LORD. And the word of Samuel came to all Israel" (1 Sam. 3:21–4:1). Through

---

6. William G. Blaikie, *Expository Lectures on the Book of First Samuel* (1887; repr., Birmingham, AL: Solid Ground, 2005), 57.

Samuel, God's Word was restored to the entire nation. The reality is that every believer who is devoted to knowing and speaking God's Word will experience God at work through him or her in remarkable and far-reaching ways. Few of us will be granted so far-reaching a ministry as Samuel, but if we will bring God's Word into whatever sphere he has placed us, we will be astonished at the transforming results.

Jesus stated this principle when he described what happens when the seed of God's Word takes root in the good soil of a heart prepared by the Holy Spirit. The harvest is different in each case, but always extraordinary: "This is the one who hears the word and understands it. He indeed bears fruit and yields, in one case a hundredfold, in another sixty, and in another thirty" (Matt. 13:23). "So shall my word be that goes out from my mouth," God said; "it shall not return to me empty, but it shall accomplish that which I purpose, and shall succeed in the thing for which I sent it" (Isa. 55:11). Given these truths, Christians will find that the Word of God in the hand of God is sufficient to do the work of God in the church and in the world.

Responding to God's Word

Some of us may be shamed by Samuel's response when God called him. Bill Arnold rightly comments that "1 Samuel 3 is meant to arouse us out of our lethargy, as it aroused Samuel from his early-morning sleep."[7] When God calls us, let us answer in the same way that Samuel spoke to Eli and to God: "Here I am, for you called me" (1 Sam. 3:5). There are callings that every Christian shares: the calling to believe in Christ, to grow in godliness, to study God's Word, and to speak God's Word to the world. But God has particular callings for different individuals: to take an interest in a certain person's salvation, to meet a ministry need in the church, to leave one's home to serve on the mission field, to enter the ordained ministry, to serve as an elder or deacon, to take up the burden of schooling one's children, and to make financial sacrifices for the support of a kingdom cause, to name a few. Such callings constitute decisive moments in our lives, and our fruitfulness in life is largely determined by our willingness to repeat Samuel's answer: "Here I am, for you called me."

7. Arnold, *1 & 2 Samuel*, 85–86.

When I was first seeking to answer God's call to preach the gospel, I was occasionally invited to speak at a Sunday gathering at the United States Military Academy, where I was teaching. Almost every time I came, the leaders were frantically seeking for someone who could play the piano. Around that time I learned that one of the regular attendees was an accomplished pianist, so I asked him, "Why do you never volunteer to play piano, when there is always such a need?" I will never forget his reply: "If I start volunteering to serve God, I am going to end up in Africa. I don't want to go to Africa, so I am not volunteering for anything!" There could hardly be a surer way to keep yourself from growing and experiencing the power of God's grace than to follow this man's example! For one thing, if God wants you to go to Africa, then Africa is where God's blessing lies for you. More importantly, God is so worthy of our obedient faith, humble submission, and awe-filled worship that we will never go wrong by going where he leads us and serving as he has called.

Are you willing to echo young Samuel's words, saying to God, "Here I am, Lord, for you called me. Speak; your servant is listening"? There is every reason why you should. Paul reminds us that God has proved his goodwill toward us by sending his own Son to die for our sins on the cross. He reasons, "He who did not spare his own Son but gave him up for us all, how will he not also with him graciously give us all things?" (Rom. 8:32). Jesus said, "Seek first the kingdom of God and his righteousness, and all [other] things will be added to you" (Matt. 6:33). He added, "Truly, I say to you, there is no one who has left house or brothers or sisters or mother or father or children or lands, for my sake and for the gospel, who will not receive a hundredfold now in this time, houses and brothers and sisters and mothers and children and lands, with persecutions, and in the age to come eternal life" (Mark 10:29–30). In light of these texts, answering Jesus' call to serve is the best investment that any believer can make.

These are very good reasons for us to answer God when he calls. But the best reason is the one that caused young Samuel to come swiftly into aged Eli's bedchamber when he thought the high priest was calling: he loved him and delighted to serve him. The apostle John wrote, "In this is love, not that we have loved God but that he loved us and sent his Son to be the propitiation for our sins" (1 John 4:10). The more clearly we realize the greatness of God's love and the preciousness of the gift of his Son to die for our sins, the more fervently we will love him and the more grateful we will be that he spoke his Word to our heart. And when he calls, we will delight to reply, "Here I am, Lord, for you called me."

7

POWER RELIGION

1 Samuel 4:1—11

The elders of Israel said, "Why has the LORD defeated us today before the Philistines? Let us bring the ark of the covenant of the LORD here from Shiloh, that it may come among us and save us from the power of our enemies." (1 Sam. 4:3)

For many Christians, the ark of the covenant holds immense fascination. The ark was a golden box of acacia wood in which the stone tablets of the Ten Commandments were kept, and that represented the presence of God within the Holy of Holies inside Israel's temple. The quest to find the lost ark has become a cottage industry, especially among Christians absorbed with premillennial end-times schemes, spawning scores of books and videos. The ark of the covenant fascinates even nonbelievers, who consider it a talisman for accessing divine or magical power. For instance, it was the belief of Marcus Brody, sidekick to Indiana Jones in the fictional movie *Raiders of the Lost Ark*, that "an army which carries the ark before it is invincible."

First Samuel 4 begins a lengthy sequence known to scholars as "The Ark Narrative," spanning 1 Samuel 4:1–7:2. Having focused so far on the birth and calling of Samuel to be Israel's prophet and judge, the story now goes on to replace him by these three chapters that tell of the fate of God's holy ark. In chapter 4, the ark is presented as a focal point for "power religion"—that is, an idolatrous attempt to harness God's power for our own purposes on earth.

A QUESTION NEEDING AN ANSWER

Having focused on the affairs of the small family of Elkanah and Hannah, and then on the concerns of young Samuel, we now have our vision broadened to consider the affairs of Israel. These affairs centered on the menacing threat of the neighboring Philistines, a seafaring people who came from the Aegean isles. Descending on the coast of Palestine in the early twelfth century B.C., the Philistines built five city-states between the sea and the hill country of Judah. In the Bible, the Philistines first appear during the judgeship of Deborah (Judg. 3:31). By the time of Samson, they had spread their influence inland and subjugated much of Israel. Samson waged bitter war against the Philistines until his betrayal and capture. In the hour of his death, Samson regained his supernatural strength in order to pull down the pillars of the Philistine temple. Dealing a major setback to the enemy, Samson killed himself along with all the Philistine lords and three thousand other people.

All this was recent history to the Israel of Samuel's time. Now the Philistines had regrouped and begun making a push into the hill country of Ephraim, not far from Shiloh and the tabernacle. Chapter 4 begins, "Now Israel went out to battle against the Philistines. They encamped at Ebenezer, and the Philistines encamped at Aphek" (1 Sam. 4:1). Aphek was an Ephraimite town near the Philistine-Israelite border. To counter this threat, Israel's army gathered at nearby Ebenezer. The account of the first battle at Ebenezer is as brief as the battle was depressing: "The Philistines drew up in line against Israel, and when the battle spread, Israel was defeated by the Philistines, who killed about four thousand men on the field of battle" (4:2).

In modern parlance, the word *Philistine* refers to a person who is lacking in or hostile to culture. But the ancient Philistines were as advanced as, if not more advanced than, any of the nearby peoples—technologically, militarily, and administratively. Thus, they were a constant nuisance and danger to Israel. Gordon Keddie writes: "Their restless expansionism therefore afforded a perennial challenge to the territorial integrity and national sovereignty of God's covenant people. . . . They were . . . the 'scourge of God', raised up to chastise the backslidings of the Lord's people." Therefore, "Israel's relationship with the Philistines was a barometer of their relationship with God. When they experienced defeat, they saw it as the withdrawal of divine favour."[1]

An example of divine disfavor is provided by the first defeat at Ebenezer: "When the troops came to the camp, the elders of Israel said, 'Why has the LORD defeated us today before the Philistines?'" (1 Sam. 4:3). The elders realized that God is sovereign over all affairs, and they also understood that under the covenant Israel's success or failure in battle was a direct sign of God's favor or disfavor. After all, when Joshua led the tribes into Canaan, it was God who gave them victory at Jericho. But when Achan sinned, it was also God who made the same army fail at Ai (Josh. 7). Experiencing this new failure, with four thousand lost in a single battle,[2] the elders turned their minds to God: "Why has the LORD defeated us?"

This defeat at Ebenezer fits in with the pattern displayed all through the book of Judges. Throughout this dark period of Israel's history, there was a predictable cycle of events. First Israel would forget the Lord and sin against his law. As a result, the Lord would give the Israelites over into the hands of their enemies. During this period of foreign oppression, the people would sooner or later repent and turn back to the Lord. He would then send the next leader in the line of judges to bring victory and save them from their enemies. Before long, the people would turn again from the Lord, engaging in even worse idolatry than before, prompting yet another judgment from God in the form of conquest and subjugation. This downward-spiraling pattern continued under the wanton leadership of Eli and his sons.

Some scholars argue that God's approach to justice in the Old Testament, known as *retributive justice*, is no longer valid in the New Testament. But

1. Gordon J. Keddie, *Dawn of a Kingdom: The Message of 1 Samuel* (Darlington, UK: Evangelical Press, 1988), 61–62.
2. Scholars debate whether this should be taken as four "thousand" or four "companies," since the word for *thousand* is also used for the Israelite equivalent of modern military small units. Kyle McCarter points out that in Numbers 1 such units contain from five to fourteen men. Using this calculation, he suggests a number of twenty to sixty-five casualties for Israel's initial defeat at Ebenezer, a number more likely given the historical setting. See P. Kyle McCarter Jr., *1 Samuel*, Anchor Bible, vol. 8 (New York: Doubleday, 1980), 105, 107.

the actual evidence of the New Testament makes it clear that things have not changed so much as one might think. When Peter decreed death to Ananias and Sapphira, God's justice took retribution on the sin of lying to the Holy Spirit. Most significant is the New Testament affirmation regarding the final judgment after the return of Christ, in which unbelievers are "judged by what was written in the books, according to what they had done" (Rev. 20:12), a clear statement of retributive justice. Given God's warnings against flagrant sin in all the Bible, the elders of Israel were right to seek an answer for the cause of God's offense. Keddie's comments regarding God's rebuke to Israel are worth considering regarding the church today: "He called them to face the consequences of their sin so that they might change their ways and enjoy the escalation of divine blessing into a future bright with the redeeming love of their Father-God."[3]

The Wrong Answer: Power Religion

Unfortunately, Israel's elders did not ponder this question long enough. Nor did they go to ask Samuel, the prophet through whom God was now speaking. Instead, they quickly turned to an action of their own devising that they thought would remedy the situation. "Let us bring the ark of the covenant of the Lord here from Shiloh," they decided, "that it may come among us and save us from the power of our enemies" (1 Sam. 4:3). Quickly agreeing, "the people sent to Shiloh and brought from there the ark of the covenant of the Lord of hosts" (4:4).

There are two main ways to look at the Israelites' action, one of which is more charitable and the other less so, though both are condemning. More charitably, it is assumed by some commentators that Israel saw the ark as a symbol of God's covenant and therefore a pledge of his commitment to their success. John Woodhouse takes this view, arguing that "the elders were probably not so crass as to think of the ark in simple magical terms, as if its presence would itself bring God's power to their side."[4] The other view asserts that this is precisely what the Israelites had in mind. In verse 4, the narrator describes God as "the Lord of hosts, who is enthroned on the cherubim." The cherubim were the two golden images of angels atop the

3. Keddie, *Dawn of a Kingdom*, 63.
4. John Woodhouse, *1 Samuel: Looking for a Leader* (Wheaton, IL: Crossway, 2008), 90.

lid of the ark. This description strengthens the idea of the elders' belief that God's presence and power were physically tied to the ark.

Remember that Israel's history was replete with dramatic occasions when the presence of the ark of the covenant brought divine power for victory. The ark was carried before the marching tribes of Israel in the exodus. Numbers 10:35 tells us that "whenever the ark set out, Moses said, 'Arise, O LORD, and let your enemies be scattered, and let those who hate you flee before you.'" When Israel crossed the Jordan into Canaan, the ark went before the people as a sign of God's promised victory (Josh. 3:10–11); in the great victory over mighty Jericho, the priests went before the ark, blowing trumpets, and the walls of Jericho fell down (6:4–20). It would be all too easy for the people to believe that it was the ark that brought miraculous power rather than God himself—his presence merely symbolized by the ark—who won Israel's victories. Especially in a time when the people did not know the Lord (1 Sam. 3:7), it is practically inevitable that the people should think of the ark as a divine power box. So the elders summoned to the rear for their ace in the hole, the ark that put (they thought) the power of God at their disposal.

The exercise of religion in an attempt to manipulate or control God is common both in the Bible and in our contemporary world. Indeed, if ever there was a time when the kind of "power religion" practiced by the elders of Israel has been especially in vogue, that time must be now. According to the Bible, the purpose of our faith is to bring us to a saving knowledge of God (John 17:3), that we might grow in holiness (Eph. 4:20–24) and that we might serve the Lord while we make our pilgrim journey to heaven (1 Peter 2:9). Knowing God, growing in holiness, and serving the Lord and his gospel are the Bible's priorities for the Christian life. But what a far cry this view is from the motivation behind much popular Christianity and its presentation to the world.

An example is a businessman who sees little value in Christianity until he is told that God has the power to keep his company afloat. A sick person is told to seek God because he has power to heal. A student facing exams turns to God in prayer because she knows that God has the power to enable her to score high marks. A politician takes a sudden interest in God when a sufficient amount of pressure is applied by Christian constituents. Apart from what God can do to meet our immediate needs, such people have little genuine interest in faith or religion. In all these cases, their actions consist of "human attempts to harness God's power."[5] Dale Ralph Davis refers to this approach to Christianity as "rabbit-foot theology": "Our concern is not to seek God but to control him, not to submit to God but to use him. So we prefer religious magic to spiritual holiness; we are interested in success, not repentance."[6]

A sure sign of those who practice power religion, or "rabbit-foot theology," is an emphasis on religious and spiritual techniques. This is how the elders of Israel thought: they had a technology that would bring God's power. They did not turn their hearts to God. They did not ask God why he had permitted their earlier defeat. They did not humble themselves and seek first God's kingdom and his righteousness, only then looking after other things (cf. Matt. 6:33). We see a similar attitude in Christians and churches that engage in monthlong prayer vigils, but never consult the Bible for how God would have them mend their ways.

An illustration of power religion is seen in the contrast between the leaders of the First Great Awakening in America (mid-eighteenth century) and the Second Great Awakening (early nineteenth century). The First Great Awakening arrived as an unexpected and mighty work of God as his Spirit attended the simple and faithful preaching of his Word. There was no particular technique or method to the First Great Awakening, and its leaders devoted themselves to personal godliness, to prayer for God's will, and to fervent if plain Bible preaching. This true revival was a sovereign outpouring of God's Spirit that fundamentally changed the character of America. But in the Second Great Awakening the emphasis shifted to the machinery of revivalism that has dominated religious culture ever since: altar calls, numbers-driven fund-raising, and frequently bizarre and manipulative evangelistic tactics. Christians today have followed the Israelite elders' lead in seeking devices for seizing God's power instead of turning to God himself and humbling ourselves in seeking his grace.

The entry of the ark of the covenant into the army camp at Ebenezer presents a telling scene: "And the two sons of Eli, Hophni and Phinehas, were there with the ark of the covenant of God" (1 Sam. 4:4). The ark was the sign of God's presence, and there as his attendants were the two men

5. Ibid., 85.
6. Dale Ralph Davis, *1 Samuel: Looking on the Heart* (Fearn, Ross-shire, UK: Christian Focus, 2000), 43.

most offensive to God: the wicked sons of Eli. Inside the ark were the tablets of God's law, which Hophni and Phinehas had brazenly broken even while serving as Israel's priests. This separation of God's holy requirements from God's blessings is characteristic of power religion; the whole point is to get God to serve us rather than for us to serve him. If the Israelites' defeat in battle had not reminded them of their need to be right with God, the presence of the ark of the covenant should surely have done so. Seeing the ark, Israel's hosts should have remembered God's law, considered their own sin, and cast themselves upon God's mercy symbolized through the mercy seat atop the ark, where the sacrificial lamb's blood—looking forward to the cross of Jesus Christ—would be sprinkled to cover Israel's sin before God's sight. Instead, Israel was so presumptuous of God's favor that the people saw no danger in having the two lawbreaking priests as escorts for God's holy ark.

Such a cavalier assumption of God's blessing is especially characteristic of nations during time of war. It is a little-known fact that the German army belt buckles issued by Adolf Hitler's Nazi regime carried the inscription *Gott mit uns*, meaning "God is with us." In the American Civil War, both sides could be commended and condemned for their appeal to God's help. Southerners cried out for God's help while they closed their own ears to the cries of their Negro slaves. Northerners prided themselves on being servants of God's will as they pillaged and burned their way through Georgia and South Carolina. The point is that if we are to seek God's mighty help in battle, we should seriously seek to honor God by heeding the rebukes, corrections, and instructions found in the Bible.

THE FAILURE OF POWER RELIGION

It is unlikely that the elders of Israel gave much thought to what God might be thinking of their actions. They had the divine rabbit's foot, and "as soon as the ark of the covenant of the LORD came into the camp, all Israel gave a mighty shout, so that the earth resounded" (1 Sam. 4:5).

The passage concludes with the results of Israel's resort to power religion without repentance before God. The first result was the false confidence of the Israelite army. Their "mighty shout," which echoed so loudly as to be heard in the Philistine camp two miles away, is reminiscent of earlier holy wars in which Israel had triumphed (cf. Josh. 6:5; Judg. 7:20). They believed that God was with them as before, when in fact God had not ordained the battle they were fighting, had not promised his presence, and would not act to protect them from their foes.

Second, the arrival of the ark had effects not only on the Israelites, inciting them to false confidence, but also in the Philistine camp:

> And when the Philistines heard the noise of the shouting, they said, "What does this great shouting in the camp of the Hebrews mean?" And when they learned that the ark of the LORD had come to the camp, the Philistines were afraid, for they said, "A god has come into the camp." And they said, "Woe to us! For nothing like this has happened before. Woe to us! Who can deliver us from the power of these mighty gods? These are the gods who struck the Egyptians with every sort of plague in the wilderness. Take courage, and be men, O Philistines, lest you become slaves to the Hebrews as they have been to you; be men and fight." (1 Sam. 4:6–9)

The Philistines had heard of the ark from the mighty power God exerted when Moses led the Israelites from Egypt. The fear of the ark came upon them, just as the Israelites intended. It was not a fear that came from God, however, but rather the fear of a mighty tactical innovation, according to their superstitious thinking. Rather than flee in terror, they resolved instead to put forth their best possible effort. The Israelites' exercise in power religion had merely incited a concentration of the Philistines' valor: "Take courage, and be men, O Philistines . . . ; be men and fight" (1 Sam. 4:9).

This episode shows that when it comes to manipulating or exciting the carnal passions of men, the world is as adept as Christians, and even more able to muster worldly power. Unless our power in cultural and spiritual warfare is truly the might of God, directed by his Word, motivated by his grace, and animated by his Spirit, then the world's power is easily able to overcome our religious pretensions.

The third result was the defeat of Israel in battle, with calamitous effects: "So the Philistines fought, and Israel was defeated, and they fled, every man to his home. And there was a very great slaughter, for there fell of Israel thirty thousand foot soldiers" (1 Sam. 4:10).[7] Alarmed by the presence of the ark,

---

7. Taking the approach suggested by McCarter in treating verse 2, this number would be revised to between 150 and 420. McCarter, *1 Samuel*, 107.

the Philistines attacked, swept the Israelite army away, and captured the ark of the covenant. But in Israel's defeat, God's purpose was established in accordance with his prophecy to Samuel: "The ark of God was captured, and the two sons of Eli, Hophni and Phinehas, died" (4:11). So ended the rule of the house of Eli. Also ended was the prominence of Shiloh as the center of God's covenant religion; in hot pursuit, the Philistines overran and destroyed Israel's religious capital. Psalm 78 laments how God "forsook his dwelling at Shiloh, the tent where he dwelt among mankind, and delivered his power to captivity, his glory to the hand of the foe. He gave his people over to the sword and vented his wrath on his heritage" (Ps. 78:60–62).

Thus ended the rule of the priests at Shiloh, just as God planned for the sake of the kingship that he would establish through Samuel. For whatever Israel and the Philistines might think, the capture of the ark and the defeat of Israel's army did not signify the overthrow of God. The elders thought that by bringing the ark they had ensured that God would defend his honor; little did they realize that God intended to defend his honor by sending the Philistines to bring judgment on his idolatrous people!

The Alternative to Power Religion

What is the alternative to power religion? It is the religion of the Bible, which Martin Luther summarized as the "theology of the cross." Biblical religion is not a series of techniques for manipulating God's goodwill or harnessing God's power. Rather, it is a humble appeal for God's mercy and grace, which he has offered through the priestly ministry of his Son, Jesus Christ. Indeed, it was because of the failure of Israel's priests, such as Hophni and Phinehas, that God sent his own Son to save us from sin and restore us to his blessing.

The ark of the covenant presented a picture of Christ in his perfect work—fulfilling God's law for us and shedding his atoning blood—so that God's presence and favor are with us through our union with Christ in faith. This is why the modern-day quests to find the ark are misguided: the ark has been fulfilled in the coming of Christ. John the Baptist announced this truth when he said of Jesus: "Behold, the Lamb of God, who takes away the sin of the world!" (John 1:29). True religion is that which comes to God humbly and confesses our sin, trusting in the Lamb of God's precious blood, shed by Christ for sin on the cross. True religion then seeks to glorify God in our lives as we do his will and not our own.

Doubtless you want God's power to help you with your struggles and trials, and in its proper place this desire is good and God-honoring. But have you realized that you must first deal with God himself? You must come before him on his terms, facing the demand for perfect righteousness that his holiness requires. This is the realization that the arrival of the ark should have inspired, for the ark was designed to house God's holy law and also to provide the means of cleansing through the shed blood of the lamb. Realizing this, the Israelite army might then have cried out not with loud shouts of carnal enthusiasm but with laments for their sins and cries to God for mercy—a sound far more terrifying to the world and to demons than the cheers that rang from Israel's camp. With Christ in our midst through faith in his cross, we truly can prevail in the holy war against Satan and sin, knowing with Paul that nothing in heaven or on earth "will be able to separate us from the love of God in Christ Jesus our Lord" (Rom. 8:39).

Israel's elders revealed their attitude in the use of a single telling word. They called for the ark, trusting "that *it* may come among us and save us" (1 Sam. 4:3). They were trusting *it* to save them—their box, their God-machine—rather than *him*, the living God. Is there an *it* that you are trusting in the place of God—some technique, some routine, some ritual, some spiritual approach of your own that in truth only keeps you from facing God? For many people today, emotionally charged music is considered essential to their spiritual life. Others seek to meet their spiritual needs primarily through the social life of the church. These are just examples of putting things—even good things—in the place of God. There is no *it*, no *thing*, by which we are saved—not even good things such as our baptism, our church membership, and our knowledge of the Bible and theology. We are never saved by an *it* or a *thing*, but only by *him*: the sovereign God of justice and mercy, who requires us to repent and be changed, to believe and seek his grace.

Are you wrestling with some struggle, some failure, some proof that you need divine power for your salvation? Turn to God for mercy and grace in Jesus Christ. "Let the wicked forsake his way, and the unrighteous man his thoughts," God says; "let him return to the Lord, that he may have compassion on him, and to our God, for he will abundantly pardon" (Isa. 55:7).

8

Ichabod!

1 Samuel 4:12–22

She named the child Ichabod, saying, "The glory has departed from Israel!" because the ark of God had been captured and because of her father-in-law and her husband. (1 Sam. 4:21)

The prophet Isaiah exclaimed, "How beautiful upon the mountains are the feet of him who brings good news" (Isa. 52:7). Perhaps the most famous example is that of Philippides, who sped the 26.2 miles from Marathon to Athens with news of the Greek victory over the Persians (490 B.C.). Arriving in Athens, Philippides cried out, "*Nenike'kamen!*" (which means "we have won!"), and then immediately fell over dead. Athletes today remember his feat by running races of the same length, known as the *marathon*.

No doubt Eli, Israel's high priest, would have rejoiced for similar good news as he waited in Shiloh for a report from the battle with the Philistines. It is said that anxious watchers could guess the news simply by watching the posture of an approaching messenger, in which case Eli and his fellow Israelites would likely have been uneasy. First Samuel 4:12 tells us, "A man of Benjamin ran from the battle line and came to Shiloh the same day, with his clothes torn and with dirt on his head." To race twenty miles over rough terrain was a remarkable athletic feat, though perhaps not as epic as that of Philippides. Yet however great his strength and valor, the Benjaminite's arrival would never be remembered with joy, since his very appearance bore testimony of bad news.

The End of a Dark Era

As Eli waited, the high priest "was sitting on his seat by the road watching, for his heart trembled for the ark of God" (1 Sam. 4:13). This is a telling remark: Eli seems always to be sitting down and waiting when he should be standing up and acting. In this instance, we might expect Eli at least to be waiting optimistically, sure of good news. After all, the ark of the covenant had gone into battle with Israel. When the ark arrived in the camp, Israel's soldiers "gave a mighty shout" (4:5), and when the Philistines learned that the ark had appeared, they "were afraid" (4:7). So what did Eli know that the army and the Philistines did not know? Why was he trembling with fear as he waited for news?

There are two answers to this question. The first is that Eli had received a prophecy from an unnamed "man of God" (1 Sam. 2:27). Because Eli had allowed his sons to sin in the tabernacle, he was told that "all the descendants of your house shall die by the sword of men. And this that shall come upon your two sons, Hophni and Phinehas, shall be the sign to you: both of them shall die on the same day" (2:33–34). This prophecy was later confirmed in God's first message through young Samuel: "I am about to punish his house forever, for the iniquity that he knew, because his sons were blaspheming God, and he did not restrain them" (3:13).

With these prophecies ringing in his ears, we understand why Eli trembled on the day that his two sons had taken the ark into battle. Could this be the day when God's judgment would fall? The hearts of sinful men are always uneasy in times of danger because their consciences testify to their guilt before God. John Calvin sagely commented, "He who is the boldest despiser of God is of all men the most startled at the rustle of a falling leaf."[1] Because of God's threatened judgment on all sin, only those whose sins have been cleansed by the blood of Christ can face the storms of life with peace in their hearts.

1. John Calvin, *Institutes of the Christian Religion*, trans. Ford Lewis Battles (Philadelphia: Westminster, 1960), 1.3.2.

There is a second reason why Eli trembled with anxiety. He was surely aware that the ark was to go forth only at God's command (Deut. 12:5, 11). In all of Israel's great victories, God sent his people into battle, promising his mighty help: the people did not rush into battle on their own, commanding God to bring his power. Even godly men and women will lose their peace when they act in ways contrary to God's Word. The only safe way for us to face the troubles of life is, first, to be justified with God through faith in Christ, and second, to act in obedience to God's Word.

The messenger arrived, racing past Eli: "When the man came into the city and told the news, all the city cried out. When Eli heard the sound of the outcry, he said, 'What is this uproar?' Then the man hurried and came and told Eli" (1 Sam. 4:13–14). "I am he who has come from the battle," he reported; "I fled from the battle today." Eli replied, "How did it go, my son?" The messenger reported his news, which grew worse with every new item: "Israel has fled before the Philistines, and there has also been a great defeat among the people. Your two sons also, Hophni and Phinehas, are dead" (4:16–17). This was terrible but not unexpected news: the Philistines had won, a great number of Israelites had been slain, and among them were both his sons. But Eli was not prepared for the last piece of news: "and the ark of God has been captured" (4:17).

The news of the lost ark stunned the high priest. Eli had been resolved to accept his own fall from office and even the death of his sons—they deserved it, after all, and God had foretold it (1 Sam. 2:31–34)—but he never imagined how God's judgment on his sins could imperil the whole nation. The shock of the news literally killed him: "As soon as he mentioned the ark of God, Eli fell over backward from his seat by the side of the gate, and his neck was broken and he died" (4:18). Thus ended Eli's life and ministry. It was the end, in fact, of a dark era going back through the entire period of the judges. This era had begun with the children of Israel forgetting the Lord and pursuing other gods (Judg. 2:10–12). It ended with the forfeiture of God's very presence, his glory having departed from the people with the lost ark of the covenant. It was, says one commentator, "a point in Israelite history lower than any since the captivity in Egypt."[2]

2. Hans Wilhelm Hertzberg, quoted in Bill T. Arnold, *1 & 2 Samuel*, NIV Application Commentary (Grand Rapids: Zondervan, 2003), 108.

The commentary of this passage regarding Eli is depressing. We are told that his heart was uneasy, that his eyes were blind, that he was old and obese (probably having benefited from his sons' theft of dedicated meats), and that he died by breaking his neck, the very judgment that God would inflict in the next chapter on the Philistine god Dagon. This is the final testament to a man who "had judged Israel forty years" (1 Sam. 4:18); his legacy was one of utter failure and despair.

How did this happen? One answer is that we do not entirely know. The Bible records neither Eli's early years as high priest and judge nor any of his accomplishments. We do not know whether he started poorly or well, or how he went astray. Perhaps it resulted from his grief over his wife, who died before the events recorded in 1 Samuel took place. Perhaps Eli was like many other men whose devotion to work causes them to neglect the raising of their children, which in Eli's case led to his utter ruin. Ultimately, we do not know.

Another answer is that Eli's disgrace and fall would have happened the way it always does: one step, one decision, one compromise at a time. Paul expressed this idea as a proverb: "Do not be deceived: God is not mocked, for whatever one sows, that will he also reap. For the one who sows to his own flesh will from the flesh reap corruption, but the one who sows to the Spirit will from the Spirit reap eternal life" (Gal. 6:7–8). First we sow; then we reap. It is said that we sow a thought and reap an action; sow an action and reap a habit; sow a habit and reap a lifestyle; sow a lifestyle and reap a character; sow a character and reap a destiny.

If this accurately explains the fall of Eli and his house, then the key to avoiding his fate is to realize that our actions and habits, our character and destiny, ultimately flow from our thoughts and beliefs. The way to be a godly people is to renew our minds with God's Word. This is the counsel given by the apostle Paul as the key to the Christian life: "Do not be conformed to this world, but be transformed by the renewal of your mind, that by testing you may discern what is the will of God, what is good and acceptable and perfect" (Rom. 12:2). What kind of positive difference would it have made, we wonder, if Eli had been more devoted to studying God's Word and teaching it to his sons? We do not know, except that the difference could only have been very great.

THE DARK BEGINNING OF A NEW ERA

The passage concludes with a moving and disturbing anecdote from Eli's family. The wife of his son Phinehas was near to giving birth. "When she heard the news that the ark of God was captured, and that her father-in-law and her husband were dead, she bowed and gave birth, for her pains came upon her" (1 Sam. 4:19). This sudden delivery proved fatal to her, and, realizing what was happening, some women tried to console her: "Do not be afraid, for you have borne a son" (4:20). The bearing of a son was the high point of any Israelite woman's life, but she was not consoled: "She did not answer or pay attention. And she named the child Ichabod, saying, 'The glory has departed from Israel!' because the ark of God had been captured and because of her father-in-law and her husband. And she said, 'The glory has departed from Israel, for the ark of God has been captured'" (1 Sam. 4:20–22).

This passage, like the chapter as a whole, is laden with symbolism and irony. Phinehas's wife is pregnant with a son, normally a cause for great rejoicing and a sign that a new era is beginning. But she is beset with the pains of birth, a detail seldom cited in biblical birth narratives, and a reminder here of God's curse on sin (Gen. 3:16). Because of sin, a scene of joy is turned to grief.

Here we see one more result of the sins of Eli and his sons: this evidently godly woman dies in sudden distress, leaving Eli's grandson an orphan, without mother or father, grandfather or grandmother, or even his uncle. Even had the woman lived, hers would still be a scene of woe, for a mother without a family to protect and provide for her was in dire straits. Yet far more significant, she saw, was the loss of God's holy ark. Thus, with her dying breath she names her newborn son *Ichabod*. The name means either "no glory" or "where is the glory?" The child is thus an image of the fate of Israel—orphaned amid a dark and dangerous world, without the benefits of God's covenant care—so his mother grants him a fitting, if terrible, name: "She named the child Ichabod, saying, 'The glory has departed from Israel!'" (1 Sam. 4:21).

For Phinehas's widow, the loss of the ark raised disturbing thoughts. She may have reasoned that Israel's link with their God had been lost, or even that the Philistines now controlled the power of God. The ark was the manifestation—the "glory"—of God's presence. Her statement that "the glory has departed from Israel" indicates that she realized that God had removed his presence and blessing from Israel; the capture of the ark was the symbol, not the cause, of God's self-imposed exile from his people. None of the other losses—the loss of a battle, soldiers, her husband and father-in-law, even her own life—compared with this loss: "the glory has departed from Israel" (1 Sam. 4:22).

Christians sometimes respond to tragic events with conclusions similar to that of Phinehas's widow. God's glory seems to have evaporated, God seems less powerful than they had thought, or his presence seems less accessible than they had hoped. The question for them, when sorrows draw near, is whether the name *Ichabod* applies to them.

The apostle Paul addresses Christians who feel that God's presence has abandoned them in times of trouble. Citing Moses, he says, "Do not say in your heart, 'Who will ascend into heaven?' (that is, to bring Christ down) or 'Who will descend into the abyss?' (that is, to bring Christ up from the dead)" (Rom. 10:6–7). His meaning is that our confidence in the Lord's gracious presence does not require some manifestation from heaven or some reversal from the realm of death. Instead, Paul reasons, " 'The word is near you, in your mouth and in your heart' (that is, the word of faith that we proclaim)" (Rom. 10:8, quoting Deut. 30:14). How is God present amid what seems to us to be the greatest darkness? He is present by his Word. God is as near to us as the Word that we speak by our mouths and believe in our hearts.

In an important sense, Phinehas's widow was right, for the ark was gone and God's chastisement was falling heavy on the people. But in a greater sense, the glory of God was not truly departed. God had given great promises to Israel that could never be broken: "I will take you to be my people, and I will be your God" (Ex. 6:7). Likewise, the Word of Christ declares to us: "I will never leave you nor forsake you" (Heb. 13:5, quoting Josh. 1:5); it testifies that nothing in all creation "will be able to separate us from the love of God in Christ Jesus our Lord" (Rom. 8:39); Jesus says, "I give them eternal life, and they will never perish, and no one will snatch them out of my hand" (John 10:28). Therefore, just as subsequent events would reveal that God had not finally abandoned his people, we, too, always have access to the glory of God, even in the darkest night, by holding fast to his Word on our lips and in our hearts. For, Paul concludes, "if you confess with your mouth that Jesus is Lord and believe in your heart that God raised him from the dead, you will be saved" (Rom. 10:9). Our challenge during trials, therefore, is to believe the Word that is in our mouths and that God would place within our hearts: if this challenge is met with faith, we will have strength to endure the other challenges associated with our trials.

When the Glory Departs

Still, the loss of the ark to Israel's enemies did signal a time of divine chastisement. The dying woman spoke the truth when she wrote *Ichabod* over the scene that she was leaving. For God was temporarily removing his blessing and protection from the people. Shiloh would soon be destroyed, and the Philistines would once again place Israel under their hated yoke.

The Old Testament shows that when God's people persist in rebellion, walking in ways of wickedness and bowing down to the idols of the world, God will inevitably withdraw his glory—that is, the power and blessing of his presence—from his people. The greatest Old Testament instance of God's glory departing was not the loss of the ark in Eli's time, but rather the removal of God's Holy Spirit before the fall of Jerusalem over four hundred years later. The prophet Ezekiel saw a vision not merely of the ark of the covenant departing the temple, but of the actual presence of God's Spirit rising up and leaving. "The glory of the LORD went out from the threshold of the house, and stood over the cherubim," Ezekiel reported. "And the cherubim lifted up their wings and mounted up from the earth before my eyes as they went out . . . And they stood at the entrance of the east gate of the house of the LORD, and the glory of the God of Israel was over them" (Ezek. 10:18–19). With this, the glory of the Lord departed from Jerusalem, and the word *Ichabod* was written over its doomed walls. Now there was nothing to protect God's people from the Babylonian army, and shortly afterward the city and temple were destroyed and the people who were not slaughtered were sent off in chains.

If we think this withdrawal of God's presence is only an Old Testament phenomenon, then we should remember the seven letters of Jesus to the churches of Asia, in which the exalted Christ threatened to remove the lampstands of wayward churches (Rev. 2–3). Individual believers are likewise warned not to "grieve the Holy Spirit of God" (Eph. 4:30) through ungodly living, suggesting that Christians may experience God's absence as a form of discipline. The Westminster Confession of Faith asserts, "True believers may have the assurance of their salvation divers ways shaken, diminished, and intermitted; as, by negligence in preserving of it; by falling into some special sin, which woundeth the conscience, and grieveth the Spirit" (WCF 18.4). In David's prayer of repentance, he begged God: "Cast me not away from your presence, and take not your Holy Spirit from me" (Ps. 51:11).

What causes God to remove the manifestation of his glory? The example of Eli and his sons shows that God is angered by sacrilege committed by his people in worship, as the wicked priests stole from the offerings brought to God and committed sexual sins at the tabernacle (1 Sam. 2:12–17, 22). Isaiah would later level a similar charge against the worship in Jerusalem: "This people draw near with their mouth and honor me with their lips, while their hearts are far from me" (Isa. 29:13). Rather than allow his own people to despise his holy presence in corrupt worship, God sent the ark into the hands of the Philistines to be despised by pagans instead. So false worship that despises God's holiness is a cause for the removal of God's glory.

At the time of Ezekiel's vision, when God gave Jerusalem over to Babylon's army, Jeremiah cited their idolatry in forsaking God for the false gods of the nations: "You defiled my land and made my heritage an abomination. . . . My people have changed their glory for that which does not profit" (Jer. 2:7, 11). Since Jerusalem had rejected God's glory for the false glory of worldly idols, God removed his glory altogether.

In his letters to the churches in Revelation, Jesus focuses on the issues of false teaching and immorality. The church in Pergamum was accosted for tolerating the heresies of Balaam and the Nicolaitans (Rev. 2:14–15). Thyatira was summoned for tolerating sexual immorality (2:20). Meanwhile, the church in Ephesus was commended for testing and rejecting false apostles (2:2), and those in Thyatira who had not entered into false teaching and sensual sins were praised (2:24–25). If Jesus were to write letters to our churches today, many of them would similarly be exposed for promoting false teaching, and a great deal more for materialism, sensualism, and a lack of zeal for missions.

We are meant to be warned by the naming of Ichabod at Shiloh, just as Jeremiah warned his generation: "Go now to my place that was in Shiloh, where I made my name dwell at first, and see what I did to it because of the evil of my people Israel" (Jer. 7:12). Jeremiah warned that if Jerusalem did not repent, "I will do to the house that is called by my name, and in which you trust, and to the place that I gave to you and to your fathers, as I did to Shiloh" (7:14).

The validity of this warning for us was vividly displayed to me when I ministered in downtown Philadelphia, which is practically filled with Shilohs. All around are cathedrals and preaching palaces built in days of yore, now immaculately maintained by financial endowments but largely empty on Sundays. I was regularly confronted by one Shiloh because I bought gas for my car at the service station that now rests at its location. The wall next door bore a mural of the church that used to be there, upon which at some point God wrote his *Ichabod*, because it is now no more than "a shadow in the city."[3]

Around a hundred years ago, mainline churches concluded that the Bible is not really God's Word and began teaching the heresies of evolution and secular humanism in place of the gospel. As a result, God wrote *Ichabod* across the liberal churches, so that their spiritual power evaporated. Today, we may wonder whether the same thing is happening to the evangelical movement, which once spoke and acted with such power from God. We witness great spiritual vigor elsewhere on the globe, with masses of converts and a holy boldness in withstanding persecution. Meanwhile, in the West, not only is our cultural influence waning, but evangelical Christians are not even persuading their own children to remain in the faith: a 2002 study by the Southern Baptist Convention showed that 88 percent of evangelical children abandon the church after age eighteen.[4] It is hard to account for such a figure without a removal of God's presence because of worldliness, heresy, idolatry, and sin. How urgent is the need of the Christian church in the West to repent of sin, to return to the truths of the Bible, and to regain a burning passion for Christ and his gospel!

FROM ICHABOD TO IMMANUEL

This leaves a final question about God's departed glory. Once the Lord has written *Ichabod* over a nation or church, or even an individual, is there anything we can do to see a return of God's glory and power? The answer

---

3. Philip Graham Ryken, *Jeremiah & Lamentations* (Wheaton, IL: Crossway, 2001), 126.
4. Reported on Baptist Press, www.bpnews.net, June 12, 2002.

is given through the prophet Zechariah: "Return to me, says the LORD of hosts, and I will return to you" (Zech. 1:3). God's purpose in withdrawing himself, causing his glory to depart, is to spur his people to seek his glory once again. This is what subsequent events will reveal in 1 Samuel. Jeremiah wrote in a similar vein to the Jews who had gone to Babylon in captivity, assuring them of God's returning grace if only they would seek him in true faith: "Then you will call upon me and come and pray to me, and I will hear you. You will seek me and find me, when you seek me with all your heart. I will be found by you, declares the LORD, and I will restore your fortunes and gather you from all the nations and all the places where I have driven you, declares the LORD" (Jer. 29:12–14).

The Israelites of Samuel's time would suffer under the Philistines for twenty years, lamenting the glory of God that had departed (cf. 1 Sam. 7:2). If God has withdrawn from you, there is no reason for so much time to pass before you seek him with all your heart. Christians will sometimes find that they lack the power and zeal of former days, and that their faith lacks the peace and joy that it once possessed. God seems distant, they will say, as if the fault lay with him. If this describes your condition, then realize that God wants you to seek him with all your heart. When you seek him, you will find him, and God will restore his glory as of old.

The greatest instance in the Old Testament of God's removing his glory was the fall of Jerusalem in the time of Jeremiah. But a later and greater instance when the dreadful name *Ichabod* might well have been spoken furnishes proof of God's saving grace for those who have fallen away: the death of Jesus Christ, God's own Son and glory, to pay for our sins on the cross. The apostle John explains Jesus' coming in these words: "The Word became flesh and dwelt among us, and we have seen his glory, glory as of the only Son from the Father, full of grace and truth" (John 1:14). If ever the glory of God dwelt among mankind, it was in the life and ministry of Jesus Christ. Yet men despised him because they loved their sins (3:20), and they put God's glory to death on the cross.

If there was ever a time when *Ichabod* may have been named, it was when Jesus died, for then the true glory of God was removed from the earth. All that the ark of the covenant symbolized—God's glory and the only way of salvation through the atoning blood—had departed from this world. This was vividly depicted in the darkness that covered the earth during the three hours that Jesus suffered on the cross (Matt. 27:45). Yet God's resolve to save his people is proved by the fact that even when his Son was rejected and put to death, Jesus was not ultimately taken away, but rose from the grave on the third day in order to bring eternal life to those who would believe in him.

Reflecting on Jesus' atoning death, we should remember Phinehas's widow's cry of "Ichabod!" and do the same. We should lament that God's glory is rightly removed from us because of our sins. But if we look up from our despair in sin and see Jesus as the Savior who died to put away our shame and reproach, and then who rose again, we see a new beginning in his forgiving grace. Our sin cries, "Ichabod!," "the glory is departed," but God's grace replies, "Immanuel," the name given to our Savior, meaning "God with us" in the grace of Jesus Christ. Though we would rightly be abandoned by God, the gospel assures us of forgiveness and acceptance in Christ. As Paul puts it, "For God, who said, 'Let light shine out of darkness,' has shone in our hearts to give the light of the knowledge of the glory of God in the face of Jesus Christ" (2 Cor. 4:6, quoting Gen. 1:3).

There is one more thing. With the gospel message that answers *Ichabod* with *Immanuel*, God sends us as heralds of his victory over sin, with good news of salvation to spread to the world. Since Jesus has come, died for our sins, and risen with new life for salvation, there need be no more downcast messengers like the Benjaminite who brought news of defeat to Shiloh. Instead, it will be said of us as we spread the joyful news of Jesus and his saving blood, "How beautiful upon the mountains are the feet of him who brings good news" (Isa. 52:7).

9

FALL OF THE GODS

1 Samuel 5:1—12

*When they arose early on the next morning, behold, Dagon
had fallen face downward on the ground before the ark of the
LORD, and the head of Dagon and both his hands were lying
cut off on the threshold. (1 Sam. 5:4)*

First Samuel 4 records Israel's defeat at the battle of Ebenezer, in which Eli's sons, Hophni and Phinehas, were slain and the ark of the covenant fell into Philistine hands. First Samuel 5 follows up by telling of the ark's fate among the Philistines. The Israelites feared that their beloved artifact had been lost forever or, even worse, that God's power might now pass to their enemies. But instead of God's falling into their hands, those who possessed God's holy vessel discovered what the writer of Hebrews warns us: "It is a fearful thing to fall into the hands of the living God" (Heb. 10:31).

PHILISTINES TODAY

The apostle Paul informs Christians that the events of the Old Testament "happened to them as an example," and "were written down for our instruction" (1 Cor. 10:11). This shows that the principles taught by this ancient episode are relevant for us today. Like Israel of old, the church in the West is in a state of weakness, having apparently been routed in the battle for our generation. Anyone who doubts this reality need only stroll through a magazine shop or watch an evening of television: our land is dominated by Philistine powers with scarcely a hint of genuine Christian influence. In a 1953 address to an international congress of Reformed Christians, Martyn Lloyd-Jones pointed out the parallels between the situation in 1 Samuel 4–5 and the modern church: "Surely it is nothing but an account of religion in a state of declension. . . . It is God, and God's cause, apparently completely routed and almost, as it were, destroyed, by the great traditional enemy. The enemy is triumphant all along the line, and is rejoicing. That is the picture."[1]

The Philistine enemy takes different forms at different times. At the vanguard of the unbelieving army today are secular philosophy and science. Philosophy has always regarded Christianity as foolishness (cf. 1 Cor. 1:23), but of late the philosophers have gone further and pronounced religion in general and Christianity in particular as dangerous to the public good. Recent best-selling titles include Christopher Hitchens's *God Is Not Great: How Religion Poisons Everything*[2] and Richard Dawkins's *The God Delusion*.[3] These books garner great public attention and shape the thoughts of many people.

If anything, the assault from science is even more intense. It is now taken for granted in secular media and public education that Charles Darwin's theory of evolution, published 150 years ago, not only shook but destroyed the biblical account of the world, thus freeing enlightened minds from the shackles of religion. While passing through London a few years ago, I found it remarkable to see Darwin's picture on England's ten-pound note. In a country that once celebrated the cultural supremacy of such Christians as Isaac Newton and John Milton, England's pride is now vested in this Philistine giant who supposedly slew the Bible. Lloyd-Jones commented that "on the surface we might very well come to the conclusion that the modern

1. D. Martyn Lloyd-Jones, *Old Testament Evangelistic Sermons* (Edinburgh: Banner of Truth, 1995), 60.
2. New York: Twelve, 2007.
3. Boston: Houghton Mifflin, 2006.

Philistines have been as successful as their ancient prototypes. Indeed, our contemporaries believe that the modern Philistine really has demolished the church and the Christian cause. . . . The secularization of the whole of life seems to be almost complete."[4]

In our twenty-first century, things are much worse even than in Lloyd-Jones's time fifty years ago, an era when Christian morality still exerted a strong influence on society. Today, the postmodern Philistine looks even more triumphant than the modernist Philistine in his battle over the church. Secular society has advanced from godless rationalism to godless hedonism. Even the basic building blocks of human society—gender distinctions and the institution of marriage—are under ferocious assault. So thorough is the postmodern Philistine victory that a large portion of the Christian church has virtually given up even trying to influence the culture and frankly admits to adopting worldly Philistine values such as pragmatism, relativism, and sensualism as being necessary to basic survival. In short, our situation is akin to that of Israel under the heel of the Philistines; the twentieth and twenty-first centuries have been for us a massive defeat not unlike the Israelite calamity at Ebenezer.

Yet it is not that the Philistines want to do away with God altogether. The actions described in 1 Samuel 5:1–2 perfectly describe the attitude toward God today: "When the Philistines captured the ark of God, they brought it from Ebenezer to Ashdod. Then the Philistines took the ark of God and brought it into the house of Dagon and set it up beside Dagon." They did not destroy the ark, but instead they put it in their own temple on a shelf near their god.

Similarly, the Philistine world today does not really want to eradicate God, but only to domesticate him. We see this truth in the desire of non-Christian people to be married in a church. Even more, we see it in the use of a Bible and the invocation of God's name when public officials are sworn into office. Not many actually believe in the Bible and its teaching is forbidden in public affairs, but if it can be taken off the shelf to lend a little sanctity to our government, then that is fine. Our courts and legislative sessions open with prayers for God to bless America, so long as God does not try to tell anyone what to do. This is what the Philistines

4. Lloyd-Jones, *Old Testament Evangelistic Sermons*, 61.

intended for the ark: God could remain if he sat behind the Philistine god and stayed quiet.

How Does God Handle the Philistines?

Most of the observations about the Bible in American public life could have been made at the end of 1 Samuel 4, as the surviving widow of Eli's house died with the word *Ichabod*—"the glory has departed"—on her lips. So what does chapter 5 have to say? We might put it this way: whereas chapter 4 shows the weakness of a spiritually corrupt and fallen church against the Philistine powers, chapter 5 asks, "What can God do about the Philistines?" The Philistines are, after all, God's enemies as well as his people's, so what will God do to the Philistines? The answer is provided in dramatic fashion: "when the people of Ashdod rose early the next day, behold, Dagon had fallen face downward on the ground before the ark of the Lord. So they took Dagon and put him back in his place" (1 Sam. 5:3). This is what happens whenever the idols are exalted against God: he humbles the false gods before the eyes of the world.

Lloyd-Jones compared God's humbling of Dagon to the early decades of the twentieth century. The nineteenth century ended with arrogant confidence. Writers spoke of a golden age of humanism: because of his science and knowledge, man was evolving into a self-made and self-glorying paradise. Now that religion had been put on the shelf, education would eradicate war and poverty. But immediately the priests went into the temple to find Dagon fallen on his face. For example, the Moroccan crisis of 1911 threatened to upend Europe's political arrangements and cast its nations into war. But Dagon was put back up and the situation was controlled, so the people moved on. In 1912 Dagon fell on his face again. The *Titanic*, purportedly the ultimate naval achievement, a ship that, according to its designer, "not even God could sink," sank in the cold North Atlantic. People aboard had been enjoying themselves and the band was playing on the deck when news of icebergs surfaced. No one worried until the ship was struck and began to go down. The modern worldview was briefly shaken, but Dagon was put back up. Finally, in 1914, the war that everyone said was impossible began. World War I was terrible and bloody, but when it was over the modernists declared it "the war to end all wars," and Dagon was set back in place.

What was happening? God was humbling the idols of modernity. When the people did not repent, God finally struck the idol a deadly blow. In the time of the Philistines, when Dagon fell, the embarrassed priests simply hauled him back up to his seat of sovereignty. But the next day, "Dagon had fallen face downward on the ground before the ark of the LORD, and the head of Dagon and both his hands were lying cut off on the threshold. Only the trunk of Dagon was left to him" (1 Sam. 5:4). This mirrored a common practice performed on the corpses of slain enemies: their heads and hands would be taken as trophies of their conquest. In effect, Dagon had been conquered and slain by the God of Israel's ark. Verse 5 tells us that years later Philistine priests still remembered the humbling of their god: "This is why the priests of Dagon and all who enter the house of Dagon do not tread on the threshold of Dagon in Ashdod to this day."

In more recent times, modernity was smashed by the coming of Nazism and World War II, then by the Communism of Stalin, Mao, and Pol Pot, and finally by the threat of planetary nuclear suicide. God does not leave the Philistine gods alone: he throws them to the ground. And when idolatrous man has put the idols back in place, God smashes the idols entirely, cutting off their heads and hands.

The great tragedy of our era is that when God destroyed the idols of twentieth-century modernity, the Western nations did not repent and turn to God but moved on to postmodernity. Postmodernity laments the obvious failings of an arrogant humanism, but instead of turning to God in faith, it merely offers a despairing humanism. We have simply stepped over the threshold and adapted new strategies for rebelling against the Lord's sovereignty, replacing one brand of humanism for another. As a result, we can expect that in the years to come God will cast down the idols of postmodernity, in due time smashing them utterly.

At the center of postmodernity is the sexual revolution of the 1960s and '70s. Americans decided to put the Bible on the shelf and write our own rules for sex, marriage, and even gender. As a direct result, the breaking of homes through divorces skyrocketed, as did the spread of pornography and sexual violence. Dagon was obviously fallen, but we put him back up and moved on. Next was the open advocacy of homosexuality and related sexual deviancies. What happened? However we choose to explain it, at the very moment when American culture was granting acceptance to sexual perversions denounced by the Bible as abominations (Lev. 18:22; 20:13), a mysterious virus appeared that spread death primarily through sexually promiscuous behavior. One might think this would spur widespread national repentance. Instead, we have devoted ourselves to health solutions while utterly refusing the moral reforms that would practically wipe out AIDS. Dagon has been set back in place and our society has resumed its moral idolatry. What now? The example of Europe is telling in this respect. There, sexual immorality, coupled with the demise of marriage and a corresponding disinterest in children, has produced a birth rate so low that numerous European ethnicities are in danger of vanishing, as Muslims rapidly move to occupy the vacant space in the European landscape. There is no other adequate explanation for the bloodbath of the twentieth century and the shocking collapse of Western society in the twenty-first century than God's judgment on our false gods and idols. What we have said about the idol of hedonistic sexuality we could also say about the gods of politics and government, of technology, and of military power. When Dagon has fallen, the lessons of the Bible and of history implore us to repent and seek the grace of the true God who makes all the false gods to fall.

GOD'S HEAVY HAND

God not only humbles and slays the idols that are set up against him, but also judges the people who worship and serve them. The first Philistines to feel God's wrath were the people of Ashdod:

> The hand of the LORD was heavy against the people of Ashdod, and he terrified and afflicted them with tumors, both Ashdod and its territory. And when the men of Ashdod saw how things were, they said, "The ark of the God of Israel must not remain with us, for his hand is hard against us and against Dagon our god." (1 Sam. 5:6–7)

Whereas Dagon's hands were cut off, the Lord's hand was heavy upon Dagon's people. It seems likely that God afflicted the Philistines with bubonic plague, the term *tumors* speaking generally about swellings and growths. This was a disease that frequented coastal regions, spread by mice and rats that came in on ships. We see a connection between the tumors and mice in 1 Samuel 6:4–5, when golden mice are offered in sacrifice. Kyle McCarter

101

notes that "a connection between rats and pestilence was recognized in early times,"[5] and the Lord may have terrified the people by having swarms of infected rodents overrun their habitations.

The Ashdodites realized that Israel's God was the cause of their calamity. They summoned a council of all the Philistine lords and asked, "What shall we do with the ark of the God of Israel?" (1 Sam. 5:8). God had gotten their attention, just as he seeks ours today. The Philistines agreed to move the ark to Gath, thinking that perhaps there were simply local circumstances behind the apparent outbreak of divine wrath in Ashdod. But the same thing happened in Gath: "The hand of the LORD was against the city, causing a very great panic, and he afflicted the men of the city, both young and old, so that tumors broke out on them" (5:9). Next "they sent the ark of God to Ekron," but the people immediately rebelled. "They have brought around to us the ark of the God of Israel to kill us and our people," they cried (5:10). The point is that God's heavy hand against the worshipers of false gods is universal and constant:

> They sent therefore and gathered together all the lords of the Philistines and said, "Send away the ark of the God of Israel, and let it return to its own place, that it may not kill us and our people." For there was a deathly panic throughout the whole city. The hand of God was very heavy there. The men who did not die were struck with tumors, and the cry of the city went up to heaven. (5:11–12)

This episode is not an isolated incident, but a warning of God's judgment on all idolaters. The experience of God's obvious judgment on the false gods of our times makes a similar point. Lloyd-Jones asserts, "Everything that is happening in this century is, in the same way, pointing to the judgment of God upon rebellious man, and announcing the final destruction of all who do not submit to him."[6]

WHY ARE CHRISTIANS DEFEATED?

The episode of the ark in Philistia speaks powerfully to God's people and to the Philistine world. What was the message to Israel and the church? The

5. P. Kyle McCarter Jr., *1 Samuel*, Anchor Bible, vol. 8 (New York: Doubleday, 1980), 123.
6. Lloyd-Jones, *Old Testament Evangelistic Sermons*, 69.

point for us is to understand rightly the cause of our defeat in the world. The fall of Dagon before the ark of the Lord shows that we suffer defeat not because our enemy is so strong, much less that the Philistine god is stronger than our God. Rather, the cause of our weakness and defeat is our estranged relationship with the Lord.

We frequently hear that Christianity is waning because today's society is too hostile to the gospel. We cannot expect educated people to seek truth from the Bible rather than from the certified results of science. We cannot hope for people who are drunk on sensual pleasures to be interested in a church service—especially worship that fails to conform to popular tastes and demands. We cannot expect today's people to give their video-short attention spans to serious Bible preaching. The Philistines of secularism, sensualism, and relativism are just too strong, and biblical Christianity lacks sufficient appeal. It is on this view that so many Christians and churches have concluded that we must join the Philistines if we are ever to win them. So it seemed for Israel: the Philistines had better technology and organization, and even bigger and stronger men. Yet how easy it was for God to cast the Philistine idol upon his face!

This shows, by the way, that it is not the church's job to cast down the Philistine gods. The job of God's people is to honor the Lord in all things, refusing to join in the world's idolatry and remaining faithful. Thus Christians are told "to stand against the schemes of the devil" (Eph. 6:11). We are not told to go on the offensive against Satan, but "to withstand in the evil day, and having done all, to stand firm" (6:13). This is not to say that Christians should not speak out against lies and evils. It simply means that the church in its spiritual mission is not called to wage worldly warfare against our enemies. In his own time, in his own ways, we can be sure that God will humble the idols of the world. We are to remember the Lord, trusting in him and spreading his gospel.

Israel's problem in the days of Eli's priesthood was that the people forgot about God. Eli's sons could not possibly have committed their sins in the temple had they remembered the Lord. The Israelites were spiritually estranged from God and his Word; their worship was false-hearted; their lives were an affront to the Lord's purity. Forgetting God, drifting from God, and offending him, Israel was easy prey for the Philistine army. And so it is with the Christian church today.

The same is true on a personal level. Consider, as one example, the struggle of men (and, increasingly, women as well) with the sin of pornography. Numerous surveys show a majority of men practically addicted to filthy fantasies, mainly by means of Internet websites. Surveys also show professing Christian men, and even pastors, addicted to pornography at rates similar to those of nonbelievers. In response to cries of alarm, we are told that we must simply face the fact that the temptation is too strong, the pictures too accessible, and men's hearts too deeply ingrained for us to expect any real change. What can an Israelite man do in the face of so mighty a Philistine?

The answer is that we can remember God. We can turn to God for his power. We can bathe our hearts and minds in the glory of God through his Word. We can gain a passion for the cause of the gospel in a dying world, so that we no longer need fantasies in order to feel important. We can get on our knees and ask our mighty, merciful God to cleanse us from our sins and make us holy. The reality is that a Christian man who is walking close to the Lord, whose active faith is empowered by the Holy Spirit through God's Word and prayer, and who is participating in a supportive community with other believers is not easily overcome by seductive pictures of naked women.

The truth is that Christians not only *must not* continue in the sinful habits of a Philistine world, but also *need not* continue in the power of sin. Yes, the Philistine is stronger than we are, but not stronger than God! The apostle John reminds us, "He who is in you is greater than he who is in the world" (1 John 4:4). This was Paul's logic when he wrote to Christians living in a world just as depraved as ours, with sinful pleasures just as accessible and culturally tolerated: "You also must consider yourselves dead to sin and alive to God in Christ Jesus. Let not sin therefore reign in your mortal body, to make you obey its passions. . . . For sin will have no dominion over you, since you are not under law but under grace" (Rom. 6:11–14). While total freedom must wait until we reach the glories of heaven, Christians may live in increasing liberty from the domination of sin because God is greater and more powerful than sin.

God's Message for the Philistine World

By casting down the Philistine idol and striking the people in his wrath, God delivered a message not only to his own people but also to the Philistine world.

First, God proved that he is *a living God*. The Philistines thought of their gods as objects—idols that they worshiped to gain an edge in the problems of life, but still objects. Israel had fallen into this kind of thinking when it put its confidence in the ark, while forgetting God himself. But God is not a thing to be manipulated and controlled, an object to be put on the shelf and taken down at our whim. He is still today what he was in Bible times: "The Lord is the true God; he is the living God and the everlasting King" (Jer. 10:10). Lloyd-Jones says, "When you think you have him defeated, then he is active; when you think you have him captive, he knocks down your god. He is God who cannot be restrained, illimitable, absolute, eternal—the living God."[7] For this reason, we all must reckon with God, before whom we "live and move and have our being" (Acts 17:28, quoting Job 12:10).

Second, the Lord taught that he is *the only true God*. God is jealous of his exclusive status: "I am the Lord your God . . . You shall have no other gods before me" (Ex. 20:2–3). God is not placated if we make a little room for him on the shelf beside our other gods. He demands exclusive sovereignty in our lives. He will not share his reign with idols, but ruthlessly casts them down and smites those who serve them. On the national level, if we make a god of government, then God will send corrupt and incompetent leaders. If we make a god of the economy, God is able to make the stock market plummet. If we use science to violate his laws, then God will make our technology a curse to our lives. God demands that all things—presidencies, corporate earnings, fighter planes, and microscopes—be submitted to his sovereign rule. "I am God, and there is no other," he decrees; "I am God, and there is none like me" (Isa. 46:9). Likewise, on the personal level, God calls for us to submit all things to his service. He is not willing to share sovereignty in our hearts with false gods such as fame, pleasure, and wealth.

Third, the living and true God proved that he is *powerful and mighty*. How swiftly and surely the Philistines were crushed when the heavy hand of God struck them, just as God struck Pharaoh and the Egyptians in the time of Moses. There is no chance of withstanding God's judgment, either now or in the end. For this reason, the odds of the evolutionary worldview's prevailing indefinitely are precisely zero. The chances of sexual liberty's producing happiness are nil. God will strike down every rebel power with his infinite might.

7. Ibid., 70.

History has borne out this reality over and over again. The French Revolution raised its fist against God and produced not fraternity but tyranny. Nineteenth-century German humanism did not produce a secular heaven but the hell of Nazism. Atheistic communism did not produce a workers' paradise but a slaves' poorhouse. Likewise, secular-humanistic, postmodern America will not achieve its promised dreams of pleasure and prosperity but only a legacy of societal ruin and lost opportunity. God lives. God demands our worship. And God is omnipotent to frustrate the plans of rebel mankind.

Finally, God reveals himself as *a saving God*. The Philistines might well have reflected on what God was doing to the enemies of his people. How faithful this God was to allow himself, via the ark, to fall into the hands of his enemies, that he might better save Israel. Reflecting on God's covenant-keeping grace, the Philistines should have cast out Dagon and every other false god in order to embrace the true God in faith.

The message God delivered to the Philistines is the message we need to give to our world today. We must insist that God is not on the shelf, that he is very much involved in events and affairs, in accordance with the principles taught in his Word. He is a living God, and we must reckon on him. Moreover, we must insist that God is jealous, warning of grave danger for all who trust in other gods. We must show people from both Scripture and God's providential dealings in history how foolish and futile it is to rebel against the true and living God, and how severe his holy judgment is against his enemies.

But we can also tell the world that the God we should all fear is also a merciful and saving God whom we can trust and adore. The incident of the ark's falling into enemy hands was only a preview of a greater work of salvation. God sent his own Son into this rebel world to deliver his people. Jesus surrendered to his enemies, but did not strike them with his heavy hand. Instead, he yielded himself to death on the cross. In this way, God struck the heaviest blow to the power and dominion of sin, taking away its curse by cleansing our guilt with the precious blood of Christ. The plague of sin that rightly should slay us fell instead on Jesus Christ. Indeed, it was for Philistine sinners like us that Jesus died. Paul writes, "God shows his love for us in that while we were still sinners, Christ died for us" (Rom. 5:8). Now, by trusting in Christ, we are reconciled to live in the light of God's love. And, remembering the Lord in obedient faith, we need never fear any Philistine foe ever again.

10

THIS HOLY GOD!

1 Samuel 6:1–7:2

Then the men of Beth-shemesh said, "Who is able to stand before the LORD, this holy God? And to whom shall he go up away from us?" (1 Sam. 6:20)

The apostle Paul addressed the philosophers in Athens, saying, "I perceive that in every way you are very religious" (Acts 17:22). The same words might be said of men in every place and time. People in our day claim to have repudiated religion, yet their pursuit of science is intensely religious, seeking the hope and meaning that have traditionally come from belief in God. Even the Philistines, the ancient enemies of God's people, Israel, were very religious. Thus they took special joy in capturing Israel's most holy object, the ark of the covenant. But when the presence of the ark brought God's wrath upon them in the form of a deadly plague, the Philistines sought answers to some of the most basic religious questions. They wondered, first, how to escape God's holy wrath. Then they sought a means for understanding God's holy ways. Finally, when the Philistines were rid of the ark, the Israelites sought the answer to yet another essential religious question. They asked, "Who is able to stand before the LORD, this holy God?" (1 Sam. 6:20).

ESCAPING GOD'S HOLY WRATH

The Philistines' first question is one that was particularly pressing given their circumstances. "The ark of the LORD was in the country of the Philistines seven months" (1 Sam. 6:1), and during this time the people of at least three Philistine cities were thrown into an uproar. It started in Ashdod when the Philistine god Dagon was found on the ground before the Lord's ark and then later with his head and hands cut off. A plague fell upon the people of Ashdod, so the ark was sent away to Gath and then to Ekron. Ekron, too, was thrown into panic, and many died or "were struck with tumors" (5:12).

Obviously, not all was well between the Philistines and the Lord! Capturing their enemy's most sacred object was something to be proud of, so at first there was opposition to simply giving up the ark. But now it clearly had to be sent away. The question was: how? "The Philistines called for the priests and the diviners and said, 'What shall we do with the ark of the LORD? Tell us with what we shall send it to its place'" (1 Sam. 6:2). Kenneth Chafin writes: "What had happened to their god Dagon, to themselves, and to their land had created a certain fear of making things worse by not observing the proper protocol."[1] The priests answered: "If you send away the ark of the God of Israel, do not send it empty, but by all means return him a guilt offering" (1 Sam. 6:3).

The Philistines' approach reveals both insight and ignorance with respect to God and his holy wrath. What insight they had came from the schooling they had been receiving: they realized that they had offended a holy God. Yet even with this insight, their desperate attempts to rid themselves of God and his wrath ultimately reveal great ignorance of God and his ways. Still, their actions help us to understand three key truths about God and his holy wrath.

The first truth is that God's wrath is brought on us by our sin, which the answer to question 14 of the Westminster Shorter Catechism defines as "any want of conformity unto, or transgression of, the law of God." Placing God's holy ark beside a pagan idol transgressed not only God's law but God's very first commandment: "You shall have no other gods before me" (Ex. 20:3). This sin alone was a sufficient explanation for the Philistines' suffering at God's hand.

1. Kenneth L. Chafin, *1 & 2 Samuel*, Preacher's Commentary, vol. 8 (Nashville: Thomas Nelson, 1989), 57.

Second, the holy God responds to sin with wrath and judgment. As Paul wrote, "The wrath of God is revealed from heaven against all ungodliness and unrighteousness of men" (Rom. 1:18). Here the apostle teaches the very thing experienced by the Philistines, that "the wages of sin is death" (6:23). The Philistines had offended God and broken his law, so God in his wrath struck them with death.

The idea of God's wrath is widely disputed today. One well-known example is Rabbi Harold Kushner, who tells of ministering in the synagogue on Yom Kippur, the Jewish Day of Atonement, and feeling distressed by the guilt that his people felt. To address these feelings of guilt, Kushner wrote a book revising the Bible's story of Adam and Eve and their fall into sin by eating from the forbidden tree. Kushner writes, "A God who punished people so severely for breaking one arbitrary rule was not a God I wanted to believe in."[2] Therefore, in Kushner's retelling, "the story of the Garden of Eden is not an account of people being punished for having made one mistake, losing Paradise because they were not perfect. . . . The story of the Garden of Eden is not a story of the Fall of Man, but of the Emergence of Humankind."[3] In short, Kushner responded to the guilt feelings of his congregation by changing the Bible's story and its teaching. Remarkably, similar arguments are being made by evangelical Christian scholars today. For instance, evangelicals Joel Green and Mark Baker write, in accord with Kushner, "The Scriptures as a whole provide no ground for a portrait of an angry God needing to be appeased in atoning sacrifice."[4]

Kushner's book would not have sold well among the Philistines; Green and Baker's argument would have gained little traction in Ashdod or Gath. The Philistines had experienced God's wrath firsthand! Whether or not they felt guilty, it was obvious that God considered them guilty and responded in anger. The Bible as a whole concurs with this view, assuring us that God's wrath burns against all unforgiven sin. To be sure, we should never think of God's wrath in terms of petulant, sinful human anger. Instead, John Stott explains, "The wrath of God . . . is his steady, unrelenting, unremitting, uncompromising antagonism to evil in all its forms and manifestations."[5]

2. Harold Kushner, *How Good Do We Have to Be?* (New York: Little, Brown, 1996), 3.

3. Ibid., 30–31.

4. Joel B. Green and Mark D. Baker, *Recovering the Scandal of the Cross: Atonement in New Testament and Contemporary Contexts* (Downers Grove, IL: InterVarsity Press, 2000), 51.

5. John R. W. Stott, *The Cross of Christ* (Downers Grove, IL: InterVarsity Press, 1986), 173.

Given the perfect holiness of God, such wrath against sin is not only inevitable but also just. J. I. Packer thus argues, "So far from the manifestation of God's wrath in punishing sin being morally doubtful, the thing that would be morally doubtful would be for Him *not* to show His wrath in this way."[6]

Given that sin produces guilt and that God responds to sin with righteous anger and judgment, the Philistines needed a way to placate or turn aside God's wrath. In other words, the third thing they realized was that they needed a suitable sacrifice to satisfy God's righteous anger toward their sin. Their priests urged this very idea, saying: "Do not send it empty, but by all means return him a guilt offering. Then you will be healed, and it will be known to you why his hand does not turn away from you" (1 Sam. 6:3). What the people needed was the right offering to satisfy God's anger, so that the plagues would stop. Therefore, they replied, "What is the guilt offering that we shall return to him?" (6:4). This is the question with which the entire Bible is concerned: what offering will satisfy God's wrath against our sin?

It was at this point that the Philistine priests revealed both insight and ignorance. Their answer is one that sounds strange to us, but involved a fair amount of understanding:

> Five golden tumors and five golden mice, according to the number of the lords of the Philistines, for the same plague was on all of you and on your lords. So you must make images of your tumors and images of your mice that ravage the land, and give glory to the God of Israel. Perhaps he will lighten his hand from off you and your gods and your land. (1 Sam. 6:4–5)

How are we to understand this offering? The priests realized that any payment to God for sin must be costly. The Philistines were paying a high price for what they had done to offend the Lord, and it was obvious that they could satisfy God's wrath only by making a costly sacrifice. Moreover, the offering must correspond in some way to the punishment they were receiving. Since God's judgment involved diseased mice and produced tumors in their flesh, they thought to offer the Lord what verse 18 assures us was a great many golden mice—one each not only for the major cities but also for each

6. J. I. Packer and Mark Dever, *In My Place Condemned He Stood: Celebrating the Glory of the Atonement* (Wheaton, IL: Crossway, 2007), 35.

of the towns—that would memorialize and pay for the dreadful judgment that God had inflicted.

From a biblical standpoint, there are some obvious problems with these offerings. Mice are among the ritually detestable animals that God forbade to be used in offerings (cf. Lev. 11:29), and the images of tumors were likewise unclean before the Lord (not to mention unpleasant to the eyes). The Philistines had learned much at the heavy hand of the Lord, but they failed to realize that saving truth does not come from the diviners and pagan priests they had consulted. Such truth comes only from those who speak the Word of the Lord.

What the Philistines should have done was to consult an *Israelite* priest, just as we should consult the Bible to learn how to satisfy God's wrath against our sins. A true priest would have told them the proper guilt offering: "bring to the LORD as his compensation, a ram without blemish out of the flock" (Lev. 5:15). The prophet Isaiah would have gone further and informed them that these animal sacrifices looked forward to the coming of the Savior whom God would send: "he was wounded for our transgressions; he was crushed for our iniquities; upon him was the chastisement that brought us peace, and with his stripes we are healed. All we like sheep have gone astray; we have turned—every one—to his own way; and the LORD has laid on him the iniquity of us all" (Isa. 53:5–6). Finally, in the New Testament we learn that this Savior is the very Son of God, Jesus Christ, of whom John the Baptist declared: "Behold, the Lamb of God, who takes away the sin of the world!" (John 1:29).

The apostle Paul gives perhaps the clearest account of the Bible's atonement theology, telling us that the sacrifice we need was so costly that only God could provide it, and that God in his grace has sent his own Son to be the sacrifice for our sins. Paul writes: "All have sinned and fall short of the glory of God, and are justified by his grace as a gift, through the redemption that is in Christ Jesus, whom God put forward as a propitiation by his blood, to be received by faith" (Rom. 3:23–25).

The Philistines' instinct in offering costly materials was right, but their estimation of the cost of forgiveness was simply too low! Our sin causes infinite offense to God's holy justice, and thus we can be forgiven and cleansed only by an infinitely valuable sacrifice. Peter says that we gain forgiveness "not with perishable things such as silver or gold, but with the precious blood of Christ" (1 Peter 1:18–19). God himself, in his infinite grace, has sent the sacrifice by which we can escape his wrath against our sins; only by relying on the blood of Christ can we receive forgiveness, not as something we have bought or earned but as a gift from God's mercy, received through faith alone.

The Philistine diviners may not have known the way of atonement accepted by God, but at least they recognized the urgency of seeking it. They warned the people: "Why should you harden your hearts as the Egyptians and Pharaoh hardened their hearts? After he had dealt severely with them, did they not send the people away, and they departed?" (1 Sam. 6:6). The story of Israel's departure from Egypt in the time of Moses was well known in the ancient world. Pharaoh hardened his heart, and as a result, death fell on the land of the Nile. This exhortation remains valid today: sinners must not harden their hearts against God's way of forgiveness through faith in Jesus Christ. To refuse to confess their guilt, or to reject the way of atonement that God has provided, is simple self-destruction. Why would anyone who realizes how holy God is and how offensive our sin is to him do anything but accept God's gift of forgiveness through faith in the precious blood of Christ?

UNDERSTANDING GOD'S HOLY WAYS

Despite all they had experienced and said, the Philistines still entertained doubts whether the plague had really been caused by the Lord. So they devised a scheme to determine God's ways: "Now then, take and prepare a new cart and two milk cows on which there has never come a yoke, and yoke the cows to the cart, but take their calves home, away from them. And take the ark of the LORD and place it on the cart and put in a box at its side the figures of gold, which you are returning to him as a guilt offering. Then send it off and let it go its way and watch" (1 Sam. 6:7–9). The making of a new cart and the use of cows not previously yoked is an expression of respect. But the Philistines added a wrinkle, using cows that had recently calved. Anyone who has been around farm animals knows that mother cows and their nursing calves are practically inseparable. Thus, if the cows went away on their own to the nearby Jewish city, it could only be a confirmation from the Lord.

The Philistines were practicing an approach to discerning God's will that is sometimes used by God's people. A famous example is Gideon, who responded to God's command by seeking supernatural confirmation (Judg. 6:36–40). Just like the Philistines, Gideon was asking God to confirm his involvement by making things happen contrary to nature. Gideon laid his fleece on the ground and asked God to make it wet with dew while the ground was dry. When this happened, Gideon asked for the ground to be wet but the fleece to be dry. His "laying out a fleece" is not an example we should follow but a sign of Gideon's weak faith.

Off went the cows, with no one guiding them and their nursing calves left behind. Sure enough, the cart went straight down the road to Beth-shemesh: "They turned neither to the right nor to the left, and the lords of the Philistines went after them as far as the border of Beth-shemesh" (1 Sam. 6:12). We can scarcely imagine the relief of the Philistines as God's holy ark finally departed from their lands.

God's accommodation to the Philistines' procedure should not encourage us to rely on superstitious approaches to discerning God's will. Subjective signs crafted out of the folly of our minds are no way to discern God's will; instead, they invite us to divinize our own hunches and sometimes provide an opportunity for Satan to deceive us. Instead, we should remember the testimony of Peter, who witnessed several clear divine revelations, including the audible speaking of God's voice. Yet Peter tells us that "we have something more sure, the prophetic word," that is, the Bible, "to which you will do well to pay attention as to a lamp shining in a dark place" (2 Peter 1:19). If we want God's revelation to us, the place to look is in the holy Scriptures, which God has given as a lamp to our feet and a light for our path (Ps. 119:105).

Apparently, God's purposes with the Philistines were finished, at least for the time being. We should not suppose that their gold trinkets successfully atoned for their sins, but that the Lord had sufficiently humbled them and made his point. The Philistines returned home, glad to be rid of this dangerous holiness. How easy it is for us to do likewise when God's hand has struck us in chastisement, glad to escape the pain of God's reproof but thinking little on the truths he has emphasized. The Philistines were like the wicked men of whom Job said, "They say to God, 'Depart from us! We do not desire the knowledge of your ways' "

(Job 21:14). How much better to treasure God's Word and to humble ourselves in trusting obedience to all that he has revealed!

STANDING IN GOD'S HOLY PRESENCE

So God's holy ark returned to Israel after seven months in Philistine hands. The Philistines had wanted only to escape God's wrath and discern enough of God's will to think themselves free from his judgment. Now, as the ark returned to Israel, we ask, "How can his people abide in the presence of so holy a God?"

The first answer is that God's people are to receive God's presence *with joy.* We see such joy modeled by the people of Beth-shemesh: they "were reaping their wheat harvest in the valley. And when they lifted up their eyes and saw the ark, they rejoiced to see it" (1 Sam. 6:13). The Philistines may have wanted only to be rid of so holy a God, but the Lord's people knew of his mighty grace. Nehemiah said that "the joy of the LORD is your strength" (Neh. 8:10). Christians are strongest when we are rejoicing in the Lord, and God is never more fully praised by us than when we most rejoice in him.

Second, God's people are to dwell with him *in reverence.* It turns out that Beth-shemesh was a Levitical city in which the clan of Kohath lived, the clan assigned to care for the ark of the covenant within the tabernacle (cf. Num. 4:2; Josh. 21:16). It is not surprising, then, for them to arrange an immediate sacrifice: "The cart came into the field of Joshua of Beth-shemesh and stopped there. A great stone was there. And they split up the wood of the cart and offered the cows as a burnt offering to the LORD" (1 Sam. 6:14).

What is surprising, however, is their failure to observe the commandment that only bulls be offered (Lev. 1:3). This was followed by a more fatal transgression. The ark was set on a great stone in the field of a man named Joshua (1 Sam. 6:18). There, God "struck some of the men of Beth-shemesh, because they looked upon the ark of the LORD. He struck seventy men of them, and the people mourned because the LORD had struck the people with a great blow" (6:19).

Remarkably, the Levites had allowed God's holy ark to become a tourist attraction. What a sight it must have been to the eyes of country folk: a large, shining golden box, adorned with such finely crafted angels that God had employed craftsmen specially anointed by the Holy Spirit (Ex. 35:30–35).

How natural it was for crowds to gather to see the great ark of the covenant, now in Beth-shemesh for the first time! But what seems natural to us is sometimes sacrilege to God. Indeed, the Lord had specified that only priests were allowed even to see the exterior of the ark, while not even the Kohathites were allowed to look inside. According to Numbers 4:20, no one was to "look on the holy things even for a moment, lest they die." This rule expressed the utter holiness of the God represented by the ark. The priests' first duty, which they would have realized with even a cursory inspection of God's Word, was to safeguard the ark from view.

The example of Beth-shemesh reminds us that we do not show reverence for God by treating him according to our own wisdom and sentiments, but only by obeying the commands and precepts of his Word. How much flagrantly carnal worship is offered up to God today, designed to appeal to the fashions of men but with no reference to biblical principles (often in direct violation of scriptural teaching), and how greatly such irreverence must account for the lack of true spiritual blessing experienced by Christians! Just as the Kohathites' remarkable ignorance in handling the ark reveals the spiritual decline of that generation, so also does the lack of reverence for God in Christian worship today signal a spiritual declension among us.

The Levites of Beth-shemesh further showed their spiritual poverty by responding to God's wrath in a fashion identical to the Philistines. They cried out, "Who is able to stand before the LORD, this holy God? And to whom shall he go up away from us?" (1 Sam. 6:20). Then, just as the Philistines of Ashdod had palmed off the ark to Gath and then Ekron, the people of Beth-shemesh "sent messengers to the inhabitants of Kiriath-jearim, saying, 'The Philistines have returned the ark of the LORD. Come down and take it up to you'" (6:21). This shows the ultimate result when God's people drift from God's Word: the church takes on the attitude of the world and ultimately rejects the holy God in unbelief.

The people of Kiriath-jearim provide a third example of how we are to dwell in the presence of the holy God, namely, *by faith*: "The men of Kiriath-jearim came and took up the ark of the LORD and brought it to the house of Abinadab on the hill. And they consecrated his son Eleazar to have charge of the ark of the LORD" (1 Sam. 7:1). William Blaikie comments, "More timid men might have said, The ark has brought nothing but disaster in its train; we will have nothing to do with it. There was faith and loyalty to God shown in their readiness to give accommodation to it within their bounds."[7]

It is noteworthy that Kiriath-jearim was a Gibeonite city (Josh. 9:17). The Gibeonites were non-Israelites who tricked Joshua into permitting them to live and who were assigned as woodcutters and water-bearers for the tabernacle (9:21–22, 27). Thus God shows that his true people are those who respond to him in faith. Though they had not been born into the covenant, these Gibeonites trusted God's Word; acting according to Scripture, they were keen to have the ark in their midst. Trusting in God's grace, humbly adhering to God's Word, they had the privilege of housing God's holy ark for a generation, until King David appeared to take the ark and bring it into Jerusalem.

Abinadab and his son apparently did everything they could to observe God's commandments for the ark. They also refused to do more than God's Word permitted. Kiriath-jearim thus was not advertised as a new national shine, replacing Shiloh, which the Philistines had destroyed. The traditional feasts were not celebrated there and the sacrificial service was not observed, there being no proper priesthood. For twenty years "the ark was lodged at Kiriath-jearim," not in the center but on the fringe of the nation, faithfully cared for by loyal foreigners who trusted God's Word but inaccessible to the nation, so that "all the house of Israel lamented after the LORD" (1 Sam. 7:2). Just as the gospel is, according to Paul, a savor of death to those who do not believe but an aroma of life to those of faith (2 Cor. 2:15–16), so also the ark was the savor of death to irreverent Beth-shemesh and the savor of life and joy to the faithful household of Abinadab.

WHO IS ABLE TO STAND?

We have considered three great questions answered in this chapter: How can we escape God's holy wrath? How can we understand God's holy ways? And how can we abide in the presence of this holy God? All three of these questions can really be wrapped up in the last of them, asked by the Israelites to whom the ark returned, and answered by the example of the faithful Abinadab: "Who is able to stand before the LORD, this holy God?"

7. William G. Blaikie, *Expository Lectures on the Book of First Samuel* (1887; repr., Birmingham, AL: Solid Ground, 2005), 85.

(1 Sam. 6:20). To stand in God's holy presence is to be cleansed from sin and freed from God's holy wrath. To believe this message of salvation is to understand the very heart of God's will for us.

Interestingly, the answer to this question is provided by the very construction of the ark of the covenant, so that if the Philistines had reflected on its unique design, they might have understood God's will and salvation far better than they did.

As we have noted, the ark was a golden box, inside of which were contained the actual tablets of the Ten Commandments given to Moses by God. Atop the ark were golden statues of two holy cherubim, angels who served as God's attendants and signified his holy presence. Looking downward, the angels saw the law of God—his holy requirements for mankind—which we have broken. This is our problem, and the source of God's wrath against us. But there was one more feature of the ark, a golden cover, known as the mercy seat, upon which the blood of sacrificed goats and lambs was sprinkled, so that the holy God no longer saw his broken law but the atoning blood of the sacrifice that he himself had ordained.

Earlier I cited Paul's teaching in Romans 3:25, which says of Jesus Christ, the true Lamb, that "God put [him] forward as a propitiation by his blood, to be received by faith." *Propitiation* refers to the turning aside of God's wrath; in the Greek language, the word is *hilasterion*. This happens to be the same word used in the Greek translation of the Old Testament for the mercy seat, the lid on which the sacrificial blood was sprinkled to turn God's wrath from our sin. With the law and the mercy seat, the ark of the covenant was designed to express God's absolute holiness that burns against all sin and his marvelous grace that provides a way for sinners to draw near through the blood of his Son, Jesus Christ.

I do not believe that the Philistines could have understood all this simply by examining the ark. But it could have gotten them thinking in the right direction. They would have immediately realized that Israel's religion was completely different from the pagan idolatry that they were used to. By seeking further, they might have put away their pagan schemes and sought to learn more about Israel's God and his mercy seat that covers the sins of those who come in faith. The fact that the ark found its home among Gibeonites proves that anyone—even a Philistine—who trusts in the atoning blood may stand in God's holy presence.

We have the benefit of God's completed revelation in the Old and New Testaments. This means not only that we can understand God's will simply by reading God's Word, but also that the story of redemption is now complete in the life and death of Jesus Christ. The ark played its role for a time, declaring God's holiness and mercy, but now, the apostle John writes, "grace and truth [have come] through Jesus Christ" (John 1:17).

How does Jesus answer the question that looms over every other human quest: "Who is able to stand before the LORD, this holy God?" (1 Sam. 6:20). He answers, "The Son of Man came not to be served but to serve, and to give his life as a ransom for many" (Matt. 20:28). The book of Hebrews tells us that Jesus came as "a merciful and faithful high priest in the service of God, to make propitiation for the sins of the people" (Heb. 2:17). Jesus came to cleanse us from our sins and robe us in the garments of his own righteousness, that we might stand unafraid in the presence of God and with great joy. "Once for all . . . he offered up himself" (7:27), and "consequently, he is able to save to the uttermost those who draw near to God through him" (7:25).

11

RAISING EBENEZER

1 Samuel 7:3–17

Then Samuel took a stone and set it up between Mizpah and Shen and called its name Ebenezer; for he said, "Till now the LORD has helped us." (1 Sam. 7:12)

wenty years had passed since the ark of the covenant was lost to Israel. Their leaders sought to use God's holy ark as a military superweapon without first humbling themselves before the Lord or seeking his will. God gave Israel over to defeat with terrible slaughter, and his ark fell into Philistine hands. Seven months later, God had inflicted such wrath in turn on the Philistines that they sent the ark back to Israel, where it remained in an obscure border village. For twenty years, the Philistines maintained their domination over God's people. Israel was reduced to virtual serfdom, forbidden by the Philistines to employ blacksmiths, lest Israelite plowshares be beaten into swords, while their enemies maintained forts deep in Israel's territory (cf. 1 Sam. 13:19–14:5).

We may wonder where Samuel was when all these events took place. He probably would have been present at Shiloh when news of Israel's defeat came and Eli the high priest died, and he perhaps returned to his home in Ramah when Shiloh was destroyed. During the long years of Israel's oppression,

Samuel must have prayed and urged Israel to return to the Lord. If so, then the last words of 1 Samuel 7:2 provide the words that Samuel was waiting for: "all the house of Israel lamented after the LORD." Twenty years of oppression finally made Israel miss God's loving care and even lament the absence of the Lord himself. The apostle Paul says that "godly grief produces a repentance that leads to salvation" (2 Cor. 7:10). To see whether Israel's was true, godly grief, Samuel came forth to urge the people to return to the Lord. "If you are returning to the LORD with all your heart . . . ," he began to call out, more as a challenge than a question (1 Sam. 7:3). Rather than remaining satisfied with a fleeting remorse, Samuel sought to lead Israel in true repentance so as to restore the people to the Lord.

RETURNING TO THE LORD

A number of years ago, a billboard was put up near my home with a message from the local diocese of the Roman Catholic Church. The billboard presented a picture of a wistful young woman looking distressed, and it read, "If you think you can't make it right, you're wrong." Protestants will no doubt quarrel with some of the theology behind that Catholic message, but its main point is one that all Christians can embrace: you can always come back to God.

As proof of this principle, we should consider Samuel's message to the fallen people of Israel. So intensely had they and their leaders offended God that he departed from them by sending away the ark of the covenant. The Lord gave them over to destruction, so that the name *Ichabod* (meaning "the glory has departed") was rightly spoken of them. They had abandoned the true God for idols, indulging in gross sins, and in consequence they had fallen into bondage and misery. So it ever is with sin. Jesus said that "everyone who commits sin is a slave to sin" (John 8:34), and Paul wrote that "the wages of sin is death" (Rom. 6:23). Sin leads to a miserable slavery that ends in death. So how can there be hope for sinners like the Israelites, who have offended God?

The answer is the mercy of God, who always welcomes sinners back when they come humbly seeking grace. God says: "Return to me, . . . and I will return to you" (Zech. 1:3). It was with this grace in mind that Samuel spoke to Israel about returning to the Lord: "And Samuel said to all the house of Israel, 'If you are returning to the LORD with all your heart . . .'" (1 Sam. 7:3). This is the appeal that God always makes to those who are fallen in sin.

Samuel understood that repentance involves far more than feeling sorry about our sin. Most people are sorry only that they got caught sinning or for the misery they have experienced as a result. But true repentance begins by being sorry over the sin itself and then goes on to forsake sin so completely as to turn to God in new obedience. Israel's chief sin had been idolatry, so Samuel exhorted the people: "If you are returning to the LORD with all your heart, then put away the foreign gods and the Ashtaroth from among you" (1 Sam. 7:3).

This command involved far more than throwing a few statues into a ditch. Idolatry, then as now, involved a whole way of life. Verse 4 refers to "the Baals and the Ashtaroth." These Canaanite "foreign gods" (v. 3) were linked to the vital matter of fertility, so that through their worship people hoped to secure rains and abundant crops. Baal was the Canaanite storm god, and Asherah was his wife. It is possible that Asherah was considered a consort to Yahweh, Israel's God. The idea of needing a feminine counterpart to the masculine god is pervasive in idolatry; a contemporary example is the Roman Catholic veneration of Mary as co-redemptrix with Christ.

To abandon the Baalim and the Ashtaroth required two difficult movements. First, the Israelites had to reject the ways that were fashionable and widespread in their time. To worship the God of the Bible required them to be separate and distinct from the idolatrous culture around them. Similarly, anyone who wants to follow Jesus Christ today simply cannot fit into the ways of the world. The world has its definition of success and its approach to the problems of life that are completely different from those of God and his people. John reminds us that "all that is in the world—the desires of the flesh and the desires of the eyes and pride in possessions—is not from the Father but is from the world" (1 John 2:16). So also, James warns believers that worldliness is idolatry: "You adulterous people! Do you not know that friendship with the world is enmity with God? Therefore whoever wishes to be a friend of the world makes himself an enemy of God" (James 4:4).

Added to the difficulty of being different is the reality that idol-worship was sensually appealing. The worship of Baal and Asherah involved offerings of ritual sex so as to leverage their powers for fertility. Many Israelites thought this was a more enjoyable way of getting crops to grow than holding a prayer meeting! Since the ways of sin so naturally appeal to our corrupt natures, Dale Ralph Davis points out that "no superficial—only a supernatural—repentance would break such bondage."[1]

This is why Samuel joined turning from idols with wholehearted devotion to the Lord: "direct your heart to the LORD and serve him only" (1 Sam. 7:3). Single-minded devotion to the Lord requires forsaking false gods and turning from sin. But Samuel realized that the power for repentance comes from a new fervor for the Lord. We not only forsake the darkness but come to walk in the light. The power to turn from sin comes from seeing the glory of the Lord as the true God and the blessing of his salvation as our only true hope.

This is why Samuel added a promise of blessing to his call to repentance, since it is the gospel hope that empowers our turning from sin. "He will deliver you out of the hand of the Philistines," Samuel promised (1 Sam. 7:3). Since God had given Israel over so as to bring the people to remorse over their sin, true repentance would restore God's blessing and help. Christians should realize that this is the way for us to enjoy the fullness of God's power and blessing: by turning from the idolatry of our sins and wholeheartedly serving the Lord.

The sincerity of the Israelites' longing for God is seen in their response: "So the people of Israel put away the Baals and the Ashtaroth, and they served the LORD only" (1 Sam. 7:4). The word *served* refers in this context to worship: they gave glory to God alone. This reminds us that our lifestyles are really matters of worship. People today worship the idols of self and pleasure, and their lifestyles show it. Jesus said, "You cannot serve God and money" (Matt. 6:24). The lifestyle of idolatry is one of taking, whereas God calls his people to giving; the gods of this world teach us to dominate others, whereas the true God calls us to a lifestyle of sacrifice and service. In such things our true religion is seen. As Israel turned back to the Lord, a long era of sinful idolatry was drawing to a close and a new day of blessing was dawning.

Samuel's call to repentance directly challenges some of the messages heard in the church today. We are living in a time when carnal entertainment and worldly inducements—some of them so sensual as to evoke

---

1. Dale Ralph Davis, *1 Samuel: Looking on the Heart* (Fearn, Ross-shire, UK: Christian Focus, 2000), 58.

comparisons with Baal and Asherah worship—are widely employed to persuade people to come to church. In one prominent church, advertisements promoted a sermon series on sexual pleasure by referring to it as a "strip club." Another well-known church has used the incentive of raffling off a house to a lucky member who came to church that day. The inevitably large crowds gathered through such worldly means are then cited as evidence of a spiritual revival, so that reluctant Christians should put aside their biblical objections and get on board. But Samuel's teaching reminds us that true spiritual renewal is always accompanied by repentance from worldliness and sin, just as true revival also bears fruit in the reformation of Christ's church according to God's Word. Without true repentance from sin and reformation in the church, we have no biblical basis for claiming to enjoy a revival. Rather than relying on marketing strategies taught by the world, how much better it would be for us to follow Samuel's example in calling forth the Word of God so as to lead sinners to repent and come for mercy in Christ.

The same is true on a personal level: spiritual revival is always joined to a passion for holiness. Thus, each of us should see our love for sin as the chief barrier to our spiritual blessing. One of the best prayers we can offer is the supplication in William Cowper's 1779 hymn "O for a Closer Walk with God":

> The dearest idol I have known,
> Whate'er that idol be,
> Help me to tear it from thy throne,
> And worship only thee.

RESTORATION AT MIZPAH

Individual sins should be confessed and repented of on an individual basis. But there are national and church sins that should be repented of as a nation and as a church. Moreover, it is proper for congregations, as they seek God's blessing in worship, to confess together the guilt of their sin. So Samuel summoned the people to assemble at Mizpah, a traditional meeting place about five miles north of Jerusalem. "Gather all Israel at Mizpah," Samuel said, "and I will pray to the LORD for you" (1 Sam. 7:5).

Once the people had gathered, they responded in a couple of actions designed to express their contrition over sin. First, they "drew water and poured it out before the LORD" (1 Sam. 7:6). The meaning of this gesture is not entirely clear. Robert Bergen supposes that they "were denying themselves liquids as a symbolic confession that the Lord's favor was more important to them than life-sustaining water."[2] William Blaikie sees it as "a symbol of pouring out before God confessions of sin drawn from the depths of the heart."[3] To this was added public fasting, the purpose of which was to express special humiliation and grief for sin (cf. 2 Sam. 12:21; 1 Kings 21:27; Dan. 10:2–3). In these ways, the Israelites came before the Lord declaring their eager readiness to receive his renewing grace. There can be little doubt of the sincerity, fervor, and grief poured out in their words of confession, spoken together as a penitent people, "We have sinned against the LORD" (1 Sam. 7:6). Blaikie writes: "They humbled themselves before God in deep conviction of their unworthiness, and being thus emptied of self they were in a better state to receive the gracious visitation of love and mercy."[4]

We can understand why the Israelites would humble themselves and confess their sins: twenty years of chastisement had prompted their contrition. But it is not obvious why God would accept their confession and forgive their sins. The same is true for us: even a brief glimpse of God's holy character makes confession of sin imperative for us. But why should God forgive?

The answer is seen at Mizpah, where Samuel mediated for Israel before the Lord. "Gather," Samuel had called, "and I will pray to the LORD for you" (1 Sam. 7:5). Serving in his priestly capacity, Samuel was appointed to represent the people to God and God to the people. Note the contrast here with the prior situation in Shiloh: it was for want of godly priests—Eli's sons' being rejected for their wickedness—that Israel had been abandoned by God. Now there is a true and godly priest, and the people are restored to God's favor.

But it was not merely who Samuel was that brought reconciliation with God; it was also what Samuel did: "Samuel took a nursing lamb and offered

---

2. Robert D. Bergen, *1, 2 Samuel*, New American Commentary (Nashville: Broadman & Holman, 1996), 107.

3. William G. Blaikie, *Expository Lectures on the Book of First Samuel* (1887; repr., Birmingham, AL: Solid Ground, 2005), 91.

4. Ibid., 91–92.

it as a whole burnt offering to the LORD. And Samuel cried out to the LORD for Israel, and the LORD answered him" (1 Sam. 7:9).

Samuel first offered a sacrifice to atone for the people's sins. This is the only way that sinners can be forgiven by God and restored to his favor. The Bible says that "without the shedding of blood there is no forgiveness of sins" (Heb. 9:22), for the simple reason that sin against God is deserving of death. When God commanded Adam not to eat from the forbidden tree, he warned that "in the day that you eat of it you shall surely die" (Gen. 2:17). Thus, every transgression of God's law requires the penalty of death, for sin cannot be permitted to abide in God's holy presence. But God in his mercy has made a way of forgiveness, through a substitute to pay the penalty for sin. That substitute—symbolized in the Old Testament by sacrificial animals—is God's own Son who came into the world to "save his people from their sins" (Matt. 1:21).

This is the message that Christians bear before the world: there is forgiveness through the atoning blood of Christ. There is no other way that will bring sinful men and women into God's favor and no other gospel that will speak true peace to our hearts. This is what Martin Luther discovered. People attempt all manner of ways to gain favor with God, and Luther tried practically all of them. He offered good works as a monk, he undertook sacred quests and made special offerings, he sought mystical highs and abased himself low before the church confessors. But none of these attempts succeeded for Luther, for the simple reason that none had God's written approval. Finally, Luther turned to the Bible, where he learned the gospel—which is, he wrote, "nothing but the story of how Christ stepped into our sins, carried them on the cross in his flesh, and destroyed them, so that all who believe in him are set free from sin through him."[5] This is the same method of atonement that the apostles taught. Paul wrote, "In [Christ] we have redemption through his blood, the forgiveness of our trespasses" (Eph. 1:7). John taught, "The blood of Jesus [God's] Son cleanses us from all sin" (1 John 1:7). Peter said, "You were ransomed from the futile ways inherited from your forefathers, not with perishable things such as silver or gold, but with the precious blood of Christ, like that of a lamb without blemish or spot" (1 Peter 1:18–19). The message of Samuel's sacrifice, and

---

5. Martin Luther, *Concerning the Letter and the Spirit*, in *Martin Luther's Basic Theological Writings*, ed. Timothy F. Lull (Minneapolis: Fortress, 1989), 84.

the message of the entire Bible, is twofold: *no sinner* may come before God's holiness without atoning blood, but also *any sinner* may come through the precious blood of Christ.

Samuel's lamb was a picture of Christ as our sacrifice, but Samuel himself was a picture of Christ as our Priest. "Samuel cried out to the LORD" (1 Sam. 7:9) so that the people would be accepted by God. Like Israel, we are reconciled to God through the mediating ministry of One sent by God—One who is both God and man, the incarnate Son of God, Jesus Christ. The writer of Hebrews reminds us that because the risen Lord Jesus lives and reigns forever, "he is able to save to the uttermost those who draw near to God through him, since he always lives to make intercession for them" (Heb. 7:25). Dale Ralph Davis comments: "In Samuel's intercession on Israel's behalf . . . we see a picture of the office of Christ as our high priest . . . Here is the true secret of our steadfastness: we rely on the prayers of Another whose prayers are always effectual. Nothing is quite so moving as knowing that I am a subject of Jesus' intercessory prayer."[6]

Christian faith is always lived out in a dangerous world that is hostile to true faith. So when the Philistines learned of the assembly at Mizpah, they were very unhappy: "Now when the Philistines heard that the people of Israel had gathered at Mizpah, the lords of the Philistines went up against Israel" (1 Sam. 7:7). The Philistines would have thought—accurately—that a spiritual renewal of Israel threatened their overlordship. Militarily superior, the Philistines confidently advanced on Mizpah, eager to snuff out this Israelite resurgence.

"When the people of Israel heard of it, they were afraid of the Philistines" (1 Sam. 7:7). It must have seemed like a replay of the earlier disaster. At the first battle of Ebenezer, the Philistines had appeared in their might. On that occasion, Israel's leaders had arrogantly sought to employ God's power through the ark. But this time they appealed to Samuel: "Do not cease to cry out to the LORD our God for us, that he may save us from the hand of the Philistines" (7:8). In the contrast between this scenario and the earlier battle, we see the difference between true and false religion. Earlier, summoning the ark, they had hoped "that *it* may come among us and save us" (4:3). Now they ask Samuel to pray to God "that *he* may save us" (7:8). False

6. Davis, *1 Samuel*, 60.

religion is always an impersonal, impious attempt to manipulate God's power for our own purpose. True religion is a personal relationship with the holy God, who reconciles us through the Mediator he has sent, cleanses us by the sacrifice he provides, and saves us by his mighty grace.

"As Samuel was offering up the burnt offering, the Philistines drew near to attack Israel. But the LORD thundered with a mighty sound that day against the Philistines and threw them into confusion, and they were routed before Israel" (1 Sam. 7:10). What a difference true religion makes! When God's people humbly come to God through the atoning blood and look to him in faith, God shows his power to save. Invigorated by God's mighty intervention, the Israelites sprang forward in new power: "The men of Israel went out from Mizpah and pursued the Philistines and struck them, as far as below Beth-car" (7:11). What a difference this was from the weakness and despair of Israel at the beginning of the chapter! The Israelites returned to the Lord, confessed their sins, and appealed to God's grace in Christ with a sincere faith.

RAISING EBENEZER

Scholars debate what really happened at Mizpah, offering all manner of creative suggestions to avoid the plain statement of the biblical text. Samuel's simple explanation was offered in the form of a memorial stone that he set in place on the site. He "called its name Ebenezer; for he said, 'Till now the LORD has helped us'" (1 Sam. 7:12). That is what happened at Mizpah: God helped his people by saving them from their enemies, just as he protects and preserves the souls of everyone who calls on his name in faith.

By erecting a memorial stone, Samuel was following in the footsteps of prior believers, especially Joshua. When God opened a way through the Jordan River for Israel to pass through, Joshua built a pile of stones to mark the event (Josh. 4:20–24). At the end of Joshua's life, when Israel gathered to renew the covenant at Shechem, Joshua set up a stone as a testimony (24:26). "The idea of these memorials," writes Gordon Keddie, "was that they be a standing witness to what God had done in the past for his people, and to what he would yet do in time to come."[7]

---

7. Gordon J. Keddie, *Dawn of a Kingdom: The Message of 1 Samuel* (Darlington, UK: Evangelical Press, 1988), 88.

The curious feature on this occasion was the name that Samuel gave to the memorial stone: *Ebenezer*. Ebenezer was the location of Israel's defeat twenty years earlier, many miles to the northwest. On that occasion the name of the place had mocked Israel's failure: *Ebenezer* means "stone of help," yet God refused to help Israel because of unbelief. Now, acting in faith, Israel had experienced God's help, and Samuel seems to want to make this point clear. Robert Bergen writes, "All that was lost through sin in the first Ebenezer event was restored through repentance in the second."[8]

Moreover, Samuel specifies, "Till now the LORD has helped us" (1 Sam. 7:12). He thus reminds Israel that this recent victory is just the latest in a long history of God's mighty redemptive acts, not the least of which was God's aid in helping the Israelites to repent. It is because of a long chain of mercies that the people of God exist in blessing. Samuel aims for the people to remember what God has done "till now," so that in the future they will again appeal to him in faith.

This account suggests that Christians should make memorials of God's grace in their own lives. There have been times when we turned to the Lord sincerely and he gave us his peace, met our need, and strengthened our faith to endure a trial. Kenneth Chafin tells us how to respond: "Often an individual can work out of a time of discouragement simply by stopping to remember all the blessings God has brought into his or her life."[9] In the future, we may find ourselves on dark paths, and we may think ourselves pushed to the limit of our endurance and tempted to despair. What we need then is to remember that "till now the LORD has helped us." God has been there for us in the past, so we are encouraged to trust him for today and tomorrow. The famous hymn drawn from this passage says, "Here I raise my Ebenezer; hither by thy help I'm come; / And I hope, by thy good pleasure, safely to arrive at home."[10] Christians do not live *in* the past, but we do live *out of* the past: we remember how God has proved his faithfulness and love, and thus we hope anew to arrive safely at home.

Of course, the great event to which we look in gratitude, memorialized by the Ebenezer stone of the Lord's Supper, is the cross of Jesus Christ. Looking to the cross, where God gave his own Son to save us from our sins, no

---

8. Bergen, *1, 2 Samuel*, 108.

9. Kenneth L. Chafin, *1 & 2 Samuel*, Preacher's Commentary, vol. 8 (Nashville: Thomas Nelson, 1989), 66.

10. Robert Robinson, "Come, Thou Fount of Every Blessing" (1758).

Christian can truly doubt God's help. With the cross in view, we say, "O to grace how great a debtor daily I'm constrained to be; / let that grace now, like a fetter, bind my wand'ring heart to thee."[11]

Just as the cross overcame our sin and gained us salvation, God's defeat of Israel's enemies led to a renewed time of peace: "The Philistines were subdued and did not again enter the territory of Israel. And the hand of the LORD was against the Philistines all the days of Samuel. The cities that the Philistines had taken from Israel were restored to Israel, from Ekron to Gath, and Israel delivered their territory from the hand of the Philistines. There was peace also between Israel and the Amorites" (1 Sam. 7:13–14). So it is when God's people are strong in the Lord. The history of revivals shows that when the gospel is advancing, vice is subdued in society. Blaikie writes: "Wherever the life and character of a godly man is such as to recall God, wherever God's image is plainly visible, wherever the results of God's presence are plainly seen, there the idea of a supernatural Power is conveyed, and a certain overawing influence is felt."[12]

Samuel's Ebenezer stone was intended to speak to such times, for prosperity and peace had often led Israel into idolatry in the past. The memorial was designed to inspire people to thanksgiving for the victory that God had graciously given and to remind them not to forsake God's help by turning away to other gods.

For the rest of his life, Samuel remained as judge over Israel: "And he went on a circuit year by year to Bethel, Gilgal, and Mizpah. And he judged Israel in all these places. Then he would return to Ramah, for his home was there, and there also he judged Israel. And he built there an altar to the LORD" (1 Sam. 7:16–17). By Samuel's traveling to different regions, his leadership served to unite the tribes of Israel, and in this way set the stage for the kingship that followed. While these words sum up years of ministry that followed the victory at Ebenezer, we can have little doubt regarding the message that Samuel continued to bring before the people, a message that is as true and urgent today as ever: "If you are returning to the LORD with all your heart, then put away the foreign gods . . . and direct your heart to the LORD and serve him only, . . . [for] till now the LORD has helped us" (1 Sam. 7:3, 12). May we never forget that grace, relying on the Lord's help in all our times of need.

11. Ibid.
12. Blaikie, *First Samuel*, 102.

PART 2

A King like All the Nations

12

A King like All the Nations

1 Samuel 8:1–22

Then all the elders of Israel gathered together and came to
Samuel at Ramah and said to him, "Behold, you are old and
your sons do not walk in your ways. Now appoint for us a king
to judge us like all the nations." (1 Sam. 8:4–5)

Samuel was one of the great leaders of the Bible, who "judged Israel all the days of his life" (1 Sam. 7:15). He played a historically pivotal role in the nation's transition from a tribal confederation to a monarchy. The years after his great victory over the Philistines saw a return to peace, prosperity, and national vigor. But there was one problem with Samuel. Being a man, he was mortal. Chapter 8 thus begins with this troubling reality: "Samuel became old" (1 Sam. 8:1).

The period of history covered by the books of Judges and Samuel was dominated by leadership crises. Judges laments, "In those days there was no king in Israel. Everyone did what was right in his own eyes" (Judg. 17:6; 21:25). God raised up judges to lead, and the people tried to make at least one of them king. Gideon rejected this offer, reminding them of the privilege of having the Lord as their only King: "I will not rule over you, and my son will not rule over you; the Lord will rule over you" (8:23). But the kingship of the invisible God strained the people's faith, so through Samuel God provided a human kingship, by which ultimately he established his sovereign rule over his people.

Churches today often suffer from leadership crises, especially during pastoral transitions. Like the Israelites of old, Christians must learn that God has appointed the means for governing his people and that God provides the leaders to do his will in the church. Relying on the Lord's provision may inspire us to take biblical qualifications more seriously and devote more effort and energy to prayer.

GIVE US A KING!

One time-honored solution to the problem of leadership is hereditary rule, whereby children follow their father into office. Samuel attempted this approach: "When Samuel became old, he made his sons judges over Israel. The name of his firstborn son was Joel, and the name of his second, Abijah; they were judges in Beersheba" (1 Sam. 8:1–2). The names that Samuel gave his sons suggest high expectations: *Joel* means "Yahweh is God," and *Abijah* means "Yahweh is our Father." We can easily understand why Samuel would want his sons to shoulder the difficult load of leading God's people. Likewise, many prominent ministries and churches engage in hereditary rule, with sons stepping directly into their fathers' shoes.

The problem is that the sons of great leaders, with some exceptions, are seldom great leaders themselves. Moreover, it is God who provides leaders for his people, and the practice of nepotism runs contrary to the idea of God's special calling in his church. Four of Israel's judges were succeeded by their sons (Gideon, Jair, Eli, and Samuel), and it is no surprise that the result was negative in three of these cases. The Bible says that Christ provides leaders by his gracious distribution of spiritual gifts (Eph. 4:7–12) and that godly character, not bloodline, qualifies men to lead the church (1 Tim. 3:1–7; Titus 1:7–9). By this standard, Samuel's sons fell desperately short: "his sons did not walk in his ways but turned aside after gain. They took bribes and perverted justice" (1 Sam. 8:3).

With these leadership concerns on their minds, the elders of Israel came to Samuel. Given the earlier debacle with Eli's wicked sons, we can understand their anxiety: "Behold, you are old and your sons do not walk in your ways"

(1 Sam. 8:5). If we remember the lessons taught earlier in 1 Samuel, we know that the elders should now await a word from the Lord by his prophet. But as so often happened in those days (and in our own), the elders did not come to listen to the prophet but to dictate their plans to Samuel.

Earlier, Israel's leaders had concocted the idea of bringing the ark of the covenant up to the battlefield, confident that God's holy box would give them a fighting edge (1 Sam. 4:4). On that occasion, God was angered and gave them into their enemies' hands. Once again, the Israelites have their own idea about what needs to happen: "Now appoint for us a king to judge us like all the nations" (8:5). Their reasoning is easy to follow: the system of periodic judges wasn't working, and now Samuel was nearing his death; the constant military threat from the Philistines and Ammonites argued for consistent executive control (see 12:12). Finally, since his sons had disqualified themselves and since a leadership vacuum could jeopardize the nation, Samuel should provide the kind of ruler that other nations enjoyed: "appoint for us a king." John Woodhouse explains that a king "offered a strong, stable, and predictable center of political authority for a nation that otherwise had to depend on an unseen God to unite them. Furthermore, the kingship held out the promise of efficient central organization to a nation that, lacking such structures, tended to lurch from one crisis to the next."[1]

The elders reasoned that the proven solutions in worldly institutions would work just as well for a divine institution such as Israel. The same logic is displayed today when the church is urged to imitate the practices that make corporations so effective and efficient. How often it is said today that by copying worldly approaches to recruitment, marketing, and product delivery, the church can expand God's market share in the world! The reasoning of Israel's elders continues to be heard among God's people: "Appoint for us a king . . . like all the nations" (1 Sam. 8:5).

How should we understand the elders' demand? Bill Arnold describes it as sinful in its motives, since their request represented a rebellion against God's rule; selfish in its timing, since they demanded God's provision at the time of their own choosing; and cowardly in its spirit, since they sought a system that would remove the need for their faith in the Lord.[2]

---

1. John Woodhouse, *1 Samuel: Looking for a Leader* (Wheaton, IL: Crossway, 2008), 145.
2. Bill T. Arnold, *1 & 2 Samuel*, NIV Application Commentary (Grand Rapids: Zondervan, 2003), 153–54.

The alternative to their demand was a true seeking after God, including their willingness to walk in his ways. But as before, it seemed easier to seek a new gimmick, a new device, rather than the repentance needed to be restored to the Lord.

SAMUEL'S PRAYER AND GOD'S ANSWER

Having learned from his years of experience, Samuel did what the elders should have done: he turned to the Lord in prayer. "The thing displeased Samuel when they said, 'Give us a king to judge us,'" but instead of acting in anger, "Samuel prayed to the LORD" (1 Sam. 8:6). He provides an example of wisdom, reminding us to respond to every challenge or need by first turning to God in prayer.

The Lord's answer was somewhat surprising, especially since he did not seem as indignant as his prophet. God had three replies for Samuel. First, he ministered to his servant by assuring him that the fault did not lie with him. Samuel had not failed Israel, and the people were not rejecting him: "they have not rejected you, but they have rejected me from being king over them" (1 Sam. 8:7). In fact, this episode was merely the latest in a long history of Israel's rejecting God's rule: "According to all the deeds that they have done, from the day I brought them up out of Egypt even to this day, forsaking me and serving other gods, so they are also doing to you" (8:8). From the moment Israel stepped free from the bondage of Egypt, the Lord had been their King. Yet Israel's unbelief and rebellion were recurrent problems, so Samuel should not think himself the cause of their disaffection. These words should console every pastor, teacher, or parent whose charges refuse to follow in the way of the Lord: so long as we have been faithful to teach and lead, the failure is not ours, and we share our sense of rejection with the Lord.

Second, with this in mind, God knew how to answer the elders: by agreeing to their request! God frequently responds this way to rebellion among his people. When we demand a substitute for God, the Lord will allow us to experience worldly and unbelieving rule, with all its harmful consequences. This is not because God was thwarted by the elders' obstinacy or that God found himself at his wits' end. Rather, God intended a humbling lesson that might result in future repentance and restoration.

This reminds us that we should not always be encouraged when God seems to answer our prayers. Here, God's relenting was a sign not of his blessing but of his chastisement. The more we realize how sinful our hearts are and how frequently our thoughts and desires run astray, the more we will humbly desire God to overrule in our prayers so that his wisdom will overcome our folly, and his holiness will correct our sin.

THE WAYS OF KINGS

God's third response was to command Samuel: "Now then, obey their voice; only you shall solemnly warn them and show them the ways of the king who shall reign over them" (1 Sam. 8:9). It was remarkably patient of God to provide his obstinate people with a detailed warning about what they were demanding. Accordingly, "Samuel told all the words of the LORD to the people who were asking for a king from him" (8:10).

What follows is an extraordinarily accurate depiction of the ordinary results of human lordship. Samuel describes human kingship not just at its most depraved but in its very nature, featuring two verbs: *take* and *serve*. The king will take, and they will serve:

> These will be the ways of the king who will reign over you: he will take your sons and appoint them to his chariots and to be his horsemen and to run before his chariots. And he will appoint for himself commanders of thousands and commanders of fifties, and some to plow his ground and to reap his harvest, and to make his implements of war and the equipment of his chariots. He will take your daughters to be perfumers and cooks and bakers. He will take the best of your fields and vineyards and olive orchards and give them to his servants. He will take the tenth of your grain and of your vineyards and give it to his officers and to his servants. He will take your male servants and female servants and the best of your young men and your donkeys, and put them to his work. He will take the tenth of your flocks, and you shall be his slaves. (1 Sam. 8:11–17)

The word *take* occurs six times. A king will "take your sons" to serve in his armies and die in his battles. When not fighting, their sons will be taken by the king as virtual serfs "to plow his ground and to reap his harvest" or to wearily work in his factories. But that is not all, for a king will "take your daughters" as well. The Israelites should not think that their daughters would be able to stay at home tending to the family. They would be needed for government work as "perfumers and cooks and bakers." Then the king "will take the best of your fields and vineyards and olive orchards," so that he can reward his most successful servants. There will be an extra tithe of all produce so that high-ranking officials can live in proper luxury. Finally, a king would take Israel's servants so that they work no longer in their fields or in their house, but in the king's fields, doing his work. In short, whenever people appeal to a human leader to save them from all their problems, the inevitable result is that they are reduced to Israel's former status in Egypt: "you shall be his slaves" (1 Sam. 8:17).

This was Samuel's message then, and it is true today as well. If they did not want divine rule, but the kind of leaders who rule "all the nations," then the Israelites would experience the usual lot of mankind: slavery to oppressive masters. Likewise today, those who want national government to provide for all their needs must be ready to sign away their rights as free people. If the government is to solve all our problems, then the government must be obeyed in all things and most of what we have must be given to it. However much a king may accomplish for the nation, it is certain that he will take more than he gives. He will take and you will serve: such is the despotism whenever sinful men are set in the place of God over our lives.

This principle is even more true when it comes to our yielding to sin, the great slave master of our world. Jesus said, "Everyone who commits sin is a slave to sin" (John 8:34). We think we will dabble in sin while retaining control over our passions, but it is not true. Sin takes and we serve, until finally sin destroys us in the holy judgment of God.

Undoubtedly, the people of Israel wanted to have their cake and eat it, too. They were willing to observe God's religion only if they had a secular government; they wanted a faith of private piety, not of public reliance. Likewise, the trappings of religion are permitted by secular governments today, enlisting God's endorsement of man's sovereign rule, so long as God agrees not to have any say in our affairs. But God does not accommodate such a scheme. He told the Israelite elders that if they wanted a human king, they would have to rely on him without help from the Lord: "In that day you will cry out because of your king, whom you have chosen for yourselves, but the LORD will not answer you in that day" (1 Sam. 8:18).

This scenario played out within two generations, as Israel experienced the very oppression that Samuel had predicted under King David's son and successor, King Solomon. Solomon spent seven years building the Lord's temple (1 Kings 6:38), but he took thirteen years building an even more spectacular palace for himself (7:1). To accomplish this feat, Solomon pressed much of Israel into forced labor (5:13–18). Solomon took and they served, and when Solomon died the elders appealed to his son Rehoboam for leniency. They pleaded, "Your father made our yoke heavy. Now therefore lighten the hard service . . . , and we will serve you" (12:4). Rehoboam responded as any king would, refusing to begin his reign with a sign of weakness. He boasted, "My little finger is thicker than my father's thighs. And now, whereas my father laid on you a heavy yoke, I will add to your yoke" (12:10–11). In this way, God gave his people over to the misery of their own unbelieving folly, and their cries for relief went unanswered. "No!" they had insisted, as they rejected Samuel's warning. "There shall be a king over us, that we also may be like all the nations, and that our king may judge us and go out before us and fight our battles" (1 Sam. 8:19–20). The Lord relented, sealing on them his judgment: "Obey their voice and make them a king." So Samuel dismissed the elders, saying, "Go every man to his city" (8:22).

TWO INTERRELATED PRINCIPLES

This episode reveals two related aspects of faith in the Lord and, correspondingly, two related forces that act against our faith. The first aspect of our faith is our calling to be exclusively devoted to the Lord. Moses commanded, "You shall love the LORD your God with all your heart and with all your soul and with all your might" (Deut. 6:5). Jesus referred to this as "the great and first commandment" (Matt. 22:37–38). At the heart of the covenant relationship was this obligation of mutual devotion: God has shown his love to you; now love and honor him in all things. Thus, the demand for a king was an affront to the very heart of Israel's covenant relationship with God.

The second great obligation of the old covenant was Israel's calling to holiness: "For you are a people holy to the LORD your God, and the LORD has chosen you to be a people for his treasured possession, out of all the peoples who are on the face of the earth" (Deut. 14:2). God's people were to be different from the nations in practically every way: their way of thinking, their patterns of behavior, their goals, and their methods were to be godly and not worldly. By demanding a king "like all the nations" (1 Sam. 8:5), the Israelite elders rejected God's call for them to be holy and set apart from the unbelieving world.

Both of these principles are fully valid for Christians today. The insight we should take from the elders' rejection of exclusive devotion to the Lord and of holiness before the world is that these two principles either stand or fall together. It is not by chance that in rejecting the Lord, the Israelite elders were demanding to be like the nations, or that by longing to conform with the world, they ended up repudiating the true God. There is a synergy between the vertical dimension of our faith—our devotion to and delight in the Lord—and the horizontal dimension—our separation from worldliness and sin. What is it, after all, that emboldens Christians to stand firm in the ways of the Lord, accepting the difficulty of always being opposed by the prevailing winds of the world? The answer is that our calling to holiness can be empowered only by our awe for God's glory and our gratitude for God's saving grace. This is why Paul says that it is "the grace of God" that teaches us "to renounce ungodliness and worldly passions, and to live self-controlled, upright, and godly lives in the present age, waiting for our blessed hope, the appearing of the glory of our great God and Savior Jesus Christ" (Titus 2:11–13). It is the wonder of grace and the glory of God that seals our hearts for holy living.

We might say the same thing backwards: by separating our hearts from the pleasures and treasures of a sin-stained world, by keeping our minds free from the lies of false religion and vain philosophy, we strengthen ourselves for faithfulness to the Lord. Faithfulness to God and holiness before the world are inseparable and mutually supportive. But in reverse they are equally supportive in spiritual failure. Israel forgot the Lord and thus pursued the false gods of the world. Idolatry then drew the people's hearts further from God and corrupted their spiritual appetite through pagan practices. In this way, God's holy people became an unbelieving nation, demanding a king "like all the nations" in the place of God.

While these two principles are mutually related, we must always give priority to the vertical dimension. The spiritual decline that led to God's rejection had begun decades earlier when "there arose another generation . . . who did not know the LORD or the work that he had done for Israel"

(Judg. 2:10). This reminds us that there is no higher or more urgent calling in the church than for preaching that begins with God and not man, that focuses on God's great saving deeds in history, culminating in Jesus Christ, and not the issues and problems reported in newspapers and magazines. What is true for the church is true for individuals: those who do not know the Lord or his saving work will inevitably fall into the ways and worship of the world. Thus, "churches that lose their focus on God inevitably become worldly in their practice, which leads them further from God until there is hardly anything distinctly Christian left. But those who make the knowledge and glory of God their prime focus are pulled back from the world with its methods and its idols and are thus drawn close in reliance on and fellowship with the Lord."[3]

Biblical Standards for Christian Leadership

Despite Samuel's negative opinion and God's own condemnation of the elders' motives, it was not strictly contrary to God's Word for Israel to have a human king. The sinfulness of the elders' attitude is obvious, yet their idea for a king may well have come from God's Word. For instance, God had told Abraham, "I will make you into nations, and kings shall come from you" (Gen. 17:6). Moreover, Moses' final directions included God's instructions for future kings in Israel. We know that God saw the elders' demand as a rejection of himself and a plea for worldliness (1 Sam. 8:7–8), yet earlier he had anticipated this very event: "When you come to the land that the Lord your God is giving you, and you possess it and dwell in it and then say, 'I will set a king over me, like all the nations that are around me,' you may indeed set a king over you" (Deut. 17:14–15). This allowance was designed to promote godliness, not worldliness, in Israel's kings. These principles are valid and vital today for establishing godly leadership in the church.

First, leaders over God's people must be chosen and called by him: "you may indeed set a king over you whom the Lord your God will choose" (Deut. 17:15). In that time, God revealed his choice through special revelation by a prophet, as would happen when Samuel later anointed first Saul and then David as Israel's king. In the New Testament, when the apostles

3. Richard D. Phillips, *Turning Back the Darkness: The Biblical Pattern of Reformation* (Wheaton, IL: Crossway, 2002), 47.

141

sought to replace Judas with a new apostle, God revealed his choice through the casting of lots (Acts 1:26). Today, God brings forth his leaders by having qualified men approved by the elders and their calling recognized as the church gives its assent. Divinely appointed men (the New Testament restricts church office to men only; see 1 Tim. 2:11–12; 3:2; Titus 1:6) do not inherit eldership or ordination, they do not apply for the job, and they do not fall into ministry for lack of anything better to do. True spiritual leaders are chosen and equipped by God, and their calling is affirmed by the Spirit speaking through the church.

Second, God ordained that Israel's kings must come "from among your brothers." "You may not put a foreigner over you, who is not your brother" (Deut. 17:15). It goes without saying that pastors and elders must be Christians, just as Israel's kings must be drawn from God's people. But by repeating the word *brother*, the Lord was making an additional point. Christian leaders must have a fellow feeling for those under their spiritual authority. They should not be aloof from the trials and hardships of their flocks, so as to have sympathy on those who err or fall.

Third, "he must not acquire many horses for himself . . . And he shall not acquire many wives for himself, lest his heart turn away, nor shall he acquire for himself excessive silver and gold" (Deut. 17:16–17). The New Testament teaches that the worldly needs of pastors should be provided for so as to enable them to focus on the spiritual care and feeding of the flock. "You shall not muzzle an ox when it treads out the grain," Paul writes, for "the laborer deserves his wages" (1 Tim. 5:18). "If we have sown spiritual things among you, is it too much if we reap material things from you?" he asks (1 Cor. 9:11). Yet there should be no trappings of excess or pursuit of worldly luxury, and the increasing practice of celebrity preachers' receiving exorbitant sums far above any reasonable need is a scandal to our generation. While ministers should be paid generously, they should always remember that their income arises from the tithes and offerings of God's often-suffering people. Peter therefore emphasizes that church leaders must serve "not for shameful gain, but eagerly; not domineering over those in your charge, but being examples to the flock" (1 Peter 5:2–3).

Finally, a God-honoring leader will be under the authority of God's Word in all things. This was God's chief provision for godly kingship. He directed that the first thing any man would do upon ascending to the throne was to "write for himself in a book a copy of this law, approved by the Levitical priests" (Deut. 17:18). He was literally to make his own handwritten copy of God's Word, acceptable to the priests, which he was then to carry with him everywhere he went. "It shall be with him, and he shall read in it all the days of his life, that he may learn to fear the LORD his God by keeping all the words of this law and these statutes, and doing them" (17:19). This, then, is the ultimate standard of Christian leadership: an observable commitment to God's Word that is reflected in careful obedience to all that the Bible teaches and commands. This standard—not a dynamic personality, not political influence, not managerial ability—is the key to all spiritual leadership. A true spiritual leader must be able to say with King David, "I will delight in your statutes; I will not forget your word" (Ps. 119:16).

THE GOVERNMENT ON HIS SHOULDERS

God's true plan for reigning over his people involved a man who would reign as King forever. Indeed, the last duty of Samuel would be to anoint young David and then guide him in his struggling first steps. But David was only a forerunner of the true and great King, who would arise from his own line. God promised David: "I will raise up your offspring after you, who shall come from your body, and I will establish his kingdom. . . . Your throne shall be established forever" (2 Sam. 7:12, 16). The very heart of the Old Testament is the promise of this saving Shepherd-King, who would fulfill the prophecies by being born both Son of David and Son of God. Isaiah sang, "For to us a child is born, to us a son is given; and the government shall be upon his shoulder, and his name shall be called Wonderful Counselor, Mighty God, Everlasting Father, Prince of Peace" (Isa. 9:6). Micah foretold: "But you, O Bethlehem Ephrathah, who are too little to be among the clans of Judah, from you shall come forth for me one who is to be ruler in Israel, whose coming forth is from of old, from ancient days" (Mic. 5:2). These prophecies were fulfilled, and our King provided, in the coming of Jesus Christ, who was born of woman and also "Son of the Most High . . . the Son of God" (Luke 1:32, 35).

What a contrast there is between Jesus and the kings described by Samuel! Jesus is not a King who takes, but a King who gives. Jesus said, "The Son of Man came not to be served but to serve, and to give his life as a ransom for many" (Matt. 20:28). He gave his own life on the cross, dying in our place, that we might be freed from the guilt of our sin. He is the King "who loves us and has freed us from our sins by his blood" (Rev. 1:5). And when our King Jesus stood before the powers of this age, with the wounds of their scourges deep in his flesh, he stated clearly to Pontius Pilate: "My kingdom is not of this world" (John 18:36). Jesus Christ is a King, but not "a king . . . like all the nations," a King who serves the least in his kingdom and gives eternal life to those who love and trust in him. If we will take him for our King—this man who is also God—then we will enter with him into the glorious realm long prepared by his Father, and he will share with us the marvels and blessings of God—treasures that are not of this world but that will endure forever in the Promised Land of the age that is to come.

13

BEHOLD, YOUR KING!

1 Samuel 9:1—10:16

*There was not a man among the people of Israel more
handsome than he. From his shoulders upward he was taller
than any of the people.* (1 Sam. 9:2)

he opening words of 1 Samuel 9 indicate that a new section of
the book has been reached. When we read, "There was a man
of Benjamin whose name was Kish" (1 Sam. 9:1), we recall
the opening words of chapter 1: "There was a certain man of Ramathaim-
zophim" (1:1). The first section of 1 Samuel (chapters 1–8) relates the rise
and rule of Samuel as Israel's judge, ending with the elders' demand for "a
king . . . like all the nations" (1 Sam. 8:5). Chapter 9 begins a new section
(chapters 9–31) by presenting this king, whose entry parallels our earlier
introduction to Samuel.

This repetition reminds us that the books of Samuel deal with the question of leadership for God's people. The elders demanded a different kind
of leadership from what God had given through the judges—men called
forth by God as need arose. Instead, they desired the kind of hereditary
kingship that the other nations possessed: "There shall be a king over us,
that we also may be like all the nations" (1 Sam. 8:19–20). Samuel warned

145

that such a king would take all that they had and reduce them to the status of slaves. But when the elders insisted, the Lord instructed Samuel to "obey their voice and make them a king" (8:22). Samuel responded by sending the elders home until God should reveal this king. In chapter 9, God provides Saul the son of Kish, through whom Israel will learn their folly in demanding to be "like all the nations."

THE SON OF KISH

The first thing we learn about Saul is his lineage: "There was a man of Benjamin whose name was Kish, the son of Abiel, son of Zeror, son of Becorath, son of Aphiah, a Benjaminite, a man of wealth" (1 Sam. 9:1). This is not a distinguished family tree—none of these names hold any distinction in the Bible—although Saul's father possessed a degree of prominence and wealth. Moreover, Benjamin was the smallest of Israel's tribes, its namesake being the last of Jacob's twelve sons. From a political standpoint, Benjamin was not a bad choice to provide a king, however, since a member of this tribe could mediate between the powerful tribes of Judah to the south and Ephraim to the north.

The name *Saul* means "asked for" or "dedicated" (cf. 1 Sam. 1:28). This corresponds to the elders' request for a king. Saul was, in fact, exactly what Israel had asked for: the kind of person admired according to worldly standards. The world admires someone who looks and acts like a leader, and Saul was "a handsome young man." Indeed, "there was not a man among the people of Israel more handsome than he" (1 Sam. 9:2). The word translated as "handsome" is simply the word *good* (Hebrew, *tov*). The point is that Saul made a very good impression, in both his appearance and bearing. Dale Ralph Davis quips, "People would have voted him Mr. Israel had there been such a contest."[1] Moreover, in a world that values physical stature, Saul was something of a giant: "From his shoulders upward [Saul] was taller than any of the people" (1 Sam. 9:2). The fact that Saul is the only Israelite identified in the Bible for his great height—physical stature always being a mark of Israel's enemies (cf. Num. 13:33; Deut. 1:28; 2:10; 9:2; 1 Sam. 17:4)—amplifies the impres-

---

1. Dale Ralph Davis, *1 Samuel: Looking on the Heart* (Fearn, Ross-shire, UK: Christian Focus, 2000), 74.

sion that Saul is precisely the kind of king who would be chosen by "all the nations."

The story of Saul begins with a common event in that agricultural world: "Now the donkeys of Kish, Saul's father, were lost. So Kish said to Saul his son, 'Take one of the young men with you, and arise, go and look for the donkeys'" (1 Sam. 9:3). Saul and his servant thus undertook a circuitous quest for the missing animals, with the result that they did not find the donkeys but did find themselves in "the land of Zuph" (9:5). Zuph was home to Israel's prophet-judge, Samuel.

Along the way, several credentials support Saul's prospects for leadership. In verse 5, Saul shows respect and concern for his father, wanting to return home "lest my father cease to care about the donkeys and become anxious about us" (1 Sam. 9:5). Second, when Saul's servant suggests that they consult with "a man of God in this city" (9:6), Saul insists that they appear before the Lord's servant only if they had a suitable gift: "But if we go, what can we bring the man? For the bread in our sacks is gone, and there is no present to bring to the man of God" (1 Sam. 9:7). This was the kind of thing expected in Israel's social world when a traveler appeared unannounced before a person of eminence,[2] and Saul was careful to act accordingly.

Furthermore, the fact that Saul and his servant came to inquire of God's prophet sets him apart from Israel's other leaders, such as those who heedlessly brought the ark of the covenant to the battlefield (1 Sam. 4:3–4) and the elders who demanded a worldly king (8:5). Saul and his servant remind us that there are no matters so trivial that God does not invite us to seek his counsel through prayer and the study of his Word. God's wisdom says, "In all your ways acknowledge him, and he will make straight your paths" (Prov. 3:6).

A second point made by this travel account is that while Saul was humanly impressive, he nonetheless was not a true spiritual leader. This is the major point made throughout chapters 9 and 10. First, Saul's aptitude for spiritual leadership is besmirched by his inability to find his father's lost donkeys. Most of Israel's famed leaders had been shepherds—Abraham, Isaac, Jacob, and Moses—so Saul's incompetence at tracking down even such large beasts (who eventually found their own way home) is unflattering, to say the least.

---

2. C. H. Gordon, cited in David Toshio Tsumura, *The First Book of Samuel*, New International Commentary on the Old Testament (Grand Rapids: Eerdmans, 2007), 269.

One of the most important qualifications of a spiritual leader is faithfulness in watching over God's flock (Heb. 13:17; 1 Peter 5:2–3), but this was not the kind of thing at which Saul excelled.

Moreover, some scholars argue that Saul's concern over a gift for "the man of God" in Zuph was not mere social courtesy but his belief that God's servants were to be hired with cash. This is precisely the attitude that worldly people have toward pastors and churches today: religion, they think, is just another business.

Additionally, the text highlights Saul's ignorance of the man of God to whom his servant referred. Here is "a man who is held in honor; all that he says comes true" (1 Sam. 9:6). We will soon find out that the servant is referring to Samuel himself. Earlier, we learned that "all Israel from Dan to Beersheba knew that Samuel was established as a prophet of the LORD" (3:20), and that "the word of Samuel came to all Israel" (4:1). Yet Saul had never heard of him! Apparently he had been too busy becoming outwardly impressive to take any interest in spiritual matters. Saul's complete ignorance of Israel's chief prophet and judge is confirmed later, when he meets Samuel and asks, "Tell me where is the house of the seer?" (9:18), only to learn that he was speaking to the man himself. Saul's spiritual blindness will play a significant role in events to come, especially as he misjudges the motives of his godly son Jonathan and sees in faithful David a threat to his throne.

Finally, we observe that while Saul was in charge, it was actually his servant who led while Saul followed. It was the servant, not Saul, who insisted that they inquire of God's prophet. Later, when he became king, Saul would frequently be influenced by the counsel of others rather than steering a course charted by his own faith and convictions.

We recognize Saul, do we not? Saul is among us today as the executive who runs the company into the ground while demanding a lavish bonus, or the politician who masters the art of public speaking but never really tells the truth. The Sauls of the world have little competence for the actual job at hand, but only the carefully cultivated impression of superiority. The Sauls have few convictions but many ambitions. They are led by the winds of changing fashion. This was the kind of king the Israelites demanded, and in a corrupt world like ours, Saul is the kind of man who often comes to prominence and power.

A final point made in the opening section of chapter 9 is God's providential control over the small affairs of our lives, according to his sovereign will. Chasing donkeys was a common affair in which Saul's will was fully engaged. Yet it was God's unfolding plan that directed the paths of men in ways completely unforeseen by them. It is obvious from the text that God had ordained every detail of this journey, even having Saul and his servant arrive at the town gates at precisely the moment Samuel walked through them (1 Sam. 9:14). Here we are reminded that God's utter sovereignty over even the smallest details of life does not conflict with the full expression of human choice and will. Through the small affairs of human lives, God fulfills his covenant promises and purposes. He had promised to provide Israel with a king like the nations, and by his appointed means this promise would be fulfilled. Moreover, this event would work toward God's own sovereign plan for his people, foreknown and ordained in eternity past: "Known to God from eternity are all His works" (Acts 15:18 NKJV). God's people seldom know how God intends to use the simple events of their lives or the great things that God will make out of our small affairs, but we do know that "for those who love God all things work together for good, for those who are called according to his purpose" (Rom. 8:28). In this respect, Saul's selection as Israel's king reminds us of God's provision of his Son, Jesus, to reign as the Savior for his people. Whereas the religious leaders in Jerusalem thought they were betraying just another rabbi in handing Jesus over to the Romans, Peter declared that God's eternal plan of redemption was truly at work. On Pentecost Sunday, Peter preached to the Jews about Jesus, whom they had "delivered up according to the definite plan and foreknowledge of God, [and] crucified and killed by the hands of lawless men" (Acts 2:23).

God's Message to Samuel

God's purpose in Saul's donkey chase is made apparent as soon as we obtain Samuel's perspective. Saul had been about to return home when his servant produced a coin to be given to the prophet (verse 9 notes that the former term *seer* refers to the prophet) in exchange for news of their lost donkeys. Saul consented, and the two went up into the city, which we may presume was Samuel's hometown of Ramah, in the land of Zuph. As they went, there just happened to be some young women coming out who knew exactly where the seer was. "Hurry," they urged. "He has come just now to the city, because the people have a sacrifice today on the high place. As soon as you enter the city you will find him, before he goes up to the high place to eat" (1 Sam. 9:12–13). The women added what Saul may not have known, that "the people will not eat till he comes, since he must bless the sacrifice" (9:13). Sure enough, when they entered the city they ran straight into Samuel.

Saul and his servant did not know that the great prophet and judge was expecting them. But Samuel had been advised through a message from God received the previous day: "Tomorrow about this time I will send to you a man from the land of Benjamin, and you shall anoint him to be prince over my people Israel. He shall save my people from the hand of the Philistines. For I have seen my people, because their cry has come to me" (1 Sam. 9:16). As Saul approached, God spoke to Samuel again: "Here is the man of whom I spoke to you! He it is who shall restrain my people" (9:17). Because of God's foreordained plan, this "chance" meeting was a momentous occasion in the history of Israel, as well as for these two important figures whose lives would henceforth be intertwined.

Samuel learned, first, that he was to anoint Saul as "prince" or "commander" over Israel. It is interesting that the Lord did not identify Saul as Israel's king, although the term might refer to Saul's status as king-designate.[3] In any case, we see that the Lord has not changed his approach based on the elders' demand: God is still raising up a man of his own choosing to lead his people in troubled times. Even though Saul would be made king by popular demand, he would still be raised up as God's choice, as had been true of the judges.

Second, God's intention was that Saul would "save my people from the hand of the Philistines" (1 Sam. 9:16). These seafaring enemies, beaten back earlier in Samuel's judgeship, had now regained much of their oppressive control over Israel. This is why the elders had demanded a king to "go out before us and fight our battles" (8:20). Saul was the kind of leader who could rally the nation for battle, and God would use him to this end.

Third, we learn God's motive: "For I have seen my people, because their cry has come to me" (1 Sam. 9:16). These are precious words when we realize

---

3. See David F. Payne, *I & II Samuel*, Daily Study Bible (Philadelphia: Westminster, 1992), 50.

how many times Israel had angered the Lord, and how at this very time the elders had rebelled against him. Paul wrote, "If we are faithless, he remains faithful—for he cannot deny himself" (2 Tim. 2:13). Davis comments: "These foolish, stubborn people do not cease to be objects of Yahweh's compassions. . . . If you are a child of God, you rejoice to see . . . that your sin does not dry up the fountain of his compassions, that his pity refuses to let go of his people."[4]

Fourth, when Saul arrived, God added, "He it is who shall restrain my people" (1 Sam. 9:17). There is debate about the meaning of the word translated here as *restrain* (Hebrew, *yaazar*). Several English versions render this as saying that Saul will *rule* God's people (KJV, NIV, NKJV, NLT), but this is not the word's meaning. Robert Bergen points out that this word is almost always used in a negative way, connoting imprisonment or hindrance. He thus argues that "the Lord had determined to use Saul's career as a means of punishing the nation. . . . As he governed Israel, his policies and behavior would hinder the welfare of the nation and act as a sort of barrier separating Israel from God's best for them."[5] The biblical record shows that this is precisely what happened during Saul's reign as king: despite his early military successes, his death in battle would leave Israel in no better condition than when he arrived.

Before moving on, we should notice that three times in his message to Samuel, the Lord refers to Israel as "my people." Saul will be prince "over my people Israel"; Saul will "save my people," since "I have seen my people, because their cry has come to me" (1 Sam. 9:16). This shows that however rebellious his people might be, God had no intention of relinquishing his ownership of or his love for them. Later, Samuel refers to Israel as the Lord's "heritage" (10:1). This expresses the permanency of God's ownership of Israel, since a heritage is "an indisputable possession that cannot be transferred to another."[6] The people would get their king, but they would never replace God with Saul or any other human ruler. What an undeserved blessing it was for Israel to be named the heritage of the Lord, held in God's love by unwavering, sovereign grace. What a blessing it is for Christians today to

4. Davis, *1 Samuel*, 77.
5. Robert D. Bergen, *1, 2 Samuel*, New American Commentary (Nashville: Broadman & Holman, 1996), 123.
6. Woodhouse, *1 Samuel*, 169.

be designated as God's "holy nation, a people for his own possession, that you may proclaim the excellencies of him who called you out of darkness into his marvelous light" (1 Peter 2:9).

SAUL ANOINTED

Saul knew nothing of God's message, nor did he know who Samuel was. But Samuel knew Saul, and he responded to the young man's greeting by summoning him to come to the sacrifice and spend the night. First, Samuel informed Saul not to worry about the donkeys, which had been found. The prophet then alluded to Saul's destiny. "For whom is all that is desirable in Israel?" he asked. "Is it not for you and for all your father's house?" (1 Sam. 9:20). This likely refers to the plea of the elders for an impressive man to be king. Saul was puzzled, given his humble origins. He answered: "Am I not a Benjaminite, from the least of the tribes of Israel? And is not my clan the humblest of all the clans of the tribe of Benjamin? Why then have you spoken to me in this way?" (9:21).

The long section from 1 Samuel 9:22 to 10:8 recounts the honor that Samuel showed to Saul, Samuel's private anointing of Saul, and Samuel's instructions for what Saul should do. Saul was surprised to be seated at the place of honor, with the choice cuts of meat set aside in advance for his coming. Samuel said, "See, what was kept is set before you. Eat, because it was kept for you until the hour appointed, that you might eat with the guests" (1 Sam. 9:24). This was followed by the special privilege of a night over at Samuel's house, followed by a private meeting at dawn. All of this was designed to impress upon Saul his elevation to so important a position.

In the morning, as Samuel escorted Saul to the town gates, he pulled Saul aside privately, "that I may make known to you the word of God" (1 Sam. 9:27). Samuel then poured a flask of oil over Saul's head, kissed him as a sign of honor, and declared to Saul, "Has not the LORD anointed you to be prince over his people Israel?" (10:1). To further explain, Samuel added, "And you shall reign over the people of the LORD and you will save them from the hand of their surrounding enemies" (10:1). This anointing signified God's authority over Saul, having installed him first as his own servant and only then as king of Israel. Anointing also symbolized the Holy Spirit's equipping for God's specially chosen servants.

The anointing was followed with three signs, which were designed to certify to Saul the truth of Samuel's message and the divine authority behind it. The first sign foretold that near the tomb of Rachel, Saul would encounter two men who would inform Saul of the finding of the donkeys and his father's concern for his safety (1 Sam. 10:2). The second sign would force Saul to acknowledge his anointed status, since it would involve three men on their way to worship at Bethel, "one carrying three young goats, another carrying three loaves of bread, and another carrying a skin of wine" (10:3). Greeting Saul, the men would give him these offerings that were designated for the Lord, and in accepting them Saul would acknowledge his newly anointed status (10:4). The third sign would happen near Saul's home at Gibeath-elohim (meaning "hill of God"):

> As soon as you come to the city, you will meet a group of prophets coming down from the high place with harp, tambourine, flute, and lyre before them, prophesying. Then the Spirit of the Lord will rush upon you, and you will prophesy with them and be turned into another man. Now when these signs meet you, do what your hand finds to do, for God is with you. (10:5–7)

This last sign would confirm that it really was God who had anointed Saul; it would also provide the divine equipping that Saul's calling demanded.

Finally, Samuel had God's instructions for Saul, showing that even under the new monarchy, Israel's kings were to be subordinate to God's Word through the prophets. Samuel had mentioned the Philistine garrison in Gibeath-elohim, and now he suggested that Saul attack it: "Now when these signs meet you, do what your hand finds to do, for God is with you" (1 Sam. 10:7). Saul was then to go to Gilgal, the place where Joshua had renewed Israel's covenant with God, to wait for Samuel's coming in a week. There, Samuel would offer burnt offerings to cover Israel's sins and peace offerings, which were presumably intended to thank God for the victory Saul would have won over the Philistine garrison (10:7–8).

Saul among the Prophets

Israel's elders had demanded a worldly king, and God sent Saul as his answer. Saul was the messiah (i.e., "anointed one") and king for unbelieving

153

Israel, and he would bring relief from the heavy Philistine hand. To this end, God sent his Spirit to equip Saul for the task ahead. 1 Samuel 10:9 says that as Saul departed from Samuel, "God gave him another heart." Then, when Saul encountered the band of prophets at Gibeah, "the Spirit of God rushed upon him, and he prophesied among them" (1 Sam. 10:10).

Those who previously knew Saul were surprised. They marveled, "What has come over the son of Kish? Is Saul also among the prophets?" (1 Sam. 10:11). This saying became a local proverb, meaning roughly the same thing as our expression "Wonders never cease!" One man mocked Saul's new association, asking, "And who is their father?" (10:12), probably alluding to the fact that Saul did not come from a family that typically produced God's prophets. At first reading, all this might encourage us to conclude that God had sent a true messiah to lead his people into a golden era of faith and spiritual power.

The failure of this view is seen in the final verses of this passage, which relate Saul's subsequent actions. According to the Bible, the way to evaluate a purported spiritual rebirth is to observe the lifestyle that follows. Ezekiel foretold that God "will remove the heart of stone from your flesh and give you a heart of flesh" (Ezek. 36:26). Is this what had happened to Saul: a true spiritual transformation? According to Ezekiel, God gives the new heart of the rebirth for a purpose: "I will put my Spirit within you, and cause you to walk in my statutes and be careful to obey my rules" (36:27). So did Saul's new heart result in a new zeal to serve God and obey his Word?

The answer is "No!" After his brief flirtation with the prophets, Saul went home. "Where did you go?" his uncle inquired (1 Sam. 10:14). Saul replied by saying nothing about Samuel's anointing or his experience with the prophets, noting only that he had not been able to find the donkeys. Saul did not tell anyone about his receipt of the Holy Spirit, nor did he lift a finger against the Philistines. This indicates that whatever else had happened to him, Saul did not receive eternal life or enter into a true saving relationship with the Lord, for the simple reason that he showed no inclination to obey God's Word.

So what did it mean that the Spirit came upon Saul? This question has occasioned no end of debate. The best answer recognizes that in the Old Testament, God sometimes sent his Spirit to enable chosen servants to perform designated tasks. God's Spirit came upon Bezalel, giving him the supernatural ability to work with metals that enabled him to make the ark of the covenant (Ex. 31:2–4), and God's Spirit gave Samson the supernatural strength with which he slew so many Philistines (Judg. 14:6). God's Spirit gave Saul a new sense of calling, so that in this limited sense we can say that he received a new heart (1 Sam. 10:9).

What about Saul's prophesying with the band of prophets? The word used here for *prophesied* occurs with both positive and negative overtones in the Bible. In some cases, it refers to ecstatic raving, as in the case of the prophets of Baal in their contest against Elijah, who "raved" in their cries and gyrations, even cutting themselves as they sought to call forth Baal's power (1 Kings 18:28). The term is also used, however, of the prophet Ezekiel (Ezek. 37:10) and in Numbers 11, when the Spirit came upon the seventy elders of Israel. On that occasion, Moses commented: "Would that all the Lord's people were prophets, that the Lord would put his Spirit on them!" (Num. 11:29). At Gibeah, the Lord enabled Saul to experience the spiritual high of prophetic utterance, yet Saul did not show the signs of a true rebirth, which comes with a new life of obedience to God's Word.

Saul provided a good illustration for Jesus' teaching about the necessity of a faith that obeys God's Word. Our good works are not the cause of our salvation, but works are a necessary consequence of true and saving faith. Jesus taught that "not everyone who says to me, 'Lord, Lord,' will enter the kingdom of heaven, but the one who does the will of my Father who is in heaven" (Matt. 7:21). This implies that a person whom Christ has saved inevitably seeks to do God's will. Some of Jesus' hearers objected to this, using the very argument that Saul might have offered: "Lord, Lord, did we not prophesy in your name, and cast out demons in your name, and do many mighty works in your name?" Jesus replied, "And then will I declare to them, 'I never knew you; depart from me, you workers of lawlessness'" (7:22–23). The evidence of salvation is not given by dramatic experiences or even great deeds, especially when there are no signs of repentance from a life of sin. Instead, the people who have been savingly known by Christ are those whose faith trusts in his Word and whose lives are marked by turning from iniquity in obedience to God's will.

The reality is that Saul's experience perfectly fits with worldly attitudes toward God and salvation. Saul typified the kind of person who seeks spiritual experiences but has little interest in cultivating a true and living faith that obeys the Lord. In religion, as in other affairs, Saul was truly "a king . . . like all the nations," one who gives lip service but not heart obedience to the Word of the Lord.

BEHOLD, YOUR KING!

Israel's elders had asked for a worldly king, and God sent Saul as his literal answer. Saul was the messiah (i.e., "anointed one") and king for unbelieving Israel. But through the bitter experiences that would follow, many among God's people would cry for a true King who does God's will and not the will of the world. In time, God would provide for them a King and Messiah, and his coming would be in stark contrast to the coming of Saul.

The day that God provided his true King to Israel is remembered as Palm Sunday, while Jesus rode into Jerusalem amid the cries of "Hosanna!" (meaning "save now!"). It is striking that while Saul came to Ramah, Israel's chief worship center at that time, he came in a way exactly opposite to Jesus' coming to Jerusalem. Jesus came riding on a donkey, Israel's royal symbol of one who brings peace. Saul arrived as one who had been unable to find his donkeys! For all his impressive qualifications, Saul simply was not able to be a true king for God's people. While Saul came to Israel with a fleshly impressiveness that masked his incompetence, Jesus appeared in a humility that cloaked his divine majesty and power.

The more foundational difference between Saul and Jesus was Saul's disinterest in righteousness before God. This is the distinguishing feature of worldly kings and empires: a concern only for the pragmatic means of earthly success, with little or no thought to what God desires or thinks. All through the reign of Saul, he will stumble over God's commands, finding his own will more suitable to his perceived needs. In the greatest contrast, Jesus is the King who perfectly obeys God's Word and is filled with a passion for righteousness. Jesus could honestly say, "My food is to do the will of him who sent me and to accomplish his work" (John 4:34). Saul had a fleeting empowerment from God's Spirit. But Jesus, as God's true Son, was fully and constantly animated by the Spirit of God. "He who sent me is with me," Jesus declared. "He has not left me alone, for I always do the things that are pleasing to him" (John 8:29). "The Spirit of the Lord is upon me," Jesus preached, "because he has anointed me to proclaim good news to the poor" (Luke 4:18, quoting Isa. 61:1).

His perfect, personal righteousness qualified Jesus to ride the royal donkey of peace into Jerusalem. Zechariah prophesied, "Behold, your king is coming to you; righteous and having salvation is he, humble and mounted on a donkey, on a colt, the foal of a donkey" (Zech. 9:9). Hebrews 1:8–9 says, "The scepter of uprightness is the scepter of your kingdom. You have loved righteousness and hated wickedness; therefore God, your God, has anointed you with the oil of gladness beyond your companions" (quoting Ps. 45:7). Jesus is the true King sent by God to establish righteousness on earth, and in that righteousness to give eternal peace to those who hail him as Savior and Lord.

The Israelites had no choice but to accept Saul as king. Their elders had rebelled against God by demanding a worldly kingship, and God gave them Saul. But we do have a choice. Everything that Saul represents is still alive today, enthroned in the worldly seats of power and holding forth enticing calls for our submission and worship. We have a choice between Saul, whose name identifies him as the king that the unbelieving world asked for, and Jesus, whose name identified him as the Savior sent by God to deliver his people from the penalty and power of their sins (Matt. 1:21). Our choice—to embrace the world or trust in Christ—will determine the kingdom in which our salvation will be found: either an earthly reign of unrighteous expedience and fleshly power or an eternal and heavenly kingdom of righteousness and peace.

Jesus our King gave his life to pay the penalty for our sins, and the Spirit he sends empowers believers to obey God's will as declared in his Word. In the righteousness that Jesus gives—forgiveness for our sins and power to live for God—we find the peace of God. Of his reign it is said: "He shall stand and shepherd his flock in the strength of the LORD, in the majesty of the name of the LORD his God. And they shall dwell secure . . . And he shall be their peace" (Mic. 5:4–5).

14

LONG LIVE THE KING!

1 Samuel 10:17–27

Samuel said to all the people, "Do you see him whom the LORD
has chosen? There is none like him among all the people." And
all the people shouted, "Long live the king!" (1 Sam. 10:24)

O n July 31, 2008, the tiny South Pacific nation of Tonga crowned
its new king, one of the world's last absolute monarchs, George
Tupou V. The three-day coronation event included a formal ball,
a military parade, a traditional kava-drinking ceremony, a fireworks display,
a rugby match, an open-air torchlight music concert, and a beauty contest.
The cost for these events was estimated at 1.6 million pounds, spurring
complaints because of the nation's 40 percent poverty rate. The government
and a majority of the people defended the expenditure, seeing it as important
to upholding the traditional culture of the island nation.[1]

The Tongans' insistence on a proper coronation is backed up in principle by the biblical example of King Saul. Israel's elders had come to
Samuel the judge demanding a king, and God had revealed to Samuel
his choice of Saul, son of Kish. But there was still a need for the public

---

1. Sophie Tedmanson, "Lavish Coronation Ceremony for New King of Tonga," *The Times*, August
1, 2008, http://www.timesonline.co.uk/tol/news/world/asia/article4440717.ece.

formalities that would install Saul in his kingship. Saul's coronation marked an ominous change in Israel's history and provided a remarkable assertion of God's sovereignty as Lord over all.

Israel's Unbelief Rebuked

Solemn ceremonies demand careful attention to protocol. Yet sometimes exceptions are warranted. In the eighteenth-century Church of Scotland, the General Assembly had power to impose an unwanted minister on a congregation. Thus, in 1773, the General Assembly directed a presbytery and its members to induct David Thomson as minister of a parish near Stirling. The presbytery's moderator, Robert Findley, addressed Thomson during the installation service. He informed Thomson that he and the other ministers were present only at the order of the General Assembly and that six hundred heads of families, along with all the elders of the church except one, had opposed his selection as pastor. Before the presbytery and congregation, Findley therefore implored Thomson to "give it up." Thomson refused, directing Findley to "obey the orders of your superiors." At this, Findley intoned the words of installation and then closed the service, without having even prayed for the new minister or his congregation.[2]

Findley violated the polite etiquette for a ceremonsial occasion such as a pastor's installation. But sometimes the truth requires a breach of protocol. Samuel reasoned this way when he gathered all Israel to an assembly at Mizpah. This was the place where Samuel had earlier led the nation in repentance before the Lord, resulting in their victory over the Philistines (1 Sam. 7:6–7). Samuel returned now to Mizpah not merely to remember the prior repentance but in the hopes that a new repentance would occur. Therefore, while a coronation would normally call for polite and formal behavior, with bland speeches and cheery affirmations, Samuel took the occasion to rebuke the nation for its unbelief in demanding a king in place of the Lord.

Samuel's rebuke had two parts, the first of which was to remind the people of God's great and saving works in their history. He told them, "Thus says the Lord, the God of Israel, 'I brought up Israel out of Egypt, and I delivered

2. Dale Ralph Davis, *1 Samuel: Looking on the Heart* (Fearn, Ross-shire, UK: Christian Focus, 2000), 85.

159

you from the hand of the Egyptians and from the hand of all the kingdoms that were oppressing you'" (1 Sam. 10:18). It is true that under God's rule, Israel had been regularly oppressed. They had been cast into slavery in Egypt, had been opposed by the Moabites and Ammonites, and were now being oppressed by the Philistines. Likewise, being a Christian enlists us into battle with the world, the flesh, and the devil. It is, in fact, because we are God's people, because we are set apart from the world and from sin to a life that is holy, that believers experience at least some of our trials and pains. But Samuel knew that God had been faithful on every single occasion when Israel had called on him. "I delivered you," God summarized—and we will find that God delivers us from all our fiery foes as well.

Nonetheless, God's people are sometimes tempted to avoid trials by fitting in with the world. If we do just a few things the world's way—falling into a worldly manner of speech or dress, or adopting the world's priorities for money, time, and talents—we can avoid sticking out. This is what Israel was doing in demanding a king. The people were not asking for a new god to worship, but only a political system to make them "like all the nations" (1 Sam. 8:20). Yet in the second part of his rebuke, Samuel insisted that to demand the latter was to imply the former. He cried out: "Today you have rejected your God, who saves you from all your calamities and your distresses, and you have said to him, 'Set a king over us'" (10:19).

If the apostle James had been at Mizpah, he would have had this to say: "You adulterous people! Do you not know that friendship with the world is enmity with God? Therefore whoever wishes to be a friend of the world makes himself an enemy of God" (James 4:4). Christians who desire to be like the world are like the Israelites in their demand for a king. For all their formal claims of fidelity to the Lord, the Israelites were committing apostasy, replacing God's rule with that of a mere man. Being God's people demanded fidelity to him and holiness before the world, and thus Israel's request for a worldly king was effectively "a desire to no longer be the Lord's people."[3] Jesus told his followers, "In the world you will have tribulation. But take heart; I have overcome the world" (John 16:33). For Christians to turn aside from the tribulations that accompany godliness is to renounce Christ's power to overcome on our behalf.

---

3. John Woodhouse, *1 Samuel: Looking for a Leader* (Wheaton, IL: Crossway, 2008), 184.

Israel's King Revealed

We are not able to tell the exact manner in which Samuel spoke the words of his rebuke—whether he was loud or soft, fast or slow—but I would not be surprised if there was a pause within verse 19. Samuel rebuked the people for rejecting the Lord in asking for a king. Might he not have paused to await some expression of repentance? "But today you have rejected your God, who saves you from all your calamities and your distresses, and you have said to him, 'Set a king over us'" . . . (pause). Samuel might have been hoping for a repeat performance of the people's repentance at Mizpah, when they had broken forth in remorse for their sins. If Samuel did take such a pause, it was in vain, greeted only by stony silence. So he continued, "Now therefore present yourselves before the Lord by your tribes and by your thousands" (1 Sam. 10:19).

This summons must have come as an unsettling surprise for the people. They may have been unsure about the procedures for the king's selection, but they knew full well what it meant to be summoned by tribes and clans for selection by lots. For this is what God had done earlier in their history in response to the sin of Achan after Israel's defeat at Ai. First a tribe was selected by lot, and then a clan, then a household, and finally the man was revealed who had brought God's wrath by his sin. Achan was thus revealed, and he, along with his entire household, was stoned to death and burned. On that precedent-setting occasion, the lots were used to identify the sinner who would receive God's wrath (see Josh. 7:14–18).

Now Samuel called the nation to assemble once more, with the lots before him. The leader of each tribe was to come forth, write the name of his tribe on a stone, and then await the selection. The lot of the tribe of Benjamin was called out. Then all the clan heads of Benjamin came forth to present their stones, and the lot of the Matrites was chosen. Finally, out of this clan, the name of Saul, son of Kish, was read. He would be the one to . . . what? Israel was being judged, and Saul's name was chosen by lot . . . for what? In the place where Achan had been chosen to receive God's wrath, Saul was chosen to be Israel's king.

Saul was selected as king by lot for two reasons. The first was to indicate that God's assent to provide a king was a form of his judgment. Usually, when a prophet denounced Israel's sin, the sentence of God's judgment immediately followed. Here, "the selection of Saul is inserted at the very point where we would expect an announcement of judgment."[4] Sometimes God's most severe judgment is to permit our sin and its consequences, and so it was here. Not that Saul was being punished by being made king, but all Israel was receiving divine discipline through his selection as king. This is confirmed by God's later statement: "I gave you a king in my anger" (Hos. 13:11).

The use of lots served a second purpose. Since this was an authorized and accepted method by which God revealed his selection, the lot identified Saul as God's choice for the kingship. Proverbs 16:33 says, "The lot is cast into the lap, but its every decision is from the LORD." The lot therefore showed that Saul was not merely Samuel's choice as king but God's choice, so the lot gave public legitimacy to Saul's kingship through divine revelation.

There was only one problem: "when they sought [Saul], he could not be found" (1 Sam. 10:21). We can imagine the scene: "And finally, God's choice to be king of Israel . . . Saul the son of Kish! . . . I said, *Saul the son of Kish!* . . . Has anyone seen Saul the son of Kish?" The answer was that "when they sought him, he could not be found" (10:21). Where was Saul? Saul knew he was going to be chosen, having received advance notice through his anointing, which was then confirmed through three divinely revealed signs. So shouldn't Saul be standing by for his grand entrance onto history's stage? Instead, the Lord informed them: "Behold, he has hidden himself among the baggage" (10:22). What are we to make of this unexpected behavior?

There are two main assessments of Saul's action. Some commentators see this as commendable humility on Saul's part. Cyril Barber, for instance, points out that many of God's best servants have sought to avoid positions of public prominence, including Athanasius, the great champion of the faith in the early church.[5] Matthew Henry asserts that Saul hoped his absence would lead to the choice of another, since Saul "was conscious to himself of unfitness for so great a trust."[6] Saul's concern, this view argues, was for the well-being of his nation, since he thought someone else would do a better job than he could.

4. Bill T. Arnold, *1 & 2 Samuel*, NIV Application Commentary (Grand Rapids: Zondervan, 2003), 167.

5. Cyril J. Barber, *The Books of Samuel*, 2 vols. (Neptune, NJ: Loizeaux, 1994), 1:118.

6. Matthew Henry, *Commentary on the Whole Bible*, 6 vols. (Peabody, MA: Hendrickson, 1992), 2:262.

More negatively, others have argued that Saul reveals cowardice by hiding under the baggage. Indeed, the context strongly suggests fear instead of humility as the reason that Saul hid himself. And who can blame him, since he was being called to step into God's place! Perhaps Saul could see that God was angry and that his selection was God's judgment on the nation. Given the difficulty of the task, we can hardly blame him for trying to get away. Nonetheless, Saul's selfish neglect of duty foreshadows a pattern that will be repeated during his kingship. The people of Israel had desired a king who would give them the leadership edge enjoyed by the worldly nations, no longer willing to rely simply on God's saving power. Here, then, is the kind of self-serving cowardice that they will have to get used to under human kings! However we may understand Saul's hiding at his coronation, this beginning does not bode well for the future kingship of Israel.

I admit that I would enjoy seeing a dramatic reenactment of this episode. For when Saul could not be found, the people wondered, "Is there a man still to come?" The Lord answered, "Behold, he has hidden himself among the baggage" (1 Sam. 10:22). So the people ran to the baggage, found Saul, and hauled him out. We read, "When he stood among the people, he was taller than any of the people from his shoulders upward" (10:23). Here is where I would love to see the look on Samuel's face as he called out: "Do you see him whom the LORD has chosen? There is none like him among all the people" (10:24). If Samuel had worn a smug look of irony, we could not blame him. He was saying, in effect, "There is the man you have sought, the man chosen by the Lord as your king, the bold leader who was hiding under the baggage during his own coronation—isn't he tall and handsome?" The people, recovering themselves as well as they could, shouted in response, "Long live the king!" (10:24). Regardless of his timid behavior, Saul looked like just the kind of king they were hoping for: tall, handsome, outwardly impressive. The issues of character and faith were easily brushed aside, and Israel acclaimed the king they craved.

Throughout these verses we see God's continuing and relentless sovereignty. The people demanded a king, but they were not able to achieve independence from God. It was the Lord who chose and revealed Saul. God's sovereignty was not set aside, even as he acceded to Israel's demand for a king to replace him. Likewise, Christians will find that no matter how we may strive to grab the reins of our own lives, deciding for ourselves how we will think and live, God remains relentlessly sovereign and apportions all our circumstances. Either in faith or in unbelief, we *will* have God as our Lord, and he *will* exercise his sovereign prerogatives!

ISRAEL'S LAW REAFFIRMED

Another way in which God emphasized his sovereignty was through Samuel's immediate application of God's law to the new kingship: "Then Samuel told the people the rights and duties of the kingship, and he wrote them in a book and laid it up before the LORD" (1 Sam. 10:25). Israel could have the desired king, though God would select and reveal this new ruler. Moreover, the kingship was to be subject to God's law and to the word of God's prophet.

A vital distinction is made in the text, which speaks of the rules, or "justice," not of the "king" but of the "kingship." In other words, Samuel was placing the new institution under the authority of God's Word; he did not highlight the authority of the king over the law, but rather the authority of the law over the king.

There can be little doubt that the commandments Samuel read aloud and then wrote down were taken from God's teaching on the kingship in Deuteronomy 17. Not only was the king forbidden to accumulate massive treasures or devote himself to excess luxury (Deut. 17:16–17), but more importantly he was devotedly to observe God's Word. The king was to handwrite his own copy of God's law to keep with him at all times and to read daily, "that he may learn to fear the LORD his God by keeping all the words of this law and these statutes, and doing them" (17:19). If the king would carefully observe God's statutes and commandments, then Israel would enjoy success and the king's reign would be long (17:20).

This passage has played an important role not merely in Old Testament Israel but also in church and state relations ever since. John Knox pointed to this passage to show that earthly monarchs are not laws unto themselves but are themselves subject to God's law. Thus, when Mary, Queen of Scots, committed adultery and abetted the murder of her husband, Knox called for her arrest and execution. Even more significant was the influence of Saul's coronation in Samuel Rutherford's 1644 classic, *Lex Rex*. Rutherford wrote *Lex Rex*, which means the "law of kingship," to oppose the idea of

Rex Lex, the king as a law unto himself. Rutherford's book was based on Deuteronomy 17, probably the very Bible verses that Samuel had set before Saul, and referred to Samuel's placing King Saul under the authority of God's Word. Rutherford asserted that the kings of Scotland did not have the right to make laws that were contrary to Scripture and declared that when a king conducted himself lawlessly, his rights over the people were forfeited. *Lex Rex*'s biblical model of separation of powers and social covenant was influential among the founding fathers of America and also provided a biblical rationale for colonial American Christians in their rebellion against the lawless English monarch. John Robbins has therefore described 1 Samuel as "the oldest textbook in political freedom," pointing out that by placing human society under God's law, "the Bible . . . furnishes us with the principles we need to defend a free society."[7]

It is not just kings who are called to obey God's commands, but all of God's people. Many Christians are confused about obeying God's law, since the New Testament teaches that we are "not under law but under grace" (Rom. 6:14). Paul says this in referring to the law as a means of righteousness. His point is that Christians do not gain salvation by the law but by the grace of God in the gospel of Christ. But Paul's point in that passage was not to promote antinomianism—the belief that grace frees us from any and all standard of conduct. Paul makes this clear by asking: "What then? Are we to sin because we are not under law but under grace? By no means!" (6:15). Christians are not saved *by* God's law, but we are saved *to* God's law: that is, our life as believers is to be in keeping with God's commands. This includes both the moral obligations of the Ten Commandments, the importance of which is stressed all through the New Testament, and the rules and regulations that God has given in his Word for all of life.

Just as God would reign over King Saul by means of the law of the kingship, God exercises his sovereignty over our lives through the statutes and rules in Holy Scripture. Christians preparing for marriage must be informed of God's rules and regulations involving the duties of husbands and wives. Just as Samuel read the rules of kingship at Saul's coronation, so also ministers must prepare couples for marriage by presenting husbands with the biblical command to love their wives with Christ's self-sacrificing and cherishing love

7. John W. Robbins, *Freedom and Capitalism: Essays on Christian Politics and Economics* (Unicoi, TN: Trinity Foundation, 2006), 30, 46.

165

(Eph. 5:25–31) and teaching wives the biblical command to help and submit to their husbands in everything (5:22–24). These are not merely traditional ideas about marriage, but God's rules and regulations for the marital state. Likewise, the Bible has rules for the relationship between the civil authority and its citizens (Rom. 13:1–7), parents and children (Eph. 6:1–4), masters and servants (Eph. 6:5–9), and pastors and church members (Eph. 4:1–3; Heb. 13:17; 1 Peter 5:1–3). Christians are to be taught to live by these rules.

God is sovereign over his people, and he reigns over us through his Word. To carefully observe God's rules is not to practice legalism but to render faithful obedience to our gracious Sovereign. Observing God's laws does not hinder our well-being, but rather is the way in which believers experience the freedom of God's richest blessing. One might argue that a map constrains the behavior of those who follow its guidance, but the map also gives us the freedom to arrive safely at our destination. For a believer in Christ, the apostle James refers to God's commands as "the law of liberty" (James 1:25), since God's commands order our life for good and administer to us his sovereign blessing.

ISRAEL'S KING INSTALLED

"Long live the king!" the people cried, establishing a tradition that continues today. With these words Israel welcomed her new king, Saul the son of Kish. Had the people consulted God's Word, however, they would have known that however long Saul might reign, his dynasty could not endure. For as Israel's patriarch Jacob had prophesied, the royal scepter was destined for the tribe of Judah. "The scepter shall not depart from Judah," Jacob said, "nor the ruler's staff from between his feet, until tribute comes to him; and to him shall be the obedience of the peoples" (Gen. 49:10).

First Samuel will tell the story of how the kingship passes from Saul to David, and from the tribe of Benjamin to Judah. Israel's kings were types—instructive forerunners—of the true King over God's kingdom, his own Son, Jesus Christ, who was born of the line of David from the tribe of Judah. In Saul's case, we see more of a foil of Christ: as a tainted king, he serves more to contrast with Jesus than to typify the reign of God's Son.

First, whatever we may think of Saul's hiding among the baggage, Jesus also hid his royal calling from the people of Israel. Mark records that when

Jesus performed miracles of healing, he instructed the recipients not to identify him. "Jesus charged them to tell no one" (Mark 7:36; cf. 1:45; 5:20, 34; 8:26) about his divine power. The reason for Jesus' "messianic secret" was not his fear or reluctance but the fact that he had come first to die for our sins and only later to return in royal glory and power.

A second contrast is Samuel's acclamation of Saul that "there is none like him among all the people" (1 Sam. 10:24). This was true outwardly of Saul, but it is true inwardly of Christ's character and being. In this respect, Saul shows us Christ by what is missing in Saul's life. Jesus alone is utterly pure and without sin; even Pontius Pilate said of Jesus during his trial, "I find no guilt in him" (John 18:38). Colossians 1:18 says that in everything Christ is preeminent. The book of Hebrews hails Jesus as greater than the angels, greater than Moses, greater than Joshua, and greater than the high priest Aaron. For this reason Scripture says to God of Christ: "You have crowned him with glory and honor, putting everything in subjection under his feet" (Heb. 2:7–8, quoting Ps. 8:5–6). There truly is none like Jesus among all the people—Hebrews 7:26 describes him as "holy, innocent, unstained, separated from sinners, and exalted above the heavens"—and he is worthy to reign over God's people as King forevermore.

Furthermore, we noted that Saul's presentation was preceded by a statement of God's judgment on the people. Saul was set forth as an expression of God's wrath against sin. Jesus, however, came to deliver God's remedy for sin. Paul says that God "put forward [Christ] as a propitiation by his blood, to be received by faith" (Rom. 3:25). A *propitiation* is a blood sacrifice that satisfies God's just wrath, and Jesus takes up his crown as our King after having first taken up the cross to die for our sins. The apostle John, witnessing the worship in heaven, records that Jesus is acclaimed worthy of taking up his royal throne: "For you were slain, and by your blood you ransomed people for God from every tribe and language and people and nation, and you have made them a kingdom and priests to our God, and they shall reign on the earth" (Rev. 5:9–10). The Bible declares Jesus' kingship as a reign of grace over sin, so that all who belong to his kingdom are those who have come to his cross for cleansing, forgiveness, and redemption from sin. Have you brought your sins to the cross to be forgiven in Christ's blood? The cross where Jesus died for our sins is the throne from which he reigns with peace for mankind.

Finally, Saul's coronation brought division to Israel. As the new king went to his home at Gibeah, there went with him a band of followers, "men of valor whose hearts God had touched" (1 Sam. 10:26). Yet there were others, "worthless fellows," who said, "How can this man save us?" These rebels "despised him and brought him no present" (10:27). The Bible's scornful description of these critics reminds us that even when God permits us to be ruled by unspiritual leaders, God's people have an obligation to submit to those rulers placed over them by God. Paul wrote, "Let every person be subject to the governing authorities. For there is no authority except from God, and those that exist have been instituted by God" (Rom. 13:1)—and if we fail to submit to all legitimate leaders placed over us, we earn the contemptuous label of "worthless fellows," given to the Israelites who opposed King Saul.

The coming of Christ has likewise divided the world. Some, their hearts touched by the gospel of God's grace, have raced to Jesus' cross to be cleansed of their sins and to live as his disciples. But many others despise Jesus and withhold both their praise and their faith. Like Saul, Jesus "held his peace" during his life. But in the day of his return in glory, "with his mighty angels in flaming fire" (2 Thess. 1:7–8), Christ will judge the nations (Matt. 25:31) and inflict eternal destruction on those who oppose his reign (2 Thess. 1:8–9).

When Saul was presented to Israel, the people cried out with all the optimism they could muster: "Long live the king!" (1 Sam. 10:24). What, then, shall we say to the Lord Jesus, who comes in the glory of his grace and power? Seeing him as One who excels all others, who died for our sins on the cross, and who reigns now forever in his resurrection life, we can surely echo the Israelites' words with much greater hope. God in his anger gave Saul to Israel, but in his mercy has he given us his Son, Jesus Christ. If our hearts are opened by God to see Jesus in the glory of his grace, we will crown him with many crowns, each of us gladly yielding our hearts, and crying out to Jesus, "Long live the King!" His reign will never fail and never end, and those who bow to his throne "will reign forever and ever" with him in glory (Rev. 22:5).

15

SALVATION IN ISRAEL

1 Samuel 11:1–15

But Saul said, "Not a man shall be put to death this day, for today the LORD has worked salvation in Israel." (1 Sam. 11:13)

merican military commanders follow a standard procedure for planning their operations that has proved effective over many years. The Operations Order consists of five paragraphs, the most important of which are the first two: the situation and the mission. Above all else, a successful battle plan requires a proper understanding of the situation and a grasp of the correct mission for the unit to perform.

It would have been a good idea for King Saul to have evaluated his situation and mission, having just been acclaimed as Israel's king. He faced two grave matters, both of which threatened the nation's existence. The first was Israel's internal division. The tribes of Israel were physically divided, some in the north and some in the south, with most of the nation to the west of the river Jordan but some tribes left on the east bank. Even worse, the tribes were morally and spiritually divided, as is shown at the end of the book of Judges. Saul's hometown in the land of Benjamin had been the cause of a brief civil war, resulting in thousands of Israelite deaths (Judg. 19:1–20:48). Moreover, there was opposition to Saul's selection as king from "some worthless fellows" who doubted his leadership and "despised him" (1 Sam. 10:27). Unless Saul could unite the tribes and work out a means of effective coordination, Israel could not hope to survive against its enemies. These outside enemies were Israel's other threat, consisting of the neighboring Philistines to the west and the Ammonites to the east, both of them fierce and well-armed foes.

These twin problems presented the situation Saul faced. His mission, then, was to heal the petty grievances that divided Israel, unite the tribes under his royal leadership, and strike a blow to Israel's enemies that would secure peace for his generation.

First Samuel chapter 11 presents Saul's response to these challenges, including a new threat from the Ammonites. Saul's effective action put his kingship on a good footing for the future. Behind Saul, however, it was the Lord who saved his people. The word for "save" or "salvation" occurs three times in this chapter, indicating its major theme. Perhaps most important is Saul's apparent realization of what every leader needs to know—whether on a large scale in society or on a small scale in the church or home—namely, that in the face of threats and danger, our hope for success lies ultimately with the Lord.

Nahash and the Siege of Jabesh-gilead

After his coronation, Saul returned home to Gibeah and resumed his normal life. Perhaps he was keeping a low profile while waiting for an opportunity, in keeping with the practice of the judges before him. But trouble was brewing in the Israelite lands east of the Jordan River: "Nahash the Ammonite went up and besieged Jabesh-gilead" (1 Sam. 11:1).

An interesting textual matter arises here, since one of the Dead Sea Scrolls (4QSam[a]) includes material missing from all other Hebrew texts. Josephus alludes to this material in his history, stating that Nahash, the Ammonite king, had reduced the Transjordan Israelite cities to slavery.[1] The Dead Sea Scroll addition states that Nahash "had been oppressing the Gadites and the Reubenites grievously, gouging out the right eye of each of them and allowing Israel no deliverer." Nahash had conquered

---

1. Josephus, *The Antiquities of the Jews*, 6.5.

the whole region across the Jordan, but seven thousand men had escaped and fled to Jabesh-gilead.

Whether this addition is authentic or not, the Bible informs us that the Israelite fugitives were desperate enough to seek terms with Nahash: "Make a treaty with us, and we will serve you" (1 Sam. 11:1). Nahash was willing, but on only one condition: "that I gouge out all your right eyes, and thus bring disgrace on all Israel" (11:2). According to Josephus, warriors of that day fought in formation with interlocked shields, so that the left eye was covered by the shield. By gouging out the right eye, Nahash rendered them unfit for battle, though still eligible for slave labor.[2] If Nahash succeeded in reducing Jabesh-gilead and disarming its garrison, Israel could have lost its territory east of the Jordan permanently. Furthermore, William Blaikie comments, "The mutilated condition of that poor one-eyed community would be a ground for despising the whole nation; it would be a token of the humiliation and degradation of the whole Israelite community."[3]

This episode reminds us what a dangerous world we live in. We often hear that it is a "dog-eat-dog world," an aphorism comparing human society to hounds fighting over food. Indeed, if one is not prepared to defend what he possesses, he may not long expect to enjoy it. George Washington departed from public life saying, "Eternal vigilance is the price of liberty." If a man is given the chance, he will kill, steal, and enslave those who are weak around him.

But Nahash also had a grudge against the Israelites, wanting to "bring disgrace on all Israel" (1 Sam. 11:2). The Ammonites were Israel's cousins via incest, having descended from the illicit union between drunken Lot and one of his daughters after their flight from the destruction of Sodom (Gen. 19:38). The Israelites did not hold the Ammonites in high honor, to say the least, so that the ill-feeling was reciprocated. During Israel's wilderness passage in the exodus, the Ammonites had refused to offer needed provisions (Deut. 23:4), and they are listed among the traditional enemies of Israel (see Isa. 11:14; Jer. 9:25–26; Ezek. 25:1–7). Finally, during the judgeship of Jephthah the Gileadite, the Ammonites made war in these same regions. Jephthah defeated the Ammonites and captured twenty of

2. Ibid.

3. William G. Blaikie, *Expository Lectures on the Book of First Samuel* (1887; repr., Birmingham, AL: Solid Ground, 2005), 172–73.

their cities (Judg. 11:33). The antipathy between Israel and Ammon was long-standing.

For these or other reasons, Nahash delighted in causing the Israelites of Jabesh-gilead to writhe in fear before him. In this, he depicts the hatred of the world for God's people in every generation. Dale Ralph Davis writes, "This arrogance, this hatred, never ceases. Nahash may become historical furniture, but the 'Ammonite mind,' that is, to maim, destroy, and strangle God's people, is always with us."[4] The classic example is the unjust murder of Jesus Christ. Jesus told his disciples, "If you were of the world, the world would love you as its own; but because you are not of the world, but I chose you out of the world, therefore the world hates you" (John 15:19).

It is because of this hostility from an evil and hateful world that God's people need a Savior. Seeking salvation, the Israelite leaders in Jabesh-gilead appealed to Nahash: "Give us seven days' respite that we may send messengers through all the territory of Israel. Then, if there is no one to save us, we will give ourselves up to you" (1 Sam. 11:3). This is the plea that Christians often make to God, as we see modeled in the Psalms: "O LORD my God, in you do I take refuge; save me from all my pursuers and deliver me, lest like a lion they tear my soul apart, rending it in pieces, with none to deliver" (Ps. 7:1–2). To be a Christian is to realize your need for God's salvation—not just forgiveness from your sins but salvation from the dangers and malice of this world—and to call out to God to deliver you in times of fear and dread.

KING SAUL KINDLED

It is probably a measure of the contempt in which Nahash held the Israelites, and his confident desire to spread terror in their nation, that the Ammonite king permitted the Jabesh-gileadites to send messengers calling for their salvation. Realizing the stakes for the entire nation, and seeking help wherever it might be found, they sent messengers "through all the territory of Israel," assuring Nahash that if no help came in seven days, "we will give ourselves up to you" (1 Sam. 11:3).

In this manner, news of the Ammonite siege arrived at Gibeah. It seems that the messengers were unaware of Saul's new kingship, since they went

4. Dale Ralph Davis, *1 Samuel: Looking on the Heart* (Fearn, Ross-shire, UK: Christian Focus, 2000), 93.

to the people in general, rather than approaching the king directly. At the news, "all the people wept aloud" (1 Sam. 11:4). Behind this grief was a particular bond between Gibeah and Jabesh-gilead. In the war against Benjamin recorded in Judges 21, Jabesh-gilead had refused to participate. As a result, all the unmarried maidens of Jabesh-gilead had been given to provide wives for the men of Gibeah (Judg. 21:12–14), so that many of the people in Saul's town were the sons and daughters of women from Jabesh-gilead. Hearing the tumult inspired by this bond, Saul inquired, "What is wrong with the people, that they are weeping?" (1 Sam. 11:5), so the news was told to him.

With this news, a decisive moment had come to newly enthroned Saul. It was the threat of invasion that had largely motivated the elders' demand for a king (1 Sam. 8:20). Now that such an invasion had occurred, it was the king's duty to save Israel. This had been the very concern raised by Saul's opponents: "How can this man save us?" (10:27). So this episode would be a key turning point for the new regime.

Fortunately for Saul, his greatest need was met at this very moment: "The Spirit of God rushed upon Saul when he heard these words, and his anger was greatly kindled" (1 Sam. 11:6). The coming of the Spirit makes a remarkable point, because it shows the Lord's favor toward this king who had been installed as a result of the people's rebellion. The Lord would give Saul every opportunity of serving in God's own strength; he was graciously willing to remain Israel's Savior through the kingship of Saul. Just as God's Spirit had rushed into Samson, giving him a supernatural strength to smite the Philistines (Judg. 14:6, 19; 15:14), and just as the Spirit had empowered Othniel, Gideon, and Jephthah in their victories, now the Spirit came to empower Saul with courage and vigor to lead Israel in this time of crisis.

The coming of God's Spirit filled Saul with an attitude of righteous anger for Nahash's evil and with a violent resolve to strike out in defense of God's people. Saul's counterattack makes an important statement that opposes the idea of Christian pacifism. Jesus taught in the Sermon on the Mount that we are to avoid striking back at those who do us personal injury. "Do not resist the one who is evil," Jesus said. "But if anyone slaps you on the right cheek, turn to him the other also" (Matt. 5:39). Some Christians have wrongly concluded that we must therefore stand by passively when others are being threatened or harmed, failing to note the difference between defending ourselves and protecting others from harm. But when God's Spirit came upon Saul, the result of this divine influence was a holy zeal to make war on the evil tormentor of his fellow Israelite. John Woodhouse writes: "This was God-inspired rage. The anger inspired in Saul by the Spirit of God was obviously directed at the threat posed to the people of Jabesh-gilead by Nahash and the Ammonites."[5] This righteous anger reflects God's own wrath against evil, for which sake the Lord has given the sword to civil officials (Rom. 13:1–4).

Saul's situation—in terms of both his need to establish his authority and Jabesh-gilead's urgent need to be rescued—called for bold and decisive action. Saul acted accordingly: "He took a yoke of oxen and cut them in pieces and sent them throughout all the territory of Israel by the hand of messengers, saying, 'Whoever does not come out after Saul and Samuel, so shall it be done to his oxen!' Then the dread of the Lord fell upon the people, and they came out as one man" (1 Sam. 11:7).

Inspired by the Spirit, Saul spoke with authority, just as God's servants should speak boldly in proclaiming divine truth today. Yet Saul was not harsh, forbearing to threaten death to those who opposed him (as had been done when Israel was summoned to make war on his own tribe and hometown, in Judges 19:29), but only imposing the civil punishment of death on their oxen. This reminds us that it is not necessary for church leaders to be harsh or insulting when reproving or exhorting God's people. Those charged with spiritual authority may be forthright but also moderate in their church discipline. It is always the Spirit who makes God's people willing to repent or obey. In this case, the Lord put his awe upon the nation and the Israelites "came out as one man."

This link between a nation's godliness and the well-being of the nation as a whole reminds us why a government is wise to encourage biblical religion, and why government intolerance for Christianity is harmful to its own good. Matthew Henry observes: "Religion and the fear of God will make men good subjects, good soldiers, and good friends to the public interests of the country. Those that fear God will make conscience of their duty to all men, particularly to their rulers."[6]

5. John Woodhouse, *1 Samuel: Looking for a Leader* (Wheaton, IL: Crossway, 2008), 197–98.
6. Matthew Henry, *Commentary on the Whole Bible*, 6 vols. (Peabody, MA: Hendrickson, 1992), 2:264.

Again, aided by God's Spirit, Saul quickly organized the people: "When he mustered them at Bezek, the people of Israel were three hundred thousand, and the men of Judah thirty thousand" (1 Sam. 11:8). Since the Hebrew word for "thousand" is also used for a company-sized military unit, it is possible that these numbers were significantly lower—three hundred Israelite units of thirty to fifty men and thirty Judean units of thirty to fifty men—though still a significant military force. Saul then sent a message to the besieged town: "Tomorrow, by the time the sun is hot, you shall have deliverance" (11:9). The Jabesh-gileadites were made confident by Saul's bold and effective leadership, and they sent a message to Nahash, stating, "Tomorrow we will give ourselves up to you, and you may do to us whatever seems good to you" (11:10). The apparent effect of this message was to lull Nahash's forces into an inattentive overconfidence. Thus, when Saul's forces arrived—well ordered in three lines of battle—"they came into the midst of the camp in the morning watch and struck down the Ammonites until the heat of the day. And those who survived were scattered, so that no two of them were left together" (11:11).

One lesson that we might draw from Saul's victory over Nahash is the importance of gifted and able leadership. But the better point to note is the vital role played by the Spirit of God in equipping such spiritual leadership and animating the people in godly obedience. Davis notes: "Salvation came not because Israel had a king but because the king had Yahweh's Spirit; it is not the institution of kingship but the power of the Spirit that brings deliverance."[7]

It is said that the great English preacher Charles Spurgeon preceded every sermon with a prayer for God to send the Spirit, which explains much of his remarkable effectiveness as a gospel herald. It is the Holy Spirit who makes the Word of God mighty for salvation (Ezek. 36:26–27), who empowers Christians for growth in holiness and grace (Gal. 5:16; Eph. 1:16–20; 3:16–19), and who bears the fruits of righteousness, peace, and joy (Rom. 14:17; cf. Gal. 5:22–23). The rule among God's people is ever that which was stated to Zerubbabel: "Not by might, nor by power, but by my Spirit, says the LORD of hosts" (Zech. 4:6). Whenever God's people resort to worldly stratagems, they begin to fail in power; but whenever God's Spirit comes to believers, we are fortified in power and grace.

7. Davis, *1 Samuel*, 95.

How, then, do Christians gain access to the power and blessing of God's Spirit? It may please the Lord to grant his Spirit unexpectedly, as he did in this case with King Saul. But the New Testament gives us two consistent rules. First, we are to pray for the ministry of God's Spirit within us. Thus, Jesus concluded his teaching on prayer in Luke 11 by saying, "How much more will the heavenly Father give the Holy Spirit to those who ask him!" (Luke 11:13). The Holy Spirit is ours for the asking.

Second, God's Spirit attends to faith in God's Word. Thus, Paul challenged the Galatians, "Did you receive the Spirit by works of the law or by hearing with faith?" (Gal. 3:2). The answer is that it was faith in God's Word that brought God's Spirit. The Spirit is the author of God's Word (2 Peter 1:21). Jesus said, "It is the Spirit who gives life; the flesh is no help at all. The words that I have spoken to you are spirit and life" (John 6:63). Therefore, the way for us to have the Spirit is to be devoted to the Word; it is those who are relying on God's Word who enjoy the blessing of the Holy Spirit's power. So if Christians hope to be renewed with power to face the challenges of sin and unbelief in our day, we will require the presence and power of the Holy Spirit, who comes to God's people through prayer and devotion to the Bible.

THE KINGDOM RENEWED

Saul's victory at Jabesh-gilead established his kingdom among the tribes of Israel. The people responded by appealing to Samuel, demanding violence against the faction that had opposed Saul at his earlier coronation: "Who is it that said, 'Shall Saul reign over us?' Bring the men, that we may put them to death" (1 Sam. 11:12). This demand may have expressed their newfound devotion to Saul, although it may also have been a calculated concern to rid the nation of internal dissent.

Whatever the motive, the answer came not from Samuel but from Saul: "Not a man shall be put to death this day, for today the LORD has worked salvation in Israel" (1 Sam. 11:13). Here was more inspired leadership from the new king, showing the restraint and magnanimity that alone can bring true unity to any people. This was the high point of Saul's entire life and reign, as he reminded the people that it was not he but the Lord who had saved them, so that the people should honor the Lord with godliness rather than honor Saul with violence against his critics. "The LORD has worked salvation in Israel," he said. Here is the only basis for true unity and strength: the confession of God's saving power and the resolve to honor his sovereignty through submission to his Word.

These events seem to have brought satisfaction to Samuel. Israel had rejected him as well as the Lord in demanding a king. But now God's Spirit had come to Saul, so that Samuel might hope for godliness and faith in the new ruler. The prophet quickly took advantage of the situation: "Then Samuel said to the people, 'Come, let us go to Gilgal and there renew the kingdom'" (1 Sam. 11:14). So the people went to Gilgal, a traditional gathering ground near Jabesh-gilead, "and there they made Saul king before the Lord in Gilgal" (11:15).

There is some question about Samuel's exact meaning when he summoned the people to "renew the kingdom" (1 Sam. 11:14). It is obvious that he meant the public confirmation of Saul, given that Saul was "made king" there (11:15). But it seems that Samuel likely meant more than this: he intended for the people to renew their fidelity to God's sovereign kingdom, under King Saul. Gilgal is where Joshua had brought Israel after crossing the Jordan River, setting up memorial stones there to God's faithfulness and renewing the nation's covenant with the Lord (Josh. 4:20–24). Samuel's purpose was to tie this new victory to God's ancient faithfulness, reminding the people that victory and blessing come only through faith in the Lord (cf. 1 Sam. 12:14).

Thus, "they sacrificed peace offerings before the Lord" (1 Sam. 11:15), reaffirming their appeal to God's grace for their blessing. No wonder this chapter ends with a statement of remarkable happiness: "There Saul and all the men of Israel rejoiced greatly" (11:15). This is also the way for our churches to be happy and blessed: for God-honoring leadership to receive the approval of God's people, as the whole church renews its commitment to God's grace, in accordance with the teaching of God's Word.

Battle Plans, Not Business Plans

Saul's victory over Jabesh-gilead presents a challenge to Christians and churches today. The first challenge is for us to realize that no matter how congenial our circumstances may seem, on the spiritual plane God's people are always on a war footing. Paul warns Christians that "we do not wrestle against flesh and blood, but against the rulers, against the authorities, against the cosmic powers over this present darkness, against the spiritual forces of evil in the heavenly places" (Eph. 6:12). These spiritual foes are just as eager to destroy and humiliate God's people today as Nahash the Ammonite was in the day of King Saul.

In fact, Nahash may be viewed as symbolic of the power of sin, so that the plight of Jabesh-gilead warns us against capitulating to the vicious power of sin and temptation. Blaikie writes: "If we regard Nahash as a type of another tyrant, as representing the tyranny of sin, we may derive from his conditions an illustration of the hard terms which sin usually imposes."[8] Nahash wanted to remove the Israelites' right eyes; likewise, sin wishes to disarm us and render us unfit to fight in God's causes. How happy we will be to realize, as the men of Jabesh-gilead realized just in time, that surrender to sin only subjects us to injuries and humiliations that may mark us for the rest of our lives.

Yet despite the warning of this text, the reality is that the church today rarely sees itself as engaged in deadly spiritual warfare. Woodhouse remarks that this reality can be seen in the fact that most churches conduct themselves according to business plans rather than battle plans. He writes:

> "Going to do battle" is *not* how we like to think of our evangelistic efforts. In many ways the business world has replaced the battle field as a source of categories for thinking about this work. Gospel work is then not war but *commerce*: we go to sell a product, not to fight a battle. We are marketers, not soldiers. We have merchandise, not weapons. We face potential customers, not an enemy. We are out to expand our market share and increase our customer base, not to capture, defeat, and destroy a foe.... The language of war, weapons, and battle is too extreme for the way we think about evangelism. We are more like advertisers than fighters.[9]

If this is how we are thinking about the work of our church, then God's Word would have us radically rethink our approach. Our challenge in evangelism is not to present an appealing product to a consumer culture. Rather, Paul says, "the god of this world has blinded the minds of the unbelievers, to keep them from seeing the light of the gospel of the glory of Christ, who

8. Blaikie, *First Samuel*, 173.
9. Woodhouse, *1 Samuel*, 192.

is the image of God" (2 Cor. 4:4). If Paul is correct and the combination of spiritual domination and depravity is the problem with unbelievers, then evangelism will have to rely on something different from worldly appeals to persuasion. After all, the gospel cannot be sold to those who are blind and even hostile to it. Instead, Christians must understand themselves as being engaged in spiritual warfare, taking up the spiritual weapons of prayer and God's Word. Paul writes: "For though we walk in the flesh, we are not waging war according to the flesh. For the weapons of our warfare are not of the flesh but have divine power to destroy strongholds. We destroy arguments and every lofty opinion raised against the knowledge of God, and take every thought captive to obey Christ" (2 Cor. 10:3–5). If Paul is right, then the sign that we have awakened to the reality of spiritual warfare will be our renewed commitment to the power of God through his Word (Heb. 4:12–13; 1 Peter 1:23).

The same is true on an individual level. We, too, are on the front lines of spiritual warfare. The reason that so many Christians live so closely to the world, casually participating in worldliness and sin, is our failure to appreciate the danger to our souls. Peter warns, "Your adversary the devil prowls around like a roaring lion, seeking someone to devour" (1 Peter 5:8). This being the case, he urges us to "be sober-minded; be watchful. . . . Resist him, firm in your faith" (5:8–9). Thus, Christians who recognize the violent threat of our spiritual enemies will eagerly make use of the means of God's grace for the growth and soundness of their faith, resisting the urges of sin that bombard our culture.

Finally, this chapter presents the theme of salvation in Israel, and thus reminds us that God's people need a Savior to deliver us from the Nahashes of this evil world. Realizing this, we should draw near to the true Spirit-empowered King whom God has sent into our world. Jesus Christ began his ministry by saying: "The Spirit of the Lord is upon me, because he has anointed me to proclaim good news to the poor. He has sent me to proclaim liberty to the captives and recovering of sight to the blind, to set at liberty those who are oppressed, to proclaim the year of the Lord's favor" (Luke 4:18–19, quoting Isa. 61:1–2). It is in the kingdom of Christ, entered through faith in Jesus, that we are defended and delivered from our spiritual foes—from Satan, sin, and the death our guilt has deserved—receiving the liberty of salvation and the blessing of sight to believe on Jesus.

Then, as we walk closely with Christ, strengthening our faith by his Word and continual prayer, and receiving the power of God's Spirit that he graciously sends to those who seek his will, we may know even in this world the joy of our salvation, as Israel celebrated her kingdom renewal at Gilgal. Jesus said, "He whom God has sent utters the words of God, for he gives the Spirit without measure" (John 3:34). Through faith in Christ and in God's Word, the God who caused the Spirit to "rush upon" Saul will empower us to stand firm in these evil days of spiritual warfare, and he will use us to bring this same salvation to others besieged by darkness and unbelief.

16

SAMUEL'S FAREWELL

1 Samuel 12:1–25

Only fear the LORD and serve him faithfully with all your heart.
For consider what great things he has done for you. But if you
still do wickedly, you shall be swept away, both you and your
king. (1 Sam. 12:24–25)

henever a great leader comes to the end of his career, his final address to his followers is usually interesting and always important. This is especially true for the great leaders of God's people in the Bible. The book of Deuteronomy presents Moses' final words to Israel, after which the great deliverer and lawgiver went up atop Mount Nebo to look upon the Promised Land and then die. His successor, Joshua, gathered all Israel to issue a challenge that still rings in our ears: "Choose this day whom you will serve," whether the false gods of their fathers or the true God of Israel. "But as for me and my house," Joshua concluded, "we will serve the LORD" (Josh. 24:15). When Paul passed through Ephesus for what he knew would be the last time, he gathered the elders to meet with him. The apostle reminded them what a true ministry is like—"I did not shrink from declaring to you anything that was profitable . . . I did not shrink from declaring to you the whole counsel of God" (Acts 20:20, 27)—and warned them against wolves that would enter the flock and tear apart the sheep (20:29–30). Most important is the final address of the Lord Jesus Christ to his disciples at what we call the "Last Supper." There, Jesus drew their attention to the work he was about to do in dying on the cross for our sins (Matt. 26:26–28), and he gave them instructions to guide them during the years of their service as apostles (John 13–16).

Considering these examples, we can see a general pattern to the farewell addresses of the Bible's great men. Most of them seek to recap and summarize their ministries, which they also vindicate as faithful to the Lord. Added to this is a charge for those who carry on to remain faithful in their own faith and practice. In response, it is common for the people to express remorse at the loss of their leader, and to express a need for intercession with the Lord that can ultimately be met only by Jesus Christ himself. This is the very pattern reflected in the final address of the great prophet and judge Samuel, as he prepares to hand over the leadership of Israel to the newly consecrated King Saul.

SAMUEL'S MINISTRY VINDICATED

It may seem strange that as exalted a figure as Samuel would need to vindicate his years of ministry. But when we remember the kind of leadership that the Israelites had previously received and the general depravity of the wider ancient world, we should not be surprised. Ministers today who come after one who fell into sin will often find themselves held under unfair suspicion. Samuel had replaced Eli and his wicked sons, so concerns about the exploitation of his office and personal morality would not have been unexpected.

Samuel therefore began, "Behold, I have obeyed your voice in all that you have said to me and have made a king over you. And now, behold, the king walks before you" (1 Sam. 12:1–2). The point of this statement is that Samuel was not ill-disposed toward the people. He was not unyielding and unwilling to answer their requests. Even though he considered the request for a king to be an insult to himself, and even more importantly an insult to God, and though he warned the people about what a catastrophe this request would bring (8:11–17), he was willing to do his best to make the demanded arrangement work. Moreover, when the Lord commanded Samuel to anoint

Saul as king, an action that Samuel found distasteful, the great judge and prophet did not hesitate to act in obedience to the Lord. In fact, Samuel's role in enthroning King Saul shows just how disinterested he was in personal gain, for Saul was his own replacement. For centuries, Israel had relied on the judges whom God would raise up to meet particular needs, rather than on a regular dynastic succession. Samuel was the last of these judges, and at the request of the people and the will of the Lord, he comes to speak his final words as he departs from the executive leadership of the nation.

Samuel also points to his manner of life: "I am old and gray; and behold, my sons are with you. I have walked before you from my youth until this day. Here I am; testify against me before the LORD and before his anointed. Whose ox have I taken? Or whose donkey have I taken? Or whom have I defrauded? Whom have I oppressed? Or from whose hand have I taken a bribe to blind my eyes with it? Testify against me and I will restore it to you" (1 Sam. 12:2–3).

Samuel knew that people tend to resent and distrust those given great authority, for the simple reason that such leaders so often misuse their power. "Power corrupts," said Lord Acton, "and absolute power corrupts absolutely." So Samuel challenges the people to testify if this could be said of him. "Here I am," he declared; "testify against me before the LORD." If Samuel had cheated anyone, if he had demanded unauthorized payments in order to perform his services, if he had used his position to harass his opponents, such persons could come forward now and disgrace his whole life in ministry. The failure of anyone to come forward with a charge against Samuel testifies to his extraordinary godliness, and it reminds all Christians of the value of a clean record and a good name. Could we stand before the church and give anyone the opportunity to speak against our integrity? If we could not, then we should remedy our spotted reputation and immediately turn to the Lord, seeking an upright and honest heart, and then do all that we can to reconcile with those who could accuse us.

In response to Samuel's plea, the people had no option but to respond positively: "They said, 'You have not defrauded us or oppressed us or taken anything from any man's hand'" (1 Sam. 12:4). Samuel pressed his case, calling both the Lord and the newly anointed king, Saul, to certify his faithfulness, saying: "'The LORD is witness against you, and his anointed is witness this day, that you have not found anything in my hand.' And they said, 'He is witness'" (12:5). In this way, Samuel was setting the people up to confess their own sin before the Lord. For, as John Woodhouse comments, "The vindication of Samuel meant the indictment of the people,"[1] since they acknowledged that they had no cause other than unbelief for their demand that Samuel be replaced by a king.

The young Scottish minister Robert Murray M'Cheyne is famous for having said that the most important gift that he could give his congregation was his own personal holiness. The reason for this is that we are greatly encouraged to believe the gospel when we see its power at work in the lives of others. Faithfulness as Christians is not important merely for ministers, but also for parents. Our children will learn from our conduct whether God is truly sovereign over our lives and whether the gospel of forgiveness is truly our rule for faith and life. Thomas Carlyle said of his poor, uneducated father that he was prouder to bear his pedigree than he would be that of a duke or a king: "for what is the glory of mere rank or accidental station compared to the glory of Godlike qualities, and of a character which reflects the image of God Himself?"[2]

The writer of Hebrews stresses the value of following the example seen in the lives of godly elders: "Remember your leaders, those who spoke to you the word of God. Consider the outcome of their way of life, and imitate their faith" (Heb. 13:7). Any mere man is bound to have weaknesses and failures, but our faith should be an example to others. The faith of spiritual leaders and their faithfulness in ministering to the flock should be held before all Christians, and the world as well, as a strong encouragement to faith.

The Lord's Cause Pleaded

The purpose behind Samuel's vindication was not his concern over his own legacy or reputation. Rather, Samuel set forth his own trustworthiness as a preamble for his main concern: Samuel wanted the people to remember what a great and faithful God they served and had offended through their request for a king. This was another purpose in citing God as a witness to

1. John Woodhouse, *1 Samuel: Looking for a Leader* (Wheaton, IL: Crossway, 2008), 215.
2. Quoted in William G. Blaikie, *Expository Lectures on the Book of First Samuel* (1887; repr., Birmingham, AL: Solid Ground, 2005), 185.

his own integrity; having spoken of the Lord as witness, Samuel elaborates on the Lord's faithfulness to Israel:

> And Samuel said to the people, "The LORD is witness, who appointed Moses and Aaron and brought your fathers up out of the land of Egypt. Now therefore stand still that I may plead with you before the LORD concerning all the righteous deeds of the LORD that he performed for you and for your fathers." (1 Sam. 12:6–7)

Samuel begins with the exodus, reminding the people of Israel that their forefathers had gone into Egypt and been brutally enslaved. But they cried out to the Lord, "and the LORD sent Moses and Aaron, who brought your fathers out of Egypt and made them dwell in this place" (1 Sam. 12:8). These words summarize all the great miracles involved in the exodus, Israel's journey from bondage in Egypt to lordship in the land of promise. "But," Samuel laments, "they forgot the LORD their God" (12:9). The result of Israel's covenant unfaithfulness was God's chastisement, giving his people over to oppression at "the hand of Sisera, commander of the army of Hazor, and into the hand of the Philistines, and into the hand of the king of Moab" (12:9). As it was true then that unrepented patterns of sin led to God's stern discipline, so it is also true now for Christians (see Heb. 12:4ff.). Yet the people "cried out to the LORD" again, saying, "We have sinned, because we have forsaken the LORD and have served the Baals and the Ashtaroth" (1 Sam. 12:10), with the result that God saved them again.

In the days of the judges, God sent such heroes as Jerubbaal (Gideon), Barak, and Jephthah—and finally Samuel himself—so that the Lord's faithfulness in saving his repenting and believing people cannot be questioned. Most recently, the people had faced the threat of Nahash the Ammonite. Instead of trusting the Lord, they had demanded that the Lord provide them a king. (Verse 12 confirms that it was fear of defeat that prompted Israel to seek a human king.) This is clearly seen as an act of unbelief and sin: "You said to me, 'No, but a king shall reign over us,' when the LORD your God was your king" (1 Sam. 12:12). Their demand for a king was a rejection of the Lord as King. Therefore, given God's consistent pattern of judging and chastising the idolatry of his people, we can see God's acceding to their request for a king as a form of judgment. God not so much provided a king as he gave the people over to their sin and its consequences: "And now behold the king whom you have chosen, for whom you have asked; behold, the LORD has set a king over you" (12:13). So long as Saul lived and reigned, he would remain "the other king," while God prepared his people through a history of failure to receive the one true King.

This prompts an observation. Whenever we turn aside to our own schemes and plans, or to the world's schemes and plans, as opposed to God's, we are heading for trouble. Such an abandonment of the Lord is seldom explicit: it is merely that we become drawn in by some worldly strategy or approach to ministry or personal growth, having lost confidence in God's Word and the methods taught there. Whenever this happens, we are heading for disaster, because God's way is the true and right way and also because God actively punishes the unbelief and disobedience of his people.

If we find that such a departure from God and his Word has happened, what should we do? Samuel answers for us:

> If you will fear the LORD and serve him and obey his voice and not rebel against the commandment of the LORD, and if both you and the king who reigns over you will follow the LORD your God, it will be well. But if you will not obey the voice of the LORD, but rebel against the commandment of the LORD, then the hand of the LORD will be against you and your king. (1 Sam. 12:14–15)

This is a remarkable statement, and remarkably encouraging to us. Samuel is saying that even though the people of God had sinned in choosing Saul, and even though Saul's kingship was an affront to the Lord, yet if they and King Saul would humble themselves before the Lord and resolve to renew their fidelity to him, and if they and the new king would really "follow the LORD [their] God," then the Lord would be gracious to bless them. They would have to be serious, though, and God would not be fooled. Notice how thorough and definitive the language is: they must *fear the Lord*, they must *serve* and *obey his voice*, they must *not rebel* against his commandments, and they must *follow the Lord* and *obey the voice of the Lord*. If they did these things, then God would make the new kingship— for all the unbelief, idolatry, worldliness, and disobedience behind it—a success that would bless his people.

This same principle holds true for us. What happens when we find that we have made a bad decision, or realize that we have fallen into sin and rebellion and have put ourselves at odds with the Lord? The Bible teaches that God allows us to start right where we are, humbling ourselves and confessing our sins, trusting in the Lord and calling on his name, and recommitting ourselves to new obedience in fidelity to God's Word.

Sometimes a Christian will find that he has made an unwise decision in accepting a job, but cannot now go back on his decision. What should he do? He should turn to the Lord, walking in fear and obedience while trusting God's promises, and God may give his blessing to him even in what he regards as a bad job. The same is true if we make a poor decision in moving to a certain city, attending a certain college, joining an unhealthy church, or even entering into a foolish marriage. In some cases, we can overrule our prior decision and go back; in other cases, we cannot. So what should we do? We turn to the Lord precisely where we are, humble ourselves before him and his Word, and begin walking in faithfulness. We can be certain, even when there will be difficulties, that God's blessing will be upon us and his help will be ready at hand. This is the remedy for those who assume they have "stepped outside God's will," and therefore neglect to turn to him for help. Christians may thank God that even when we turn in wrong directions, he is gracious to help us when we pray.

There is no situation and no problem in which Christians cannot be blessed by God's mighty help, if only we will turn to the Lord in sincere faith, humble ourselves before him as our Lord and God, and renew our commitment to walk in his Word. This is the all-purpose solution to every problem, and it works because God is so gracious and ready to receive his erring children as to put his blessing upon our heads. Repentance, faith, and new obedience are the way forward for every Christian from wherever we are, good or bad, right at this moment. David expressed this principle in Psalm 28:7, which begins with a statement of renewed reliance on God's saving power that expresses faith in him, receives God's help, and therefore responds with joyful thanks: "The Lord is my strength and my shield; in him my heart trusts, and I am helped; my heart exults, and with my song I give thanks to him."

On one occasion when I was evangelizing among Muslims in Africa, I was challenged by an impoverished woman as to the power of the Christian

God. She demanded that before I witnessed to the gospel, I perform a miracle to persuade her. I replied that I was not aware of possessing any power to perform miracles, nor did I need to do so. Rather, I came bearing the good news of God's forgiving grace through his Son, Jesus Christ. She responded that her people were poor, sick, downtrodden, and oppressed: they needed a God who would solve their problems. I answered that if she believed in Jesus, she would still have all those problems. But her greatest problem—the holy God's wrath upon her sin, for which her soul would go to hell—would be remedied by the atoning blood of God's Son. Moreover, she would become a dearly beloved child of God, and God would take upon himself the duty of caring for her. If God did not change her conditions, then he would give her the power to endure them cheerfully, and God our Father would ensure that everything she truly needed would be provided. But in order for this to happen, she must renounce the false god Allah, she must humble herself before the true God in repentance and faith, and she must walk with him in sincere obedience, lest her Father find it necessary to painfully discipline her in his holy love. This explanation was followed by a long conversation in which I explained the good news of salvation through Jesus. By God's grace the woman believed, along with a number of her friends who were there, and they made the significant public statement of joining us for worship at the nearby Christian church.

Whatever our circumstances—whether we seem to be on top of the world or under its foot—we have just as much reason as that poor African woman to believe in Jesus Christ. The people of Israel's biggest problem was not Nahash the Ammonite and his threat to gouge out all their right eyes (1 Sam. 11:2), but rather the holy God who threatened their souls with just condemnation for their sins. Jesus said, "Do not fear those who kill the body but cannot kill the soul. Rather fear him who can destroy both soul and body in hell" (Matt. 10:28). Moreover, the way for us to lead joyful, pure, and godly lives—lives that have real significance in this world and in the next—is to come to God for his fatherly care and devote our lives in faith to him through his saving Son.

This was Samuel's message to Israel, as it is the Bible's message to us. The Bible does not say that our lives will be trouble-free. Jesus said, "In the world you will have tribulation." But he added, "Take heart; I have overcome the world" (John 16:33). It is that latter statement that enables us to endure the former. Yet if Israel were to refuse Samuel's offer—"if you will not obey the voice of the LORD, but rebel against the commandment of the LORD"—then not only would God's blessing be forfeited, but "the hand of the LORD will be against you and your king" (1 Sam. 12:14–15).

The Israelites were God's covenant people, by God's choice and not theirs, so whether they had a king or not, they still came under God's covenant rule. The same is true for believers, who are all called to Christ by God's sovereign grace just as Israel was: we may live foolishly or faithfully, but we cannot live without the holy and almighty government of God over our lives. God's hand will be upon us for blessing or against us in unpleasant discipline, but God's hand will never be removed. How much better, then, for Christians simply to resolve to fear, honor, trust, and obey the Lord; then, under whatever circumstances we find ourselves, we can be confident of lives that bear the mark of peace with God and the joy of the strength of the Lord.

SAMUEL'S INTERCESSION SOUGHT

Unlike me, Samuel *did* have power to perform miracles, and he judged this farewell address a good time for a demonstration that would place an exclamation point on his message:

> "Now therefore stand still and see this great thing that the LORD will do before your eyes. Is it not wheat harvest today? I will call upon the LORD, that he may send thunder and rain. And you shall know and see that your wickedness is great, which you have done in the sight of the LORD, in asking for yourselves a king." So Samuel called upon the LORD, and the LORD sent thunder and rain that day, and all the people greatly feared the LORD and Samuel. (1 Sam. 12:16–18)

First, Samuel reminded the people that it was a time of year when no strong rains fell, and then he promised a miracle that should set a seal on his call for their repentance. When he called on the Lord, a violent thunderstorm immediately came upon them, "and all the people greatly feared the LORD and Samuel" (1 Sam. 12:18). We do not know whether Samuel enjoyed going out from his rule over Israel in such style, but his point was well made! The prophet was not, after all, departing completely from the affairs of Israel. Though no longer a ruling judge over the people, he remained a prophet of the Lord, and therefore one who spoke with authority and power to both people and king.

The terrified people responded by calling on Samuel to intercede for them with God: "All the people said to Samuel, 'Pray for your servants to the LORD your God, that we may not die, for we have added to all our sins this evil, to ask for ourselves a king'" (1 Sam. 12:19). Here was a sincere confession of sin, if not one that had been readily given. The people acknowledged that their whole history was one of disobedience and rebellion, and that they had entered into the ungodly line by asking for a king like all the other nations, in the place of God. "Better late than never!" we say. They did the right thing in confessing their sin, and also in asking Samuel to mediate with God on their behalf.

On the one hand, the plea for a mediator indicated a great problem. We need a mediator to speak on our behalf with a Lord from whom we ourselves fear judgment. Notice that the people spoke to Samuel, referring to the Lord as "your God," and that instead of going to the Lord in prayer themselves, they asked him to "pray for your servants to the LORD" (1 Sam. 12:19). This is practically a quote from the lips of Pharaoh, after God had broken his will through the angel of death that slew his firstborn son. When Moses and Israel were finally permitted to leave Egypt, Pharaoh approached Moses for a favor. "Take your flocks and your herds, as you have said, and be gone," Pharaoh ordered, and then asked, "and bless me also!" (Ex. 12:32). Pharaoh had no basis for approaching God himself and no standing in God's presence, so he had to ask someone who *did* have God's favor to pray to God for him. Now all the people of Israel, through their own idolatry and wickedness, had degraded themselves to the status that Pharaoh occupied before God's wrath, and they could only ask the man of God in their midst to pray to the Lord on their behalf.

Samuel responded as all of God's servants respond to an earnest plea for spiritual help, and thus he sets an instructive example for how we should respond to non-Christian people who ask for our spiritual aid. Samuel was more than willing to pray for them: "as for me, far be it from me that I should sin against the LORD by ceasing to pray for you," this being the duty of any man of God. But he offered more: "and I will instruct you in the good and the right way" (1 Sam. 12:23). This is precisely how we should answer unbelieving family and friends who ask for our prayers: "I will pray for you, but I also want to tell you how you may have the right to prayer for yourself." This answer provides us with an opening to explain how personal faith in Jesus offers personal access to God the Father for help and salvation.

Second, Samuel reassured them of God's gracious goodwill: "Do not be afraid" (1 Sam. 12:20). We likewise have the privilege of informing people of God's kindness and love for them in Jesus Christ. Third, Samuel acknowledged their sin but directed them to its remedy: "You have done all this evil. Yet do not turn aside from following the LORD, but serve the LORD with all your heart. And do not turn aside after empty things that cannot profit or deliver, for they are empty" (12:20–21). Samuel was referring to the false and empty gods, reminding the Israelites and us that we cannot follow the Lord while still pursuing the idolatries of the world, including greed, lust, pride, and malice.

Fourth, Samuel reminded the people of God's covenant promises: "For the LORD will not forsake his people, for his great name's sake, because it has pleased the LORD to make you a people for himself" (1 Sam. 12:22). God would honor his promises of salvation primarily for the honor of his own name, so they could be sure that he would be true to all that he had pledged to them. Likewise, we can be certain that God will fulfill his gospel pledge to everyone who believes: Jesus said, "Truly, truly, I say to you, whoever hears my word and believes him who sent me has eternal life. He does not come into judgment, but has passed from death to life" (John 5:24).

These are messages that we must believe for ourselves, as well as tell to others: we must remember God's goodwill for sinners through Jesus Christ, confess our sins, turn to him for salvation, and believe his gospel promises that pledge his unfailing mercy and grace to those who follow him in sincere faith. This was Samuel's final message as he laid down his judgeship, though retaining his office as prophet of the Lord: "Only fear the LORD and serve him faithfully with all your heart. For consider what great things he has done for you. But if you still do wickedly, you shall be swept away, both you and your king" (1 Sam. 12:24–25). King or no king was not really the issue: faith in the Lord or rebellion against his sovereign will is the single matter that decides our eternal destiny and our relationship with God during this life.

Our True Mediator

With these words, the narrative of 1 Samuel transitions from its focus on Samuel to a new focus on King Saul. Samuel had been a faithful servant of the Lord, as the people attested, and a truly great man of God. When the Ammonite horde began pouring into the eastern regions of Israel, the elders of Israel looked on aged Samuel, and on his unruly sons, and decided they needed to look elsewhere for salvation, demanding the king whom God had now given in Saul the son of Kish.

We might honor Samuel's legacy by recounting all the things that made him great. But a better way to honor him would be to look through him to see reasons why Jesus Christ is a better Savior, King, and Mediator, in whom we may find all that we need for the eternal salvation of our souls.

First, while the people asked Samuel to mediate on their behalf with God, we have the better privilege of approaching God's throne through the mediation of Jesus. For all his virtue, Samuel remained a sinner; even he could not ultimately stand before God on his own merits. In the end, like Israel and like us, Samuel would have to take up the words that evil Pharaoh had begged of Moses: "Would you please bless me and intercede for me with God?" Jesus is no mere holy man; he is the God-man, *Immanuel*, which means "God with us," God the Son who took up flesh to bring his people to God (Isa. 7:14; Heb. 2:14–17). By virtue of who Christ is and what he has done, Paul states, "There is one mediator between God and men, the man Christ Jesus" (1 Tim. 2:5). Jesus is the one completely sinless man, who does not need his own Savior before the holy law of God, and who as the Son of God is therefore able to offer his death for the forgiveness of everyone who believes in him and calls on God's name through his salvation.

Second, Jesus is a better mediator than Samuel because he never grows old and feeble. Under Israel's monarchy, even the best of kings grew old and ultimately died, so that the people had to tremble at what awaited under the new regime. But the kingdom of God knows no such anxiety. Jesus our King, who died for our sins, has risen from the grave into eternal resurrection life. The writer of Hebrews thus exults that Jesus' priesthood is eternal, and the same is true of his offices as Prophet and as King: he reigns "permanently, because he continues forever. Consequently, he is able to save to the uttermost those who draw near to God through him, since he always lives to make intercession for them" (Heb. 7:24–25).

Finally, while Samuel displayed a power of rhetoric and prophetic preaching that stirs the soul, and backed it up even with a striking miracle that awed his hearers, yet his words lacked the power in themselves to change the heart. How different is the Lord Jesus Christ, who speaks and preaches with the power and persuasion of the Holy Spirit. Jesus alone can say, "[My] words . . . are spirit and life" (John 6:63). If we will call on his name—the name of God's only Son and the Savior of the world—if we will enter into his kingdom through faith, and if we will open our hearts to his living and mighty words, Jesus says that we will have eternal life. Faithful Samuel pointed us to the Lord, saying, "Fear the Lord and serve him faithfully with all your heart" (1 Sam. 12:24). Jesus, the very Lord to whom Samuel pointed, calls to us, saying, "I am the light of the world. Whoever follows me will not walk in darkness, but will have the light of life" (John 8:12).

17

AFTER GOD'S OWN HEART

1 Samuel 13:1–23

The LORD has sought out a man after his own heart, and
the LORD has commanded him to be prince over his people,
because you have not kept what the LORD commanded you.
(1 Sam. 13:14)

irst Samuel 13 begins with a textual problem that has puzzled the commentators. The Masoretic Text, generally regarded as the most authoritative Hebrew text of the Old Testament, reads that "Saul was one years old when he began to reign, and he reigned for two years over Israel" (1 Sam. 13:1). There are three main approaches to dealing with this statement. The first, and most common, is to assume that something has been lost in the scribal transmission of the text.[1] It is on this assumption that some English versions correct the verse on the basis of other records. The New International Version reads, "Saul was thirty years old when he became king, and he reigned over Israel forty-two years." This reading is based on the Septuagint, the third-century B.C.

1. For this view, see P. Kyle McCarter Jr., *1 Samuel*, Anchor Bible, vol. 8 (New York: Doubleday, 1980), 222. McCarter sees this as an instance of "scribal suppression of an obviously corrupt text."

Greek text of the Old Testament, as well as on Paul's statement in Acts 13:21 that God gave Saul to Israel for forty years. The problem with this reading is that Saul's son Jonathan plays a prominent role as a general in Israel's army, which is hard to imagine if Saul, his father, was only thirty years old. With this in mind, the New American Standard Bible (prior to the 1999 update) changed verse 1 to say that Saul was forty years old when he started to reign.

A second approach assumes that this problem resulted not from a scribal error but from the original author. It may be, some argue, that the editor who put 1 and 2 Samuel into their final forms may not have known how old Saul was or how long he reigned, and thus left the text blank until he could find records to supply the information.[2]

A third approach assumes that the text reads as it was meant to read, however awkward it may appear. For instance, the expression "son of a year," which is normally translated as "one year old," could mean "at a certain age."[3] More likely is the view of John Woodhouse, who suggests that the text means that it had been a year since Saul's anointing when the events of chapter 13 took place. Likewise, while it is certain that Saul reigned for more than two years—the New Testament puts the number at forty—the text seems to be stating that Saul's legitimacy as king lasted only during the period recorded in chapters 13–15, after which he was rejected by the Lord, a period that would then have lasted two years.[4] This final solution is the best, since it makes workable sense of what the biblical text actually says: "When it had been a year, Saul began reigning over Israel, and he reigned for two years."

Saul's Philistine War

If that is the correct introduction to this chapter, it is a depressing one. Nonetheless, 1 Samuel 13 proceeds with an upbeat note, as Saul takes the offensive against the Philistine forces who maintained fortresses on Israelite territory:

2. An example of this view is found in Bill T. Arnold, *1 & 2 Samuel*, NIV Application Commentary (Grand Rapids: Zondervan, 2003), 497.

3. For this view, see David Toshio Tsumura, *The First Book of Samuel*, New International Commentary on the Old Testament (Grand Rapids: Eerdmans, 2007), 330–33.

4. John Woodhouse, *1 Samuel: Looking for a Leader* (Wheaton, IL: Crossway, 2008), 227–29.

> Saul chose three thousand men of Israel. Two thousand were with Saul in Michmash and the hill country of Bethel, and a thousand were with Jonathan in Gibeah of Benjamin. The rest of the people he sent home, every man to his tent. Jonathan defeated the garrison of the Philistines that was at Geba, and the Philistines heard of it. And Saul blew the trumpet throughout all the land, saying, "Let the Hebrews hear." And all Israel heard it said that Saul had defeated the garrison of the Philistines, and also that Israel had become a stench to the Philistines. And the people were called out to join Saul at Gilgal. (1 Sam. 13:2–4)

Here Saul responds to the greatest of the problems facing him: the Philistine domination of the Israelites. To this end he forms a standing army, which he locates centrally, under his own command and that of his son Jonathan. Michmash and Gibeah were central locations on the west side of the Jordan River, from which Saul could respond in virtually any direction. With this arrangement, the king sent the rest of the people—the citizen militia—back to their homes to await a call to mobilization. After these arrangements had been made, Jonathan struck out at the nearby Philistine garrison (*Geba* is either a variant of *Gibeah* or the name of a nearby location to the northeast[5]), setting in motion the conflict that followed.

The key to understanding this chapter is to realize that, intentionally or not, Saul had finally gotten around to obeying Samuel's instructions, given to him at the time of his anointing a year earlier. After providing Saul with three supernatural confirmations of his anointing, Samuel commanded him: "Now when these signs meet you, do what your hand finds to do, for God is with you. Then go down before me to Gilgal. And behold, I am coming to you to offer burnt offerings and to sacrifice peace offerings. Seven days you shall wait, until I come to you and show you what you shall do" (1 Sam. 10:7–8).

The command to "do what your hand finds to do" was a way of directing Saul to attack the Philistines, a command that Saul did not keep at the time. How much had happened in the meantime! Saul had been selected by lot to be Israel's king. Samuel, in his farewell address to the nation, had called on both people and king to be careful in obeying God's Word: "Only fear the LORD and serve him faithfully with all your heart. . . . But

---

5. For a discussion of the former possibility, see McCarter, *1 Samuel*, 225. For the latter view, see John Bright, *A History of Israel*, 3rd ed. (Philadelphia: Westminster, 1981), 188–89.

if you still do wickedly, you shall be swept away, both you and your king" (1 Sam. 12:24–25).

Perhaps it took a year of thinking about this to work up his courage, and perhaps it was Jonathan's initiative that forced his hand, but Saul finally committed himself to do as the prophet had directed. Gibeah was the location of the Philistine garrison that Samuel had ordered Saul to capture, and Jonathan's victory there started Saul down the road appointed by the prophet. When the Philistines were aroused by this break in the truce, Saul responded by sounding a trumpet throughout the land and calling for national mobilization, saying, "Let the Hebrews hear." "And all Israel heard it said that Saul had defeated the garrison of the Philistines, and also that Israel had become a stench to the Philistines. And the people were called out to join Saul at Gilgal" (1 Sam. 13:3–4).

Some commentators malign Saul for what they consider to be his rash militarism. Gordon Keddie compares Jonathan's strike at Geba to Japan's attack on the United States at Pearl Harbor, the result of which was the stirring up of a massive enemy to full-scale war. Keddie writes, "In embarking upon a war of aggression, Saul had made his first major mistake and brought the judgement of God upon his people."[6]

This is an erroneous view, however. For one thing, Old Testament holy war did not accommodate the idea of a truce with pagan nations occupying Israel's holy land. For another, Saul was finally getting around to obeying the commands of God's Word. It is never wrong for believers to begin practicing what God has commanded—in this matter, it truly is better late than never—and Saul was following the words of the prophet given at the time of his anointing to be Israel's king. Likewise, while believers and churches should not always take a politically militant attitude toward our society and its prevailing sins, we should nonetheless embrace the boldness of Saul and Jonathan by speaking out against idolatry, gross immorality, and falsehood. For the church to seek cultural victory by worldly means would involve a mistaken militarism. But by muting our witness of God's Word—for instance, refusing to speak out about controversial topics such as abortion and homosexuality—we betray the Lord through accommodation with his Philistine foes.

6. Gordon J. Keddie, *Dawn of a Kingdom: The Message of 1 Samuel* (Darlington, UK: Evangelical Press, 1988), 122.

It is true, as we will see, that Saul's action—or perhaps Jonathan's brave assault—immediately brought Israel into desperate straits, just as obeying the Lord will sometimes lead us into short-term difficulties. But Saul was following the plan that God had commanded through the prophet, so the ultimate result of the attack he launched at Geba would be the deliverance of Israel from its oppressive foes, at least for a time. When in doubt, we should always simply obey God's Word as it applies to our situation. This is what Saul did, and while it gained him the scorn of both ancient and modern observers, we cannot fail to view this as the high-water mark of Saul's entire life and reign.

SAUL'S FAILURE AND REBUKE

The Philistines responded to Saul and Jonathan's assault with immediate, savage, and overwhelming force: "The Philistines mustered to fight with Israel, thirty thousand chariots and six thousand horsemen and troops like the sand on the seashore in multitude. They came up and encamped in Michmash, to the east of Beth-aven" (1 Sam. 13:5). This was a vast array far beyond what Israel could handle. Even if we take the Hebrew word for "thousand" to mean "regiment," as is probably warranted (so that the Philistines advanced with thirty regiments of chariots), their host completely overwhelmed the Israelites. As a result, when Saul blew his trumpets, calling for mobilization, the people fled from the war zone as fast as they could:

> When the men of Israel saw that they were in trouble (for the people were hard pressed), the people hid themselves in caves and in holes and in rocks and in tombs and in cisterns, and some Hebrews crossed the fords of the Jordan to the land of Gad and Gilead. Saul was still at Gilgal, and all the people followed him trembling. (13:6–7)

Meanwhile, Saul had gone to Gilgal, precisely in accord with Samuel's directions, to begin the seven-day wait until the prophet arrived. This must have involved an extraordinary trial on Saul's already tentative faith. He had decided to obey the Lord, putting God's faithfulness to the test, and it seemed that a major catastrophe was resulting. Still, Saul's orders required him to wait for "seven days, the time appointed by Samuel," during which time "the people were scattering from him," and "Samuel did not come to Gilgal" (1 Sam. 13:8).

How are we to understand God's purposes at work through Saul? In his farewell address, Samuel had admonished Saul and the people to "fear the Lord and serve him faithfully with all your heart" (1 Sam. 12:24), remembering the great things that God had done for them. Saul was trying to do this very thing, but everything was going wrong and now his destruction seemed near. Does this mean that God never intended for Saul to succeed, so the Lord gave him a test that would strain anyone to the breaking point? Such an idea poorly represents God's integrity, and fails to note the clear terms with which God had offered his blessing to Saul if he should obey (12:14). The reality is that God does test his people with severe trials, giving grace to those who trust in his might. Moses learned to trust the Lord with his back to the Red Sea—which God parted to save his people and destroy the Egyptian army. Likewise, Saul would need to trust the Lord in trying times if he wanted to see God's salvation.

Yet the test proved too much for Saul. We can sympathize with him: the enemy he had provoked was drawing near, his own forces were melting away, and he was stuck waiting for Samuel to come and offer the sacrifice so that he could be sure of God's favor. What would we do in such a situation? Would it not be tempting to face the practical realities without regard for the seemingly unreasonable requirements of obedience and faith? Few of us can look with contempt on King Saul as he decided to take matters into his own hands: "So Saul said, 'Bring the burnt offering here to me, and the peace offerings.' And he offered the burnt offering" (1 Sam. 13:9).

How often God's people fail when a little more obedience would have won through to success! In Saul's case, he broke down and offered the sacrifice just as Samuel was finally approaching: "As soon as he had finished offering the burnt offering, behold, Samuel came. And Saul went out to meet him and greet him" (1 Sam. 13:10). The prophet immediately accosted Saul: "What have you done?" (13:11). We are reminded of the voice of the Lord speaking to Adam and Eve after their sin in the garden (Gen. 3:9–13). Like Adam with his fig leaves, Saul sought to cover his disobedience in a cloak of religiosity:

> When I saw that the people were scattering from me, and that you did not come within the days appointed, and that the Philistines had mustered at

Michmash, I said, "Now the Philistines will come down against me at Gilgal, and I have not sought the favor of the LORD." So I forced myself, and offered the burnt offering. (1 Sam. 13:11–12)

If we are surprised by the ferocity of the rebuke that followed, imagine how Saul must have felt. Samuel replied:

You have done foolishly. You have not kept the command of the LORD your God, with which he commanded you. For then the LORD would have established your kingdom over Israel forever. But now your kingdom shall not continue. The LORD has sought out a man after his own heart, and the LORD has commanded him to be prince over his people, because you have not kept what the LORD commanded you. (1 Sam. 13:13–14)

Saul was reminded, as we need to be, that God is interested in the motives of the heart. What Saul completely failed to grasp was that character is the issue, and that in this respect he had been weighed and found wanting.

According to Samuel, had Saul obeyed this simple test, then his kingdom would have been embraced by the Lord and established forever. We must take this statement at face value, however unlikely its fulfillment was. Since Saul failed to obey God's Word, his kingdom would not continue. This was the beginning of the Lord's rejection of Saul, after which Saul should consider his reign to be illegitimate. At a minimum, Samuel's rebuke means that Saul would not produce a perpetual dynasty, his kingdom not being established forever.

Why would God reject Saul for what may seem to us as such a small failing? Some might consider Saul's actions as an "almost obedience" that was worthy of some appreciation. Hadn't he "almost" obeyed, and wouldn't that count for something with God? Samuel answered Saul in a way that tells us that God desired more than halfhearted, halfway obedience, that the Lord was seeking a man "after his own heart" (1 Sam. 13:14). This statement can—and perhaps should—be taken two ways. On the one hand, it can mean that God desired a king whose heart was wholeheartedly committed to him in faith. Saul's disobedience revealed a problem regarding his heart, which was not wholly dedicated to God. That is why he thought an "almost obedience" would be enough for the Lord. The expression "after [God's] own heart" can also mean that God desires a king of his own choosing. Saul was the king "like all the nations" (8:5), chosen by the unbelieving people. God desired a king of his own choosing, a king whose heart would express true devotion to the Lord through his faith and obedience.

The Lessons of Saul's Sin

What, exactly, was Saul's sin? The obvious answer was that he made the sacrifice without authority to do so. Only a properly ordained priest could offer the burnt offering that would secure God's favor. But given the dire national circumstances that Saul was facing, is it possible that God would be more concerned with the proper ritual for the offering of his sacrifices than with Saul's need to get moving with organizing the war? The answer is "Yes." The sacrificial offerings of the priesthood were more important than the king's pursuit of the war. What we do in worship reveals our beliefs about who God is and what he wants, so that our obedience in worship should receive priority in our lives. The sacrifices Saul desecrated were holy, and they dealt with holy things, such as God's wrath against our sin and his atoning work in Christ for our forgiveness. Objectively, it was more important for God to be worshiped properly than for Israel to survive its war.

At the same time, Saul's obedience to God's command would have gained the help of the Almighty, who is more than able to defend his people against all enemies. Had not Samuel warned them, above all else, to fear the Lord (1 Sam. 12:24)? William Blaikie writes: "God was willing to defend and rule His people as of old, *if only they had due regard to Him and His covenant.*" This realization "should have made Saul doubly careful to act at this crisis in every particular in the most rigid compliance with God's will."[7]

Several aspects of Samuel's rebuke apply to us. First, we notice that foolishness consists of violating the command of the Lord. The proverb states, "Trust in the LORD with all your heart, and do not lean on your own understanding" (Prov. 3:5). Saul violated this very precept in making the offering himself. Given the circumstances, it seemed best to him—even necessary—to violate the command of God. But it is never right to violate the command of God, who is sovereign over all circumstances and saves his people who trust in him. This applies to Christians today in matters such as child-raising,

---

7. William G. Blaikie, *Expository Lectures on the Book of First Samuel* (1887; repr., Birmingham, AL: Solid Ground, 2005), 210 (emphasis in original).

dating, marriage, and the use of time and money. Whereas our society encourages independence in children, the Bible commands obedience to parents. Whereas the world applauds sexual indulgence in dating, God requires purity and self-control. So it goes in virtually every other aspect of life. When secular ideas conflict with the teaching of God's Word and especially with its clear commands, they are to be seen as dangerous folly. As Samuel said to Saul, so it could be said of us when our "wisdom" leads us to violate God's Word: "You have done foolishly. You have not kept the command of the LORD your God, with which he commanded you" (1 Sam. 13:13).

Second, we see that obedience to God is obedience to God's Word. The reason Saul was guilty of breaking God's command is that he violated the word that Samuel had given him. Today, we receive God's Word in the Holy Scriptures. Some people complain that to revere the Bible is to make it an idol. But the Bible is God's Word, and the way that we worship and obey God is by obeying the teachings of the Bible. It was because Saul treated God's Word without reverence that he was rebuked by the Lord.

Third, Samuel reminds us that if we want to do God's work, we must do it in accordance with God's Word. Saul was not on some agenda of his own; he was serving Israel against its enemies. So what was the problem? The problem was that he did not serve God in accordance with God's Word, so that he was rebuked and rejected by the Lord. Christians and churches risk the same result today when they adapt the worship of the church and plans for church growth to worldly models derived from the entertainment and business worlds, rather than faithfully applying the kinds of ministry taught and modeled in the Bible.

Fourth, we may be tempted to think that Samuel, and therefore God, was excessive in his rebuke of Saul. But this example shows that what we consider to be small matters of negligence are often considered by God to be major indicators of a heart that is not devoted to him. God looks on the heart (1 Sam. 16:7), and it is in the small matters of our lives that our heart's true attitude is often revealed.

SAUL'S DESPERATE STRAITS

As Saul departs from Samuel, the scene is one of despair. Everything had gone wrong, even Saul's fleshly attempt to honor the Lord. His mission at

Gilgal having resulted in failure and rebuke, Saul returned to the army. When he numbered those who remained to face the Philistine juggernaut, they amounted to little more than a single regiment, "about six hundred men" (1 Sam. 13:15). This little force remained on the field of their victory over the Philistine fortress at Geba, while the enemy army fanned out to seize total control of the populace: "Raiders came out of the camp of the Philistines in three companies. One company turned toward Ophrah, to the land of Shual; another company turned toward Beth-horon; and another company turned toward the border that looks down on the Valley of Zeboim toward the wilderness" (1 Sam. 13:17–18).

Meanwhile, having thus extended their occupation of the Israelite towns, the Philistines tightened their grip:

> Now there was no blacksmith to be found throughout all the land of Israel, for the Philistines said, "Lest the Hebrews make themselves swords or spears." But every one of the Israelites went down to the Philistines to sharpen his plowshare, his mattock, his axe, or his sickle, and the charge was two-thirds of a shekel for the plowshares and for the mattocks, and a third of a shekel for sharpening the axes and for setting the goads. (1 Sam. 13:19–21)

These words describe a people who had been piteously reduced to serfdom, denied the basis even of maintaining their own economy lest they present a military threat to their conquerors. We can imagine, in such a state of humiliation, the miserable jeers directed at Saul for his pitiful attempt to obey God's command. Today, people would complain, "This is what happens when you become fanatical about the Bible!" Because of Saul's failed attempt at obedience, the nation was in worse straits than ever and God's honor was even more disgraced. As the chapter ends, Saul is cornered in the garrison fortress he has taken, the nation is utterly subjugated once more, and the people are deprived even of the means of resistance, with "neither sword nor spear found in the hand of any of the people" (1 Sam. 13:22).

Little did Saul imagine how near was the help of the Lord, and how soon it would be before God struck out against the oppressors to save his people. Saul may have failed the Lord, but he was still the king of Israel, however illegitimate, and Israel was still the people of the Lord. As the angel would say to a later generation of Israelites, "he who touches you touches the apple of his eye" (Zech. 2:8). And as the apostle Paul discovered in his own time of need, God says, "My grace is sufficient for you, for my power is made perfect in weakness" (2 Cor. 12:9).

AFTER GOD'S OWN HEART

The statement for which 1 Samuel 13 is justly famous is Samuel's teaching regarding God's desire for a man "after his own heart." Samuel told Saul: "The LORD has sought out a man after his own heart, and the LORD has commanded him to be prince over his people, because you have not kept what the LORD commanded you" (1 Sam. 13:14).

This statement anticipates the calling of David as king, yet it is primarily a general statement of God's purpose. God is seeking "a man after his own heart." This is what God is looking for in this world: obedience to his will. A true king and leader receives God's approval through faithful submission and service.

This shows us the importance of the test that Saul received. God was giving him a chance to be such a person: under the stress that Saul experienced, his reliance on God would be tested and revealed. If Saul would hold fast to God's Word, even with his followers scattering and the Philistines advancing in great strength, this perseverance would show that his heart was wholly given to the Lord. As it happened, Saul's test revealed the opposite, namely, that he was proved unfit to reign over God's people.

Saul's test was not the first such trial given by the Lord, nor would it be the last. The first is recorded at the beginning of the Bible, when Adam underwent a similar trial on behalf of our entire race:

> The LORD God took the man and put him in the garden of Eden to work it and keep it. And the LORD God commanded the man, saying, "You may surely eat of every tree of the garden, but of the tree of the knowledge of good and evil you shall not eat, for in the day that you eat of it you shall surely die." (Gen. 2:15–17)

Like Saul, had Adam kept this covenant under the duress of Satan's temptation, then the principle of what God said of Saul would have been true for Adam as well: "For then the LORD would have established your kingdom over Israel forever" (1 Sam. 13:13). But Adam failed the test, plunging our race under the curse of sin, leaving God still searching for a man after his own heart.

As we continue in 1 Samuel, we will see that David answers God's quest, at least provisionally, when he is enthroned as the king after the Lord's heart. When it comes to David's trial with Goliath the giant (1 Sam. 17) or with King Saul in the cave at Adullam (1 Sam. 24:6), David obeys the Word of God under the greatest stress. In this, David, a sinner saved by grace, is a type of his greater descendant Jesus Christ, who receives the throne of God's eternal kingdom because of his perfect obedience in fulfilling God's law. God thus promised to establish David's house as the eternal kingdom, not through sinful David but through the Son whom God would give: "I will raise up your offspring after you, who shall come from your body, and I will establish his kingdom. He shall build a house for my name, and I will establish the throne of his kingdom forever" (2 Sam. 7:12–13). That Son and eternal King would later come in fulfillment of God's prophecy to David's hometown of Bethlehem: "From you shall come forth for me one who is to be ruler in Israel, whose coming forth is from of old, from ancient days" (Mic. 5:2).

The New Testament reveals this promised Son, the man truly and fully after God's own heart, as Jesus our Savior. Like King Saul, Jesus began his ministry with a sore trial: his temptation in the wilderness. How greatly it must have rejoiced the Father's heart when his Son honored him under the trials of Satan, passing every test through obedience to the Word of God: "It is written, 'Man shall not live by bread alone'" (Luke 4:4, quoting Deut. 8:3); "It is written, 'You shall worship the Lord your God, and him only shall you serve'" (Luke 4:8, quoting Deut. 6:13); "It is said, 'You shall not put the Lord your God to the test'" (Luke 4:12, quoting Deut. 6:16).

Jesus' success as the man after God's own heart means that *we have a king who reigns secure from an eternal throne.* Hebrews 1:8–9 rejoices: "Of the Son he says, 'Your throne, O God, is forever and ever, the scepter of uprightness is the scepter of your kingdom. You have loved righteousness and hated wickedness; therefore God, your God, has anointed you with the oil of gladness beyond your companions'" (quoting Ps. 45:6–7). Furthermore, through Jesus' righteousness *we have a Mediator who reconciles the fallen children of Adam through his own perfect obedience.* Paul explains: "As one trespass led to condemnation for all men, so one act of righteousness leads to justification and life for all men. For as by the one man's disobedience the many were made sinners, so by the one man's obedience the many will be made righteous" (Rom. 5:18–19). This says that Jesus is the "man after [God's] own heart" in our place. Theologians refer to Christ's "active obedience" in perfectly fulfilling the law of God in our place. Casting ourselves upon Jesus in faith, we have the comfort of knowing that whereas our sin must leave us eternally alienated from God and subject to his wrath, Christ's active obedience in life and his sacrificial atonement in death reconcile us to the embrace of our loving God.

Jesus' obedience therefore establishes the pattern for his own work in our lives. *He leads us into his own likeness*, so that we might be men and women after God's own heart in him, through obedience to God's Word and by the power of the Holy Spirit that Jesus sends: "For this is the covenant that I will make with the house of Israel after those days, declares the Lord: I will put my laws into their minds, and write them on their hearts, and I will be their God, and they shall be my people" (Heb. 8:10, quoting Jer. 31:33). God's work in the followers of his royal Son is to make us men and women after God's own heart. As we trust God, we will have nothing to fear from the Philistines of this world, knowing that like his Son, in whom God is well pleased, we are the apple of his eye and he will let nothing touch us apart from his own good will for our salvation.

18

By Many or by Few

1 Samuel 14:1–23

Jonathan said to the young man who carried his armor, "Come,
let us go over to the garrison of these uncircumcised. It may be
that the LORD will work for us, for nothing can hinder the LORD
from saving by many or by few." (1 Sam. 14:6)

First Samuel 14 introduces us to one of the most beautiful characters in all of Scripture, Jonathan the son of King Saul. Jonathan is not one of the primary figures in 1 Samuel, but he plays an important role in so many different situations that we get to know him well. In none of these accounts does Jonathan display the least vice; always he acts according to a bold faith and a keen devotion to the Lord and his servants. We know that Jonathan must have been a sinner, yet in his biblical portrayal we see a shining model of Christian manhood, faithful friendship, and devoted service to the cause of the Lord.

FAITH CONTRASTED

The writer of Samuel often makes his points through the use of contrast and comparison. He will frequently place two figures side by side, providing parallel details that make clear the issues of faith and unbelief, virtue and sin. In this chapter, the two contrasting figures are King Saul and Jonathan.

First, King Saul "was staying in the outskirts of Gibeah in the pomegranate cave at Migron. The people who were with him were about six hundred men, including Ahijah the son of Ahitub, Ichabod's brother, son of Phinehas, son of Eli, the priest of the LORD in Shiloh, wearing an ephod" (1 Sam. 14:2–3). This description is a portrait of official spiritual malaise. Having attempted to lead the people on God's behalf, Saul had failed utterly. His first strike against the Philistines had provoked their massive retaliation, and his failure to obey God's Word had led to his rejection by the Lord (13:13–14). His present setting reflects both of these sad realities. Beset with an enemy vastly superior in both numbers and armament, Saul is cornered on the outskirts of his capital with a mere six hundred soldiers who, according to 1 Samuel 13:22, lack even the basic weaponry of swords or spears. Accordingly, Saul takes no military initiative; Jonathan's ability to slip from his camp unobserved suggests that Saul's followers were so dispirited that they failed even to post proper sentries.

On the spiritual plane, Saul's situation is even worse. Saul has set up his court, following tradition by taking his seat beneath or beside a notable tree. With him is Saul's royal chaplain, a proper descendant of the high-priestly line wearing the sacred ephod, the holy apron with its Urim and Thummim for seeking the Lord's will. So far, so good—until we learn the identity of this priest: Ahijah, the grandson of wicked Phinehas, of the rejected and cursed house of Eli, the nephew of "the glory has departed" Ichabod. These details are not randomly inserted into the biblical text. Rather, they make a point about Saul's standing. David Jobling writes, "His own royal glory gone, where else would we expect Saul to be than with a relative of 'Glory gone'?"[1] Saul, having replaced the dynamic counsel of Samuel with the disgraced counsel of the house of Eli, has lost his way and is able to do little more than grasp at the tattered shreds of his lost credibility.

In contrast is Saul's son Jonathan. Jonathan does not surround himself with royal courtiers but goes only in the company of his armor-bearer. Jonathan is the one man other than Saul in Israel's army to possess proper

---

1. Quoted in Bill T. Arnold, *1 & 2 Samuel*, NIV Application Commentary (Grand Rapids: Zondervan, 2003), 209.

battle equipment, and he employs his sword not by sheathing it in besieged safety but by wielding it in daring faith. While Saul sits, Jonathan acts. While Saul's pious inactivity inspires no help from the Lord, Jonathan's faith-driven initiative receives God's mighty aid. "Whereas Saul the commander publicly dishonored the Lord through fear-inspired disobedience, Jonathan the warrior would bring honor to the Lord through his fearless faith."[2]

FAITH DARING

Jonathan's famous deed, resulting in so great a deliverance for his people, began with the royal prince's simple desire to do something for the sake of the Lord and his people. "One day Jonathan the son of Saul said to the young man who carried his armor, 'Come, let us go over to the Philistine garrison on the other side'" (1 Sam. 14:1). Jonathan had no definite plan. Rather, wearied by inactivity, he simply went out to look for an opportunity to take action.

The opposing armies were situated across a valley several miles north of Jerusalem at a place where the ascent on both sides was particularly daunting. It was probably because of this difficult terrain that Saul had caused his force to retreat here and also why the Philistines had contented themselves with besieging rather than assaulting the Israelites. This is what Jonathan observed when he went forth: "There was a rocky crag on the one side and a rocky crag on the other side. The name of the one was Bozez, and the name of the other Seneh. The one crag rose on the north in front of Michmash, and the other on the south in front of Geba" (1 Sam. 14:4–5). The names for these crags, roughly equivalent to Slippery (Bozez) and Thorny (Seneh), describe their inaccessibility. Between these steep ascents the Wadi Suwneit cuts its narrow and deep trough toward the Jordan River. In short, any military assessment of the approaches to either camp would declare them inaccessible.[3]

It is obvious that everyone else on both sides viewed this situation as shutting out any possibility for effective action against the other. But Jonathan

2. Robert D. Bergen, *1, 2 Samuel*, New American Commentary (Nashville: Broadman & Holman, 1996), 155.

3. Dale Ralph Davis, *1 Samuel: Looking on the Heart* (Fearn, Ross-shire, UK: Christian Focus, 2000), 112.

thought differently. He was of the daring sort who imagines possibilities where others see only barriers. Thus, Jonathan said to the young man who carried his armor, "Come, let us go over to the garrison of these uncircumcised. It may be that the LORD will work for us, for nothing can hinder the LORD from saving by many or by few" (1 Sam. 14:6).

Behind Jonathan's daring actions was the simple conviction of his faith: "nothing can hinder the LORD from saving by many or by few." In other words, Jonathan realized that salvation is not a matter of human factors but of divine grace and power alone. If the Lord was pleased to use Jonathan to gain a victory for Israel, then it did not really matter what forces were arrayed against him or the difficulty of the terrain. His faith did not rely on favorable circumstances but looked to God and his might.

Where did Jonathan gain this bold perspective on God? The answer: probably from the record of God's dealings with his people over the years. The whole record of the period of the judges, Israel's recent history, showed that when it pleased the Lord to deliver Israel, he could very well arrange it by a few good men or even a single bold believer. Ehud had gone alone into the stronghold of Eglon of Moab and slain the oppressor of his people (Judg. 3:16–30). Then arose Shamgar, "who killed 600 of the Philistines with an oxgoad, and he also saved Israel" (3:31).

Perhaps most famous was God's deliverance of Israel from the Midianites through Gideon. Israel's situation under the Midianites had been similar to their present plight under the Philistines: "because of Midian the people of Israel made for themselves the dens that are in the mountains and the caves and the strongholds," for the Midianite raiders would descend to steal all their crops and run off with their livestock, laying waste the land (Judg. 6:2–5). Saul's present stronghold may well have been constructed during that time. Gideon himself had been hiding in a winepress when an angel called him forth to lead Israel. Then, after Gideon's first strike, against an altar to Baal, thirty-two thousand Israelites gathered to his call. But the Lord considered this too many for his purposes, so that twenty-two thousand departed. This was still too many, so the Lord sent them down to the water nearby to be tested: everyone who lapped the water from their hands would remain; those who knelt to drink directly from the stream would go home (7:5–6). This reduced the number to a mere three hundred stalwart Israelites, and with them the Lord utterly routed the vast Midianite host.

There are so many parallels in this chapter to Gideon's victory over the Midianites that Jonathan may perhaps be referring to that earlier episode, concluding from it and other examples that "nothing can hinder the LORD from saving by many or by few" (1 Sam. 14:6).

This comparison suggests that one way for us to strengthen our faith is to consider how our situation mirrors that of others in the Bible, and to remember how God delivered his people of old. Moses and the Israelites had their backs to the Red Sea with the army of Pharaoh bearing down, and the Lord parted the waves to pass his people through, then to crash down on their pursuing enemies. Likewise, God will often provide an unforeseen way of escape for his beleaguered people today. Sennacherib's host surrounded Jerusalem, but when Hezekiah took their taunts before the Lord in prayer, the angel of God came to strike down the Assyrian army of one hundred eighty-five thousand (Isa. 37:36). So today, "the prayer of a righteous person has great power" (James 5:16). Earlier still, when Joseph refused to offend the Lord by sinning with his master's wife, for which he was thrown into Pharaoh's dungeon under false accusation, God not only arranged for his release but used this dark trial to elevate Joseph to a place of high influence in the nation. Likewise, we should trust God to use our afflictions to reveal his grace and power. These and many other biblical examples have parallels in the affairs of God's people today, great and small, and should fuel the fires of a bold and daring faith.

Recalling the examples of the judges and focusing his faith on God's sovereign might, Jonathan resolved to make himself available for the Lord's use. He was undoubtedly aware of the demoralization of the Israelite army, and he set forth to see whether the Lord would use him to change the situation. This is the kind of daring initiative that is so needed in the church. Jonathan combined personal initiative with trustful hope in the Lord's blessing as he sought to advance the cause of God and his people.

It is too easy, and too common, today for churches to do nothing in the face of great needs, waiting for increased staffing, improved funding, enlarged membership, and denominational approval. Like Saul under the pomegranate tree, such Christians will always find their challenges too daunting to encourage action. Better for Christians to act daringly, acknowledging the possibility—even the certainty—of failure should the Lord not help, but knowing that God is often pleased to bless bold initiative in faith.

William Carey launched a generation of missions with his message: "Attempt great things for God; expect great things from God." Carey himself overcame great odds and official discouragement to launch the first successful mission to India. Likewise, William Wilberforce faced down the entrenched and moneyed political forces of England to stamp out the trading of slaves. George Müller considered the vast plight of orphans in nineteenth-century England—an overwhelming problem—and by the power of prayer he succeeded in raising and educating over twenty-three thousand orphans in a Christian environment. Today, it is because of the Jonathan-like daring of God-trusting believers that Christians are answering the crisis of AIDS and orphans in Africa, responding to the epidemic of unwanted pregnancies in America, and delivering the gospel of God's grace deep into Muslim lands at the risk of their lives.

Jonathan reminds us that Christians do not have to have the answers to our prayers before we act daringly in faith. All we truly need is a faith that believes that our God is able to triumph by many or by few. It is by this faith that Christians have dared great things for God and have shaken the nations. All Christians should dare to live boldly for God, at all times standing firm for truth and bearing witness about Christ and his gospel of salvation. William Blaikie writes that "the true secret of all spiritual success lies in our seeking to be instruments in God's hands, and in our lending ourselves to Him, to do in us and by us whatever is good in His sight."[4]

Faith Triumphing

It is important that we realize that Jonathan was not claiming for himself some special place in God's plan of salvation. Jonathan did not take up the mantle of a Gideon and place it on his own shoulders. Rather, he simply said, "It may be that the LORD will work for us" (1 Sam. 14:6). Jonathan was offering himself to the Lord, not demanding of the Lord. Such a faith will often attract worthy followers, and Jonathan's armor-bearer was eager to accompany him: "Do all that is in your heart. Do as you wish. Behold, I am with you heart and soul" (14:7).

4. William G. Blaikie, *Expository Lectures on the Book of First Samuel* (1887; repr., Birmingham, AL: Solid Ground, 2005), 228.

As the two men approached the Philistine side of the wadi, Jonathan proposed a resolution: "Behold, we will cross over to the men, and we will show ourselves to them. If they say to us, 'Wait until we come to you,' then we will stand still in our place, and we will not go up to them. But if they say, 'Come up to us,' then we will go up, for the LORD has given them into our hand. And this shall be the sign to us" (1 Sam. 14:8–10).

Does this indicate that Jonathan had some revelation from God, either in advance or as he was approaching the Philistines? Nothing in the text suggests that this is the case, although remembering Gideon's fleece (Judg. 6:34–40), Jonathan may have been asking the Lord for a sign of his aid. Moreover, it is likely that Jonathan combined this request for a sign with some military savvy. If the Philistines were to allow Jonathan to come into their midst in the narrow and difficult path, then he might have a chance to deal with them one by one in a place where numbers could yield little influence. Oliver Cromwell famously commanded his troops: "Trust the Lord, and keep your powder dry!" Likewise, Jonathan was looking to the Lord for help, but he anticipated that this help would arrive in ways that would provide a practical advantage to his arms. An analogy for us today might be for us to ask in prayer for an opening to our ministry or our witness, being eager to see God's hand in our early success and being ready to leap into the opportunities that God provides. Jonathan's sign amounted to a prayer that the Lord would give him a military advantage, and by expecting God's help he was ready to act boldly when it came.

In accordance with this plan, Jonathan and his armor-bearer "showed themselves to the garrison of the Philistines" (1 Sam. 14:11). Seeing these mere two Israelite soldiers, the haughty Philistines mocked them: "Look, Hebrews are coming out of the holes where they have hidden themselves" (14:11). It was this very disgrace that Jonathan hoped to rectify with his bold attack. Sure enough, "the men of the garrison hailed Jonathan and his armor-bearer and said, 'Come up to us, and we will show you a thing'" (14:12). Why wouldn't the Philistines jeer and mock the Israelites, who had shown nothing but cowardice? But Jonathan was elated—God had granted his sign! To his comrade, he cried, "Come up after me, for the LORD has given them into the hand of Israel" (14:12).

Picture Jonathan now, as he begins his two-man assault on the Philistine heights. Having presented himself to the sentries, he now disappears from their sight as he begins climbing "on his hands and feet" (1 Sam. 14:13) up the steep face. Meanwhile, the Philistines have returned to their affairs, not worrying about the threat of two men along this unlikely route of approach. But then Jonathan scales over the top of the crag named Slippery, and before the Philistines know what has hit them, Jonathan assails them with his sword. One by one, the Israelite hero fells his enemies, with his armor-bearer coming behind to finish them off. Before long, there were "twenty men who would never teach a Hebrew another lesson."[5]

So it is that the faith that dares often triumphs. Jonathan's commando raid might be explained by entirely human factors: one well-trained and well-armed assailant comes by a difficult route, springs on his enemies, and gains an immediate advantage. Jonathan, of course, would have nothing of this view. His theological perspective was immediately reinforced by more dramatic help from the Lord: "And there was a panic in the camp, in the field, and among all the people. The garrison and even the raiders trembled, the earth quaked, and it became a very great panic" (1 Sam. 14:15). Notice that Jonathan's assault brought about a general panic among the Philistines. Notice, too, that God added the dramatic effects of an earthquake to spur the Philistines into "a very great panic." Military history recalls many flank attacks that broke an army, but none of them were launched by a single man and his armor-bearer! This was God at work with Jonathan as he had been with Gideon before, clouding the minds of Israel's foes and driving them away in panicked fear.

Faith Rallying

Jonathan's faith gave him a daring boldness. That faith produced an important triumph for God's people. Furthermore, Jonathan's faith succeeded in rallying the flagging hearts of all Israel, so that the nation was inspired to action. Faith dares, faith often triumphs, and faith rallies the people of God.

With this in mind, the scene returns to Saul's camp: "The watchmen of Saul in Gibeah of Benjamin looked, and behold, the multitude was dispersing here and there" (1 Sam. 14:16). These sentries had not been vigilant

---

5. Davis, *1 Samuel*, 114.

enough to notice Jonathan's departure, but the stampede of Philistines was too obvious for even them to miss. Saul responded by seeking out who was responsible: "Count and see who has gone from us" (14:17). The muster revealed that Jonathan and his armor-bearer were gone.

At this point, we see yet another contrast between Saul and his son. Saul no doubt remembered the trouble he had gotten into previously when he did not follow the proper procedures for dealing with the Lord. He knew as well that Israel was not to advance into battle without divine confirmation through the high priest (Deut. 20:4–5). "So Saul said to Ahijah, 'Bring the ark of God here'" (1 Sam. 14:18). We can imagine Saul pacing, casting his eye first to the priest and then across the wadi where Jonathan was routing the Philistines. Finally, "while Saul was talking to the priest, the tumult in the camp of the Philistines increased more and more. So Saul said to the priest, 'Withdraw your hand'" (14:19), meaning that the priest should cease his activity. God was not speaking to Saul, and the priestly rituals were taking too long! By biblical standards, this interruption in divinely ordained procedures provided one more proof of Saul's spiritual incompetence. Gordon Keddie puts his finger on the problem: "Saul gives us the impression that he felt he was supposed to be 'religious' and observe certain conventions at the appropriate times, but really had not deep convictions of his own. He used religion, as opposed to living a personal faith in the Lord."[6] What a contrast there is between Saul's religion and Jonathan's bold faith!

But even Saul's royal incompetence was not enough to stem the tide of victory for the Israelites that day. Saul's confidence was rallied by Jonathan's faith, so that the king sprang to action with all his forces (1 Sam. 14:20). Among the Philistines had been a number of Hebrews who had previously joined the enemy's host, but who now joined with Jonathan. Likewise, "when all the men of Israel who had hidden themselves in the hill country of Ephraim heard that the Philistines were fleeing, they too followed hard after them in the battle" (14:21–22). What a victory faith had won for Jonathan! He not only had won against the Philistines but had won the Israelites back to the cause of the Lord. How often the faith of just one man or woman will rekindle the faith of others! Indeed, there can never be a shortage of bold,

6. Gordon J. Keddie, *Dawn of a Kingdom: The Message of 1 Samuel* (Darlington, UK: Evangelical Press, 1988), 133.

Jonathan-like examples of daring faith in the church, spurring God's people to act boldly in reliance on his might.

Most importantly, Jonathan's faith had brought the Lord's help. Here we see yet another parallel between Jonathan and Gideon. When Gideon's small force encircled the Midianite army, brandishing their torches and shouting on command, the Midianites fled in panic and even assailed one another in the confusion. Likewise, Jonathan's God-empowered assault brought a self-destructive confusion upon the Philistines: "Behold, every Philistine's sword was against his fellow, and there was very great confusion" (1 Sam. 14:20). The situation began with the dismal fact that in all Israel only Saul and Jonathan possessed swords. But while Saul kept his sword sheathed, Jonathan offered his sword in faith to the Lord. The Lord, in reply, was able to bring all the swords that Israel needed into the battle, even those that would be wielded by the Philistines against themselves. Truly, Jonathan's faith was rewarded when he said, "Nothing can hinder the LORD from saving by many or by few" (14:6).

ONE MAN WITH GOD

The passage concludes with the proper postscript: "So the LORD saved Israel that day" (1 Sam. 14:23), driving the enemy far away. While the praise rightly redounds to God alone—for who authored Jonathan's faith if not the Lord, who answered his prayer, and who used his otherwise suicidal assault to rout a whole army?—we are nonetheless invited to reflect on the faith of young Jonathan. Do we believe, as he believed, that circumstances do not determine outcomes when God is involved? Do we believe in the possibility of God's acting in our circumstances: opening doors for evangelism, providing resources for ministry, offering his might to give success where otherwise there would be only failure? If we believe these things, then we will not sit in idle despondency as forces hostile to Christianity sweep our generation. We will not play the part of Saul in his inaction or in his pragmatic, unprincipled religion. Rather, if we are inspired by Jonathan's faith, we will do as Jonathan did in offering ourselves to the Lord's service, stepping forward into the scene of action, praying for the Lord to give openings and strength, and leaping into the opportunities that the Lord provides, confident of his grace to empower our efforts.

One man who stood forth for the Lord in his generation was John Knox. An early adherent to the Reformation gospel in Scotland, Knox joined forces with the persecuted band of gospel preachers, narrowly escaping with his life. Exiled to Geneva, he grew strong in faith under the ministry of John Calvin, seeing firsthand the power of God to transform a whole society. Returning to his homeland, he boldly advanced the Reformation cause, sending forth the gospel message and aggressively opposing the religious perversions that dominated in the land. Under his leadership, Scotland emerged from the darkness of medieval Roman Catholicism.

How did John Knox accomplish so much? His own answer was given in memorable words, recalling the earlier example of faithful Jonathan. Knox declared that "one man with God is always in the majority." So it was for Jonathan: one man, accompanied by only one comrade, but aided by the thunder of almighty God, routed a vast host set against his people.

What will God do today through single men and women who stand in the power of God for the cause of gospel truth and grace in our times? We will never know unless we, like Jonathan, step forward into the world, offering ourselves to God, believing that he can save with few just as well as with many, saying, "It may be that the LORD will work for us" (1 Sam. 14:6), as he has so often worked for his daring people before. Jonathan's example challenges us to be daring in giving and bold in our commitment to worldwide missions, church-planting, and other works of gospel growth. It speaks to our boldness in bearing witness to the gospel, as a church and as Christian individuals. It speaks boldly to our stand against the powers of sin and the advance of spiritual darkness in our times. Let us not sit under the tree, despondent over evil. But let us go forth in faith, knowing that with God we will certainly be a majority, for if it is his gracious will, "nothing can hinder the LORD from saving by many or by few" (14:6).

19

SAUL'S FOLLY

1 Samuel 14:24—46

Saul had laid an oath on the people, saying, "Cursed be the man who eats food until it is evening and I am avenged on my enemies." (1 Sam. 14:24)

*I*n the 1850s, the name of John Banvard was one of the most famous in America. He was the world's most renowned painter, and his innovative, moving panoramas of landscapes from the American West made him an exceptionally rich man. Returning home from his triumphant tour of Europe, Banvard celebrated his elevation in the world by building himself a replica of Windsor Castle on Long Island, New York. One biographer says of him, "Acclaimed by millions and by such contemporaries as Dickens, Longfellow, and Queen Victoria, his artistry, wealth, and stature all seemed unassailable."[1] Yet within a short period of time, Banvard would be penniless and his reputation disgraced. What happened? As is outlined in the book *Banvard's Folly: Thirteen Tales of People Who Didn't Change the World*, Banvard committed the crucial mistake of staking all his money and prestige in a venture that quickly got him in over

---

1. Paul Collins, *Banvard's Folly: Thirteen Tales of People Who Didn't Change the World* (New York: Picador, 2002), 1.

his head. Building a vast museum in New York City, Banvard launched into a head-to-head battle with the great showman and promoter P. T. Barnum. In this duel, Banvard was continually outmaneuvered, until Banvard's folly was fully exposed in the demise of his museum and collapse of his fortune.

If Paul Collins, the biographer who chronicled Banvard's and others' sudden demises, had expanded his study to include the ancient world, he could hardly have found a better subject than Israel's King Saul. When it comes to gross and self-destructive folly, few can surpass Saul. His foolish actions and fall from national respect are chronicled in 1 Samuel 14, a chapter that reminds us of our need to be guided by the teaching of God's Word, followed in a humble spirit of prayer.

SAUL'S FOOLISH OATH

The effect of Saul's folly on Israel is seen in the transition between the first half of chapter 14 and the second half: "So the LORD delivered Israel that day . . . Now the men of Israel were hard-pressed on that day" (1 Sam. 14:23–24 NASB).[2] The first statement refers to Jonathan's bold assault, which received God's blessing. The second part resulted from Saul's assumption of leadership. Saul's efforts served almost to snatch defeat from the jaws of victory, and by his folly the Philistines were able to survive their stunning defeat.

Jonathan's heroic assault drove the Philistines from the battlefield in panic and confusion. Now a relentless pursuit was called for so as to destroy their forces utterly. To this end, Saul, who had roused himself from the lethargy of fear, gave orders to motivate his soldiers. "The men of Israel had been hard pressed that day, so Saul had laid an oath on the people, saying, 'Cursed be the man who eats food until it is evening and I am avenged on my enemies.' So none of the people had tasted food" (1 Sam. 14:24).

The text does not inform us of Saul's precise motive in making this oath, but two possibilities seem most likely. First, the king may have had a legitimate concern that the pursuit of the Philistines would lag if Israel's soldiers turned aside to loot the enemy camp for food and other valuables. Ancient soldiers had to provide their own food, so the temptation of turning aside

---

2. The presence of the Hebrew *waw* preceding a noun gives a disjunctive force, not a conjunctive force, to verse 24. Thus, instead of continuing the prior narrative, the writer is introducing a new section, the point of which is given by this introductory verse.

from the fight to gain the spoils of victory was a real one. Instead of this, Saul wanted every soldier to press the fight unceasingly and destroy the enemy completely.

If this was Saul's intent, then his oath was foolishly harsh, both in forbidding the soldiers from eating and in binding them with a vow. Matthew Henry derides Saul's oath as *impolitic*, "for, if it gained time, it lost strength for the pursuit"; *imperious*, for "to forbid them to feast would have been commendable, but to forbid them so much as to taste, though ever so hungry, was barbarous"; and *impious* "to enforce the prohibition with a curse and an oath. Had he no penalty less than an anathema wherewith to support his military discipline?"[3] It was because of Saul's foolish oath that "the men of Israel were hard-pressed on that day" (1 Sam. 14:24 NASB).

An additional motive behind Saul's oath becomes more likely when we consider the context of his recent experiences. Saul was becoming more religious since his rejection by Samuel for the sin of improperly offering the sacrifice at Gilgal. After Saul's initial battle that began this war with the Philistines, Samuel had directed the king to go to the ancestral meeting place and wait for seven days for the prophet to arrive and make the sacrifice that would bring God's favor. As the period drew to its end without Samuel's having arrived, and as his military situation got worse by the minute, Saul had impetuously offered the sacrifice himself, in violation of God's commands. For this Samuel rebuked Saul and informed him that the Lord had rejected his kingship (1 Sam. 13:8–14). In the aftermath of this rebuke, Saul seems to have devoted himself to religious observance at the same time that his heart grew more reckless and hard. One example is the way in which Saul first sought divine guidance after Jonathan had attacked and then impatiently interrupted the priests when God refused to answer (14:18–19). As a further example of this renewed commitment to religious observance, Saul ordered the Israelite soldiers to fast during their battle, perhaps as an attempt to regain the favor of the Lord, who was silent to him.

The Bible's commentary on Saul's rash vow is given by means of an episode involving his son Jonathan, the hero of this chapter. Jonathan was leading the vanguard of the assault against the fleeing Philistines. At one point,

3. Matthew Henry, *Commentary on the Whole Bible*, 6 vols. (Peabody, MA: Hendrickson, 1992), 2:277.

Jonathan and the soldiers following him came upon a forest where "there was honey on the ground" (1 Sam. 14:25). Apparently, the beehives were so thick in this spot that "the honey was dropping" from them (14:26). Saul's soldiers, fearing the threat of his oath, painfully passed through without eating. "But Jonathan had not heard his father charge the people with the oath, so he put out the tip of the staff that was in his hand and dipped it in the honeycomb and put his hand to his mouth" (14:27). This was no act of rebellion, and Jonathan's zeal for battle was unflagging. In fact, the honey had an immediately positive effect on his battle-readiness: "his eyes became bright" (14:27). But right when Jonathan was flushed with this new source of energy, a soldier stopped him, saying, "Your father strictly charged the people with an oath, saying, 'Cursed be the man who eats food this day'" (14:28).

Jonathan responded candidly: "My father has troubled the land" (1 Sam. 14:29). This was a provocative statement because it is the same terminology used previously in the Bible for an individual whose sin causes Israel to lose God's blessing. In the book of Joshua, Achan brought "trouble" on Israel by his sins of stealing consecrated items from the ruin of Jericho (Josh. 7:25–26). Jonathan, who surely knew his father's heart and motives well, plainly stated that his father's sin and folly were hindering Israel from enjoying God's full blessing in battle. This was the practical effect of Saul's oath, for "the people were faint" (1 Sam. 14:28). Jonathan sadly exclaimed, "See how my eyes have become bright because I tasted a little of this honey. How much better if the people had eaten freely today of the spoil of their enemies that they found. For now the defeat among the Philistines has not been great" (14:29–30).

As a spiritual leader, Saul erred by requiring more of God's people than God himself had asked, which Saul did by demanding a fast in the midst of battle. Moreover, Saul's unbiblical requirements resulted in unintentional evils (as extrabiblical requirements have a tendency to do!). William Blaikie comments: "It was cruel in Saul to impose a fast at such a time, all the more that, being commander-in-chief of the army, it was his duty to do his utmost for the comfort of his soldiers."[4] Saul's example reminds parents, for example, that harsh and unfeeling commands, especially in the name of religious observance, merely embitter children against the parents' rule

---

4. William G. Blaikie, *Expository Lectures on the Book of First Samuel* (1887; repr., Birmingham, AL: Solid Ground, 2005), 233.

and religion. Likewise, church leaders who invent their own extrabiblical rules for conduct do more to hinder than to advance the cause of the gospel.

SAUL'S FOOLISH ORDERS

One of the unintended evils of Saul's foolish vow involved the sin of his famished soldiers in violating Israel's food regulations. Despite their physical weakness, the Israelites had pursued the enemy from Michmash to Aijalon (1 Sam. 14:31), a distance of twenty miles over rugged terrain. By the day's end, the soldiers were so starved that they "pounced on the spoil and took sheep and oxen and calves and slaughtered them on the ground." The problem was that they "ate them with the blood" (14:32). Because blood was a symbol of life, the Israelites were not permitted to eat meats that had not yet had the blood drained out of them (this was usually done by hanging the meats: see Lev. 19:26). Moreover, "the blood of an animal was the part that made atonement in sacrifices," so Israelites could not eat blood-filled portions (cf. Lev. 17:10–14).[5]

Once again, Saul was keen to make an impression by his outward show of religion. This was, as he saw it, a perfect opportunity to display his religious worthiness. Accordingly, when he was informed that "the people are sinning against the LORD by eating with the blood" (1 Sam. 14:33), Saul responded with zeal. Scolding as "treacherous" the soldiers who had violated God's law in sheer desperation because of Saul's oath, the king immediately took charge. Every man was to "bring his ox or his sheep and slaughter them" on the great stone that Saul had rolled into their camp. "Do not sin against the LORD by eating with the blood," he adjured them. Finally, after the fast had provoked the mess of his army's sin against the Lord, Saul made proper mess facilities, "so every one of the people brought his ox with him that night and they slaughtered them there" (14:34).

Flush with this success in external religious observance, Saul "built an altar to the LORD," presumably using the stone on which the animals had already been slaughtered. The text adds the suggestive note: "it was the first altar that he built to the LORD" (1 Sam. 14:35). Henry offers the sage comment that "Saul was turning aside from God, and yet now he began to build

---

5. David Toshio Tsumura, *The First Book of Samuel*, New International Commentary on the Old Testament (Grand Rapids: Eerdmans, 2007), 374.

altars, being most zealous (as many are) for the form of godliness when he was denying the power of it."[6] In all these actions, Saul showed no sign of penitence toward God, grieving over sin, or a real zeal in honoring the Lord. "He feels only that his own interests as king are imperiled. It is this selfish motive that makes him determine to be more religious."[7]

Feeling that he once more had his legs under him, Saul proposed a new endeavor against the Philistines: "Let us go down after the Philistines by night and plunder them until the morning light; let us not leave a man of them" (1 Sam. 14:36). The wisdom of this order is questionable, given the fatigue and evident raggedness of the army. Moreover, this plan was roughly the opposite of Saul's orders during the day. Earlier, the Israelites must not eat lest their plunder of the Philistines cease the pursuit; now, Saul presents the chance of plunder as the motivation for their nighttime assault.

Saul was a man who desired to succeed, but who was guided by no strong or deep convictions. The soldiers followed him with a lack of conviction appropriate to such leadership: they replied, "Do whatever seems good to you" (1 Sam. 14:36). What a contrast between this response and the earlier words of Jonathan's armor-bearer, who benefited from the inspiring convictions of the warrior prince. Offering one set of foolish orders after another, Saul would never hear the words that were eagerly spoken to his son: "Behold, I am with you heart and soul" (14:7). Saul and Jonathan instruct us that true spiritual leadership requires more than expedient opportunism and outward religious observance, but that the people of God are to be led by true biblical convictions expressed with consistency and a passionate, principled faith.

SAUL'S FOOLISH LOT

Earlier, we heard Jonathan's frustration with his father's expedient folly. Now, it is another of the men closest to the king who expresses concern over the wisdom of his commands. The priest, presumably Ahijah the high priest, said, "Let us draw near to God here" (1 Sam. 14:36). This was his polite way of suggesting that they consult with the Lord before acting on Saul's plan. Saul, perhaps deriving new hope from his most recent religious observance, agreed to seek a revelation from God: "Shall I go down after the Philistines?

6. Matthew Henry, *Commentary on the Whole Bible*, 2:277.
7. Blaikie, *First Samuel*, 230.

Will you give them into the hand of Israel?" We can only imagine his frustrated anger when the Lord "did not answer him that day" (14:37).

We do not know exactly what the Urim and Thummim (the high priests' objects for divining God's will) were, or precisely how they functioned. Presumably, they were some form of lots, and given the example here, they must have had the ability not only to answer "Yes" and "No," but also to signify that God offered no revelation. Imagine the effect this failure must have had on Saul's troops, standing by to renew the assault, to witness God's silence toward their king and high priest! God's refusal to give an omen was an ominous omen in itself!

God's refusal to speak to Saul or Ahijah subjected the king's religious observance to public ridicule. Saul obviously felt it necessary to provide a rationale for this failure, and remembering Israel's earlier lesson in which Achan's sin had hampered the whole nation (which Jonathan had likewise recalled earlier that day), "Saul said, 'Come here, all you leaders of the people, and know and see how this sin has arisen today'" (1 Sam. 14:38). Is it possible that Saul was this hard-hearted in refusing to acknowledge himself as the source of God's disfavor? More likely, as his actions suggest, Saul was simply blind to his real spiritual standing. How ironic, and tragically foolish, for the king to seek to identify the sin that had alienated the Lord, while refusing to address the Lord's condemnation of his own sin!

Thus the setting was provided for the third of Saul's almost comical follies in this chapter. Calling for the lots again, he bombastically uttered yet another oath: "Come here, all you leaders of the people, and know and see how this sin has arisen today. For as the Lord lives who saves Israel, though it be in Jonathan my son, he shall surely die" (1 Sam. 14:38–39). Just as Jonathan embodied the triumphant faith of Gideon of old, Saul imbibed the folly of Jephthah, the judge whose vow resulted in the needless death of his daughter (Judg. 11:30–40). Standing by, the people were speechless: "There was not a man among all the people who answered him" (1 Sam. 14:39).

Saul proceeded by establishing the context for his inquiry: "He said to all Israel, 'You shall be on one side, and I and Jonathan my son will be on the other side.'" Once again, the people responded with unenthusiastic submission: "Do what seems good to you" (1 Sam. 14:40). Saul then turned again to the Lord: "O Lord God of Israel, why have you not answered your servant this day? If this guilt is in me or in Jonathan my son, O Lord,

God of Israel, give Urim. But if this guilt is in your people Israel, give Thummim" (14:41).

It is not obvious why Saul divided the lots between himself and his son on the one hand and the rest of Israel on the other. Perhaps this reflected his guilty need to exonerate himself, and he added Jonathan in an attempt to bolster his case. Having exonerated himself, he could then safely play the role of Joshua in calling for the new Achan to emerge and face judgment. But this plan, too, was frustrated by the Lord. The lots were cast and "Jonathan and Saul were taken, but the people escaped" (1 Sam. 14:41). Saul now had no choice but to go forward: "Cast the lot between me and my son Jonathan," he demanded. "Jonathan was taken," so Saul said to him, "Tell me what you have done" (14:41–43).

Imagine the quandary of Jonathan, having committed no open sin against either Saul or the Lord, yet now being identified as Israel's transgressor. Again, in perfect candor, Jonathan set forth his heinous crime: "I tasted a little honey with the tip of the staff that was in my hand. Here I am; I will die" (1 Sam. 14:43). Saul, a mere mockery of the kind of spiritual leader that Joshua had been, immediately let loose yet another oath: "God do so to me and more also; you shall surely die, Jonathan" (14:44).

Was it the Lord who spoke through Saul's lots to identify godly Jonathan? It is possible that the Lord did answer this one plea from Saul, as a way of increasing his judgment. Jonathan did violate the oath of Israel's king, however innocent his intentions may have been, so it is conceivable that the Lord spoke so as to uphold the formalities of justice. This explanation, however, runs against the current of everything we read in this chapter, in which God's blessing rests not on religious formality but on the sincerity evidenced by Jonathan. The king's son was not the cause of the Lord's disfavor; indeed, it was only in response to Jonathan's bold faith that the Lord had exerted his power for Israel's victory that day. Therefore, a second explanation makes better sense. Without God's presence, the Urim and Thummim simply were not able to function properly. Jonathan's selection by lot for judgment—when Jonathan was the one faithful man on that day—merely proves the vanity of the religious observance without the endorsement of God's presence. Blaikie comments that even "Saul ought to have seen it. And he ought to have confessed that he was entirely out of his reckoning. Frankly and cordially he should have taken the blame on himself, and at once exonerated

225

his noble son."[8] Such an action, however, required a quality of character and godliness that Saul did not possess.

This chapter witnesses the folly of King Saul in both frustrating Israel's success and alienating the king from all his most loyal followers. His foolish vow alienated him from his son, who could not help but criticize his father before the army. His foolish orders alienated the priest, who awkwardly suggested that Saul seek divine counsel before acting on his plans. Now, Saul's foolish lots alienated him from the mass of the people themselves, who simply would not allow such a travesty of justice to take place.

Just as God's faithful people have sometimes risen up from their pews against an unfaithful pulpit, now Saul's army countered the king's oath with one of their own: "As the LORD lives," they answered to Saul, "there shall not one hair of his head fall to the ground" (1 Sam. 14:45). Saul may be king, so that the soldiers had done their best to obey his foolish commands, but there were limits to what he could demand of them. They would not stand for Jonathan's execution. "Shall Jonathan die, who has worked this great salvation in Israel?" they demanded. In an obvious affront to their king, they added, "He has worked with God this day." Thus "the people ransomed Jonathan, so that he did not die" (14:45). Saul's credibility was now completely shattered—a remarkable achievement for a king on a day when God had granted so great a victory over his enemies—with the effect that the pursuit came to a complete halt: "Saul went up from pursuing the Philistines, and the Philistines went to their own place" (14:46). The Philistines would survive to fight again, and Saul would never again possess so great an opportunity from the Lord to defend his people.

SAUL'S FOLLY AND FALL

Modern examples of calamitous folly and precipitous fall, such as the one supplied by John Banvard, pale in comparison to the folly and fall of Israel's King Saul. His willful sin had resulted in his rejection by the Lord (1 Sam. 13:13–14). Now, his willful folly had resulted in his fall from any hold on credibility as the leader over his nation, even while Saul remained enthroned as king. God would continue to bless the faithful people, as he

8. Ibid., 237.

had blessed Jonathan in this battle, so that Saul's reign would yet witness many successes. But for Saul, all that now remained was a final rejection from the Lord, followed by years of bitter, rebellious power as the king awaited his inevitable judgment.

What lessons should we derive from Saul's foolish behavior? The first lesson is that our religion must begin with a true saving relationship with the Lord. The recovery of God's favor requires those who have sinned to humble themselves before God, seeking his grace. The absence of such humble contrition, with a frank admission of his sins and failures, is the glaring omission from the many accounts of Saul's reign.

The difference between sinful Saul and the sinful David who will follow him as king is the same as the difference between the apostate disciple Judas and the sinful apostle Peter, both of whom betrayed Jesus on the night of his arrest. The difference between David and Peter, on the one hand, and Saul and Judas on the other is a humility that repents of sin and seeks the Lord's mercy and grace. David's great prayer of repentance begins with both a fervent plea for mercy and a trusting faith in God's offer of forgiveness through the sacrificial blood: "Have mercy on me, O God, according to your steadfast love; according to your abundant mercy blot out my transgressions. Wash me thoroughly from my iniquity, and cleanse me from my sin!" (Ps. 51:1–2). David's faith was looking forward to the true Lamb of God, Jesus Christ, represented by the blood of lambs and goats, who takes away our sin (John 1:29) and restores us to God's grace. There was nothing keeping Saul from this same kind of sincere repentance and faith, with the result that he would have been restored to the Lord's favor, except for the hardness of his unbelieving heart. Here we see Saul's chief and greatest folly: at every point he resorted to outward shows of religious observance, which served only to avoid the opening of his heart in humble contrition before the Lord.

This is a lesson that applies to every sinner beset by the folly of his or her own sin. Do not think that God can be bought off with petty good works, religious formalism, or cash payments. God calls on every sinner to confess his or her sin and appeal to the blood of the Savior whom God has sent, Jesus Christ. He promises, "If we confess our sins, he is faithful and just to forgive us our sins and to cleanse us from all unrighteousness" (1 John 1:9). Jesus renders the verdict on Saul's failed religion: "Everyone who exalts himself will be humbled, but the one who humbles himself will be exalted" (Luke 18:14). Since Saul was seeking always to exalt himself, his proud progress was all downward, whereas if he had lowered himself in humility, the Lord would surely have brought him upward in true spiritual progress and strength.

Second, Saul shows the need for spiritual leaders to be sincerely motivated for God's will and the salvation of God's people, and not for mere self-interested gain. Christian leaders of all kinds, including pastors and parents, who rely solely on the authority of their position, without an inspiring example of faith and a living ministry of God's grace, are as likely to harden their followers against the Lord as they are to lead them into salvation. Consider the remarkable fidelity exhibited by Jonathan and the faithful endurance of Israel's soldiers, who did their best to keep Saul's foolish oath. Yet in the end, the bitter effects of hard-hearted spiritual leadership can only alienate true-hearted followers, so that unfaithful rulers find their strongest opposition in the most faithful servants.

Third, Saul reveals the course of affairs for even the best of us if we are not guided by the revealed Word of God. Notice the absence of the prophet Samuel and the silence of God! Herein lay the Lord's chief judgment on Saul's unbelief. How tragic it is when we believers foolishly place ourselves in the same position by failing to consult and daily meditate on the precepts of God's Word. Blaikie states the final lesson of Saul's folly, warning us: "Who does not see what a fearful thing it is to leave God and His ways, and give one's self up to the impulses of one's own heart? Fearful for even the humblest of us, but infinitely fearful for one of great resources and influence, with a whole people under him!"[9] Let us fear, indeed, that such a calamity should befall us, our families, or our churches. Instead, let the wisdom of the Psalms speak the desire of our hearts:

> Make me to know your ways, O LORD;
>   teach me your paths.
> Lead me in your truth and teach me,
>   for you are the God of my salvation;
>   for you I wait all the day long.
> Remember your mercy, O LORD . . . ;
>   according to your steadfast love remember me,
>   for the sake of your goodness, O LORD! (Ps. 25:4–7)

9. Ibid., 240.

20

To Obey Is Better

1 Samuel 14:47–15:23

Behold, to obey is better than sacrifice, and to listen than the fat
of rams. (1 Sam. 15:22)

irst Samuel 14 concludes with a rapid summary that chronicles in brief the long reign of King Saul. We find that Saul was more or less constantly beset with enemies on every side, fighting "against Moab, against the Ammonites, against Edom, against the kings of Zobah, and against the Philistines." All four directions find their representative on that list, and Saul prevailed over them all: "Wherever he turned he routed them. And he did valiantly and struck the Amalekites and delivered Israel out of the hands of those who plundered them" (1 Sam. 14:47–48). "There was hard fighting against the Philistines all the days of Saul." For this reason, Saul was constantly recruiting expert fighters: "When Saul saw any strong man, or any valiant man, he attached him to himself" (14:52).

Saul's domestic life was equally active. He had three sons, "Jonathan, Ishvi, and Malchi-shua," and God blessed him with two daughters, Merab and Michal (1 Sam. 14:49). In a passage that today would read like an obituary, the narrative recounts the name of Saul's wife, Ahimaaz, and his uncle

Abner, who commanded the army, along with Saul's father, Kish, and Abner's father, Ner, and grandfather Abiel.

Thus was the life of Saul, king of Israel—a great life, to be sure. But what is the point of this summary, when so much of Saul's reign is yet to be told? The apparent reason is one of charity and appreciation. This is the positive record that can be attributed to Saul: his battles, his family, and his army of followers. If only these things provided the sum of a man or woman! But they do not, and the lesson taught to us by Saul's decrepit end is that a person's life is finally assessed not by worldly achievements but by its relationship to the Lord. How many people today possess glowing résumés and glittering accomplishments, yet none of it ultimately matters because they are estranged from their Maker! To be a man or woman of God is better than to be a great king like Saul. Or, to put it in terms of the lesson of 1 Samuel 15, "to obey is better than sacrifice" (1 Sam. 15:22).

SAUL COMMANDED TO HOLY WAR

Chapter 15 is a pivotal account in 1 Samuel, since it closes the book of Saul's kingship and opens the book for his successor, King David. From the very start of the chapter, the matter at hand is obedience to the Lord. Samuel appears before Saul, saying, "The LORD sent me to anoint you king over his people Israel; now therefore listen to the words of the LORD" (1 Sam. 15:1). Since Saul became king through God's anointing, Saul had an obligation to follow the instructions that came from the prophet Samuel. Literally, Samuel says, "Listen to the voice of the words of the LORD." As king, Saul must hearken to God's words and obey what the Lord tells him.

The particular command that Samuel brought to Saul pertained to one of Israel's ancient and hated enemies, the Amalekites: "Thus says the LORD of hosts, 'I have noted what Amalek did to Israel in opposing them on the way when they came up out of Egypt. Now go and strike Amalek and devote to destruction all that they have. Do not spare them, but kill both man and woman, child and infant, ox and sheep, camel and donkey'" (1 Sam. 15:2–3).

Saul was to attack and destroy the Amalekites, a nomadic people to the south and southeast of Israel, living in the Negeb and the Sinai desert. When Israel was passing through Sinai during the exodus from Egypt, the

Amalekites attacked them. While Aaron and Hur held up Moses' hands, the Israelites triumphed in this battle (Ex. 17:8–16). Later, the Lord commanded his vengeance: "Remember what Amalek did to you on the way as you came out of Egypt, how he attacked you on the way when you were faint and weary . . . Therefore . . . you shall blot out the memory of Amalek from under heaven" (Deut. 25:17–19).

In the timing of the Lord, the day had come for Amalek's long-awaited judgment, at the hand of King Saul. We are reminded that the counsels of the Lord are known only to him, and that while wicked men scoff at God's delays, the day of judgment comes with terrible and sudden swiftness according to God's timetable.

Saul was commanded to put the Amalekites under God's ban, the holy-war provision of devoting to destruction "all that they have" (1 Sam. 15:3). None were to be spared: not women, children, and infants, and not even the Amalekite livestock. The purpose of Saul's offensive was divine judgment; the entire Amalekite nation was to be offered to the Lord in a display of perfect divine justice. Having earlier opposed Israel during her weakness in the exodus, Amalek had continued in wickedness, and the measure of God's wrath was now full.

Many commentators struggle to accept the ethics of Samuel's command to Saul, with some dismissing it as "the provisional morality of the Old Testament."[1] David Payne expresses concern that Israelites who practiced such all-out holy war "had yet much to learn about the character of God."[2] The problem with both of these views is that it was God himself who issued the ban against the Amalekites and required Saul to practice holy-war genocide. The ethics of God's unchanging character are never provisional, nor can we plausibly declare that God was speaking in ignorance of his own morality.

The only arena in which God's people today practice holy war is spiritual warfare, as instructed in passages such as Ephesians 6:10–18. No nation today—neither an Iran nor an America—can ever claim the mantle of God's people engaged in legitimate holy war and thus claim the right to the kind of comprehensive destruction of an enemy that we witness in the Old Testament. The two purposes of such all-out Old Testament holy war were

---

1. R. P. Gordon, quoted in David Toshio Tsumura, *The First Book of Samuel*, New International Commentary on the Old Testament (Grand Rapids: Eerdmans, 2007), 391.

2. David F. Payne, *I & II Samuel*, Daily Study Bible (Philadelphia: Westminster, 1992), 76.

the preservation of Israel and the execution of God's judgment on wicked nations that had fallen under his wrath.

Today, reflecting on the horrors of Old Testament holy war, we must remember the reality of God's coming judgment, which will be, if anything, much worse. God is a holy God, and his fierce anger burns against all uncleansed evil. Revelation 19:15 tells us that when Jesus returns in judgment, "he will tread the winepress of the fury of the wrath of God the Almighty." William Blaikie reminds us:

> That God will execute wrath on the impenitent and unbelieving is just as much a feature of the gospel as that He will bestow all the blessings of salvation and eternal life on them that believe. . . . It is most wholesome for us all to look at times steadily in the face of this solemn attribute of God [perfect justice], as the Avenger of the impenitent [for] it shows us that sin is not a thing to be trifled with. It [also] shows us that God's will is not a thing to be despised.[3]

Saul responded to God's command with energy: "Saul summoned the people and numbered them in Telaim, two hundred thousand men on foot, and ten thousand men of Judah" (1 Sam. 15:4). Saul amassed a great army, although, remembering that the Hebrew word for "thousand" can also mean "military unit," it is possible that Saul's force did not number in the hundreds of thousands, though by ancient standards its strength was still very great. With this force Saul set out.

Drawing near to the Amalekites, Saul came upon the Kenites, a tribe of Midianite metalworkers who dwelt among the Amalekites. It speaks well of Saul that for the sake of their kindness to Israel during the exodus (the memory of which the Bible does not record, except that Moses' father-in-law, a Kenite [Judg. 4:11], gave aid to Moses after the battle with the Amalekites, Ex. 18:1–12), Saul gave the Kenites the opportunity to escape the battle (1 Sam. 15:6). Saul then proceeded to defeat and pursue the Amalekites as far as "Shur, which is east of Egypt" (15:7).

Yet for all of Saul's swift response to God's command, Israel's king did not fully obey it. We see this in Saul's response to the enemy king and his possessions: "And he took Agag the king of the Amalekites alive and devoted

---

3. William G. Blaikie, *Expository Lectures on the Book of First Samuel* (1887; repr., Birmingham, AL: Solid Ground, 2005), 242–43.

to destruction all the people with the edge of the sword. But Saul and the people spared Agag and the best of the sheep and of the oxen and of the fattened calves and the lambs, and all that was good, and would not utterly destroy them. All that was despised and worthless they devoted to destruction" (1 Sam. 15:8–9). How typical of Saul that even in doing the will of the Lord, he managed to self-willfully disobey!

The Lord Repents of Saul

In 1 Samuel 13, Saul failed in the first task given to him as Israel's king, offering the sacrifice to the Lord on his own rather than waiting for the prophet as he had been told to do. This failure meant that Saul would not be permitted to found a dynasty of kings. Saul's failure in chapter 15, disobeying God by sparing the life of Agag and his livestock, resulted in the Lord's complete rejection of Saul as Israel's king: "The word of the LORD came to Samuel: 'I regret that I have made Saul king, for he has turned back from following me and has not performed my commandments'" (1 Sam. 15:10–11).

This statement raises some legitimate questions, particularly as to how God can be said to "regret" or "repent" of his actions. For some readers, this and other statements of divine regret in the Bible (there are twenty-nine of them that use a verbal construction similar to that of verse 11) undermine the traditional Reformed teaching of God's foreknowledge and sovereignty. This has been the recent position of scholars promoting what they call *open theism*. Open theism results from a radical emphasis on human free will, teaching that God does not know future events until they happen, since events do not exist until created by human choices. Thus God is said to be "open" to future events, learning them along with us as our sovereign choices determine—at least in large part—the course of history. Open theism thus not only undermines the Bible's overall portrait of God, which emphasizes God's predestinating sovereignty over all things (Isa. 46:9–10; Rom. 9:1–23; Eph. 1:4–11), but radically undercuts believers' confidence in God's ability to fulfill his promises and triumph in the end for our salvation.[4]

God's repentance over his choice of Saul as king is seen by open theists as a classic text that proves their point regarding God's ignorance of the future.

---

4. A comprehensive assessment of open theism's impact on Christian faith can be found in Bruce A. Ware, *God's Lesser Glory* (Wheaton, IL: Crossway, 2000), chap. 1.

John Sanders says this passage proves "that the future is in some respects an indefinite event for God. . . . God is not following a blueprint in working with us."[5] Gregory Boyd writes that God's regret proves that God was not sovereign over Saul's choices. He writes, "Common sense tells us that we can only regret a decision we made if the decision resulted in an outcome other than what we expected."[6]

The problem with openness theology is that it conflicts with so many clear statements regarding God's perfect foreknowledge of and sovereignty over all things. Consider, for instance, Isaiah 46:9–10, where the Lord says, "I am God, and there is none like me, declaring the end from the beginning and from ancient times things not yet done, saying, 'My counsel shall stand, and I will accomplish all my purpose.'" Such a statement would be impossible under open theism, since God could not declare from the beginning an end of which he had no knowledge, and he could not claim to accomplish all his purpose if he does not know how history ends (on the macro and micro scale). Likewise, Jesus assures believers of God's care for their souls by asking: "Are not two sparrows sold for a penny? And not one of them will fall to the ground apart from your Father" (Matt. 10:29). God is sovereign in the smallest of details in his creation so that small birds live and die according to his will, predestining and actively controlling history so that Paul is able to say that God "works all things according to the counsel of his will" (Eph. 1:11).

How, then, do we handle the Bible's statements of God's sorrow or repentance over sinful events? Bruce Ware provides three answers. First, he notes that such statements indicate that God is aware of and involved in changes to the human situation and responds in appropriate ways. Thus, when Saul persistently fails to obey, God responds by repenting of Saul as Israel's king.

Second, divine repentance "indicates [God's] real experience, in historically unfolding relationships with people . . . Just because God knows in advance that some event will occur, this does not preclude God from experiencing appropriate emotions and expressing appropriate reactions when it actually happens."[7] This is why it is not sufficient to dismiss God's statements of repentance as instances of anthropopathism—which means

---

5. John Sanders, *The God Who Risks* (Downers Grove, IL: InterVarsity Press, 1998), 73.

6. Gregory Boyd, *God of the Possible* (Grand Rapids: Baker, 2000), 56.

7. Ware, *God's Lesser Glory*, 91.

that even though God does not really feel the way the Bible says he does, human descriptions are used as an accommodation to us. But the Bible says that God really did sorrow and really did repent over Saul's selection as king, just as he was sorry he had made the human race prior to Noah's flood (Gen. 6:6) and just as God relented in his judgment when Nineveh repented through Jonah's ministry (Jonah 3:10). Dale Ralph Davis rightly comments: "Nonchalance is never listed as an attribute of the true God. . . . Verse 11 does not intend to suggest Yahweh's fickleness of purpose but his sorrow over sin; it does not depict Yahweh flustered over lack of foresight but Yahweh grieved over lack of obedience."[8]

Third, Ware notes that God often expresses repentance and sorrow in order to elicit a response that he desires from his audience. God was making a point to his readers—including us—by expressing his repentance over making Saul king.[9] What was God's point in telling us this? His point was that he demands careful obedience to his commands from those who would serve on his behalf. One of the chief points of the Bible's record of Saul's reign was to make clear to God's people their obligation to obey the Lord. Saul "has turned back from following me and has not performed my commandments," lamented the Lord (1 Sam. 15:11). The message for us is that faith in the Lord obliges us to careful obedience to the whole of his Word.

Probably the best commentary on God's repentance is given by Samuel toward the end of this very chapter. Verse 11 tells us that Samuel responded to God's message with great passion: "Samuel was angry, and he cried to the LORD all night." What distressed Samuel? At a minimum, the prophet shared God's remorse that the man who enjoyed such privileges as Israel's anointed king should respond with disobedience. But he may also have struggled to accept God's statement of repentance and sorrow over Saul. In the end, Samuel is reconciled to God's unchanging sovereignty, for he declares that "the Glory of Israel will not lie or have regret, for he is not a man, that he should have regret" (1 Sam. 15:29). This is a fascinating statement, for when Samuel says that the Lord does not regret, he uses the same verb that the Lord used when he said that God did regret making Saul king.

---

8. Dale Ralph Davis, *1 Samuel: Looking on the Heart* (Fearn, Ross-shire, UK: Christian Focus, 2000), 130.

9. Ware, *God's Lesser Glory*, 91–92.

Some object to this apparent contradiction, arguing that it seems that God really does not feel repentance and regret the way that humans do. This is, of course, true. For he is, after all, God and not a man. John Piper writes, "He is not a man to experience 'repentance' [the way that humans do]. He experiences it his way—the way one experiences 'repentance' when one is all-wise and foreknows the entire future perfectly. The experience is real, but it is not like finite man experiences it."[10]

The God who predestines and foreknows the future had ordained all the events of this chapter, including his own regret and sorrow over Saul's disobedience. These events were a small part of a much greater history, also predestined and foreknown by God—a history centered not only on God's regretting sin but on God's bearing sin for his people on the cross in the person of his Son. For while the penal sacrifice of the blessed and sinless Son of God, Jesus Christ, was the most loathsome and hateful event ever to occur on planet Earth—so that the furies of God's wrath poured out on the hard-hearted city that rejected Jesus—it also took place "according to the definite plan and foreknowledge of God" (Acts 2:23). The full purpose of history is that God might be glorified, so that the perfections of the glories of all the attributes of God might be known and displayed to men and angels—attributes such as holiness, mercy, justice, forbearance, love, and wrath. God is glorified by means of a history in which he displays his full hatred of sin even while displaying such boundless grace in saving sinners through the death of Christ.

SAUL REBUKED FOR DISOBEDIENCE

Samuel was bitterly grieved by Saul's failure to obey the clear command of the Lord. Therefore, his anguished night of prayer was followed by "one of the most spectacular confrontations in the pages of the Bible, when the prophet Samuel met the defiant King Saul."[11] In a masterpiece of providential irony, Saul had been all this time building a monument to his obedience in attacking the Amalekites. The king then returned to Gilgal, along with his spoils, eagerly awaiting his expected praise from the prophet.

The exchange that takes place almost belongs in a slapstick-comedy routine. There waits Saul as Samuel strides up the road. The king greets him

---

10. Quoted in ibid., 97–98.
11. John Woodhouse, *1 Samuel: Looking for a Leader* (Wheaton, IL: Crossway, 2008), 264.

with well-prepared and smug self-congratulation: "Blessed be you to the LORD. I have performed the commandment of the LORD" (1 Sam. 15:13). It is almost too much for us to believe that Saul could say this, until we remember how common it is for us to pat ourselves on the back for obeying our own commandments rather than God's. Samuel retorted with one of the greatest one-line comebacks in the Bible: "What then is this bleating of the sheep in my ears and the lowing of the oxen that I hear?" (15:14).

What follows is a potent primer on obedience to God. Samuel first points out that *obedience to God involves keeping his actual commands.* Saul had his own understanding of his mission against the Amalekites, and it was not precisely in line with the actual requirements that God had given through Samuel. If Saul desired to celebrate his performance of God's commands, then he should have been careful to study those commands, remembering them always, and judging his own actions according to the standard given in God's Word. His failure to do this was clearly evidenced by the braying of sheep and oxen, all of which God had ordered to be slaughtered and thus devoted to himself.

Saul's fundamental error is extremely common today. Christians will often declare themselves obedient to God in any number of matters—in the doctrine they espouse, their approach to financial stewardship, sexual purity, marital faithfulness, church membership, worship, evangelism, Sabbath observance, and more—when in fact their conduct does not line up with the Bible's teaching. Very often, then, we will wonder why God's blessing does not seem to be upon us, when a simple study of God's Word will reveal our blatant disobedience to the command of the Lord.

In order to be praised by God, we need to obey what he has actually commanded. This is what Genesis 6:22 says regarding Noah: "He did all that God commanded him." Had Noah not built his ark in careful observance of God's instructions, it might not have floated during the great flood. Likewise, a failure by Christians today to preach and observe the actual doctrines and commandments of God's Word not only undermines our ministry but may well be our undoing altogether. Saul pointed out that he had not completely rebelled: "I have obeyed the voice of the LORD," he asserted. "I have gone on the mission on which the LORD sent me" (1 Sam. 15:20–21). This was true. Moreover, he had devoted the vast majority of Amalekites to destruction. But by sparing Agag, the Amalekite king, along with the sheep and oxen, he had still flagrantly disobeyed the clear command of God's Word, undoing the value of what he had done.

Second, Saul's defense of his actions reminds us that *obedience to God requires unpopular actions.* When Samuel pointed out the bleating of sheep and the lowing of oxen, Saul replied, "They have brought them from the Amalekites, for the people spared the best of the sheep and of the oxen to sacrifice to the LORD your God, and the rest we have devoted to destruction" (1 Sam. 15:15). Notice how Saul speaks of "the people" and "they" when it comes to disobedience, but when it comes to obedience, the terminology suddenly becomes inclusive: "we"! In this way, Saul argues that he had devoted *most* of the Amalekite possessions, except those that the people thought should be kept for themselves, which happened to be "the best of the sheep and of the oxen." In a suspicious explanation, Saul piously adds that these were spared so as to be offered as a sacrifice to the Lord (that is, a thank offering, the kind of sacrifice that permitted the people to enjoy eating at least part of what was offered).

Saul's behavior reminds us that spiritual leaders who would seek God's blessing must be willing to obey the Bible's commands even when they are unpopular. Paul exhorted Timothy that along with false teachers and impostors, the church will be plagued with people who "will not endure sound teaching, but having itching ears they will accumulate for themselves teachers to suit their own passions, and will turn away from listening to the truth and wander off into myths" (2 Tim. 4:3–4). Timothy should nonetheless "continue in what you have learned and have firmly believed" (3:14), and faithfully "preach the word" (4:2). An example to avoid was given by Aaron, Moses' brother and Israel's first high priest, when he presided over the making and worship of the golden calf. When Moses returned from the mountaintop, livid, Aaron provided an immortal and perennial explanation for his leadership failure: "You know the people, that they are set on evil" (Ex. 32:22).

Saul was cut from the same cloth as Aaron and many other failed leaders who did not obey the Lord because they feared the scorn of the people. Saul would have honored God in obedience only if he had forbidden the people to take the Amalekites' sheep and oxen and insisted that all things be done in accordance with God's actual commands. The same is true of pastors, parents, and individual Christians today, who honor God truly when they insist that all things be done in accordance with God's clear commands in the Bible.

Third, Samuel answered Saul's objection by pointing out that *obedience is the only thing that truly pleases the Lord*. Saul argued that the sheep and oxen were for a special offering to God. Samuel answered: "Has the LORD as great delight in burnt offerings and sacrifices, as in obeying the voice of the LORD? Behold, to obey is better than sacrifice, and to listen than the fat of rams" (1 Sam. 15:22). This is the way for God's people to worship and honor him: by obeying his commands. This is true when it comes to the gathered worship of God's people in church, the acceptability of which is regulated by God's Word (Heb. 12:28), and it is true of the living worship that each believer is to offer to God day by day (Rom. 12:1–2). God is worshiped when he is obeyed. It is better for us to obey God than to perform songs and offer prayers in his behalf.

Saul's failure on all three of these points brought Samuel's stinging rebuke. First, the prophet berated Saul, reminding him that "though you are little in your own eyes," he was still the king over Israel by God's anointing (1 Sam. 15:17). God had given Saul a crystal-clear mission: "Go, devote to destruction the sinners, the Amalekites, and fight against them until they are consumed" (15:18). With these stubborn facts in mind, Samuel pressed his point: "Why then did you not obey the voice of the LORD? Why did you pounce on the spoil and do what was evil in the sight of the LORD?" (15:19). Samuel, of course, saw through greedy Saul's pathetic statement that the sheep and oxen had been intended for God, when they were in fact intended for Saul. Saul was an extremely privileged person among God's people, anointed into an office of the highest responsibility, so he is held to high account. But all believers hold places of stewardship before the Lord, and we should be no less surprised to find ourselves accountable for disobedience and chastised by the Lord for our failures to keep the commands of his Word.

Obedience and Kingship

Saul might discount the significance of his compromises, but to God Saul's disobedience had the gravest repercussions. Therefore, Samuel revealed his correspondence with the Lord. "Stop!" he commanded Saul; "I will tell you what the LORD said to me this night" (1 Sam. 15:16). Could Saul still have hoped for a commendation to match the memorial he had already erected for himself? If so, how mortified he was at hearing what Samuel had to report:

"For rebellion is as the sin of divination, and presumption is as iniquity and idolatry. Because you have rejected the word of the LORD, he has also rejected you from being king" (15:23).

Samuel states that "rebellion is as the sin of divination." In other words, to flagrantly reject the clear teaching of God's Word is practical apostasy. Saul might as well have gone to occult mystics to gain divine revelation (as he later will do), if he was going to follow his own inventions. Moreover, to presume on God's commands—as Saul and the people had done by considering their own wisdom an improvement on God's command (and by seeking to cover their greed in pious lies about offering sacrifices to God)—"is as iniquity and idolatry." Gordon Keddie comments that given Saul's arrogant rebellion, "he might as well have been worshipping other gods. Saul's will was his real god. In practice he had dethroned the Lord in his heart."[12] What a warning this is to our generation in the church, which presumptuously assumes that our taste in spiritual consumerism must always correspond with God's approval and blessing. Instead, the only way to be sure that we are pleasing and truly serving the Lord is to act in clear obedience to the precepts and commands of his Word.

The ultimate contrast with Saul is the true King of God's people, the righteous Lord Jesus Christ. When Jesus presented himself to God at the end of his earthly ministry, he could give a report very different from King Saul's. Jesus prayed to the Father, "I glorified you on earth, having accomplished the work that you gave me to do" (John 17:4). Perfect obedience was the memorial that Jesus erected to his life. This is why God accepted Jesus and his ministry on behalf of those who trust in him. The writer of Hebrews explains:

When Christ came into the world, he said,

"Sacrifices and offerings you have not desired,
    but a body have you prepared for me;
in burnt offerings and sin offerings
    you have taken no pleasure.
Then I said, 'Behold, I have come to do your will, O God,
    as it is written of me in the scroll of the book.'"
           (Heb. 10:5–7, quoting Ps. 40:6–8)

12. Gordon J. Keddie, *Dawn of a Kingdom: The Message of 1 Samuel* (Darlington, UK: Evangelical Press, 1988), 147.

For Jesus, to obey really was better than sacrifice—this is why Jesus needed no one to die on his behalf—and it was obedience that enabled him to sacrifice for us. Our Lord presented himself in the glory of his perfect obedience, to which God responded: "This is my beloved Son, with whom I am well pleased" (Matt. 3:17). Therefore, sinners who trust not in Saul but in Christ have a Savior, a King in whose name we find salvation. Represented by Christ, we now are called to "the obedience of faith" (Rom. 1:5; 16:26), so that by faith we might be in Christ, "whom God made our wisdom, our righteousness and sanctification and redemption" (1 Cor. 1:30 RSV).

What, then, do we give in gratitude to the God who already has everything? Does God need sheep or oxen from us? Does he need money or songs or prayers? We should indeed offer these to God in thanks and love. But if we really want to please God—and what could be more worthwhile in all of life?—we will do his will, as it is written in his Book, in the name of Jesus Christ, the true and perfectly righteous King who offered no other sacrifice to God than his own obedient life, shedding his precious blood for our sins.

21

TORN AWAY

1 Samuel 15:24—35

Samuel said to Saul, "I will not return with you. For you have rejected the word of the LORD, and the LORD has rejected you from being king over Israel." (1 Sam. 15:26)

A passage in the book of Hebrews sheds a great deal of light on the situation of King Saul at the end of 1 Samuel 15. The writer of Hebrews is greatly concerned that his Jewish Christian readers not fall away from Christ under persecution. To this end, he recalls Israel's exodus generation, which departed from Egypt with Moses but died in the wilderness because of unbelief. Elaborating on this danger, the writer warns:

> For it is impossible, in the case of those who have once been enlightened, who have tasted the heavenly gift, and have shared in the Holy Spirit, and have tasted the goodness of the word of God and the powers of the age to come, and then have fallen away, to restore them again to repentance, since they are crucifying once again the Son of God to their own harm . . . (Heb. 6:4–6)

This is an accurate description of the exodus Israelites, who experienced firsthand the Lord's power, goodness, and glory, yet still did not believe.

It is also a good description of King Saul, on whom the Spirit of God had come to equip him for kingship, who was shown the light of truth, tasted God's gifts, and personally encountered divine power. Yet at no time in the long account of Saul's reign do we find that he trusted himself to the Lord for salvation. As a result, the time came when Saul was no longer able to be brought to repentance, so that the Lord turned his back on the man whom Israel had demanded as king. The judgment that had long been warned about finally fell on Saul, and even as he tore the skirt of Samuel's robe, the prophet declared: "The LORD has torn the kingdom of Israel from you this day and has given it to a neighbor of yours, who is better than you" (1 Sam. 15:28).

SAUL'S SUPERFICIAL REPENTANCE

Having failed to obey the Lord on an earlier occasion (chapter 13), Saul was given a fresh opportunity. Samuel had brought him God's command to exact vengeance on the Amalekites. The entire nation was to be devoted to destruction, with all the people and livestock slaughtered in a just, divine judgment. Saul attacked the Amalekites, then congratulated himself and went to Gilgal to await Samuel's praise. But the prophet arrived amid the bleating of sheep and lowing of oxen, which along with the captured Amalekite king proved Saul's failure to obey God's instructions. When Saul pleaded that he had spared the choice livestock to make an offering to the Lord, Samuel memorably replied, "To obey is better than sacrifice, and to listen than the fat of rams" (1 Sam. 15:22).

In the face of Samuel's blistering rebukes, Saul realized that he must confess his sin: "Saul said to Samuel, 'I have sinned, for I have transgressed the commandment of the LORD and your words, because I feared the people and obeyed their voice. Now therefore, please pardon my sin and return with me that I may worship the LORD'" (1 Sam. 15:24–25). On the surface, we might be satisfied to note most of the essential elements of true repentance. Saul said the key words, including the straightforward confession, "I have sinned." He admitted that he had "transgressed the commandment of the LORD," and he pleaded for pardon and restoration.

Yet for all these positives, there remains doubt as to the sincerity of Saul's repentance. One clue is that neither Samuel nor the Lord seemed to accept it as genuine. Augustine commented, "While to the human ear the words were the same, the divine eye saw a difference in the heart."[1] First John 1:9 says, "If we confess our sins, [God] is faithful and just to forgive us our sins and to cleanse us from all unrighteousness." But Saul's confession receives neither praise nor forgiveness. This suggests that his repentance was superficial and insincere.

Another bad sign is that Saul did not confess his sin until Samuel's insistent accusations left him with little choice. He confessed because he had been caught—the bleating sheep and the Amalekite king provided irrefutable evidence of his disobedience. This circumstance does not necessarily invalidate Saul's confession—after all, David confessed and was forgiven after being confronted by the prophet Nathan (2 Sam. 12:13)—but it is not the best start to a true repentance. How much better is any confession when it is prompted by inner conviction rather than public exposure.

A third bad sign is that Saul shows a strong orientation to Samuel and his opinion rather than an exclusive focus on God. "I have transgressed the commandment of the LORD and your words," he tells Samuel (1 Sam. 15:24). Likewise, Saul's plea for forgiveness and restoration is made to Samuel, not to God: "Now therefore, please pardon my sin and return with me that I may worship the LORD" (15:25). In contrast, David prayed directly to God: "Against you, you only, have I sinned" (Ps. 51:4). This does not mean that David denied the harm that his sins had done to other people. But he was so consumed with his offense to God that nothing else could be considered before confessing to the Lord.

Fourth, note that even as Saul confesses, he makes excuses for his conduct. The unfortunate event happened "because I feared the people and obeyed their voice" (1 Sam. 15:24). In contrast, when David confessed his sin, he added that God was "justified in your words and blameless in your judgment" (Ps. 51:4). "I deserve to be condemned" may not be easy for us to say, but those who truly confess their sin acknowledge their personal guilt before God.

Finally, note that Saul lacks concern for God's offended honor and the practical harm of his sins, but focuses only on his own restoration to honor and authority. This comes through clearly after Samuel has rejected Saul's

---

1. Augustine, "Against Faustus, a Manichaean," in *Joshua, Judges, Ruth, 1–2 Samuel*, ed. John R. Franke, Ancient Christian Commentary on Scripture, Old Testament vol. 4 (Downers Grove, IL: InterVarsity Press, 2005), 258.

empty confession, and Saul replies, "I have sinned; yet honor me now before the elders of my people and before Israel, and return with me, that I may bow before the LORD your God" (1 Sam. 15:30). Cyril Barber comments: "The confession . . . was not so much the result of inward conviction as it was an evidence of Saul's fear of losing the acclaim of the people."[2] Contrast Saul's plea with that of the penitent son in Jesus' parable of the prodigal, who argues for his loss of status rather than his right to retain it: "Father, I have sinned against heaven and before you. I am no longer worthy to be called your son. Treat me as one of your hired servants" (Luke 15:18–19).

The point of this analysis is not that we should practice how better to perform repentance, in order to increase our odds of being forgiven and restored by God. Instead, the point is to show what constitutes true and genuine repentance, which is the only kind that God accepts. True repentance is motivated not merely by a wish to escape the consequences of sin but by conviction about the sin itself. True confession is made to the Lord himself and seeks God's forgiveness by the blood of Christ, believing God's promise of salvation (1 John 1:9). Genuine repentance makes no excuses for the sin, but pleads only to be restored, without concern for worldly honor and positions that might have been lost by the sin. Proverbs 28:13 advises us as to the benefits of such true repentance: "Whoever conceals his transgressions will not prosper, but he who confesses and forsakes them will obtain mercy."

SAUL'S FINAL REJECTION

Samuel, speaking for both himself and the Lord, categorically rejected Saul's superficial confession: "Samuel said to Saul, 'I will not return with you. For you have rejected the word of the LORD, and the LORD has rejected you from being king over Israel'" (1 Sam. 15:26). After Saul's first disobedience, the Lord denied him the prospect of a long-lasting dynasty. His son Jonathan would not become king because of Saul's sin (13:13–14). But now Saul himself is rejected as one who serves on God's behalf as king over Israel.

As is true throughout the Bible for those who do not know God's grace, it is Saul's own words that condemn him: "I feared the people and obeyed their voice" (1 Sam. 15:24). But that is precisely the opposite of what God's kings

2. Cyril J. Barber, *The Books of Samuel*, 2 vols. (Neptune, NJ: Loizeaux, 1994), 1:175.

were supposed to do. During Saul's commissioning in chapter 12, Samuel warned him to "fear the LORD" (12:14), yet by his own admission, Saul had "feared the people" (15:24). Saul was to "obey his voice" (12:14), but instead he "obeyed their voice" (15:24). Thus, as Benjamin Franklin remarked: "He that cannot obey, cannot command."[3]

Having rejected Saul, Samuel turned to go away. But Saul, desperate, "seized the skirt of his robe, and it tore" (1 Sam. 15:27). We can imagine the tragic scene. The same Saul who had only recently been going about building monuments to the glory of his kingdom now clings to the robe of the prophet who had just removed him from office. Samuel saw the tearing of his robe as highly appropriate to the occasion: "Samuel said to him, 'The LORD has torn the kingdom of Israel from you this day'" (15:28). Numbers 15:38–39 commanded Israelites to weave tassels into the corner of their garments, reminding them to "remember all the commandments of the LORD, to do them, not to follow after your own heart and your own eyes." By tearing off one of these tassels from Samuel's robe, Saul "dramatically symbolized his breach of the Lord's command."[4] Having torn away God's command, Saul would now be torn away by God's hand, which is precisely what Samuel had earlier warned against (1 Sam. 12:15).

Not only would the kingdom be torn from Saul, but it would also be given to another, "a neighbor of yours, who is better than you" (1 Sam. 15:28). These words form a transition in 1 Samuel: from this point forward, the narrative will focus on the calling and rise of the "man after [God's] own heart" (13:14), who is "better than" Saul, namely, King David. Samuel testifies that David is "better than" Saul after he has earlier explained that obedience is "better than" sacrifice (15:22). As we will learn, David was far from a perfect man, but he was a man of obedient faith, and this made all the difference between him and Saul.

There is another difference between Saul and David, namely, the source of their kingship. Saul was anointed king when the people rebelled against God's rule through the judges (1 Sam. 8:8). But David, in contrast, is a king whom God provides for himself (see 16:1). This difference is probably

3. Quoted in ibid.
4. Robert D. Bergen, *1, 2 Samuel*, New American Commentary (Nashville: Broadman & Holman, 1996), 174.

reflected in the statement that Samuel adds: "The Glory of Israel will not lie or have regret, for he is not a man, that he should have regret" (15:29). In the previous chapter, we pointed out that although God could regret having made Saul king, his remorse is not like human regretting. God is not a man, that he should change his mind or repent, even though the Lord did respond to the situation of Saul's kingship with holy remorse—the very sentiment it deserved.

But verse 29 seems to refer most directly to Samuel's declaration of David's kingship. Unlike Saul's reign, which originated in the word of men and thus did not endure, David's reign originated in the sovereign will of God, and therefore God's commitment to David's house will be unshakable. Whereas Saul's human-based kingship remained conditional before God because it depended on Saul's performance, the "Davidic kingship would rest on God's unconditional commitment."[5] This statement is borne out in 2 Samuel 7, where God grants his covenant to David, promising to "establish the throne of his kingdom forever" (2 Sam. 7:13). As Psalm 132:11 states, "The Lord swore to David a sure oath from which he will not turn back."

We might see Saul as representing the works principle of God's law. Set forth by the voice of the people, Saul would be accepted by God so long as Saul obeyed God's commands. David, on the other hand, speaks for God's gospel grace, and thus is upheld not by his own performance but by God's grace. Jesus speaks similarly of anyone who comes to God not by the law but by means of his gospel: "everyone who looks on the Son and believes in him [will] have eternal life, and I will raise him up on the last day" (John 6:40).

Saul responded to this news in characteristically worldly fashion: "Then he said, 'I have sinned; yet honor me now before the elders of my people and before Israel, and return with me, that I may bow before the Lord your God'" (1 Sam. 15:30). Knowing nothing of God's grace, Saul sought only to shore up his public appearance. Samuel relented at this plea, either because he had compassion on wretched Saul or else because he had concern for the power vacuum that might occur if Saul were deposed before the new king was revealed. "So Samuel turned back after Saul, and Saul bowed before the Lord" (15:31).

5. David Toshio Tsumura, *The First Book of Samuel*, New International Commentary on the Old Testament (Grand Rapids: Eerdmans, 2007), 408.

SAMUEL'S EXAMPLE OF FAITH AND OBEDIENCE

Samuel was cut out of an entirely different cloth from King Saul, as is made plain at the end of this chapter. Whereas Saul concerned himself only with his own public reputation, Samuel looked to the Lord as "the Glory of Israel" (1 Sam. 15:29). This reminds us of God's promise to a later generation: "I will be to her a wall of fire all around, declares the LORD," speaking of faithful Jerusalem, "and I will be the glory in her midst" (Zech. 2:5). This same idea should be evident among God's people today: the glory that men and women should see in the church is not the glory of the preacher's ability or the fund-raising prowess of the church, but rather the glory of God amid his people in the power of his Word that is believed and obeyed.

With this view of God in mind, Samuel called for the Amalekite king to be brought before him. Whereas Saul had torn off the tassel of Samuel's robe that symbolized obedience to God's law, Samuel showed his spiritual commitment by tearing apart the Amalekite king in fulfillment of God's command. Agag, Samuel's victim, hoped that passions had now cooled: "Surely the bitterness of death is past," he reasoned (1 Sam. 15:32). Samuel reminded him not merely of his people's ancient guilt, but also of his personal sins: Agag had "made women childless," and now "shall your mother be childless among women" (15:33). With these words, Samuel hacked Agag to pieces—revealing the destruction facing all who face God's judgment without being forgiven. Agag was violently judged only after a long period in which repentance and faith had been held out to him. Likewise, God is giving sinners a long age to repent and believe in Jesus Christ for salvation. Yet when Jesus returns at an hour known only to God, "then he will sit on his glorious throne" of judgment (Matt. 25:31).

The chapter concludes with information that shows the grace in Samuel's character. Saul was rejected by the Lord, so the Lord's prophet no longer sought Saul out. According to verses 34–35, Samuel went his way to Ramah and Saul to Gibeah. Despite the close proximity of these towns (less than ten miles apart), "Samuel did not see Saul again until the day of his death" (1 Sam. 15:35). Yet "Samuel grieved over Saul. And the LORD regretted that he had made Saul king over Israel" (15:35).

This tells us where Samuel's heart had been all along. The prophet had never been rooting for the king to fail. The true servant of God grieves over those who remain lost in sin, even while sincerely laboring for their future salvation. Gordon Keddie writes, "No true messenger of God loves to bring a message of judgment."[6] Along with Samuel, the Lord himself was grieving: "And the LORD regretted that he had made Saul king over Israel" (1 Sam. 15:35). This example shows that Christians who look on the lost with compassion and love, eagerly extending God's message of salvation to sinners, are those who most truly represent the heart of God to the world.

SAUL'S WRETCHED END

Saul's rejection shows how wretched the king had become because of his persistent unbelief. We can gauge Saul's lost condition by comparing his words to Samuel with the words of Pharaoh to Moses after the wrath of God had fallen on Egypt. The Lord's plagues had temporarily broken Pharaoh's will, so that he begged the man of God to call off the Lord's judgment: "I have sinned against the LORD your God, and against you." Pharaoh then begged Moses to forgive his sins and asked Moses to plead with God to remove the plague (Ex. 10:16–17). But at no point did Pharaoh plead with God for forgiveness, nor did it occur to Pharaoh to pray to the Lord at all. Similarly, when the angel of death had slain all the firstborn sons of Egypt, including Pharaoh's, the Egyptian king met with Moses, urging him to leave the land. Then he added, "Bless me also!" (12:32). Pharaoh had learned the rather obvious point that Israel's Lord is the true God, but at no point did he surrender himself to the Lord, worship him, renounce his false gods, or even ask the Lord to forgive and bless him. Rather, Pharaoh merely hoped that the men who knew the Lord might arrange a blessing for him.

Consider, in that light, Saul's words to Samuel. He asks the prophet, "Please pardon my sin," and urges Samuel to come to be with him when he goes through the rituals of worship again (1 Sam. 15:25). Saul begs Samuel to honor him before "the elders of my people" and thus to allow Saul again to "bow before the LORD your God" (15:30). Saul speaks of "my people" and "your God." He was a calloused politician but not a believer with a personal relationship with the Lord.

6. Gordon J. Keddie, *Dawn of a Kingdom: The Message of 1 Samuel* (Darlington, UK: Evangelical Press, 1988), 149.

Many observers wonder whether Saul is an example of a believer who falls away and loses his salvation. The answer is that Saul was never a believer—at no point is there any clear evidence that the king came to saving faith and knew the Lord—and thus for all his remarkable privileges and experiences he never received salvation, which always comes through faith alone. Saul fell away, not from salvation, but from his outward position of privilege.

Because he would not confess his sin sincerely, because he would not humble himself before God, seeking forgiveness and grace—wanting instead only to redeem his reputation—Saul placed himself in the dreadful condition of apostasy. In this way, Saul provides a classic illustration of the apostate described in Hebrews 6:4–6. In the language of that New Testament book, Saul had "once been enlightened"—that is, he had seen the light—but had chosen darkness instead; he had "tasted" but not taken "the heavenly gift"; he had "shared in the Holy Spirit" without being spiritually renewed; Saul had "tasted the goodness of the word of God" but not obeyed it; and he had experienced "the powers of the age to come" without ever relying on the saving grace of God. Hebrews tells us that "it is impossible" to restore such a person "again to repentance" (Heb. 6:4–6), and for this reason Samuel did not expend any further effort in seeking to restore Saul.

This presents a dire warning to all who profess Christianity but presume upon God's grace. In *The Pilgrim's Progress*, John Bunyan depicts a man in an iron cage, who once was an outward professor of religion but now was locked in despair. When Christian asked how this had happened, the man replied: "I laid the reins on the neck of my lusts. I sinned against the light of the word, and the goodness of God. I grieved the Spirit, and he is gone. I tempted the devil, and he came to me. I provoked God to anger, and he left me. I hardened my heart so that I cannot repent."[7]

But what about the eternal security of believers? Did not Jesus say that believers "will never perish, and no one will snatch them out of my hand" (John 10:28)? But this security is only for believers. Those who do not believe have no such grounds for assurance of salvation. But did not Paul write that "he who began a good work in you will bring it to completion at the day of Jesus Christ" (Phil. 1:6)? Yes, but this is true only of a work begun by God. Saul's reign was a work begun by unbelieving Israel. God's preserving grace

---

7. John Bunyan, *The Pilgrim's Progress* (Nashville: Thomas Nelson, 1999), 31.

is promised to those who are born again to a true and living faith. The Saul who refused to treat with God, who excused his sin, and who wanted only the worldly benefits of what religion could give him was never a believer and therefore was never saved.

We need the Bible's teaching of the assurance of salvation for those who believe. But we also need the warning of King Saul, lest we harden our hearts against the gospel and give full vent to our sinful passions. Just as we need to hear Jesus say, "I [will] lose nothing of all that [God] has given me" (John 6:39), we also need to read the apostle Paul's exhortation that we are saved only if we "continue in the faith, stable and steadfast, not shifting from the hope of the gospel" (Col. 1:23). Great promises of eternal salvation are given to the elect of God, but the mark of the elect is faith in Christ and his gospel. None who harden their hearts in unbelief may take refuge in the biblical teaching of assurance. Instead, we should heed the grave warning of King Saul, and the commentary of Hebrews 6:4–6: "It is impossible, in the case of those who have once been enlightened . . . and then have fallen away, to restore them again to repentance." Above all else, then, let us never harden our hearts against whatever light God has given us.

Cyril Barber tells of meeting a woman at a church where he had been the visiting preacher. She told him all about how incredibly active she was in the church and then shared her distress over her spiritually lax husband. She also confided to having been attracted to another man she had met at her children's school. "He's a Christian, a widower," she explained. "I've seen him a few times and cannot but think how happy I would be if . . . well, you know . . . if I were married to him instead of Stan." Being the visiting preacher permitted Barber to speak bluntly: "Have you been sinfully involved with this man?" he asked. "Yes," she admitted, and then recounted all her active service in the church, which surely ought to grant her the right to this one understandable indiscretion. Barber sought to reason with her from the Scriptures as to the folly and sin of her thoughts and actions, but without effect.

Years later, Barber returned to the church, and he asked the pastor about the woman. It was a sad story. She had divorced her husband and married the widower. Stan and their children stopped going to church and had a very difficult time in the years that followed. Meanwhile, the woman and her new husband had joined a different church, where they sang in the choir. The relationship lasted a few years, until her new husband divorced her. This led to her disappearance from church and to a drunken car accident that took her life. Her original husband and children came back to the church to have a private burial service.

What was the key moment in this terrible progression? It was when this Christian woman saw and understood the Word of God but hardened her heart to reject it. She had her reasons and her motives. So she rejected the truth that God had shown her and fell into a depravity from which she found no repentance.

Is it ever too late for someone to repent? Clearly it was for Saul, just as Hebrews says it is possible for people to arrive at the place where they have irrevocably rejected the light. Yet the Scriptures hold out the promise of forgiveness and salvation for all who come to Christ with their sins. The promise stands: "Believe in the Lord Jesus, and you will be saved" (Acts 16:31). John exhorts, "If we confess our sins, he is faithful and just to forgive us our sins and to cleanse us from all unrighteousness" (1 John 1:9). But do we repent? Here is the question, the answer to which determines many an eternal destination: are we willing to admit our sin, forsake it, and seek the forgiveness offered in Christ? The Christian faith is not a religion for people who do not sin. But it is also not a religion for those who will not repent.

Samuel knew—perhaps by God's revelation—that Saul was too far gone, so he reached out to him no more but only grieved. We, however, can never know that someone is finally lost. Therefore, we must continue to extend gospel grace to hardened hearts, even as we grieve over their apparent rejection of the gospel. Paul urged Timothy, "God may perhaps grant them repentance leading to a knowledge of the truth" (2 Tim. 2:25). He writes in Galatians, "Brothers, if anyone is caught in any transgression, you who are spiritual should restore him in a spirit of gentleness. Keep watch on yourself, lest you too be tempted" (Gal. 6:1). Saul's wretched end urges us to take Paul's exhortation to heart, watching over our own souls lest we become hardened in unbelief. In our fellowship in the church, Christians should also be fervent in prayer for one another and tender in ministry to those who may be drifting from the Word of God. The writer of Hebrews urges us: "Take care, brothers, lest there be in any of you an evil, unbelieving heart, leading you to fall away from the living God. But exhort one another every day, as long as it is called 'today,' that none of you may be hardened by the deceitfulness of sin" (Heb. 3:12–13).

PART 3

A Man after God's Own Heart

22

LOOKING ON THE HEART

1 Samuel 16:1–13

The LORD said to Samuel, "Do not look on his appearance
or on the height of his stature, because I have rejected him.
For the LORD sees not as man sees: man looks on the outward
appearance, but the LORD looks on the heart." (1 Sam. 16:7)

Chapter 16 marks a major transition in the books of Samuel, but more than that, it begins one of the most extraordinary accounts in all the Bible or any other literature. The coming of David has been alluded to earlier in Samuel, but now the sacred text turns directly to the story of Israel's great champion, poet, prophet, and king. Three millennia after David lived, his memory still burns brightly in the hearts of God's people and his passion and faith continue to inspire. Walter Chantry writes:

> Only the supreme providence of God and the unfathomable depths of divine grace could have conceived and forged the life of David. God made the son of Jesse into the emblem of the kingly office which only Christ would fulfill more gloriously. He embodied all the qualities of manly nobility and charm.[1]

1. Walter Chantry, *David: Man of Prayer, Man of War* (Edinburgh: Banner of Truth, 2007), vii.

Vestiges of David's story can be seen in practically every noble myth beloved by Christendom, such as those of King Arthur and Saint George. But no accolade could possibly be higher than the one given by God himself. For when Israel's Messiah finally appeared, the Savior was identified as God's own Son, "who was descended from David according to the flesh" (Rom. 1:3).

God Provides a King

No playwright could excel the opening scene in which David first takes the stage. As the curtain rises, a dim light reveals an aged man. He is the greatest man of his time, one of the mightiest of God's servants. At one time, this man had been God's instrument to rescue his people in one of their darkest hours. But now Samuel, Israel's former judge and still God's prophet, trembles and weeps. The cause for Samuel's grief is Israel's king, whom for decades Samuel had tried to serve and help. King Saul, chosen by the people because of his worldly qualifications, proved to have none of the spiritual qualities needed for leading God's people. Saul would not obey the voice of the Lord, so that Samuel was called by God to rebuke and ultimately reject Saul. In the end, "the LORD regretted that he had made Saul king over Israel," and "Samuel grieved over Saul" (1 Sam. 15:35).

Perhaps Samuel realized what would soon become evident to everyone: Israel's king was going mad. Samuel's last bitter meeting with Saul had revealed an evil spirit within the king. This grim situation seems to have sapped Samuel's spirit, since the once-bold servant of God was reduced to grief and fear. After his long and great life as Israel's judge and prophet, Samuel felt defeated by the sin at work among God's people.

Many others have concluded life with the sense of grief and dread that Samuel now felt, but the prophet had one great advantage over other people: he was a man who heard the Word of God. This is the advantage that all of God's people today have through our Bibles. Where do we look to find a light in darkness? The answer is always the Word of God. Paul explains what it means to possess and know the Holy Scriptures: "For God, who said, 'Let light shine out of darkness,' has shone in our hearts" (2 Cor. 4:6, quoting Gen. 1:3). Thus, in grief, Samuel finds comfort. In fear, he is given faith. In his darkness, God shines the light of good news. God told Samuel the very good news he needed: "I have provided for myself a king" (1 Sam. 16:1).

We are reminded here of the sovereignty of God. Just as Israel was the people of God's own choosing (Deut. 7:7–8), and as believers today are those chosen by God for salvation (Eph. 1:4), so also Israel's proper king was to be chosen by the Lord. It is noteworthy that the word translated as "provided" is a form of the word ordinarily meaning "to see." By his sovereign provision, God sees what his people in darkness cannot see, just as later on we will note that while man can see only appearances, God can see the heart. God sees the true king he has desired because God has himself provided this king: he is the product of God's providential oversight and God's gift to his people: the king whom God has himself chosen.

We should notice two effects of this message of good news, both of which are usually seen when God's good news is heard and believed. The first was that God brought comfort to his grieving people. Samuel was not grieving, after all, over matters of merely personal concern. Samuel was not depressed in the way that we so often are: because our sports team has done poorly, our car needs repairs, or our lifestyle is not as high as we would like. Samuel was grieving over the sin of God's people and the misery that they were sure to experience. Samuel was grieving over a man in whom he had invested his life, the king of God's holy nation, who had now made it clear that he would chart his own direction, apart from God's will. Do we know what it is like to grieve over the indifference to God and his glory in our generation, the ignorance of the Bible even among professing Christians, and the lack of holiness or zeal for gospel missions within our churches? When Jesus said, "Blessed are those who mourn, for they shall be comforted" (Matt. 5:4), he was speaking about people who grieved from a heavenly perspective. Samuel was such a person, and to him the Lord came with good news of what he was providing for his people.

One insight we may glean from this episode is that the first sign that God intends to act out of his mercy is that he places a burden on his people for the distress of their times. Many Christians today ask when God will reach out with grace and power to reverse the spiritual collapse of our times. A better question might be this: Do we, who long for revival, feel a burden of sorrow for unbelief and evil? Roger Ellsworth asks, "Are we burdened and distressed over the condition of the church today? Until we are conscious of such a burden we need not scan the horizon for the thunderclouds of God's mercy. They only break upon the heads of those who feel the burden of the times."[2] We will know that the burden of today's darkness is felt by Christians when they turn anew to the Lord in the kind of fervent prayer for reformation and revival that is so lacking today.

With this grief, Samuel's life has come full circle, for his own story began with the tears of his mother, Hannah. Her song of praise, when God answered her prayer with the promise of a son, set the theological agenda for the books of Samuel, providing one of the main themes of the Bible's gospel. She sang that the Lord "raises up the poor from the dust; he lifts the needy from the ash heap to make them sit with princes and inherit a seat of honor" (1 Sam. 2:8). When Hannah prayed, God heard and answered. Now, in Samuel's grief for God's people, the Lord's mercy came again with good news of a king whom he would choose to provide.

God's good news has a second effect that we also see on this occasion: it challenges those who have lived in fear to renew their courage in faith.

God had a new mission for Samuel: he was to fill his horn with oil and go to the house of Jesse the Bethlehemite, "for I have provided for myself a king among his sons" (1 Sam. 16:1). Samuel responded to this calling with an almost craven fear. When we remember how intrepid this prophet had been on many prior occasions, his reaction now suggests that he had perhaps overindulged in his sorrow over King Saul. The Lord seems to rebuke him for this, even as his good news offers comfort: "How long will you grieve over Saul, since I have rejected him from being king over Israel?" (16:1).

This reproof reminds us that while grief is natural and proper at times, it should never be indulged with unbelief or a fear of man. This seems to have been Samuel's problem, for he answers the Lord: "How can I go? If Saul hears it, he will kill me" (1 Sam. 16:2). Samuel's sorrow has clearly gone amiss: if he, one of the great and courageous heroes of the faith in the Old Testament, could respond to God's call with such fear, how greatly must we all guard our hearts against a craven spirit of unbelief.

In addition to his reproof, God also kindly offered Samuel a way around his difficulty: "The LORD said, 'Take a heifer with you and say, "I have come to sacrifice to the LORD." And invite Jesse to the sacrifice, and I will show you what you shall do. And you shall anoint for me him whom I declare to you'" (1 Sam. 16:2–3). Some readers are agitated over God's apparent

2. Roger Ellsworth, *The Shepherd King: Learning from the Life of David* (Darlington, UK: Evangelical Press, 1998), 17–18.

deceit in urging Samuel to travel to Bethlehem under false colors. What they fail to realize is that Samuel was merely concealing his purpose, not denying an honest answer to someone with a right to the information. It would be perfectly legitimate for Samuel to travel to the home of Jesse with an ox brought along for a sacrifice, and this was a convenient way to avoid trouble with Saul.

Even though the Lord accommodated Samuel's fear, his message of good news was intended to drive his servant from fear to faith. We think of similar episodes, such as when stammering Moses was given a staff with which to work wonders before Pharaoh (Ex. 4:1–5), or when Gideon fretfully laid out his fleece not once but twice in order to confirm his calling to lead Israel (Judg. 6:36–40). In these cases, as with Samuel's, God helped the weakness of his servants but also roused them to a holy boldness through renewed faith in his Word. Likewise, Christians today who imbibe from the Bible's promises of good news in Christ will be those who are comforted in their grief and roused from fearful doubt to a bold belief.

Selecting from Jesse's Sons

If Samuel had been afraid to travel to Bethlehem, the men of Bethlehem were even more afraid to see him. This town was not on Samuel's normal circuit (1 Sam. 7:16), so "the elders of the city came to meet him trembling and said, 'Do you come peaceably?'" (16:4). Samuel answered, "Peaceably" (16:5). Why the elders were so frightened is not stated, although the arrival of so high and holy a figure as Samuel would naturally evoke fear of God's rebuke for some sin. But Samuel explained that he had come to make a simple pastoral inspection and give the Lord's blessing. "Consecrate yourselves," he told them, "and come with me to the sacrifice" (16:5).

Most likely, Samuel next slaughtered the heifer he had brought and sacrificed it to the Lord. The meat would then be used for a feast, which would take some time to prepare. This gave Samuel the opportunity to perform the crucial task for which he had also come. He asked to see the sons of Jesse, so as to consecrate them for the feast. As the sons were presented to Samuel, the first, and we may presume the oldest, Eliab, was extremely impressive. Samuel thought to himself, "Surely the Lord's anointed is before [me]" (1 Sam. 16:6).

According to the Lord's response, Samuel's problem is seen in the description that "he looked on Eliab and thought" (1 Sam. 16:6). That is, his thinking was based on what he could see. Undoubtedly, Eliab was "a handsome young man," and it might have been said that "from his shoulders upward he was taller than any of the people" (9:2). These words describe what Israel had seen in King Saul the last time Samuel had anointed a king. We would think he would now be on his guard against such a quick, external impression. But how common is this way of thinking! Kenneth Chafin writes: "Like Samuel, we are too impressed by the things that can be seen with the physical eyes. Consequently we live in a world where physical beauty outranks spiritual depth, where success in business and in church tends to be defined in materialistic terms, and where charisma is prized above character."[3]

We can well imagine Samuel reaching for his anointing horn of oil, when the Lord spoke to halt him: "But the LORD said to Samuel, 'Do not look on his appearance or on the height of his stature, because I have rejected him. For the LORD sees not as man sees: man looks on the outward appearance, but the LORD looks on the heart'" (1 Sam. 16:7). Here, the Lord rebukes the entire worldly approach to evaluation. "This is your problem," he says to Samuel, "that you look only at outward appearances!" This is why we so often suffer from bad leadership today: because we consider only how someone appears, in the cultivation of an image, the practice of clever sayings, the pandering to baser motives—all of which the Sauls of this world are easily able to master. But God is not hampered by our limitations or folly: he looks on the heart and sees the truth about a man's or a woman's character, faith, values, and desires.

It is because of his superior insight and wisdom that God wanted to be the One to provide Israel's king! This is also why God wants to raise up leaders for the church today by his own calling. When churches are approving leaders, we need to strictly follow the criteria given in God's Word, all of which are spiritual qualifications. Lacking our own wisdom, we need to obey God's Word. In doing this, we are especially warned against the impressiveness of external appearances. How difficult it is for us to see through a carefully managed first impression, attractive clothes, or the appearance of success! To follow the biblical guidelines is not easy, and it takes time and discernment

3. Kenneth L. Chafin, *1 & 2 Samuel*, Preacher's Commentary, vol. 8 (Nashville: Thomas Nelson, 1989), 122.

to assess character, values, and true beliefs (see 1 Tim. 5:23–25). We need to pray for God's help and wisdom, and we need to seek to look upon the heart.

Having been rebuked by the Lord, Samuel passed from Jesse's first son to the next. Abinadab was sent forth and also rejected. Next came Shammah: "Neither has the LORD chosen this one" (1 Sam. 16:9). Altogether, seven sons of Jesse came before the prophet, to which Samuel replied: "The LORD has not chosen these." So he asked Jesse: "Are all your sons here?" (16:11). After all, God had told him to anoint one of Jesse's sons, but none had gained approval. We can sense the reluctance in Jesse's demeanor when he admits that there is yet one more son: "There remains yet the youngest, but behold, he is keeping the sheep." Samuel said to Jesse, "Send and get him, for we will not sit down till he comes here" (16:11). Samuel knew how to motivate action, and the company would not get to eat until this youngest son had been fetched and brought before the prophet.

Dale Ralph Davis points out that what happened next is "the stuff songs are made of."[4] In comes David, fresh from the fields, unwashed and still smelling of the sheep. From what we learn later of his family life, his older brothers perhaps stood aloof as he drew near, looking down on the runt of their pack. Our text tells us that he "was ruddy and had beautiful eyes and was handsome." As soon as he appeared, the Lord spoke to Samuel: "Arise, anoint him, for this is he" (1 Sam. 16:12). So "Samuel took the horn of oil and anointed him in the midst of his brothers" (16:13). In the most unlikely and humble place, God had found the king of his own choosing: the youth whom God himself had fashioned for his own purpose of grace.

LEARNING FROM DAVID'S ANOINTING

In reflecting on the anointing of David, we need to consider both the event itself and the instructive word that God gave as his explanation: "man looks on the outward appearance, but the LORD looks on the heart" (1 Sam. 16:7). First, we should see this event as God's *rebuke to a principle at the heart of idolatry*: a focus on outward appearance. There is nothing wrong with a good appearance: we are told that David himself was handsome and bright-eyed. But the essence of the matter is what takes place in the heart.

4. Dale Ralph Davis, *1 Samuel: Looking on the Heart* (Fearn, Ross-shire, UK: Christian Focus, 2000), 139.

This focus on the heart is vital, for instance, in the worship of the Lord. There is a tendency for worship to be focused on right appearances and forms. William Blaikie writes: "Let everything be outwardly correct, the church beautiful, the music excellent, the sermon able, the congregation numerous and respectable—what a pattern such a church is often regarded! Alas! How little satisfactory it may be to God." What does God look for in a gathering of his people? Blaikie answers by directing us to the heart, where true worship takes place:

> The lowly sense of personal unworthiness, the wondering contemplation of the Divine love, the eager longing for mercy to pardon and grace to help, faith that grasps the promises, the hope that is anchored within the veil, the kindness that breathes benediction all round, the love that beareth all things, believeth all things, hopeth all things, endureth all things—it is these things, breathing forth from the hearts of a congregation, that give pleasure to God.[5]

What is true of worship is true of life in general, that we must repent of the idolatry of "keeping up appearances." How many people in our society place themselves deeply into debt simply so that their lifestyle may give the false appearance of affluence? How many worthless (or nearly so) products are dressed up before consumers with false and misleading advertisements? Of all the world's many idolatries, few are greater than the idolatry of outward appearances. God's people are called to repent of this way of thinking, which if allowed to persist may endanger our very souls. After all, it was the Pharisee in Christ's parable who went home unjustified because he paraded his appearance of righteousness before the Lord, as if God could not see his unclean heart (Luke 18:11–14). Focusing on his outward appearance, he never sought the righteousness that comes only through faith in Christ.

More positively, we gain much instruction from young David's anointing as Israel's king. We do not know how much Samuel told David or his father on this occasion, but we do know that God had David anointed many years before he would actually take up the royal office. Why would the Lord do this? The best answer is that God knows that *high callings require early preparation.*

---

5. William G. Blaikie, *Expository Lectures on the Book of First Samuel* (1887; repr., Birmingham, AL: Solid Ground, 2005), 258.

Regardless of how much or little Samuel let David know about the meaning of his anointing, David would go back to his fields with holy matters for reflection. Saul came to his royal ambitions in the middle of life, when his character and habits had been long formed. David was still a youth, and his further upbringing in a godly family could be directed toward his anointed appointment for service to God.

In this respect, it cannot be coincidental that the young man whom God was providing as his king was found serving as a shepherd in the fields. Shepherding was a lowly occupation, yet one that commended itself to God and was likely to instill the most noble virtues. Blaikie writes, "The duties of the shepherd, to watch over his flock, to feed and protect them, to heal the sick, bind up the broken, and bring again that which was driven away, corresponded to those which the faithful and godly ruler owed to the people committed to his scepter."[6] Ultimately, God's promised Messiah, his own Son, would take up the emblem of the shepherd to depict his rulership of love: "I am the good shepherd," declared the Lord Jesus Christ (John 10:11). When Jesse and his older sons deemed it unfit to include David among those brought before the prophet, not only were they looking only at appearances, but they also revealed the most complete ignorance of God's ways and desires. Far from being thought ineligible because he was tending flocks in the fields, David was being specially prepared for God's selection as king.

This principle applies to all Christians: if we would desire to be useful to the Lord, we should devote ourselves to preparing our character and tending our spiritual growth. We prepare ourselves to serve the Lord in the school of Scripture, in the discipline of prayer, and in the practice of serving Christ's church in even the most menial of ways.

The anointing of David especially instructs us in the preparing of young people for Christian service. Young David was given responsibility and honed real-life skills that would serve him well in the near future. Later, when Saul sought to deny David the right to challenge the Philistine giant, Goliath, David answered by appeal to his youthful shepherding experience: "Your servant used to keep sheep for his father. And when there came a lion, or a bear, and took a lamb from the flock, I went after him and struck him and delivered it out of his mouth" (1 Sam. 17:34–35). From his early years,

6. Ibid., 260.

David had been challenged to live sacrificially and accomplish meaningful tasks for his family and for the Lord. In this way God was arranging his preparation for great things. Can we not expect God likewise to employ our youths if they are challenged not merely to meet the low standard of "staying out of trouble," but instead to live boldly for Christ in our dark generation?

Another lesson of David's anointing is one that we see all through Scripture: *God's delight in elevating servants from lowly places.* God delights to bless those who are poor and low in the world, and it magnifies his glory to employ servants who possess little or no advantage save his gift of grace. We find this principle to hold true time after time in Scripture, just as it is generally true for God's calling of the humble and poor to find their salvation in Christ. Paul thus reminded the early Christians that "not many of you were wise according to worldly standards, not many were powerful, not many were of noble birth. But God chose what is foolish in the world to shame the wise; God chose what is weak in the world to shame the strong" (1 Cor. 1:26–27).

Moreover, David's anointing shows us that *the most important qualities are those that commend us to God.* In choosing spiritual leaders, in hiring employees, and in personal matters such as the selection of a husband or a wife, how urgent is our need to remember the instruction of 1 Samuel 16:7: "Man looks on the outward appearance, but the LORD looks on the heart." The Bible commends many qualities, such as those we find in the book of Proverbs, in Jesus' Beatitudes, and in Paul's list of the fruit of the Spirit: "love, joy, peace, patience, kindness, goodness, faithfulness, gentleness, self-control" (Gal. 5:22–23). None of us score very highly by these biblical standards, of course. But the quality that we can and must possess if we wish to be faithful and godly servants, employees, spouses, parents, and friends is a willingness and desire to obey the Word of God. Remember what Samuel stated in his rebuke to King Saul: "Has the LORD as great delight in burnt offerings and sacrifices, as in obeying the voice of the LORD? Behold, to obey is better than sacrifice, and to listen than the fat of rams" (1 Sam. 15:22).

Finally, David's anointing reminds us that the qualities that God desires in his servants are those *he grants by the sending of his Holy Spirit.* This is why, after Samuel anointed David, "the Spirit of the LORD rushed upon David from that day forward" (1 Sam. 16:13). Today, God's Spirit works in our lives through God's Word and through prayer. Jesus promised to send the Spirit to all his disciples, the divine Helper who "will guide you into all the truth" (John 16:13) and by whose ministry we "are being transformed" into the image of Christ (2 Cor. 3:18). The way for Christians to grow in grace and prepare ourselves for future service to the Lord is to "walk by the Spirit" (Gal. 5:16) through faith in Christ and in obedience to his Word.

LIKE DAVID, LIKE JESUS

The anointing of David marked a significant advance in God's redeeming plan for history. Moreover, it pointed forward to the greatest advancement in God's salvation, which would come with the entry of his own Son, Jesus Christ. Of all the types of Christ in the Old Testament—that is, people, events, and institutions intended to foreshadow the coming of Christ—David is the greatest and clearest. That Jesus is known as "the Son of David" was originally intended as a compliment to Jesus, although from our vantage point we see it as an instance of amazing grace to David.

The selection of David points us forward to several features that draw us to faith in Jesus Christ. Jesus was not distinguished by his outward attractions. Neither did Jesus conduct himself so as to appeal to the fads and fashions of his day in Jerusalem. He did not take the expected route of first attaining the approval of the religious power brokers. He did not set out to win over the people by flashy eloquence or studied expressions. Even while Jesus performed miracles that set forth his divine power, he accompanied them with teaching that confounded the wisdom of the age. His oratory, though indeed profound, was directed to the deep matters of the heart and the stirring realities of God. "He conquered by gentleness, by forbearance, by love, by sympathy, by self-denial. He impressed men with the glory of sacrifice, the glory of service, the glory of obedience . . . to the will of God . . . He inspired them with a love of purity of heart."[7]

Most importantly, Jesus came to obey the will of God his Father. For this reason, he did not receive the accolades of the world, and for this same reason, he did receive the power of God's Holy Spirit. "This is my beloved Son, with whom I am well pleased" (Matt. 3:17), God said, on the occasion when the Spirit fell on Jesus like a dove. Jesus was, after all, the Savior whom

7. Ibid., 262.

God himself provided for his people, who brings the salvation that comes from God and restores us to God's favor.

As we honor Jesus and trust his Word, let us follow his example in believing and doing God's will. We may lack the approval of the world and we may be denied the world's methods of advancement and success, but if we have the anointing of God's Holy Spirit, then God will see in our hearts those things that cause him pleasure and prepare us to be useful to him. And if, like Samuel, we are downcast and defeated by the influence of sin and darkness around us, perhaps thinking that all is lost, God has good news to lift our hearts and challenge us to renewed boldness in faith. Speaking of his own Son, of whom even great David was but a type and symbol, God says, "I have provided for myself a king" (1 Sam. 16:1). Believing in Jesus, our true King, we may be uplifted in spirit and renewed in faith to serve his kingdom boldly in this world.

23

In Service to King Saul

1 Samuel 16:14–23

*One of the young men answered, "Behold, I have seen a son of
Jesse the Bethlehemite, who is skillful in playing, a man of valor,
a man of war, prudent in speech, and a man of good presence,
and the LORD is with him." (1 Sam. 16:18)*

*I*t is often said that "things happen for a reason." This expression does not necessarily indicate a biblical faith in God; it may reflect Eastern religious ideas of fate or karma. But Christians learn from the Bible that the saying really is true. Things do not merely happen for a reason in general, but the events of our own lives happen for God's holy, wise, and infinitely good purposes. Things especially happen in order that God's saving plan for history will be accomplished through the gospel of Christ. According to the apostle Paul, everything happens "according to the purpose of him who works all things according to the counsel of his will" (Eph. 1:11).

We cannot always see God's sovereign hand guiding our own lives, but we do see him at work in the lives of great figures in the Bible. The life of young David provides one example. David was tending his father's flocks in the fields outside Bethlehem when a summons came to appear before the prophet Samuel. When David arrived, the great spiritual leader anointed him by pouring oil over his head. This happened for a reason; the Lord had stated to Samuel: "I have provided for myself a king" (1 Sam. 16:1).

We are not told what immediately happened in David's life. Presumably, he went back to his fields, although we can imagine his father taking more of an interest in his youngest son and Samuel interacting with him as the opportunity arose. But in time a new summons arrived for David, this time from King Saul. As David entered into Saul's service as court musician, the youth may not have understood how or why this was happening. But David could be sure that this summons had arrived for a reason, since God's gracious purposes always guide the events of his people's lives. So it is on the grand stage of history: it was while the earth was sleeping that God's Son was born and placed in the Bethlehem manger. A thousand years before Christ's coming, God summoned young David from Bethlehem into the service of King Saul.

SAUL'S EVIL SPIRIT

When last we considered Saul, Israel's king had run afoul of God and his prophet Samuel. The Lord had given Saul one last chance to obey his Word, but Saul had followed the counsel of his and the people's greed instead of God's commands. As a result, Samuel told him: "You have rejected the word of the LORD, and the LORD has rejected you from being king over Israel" (1 Sam. 15:26).

To all appearances, this spiritual dismissal had little effect on the practical affairs of Saul and his kingdom. God had rejected Saul, but Saul remained king. People today likewise tend to think that the spiritual arena has little influence over worldly matters—such things as who is in charge and who is getting ahead in life. But Saul's experience reminds us that, in fact, the spiritual realm is primary over the material realm, and that God's spiritual arrangements will unfailingly determine earthly outcomes.

God's rejection of Saul had two immediate results. The first was that "the Spirit of the LORD departed from Saul" (1 Sam. 16:14). Saul had received God's Spirit at the time of his anointing by Samuel (10:10). This does not mean that Saul had been born again to a saving faith, but rather that God's Spirit was providing him with supernatural equipping for the calling that

God had given him. Now, however, Saul had been rejected by the Lord, and David had been anointed in his place. When David was anointed, "the Spirit of the LORD rushed upon David from that day forward" (16:13). In coming to David, the Spirit had departed from King Saul.

No longer blessed with God's supernatural equipping, Saul would now have to face his challenges in his own strength. This departure should remind us that there is no greater blessing than the indwelling presence of God's Holy Spirit. It is by the Spirit that sinners believe in Jesus and receive salvation (John 3:3–8; 1 Cor. 2:14). In his teaching on prayer, Jesus presented the Holy Spirit as the chief of all God's blessings. "If you then, who are evil, know how to give good gifts to your children," Jesus taught, "how much more will the heavenly Father give the Holy Spirit to those who ask him!" (Luke 11:13). Nothing can replace the power and blessing of God's Holy Spirit. Without the Spirit we may possess all things, but we will have them without blessing; with the Spirit we may lack everything else and yet be filled with the joy of God. Paul wrote, "The kingdom of God is not a matter of eating and drinking but of righteousness and peace and joy in the Holy Spirit" (Rom. 14:17).

What is true of individuals is also true of the church: our ministry is nothing without the Holy Spirit. What can the church accomplish if it has the most effective programs, the most well-financed advertising, the most polished musical performers, and the most attractive celebrity speakers? Such churches can accomplish much in a worldly sense, but virtually nothing of spiritual value. Meanwhile, a church that has no worldly advantages, but faithfully ministers God's Word, prayer, and the sacraments, may accomplish great things in the light of eternity through the power of God's Spirit. "Apart from me you can do nothing," Jesus declared (John 15:5). We can do many things apart from Christ, but in spiritual and eternal terms, they are nothing. Yet with God's Spirit, Paul says, "I can do all things through him who strengthens me" (Phil. 4:13). Realizing this, we should count the withdrawal of God's Spirit as the worst possible calamity and the presence of God's Spirit as the greatest possible help. Nothing of the world can compensate for the loss of God's Spirit, but with the Spirit's power, even the weakest of God's people can do mighty things.

It was bad enough for Saul to have God's Spirit depart from him. But the second result of the Lord's rejection was even worse. God also punished

Saul for the sins that had caused his rejection: "and a harmful spirit from the LORD tormented him" (1 Sam. 16:14). This statement has troubled many readers, especially since it is translated in some versions as "an evil spirit" that God sent to Saul. Does this mean that God was in collusion with evil, perhaps demonic powers, and that he used them to do violence against his enemies?

Commentators have tried to resolve this apparent difficulty. Some have argued that Old Testament writers tended to ascribe everything to God, to the neglect of human causation. Walter Brueggemann complains that "the world of biblical perspective is a world without secondary cause. All causes are finally traced back to the God who causes all."[1] From this perspective, Andrew Blackwood argues that what the primitive biblical writers ascribed to God and spirits was really no more than "intermittent mental aberrations."[2] Saul's problem was therefore psychological, not supernatural. The problem with this reasoning is that the Bible does in fact acknowledge both ultimate and secondary causes, and also contains a sophisticated, if not modern, psychological understanding.

A second approach to explaining this text does not deny the spiritual or even supernatural cause, but does deny that God was the source. This view states that the Holy Spirit's departure merely opened the way for demonic affliction, since any person without the Spirit "is easy prey for Satan."[3] The problem with this explanation is that the text explicitly states that the spirit tormenting Saul was "from the LORD."

In understanding the text, we need not understand the spirit as "evil," but rather as "harmful" (as the English Standard Version renders it).[4] The spirit—presumably an angel—was not himself evil, but rather he was sent by the Lord to bring harm upon King Saul. To some, this may not seem to resolve much of the difficulty, since whether the spirit was himself evil or not, we still have God harming someone, despite the Bible's teaching that "God is love" (1 John 4:8).

---

1. Walter Brueggemann, *First and Second Samuel*, Interpretation (Louisville: John Knox, 1990), 125.

2. Andrew W. Blackwood, *Preaching from Samuel* (New York: Abingdon-Cokesbury, 1946), 123.

3. Gordon J. Keddie, *Dawn of a Kingdom: The Message of 1 Samuel* (Darlington, UK: Evangelical Press, 1988), 166.

4. For a careful argument in favor of a "harmful" spirit, or "a spirit which brings forth disaster," see David Toshio Tsumura, *The First Book of Samuel*, New International Commentary on the Old Testament (Grand Rapids: Eerdmans, 2007), 427.

The answer is that this spirit of harm was sent by the Lord as an act of judgment on Saul's sin. Robert Bergen explains: "Saul's tortured state was not an accident of nature, nor was it essentially a medical condition. It was a supernatural assault by a being sent at the Lord's command, and it was brought on by Saul's disobedience."[5] Saul's repeated rebellion against God's commands had brought not only his rejection as king but also God's judgment in the form of this heaven-sent spiritual torment. God is love, and therefore he hates all evil, including Saul's sins. Saul's judgment is a warning of the far greater torment that souls in hell will experience as a result of God's deliberate and, in that case, eternal punishment for sin.

Without doubt, Saul's harmful spirit manifested itself in psychological aberrations that were unstable, hostile, and sometimes even dangerous (see 1 Sam. 18:10–11). Saul, once so impressive a young man, has now become gloomy and unstable. This was, of course, noticed by his court. Saul's followers thus sought a remedy to his torment and, no doubt, their own: "Let our lord now command your servants who are before you to seek out a man who is skillful in playing the lyre, and when the harmful spirit from God is upon you, he will play it, and you will be well" (16:16).

The advisers recognized that the source of Saul's problem was his alienation from God: "Behold now, a harmful spirit from God is tormenting you," they said (1 Sam. 16:15). Yet their remedy was superficial. The playing of the lyre was widely held in the ancient world to combat evil spirits, and even today we know the soothing power of soft music. Yet Saul's true problem was his sin against the Lord. Spiritually sound advice would urge the king to turn to the Lord in sincere and heartfelt repentance. God's grace is always available to anyone who will repent and believe: "Return to me, . . . and I will return to you," is God's rule for sinners suffering misery and judgment (Zech. 1:3).

Biblically minded counselors seem to have been absent from Saul's court, and his advisers could think only of addressing the psychological symptoms of what was fundamentally a spiritual problem. Gordon Keddie writes: "Having diagnosed the need for heart surgery, they proceeded to prescribe a sedative!"[6] While we should acknowledge that not all psychological struggles

5. Robert D. Bergen, *1, 2 Samuel*, New American Commentary (Nashville: Broadman & Holman, 1996), 182.
6. Keddie, *Dawn of a Kingdom*, 166.

stem directly from spiritual roots, it remains the case that unrepented sin is often the cause for emotional, psychological, and even physical distress. Yet Saul, thinking on no higher a plane than his advisers, consented to their plan: he ordered, "Provide for me a man who can play well and bring him to me" (1 Sam. 16:17).

DAVID IS SOUGHT FOR SAUL'S SERVICE

It was at this point that God's providence openly entered the scene. We can imagine the huddle of Saul's advisers wondering who they would get to play the lyre (a stringed instrument that looked like a small harp) for the king. It turned out that one of them had "seen a son of Jesse the Bethlehemite" who he believed was "skillful in playing." Now that he thought about this son of Jesse, he realized how ideal the young man would be for Saul's court, describing him as "a man of valor, a man of war, prudent in speech, and a man of good presence" (1 Sam. 16:18). We do not know what circumstances produced this high recommendation. But we do know the last thing said about David, which accounts for it all: "the LORD is with him" (16:18).

Each of these statements should characterize not only David but any young man or woman with a living faith in the Lord. First, David was commended for his courage and ability: "a man of valor, a man of war." David did not grow up in peaceful times. Philistine forces were often seen within a few miles of Bethlehem, a situation that "might afford him opportunities of boyish valour."[7] In the next chapter, which recounts David's famous victory over the giant Goliath, David remarks to King Saul that he has fought bears and lions in his duties as a shepherd (1 Sam. 17:37). Later, after killing the giant, David took his severed head and displayed it before the city of Jerusalem, which at that time was an unconquered Jebusite fortress (17:54). This action is never explained, but it suggests that David had dealings with that nearby enemy stronghold and had taken it upon himself to issue them a challenge on behalf of Israel. All of this material pictures an idealistic, resourceful, and courageous young man, which is exactly what a living faith in the Lord should produce. In their character-forming years, Christian youths should begin to participate in the spiritual warfare of the church by standing up

---

7. William G. Blaikie, *Expository Lectures on the Book of First Samuel* (1887; repr., Birmingham, AL: Solid Ground, 2005), 267.

for what is right, praying against what is wrong, and sharing with others the good news of Jesus Christ.

Next, David was "prudent in speech." This, too, should be emphasized in the training of Christian youths. The Bible consistently links the mouth and the heart, so that the way we speak indicates the tenor of our spiritual life. The book of Proverbs says that we must guard our hearts as the wellspring of life, and then immediately adds: "Put away from you crooked speech, and put devious talk far from you" (Prov. 4:23–24). Jesus likewise said that "out of the abundance of the heart the mouth speaks" (Matt. 12:34). Godly speech is learned through the Word of God and is a fitting theme for our prayers. David thus asked the Lord, "Let the words of my mouth and the meditation of my heart be acceptable in your sight, O LORD, my rock and my redeemer" (Ps. 19:14).

A person who is prudent in speech will usually also possess a "good presence," which is the next compliment given to young David. This seems to indicate a confident and positive demeanor. Some of us are blessed with natural beauty and some of us are not. But we can all bear ourselves with godly dignity and respect for others, and if we do, our good presence will commend the grace of God in our lives.

Given this description of David, we would not be surprised to learn that a spiritual giant, Samuel, had been involved in mentoring him after his anointing. Godly discipleship is of great value to any believer, and young people should seek role models first in their believing parents and then in other mature believers. We remember that a godly legacy extended down through David's family. His great-grandmother was Ruth the Moabitess, and the kind of loyalty she showed her mother-in-law, Naomi, is evidenced in the life of David. His great-grandfather was Boaz, the redeemer-kinsman who had acted with both charity and strength in taking Ruth for his wife. David may well have grown up in the house where Ruth and Boaz formerly lived, and their spiritual legacy would have been deeply impressed within those rooms.

The description given of young David is a good agenda for the mentoring of any Christian, especially a young one. Youthful David has been described as valiant, prudent, and well composed. The key to it all, however, is David's last accolade: "the LORD is with him" (1 Sam. 16:18). Today, in the gospel age, the Lord is with everyone who trusts in Jesus Christ, just as the Lord's voice is heard in his Word and the Lord's presence is felt in believing prayer. Jesus is present among his disciples today through the ministry of the Holy Spirit; when he was departing for the cross, Jesus told the disciples: "I will ask the Father, and he will give you another Helper, to be with you forever, even the Spirit of truth" (John 14:16–17). The way for us to experience spiritual growth and to develop a gracious character is to open our lives to the leading of the Holy Spirit in obedience to the Scripture, knowing through faith that the Lord Jesus is with us always.

SERVING KING SAUL

Based on this outstanding recommendation, "Saul sent messengers to Jesse and said, 'Send me David your son, who is with the sheep'" (1 Sam. 16:19). Receiving the summons, David's father obeyed, sending David along with bread, wine, and a young goat. In this way, "David came to Saul and entered his service" (16:21).

Remarkably, it was by Saul's own command that the man anointed by God to replace him was brought to the royal court. Remember, things were happening for a reason! In Saul's presence, David would be schooled in matters of state and have opportunities to reflect on the practice of leadership. The change of scenery must have been a major adjustment for young David, moving from the pastoral setting outside Bethlehem to the intense and spiritually challenged setting of Saul's court. If the Psalms are any reflection, the experience deepened David's faith and exposed him to the wide varieties of human experience, all of which may be brought before the Lord in prayer.

David's job was to play the lyre when Saul was in an evil mood, and David performed this well: "Whenever the harmful spirit from God was upon Saul, David took the lyre and played it with his hand. So Saul was refreshed and was well, and the harmful spirit departed from him" (1 Sam. 16:23). Saul could be truly restored only through repentance, but in the meantime, David's ministry helped bring a measure of calm to the king and to those who needed to interact with him.

Seeing firsthand the effects of Saul's hardened heart toward the Lord must have made a great impression on David. Perhaps it was the warning received in these early days that made David so willing in later years to humble himself before the Lord and repent of his sins. David would learn what it meant to have God's hand heavy upon him, with his spirit groaning day and night because of sin (Ps. 32:3–4). But David had learned what to do when this happened. He relates, "I acknowledged my sin to you, and I did not cover my iniquity; I said, 'I will confess my transgressions to the LORD,' and you forgave the iniquity of my sin" (32:5).

In the meantime, David was a servant of God's restraining grace in Saul's life. One commentator says: "Thus David was a blessing to Saul and thereby also to Israel. Because of David's presence, Saul's mind was not immediately and wholly disabled, and Israel's affairs were not completely thrown into confusion."[8] David sets an example for believers today who find themselves in service to a difficult employer or responding to troubled parents. Even when we must submit to higher authorities, Christians can make a great difference, bringing light into darkness and providing salt to preserve life and bring a pleasant flavor to any situation (see Matt. 5:13–14). Meanwhile, David received an education in the wages of sin and the peril of disobedience to the Lord, along with exposure to the art of kingcraft as practiced by Saul. His later conduct indicates that he respected Saul and learned to hold the office of king in high esteem. Christians also should convey respect to those who are placed by God in authority over us, seeking to profit from both their good and bad examples, and to prepare ourselves for later service as the Lord may be pleased to employ us.

David served Saul so well that the king "loved him greatly, and he became his armor-bearer" (1 Sam. 16:21). We need not understand that Saul held an intense personal affection for David, since this statement may simply mean that Saul liked what he saw in David. The next chapter will show that when removed from the court setting, Saul did not recognize David or remember his name. The young shepherd was, however, given the position of Saul's armor-bearer, which made him one of the king's comrades-in-arms. David thus lived out the words later written by the apostle Paul, who taught that Christian servants should serve "with a sincere heart, as you would Christ, not by the way of eye-service, as people-pleasers, but as servants of Christ, doing the will of God from the heart, rendering service with a good will as to the Lord and not to man" (Eph. 6:5–7). Believers who follow David's example

8. S. G. DeGraaf, quoted in Roger Ellsworth, *The Shepherd King: Learning from the Life of David* (Darlington, UK: Evangelical Press, 1998), 26.

in the workplace will often find themselves growing in the esteem of their leaders and advancing into positions of greater authority and responsibility.

"The Lord Is with Him"

The point of these verses is not merely to hold David up as a model employee, however. More importantly, David shows what a difference it makes for God to be with us. "The Lord is with him" is the decisive statement for understanding young David (1 Sam. 16:18). In fact, it was because of his God-given faith that David served as such a good role model for Christians and, more significantly, that he typified for us the character and ministry of the Lord Jesus Christ. Jesus, too, was able to live his perfect life, teach his divine words, and work his mighty miracles because the Lord was with him. This was the point of the very first sermon that Jesus preached: "The Spirit of the Lord is upon me, because he has anointed me to proclaim good news to the poor" (Luke 4:18, quoting Isa. 61:1).

God was with David because the Lord had determined to provide a king for himself to rule over Israel. Likewise, God was with Jesus Christ, since the Father was providing his Son to be the Savior of the world. Jesus is in fact much greater than David, since not only was God's Spirit in him, but the apostle John could say of him: "The Word became flesh and dwelt among us, and we have seen his glory, glory as of the only Son from the Father, full of grace and truth" (John 1:14). In Jesus Christ, not only did God's Spirit come upon a man, but through the Holy Spirit, God's eternal Son took up human flesh and was called "Immanuel," "God with us" (Matt. 1:23).

David's sweet music was able to soothe Saul's troubled mind for a while. But the sweetest music ever heard in this troubled world was the angel song announcing the coming of the Savior Jesus Christ: "Glory to God in the highest, and on earth peace among those with whom he is pleased!" (Luke 2:14). Jesus came not merely to soothe us in our sinful misery but to deliver us from our sin (see Matt. 1:21). Saul was blessed to listen to David's playing, but he failed to follow up on those moments of clarity and seek a deeper and true healing for his ills. It is only by believing on the Savior whom God has sent that sinful men and women will be blessed with peace that only God can give.

Are you troubled? Are you gripped by cravings and godless passions? Are you worried by the anxieties of life or concerned for the guilt of your sins? Jesus calls us to listen to his voice and through faith in him to receive the true healing that our souls require: to be forgiven of our sins, to be renewed by the Holy Spirit, to be embraced by God as dearly beloved children, and to receive from God the free gift of new and eternal life. Not only does Jesus, like David, possess God's Spirit, but he gives God's Spirit in abundance to those who receive him in faith. Jesus said, "The words that I speak to you are spirit, and they are life" (John 6:63 NKJV). The sweet music of his gospel speaks true peace to our troubled souls.

Remember: everything happens for a reason. The reason the message of salvation in Christ is preached today is that many who are troubled by the misery of sin will hear his voice, believe in him, and be saved. Jesus said, "Whoever hears my word and believes him who sent me has eternal life. He does not come into judgment, but has passed from death to life" (John 5:24).

24

A Man to Fight

1 Samuel 17:1–30

The Philistine said, "I defy the ranks of Israel this day. Give me
a man, that we may fight together." (1 Sam. 17:10)

The Bible frequently teaches issues of faith and virtue by using
contrasts. This is especially true in historical narratives such as
those in 1 Samuel. Unlike Paul's epistles in the New Testament,
for example, with their plain statements of propositional truth, historical
narratives set different people before us, tell us their stories, and show how
God interacted with them.

Of all these contrasts, none is more potent than that between Saul and
David. Ever since the first anointing of David in chapter 13, he has been
presented as Saul's opposite. Chapter 17, made famous by the battle between
David and Goliath, begins in earnest a contest between David and Saul
that will take up the remainder of 1 Samuel. Here, in David's first public
appearance, Saul and David are contrasted by their response to the Philistine
giant's challenge: "Give me a man, that we may fight together" (1 Sam. 17:10).

The account of David slaying the giant Goliath is a classic tale, having
"the ingredients of drama and excitement, anticipation and the satisfac-

tion of the good guy defeating the bad guy against all odds."[1] "David and Goliath" has become a stock phrase for any "little guy" who takes on and defeats a bigger, stronger foe, whether in war, sports, business, or politics. The prominence of this story is not accidental. This is the longest of all the accounts in Samuel, including more quotations than any other (twenty-two), and featuring the longest and most vivid speech from one of Israel's enemies. Careful attention is paid to small details, such as the number of cheeses brought by David, the pieces and weight of Goliath's armor, the number of small stones picked up by David, and so on. These details slow the reader down to ponder the narrative "and thus make the story more memorable and more likely to be studied further."[2]

As we approach this great chapter, we should realize that David's victory does not primarily foretell triumphs that we will achieve by faith but rather the victory of Christ for our salvation. David as hero and king presents a foreshadowing portrait—what theologians refer to as a *type*—of his greater Son, Jesus. Moreover, while we may recognize David's faith, character, experience from shepherding, and application of biblical principles as having played a role in his success, David triumphed mainly because he was indwelt by the Holy Spirit, God's Spirit having "rushed" upon him at his anointing (1 Sam. 16:13). Thus, David's actions remind us that faith, godliness, and courage should always result from a Spirit-led life and that they will often be used by God against our spiritual foes today.

Israel's Giant Reproach

Israel in the time of Saul and David sat in the midst of enemies on all sides. Their main foes were the Philistines to the west and the Ammonites to the east. Saul's earliest battles were against the Philistines, and after his son Jonathan's victory at Michmash (1 Sam. 14:1–23), the Philistines were driven out of Israel and back to their coastal fortresses. These resourceful enemies were not easily daunted, however, so in time they returned in force to wage war against Saul's kingdom. "The Philistines gathered their armies for battle. And they were gathered at Socoh, which belongs to Judah, and

1. John Woodhouse, *1 Samuel: Looking for a Leader* (Wheaton, IL: Crossway, 2008), 301.
2. Robert D. Bergen, *1, 2 Samuel*, New American Commentary (Nashville: Broadman & Holman, 1996), 188.

encamped between Socoh and Azekah, in Ephes-dammim" (17:1). These geographical references place the battle line about thirteen miles west of Bethlehem. Saul mobilized his army to meet the invaders, encamping in "the Valley of Elah" (17:2). This site has been identified by historians and archaeologists; through its center runs a deep ravine where winter rains flood. The Philistines moved forward to meet Israel, and the two forces faced each other on either side of the ditch.

This battle would serve as a watershed for Saul's reign, being the first battle he would face after being rejected by the Lord and abandoned by the Holy Spirit. In the past, Saul could rely on God's saving help, but now Saul and Israel would have to manage things on their own. It was a good thing, then, that Saul was such an impressive person: he was handsome and "from his shoulders upward he was taller than any of the people" (1 Sam. 9:2). It was these qualifications that made Saul so agreeable to the Israelites as their king. The people of Israel had demanded a king "like all the nations," and one of the things they wanted him to do was to "go out before us and fight our battles" (8:20). Who better to do this than the man with the largest stature in all Israel?

These thoughts may have been in the mind of Saul and his army as the two forces drew together. The Philistines had superior armament and usually possessed superior numbers, but Saul would not have been daunted. Given his own leadership, Israelite valor, and the strong defensive terrain, he should be able to hurl back any assault across the ravine. But then the din among the Philistines began to subside and their ranks parted. Out strutted the enemy's latest military innovation, a gladiator-champion of gigantic proportions.

The inspired author of Samuel takes pains to describe the Philistine champion. His name was "Goliath of Gath," and the first thing one noticed about him was his awesome size: his "height was six cubits and a span" (1 Sam. 17:4). Converting these ancient measurements yields a height of about nine feet six inches. Although the text never refers to Goliath as a giant, it doesn't need to: he was a mountain of a man, rising far above the head of any Israelite warrior.

No one familiar with biblical scholarship will be surprised to learn that this measurement has been sharply challenged. Such criticism is apparently quite ancient, since the third-century B.C. Greek translation of the

Old Testament, the Septuagint, puts Goliath at four cubits and a span, for a more believable height of six feet nine inches. But unless we operate with the assumption that things have always been as they are now—for there is still no record of any human this tall—there is no reason to doubt the Hebrew text. Moreover, Goliath's height is not without comparison. The *Guinness Book of World Records* reports that in 1940 an Illinois man named Robert Wadlow was verified to be eight feet eleven inches tall—a mere seven inches shorter than Goliath. The tallest man known in the world today is eight feet five inches.[3]

There are also good biblical reasons to take this measurement seriously. When Israel drew near to the Promised Land at the end of the exodus, Moses sent spies to investigate the land of Canaan. These spies reported seeing "descendants of Anak" (Num. 13:22), "a people great and tall" (Deut. 9:2), who terrified the Israelites, having "come from the Nephilim" (Num. 13:33). The only other reference in the Bible to the "Nephilim" comes from before Noah's flood; it states that they were "mighty men . . . , the men of renown" (Gen. 6:4). How these giants would have survived Noah's flood is a mystery (although great height would have helped!). In the time of Joshua's conquest of Canaan, the Anakim were driven out of Israel (see Josh. 15:13–14). The only other reference we have is the statement of Joshua 11:22: "There was none of the Anakim left in the land of the people of Israel. Only in Gaza, in Gath, and in Ashdod did some remain." This record links up with the account in Samuel, since the Philistines' giant was identified as "Goliath of Gath" (1 Sam. 17:4).

As is often the case, debating scholarly criticism threatens to distract us from the point of the biblical text. Remember why Saul was so impressive to Israel, and why they wanted him as king to go before them into battle? Saul's chief feature was his tall stature. Now Israel, and Saul, would learn the problem with relying on worldly sources of strength. If you are counting on money, there is always someone richer. If you are trusting to brains, there is someone smarter. And if you are relying on size, there is always someone bigger. Goliath was *a lot* bigger than Saul or anyone else in Israel's army! In situations like this, it would certainly be good to be able to call upon the Lord! But this was a privilege that Saul no longer enjoyed or apparently even sought.

---

3. This information was gathered from www.guinnessworldrecords.com, accessed August 22, 2009.

There is more to the description of Goliath. Not only was his height imposing, but his armor was intimidating: "He had a helmet of bronze on his head, and he was armed with a coat of mail, and the weight of the coat was five thousand shekels of bronze. And he had bronze armor on his legs" (1 Sam. 17:5–6). Unless things had changed since a few years earlier, most Israelites would have gone into battle with little or no armor (see 13:22). Goliath, by contrast, was armored from head to toe. And it was very heavy armor at that. His mail coat weighed five thousand shekels, that is, about 126 pounds. His massive legs were covered by bronze greaves. Goliath was effectively impregnable, and all the more so since a shield-bearer went before him. The fact that one man was required just to lug Goliath's shield suggests that it was appropriately huge.

Finally, we are told of Goliath's impressive weaponry. He had "a javelin of bronze slung between his shoulders. The shaft of his spear was like a weaver's beam, and his spear's head weighed six hundred shekels of iron" (1 Sam. 17:6–7). The hugeness of Goliath's spear is indicated by its fifteen-pound iron point. Robert Bergen summarizes the first impression Goliath made as "awesome and psychologically overpowering,"[4] the very picture of martial invincibility.

Goliath was more than a fearful spectacle; he was also a specialist in single combat. Goliath was a "champion" (1 Sam. 17:4): the Hebrew expression literally means a "man between the two." He was trained, equipped, and naturally endowed to step forth between competing armies and challenge an opponent to single combat. This strategy had the virtue of sparing the vast bloodshed of armies locked in battle, and it reflected the commonly held idea that the battle was a contest between the gods of the two nations, since single combat could prove a god's supremacy just as well as a full battle.

It was to challenge the Israelites and their God that Goliath had come forth. He stood before their ranks and jeered: "Why have you come out to draw up for battle? Am I not a Philistine, and are you not servants of Saul? Choose a man for yourselves, and let him come down to me" (1 Sam. 17:8). Whoever won this personal combat, Goliath offered, the other side would surrender and be slaves of the other.

4. Bergen, *1, 2 Samuel*, 189.

Goliath represents for us spiritual opposition to God and his people, especially as manifested by Satan and his demonic forces. A. W. Pink writes: "Goliath pictures to us the great enemy of God and man, the devil, seeking to terrify, and bring into captivity those who bear the name of the Lord."[5] Not only did his prodigious size reflect the great power of Satan, but Goliath's mocking jeers depicted Satan's hostility and hatred against the Lord and his people: "Why have you come out to draw up for battle? Am I not a Philistine, and are you not servants of Saul? . . . I defy the ranks of Israel this day. Give me a man, that we may fight together" (1 Sam. 17:8–10).

The natural candidate to fight Goliath was King Saul, since going before Israel into battle was his job (1 Sam. 8:20). But Saul was "dismayed and greatly afraid" (17:11). What about Saul's many valiant captains, Abner, his son Jonathan, or one of the other "valiant" men whom Saul had been collecting (see 14:52)? As a rule, the men below will reflect the spirit of their leader. Herein lay the problem, for God's Spirit had departed from Saul and he was left to his own limited resources. As Saul gazed slack-jawed and glassy-eyed at Goliath, the army fed off his giant-sized panic. Not one of them had the heart to answer Goliath's challenge. Proverbs 28:1 says that "the righteous are bold as a lion." Saul proved the opposite, showing that once a person is severed from God and his saving help, the world and its threats become terrifying, so that the person is easily dismayed.

ISRAEL'S ROYAL FAILURE

With the vision of a terrified and dispirited Saul and his army fresh in our minds, another figure enters the scene. His introduction is carefully crafted. Some scholars have been puzzled about why David is introduced all over again, his family connections already having been stated in the previous chapter, but a point is being made. While the giant's physical features are highlighted to impress us, it is David's covenant lineage that sets him apart: "Now David was the son of an Ephrathite of Bethlehem in Judah, named Jesse" (1 Sam. 17:12). These are the opposing powers in the contest between David and Goliath: raw worldly (and perhaps demonic) strength versus a covenant bond with the living and true God.

5. A. W. Pink, *A Life of David*, 2 vols. (Grand Rapids: Baker, 1981), 1:31.

Ordinarily, David would not have even been present on this battlefield, since he did not meet Israel's age requirement for military service of twenty years (Num. 1:3, 20). But God's providence ordained otherwise. The three oldest sons of Jesse were in the army, and in those days families had to support the soldiers and, to a certain extent, the king and his officers. Thus David was summoned from his fields. While he was the youngest, his position as lyre-player in Saul's court made him the obvious choice to take provisions to his brothers and return with news from the battlefront. So Jesse summoned David and directed him to take to his brothers "an ephah of this parched grain, and these ten loaves," along with "these ten cheeses to the commander of their thousand," and report back about his brothers (1 Sam. 17:17–18).

David's experience reminds us that we do not know what challenges may await us on any given day. Little did David realize, as he "rose early in the morning and left the sheep with a keeper and took the provisions and went" (1 Sam. 17:20), that the defining challenge of his life was a mere few hours ahead. William Blaikie comments on how greatly we may be sifted and tried on any day, asking, "Should we not pray more really, more earnestly if we did realize these possibilities? . . . Is it not a good habit, as you kneel each morning, to think, 'For aught I know, this may be the most important day of my life. The opportunity may be given me of doing a great service in the cause of truth and righteousness; or the temptation may assail me to deny my Lord and ruin my soul. O God, be not far from me this day; prepare me for all that Thou preparest for me!' "[6]

David arrived at the battlefield right as the respective forces were assuming their positions across the defile, each shouting their war cry. No teenage boy could stay back and miss seeing such a scene. Therefore, David dropped his goods at the baggage depot and "ran to the ranks and went and greeted his brothers" (1 Sam. 17:22). At just that moment, "the champion, the Philistine of Gath, Goliath by name, came up out of the ranks of the Philistines and spoke the same words as before" (17:23).

This scene had repeated itself for forty days, each resulting in the same humiliation for Israel because no one was brave enough to take up Goliath's challenge. The Bible uses the number forty for a definite period of testing—we think of Israel's forty years in the wilderness and Jesus' forty days

---

6. William G. Blaikie, *Expository Lectures on the Book of First Samuel* (1887; repr., Birmingham, AL: Solid Ground, 2005), 281.

of temptation—so David's arrival occurs at the point when Israel's army had completely failed the challenge set for them by Goliath. They had had almost six weeks for even one Israelite soldier to muster enough courage to take on the giant, and if none had stepped forward by now, none was ever going to do so. David therefore arrived at the moment when the Spirit-less Saul and his dispirited army had suffered a comprehensive moral defeat.

This failure also proved Israel to be devoid of faith in their God. Goliath's challenge of verse 8 was really a test of their confidence in the Lord. Roger Ellsworth paraphrases Goliath's taunt: "Am I not a pagan, God-hating Philistine? Then why won't any of your men of 'the living God' fight me? You must not really believe in him at all! In fact, you must believe that a nine-foot warrior is actually stronger than your 'living God' when it comes to a real battle."[7] This is the kind of test that the world still delights to pose for Christians, often with Goliath-like mockery: "We know what you teach in Sunday school, but let's see how you do when faced with a real-life sensual temptation, or an opportunity to gain riches by cheating. Let's see the look on your God-praising face when you receive a terrifying medical diagnosis or your stock portfolio crashes! Let's see how you respond when given an opportunity to cheat on an important college exam!" Behind Goliath was the same devil who wages spiritual warfare today. The issue is always the same: "Do you *really* trust in a loving God of power and grace?"

Perceiving this spiritual dynamic helps us to understand David's horrified reaction to the sight before him. This may well have been the first time that David had ever heard anyone blaspheme the name of the Lord. How mortified he was to witness as "all the men of Israel, when they saw the man, fled from him and were much afraid" (1 Sam. 17:24). Perhaps smarting from the look on David's face, the soldiers were eager to justify their cowardice: "Have you seen this man who has come up? Surely he has come up to defy Israel" (17:25).

The obvious question was what Israel's king was doing in response to this defiant blasphemy, so Saul's response was reported to David. While the king would not risk his own neck against the formidable Philistine, he was willing to richly reward anyone who would do so on his behalf. The soldiers told David, "And the king will enrich the man who kills him with

---

7. Roger Ellsworth, *The Shepherd King: Learning from the Life of David* (Darlington, UK: Evangelical Press, 1998), 30.

great riches and will give him his daughter and make his father's house free in Israel" (1 Sam. 17:25). This was a princely reward: great riches, membership in the royal family via the hand of Saul's daughter, and lifelong family exemption from taxes and other civic duties. Surely men would be lining up for a chance at a bonanza like this!

Yet not a single Israelite had signed up to be Israel's champion. Saul's offer shows that he accepted Goliath's challenge in principle. But Saul lacked the resources to accept the challenge, having not one soldier sufficiently inspired to face the Philistine giant. Saul's royal failure is now complete: not only has he failed in his calling to be Israel's champion, but his leadership has not inspired a single soldier to defend the cause of his king, his nation, and, implicitly, his God.

The real problem was that Saul, and after him the army, had indeed lost their faith in God. Not that they formally denied the Lord, of course. We read nothing here of a Philistine theological society forming in the Israelite army or of offerings made to idols. So far as we know, Saul and the army still made an orthodox profession of faith. But the test of faith is not ultimately one of words, but of action in the face of earthly trials and spiritual warfare. Do we act as if we know and serve a God who is greater than every other power, a Savior who is willing and able to save us from all dangers? This question was answered by Saul and his army by their failure to face Goliath, just as it is answered by every Christian today in his or her day-to-day actions and response to threats and temptations. Which do we believe is greater and stronger: the sin that mocks us and the fear that shoots into our hearts, or the God whose faith we profess? If we believe in God, we will at least step onto the battlefield and make a trial of his power to preserve us from sin and deliver us from fear.

David's Faithful Reply

David seems to have been stupefied that Israel's king could think of no higher incentive for his soldiers than the material riches he offered. A dead man could never spend the money Saul offered, after all, or enjoy the pleasures of marriage to the royal princess. David's response serves as a sort of double take: "What shall be done for the man who kills this Philistine and takes away the reproach from Israel? For who is this uncircumcised Philistine, that he should defy the armies of the living God?" (1 Sam. 17:26).

These words offered the first biblical, theological perspective on the battle at Elah. David's question centers on key ideas lacking in everyone else's thinking: Goliath was a "reproach" to Israel; the giant was only an "uncircumcised Philistine"; and by contrast, the God Israel served was not some mere idol, but "the living God." Dale Ralph Davis comments:

> David brings a whole new world view. To this point the narrative has been "godless" . . . , but now David injects the godly question into the episode. Doesn't having a living God make a difference in all this? This fellow has mocked "the ranks of the living God." If God is so identified with Israel, do you think he is indifferent toward such slurs on his reputation? Do you expect a living God to allow an uncircumcised Philistine to trample his name in military and theological mud?[8]

As David understood things, not only did the army of Israel have no *need* to cower before a God-denying pagan warrior, but as the people of the living God they had no *right* to flee in terror before Goliath. "Rather," writes Gordon Keddie, "they should have claimed the promise of the presence and power of the Lord and taken the field in holy boldness in dependence on the Lord."[9]

Whether it was the tone of David's question or his interjection of biblical truth among these despondent and pride-injured soldiers, it was more than his eldest brother could take. The opening portion of the chapter concludes with Eliab's unjust accusation against David: "Eliab's anger was kindled against David," so he mocked David's motives in coming: "I know your presumption and the evil of your heart, for you have come down to see the battle" (1 Sam. 17:28). Just as faith is challenged by open enemies such as Goliath, faith is often assailed by family and friends who cast aspersions on anyone who seeks to honor God and follow the faith that he has espoused. It was easier for Eliab to criticize his brother than to repent, his heart hardening with perceived reproach in David's words.

8. Dale Ralph Davis, *1 Samuel: Looking on the Heart* (Fearn, Ross-shire, UK: Christian Focus, 2000), 149.

9. Gordon J. Keddie, *Dawn of a Kingdom: The Message of 1 Samuel* (Darlington, UK: Evangelical Press, 1988), 169.

David's response to the situation at Elah teaches us that the great affairs of life are all essentially theological. What we do with our lives, how we decide whom to marry, or not, what priorities we pursue, or whether we witness the gospel to friends and neighbors all reveal what we really believe about God. Regardless of our formal profession of faith, if we seldom act on the basis of biblical truth, we show that the world holds greater sway over our minds and hearts than God does. If we shrink from doing difficult things for God, we show that we think him weak, distant, or indifferent.

Moreover, David shows how important it is for Christians to know the truth about God. This points to a great tragedy in the church today, for at the very moment when a host of cultural and spiritual Goliaths are assailing the church, Christians are being told—often from the pulpit—that theology lacks relevance for life! At the very moment when believers most need to use their minds and most require the strength that comes from biblical truth, Christians increasingly do not know their Bibles and churches do not care to teach God's Word. Just as David was assailed by his brother for his God-centered perspective on the Philistine champion, those who call the church to renew a God-centered theology are routinely castigated by fellow Christians for arrogance and meddling.

Yet how are young people today to stand up to the giant temptations facing them and the radical assaults on their faith unless they are solidly established in biblical truth? How many Christians suffer from doubt and fear, thinking of God as unfeeling, uncaring, or disapproving because of their poor spiritual performance, despite the Bible's clear testimony to God's abounding grace and delight for his people in Christ? How few believers are thus able to stand firm in the sure knowledge of God's promised power over sin?

This emphasis on faith and truth is seen in the apostle Paul's teaching about spiritual warfare. Having reminded believers that we face hostile powers in the spiritual realm, Paul urged us to "take up the whole armor of God, that you may be able to withstand in the evil day, and having done all, to stand firm" (Eph. 6:13). Without dwelling in detail on the various pieces of this "armor of God," we can observe that they center on faith in God's Word: "the belt of truth, . . . the breastplate of righteousness, . . . shoes [of] . . . the gospel of peace, . . . the shield of faith, . . . the helmet of salvation, and the sword of the Spirit, which is the word of God" (Eph. 6:14–17). Armed with truth and strengthened by faith, David was able to stand firm against the Philistine giant. Goliath had challenged Israel for a man to fight, and David alone was willing to answer those taunts because he knew his Bible and he knew his God.

Fighting in Faith

Remember the message of chapter 16: "The Lord sees not as man sees: man looks on the outward appearance, but the Lord looks on the heart" (1 Sam. 16:7). In this light, we might view the saga of Goliath as an extended illustration of the 1 Samuel 16:7 principle. The author's description of the Philistine champion is the single most detailed description of any warrior in the Bible. The point was how fearful he appeared, and the question was whether or not God's people would look on him through faith in God.

We should apply this passage by asking: What appearances have the tendency to daunt us and undo our faith? Are we dominated by how others think about us? Are we overcome by circumstances and their apparent effects? Do we shrink from obeying God, refusing sin, and witnessing about Christ, for fear of the giant hostility of the world? Trusting the God we know from the Bible, David challenges us not to cower before the Goliaths we may face, but to stand firm and step forward in the name of the living God and in the power of the Spirit he has sent.

We can approach our challenges with faith, not merely because we have the example of young David, but primarily because we have the saving work of Jesus Christ applied on our behalf. If David was disturbed by the taunts of Goliath, the Son of God was even more distressed over the reign of sin, the discomfort of God's people, and the insult to God's honor through the power of Satan and of sin. Armed with the name of the Lord even more potently than David would be in his battle with Goliath, Jesus struck down our enemies. In going forth without armor, David was offering himself as a sort of sacrifice to Goliath, if that was God's will. Only Jesus could serve as the true sacrifice, however, and it was by the death of God's Son that death itself was defeated.

Speaking of Christ's triumph through the cross and the open tomb, Paul threw the taunts back into the teeth of God's enemies: "'Death is swallowed up in victory.' 'O death, where is your victory? O death, where is your sting?' The sting of death is sin, and the power of sin is the law. But thanks be to God, who gives us the victory through our Lord Jesus Christ" (1 Cor. 15:54–57, quoting Isa. 25:8). David looked on the giant as an unclean foe who surely *would be* vanquished if only someone would step forward, trusting in the Lord. But we look on Satan, sin, and death as enemies that *have been* defeated by the conquering triumph of Jesus in his death and resurrection. As God's people believe these gospel truths, the Goliaths of our time will not fail to have godly men and women to fight them in the power of God that will fell the giants even today.

25

KING SAUL'S ARMOR

1 Samuel 17:31—40

*David strapped his sword over his armor. And he tried in vain
to go, for he had not tested them. Then David said to Saul, "I
cannot go with these, for I have not tested them." So David put
them off.* (1 Sam. 17:39)

efore Goliath, there was King Saul. That is, before going forth
to fight the giant Philistine, David first had to overcome
his own lethargic and unbelieving king. Saul was, after all,
Israel's Goliath: the tall and impressive champion, the one whose prowess
would gain the nation victory. But Saul had been bested by the taller Philistine, and now he was cowering in fear. So just as David first had to pass
through the gauntlet of his older brother's scorn (1 Sam. 17:28), he also had
to stand before the king's cynicism to get a shot at felling Goliath. So it is
that those who would fight the Lord's enemies must often first overcome
the doubt and skepticism of family and friends.

Much was at stake as David answered the summons to appear before
King Saul. Israel's army trembled before the uncircumcised Philistine, and
it seemed that not even one man of faith would defend the Lord's honor.
Were God's promises for Israel suddenly overthrown? Was this hostile power

too great for Israel's covenant Lord? David answered with a resounding "No!"—but first he had to persuade King Saul that there really was a champion in Israel.

Saul had heard of David's outrage over the Philistine's defiance and sent a summons for David to come before him. Up strode a youth not even dressed for battle, clothed as a shepherd straight from the fields. Yet it seems that his zeal and confidence overcame his appearance. It was David who spoke first, the true anointed leader respectfully brushing aside protocol as he addressed the failed ruler. Approaching the king, David assured him, "Let no man's heart fail because of him. Your servant will go and fight with this Philistine" (1 Sam. 17:32). Matthew Henry sums up the scene: "A little shepherd, come but this morning from keeping sheep, has more courage than all the mighty men of Israel."[1]

DAVID'S READINESS FOR BATTLE

David might have courage, but he still needed the king's approval before facing the Philistine giant. Yet Saul was not impressed with what he saw: "You are not able to go against this Philistine to fight with him, for you are but a youth, and he has been a man of war from his youth" (1 Sam. 17:33). To Saul, quite understandably, the idea of this young shepherd dueling with Goliath was preposterous. Saul may or may not have recognized David as the harpist whose playing had soothed his soul, but the battlefield was a different venue from the throne room, and David's boasting was just wasting the king's time.[2]

First, David must face the question of his readiness for battle. Saul declared him obviously unqualified. David could not fight Goliath, since a boy cannot do a man's job—and fighting Goliath was definitely a man's job. Reading ahead, we realize that Saul expresses the very same opinion that Goliath will state later, looking on David as a runt of a youth (1 Sam. 17:42–43). Saul and Goliath have much in common, including an ungodly way of seeing that looks only at appearances. The giant relied on his appearance to

1. Matthew Henry, *Commentary on the Whole Bible*, 6 vols. (Peabody, MA: Hendrickson, 1992), 2:293.
2. Saul's question to Abner in 1 Samuel 17:55–56 is often taken to mean that Saul did not recognize David. But the question was not "Who is he?" but "Whose son is this youth?"—which does not necessarily mean that Saul did not recognize David.

frighten his enemies into submission. Saul looked on David's appearance, seeing anything except a warrior champion. "David does not *look* the part of a hero, and so he must not *be* one."[3] Old habits die hard, and Saul was simply unable to look deeper than the outward appearance, seeing nothing of David's heart.

David, respectful in his demeanor before the king, nonetheless disputed this poor assessment of his fitness. He asserted that his experience as a shepherd was undervalued when it came to preparing him for battle. "David said to Saul, 'Your servant used to keep sheep for his father. And when there came a lion, or a bear, and took a lamb from the flock, I went after him and struck him and delivered it out of his mouth. And if he arose against me, I caught him by his beard and struck him and killed him. Your servant has struck down both lions and bears'" (1 Sam. 17:34–36). Whether the lion or bear had sought to steal off with one of David's sheep or whether the animal turned on the shepherd to seek his life, he had struck the beast and delivered the sheep back to safety.

Many people fail to learn lessons from their experience, or even learn the wrong lessons, so it matters how we reflect on our past actions. David might have come away from his experiences with an arrogant overconfidence in himself. At first it may seem that he is speaking this way, saying, "Goliath is no different from the lions and bears I have fought. I can whip him just as I slew them." But that was not David's attitude: he had learned to trust not in himself but in the Lord. True, David thought of the Philistine warrior as little more than a beast—he said that "this uncircumcised Philistine shall be like one of them" (1 Sam. 17:36). But he had realized in defending his father's sheep that it was God who was with him, protected him, and gave him success in the fight. This is the lesson that David applies to this new challenge: "The LORD who delivered me from the paw of the lion and from the paw of the bear will deliver me from the hand of this Philistine" (17:37).

David shows how we should use our past experiences of God's faithfulness to embolden us in faith for the future. Dale Ralph Davis comments: "Looking back in faith enables him to look forward in faith . . . What Yahweh

3. Richard D. Phillips, *The Heart of an Executive: Lessons on Leadership from the Life of King David* (New York: Doubleday, 1999), 60.

has done in the wilderness of Judah he will do in the Valley of Elah."[4] This is how our Bible study should fortify our faith: not only do we look to what God has done for us personally, but we see in Scripture how faithful he was to deliver his people time and again, against the most extreme dangers, and we are emboldened to trust the Lord for our own battles in his name.

David's readiness to fight Goliath stemmed from his past experience in fighting, but it consisted of his certainty of God's power and willingness to save him against his ungodly foe. Here is David's gospel message for unbelieving King Saul: "The LORD who delivered me from the paw of the lion and from the paw of the bear will deliver me from the hand of this Philistine" (1 Sam. 17:37). A. W. Pink comments: "The language used by [David] in the presence of the king was not the bravado of a boaster, but the God-honoring testimony of a man of faith."[5]

While Saul languished in despair, looking on the situation only through its appearances, David gazed on the giant with the eye of faith and the lens of his own experience as it validated the testimony of the Scriptures. David's experience taught him to believe the old stories of God's mighty deliverance—stories that Saul had forgotten or disregarded. David saw things theologically, from God's perspective, and his faith made him ready to face the giant in battle. A similar perspective on our situations, and a confidence in the Lord based on his proven faithfulness in our own lives, will prepare us to stand firm in battle against the spiritual enemies of tomorrow.

Along with David's faith, one more feature showed his readiness to fight the Lord's battles. To see this, we need to return to Saul's initial scorn: "you are but a youth" (1 Sam. 17:33). Saul dismissed David because of his weakness, but this weakness, coupled with great faith, especially readied David to stand against God's enemy. Perhaps it was because David was the youngest of many brothers, the overlooked one sent out to tend the sheep, that he had turned to the Lord for his hope and salvation. Being the least significant member of his family and possessing few privileges, David had come to realize that he needed a Savior. This awareness drove him to faith, and paradoxically, his weakness ended up making him strong. K. Scott Oliphint writes:

4. Dale Ralph Davis, *1 Samuel: Looking on the Heart* (Fearn, Ross-shire, UK: Christian Focus, 2000), 150–51.

5. A. W. Pink, *A Life of David*, 2 vols. (Grand Rapids: Baker, 1981), 1:35.

So it is with us. If we ever think that we are capable, in and of ourselves, to fight the Lord's battle, we lose the battle altogether. The Lord uses the weak in the world to shame the strong: he uses the simple to confound the strong and mighty. He does that, as Paul reminds us, so that no one will have occasion to boast. (1 Corinthians 1:27–29)[6]

DAVID'S REASONS FOR BATTLE

If we wish to fight in the Lord's battle today, it is not sufficient for us to be ready. We must also enter the fight for the right reasons. Just as David differed from King Saul in his readiness—David was qualified to fight by his faith, not by his stature—the shepherd-youth also differed from Saul in his reasoning about fighting the Philistine. David makes his reasoning clear: "This uncircumcised Philistine . . . has defied the armies of the living God" (1 Sam. 17:36).

The first reason that David stepped forward to fight the Philistine was his outrage over an idolatrous pagan's defiance toward the true and living God. In other words, David was motivated by a zealous concern for God's glory and honor. David was awestruck by Goliath, but for a different reason from everyone else: David was stupefied not that someone could be so big, but that the uncircumcised Philistine could so defy the glory of God! Moreover, the giant had challenged Israel's faith in the Lord, as if God's people would be more impressed by fear of Goliath than by fear of God. This was an outrage, an affront to God's honor, a smear on Israel's covenant name, and a cause that the Lord would surely take up himself as David put the Philistine in his place, namely, in the grave. Thus, when David finally stood before the giant, his challenge rang with passion for God's glory: "You come to me with a sword and with a spear and with a javelin, but I come to you in the name of the LORD of hosts, the God of the armies of Israel, whom you have defied" (1 Sam. 17:45).

Notice that David made no mention to Saul about the great treasure that the king had offered anyone who would strike down the giant. In light of David's outraged concern over God's honor, the rewards of vast treasures, a royal marriage, and family privileges simply had no hold on his mind. Even now, before the king, there is no "by the way" reminder of Saul's promised

6. K. Scott Oliphint, *The Battle Belongs to the Lord* (Phillipsburg, NJ: P&R Publishing, 2003), 11.

reward. This battle simply was not about David: his concern was neither for his safety nor for his later advancement. "Goliath's challenge was a challenge to the glory and power and honor of the Lord of hosts,"[7] and for that reason alone David was determined to slay the defiant enemy and see God's glory properly restored.

This is God's own first motivation in our salvation: to display the glory of his grace. Paul writes that God "predestined us for adoption as sons through Jesus Christ, according to the purpose of his will, to the praise of his glorious grace, with which he has blessed us in the Beloved" (Eph. 1:5–6). We are redeemed from our sins, Paul adds, "so that we . . . might be to the praise of his glory" (Eph. 1:12). It is a comforting thought that the first and primary purpose of our salvation is God's glory, because the glory of God is a cause in which we can believe! Just as "man's chief end is to glorify God,"[8] so also the chief end of God is his own glory, and we who have looked in faith to Christ may be confident of our ultimate salvation because it is to the praise of God's marvelous grace. As Martyn Lloyd-Jones said:

> The whole purpose of your salvation and mine is that we should glorify the Father. . . . People come and talk to me, and it is generally put in that way: "What will salvation do for me?" they ask. And the answer that is given so often in our evangelism is, "Believe the gospel, and it will do some marvelous things for you." I say, thank God that that is true, but, my dear friends, we should not put that first. The ultimate aim and object of our salvation is that we may glorify God. . . . The essence of salvation is to bring us into the state in which we do glorify God.[9]

Notice, therefore, that while David was distressed over Israel's cowardice, he gave no sign of seeking that Israel would be glorified through his victory. So also in our spiritual labor, we should be motivated not for personal gain, or for the prestige of our church or our theological position, or even for the reputation of Christians in general. We fight for God's truth because those who defy the Word of God are an affront to God's glory. We fight to defend God's name and to pursue his glory in the world. Waging war for this reason, we can be as confident as David of God's Goliath-slaying power.

7. Ibid., 8.
8. Westminster Shorter Catechism, answer 1.
9. D. Martyn Lloyd-Jones, *Saved in Eternity* (Wheaton, IL: Crossway, 1988), 44–45.

Another reason David sought to fight was to deliver God's people from danger. He was a shepherd, after all, and God's flock was intimidated, disgraced, and about to be ravaged. Goliath was a bear from whose mouth God's lambs needed to be set free. If the foe turned to fight, he would have to be slain. Finally, we may add David's full confidence in God's deliverance—"The LORD . . . will deliver me from the hand of this Philistine" (1 Sam. 17:37)—as his final reason for entering the battle. We likewise should step forward in battle today with a primary motivation of defending God's honor, while also desiring to defend God's people and counting fully on God's faithfulness and power to save.

DAVID'S RESOURCES FOR BATTLE

It is difficult to state that Saul believed David's message of faith, for if the king had really believed, he would have gone out to face Goliath himself. True and saving faith believes in God's grace for ourselves and not merely for others! More accurately, Saul was impressed with David's passion and resolve: "Saul said to David, 'Go, and the LORD be with you!' " (1 Sam. 17:37). This statement is loaded with irony, since the Lord had already departed Saul in order to be with David. Saul desired the Lord's presence and blessing for *someone* who would fight Goliath, but his heart was too hardened to repent and seek the Lord himself. Saul reminds us that biblical religion offers God's saving grace only through personal faith and repentance: the true and living God does not sell indulgences through third-party vendors! The Lord was already with David because of the faith that he had proclaimed to Saul—a faith that Saul admired in David but rejected for himself.

As will often be the case with unbelievers who seek to benefit from the faith of others, Saul then offered to be an investor in David's saving enterprise. In verses that are dripping with symbolic and spiritual irony, the king offered to send David into battle wearing his own armor: "Saul clothed David with his armor. He put a helmet of bronze on his head and clothed him with a coat of mail, and David strapped his sword over his armor" (1 Sam. 17:38–39).

We might view this action in a number of ways. Ronald Youngblood suggests that Saul was trying to take credit for David's valorous feat. He writes that the king's action was "probably calculated to so bind Saul to David that Saul would be able to take credit for, or at least share in, David's

297

victory over the Philistine giant."[10] Alternatively, John Woodhouse sees "a symbolism to this act that corresponded to the truth that we already know. Saul was the king on the way out. David was his designated replacement."[11] However true these assessments may be, I think the basic reality was that Saul was conveying goodwill to David and providing his help, but in a way that expressed his own reliance on worldly strength. We might depict Saul's offer in these words: "Here, let me help you . . . Let me give you *my* seal of authority—discredited though it is. Take *my* weapons—useless as they have shown themselves. Go forth in *my* name—though it is a curse on the lips of every man in the army."[12]

What is amazing is that David began to put Saul's armor on. Over David's torso went Saul's heavy armor. On David's head went Saul's bronze helmet. Strapped to David's side was Saul's heavy sword. What a picture David made: a Saul in miniature! This was a defining moment in the young shepherd's life. Would he step into the persona, unbelief, and worldly reliance of King Saul? There could be only one answer: "David said to Saul, 'I cannot go with these, for I have not tested them.' So David put them off" (1 Sam. 17:39). David's formal reason for removing the armor was that he could not fight in gear with which he was unpracticed. But this cannot be the only or even the main reason for David's polite refusal. Pink explains: "David quickly perceived that such was unsuited to him: the one who has much to do with God in secret cannot employ worldly means and methods in public; the man of faith has no use for carnal weapons."[13]

We should probably consider the offer of Saul's armor as one of the greatest trials of David's faith. The sight of Goliath did not daunt the young hero: he knew how God would handle a blaspheming Philistine, just like a bear or lion seeking after God's sheep. But by far the more subtle temptation was the offer to step into the shoes—that is, the armor—of the disgraced king. David's faith knew how to say "Yes" to a daunting challenge: it was equally important that his faith knew how to say "No" to worldly compromise and unbelieving help.

10. Ronald F. Youngblood, *1 & 2 Samuel*, Expositor's Bible Commentary, vol. 3 (Grand Rapids: Zondervan, 1992), 700.
11. John Woodhouse, *1 Samuel: Looking for a Leader* (Wheaton, IL: Crossway, 2008), 332.
12. Phillips, *Heart of an Executive*, 63.
13. Pink, *Life of David*, 1:36.

Divested of Saul's armor, David turned to face the Philistine giant: "Then he took his staff in his hand and chose five smooth stones from the brook and put them in his shepherd's pouch. His sling was in his hand, and he approached the Philistine" (1 Sam. 17:40). But it was not with these only that David went forth to fight Goliath: "He went to the conflict with a blazing concern for the honour of God, with confidence in the certainty of his promises and with the power of the Spirit of God."[14] David advanced against the Philistine not in the armor and identity of "a king . . . like all the nations," which Saul was (1 Sam. 8:5), relying on nothing really different from the armor and weaponry of evil Goliath, but as a shepherd-servant of the Lord, defending God's honor and protecting God's people in the power of the Lord himself. In this way, whether he realized it or not, David identified with God's great champions of prior years, shepherd-leaders such as Abraham, Isaac, Jacob, and Moses, men of spiritual valor who lived and fought by faith in the promises of God.

Reflecting on this vital turning point in his life, we cannot help but think of psalms that David penned, probably later in life. Was David thinking back on this event as he wrote the words of Psalm 3, or might David have had this prayer in his heart as he turned from Saul, leaving behind the armor, and turned to slay Goliath?

> O LORD, how many are my foes!
>   Many are rising against me;
> many are saying of my soul,
>   there is no salvation for him in God.
> But you, O LORD, are a shield about me,
>   my glory, and the lifter of my head. (Ps. 3:1–3).

THE ARMOR OF SAUL TODAY

How does the interplay between Saul and David translate to the battles of our time? What weapons of the world are Christians and churches tempted to employ in our attempt to beat back the advance of darkness, worldly unbelief, sin, and evil? The answer does not stretch our imaginations. The Sauls of

14. Roger Ellsworth, *The Shepherd King: Learning from the Life of David* (Darlington, UK: Evangelical Press, 1998), 31.

today urge Christians of the need to seize political power, so that believers can install godly laws with the same worldly power used by unbelievers to advance their secular agenda. Godly laws are greatly to be desired, yet the kingdom of Christ does not advance through secular legislation. Others would insist that preachers must embrace the advertising prowess of Madison Avenue, creating celebrity speakers whose messages are crafted with data from surveys designed to tickle the ear. Other Sauls will turn to the electricity of Hollywood entertainment, urging the church to recast sacred worship as worldly entertainment and to replace the preaching of God's Word with video clips and skits.

Behind each of these well-meant suggestions—just as Saul's armor was offered with goodwill—is the conviction that the battle must be won by the strength of our own hands. Goliath is mighty and terrible. He has lawyers, so the church must hire its own. Goliath is served by political action committees, so the army of God must send its legions to Washington, DC. The Philistine is able to recruit large numbers by offering desired goods and services, so we must make use of the same marketing data to enlist an army of our own. The worldly advance is fueled by sensual thrills, so the church must fight back amplifier for amplifier and emotional high for emotional high.

What would David say if he surveyed the spiritual challenge facing Christians today? Would he say that God's church must conform its message and methods to match the weapons of the world? Surely David would challenge the assumption that Goliath must be slain with our own power. Surely he would answer, as he declared to Goliath himself, "You come to me with a sword and with a spear and with a javelin, but I come to you in the name of the LORD of hosts, the God of the armies of Israel, whom you have defied. . . . The LORD saves not with sword and spear. For the battle is the LORD's, and he will give you into our hand" (1 Sam. 17:45, 47).

If the battle is the Lord's, what are the weapons with which God would have his people step forward into battle? The apostle Paul answered, pointing to the Word of God: "For though we walk in the flesh, we are not waging war according to the flesh. For the weapons of our warfare are not of the flesh but have divine power to destroy strongholds. We destroy arguments and every lofty opinion raised against the knowledge of God, and take every thought captive to obey Christ" (2 Cor. 10:3–5). Coupled with God's Word is the power of prayer. Paul writes of spiritual warfare:

"Take the helmet of salvation, and the sword of the Spirit, which is the word of God, praying at all times in the Spirit, with all prayer and supplication" (Eph. 6:17–18).

This is precisely how God's champions have shaken the world and cast down strongholds in generations past. John Calvin stood in Geneva's pulpit with a Bible alone, and God raised up a new Jerusalem for the Reformation. John Knox prayed, and Mary, Queen of Scots, trembled. William Wilberforce stood fast on biblical truth before the assembled powers of political calculation and commerce, and God used him to break the slave trade in England. Like the heroes who have gone before us, and like David departing from Saul to face giant Goliath, our great need today is simply faith: faith in God's Word, faith in God's grace to answer prayer, faith in God's power to uphold his people and preserve the honor of his name, and faith that the battle belongs to the Lord and must be fought with his weapons. Oliphint writes: "What is needed in the Lord's battle are weapons that will cause people to bow down, to bend the knee and acknowledge that the Lord, and he alone, is God. Only supernatural weapons can accomplish that task." With our eyes fixed on God's power and our aim directed to God's glory, "we will not use the weapons of the world. We will fight, if we fight the Lord's battle, with his weapons. And the chief weapon that he has given to us is his sword, the Word of God itself."[15]

This principle applies to our personal lives as well. What are analogies to Saul's armor for us as individuals? Perhaps success, material affluence, worldly stature, and popular approval. Do we trust in these for our security, happiness, and blessing? The reality is that only with God's Word and with prayer can we possess blessing, joy, strength of heart, and peace of mind. We do not need worldly success in order to persevere in life with blessing, but we absolutely need God's Word and prayer, wielded by faith.

In the end, if we fight in God's battles using God's weapons, relying on God's faithfulness and seeking to exalt God's glory, we will have the satisfaction of hearing the cheers and appreciation of heaven itself. This is what we find in the book of Revelation, where the conquest of God's enemies is celebrated, through the valiant warfare of God's people: "they have conquered him by the blood of the Lamb and by the word of their testimony, for they

15. Oliphint, *The Battle Belongs to the Lord*, 13.

loved not their lives even unto death. Therefore, rejoice, O heavens and you who dwell in them!" (Rev. 12:11–12).

THE BATTLE BELONGS TO THE LORD

We cannot reflect on David's heroism without realizing that his example points us forward to the coming of God's true champion, the royal Savior of the house of David, God's Son, Jesus Christ. From the earliest days of the church, God's people have seen David's victory over Goliath as a picture of our deliverance from Satan and the bonds of sin and hell. Caesarius of Arles wrote in the sixth century A.D.: "All that we read prefigured in David at that time, dearly beloved, we know was accomplished in our Lord Jesus Christ; for he strangled the lion and the bear when he descended into hell to free all the saints from their jaws."[16]

Like David, Jesus had his readiness to serve as Messiah doubted by those who noted his lack of earthly stature or worldly power. Pontius Pilate spoke for many when he incredulously asked, "Are you the king of the Jews?" (John 18:33). Jesus answered, "My kingdom is not of this world" (18:36). Jesus' fitness to save had been expressed in his prayer to the Father the previous night: "I glorified you on earth, having accomplished the work that you gave me to do" (17:4).

Like David, Jesus had a reason for battle that the world did not understand. Jesus prayed, "Father, the hour has come; glorify your Son that the Son may glorify you, since you have given him authority over all flesh, to give eternal life to all whom you have given him" (John 17:1–2).

Finally, like David, Jesus conquered Satan, sin, and death with resources that are not of this world. Peter explained, "You were ransomed . . . not with perishable things such as silver or gold, but with the precious blood of Christ, like that of a lamb without blemish or spot" (1 Peter 1:18–19). Jesus wages war today, throwing back darkness and gathering his flock with the power of God in his Word. He comes not as an earthly king but as a Shepherd-Savior. "I am the good shepherd," he declares. "My sheep hear my voice, and I know them, and they follow me. I give them eternal life, and they will never

---

16. Caesarius of Arles, Sermon 121.4, in *Joshua, Judges, Ruth, 1–2 Samuel*, ed. John R. Franke, Ancient Christian Commentary on Scripture, Old Testament vol. 4 (Downers Grove, IL: InterVarsity Press, 2005), 271.

perish, and no one will snatch them out of my hand" (John 10:14, 27–28). Jesus still wages war today, as John saw him in the book of Revelation: "In his right hand he held seven stars, from his mouth came a sharp two-edged sword, and his face was like the sun shining in full strength" (Rev. 1:16).

Do we need the armor of Saul or the weapons of the world with so great a Savior at our head? If the battle is the Lord's, do we need any weapons except those he places into our hands, strengthened by grace through faith? Readied by faith in him, fighting by reason of his glory, and armed with the resources of heaven's armory, we will surely succeed as the Lord grants us to stand and to advance.

> Fierce may be the conflict, strong may be the foe,
> But the King's own army none can overthrow;
> Round his standard ranging, vict'ry is secure;
> For his truth unchanging makes the triumph sure.
> Joyfully enlisting by thy grace divine,
> We are on the Lord's side, Savior, we are thine.[17]

---

17. Frances R. Havergal, "Who Is on the Lord's Side?" (1877).

26

In the Name of the Lord

1 Samuel 17:41–54

You come to me with a sword and with a spear and with a
javelin, but I come to you in the name of the Lord of hosts,
the God of the armies of Israel, whom you have defied.
(1 Sam. 17:45)

he story of David's victory over Goliath has launched many
five-point sermons, one point for each of the smooth stones
that David took from the brook and put into his pouch. Usually these sermons list principles or behaviors by which even the skinniest
Christian can take down the brawniest spiritual enemy.

David's victory, however, was anything but the triumph of an "every-
man." David was not just anyone in Israel, but the one man whom God
had specially anointed to lead and deliver his people, for which God had
equipped him with the Holy Spirit (see 1 Sam. 16:13). Thus, when David
declared to the giant, "I come to you in the name of the Lord of hosts"
(17:45), he meant in part that he came as God's specially anointed deliverer.
This reminds us that David's gospel—his message of salvation—was not
merely the good news that those who trust in the Lord will be saved. His
good news also declared that those who trust in the Lord will be saved by

the Anointed One—the Messiah—that God has promised. In the Valley of Elah, this anointed deliverer was none other than young David, and it was through his arm that God revealed his power in slaying the giant Philistine.

The message for Israel's army, therefore, did not consist in what each of them should and could have done. True, they should have defended God's honor and they could have triumphed had they acted in David's bold faith. The problem was that they lacked the Holy Spirit, whereas David had been filled with the Spirit at his anointing. In the reality of their weakness and sin, the message for the people of Israel was that they needed a Savior, which God provided by the man after his own heart. On the heels of David's victory, following as his disciples, we might say, the Israelites rose up and slew the enemy host. David's victory points to our need of a champion, as we face the greater foes of sin and death. For this, David typifies the true and greater Messiah, God's Son, Jesus Christ, of the house of David, in whose power we may enter the victory he has won by God's grace.

Going Forth in the Lord's Name

After gaining King Saul's blessing to go forth as Israel's champion, David took five smooth stones and with sling in hand approached the giant Goliath. The Philistine had been coming out twice a day for forty days, challenging Israel to single combat, so we might think he would be relieved that someone had finally answered. But seeing only a youth, with a staff and sling, Goliath was infuriated with the greatest contempt. Like King Saul before him, Goliath looked only on the outward appearance, not considering the heart: "He disdained him, for he was but a youth, ruddy and handsome in appearance" (1 Sam. 17:42). The battle-hardened Philistine "sought a warrior to fight with; he gets a boy to annihilate."[1] Moreover, David's meager weaponry insulted Goliath: "Am I a dog," he jeered, "that you come to me with sticks?" (1 Sam. 17:43). The giant then cursed David by his gods, promising to skewer him and leave his body as scavenger-fodder: "Come to me, and I will give your flesh to the birds of the air and to the beasts of the field" (17:44). We see in Goliath the literal fulfillment of Proverbs 16:18, that "pride goes before destruction, and a haughty spirit before a fall."

---

1. William G. Blaikie, *Expository Lectures on the Book of First Samuel* (1887; repr., Birmingham, AL: Solid Ground, 2005), 286.

Undaunted, David not only approached the menacing giant, but gave one of the classic speeches in all the Bible, one that rebuked the Philistine for his mocking, expressed David's confidence in the Lord's power to save, and announced his purpose in slaying the giant champion.

First, David rebuked the giant for his blasphemies against the true God: "David said to the Philistine, 'You come to me with a sword and with a spear and with a javelin, but I come to you in the name of the Lord of hosts, the God of the armies of Israel, whom you have defied'" (1 Sam. 17:45). In short, David was pronouncing sentence on Goliath for the capital crime of blasphemy: "This day the Lord will deliver you into my hand, and I will strike you down and cut off your head" (17:46). Goliath might think that he could blaspheme the true God, but David had come on God's behalf to inform him otherwise. Leviticus 24:16 ordained the penalty of death by stoning for blasphemy, and David had come to single-handedly enforce that censure.

Even more notably, David expressed his confidence in the Lord to deliver him in this battle. Goliath had impressive weapons as Philistines saw such things—a sword, a spear, and a javelin. But an Israelite who looked with the eyes of faith was not impressed: these were hardly weapons with which to stand against the Lord. Disdaining all such mighty weapons, David expressed his full confidence in "the name of the Lord of hosts, the God of the armies of Israel" (1 Sam. 17:45). By referring to the Lord's "name," David spoke of God's character and being. We grasp David's idea when we consider the Aaronic blessing that the priests regularly invoked over Israel: "The Lord bless you and keep you; the Lord make his face to shine upon you and be gracious to you; the Lord lift up his countenance upon you and give you peace" (Num. 6:24–26). When God first gave this blessing, he said, "So shall they put my name upon the people of Israel, and I will bless them" (6:27). To bear God's name, therefore, is to live under his blessing, which includes his promise to "keep" his people from their foes.

In proclaiming the Lord's name, David was invoking God's promise to protect those who trust in him, a blessing that David considered a mighty armament in the face of Goliath's mere bronze and iron. Robert Bergen comments: "As David viewed it, Goliath was outnumbered and would soon be overpowered, for the Lord would fight with David against the giant."[2]

---

2. Robert D. Bergen, *1, 2 Samuel*, New American Commentary (Nashville: Broadman & Holman, 1996), 196.

David's expression "the LORD of hosts, the God of the armies of Israel" (1 Sam. 17:45), recalls God's command of the legions of heaven and God's past demonstrations of power to overthrow his enemies. The God who parted the Red Sea for the Israelites under Moses, swallowing the host of Pharaoh, would overwhelm one Philistine giant easily enough. So certain was David of victory over Goliath that he vowed to cut off the giant's head with a sword, even though the only sword was in the hand of the Philistine: "This day the LORD will deliver you into my hand, and I will strike you down and cut off your head" (17:46).

In our battle with the greater powers of sin, death, and other spiritual enemies, Christians are likewise to rely on the name of the Lord in the place of worldly weapons. Paul described Christians as those who "worship by the Spirit of God and glory in Christ Jesus and put no confidence in the flesh" (Phil. 3:3). This means that we have laid aside every worldly merit in claiming God's favor. Paul looked upon his attitude before embracing Christ and recalled how he had once relied on the merits of his lineage, his covenant membership, his ritual performance of religion, and his persecution of the first Christians. Looking at himself as a kind of spiritual Goliath, Paul repented so as to declare that "whatever gain I had, I counted as loss for the sake of Christ. Indeed, I count everything as loss because of the surpassing worth of knowing Christ Jesus my Lord . . . , not having a righteousness of my own that comes from the law, but that which comes through faith in Christ, the righteousness from God that depends on faith" (Phil. 3:7–9). Paul renounced all the weaponry of self-righteousness before God and instead trusted in the name of the Lord, that is, in the promised salvation by grace that comes through faith in Christ.

THAT ALL MAY KNOW

David's proclamation of Israel's salvation to Goliath was matched in importance by the following statements, which convey his purpose and goal in standing forth to slay Goliath. David had multiple goals in defeating the giant, the first of which was evangelistic. David wanted all the world to know about Israel's God: "I will give the dead bodies of the host of the Philistines this day to the birds of the air and to the wild beasts of the earth, that all the earth may know that there is a God in Israel" (1 Sam. 17:46).

David had good news to spread. The famous God who had delivered Israel so many times in the past with such great displays of power was still present with his people to deliver them from defeat. The further good news was that in the person of David, an anointed king had come who would bear the name of the Lord against the enemies of God's people. The bad news for Goliath was that, as the mocking defier of the Lord and the satanic enemy bent on Israel's destruction, he would be slaughtered and disgraced at the hand of the Lord's anointed. The aim of this gospel call was to summon the nations to cease their foolish violence against Israel and their defiance against Israel's God, lest they, too, should suffer God's just verdict and the judgment of death. Walter Brueggemann summarizes: "The purpose of David's victory is not simply to save Israel or defeat the Philistines. The purpose is the glorification of Yahweh in the eyes of the world."[3]

David's slaying of Goliath was intended to have a message for Israel as well: "that all this assembly may know that the LORD saves not with sword and spear. For the battle is the LORD's, and he will give you into our hand" (1 Sam. 17:47). Despite his youth, David understood his times. He knew that the people of Israel had sought for Saul to be king because they were seeking after tangible, worldly sources of salvation. Israel had wanted "a king . . . like all the nations" because Israel itself wanted to be like the nations—at least when it came to salvation. The Israelites wanted to hold sharp iron in their own hands and look up to see their own tall king before them. These idols had failed Israel miserably in the Valley of Elah, as idols must always fail God's people when they turn from the salvation of the Lord and reliance on his holy methods. The Lord wanted his people to rely not on having the best of weaponry, but on having the best of Saviors. Likewise, he wants his church to succeed today through humble, holy methods by which only he can be praised. The prophet Jeremiah would sum up the one principle that David sought to demonstrate before Israel and the nations:

> Let not the wise man boast in his wisdom, let not the mighty man boast in his might, let not the rich man boast in his riches, but let him who boasts boast in this, that he understands and knows me, that I am the LORD who

3. Walter Brueggemann, *First and Second Samuel*, Interpretation (Louisville: John Knox, 1990), 132.

practices steadfast love, justice, and righteousness in the earth. For in these things I delight, declares the LORD. (Jer. 9:23–24)

In this way, David was calling Israel "away from its imitation of the nations," even as he called "the nations away from their foolish defiance of Yahweh."[4]

The Head of Goliath

The battle itself between David and Goliath was so brief as hardly to be worth the admission price. The main action had in fact been David's speech: the felling of the giant was merely a necessary but inevitable conclusion.

After David's words, Goliath began his ponderous advance on the Israelite youth. Yet David, being lightly equipped, moved quickly toward the Philistine. Without further ado, "David put his hand in his bag and took out a stone and slung it and struck the Philistine on his forehead" (1 Sam. 17:49).

David wielded a deadly weapon. After whirring the sling around his head, David released one loop and sent a tennis-ball-sized stone—two to three inches in diameter—at a speed ranging from 100 to 150 miles an hour at the Philistine. David's weapon might not have inspired fear, but it certainly rained death! With the accuracy that came with long practice and a hand calmed by faith, David's stone sped toward Goliath and struck him in the forehead, blasting its way past the bronze helmet the Philistine wore: "The stone sank into his forehead, and he fell on his face to the ground" (1 Sam. 17:49). The narrator's comment is as brief and direct as was the battle itself: "So David prevailed over the Philistine with a sling and with a stone, and struck the Philistine and killed him." Of special note is the absence of any heavy weaponry: "There was no sword in the hand of David" (17:50). Goliath was almost certainly dead before his great bulk smashed against the ground. But just in case, David sprang forward, drew the Philistine's sword, and immediately hacked off the giant's head.

Reading this, we realize that Goliath really did not have David outweaponed, for in this kind of fight David's sling conveyed to the youth an actual

4. Ibid.

advantage. As long as David could make the shot, he should have slain the ponderous infantryman. So it has often been when Christians have faced the weapons of the world. Believers quail at the thought of wrongful arrest at the hands of wicked governments. But Christians under persecution have learned not to fear such mere worldly reprisals. This has been the recent experience of the house churches in China, whose Christians think little of facing arrest and imprisonment, happily pitting against their secular enemies the power of prayer and the preaching of God's invincible Word. Like the weapon of David in his battle with Goliath, the weapons that God has given the church are actually more potent than the weapons wielded by our unbelieving, worldly foes. Even more important than the relative potency of our weapons, those who trust in the Lord have the power of God on their side: it was God's hand that truly wielded David's sling and gave it unerring accuracy. Dale Ralph Davis comments: "What matters is not whether you have the best weapons but whether you have the real God."[5] With this in mind, we see that David's victory was as unsurprising as he declared it to be inevitable.

Likewise, Christians who enter into spiritual battle trusting the Lord are armed with divine equipping. Paul described the "whole armor of God" (Eph. 6:13) as consisting of the belt of truth, the breastplate of righteousness, shoes made fleet by the gospel, the shield of faith, the helmet of salvation, and the sword of the Spirit, which is the word of God (6:14–17), along with the mighty resource of prayer. Perhaps more important than the details is the overall impression: we are protected by our salvation in Christ, with our head and chest strongly guarded, and we wield faith to block arrows and the Word of God to strike and smite our foes, held together with truth and made as agile as young David by our gospel good news. Christians thus armed, who know and trust the saving power of our Lord, not seeking worldly armor and weaponry, are fully equipped for spiritual battle and able to see many victories by the power of God.

So it was in the Valley of Elah, for when David displayed Goliath's severed head, the shocked Philistine army rose up and fled in panic. The Israelites, suddenly energized by the triumph of their unlikely champion, also rose up and pursued the fleeing enemy, strewing the paths between Elah and

5. Dale Ralph Davis, *1 Samuel: Looking on the Heart* (Fearn, Ross-shire, UK: Christian Focus, 2000), 153.

the Philistine cities with enemy bodies. Then they returned to plunder the enemy camp.

David, curiously, left the pursuit to the other soldiers. In an action that has puzzled commentators, "David took the head of the Philistine and brought it to Jerusalem, but he put his armor in his tent" (1 Sam. 17:54). We are so accustomed to the name of Jerusalem that we may not realize that this fortress city was not yet in Israel's hands. It had been given by Joshua for both the tribes of Benjamin and Judah (between which it lay) to conquer and drive out the entrenched Jebusites there. The lingering presence of this Canaanite fortress was an embarrassment to Israel and a sign of the unfulfilled legacy of the original conquest of the Promised Land. David, plainly realizing this, took advantage of his victory over the giant to declare future triumphs that would follow in due time, as Israel once more took up the mantle given by the Lord in earlier days. His declaration of coming destruction to the Canaanites in the fortress on Mount Zion served notice that Israel would be returning in faith to the Lord and that with the Lord its destiny would finally be fulfilled.

So Great a Savior

There are at least two different ways for us to draw conclusions from David's triumph over the giant Goliath. The first, and most important, is to focus our faith in the anointed Savior that God has sent to us in our battles, the true Champion and Messiah, Jesus Christ.

William Blaikie lists a series of comparisons by which we may better see Jesus through the lens of young David. First, "we find an emblematic picture of the conquests of Messiah and His Church." The arrogant disdain of Goliath is the very spirit with which the world opposes the church today: "the contempt shown for the lowly appearance of David, the undisguised scorn at the notion that through such a stripling any deliverance could come to his people, has its counterpart in the feeling towards Christ and His Gospel." Second, the "calm self-possession of David," coupled with a thorough reliance on the faithful intervention of God, mirrors the demeanor of Jesus toward the spiritual enemies of his own day, even as they nailed him to the cross. Third, "the sword of Goliath turned against himself, the weapon by which he was to annihilate his foe, employed by that very foe to sever his head from his body, was an emblem of Satan's weapons turned by Christ against Satan."[6] Hebrews 2:14–15 thus states of Christ: "through death he [destroyed] the one who has the power of death, that is, the devil, and deliver[ed] all those who through fear of death were subject to lifelong slavery."

Furthermore, we see the fourth and vital comparison in that, like David, Jesus waged war against Satan, sin, and death in a representative capacity. David fought not only for himself but for the whole of his people. Likewise, in Christ's triumph his followers gain our salvation, received through faith alone.

Fifth is the salvation joy achieved by God's anointed Savior. Blaikie writes:

> The shout that burst from the rank of Israel and Judah when they saw the champion of the Philistines fall, and the enemy betake themselves in consternation to flight, foreshadowed the joy of redeemed men when the reality of Christ's salvation flashes on their hearts, and they see the enemies that have been harassing them repulsed and scattered—a joy to be immeasurably magnified when all enemies are finally conquered and the loud voice is heard in heaven, "Now is come salvation, and strength, and the kingdom of our God and the power of His Christ, for the accuser of our brethren is cast down, that accused them before our God day and night."[7]

This Is the Victory

Looking upon David's victory in Holy Scripture and knowing the victory already achieved for us by the greater triumph of the cross of Christ, we may look on our future and final salvation with certainty and joy. Knowing ourselves "more than conquerors through him who loved us" (Rom. 8:37), we are all the more eager to follow Jesus, remaining as close as possible to him.

At the same time, we should realize that being joined to Christ in saving faith and having been sealed by the same Holy Spirit that filled young David, we now are anointed by God and equipped to fight in his cause. Thus, we should live with the same confidence that emboldened David in his approach to the Philistine champion, declaring to every foe and temptation: "You

6. Blaikie, *First Samuel*, 289–90.
7. Ibid.

come to me with a sword and with a spear and with a javelin, but I come to you in the name of the LORD of hosts, the God of the armies of Israel, whom you have defied" (1 Sam. 17:45). Through saving faith, the benediction of God now rests on us, and he has promised to keep us from all harm. David's triumph calls for us to know the same power of God available to us in Christ, so that through this same faith we may be strong against our foes.

Meanwhile, David's stated purpose in fighting Goliath supplies us with a noble purpose for our own battles of faith: that God might be glorified among the nations and that God's own people would be strengthened in their faith. David sought "that all the earth may know that there is a God in Israel" (1 Sam. 17:46). We likewise should seek that through our holy lives, joy amid trials, love among believers, and fidelity to truth, the world may know that the cross of Christ is no mere relic of history. We should endeavor to prove to our neighbors and other onlookers that the Christian faith continues to give life, that the spiritual power unleashed in the early church continues to win converts today, and that David's spirit of conquering faith lives on among God's people. Most of all, we desire for many to see that all this is true because the Lord of hosts is truly in our midst, that there is a God in our churches, and that we have a living Savior, Jesus Christ, whose death has won forgiveness and who in undying life continues to reign from heaven. Let this be our goal, and we may go forth into every battle confident in the power of the name of the Lord of hosts.

Furthermore, let us seek to embolden many a disheartened Christian, showing that even in our weakness the Lord remains mighty to save. Instead of fretting over our own well-being, knowing that our eternal safety is secured in Christ, let us seek to strengthen the faith of other believers. Let us seek to make known to other Christian churches that the Word of God remains mighty to convert the lost, build up the saints, and guide the church. Let each of us, through the battles that God places before us, encourage one another, and let us together raise tall the banner under which so many believers have stood before us, knowing that "this is the victory that has overcome the world—our faith" (1 John 5:4).

27

A Covenant of Love

1 Samuel 17:55—18:5

As soon as he had finished speaking to Saul, the soul of
Jonathan was knit to the soul of David, and Jonathan loved him
as his own soul. (1 Sam. 18:1)

Some time ago I saw an interview with a professional golfer who had won his first U.S. Open. He was talking about how this one event had changed his life forever. Suddenly he was known by thousands of people and the product endorsements were rolling in. At the same time, he found his privacy slipping away and his life taking a course all its own.

David's victory over Goliath was like this, only more so. By removing a dire threat to the nation and setting a remarkable example of valor, the shepherd-youth captured the nation's heart with one stone's throw. No longer would he experience the solitary labor of tending his father's sheep; David's pasture would be growing rapidly, bringing both opportunity and danger, joy and sorrow. As is so often the case for those who achieve sudden fame, David found success harder to swallow than hardship. David's great victory did not lead him beside still waters, but lurched him into the rapids of intrigue and deceit.

One immediate result of David's triumph, however, was that it brought him into friendship with Jonathan, King Saul's son and heir apparent to the throne. Jonathan was one of those rare individuals who stand out in their own time. As a fully grown man, Jonathan was quite a bit older than the teenage youth, and as a great hero to the nation he may have been a personal hero to David. Jonathan was a man of courage and vision, whose bold leadership and faith had previously saved the nation (1 Sam. 14:1–23). Perhaps the best result for David of his victory over Goliath was that Jonathan "loved him as his own soul" (18:3) and entered with David into a covenant league of friendship and brotherly love.

Saul's Puzzling Query

Before telling us about Jonathan's love for David, the Bible first reveals a conversation between Saul and his calculating lieutenant, Abner. First Samuel 17:55 takes us back to a time before David's victory, when he was going forth from Saul to meet the Philistine. King Saul "said to Abner, the commander of the army, 'Abner, whose son is this youth?'" (1 Sam. 17:55–58).

Liberal scholars have argued that Saul's question represents a "discrepancy" in the Bible, presenting a second tradition "concerning David's debut at court."[1] They point out that another passage, 1 Samuel 16:18, presents Saul's earlier learning of David and his family background, before his summons to play the lyre. Here, they argue, we have an alternative version about how David first came to Saul's court. The problem with this approach is not only that it has a low view of biblical inspiration, but that this reading is not the best understanding of Saul's question to Abner. Saul did not ask Abner who David was, since David had just presented himself to the king. He asked, "Whose son is this youth?"

Saul had promised high rank to the man who slew the giant Goliath, along with marriage to his daughter, so it is understandable that he would inquire about David's family background and social status. What was David's pedigree and family upbringing? Moreover, if David succeeded, Saul's promised reward would involve David's joining the king's court permanently. This is, in fact, precisely what Saul arranged after David's life-changing victory.

1. Robert P. Gordon, *I & II Samuel: A Commentary*, Library of Biblical Interpretation (Grand Rapids: Zondervan, 1986), 159.

First Samuel 18:2 says that "Saul took him that day and would not let him return to his father's house." Moreover, part of Saul's promised reward was an exemption from taxes for the victor's whole family. All this would require some arrangements with David's father, and it is understandable that Saul could not remember who this was.

Since Abner did not know the answer to Saul's questions, he fetched David to stand before the king. The scene may have been both startling and amusing, since the blood-splattered David was holding Goliath's great head in his hands. Saul offered no word of thanks or praise but only the question, "Whose son are you, young man?" David answered, "I am the son of your servant Jesse the Bethlehemite" (1 Sam. 17:58).

One point in showing this "backstage" conversation between Saul and Abner is to contrast the king's calculating spirit with the warm spiritual fervor of his son Jonathan. First Samuel, like the Bible's historical narratives in general, often makes a point by means of comparison and contrast. Instead of giving David warm thanks and a joyful embrace, Saul sizes David up, looking upon the hero as little more than a piece on a chessboard. How different was his son Jonathan, whose heart burned with a fervent faith, a love for God's people, and a zeal for the Lord's glory. Jonathan's soul, rejoicing in David's victory over Israel's enemy, whom he and Saul's other champions had trembled to face, leapt up at the sight of young David and saw neither a political asset nor a threat but a fellow believer who was worthy of his highest love and devotion.

Jonathan's Shining Spirit

In considering Jonathan's remarkable expression of love for David, we should examine both his attitude and his actions. Concerning his attitude, we first observe the spiritual priorities that governed Jonathan's response. First Samuel 18:1 says that "as soon as [David] had finished speaking to Saul, the soul of Jonathan was knit to the soul of David, and Jonathan loved him as his own soul."

There are several reasons why this was a most unlikely response from someone in Jonathan's position. Saul's son stood in the second position of the kingdom as the royal prince, having well earned his stature and the admiration of the people through his prior faith and valor. Moreover, he and David were of different ages, from different tribes and backgrounds, and with different past experiences. Jonathan would have understandable reasons for resentment and jealousy toward David's sudden rise. In short, while David had much to gain, Jonathan had much to lose. In such situations, it is common for a man in Jonathan's position to subtly undermine and criticize a David, making things difficult for him, turning him a cold shoulder, or leading him astray. Yet Jonathan's attitude toward David was completely different from what we might expect. Instead of resenting David, he "loved him as his own soul." Instead of standing aloof from the upstart, his soul "was knit to the soul of David" (1 Sam. 18:1). Undoubtedly, Jonathan was simply responding to the evident grace in David's conduct. Six times in chapter 18 we read that someone loves David. But Jonathan's response to David's success revealed the prince's commitment to spiritual principles and values instead of worldly and self-serving priorities.

In particular, it is evident that Jonathan's passion was devoted to the well-being of God's people and the upholding of God's honor. He had not been fighting in Saul's army to gain a reputation for himself or to win riches and honor. Jonathan was burdened for Israel and for Israel's Lord. This had been the case in the earlier passage where Jonathan's exploits were highlighted. While Saul's erratic commands had hindered Israel's soldiers, and when Saul took credit for a victory that Jonathan's faith had won, his virtuous son showed no concern for these matters. He remained faithful to his duty and freely gave himself in service to the cause that he loved. Even when Saul's foolish vow had threatened Jonathan's life (1 Sam. 14:43–45), so that the soldiers rose up in defense of Saul's son, Jonathan himself did not oppose his father's will.

The lesson is that envy, resentment, and hatred spring from worldly and selfish priorities, whereas godly love springs from a concern for the kingdom of God and his gospel. Christians whose concern is for the glory of Christ will not oppose the labors of fellow Christians based on considerations of race, nationality, or economic class. We will avoid a party spirit that divides us from fellow believers, showing concern instead for biblical integrity, holiness, and grace. If our goal is to reach the lost with the gospel, we will not worry much about whom God blesses to use in that work, so long as God blesses the labors of his church. Rather than envying the gifts and callings of others, like Jonathan we will rejoice over all the gifts that God gives, and our souls will be knit with all others who are working in God's kingdom.

A contrary example will help us to appreciate Jonathan's priorities. On one occasion, Jesus and the disciples went into the region of the Gadarenes, where they were confronted by a man possessed by many demons. This man, who called himself "Legion" for the great number of demons within him, had been a menace to the region, and the demons had afflicted him terribly. When Jesus came upon the man and cast out the demons, we would expect the people nearby to rejoice. A soul had been freed from Satan! Instead, the people were upset that Jesus had cast the demons into their herd of swine, and they demanded that the Savior of the world depart from their lands, since they valued their money more than their souls (cf. Mark 5:1–20). In contrast, Jonathan was burdened by no such concerns over his own advancement or petty concerns of any kind. In response to the power of God at work through true and saving faith, his soul rejoiced.

On a similar note, when we consider the bond of friendship that grew between Jonathan and David, there was not much of a natural basis for their close relationship. They were not close in age, background, or experiences. What was their common bond? They were bound together by their faith in the Lord. Jonathan's heart was knit to David because David embodied the things most precious to his heart. David had stood before the giant in the name of the Lord, determined to silence his blasphemies and eager for Israel to know the truth of God's power. These were themes that stoked the fires of Jonathan's admiration and drew out his love for the shepherd-youth.

What we see in Jonathan is nothing less than a man who has been set free from worldly thinking and selfish concerns so as to truly love God and others. His treatment of David is a living embodiment of the two great commandments highlighted by Jesus: "You shall love the Lord your God with all your heart and with all your soul and with all your strength and with all your mind, and your neighbor as yourself" (Luke 10:27, quoting Deut. 6:5). This is what God desires of us, that we live out a chief concern for his glory and work and that we love others before ourselves. Jonathan was able to keep these commandments because he had given himself over to the Lord and had trusted God to provide for all his own needs. "It is only those people who, like Jonathan, have given themselves away to something greater than themselves, who possess such freedom to love."[2] This is why the New Testament sees genuine love as the summation of our faith. As Paul put it, "in Christ Jesus neither circumcision nor uncircumcision counts for anything, but only faith working through love" (Gal. 5:6).

Trusting the Lord to meet his own needs, and offering his life in sacrificial service to God's kingdom, Jonathan was no longer fettered by the chains of petty selfishness and pride. What a difference it would make in our lives if we were set free from a worldly attitude of greed and envy, trusting God to provide for all that we need and giving our hearts wholly to the cause of God's kingdom and Christ's gospel. As a result of such a God-centered faith, we would find ourselves free to truly love one another and to rejoice in the achievements of those around us. Looking on Jonathan's faith-inspired liberty to give of his soul in love, William Blaikie writes:

> Is there anything so beautiful as a beautiful heart? After well-nigh three thousand years, we are still thrilled by the noble character of Jonathan, and well were it for every young man that he shared in some degree his high nobility. Self-seekers and self-pleasers, look at him—and be ashamed.[3]

Jonathan's Covenant of Love

Jonathan's attitude inspires us, but we should also consider his actions. It is well observed that love is not ultimately a feeling but an action. *Love* in its active sense is a verb: it is something we do and bestow on others. In this respect, Jonathan's love for David sets an example that we can follow in our love for others.

The love between these men was that of companionship and brotherhood: recent attempts by liberal scholars to paint sexual overtones onto this passage are both perverse and preposterous. There are different kinds of love, with different levels of intensity and different kinds of expression: the love of a man and woman in marriage, the love of parents for their children, Christian love between fellow believers, and the love of close friends. While Jonathan's love for David falls into the latter category, his

2. Richard D. Phillips, *The Heart of an Executive: Lessons on Leadership from the Life of King David* (New York: Doubleday, 1999), 81.

3. William G. Blaikie, *Expository Lectures on the Book of First Samuel* (1887; repr., Birmingham, AL: Solid Ground, 2005), 203.

actions inform the love we give to others in every category. In particular, Jonathan's was a love that rejoices, a love that gives, and a love that blesses.

The manner in which Jonathan responded to David shows that his love rejoiced in David's faith and achievements. It was "as soon as [David] had finished speaking to Saul," that is, immediately after his slaying of the giant, that "the soul of Jonathan was knit to the soul of David" (1 Sam. 18:1). In the prior battles, Jonathan had stood in faith alone (except for his armor-bearer) against Israel's enemies. Now he rejoiced to see someone of like heart—indeed, a man with even greater faith, since Jonathan had not been able to stand against Goliath. It is clear that Jonathan did not feel condemned by David's superiority. Rather, he rejoiced in David's greater faith.

How do we react when someone comes along who exceeds us in ability, faith, or gifts? Do we become sour in spirit and find petty ways to undermine him or her? The well-regarded English preacher F. B. Meyer realized that he resented the ability and acclaim of G. Campbell Morgan, a like-minded preacher who like Meyer pastored a prominent church in London. Meyer's church was well attended, but Morgan's overflowed. Meyer and Morgan often preached together at conferences, but those who listened eagerly to Morgan's brilliant sermons sometimes were not present when Meyer took the pulpit. A godly pastor, Meyer was disturbed to realize the envy and resentment brewing in his heart for his colleague, and he noted that he had gotten into the habit of pointing out Morgan's flaws and mistakes, while minimizing his gifts and achievements. In response, Meyer determined that he would start praying for God's blessing on the ministry of Campbell Morgan, reasoning that he could not continue to envy a man for whose blessing he prayed. Soon, Meyer could be heard rejoicing in Morgan's preaching. "My, did you hear Campbell Morgan preach today!" he would exult. Not only did Meyer's prayer enable him to love his colleague with the gift of rejoicing, but in answer to his prayers God so overflowed Morgan's church that many of the people had no choice but to attend where Meyer preached!

How encouraging it must have been for David to see such a high-profile leader and potential enemy as Jonathan rejoicing in his victory! Yet Jonathan's was not only a love that rejoiced, but also a love that gave. What a remarkable scene it was when Israel's prince and captain approached David after his victory and "stripped himself of the robe that was on him and gave it to David, and his armor, and even his sword and his bow and his belt" (1 Sam. 18:4). Some commentators view this as a formal abdication on Jonathan's part, although this is probably reading too much into the incident. Still, Jonathan was knowingly lending his own prestige and giving his endorsement to the only practical rival to his own success. Why would Jonathan do this? S. G. DeGraaf answers: "This deed on his part was an act of faith. Only faith makes us willing to be the lesser. Faith causes us to surrender the rights we pretend to have."[4] In short, where sin would have made enemies, faith made brothers.

Materially, the military equipment that Jonathan gave to David was of great value, especially since it was no doubt of very high quality. What Jonathan really gave David, however, was the honor of his endorsement before the army. How easy it would have been for the soldiers to respond as had David's brothers (1 Sam. 17:28), who resented being shown up by this young upstart. Some of them, in loyalty to their hero Jonathan, may have resented the supplanting of Saul's son. Others would have looked for flaws in David and demeaned his overall lack of military experience. But none of this would be possible once Jonathan, the darling of the army, had placed his robe, armor, and weapons onto David.

Jonathan's gift seems to have been spontaneous, but he must also have appreciated how valuable his gifts were to David. Likewise, we love by understanding the vulnerabilities, fears, and weaknesses of others, and then reaching out with help and strength at precisely these points. To those who are discouraged, love gives encouragement. To those who are wayward, love gives kind, biblical counsel. To those who are overworked, love gives understanding and practical help. To those who are broken in suffering, love gives compassion and tears.

Jonathan thus declared his personal fidelity to David in friendship, a pledge that he kept to the day of his death, often at considerable risk and cost to himself. Some commentators argue that this covenant possesses the overtones of a political partnership, and we know that King Saul later regarded this covenant as just such a conspiracy. Jonathan freely gave what he was not obliged to give, yet he must take seriously his pledge of partnership and fidelity once it was given. No doubt this

---

4. Quoted in Dale Ralph Davis, *1 Samuel: Looking on the Heart* (Fearn, Ross-shire, UK: Christian Focus, 2000), 156.

covenant reflects the extraordinary blessing of God's Spirit on David, as the true anointed king of Israel. Walter Chantry writes of Jonathan's covenant love with David:

> The crown prince of Israel made a covenant with the shepherd. He gave his clothing and weapons to David as symbols of his devoted comradeship. One day Jonathan would even express agreement with God's will that David should have the crown intended for him! It was a selfless, sacrificial, loyal love for David that would endure until death. Mutual fidelity was pledged that very day, and it proved to be a most satisfying fellowship to both men for a lifetime.[5]

Jonathan models the way a believer is knit in a bond of covenant faith with Jesus Christ. Saving faith not only involves assenting to truths regarding Jesus, but includes the gift of our allegiance and the surrender of our will to his sovereign reign. How much more worthy is the Lord Jesus Christ of our covenant fidelity and love than David was, and how much more blessed will our fellowship with him be, not merely for this life but for eternity to come.

The passage concludes with a simple statement of David's immediate success in service to Saul, which was in part the result of Jonathan's love blessing his friend: "And David went out and was successful wherever Saul sent him, so that Saul set him over the men of war. And this was good in the sight of all the people and also in the sight of Saul's servants" (1 Sam. 18:5). In no small part because of Jonathan's encouragement, endorsement, and ongoing loyalty, David was able to succeed in meeting difficult demands. Our love should likewise seek to enable others to fulfill the calling that we all share as followers of Christ, as well as to find blessing in the fulfillment of the particular callings that God has placed on our own lives. Faced with many challenges in life, what a blessing the love of such friendship is to any of us. Ecclesiastes 4:9–10 says:

> Two are better than one, because they have a good reward for their toil. For if they fall, one will lift up his fellow. But woe to him who is alone when he falls and has not another to lift him up!

5. Walter Chantry, *David: Man of Prayer, Man of War* (Edinburgh: Banner of Truth, 2007), 37.

What a Friend!

Ultimately, we should see Jonathan's love for David as God's special gift to his anointed servant. All Christians, especially Christian men, should see Jonathan's example as a calling to seek such friendship and even more to give such brotherly love to one another. Chantry writes: "As the trials began, God gave [David] the precious gift of a friend. A faithful friend is a strong defence in adversity, a soothing medicine when one is deeply wounded. Men need friends well chosen from the number who love the Lord. It is clear that Jesus wants to see our love for him worked out in love for the brethren."[6]

Even more important for us is to receive the greatest friendship ever known in this world, the brotherly love of God's Son, Jesus Christ. Jonathan knit his heart to David after witnessing his awesome spectacle of triumphant faith. But Jesus loved us in our weakness, sin, and shame. Jonathan's love for David was remarkable in that a superior surrendered his devotion to a lesser citizen. But though he is God's own Son, Jesus has loved us and made himself our servant on the cross, calling us to serve one another in return (John 13:15). Jonathan made a covenant of faithful friendship and loyalty with David. But Jesus accepted from the Father a covenant that required the shedding of his own life's blood for our sins. "Greater love has no one than this," Jesus said of his own gift of love, "that someone lay down his life for his friends" (15:13).

Moreover, just as Jonathan kept his covenant of love for David to the end of his life, after which David was shorn of this precious friendship, John's Gospel tells us that Jesus' "having loved his own who were in the world, he loved them to the end" (John 13:1). For Jesus to love us to the end of his life is to bless us with his love forever, since he has conquered death with his power of eternal life. Thus, if we accept his covenant of love through faith in him, there will never be a time in all eternity when we may not lean upon his love as it rejoices, gives, and blesses us. Hebrews 7:25 thus states: "Consequently, he is able to save to the uttermost those who draw near to God through him, since he always lives to make intercession for them."

Finally, while Jonathan stripped himself of royal badges of honor and office, Jesus placed upon us his own righteousness, woven by a life of perfect obedience to God's law, that we might stand acceptably in the holy sight of

6. Ibid.

God. Matthew Henry comments that "our Lord Jesus has thus shown his love to us, that he stripped himself to clothe us, emptied himself to enrich us; nay, he did more than Jonathan, he clothed himself with our rags, whereas Jonathan did not put on David's."[7] Placing our sinful rags upon himself, Jesus took our sins away to the cross. Here is the love above all others, as John the apostle declared: "In this is love, not that we have loved God but that he loved us and sent his Son to be the propitiation for our sins. Beloved, if God so loved us, we also ought to love one another" (1 John 4:10–11). If David rejoiced in Jonathan's love with great blessing, how much more ought our hearts to be knit to Jesus in response to his covenant love for us.

As David's victory over Goliath changed his life, so also our receipt of victory over sin through faith in Christ will be the day that changes our lives forever. Receiving Christ's forgiveness through faith in his blood, we also gain his love that is stronger than death and that secures for us his gift of eternal life.

---

7. Matthew Henry, *Commentary on the Whole Bible*, 6 vols. (Peabody, MA: Hendrickson, 1992), 2:296.

28

THE MADNESS OF KING SAUL

1 Samuel 18:6—30

*The next day a harmful spirit from God rushed upon Saul, and
he raved within his house while David was playing the lyre, as
he did day by day. Saul had his spear in his hand. And Saul
hurled the spear, for he thought, "I will pin David to the wall."*
(1 Sam. 18:10–11)

History reveals that it is not always safe to live in the company of kings. Consider the case of Black Cleitus. Cleitus was one of Alexander the Great's leading generals and a commander in his famed Companion Cavalry. At the battle of the Granicus River, Cleitus saved Alexander's life when the king was disarmed by his enemies. A few years later, after Alexander had conquered the Persian Empire, Cleitus was one of many Macedonians who were disgruntled by Alexander's embrace of Eastern court practices and his never-ending lust for conquest. During one drunken party in Alexander's tent, the two men clashed, with Cleitus hurling several insults at the king. Friends separated the two men, but when Cleitus returned to give Alexander one last piece of his mind, the young conqueror grasped his spear, hurled it into his general's chest, and killed him. When the drunken fit was over, Alexander was filled with remorse and the army was filled with horror.

Little did Alexander realize that he was taking a page right out of Saul of Israel's book. That king's jealous hatred for David was even worse than Alexander's violent fit, since at no time did David display anything but respect and loyalty to his king. But unlike Alexander, Saul did not succeed in slaying David, for God was with him. Even Saul's persecution led to David's advancement.

This episode begins a long period of trouble and hardship for young David. It may be ironic that hatred for David appeared immediately after his great achievement in the Valley of Elah and his sudden elevation to prominence, but it is not coincidental. We can see in David's long period of trial and testing, which will continue to the end of 1 Samuel, the hand of God in preparing his servant. William Blaikie writes: "It pleased God, in infinite love, to make David pass through a long period of hard discipline and salutary training for the office to which he was to be raised."[1] We should also note from Saul's reaction to David how little we may rely on the world's approval and reward. In the days immediately after his triumph over the Philistine giant, Goliath, David began learning the lesson that he later memorialized in Psalm 146:3: "Put not your trust in princes, in a son of man, in whom there is no salvation."

Saul's Jealous Rage

The seeds of trouble were sown before either Saul or David returned from the battlefield. "As they were coming home, when David returned from striking down the Philistine, the women came out of all the cities of Israel, singing and dancing, to meet King Saul, with tambourines, with songs of joy, and with musical instruments" (1 Sam. 18:6). The outpouring of joy was similar to today's ticker-tape parade. As the women greeted the king, they began singing, "Saul has struck down his thousands, and David his ten thousands" (18:7).

There is much to criticize in this song, beginning with how injudicious it was. We can understand why David was included in their praise, since he

---

1. William G. Blaikie, *Expository Lectures on the Book of First Samuel* (1887; repr., Birmingham, AL: Solid Ground, 2005), 295.

had dispatched the enemy giant, and it was obligatory that Saul be praised as well. The problem was the comparison made between the two and the prominence given to David over Saul. The women were not claiming that Saul had literally killed thousands and David ten thousands. The point was their respective might in slaying Israel's enemies, and the effect was to picture David as a mightier man than the king. The slight to Saul, though probably unintended, was inevitable.

The women's song reveals more than political ineptitude, however. Israel's low spiritual state is revealed in the fact that no praise was given to God, but only to men. Compare this with the Song of Miriam and the women of Israel after the destruction of Pharaoh's host in the Red Sea, when Miriam sang, "Sing to the LORD, for he has triumphed gloriously; the horse and his rider he has thrown into the sea" (Ex. 15:21). No praise was devoted to Moses, who had stretched out his hand over the Red Sea so that it parted, because the people knew that the power and the glory belonged to God alone. It generally reveals a low spiritual level when Christians take after the world in praising men instead of God. Yet this is the very tendency in evidence today in the marketing of celebrity ministers and their empires. We should, of course, give thanks for able and faithful Christians, but glory should be reserved for God alone.

Hearing the slight praises for himself and the strong praise for David, "Saul was very angry, and this saying displeased him. He said, 'They have ascribed to David ten thousands, and to me they have ascribed thousands, and what more can he have but the kingdom?'" (1 Sam. 18:8). Saul's proud heart, darkened in sinful brooding, could not bear a comparison that was tilted toward another. Far from enjoying the acclamation of the younger hero, who was after all his own servant, Saul looked upon David as a threat to his own regime. The praise for the young hero changed his relationship to the king immediately, and "Saul eyed David from that day on" (18:9).

We should watch carefully against the appearance of an envying spirit within our own hearts. As sinners, we are all prone to such thinking, which corrupts our capacity for joy and sets us needlessly against people who ought to be our friends. If we find ourselves thinking spitefully against others whose gifts surpass our own or resenting praise given to others' achievements, we should mortify this sinful attitude. We chiefly do this by taking

327

the matter to God in prayer, leaving no room for such wickedness to settle in our hearts. Matthew Henry observed: "It is a sign that the Spirit of God is departed from men if they [are] peevish in their resentment of affronts, envious and suspicious of all about them, and ill-natured in their conduct; for the 'wisdom from above' makes us quite otherwise."[2]

The safest habit is for us to leave others' opinions of us to themselves, concerning ourselves more deeply with what God thinks of our character and actions. Saul shows us what becomes true of anyone who craves personal praise: he loses the capacity for both joy and love. Not long previously, we were told that "Saul loved [David] greatly" (1 Sam. 16:21). Now, because of his own proud and insecure spirit, Saul begins to loathe and fear a young man who has been nothing but faithful in service to him.

Sin cherished in the heart will invariably express itself through the mouth and the hands, and Saul's heart burned so bitterly that it took only a single day for his envy to vent itself against David: "The next day a harmful spirit from God rushed upon Saul, and he raved within his house while David was playing the lyre, as he did day by day. Saul had his spear in his hand. And Saul hurled the spear, for he thought, 'I will pin David to the wall.' But David evaded him twice" (1 Sam. 18:10–11).

It says much about David's humility that after his public triumph in slaying Goliath, and despite the praise of the nation, he remained in humble service to Saul, continuing to play the lyre in his court. In the past, David's playing had soothed Saul's evil mood, but now the mere sight of David drove Saul into a violent rage. With a mad impulse, Saul hurled his spear at David, but the athletic youth who had earlier faced Goliath's great spear was able to evade Saul's.

The picture of a darkly brooding Saul, walking around his house holding a spear, is one we should consider. Many people live in a similar way, nurturing evil, jealous, or resentful thoughts, and bearing an attitude that is as sharp and almost as dangerous as Saul's spear. It is no accident when words are thrown at spouses or children that resemble Saul's weapon hurled against David. How much emotional pain is suffered in homes today by those who permit their minds to dwell in darkness! James wrote, in contrast, that "the wisdom from above is first pure, then peaceable, gentle, open to

---

2. Matthew Henry, *Commentary on the Whole Bible*, 6 vols. (Peabody, MA: Hendrickson, 1992), 2:297.

reason, full of mercy and good fruits, impartial and sincere" (James 3:17). What Alexander Maclaren wrote of envy can be said of other dark and angry thoughts: "Let us suppress its beginning. A tiger pup can be held in and its claws cut, but a full-grown tiger cannot."[3]

The most important thing for us to realize about Saul is that he is an advanced and concentrated portrait of man in rebellion to God. Saul is just like people today who focus their resentment and frustration on other people when their real problem is God. Saul's true problem was not David's popularity, the foolish song of the women, or even the Philistines. Saul's problem was his hostile relationship with the Lord. We see proof of this in verse 12, which says that Saul perceived that David was blessed by God in a way that he was not. Saul had set his will against the Lord and hardened his resentful heart against God's commands. God was therefore against Saul, as seen by the "harmful spirit" that fed into the king's jealous rage (1 Sam. 18:10).

Walter Chantry notes that "God's words and acts cannot be denied and opposed without dire consequences to those who hate what the Lord has established."[4] Our secular-humanist society proves this point, as rebellion against God's moral commands inflicts suffering on more and more people whose lives are shattered by abusive homes, sexual promiscuity, or addictions to drugs, alcohol, and gambling. Psalm 1, which speaks of the blessedness of those who love God and his Word, also notes that "the wicked are not so, but are like chaff that the wind drives away. Therefore the wicked will not stand in the judgment, . . . but the way of the wicked will perish" (Ps. 1:4–6).

This misery that is God's down payment on the future judgment of sin was well advanced in King Saul. Unable to call on God's help, he had cringed in the presence of mighty Goliath, just as secular people today live in anxiety and fear before powers greater than themselves. Then, when David showed the power of God to save those who trust him, Saul hated him for the praise that he won. These are just some of the ways that Isaiah's principle about those in rebellion to God is true: " 'The wicked are like the tossing sea . . . There is no peace,' says my God, 'for the wicked' " (Isa. 57:20–21).

3. Alexander Maclaren, *Expositions of Holy Scripture*, 17 vols. (Grand Rapids: Baker, 1982), 2:352.
4. Walter Chantry, *David: Man of Prayer, Man of War* (Edinburgh: Banner of Truth, 2007), 38.

David's Blessed Humility

Saul was enraged not merely by David himself but even more so by his awareness that God was with David. The episode with his hurled spear—which, remarkably, happened twice, indicating that David continued to serve Saul under oppressive circumstances—inspired fear not in David but in Saul, since the king rightly reasoned that God's hand was protecting the young hero. Just as Joseph's bearing in Potiphar's household was such that "his master saw that the LORD was with him" (Gen. 39:3), it was evident to Saul that the Lord was with David. This awareness ought to have caused repentance, but instead it only hardened Saul's mad resolve to end David's life.

With this in mind, Saul removed David from his personal service and put him in command of a military force engaged against the Philistines, reasoning that the odds of David's demise in battle were relatively high. But "David had success in all his undertakings, for the LORD was with him" (1 Sam. 18:14). As a result, the people acclaimed David all the more, so that "when Saul saw that he had great success, he stood in fearful awe of him" (18:15). The text literally states that he "dreaded his face," and suggests that Saul suspected that David must be the man after God's own heart who Samuel had said would replace Saul as king (13:14).

Given David's soaring popularity, Saul could hardly continue open assaults on his life. But there were other ways to arrange a funeral, and one of them was by dangling the prospect of marriage before the young hero. "Then Saul said to David, 'Here is my elder daughter Merab. I will give her to you for a wife. Only be valiant for me and fight the LORD's battles.' For Saul thought, 'Let not my hand be against him, but let the hand of the Philistines be against him'" (1 Sam. 18:17). This statement reveals Saul's advanced depravity both through its pious mask in seeking David's death and also through his callous treatment of his daughter's heart. Blaikie comments that "nothing shows a wickeder heart than being willing to involve another, and especially one's own child, in a lifelong sorrow in order to gratify some feeling of one's own."[5]

We remember that it was at least rumored that the man who slew the Philistine champion would gain the hand of Saul's daughter (1 Sam. 17:25). Far from demanding his right to this prize, however, David humbly pleaded

5. Blaikie, *First Samuel*, 303.

his unworthiness to be elevated into the royal family. "David said to Saul, 'Who am I, and who are my relatives, my father's clan in Israel, that I should be son-in-law to the king?'" (18:18). There is every reason to see this statement as a genuine expression of self-effacing humility. Coming from a poor family, and one in which there was recent non-Jewish blood (as the book of Ruth reveals), David sincerely thought it awkward for him to be married to a woman of such high standing as Merab. In response, Saul gave her hand to someone else, no doubt seeking to drive home an emotional knife: "At the time when Merab, Saul's daughter, should have been given to David, she was given to Adriel the Meholathite for a wife" (18:19). It is a significant side note that the five sons of this union were all put to death in later years as payment for Saul's sins against the Gibeonites (2 Sam. 21:8–9), a detail providing more evidence of God's curse that lay upon Saul and his family.

Sometime after this, Saul learned that another of his daughters, Michal, was in love with David. "The thing pleased him. Saul thought, 'Let me give her to him, that she may be a snare for him and that the hand of the Philistines may be against him'" (1 Sam. 18:20–21). Saul evidently believed that Michal's marriage to David would undermine his character or otherwise hinder him. The phrase "be a snare" is used in other passages for the practice of idolatry (see Ex. 23:33; 34:12; Deut. 7:16). Perhaps, then, Saul thought Michal would tempt David into idol-worship and thus ruin his relationship with God.

This time, Saul's offer was prefaced with words of approval: "Behold, the king has delight in you, and all his servants love you" (1 Sam. 18:22). The messengers' purpose was apparently to alleviate David's reservations about his lower social status. But David was still unsure, especially in light of his impoverished background: "Does it seem to you a little thing to become the king's son-in-law, since I am a poor man and have no reputation?" (18:23).

There is a sharp contrast in this response to the attitude seen in King Saul. Whereas Saul depicts the pride and fear of a man who is alienated from God, David shows the humility of a true servant of the Lord. At this stage, it seems that David does not realize that Saul is really planning a funeral, not a wedding. Yet his humility—which Saul can no more fathom than attain—protected David and confounded the king's wicked schemes. Henry notes, "It well becomes us, however God has advanced us, always to have low thoughts of ourselves. . . . And, if David thus magnified the honour

331

of being son-in-law to the king, how shall we magnify the honour of being sons (not in law, but in gospel) to the King of kings!"[6]

Since prominence and popularity brought David little more than misery, it is hard to see why Christians would desire to be elevated in the world. Instead, humbly reckoning on our unworthiness, estimating others higher than ourselves, and desiring for any advancement to come from God's hand alone, wise Christians will resist putting their own names forward for rank and privileges. God asks in Jeremiah 45:5, "Do you seek great things for yourself? Seek them not." Moreover, "God opposes the proud, but gives grace to the humble" (James 4:6, quoting Prov. 3:34). Humility results not merely from an accurate appraisal of our deficiencies, but also from our contentment in God's provision for our lives. Henry applies this truth to believers:

> If we commit our souls, and bodies, and characters, and interests, our way and work into the hands of the Lord, he will bring all to pass that is good for us, and carry us safely through all, to that blessed world where treachery, envy, and malice finds no admission, but perfect love will prevail for evermore.[7]

GOD'S PRESERVING CARE

Saul was determined to enmesh David in marriage to his daughter Michal and in the process to ensure that David remained committed to dangerous service in the war. Therefore, Saul responded to David's plea that he lacked the money to pay a sufficient bride-price for the king's daughter. His servants told David, "The king desires no bride-price except a hundred foreskins of the Philistines, that he may be avenged of the king's enemies." We further read what is already obvious: "Now Saul thought to make David fall by the hand of the Philistines" (1 Sam. 18:25).

Saul desired this unusual wedding gift not only because of the danger involved in slaying and then removing the foreskins from a hundred Philistine soldiers—this act showing the Israelites' detestation of their enemy's uncircumcised status—but also because even in success David would be so obnoxious to the Philistines that his life would be in grave

---

6. Henry, *Commentary on the Whole Bible*, 2:299.
7. Quoted in Gordon J. Keddie, *Dawn of a Kingdom: The Message of 1 Samuel* (Darlington, UK: Evangelical Press, 1988), 180.

jeopardy. Not only would the Philistines resist David in battle to their utmost strength, but they would be outraged in offense at this desecration of their dead soldiers.

On these terms, however, David was pleased to enter Saul's family. Many grooms seek a way to leverage their relationship with their future father-in-law, but the challenge given to David was ideal for a man of his skills and abilities. Before the end of the unspecified time allotted for this bride-price, David returned to King Saul and presented his bouquet of not one hundred but two hundred Philistine foreskins. By this means, David had earned his higher status, and thus he claimed Saul's daughter in marriage.

Saul was mortified, not by the bride-price itself but by the implication of David's achievement. Now he knew more than before "that the LORD was with David" and that David had stolen the heart even of his own daughter (1 Sam. 18:28). As a result, "Saul was even more afraid of David. So Saul was David's enemy continually" (18:29). David's exploit so insulted the Philistines that their princes came forth to make war, but "as often as they came out David had more success than all the servants of Saul, so that his name was highly esteemed" (18:30).

This passage reveals the third person who is present—the One whose actions dominate this chapter. We have considered Saul as a classic picture of the mad anxiety that accompanies life without God. David, on the other hand, demonstrates the humility that leads to God's protection and blessing. Finally, we are compelled to see God himself as the prime actor in these events. Thus, David shows us what a difference it makes to be right with God. Whereas Saul is driven through fear and envy into madness, David is led through success to the high esteem of God's people.

We become right with God not by fulfilling a quest or by doing enough good works, but by accepting his mercy as revealed in Jesus Christ. We are justified by looking back in faith to the Lamb of God, who died for our sins, just as David was justified by looking forward to the blood of Christ (cf. Ps. 51:7). Then we are to live by an active faith, of which David was an outstanding example. Through this life of faith we are richly blessed by God. Psalm 1 says of the man of faith: "In all that he does, he prospers" (v. 3). Jesus taught, "Whoever abides in me and I in him, he it is that bears much fruit" (John 15:5). Jesus is the blessed Son of God in whom sinners are made to prosper spiritually, bearing good fruit to the glory of God.

This is not to say that Christians do not sin, or that those who trust the Lord do not experience trials, failures, and many other hardships, because we do. When it comes to their sins, believers are distinguished from King Saul in that they confess and repent of their sins. In later years, when David fell into great sin, he was willing to repent and thus had his relationship with God restored. "I have sinned against the LORD," he confessed, and God's messenger replied, "The LORD . . . has put away your sin" (2 Sam. 12:13).

What about more practical blessings? Does God's favor mean that all Christians are certain to be rich? The answer is not merely "No," but also that Christians have something better than material riches: we do not need to be rich in order to be content and satisfied, because God himself fills our hearts. Does this mean that believers will always triumph over the Philistine foes in this world? The answer is "No," but God has promised to use even our defeats, as well as our victories, to "work together for good to those who love God" (Rom. 8:28 NKJV). Believers often have cause to repeat the explanation that Joseph gave to his brothers: "You meant evil against me, but God meant it for good" (Gen. 50:20).

This is why Saul was so unnerved by David: the Lord was with David and for David. It was for the same reason that the Roman Empire grew to fear and hold the early Christians in awe. Justin Martyr explained to the emperor in his *First Apology*, "You can kill, but not hurt us."[8] This is why savage official persecution of Christians in China not only has done nothing to slow the gospel's spread, but has actually spurred the expansion of the church, as people have witnessed the power of God to bless his people even against such affliction.[9] So it was that the more Saul sought evil for David, the more he feared him. Why? Because the promise of Psalm 121 was true for David, as it is true for all others who are owned by God through saving faith: "The LORD is your keeper . . . The LORD will keep you from all evil; he will keep your life" (Ps. 121:5–7). Imagine trying to oppose a people who have God for their keeper! Most precious to believers is the even greater promise that though the world may sometimes wrongfully

8. Justin Martyr, *First Apology*, chap. 2, in *Ante-Nicene Fathers*, ed. Alexander Roberts and James Donaldson, 10 vols. (Peabody, MA: Hendrickson, 1999), 1:163.
9. An outstanding account of the recent growth of Christianity in China can be read in David Aikman, *Jesus in Beijing* (Washington, DC: Regnery, 2003).

hate us, as Saul envied and hated David, "neither death nor life, nor angels nor rulers, nor things present nor things to come, nor powers, nor height nor depth, nor anything else in all creation, will be able to separate us from the love of God in Christ Jesus our Lord" (Rom. 8:38–39). The experience of seeking to harm a man bound in such unfailing love drove mad Saul into even deeper distress, and the same reality today should cause the opponents of Christ to fear the Lord.

BLESS THE LORD, O MY SOUL!

If we put together all the sides of the portrait presented in this chapter, we see the strongest motivation for each of us to seek the Lord. Saul had his will set against God. He was unwilling to obey God's commands and resented God's judicial opposition in his life. The result of this hardened attitude to God produced the furthest thing from happiness, peace, joy, and success for Saul. Even the things that he possessed—most notably the kingship—he could not enjoy, seeing dangerous threats all around. Moreover, as he cultivated wicked passions, he was driven by God further into madness (1 Sam. 18:10). Saul then discovered that his self-will and spiritual rebellion led him to perform shocking actions. In a similar way, men and women today who live without the blessing of God on their lives do not find satisfaction in life, and they often find themselves being led by sin into behaviors they once had scarcely thought themselves capable of engaging in. Like Saul, their true problem is with God. They are not at peace with God and God is not at peace with them, so they will not and cannot find peace with themselves or anyone else.

While the problem of unbelieving men and women is with God, he is also the solution. The whole message of Christianity is that God sent his Son to die for the sins of his enemies. Paul says, "God shows his love for us in that while we were still sinners, Christ died for us" (Rom. 5:8). Therefore, if Saul would not return to God and his blessing, through sincere repentance and renewed faith, it would not be because God was unwilling to receive him. Many of the greatest sinners in the Bible were accepted by God when they humbled themselves to him in faith.[10] Paul thus wrote: "The saying is

---

10. Prime examples are King Manasseh in the Old Testament (2 Chron. 33:12–13) and Saul/Paul in the New Testament (Acts 9:1–16).

trustworthy and deserving of full acceptance, that Christ Jesus came into the world to save sinners, of whom I am the foremost" (1 Tim. 1:15).

We then look at David and see what it looks like to live in the blessing and favor of God. David's real victory was his humble confidence and delight in the Lord, a blessing that God makes available to all who trust in him. In many respects, of course, David held a unique place in God's plans, so few others will experience the magnitude of his success. David depicts for us another man who was hated without a cause and who was not only unjustly threatened but also unjustly put to death by his own people. David's greater Son, Jesus Christ, achieved a victory over enemies greater than the Philistines, conquering the evil forces of Satan, sin, and death. In his victory, received by faith alone, we have every blessing, starting with the forgiveness of our sins.

As a result, in the case of Jesus we have an exception to the rule that we should praise God and not man, since he is both man and God. When we consider all that this chapter has shown us about God's saving presence for his humble people, we have things to praise indeed. We are told three times in this chapter that the Lord was with David, and this made all the difference. Jesus is called *Immanuel*, "God with us," and he promises to be with all who look to him in faith (Heb. 13:5). With David, we therefore praise Christ, not merely saying that he has slain thousands or ten thousands, but also singing, "Bless the LORD, O my soul, . . . who forgives all your iniquity, who heals all your diseases, who redeems your life from the pit, who crowns you with steadfast love and mercy" (Ps. 103:2–4).

29

To Kill David

1 Samuel 19:1—24

He too stripped off his clothes, and he too prophesied before
Samuel and lay naked all that day and all that night. Thus it is
said, "Is Saul also among the prophets?" (1 Sam. 19:24)

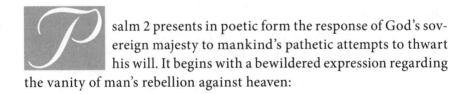salm 2 presents in poetic form the response of God's sovereign majesty to mankind's pathetic attempts to thwart his will. It begins with a bewildered expression regarding the vanity of man's rebellion against heaven:

> Why do the nations rage
> and the peoples plot in vain?
> The kings of the earth set themselves,
>   and the rulers take counsel together,
>   against the LORD and against his Anointed, saying,
> "Let us burst their bonds apart
>   and cast away their cords from us." (2:1–3)

God responds to this challenge in a way that neither shows the slightest respect nor gives the least credit to man's raised fist:

He who sits in the heavens laughs;
 the Lord holds them in derision.
Then he will speak to them in his wrath,
 and terrify them in his fury, saying,
"As for me, I have set my King
 on Zion, my holy hill." (Ps. 2:4–6)

If ever there was a biblical example of God's mocking rebuke of man's pretension in sin and unbelief, it is that of Israel's King Saul. Mad though he may have been, Saul possessed all the power the world can offer. He was crazed by a jealous desire to kill David, his own faithful servant and the anointed one of the Lord. Saul's hatred was ultimately directed against the gospel of God's grace, that he might snuff out God's kingdom so as to preserve his own. In this way, Saul is the direct precursor to the Pharisees and other religious leaders in Jerusalem who later sought so madly to take the life of Jesus Christ, God's true anointed Messiah. Like them, Saul would learn just how able God is to preserve his Anointed One. And as David noted in Psalm 59, which is reputed to have been penned on this occasion, Saul would learn how easy it is for God to overthrow his enemies. "Make them totter by your power and bring them down, O Lord, our shield!" David prayed. "Let them be trapped in their pride. . . . Consume them in wrath; consume them till they are no more" (Ps. 59:11–13).

SAUL'S SIN THWARTED BY GOD'S WORD

Saul's downward-spiraling rage against David shows the peril of an unrepentant heart. No doubt the thought of repenting of his obviously evil disposition was repulsive to Saul, but how much trouble it would have spared him! Instead, as his mad plans failed, he merely devised new schemes for destroying his righteous nemesis. So it was that "Saul spoke to Jonathan his son and to all his servants, that they should kill David" (1 Sam. 19:1).

This direct appeal was remarkably imprudent on Saul's part. He knew that Jonathan had sworn a covenant of loyalty and friendship to David and that his heart was knit to the younger hero. Moreover, Saul must have realized how greatly all Israel admired David's virtues and accomplishments. How could he expect his staff to enter a league to murder David? The answer is that those who are gripped by evil often imagine that others are as easily corrupted as themselves. The appeal to Jonathan was obvious, Saul would have reasoned, since David's popularity endangered Jonathan's ascent to the throne. Likewise, Saul's officials stood to lose their prestige in any regime change, and a man such as Saul could only imagine that such a thought overrode all other considerations.

Jonathan's faithfulness to David was tested by Saul's advance, and such was his heart that he passed the test easily. For him, the grace of God at work in the life of David was far more compelling than any worldly advancement for himself. For this reason, "Jonathan, Saul's son, delighted much in David" (1 Sam. 19:1). As a result, Jonathan immediately gave a warning to David, giving little thought to his own well-being and providing yet another example of true friendship: "Jonathan told David, 'Saul my father seeks to kill you. Therefore be on your guard in the morning. Stay in a secret place and hide yourself'" (19:2). Meanwhile, Jonathan would seek to reason with his father, still hoping for Saul's return to sanity.

With this goal in mind, Jonathan spoke to his father. His approach provides a positive example of how a child of God should respond with truth and grace to conspiracies of sin and unbelief. Jonathan's address to his father was simultaneously courteous and bold, offering counsels of prudence together with direct appeals to the Word of God. His purpose was to press upon Saul the evidence of David's innocence, along with the sinful folly of his murderous plan.

We might classify Jonathan's initial approach to Saul as an appeal to common grace. This term refers to the way that God works in the world in a common or preservative way, promoting virtue and truth so as to restrain evil for the sake of his gospel. Common grace is not saving grace; it does not directly save anyone. Yet by God's good influence on human society, it preserves those whom God will later save by special, saving grace through faith in Christ. Jonathan was relying on God's common grace when he appealed to Saul's better judgment: "Jonathan spoke well of David to Saul his father and said to him, 'Let not the king sin against his servant David, because he has not sinned against you, and because his deeds have brought good to you. For he took his life in his hand and he struck down the Philistine, and the LORD worked a great salvation for all Israel. You saw it, and rejoiced'" (1 Sam. 19:4–5). Under the influence of God's moral order, and faced with a general appeal to prudence, Saul's evil was restrained, though not conquered.

Christians should likewise reason with the sinful world on the basis of common morality and the obvious blessings of right thinking. But it will also be necessary to confront evil with direct appeals to the Word of God. Jonathan did this frankly, informing Saul that his proposals amounted to sin: "Let not the king sin," he warned (1 Sam. 19:4). "Why then will you sin against innocent blood by killing David without cause?" (19:5). The warning about "innocent blood" referred to Deuteronomy 19:10, which curses the "guilt of bloodshed" for all who slay the innocent; Deuteronomy 27:24–25 also applies God's curse against "anyone who strikes down his neighbor in secret" or conspires "to shed innocent blood." In our response to evil today, Christians should unveil the naked warnings of God in the Bible, seeking to thwart the plans of evil with divine rebuke.

God made this world, which continues under his providential rule even in sin, so it is not surprising that Jonathan's appeal had an initial success in turning Saul from his sinful intent: "Saul listened to the voice of Jonathan. Saul swore, 'As the LORD lives, he shall not be put to death'" (1 Sam. 19:6). God preserves his gospel and his church today by similar means. Roger Ellsworth comments: "God primarily preserves his cause through his children testifying of the grace of God to a dark world. We can say of Christianity what Jonathan said of David: 'It has done you good. Why should you do it harm?'"[1]

SAUL'S SIN DISPLAYED IN GOD'S JUDGMENT

In response to Saul's vow not to put his servant to death, David returned to the king's service. "Jonathan brought David to Saul, and he was in his presence as before. And there was war again. And David went out and fought with the Philistines and struck them with a great blow, so that they fled before him" (1 Sam. 19:7–8). Thus Saul was richly rewarded for heeding the counsel of his son, as God continued to work salvation for Israel through the sword of David. Undoubtedly, however, this produced a renewed outbreak of praise for the young hero, the result of which was the swift return of Saul's mad jealousy.

1. Roger Ellsworth, *The Shepherd King: Learning from the Life of David* (Darlington, UK: Evangelical Press, 1998), 50.

Saul's part in the story of David displays the corruption and torments of a man in rebellion versus God. Notice Saul's inconsistency. Under the influence of his godly son, Saul had recently taken a vow not to seek David's life. But when David returned from the war and, with remarkable humility, resumed his ministry of music in Saul's presence, he would surely have noticed a telltale sign of trouble: "Saul . . . sat in his house with his spear in his hand. And David was playing the lyre" (1 Sam. 19:9). Consumed by fear of phantoms that existed only in his mind, Saul found that his "fear and jealousy made him a torment to himself, so that he could not sit in his house without a javelin in his hand."[2] David was no doubt ready when the inevitable happened: "And Saul sought to pin David to the wall with the spear, but he eluded Saul, so that he struck the spear into the wall" (19:10).

How are we to explain Saul's behavior? First, like all other men apart from God's rule, Saul was torn apart by competing powers. On the one hand, Saul plainly knew how wicked his behavior was, which is why all through these chapters of 1 Samuel he repents repeatedly. But on the other hand, Saul was under the influence of the mad passion of sin. Gordon Keddie writes, "Saul was living a lie. That is why he could so easily make pious vows and contradict them almost in the same breath." In this respect, Saul presents in concentrated form what must be true of everyone who is restrained by the knowledge of right and wrong, yet is ultimately conquered by anger, lust, or other evils. "Without a saving change, a sinner is a mess. He hardly knows himself. . . . And even though he knows that God will judge wickedness, he goes on doing it as if he had a death-wish and encourages others along the same fatal road."[3]

If any man ever proved our need for the saving grace of Jesus Christ, that man is King Saul. What was concentrated in him is true of every person apart from the saving power of Christ: we are unable to live up to our moral pretensions and are capable of sins that we would eagerly condemn in others and that must finally condemn us before God. This is why appeals to common grace and rational prudence ultimately fail in restraining sin: the power of sin so infects the mind that men and women are suicidally irrational in their pursuit of wealth, power, lust, or hatred.

2. Matthew Henry, *Commentary on the Whole Bible*, 6 vols. (Peabody, MA: Hendrickson, 1992), 2:301.

3. Gordon J. Keddie, *Dawn of a Kingdom: The Message of 1 Samuel* (Darlington, UK: Evangelical Press, 1988), 185.

But irrationality was not the only problem with King Saul. The Bible is candid in speaking of God's ongoing judgment in the form of a tormenting spirit, which presumably was an angelic messenger who afflicted Saul's mind: "A harmful spirit from the LORD came upon Saul" (1 Sam. 19:9). The reality of such spiritual chastisement is shocking to those who see God as a doting grandfatherly gentleman in heaven. That view is false, for as the Bible tells us, "It is a fearful thing to fall into the hands of the living God" (Heb. 10:31). Saul was a reprobate, whose heart had hardened against God. Therefore, of all his problems in life, chief among them was the fierce judgment of the Almighty. Not only would Saul's divided nature not permit him to lead a wholesome, godly life, but *God* would not permit Saul to lead a wholesome, godly life.

Undoubtedly there was an interplay between Saul's jealousy of David and the torments of the evil spirit, just as Paul warned us "not [to] let the sun go down on your anger, and [to] give no opportunity to the devil" (Eph. 4:26–27). Even apart from the kind of chastisement that Saul received from God, there are enough evil influences in our world that we are well warned to guard our hearts and minds at all times, not permitting the growth of bitter seeds, lusts, or anger, which open us up to evils far beyond anything we imagined.

Saul's sin not only *caused* God's judgment, but also was to be *displayed* by God's ongoing judgment and chastisement. God continued to preserve his servant David—which is why Saul's spear continued to miss the young hero even at short range—while God's judgment of Saul revealed his apostasy before all Israel. Paul likewise writes of God's turning idolaters over to their sins. Speaking of sinful men and women who will not acknowledge God or obey his commands, Paul says that God "gave them up to dishonorable passions . . . [and] to a debased mind to do what ought not to be done" (Rom. 1:26–28). When men, women, and societies have utterly turned from God, he unleashes his judgment upon them in the form of unrestrained passions, displaying by his judgment the sin, folly, and torment of those who have turned from God and reaped godlessness in return.

When David had had enough of Saul's spears, he fled the court for his home. Saul, however, sent his agents to watch David's house and take his life in the morning. But word of this plot reached David's wife, Michal, who was also Saul's daughter, and through her loyalty God once again spared

David's life. In Psalm 59, David depicts Saul's cutthroats as "bloodthirsty men" (v. 2). "For behold, they lie in wait for my life; fierce men stir up strife against me. For no transgression or sin of mine, O LORD, . . . they run and make ready" (v. 3). David was not saying that he had never committed a sin, but rather that in this situation he was being oppressed for no fault of his own. The truth of this claim makes Saul's sin all the more grievous.

Here, as elsewhere, David's affliction foreshadows the irrational hatred of Israel's religious leaders against Jesus Christ. We see in David's situation the two reactions of our world to Jesus, of whom David was a type. There are those with eyes to see him in his glory, just as Jonathan delighted in David through his faith in God. But others see Jesus only as a threat to their self-rule and especially to their sinful desires. This is how Saul looked upon David: God's anointed was a continual threat to him, his righteous character an offense to Saul's tortured soul. How do you respond to the biblical portrait of Jesus? Is he a threat to your self-rule and worldly desires? Or do you see in him the very desire of your heart, the summation of all that is good and the Savior who will lead you to your destiny in glory? There is no more important question in all of life.

God was committed to protecting his anointed servant, David, just as Jesus could not be taken by his enemies until the time appointed for his crucifixion. Here, God uses Saul's own daughter, Michal, to save his nemesis, just as he had earlier used Saul's son Jonathan. "Michal, David's wife, told him, 'If you do not escape with your life tonight, tomorrow you will be killed.' So Michal let David down through the window, and he fled away and escaped" (1 Sam. 19:11–12).

Unlike Jonathan, Michal does not seem to be a true follower of the Lord. This will become evident later in David's life, when she despises him for his enthusiastic worship of God when the ark of the covenant is brought into Jerusalem (2 Sam. 6:16). On this earlier occasion, Michal aided David's escape—commending herself at least as a loyal wife—by means of an idol that she kept in her house:

> Michal took an image and laid it on the bed and put a pillow of goats' hair at its head and covered it with the clothes. And when Saul sent messengers to take David, she said, "He is sick." Then Saul sent the messengers to see David, saying, "Bring him up to me in the bed, that I may kill him." And

when the messengers came in, behold, the image was in the bed, with the pillow of goats' hair at its head. (1 Sam. 19:13–16)

This idol was a *teraphim*, a life-sized object probably employed for false worship of the Lord, though perhaps for the worship of other gods. It is hard to understand how such an object could be in David's house, except that he and his wife were at odds as to their fidelity to the Lord. We remember that this had been Saul's intention in offering her hand in marriage: he hoped that his daughter would "be a snare for him" (1 Sam. 18:21). This perhaps explains the lack of warmth revealed in this marriage from this time forward. Moreover, as Saul's daughter, Michal was caught in a tug-of-war that is revealed in her explanation to Saul when he discovered her duplicity in aiding David's escape: "Saul said to Michal, 'Why have you deceived me thus and let my enemy go, so that he has escaped?' And Michal answered Saul, 'He said to me, "Let me go. Why should I kill you?"'" (19:17). This was a wholly unnecessary lie, in which Michal showed less concern for David's reputation than she had shown for his life. Walter Chantry wonders, "Is it possible that these conversations strained [David's and Michal's] relationship in ways that never healed?"[4] David's sin of polygamy in years to come, inexcusable in itself, may have found a motivation in the poorly yoked relationship of his marriage to Saul's daughter.

Saul's Sin Overcome, Resulting in Praise to God

Beleaguered by Saul's persistent hostility, David fled Gibeah altogether, running for his life to nearby Ramah, where Samuel the prophet still lived. If Psalm 59 was in fact written during this journey, it reveals that David's was not a panicked flight, but that his mind was composed through faith in the Lord: "Deliver me from my enemies, O my God; protect me from those who rise up against me" (Ps. 59:1). Whereas Michal had told David that he was to be slain in the morning, David countered with faith in the Lord: "I will sing aloud of your steadfast love in the morning. For you have been to me a fortress and a refuge in the day of my distress" (Ps. 59:16). As often happens for God's people, the hatred of the world drove David into

4. Walter Chantry, *David: Man of Prayer, Man of War* (Edinburgh: Banner of Truth, 2007), 49.

the arms of God, thus providing the greatest service to his faith. William Blaikie comments: "In Samuel's company he would find congenial fellowship, and from Samuel's mature wisdom and devotion to God's law learn much that would be useful in after life."[5]

David's successful flight to Ramah reminds us that God protects his gospel and his cause, and that those who seek refuge in him will be kept safe. In fleeing to Samuel, David was casting himself on the Lord's mercy, since Samuel was the true leader of God's faithful people in Israel. There he would witness a scene that was both intriguing and instructing regarding God's salvation of those who trust in him.

Before long, news came to Saul: "Behold, David is at Naioth in Ramah" (1 Sam. 19:19). Naioth may have been a local place or even a homestead where Samuel lived with the prophets. Hearing this, "Saul sent messengers to take David, and when they saw the company of the prophets prophesying, and Samuel standing as head over them, the Spirit of God came upon the messengers of Saul, and they also prophesied. When it was told Saul, he sent other messengers, and they also prophesied. And Saul sent messengers again the third time, and they also prophesied" (19:20–21).

The description that the prophets, and then Saul's messengers, were "prophesying" seems to refer to an ecstatic state in which these men would speak with messages from God. The main point is that David was saved by the direct intervention of God's Spirit. Matthew Henry comments that God "showed how he can, when he pleases, strike an awe upon the worst of men, by the tokens of his presence in the assemblies of the faithful, and force them to acknowledge that God is with them of a truth."[6] This precept reminds us that it is the worship of God that best protects God's people, especially when the Word of God is preached in the power of the Holy Spirit. Paul stated that when the prophetic Word goes forth in power, even the observing unbeliever "will worship God and declare that God is really among you" (1 Cor. 14:25). It is by the power of the Spirit through God's Word that God's enemies are converted into believers and thus our friends. But even when the world is not converted, the Spirit's power through the Word and prayer in the sacred assembly of Christian worship

---

5. William G. Blaikie, *Expository Lectures on the Book of First Samuel* (1887; repr., Birmingham, AL: Solid Ground, 2005), 312.

6. Henry, *Commentary on the Whole Bible*, 2:303.

instills a fear and awe that protects God's people from the tongues and even the swords of their foes.

We are reminded here of God's seizing the lips of Balaam, the prophet hired to curse Israel in the days of the exodus, from whose mouth God would allow only blessings to fall on his people, and only curses on his enemies (Num. 24:1–9). We are not told what prophecies were made by Saul's agents, but we can easily imagine that under the Spirit's control they, like Balaam, spoke great truths concerning God's protection of the righteous and his promises for the success of his Messiah and the gospel.

Finally, Saul himself came to Ramah seeking David: "And the Spirit of God came upon him also, and as he went he prophesied until he came to Naioth in Ramah. And he too stripped off his clothes, and he too prophesied before Samuel and lay naked all that day and all that night. Thus it is said, 'Is Saul also among the prophets?'" (1 Sam. 19:23–24). Evidently, under control of God's Spirit, Saul was entranced in such a way that he completely disarmed himself and disrobed from all the emblems of his royal office. Saul was thus humiliated by God as he threatened the life of God's anointed servant, and God overcame his enemy in such a way as to bring praise to his name. The proverbial saying that resulted, "Is Saul also among the prophets?," was not an expression of praise but of bewilderment at the erratic conduct of the godless ruler. Keddie writes, "God sovereignly intervened and manifested his power in such a way as to express his disapproval of Saul's intent towards David and to expose him to the self-destructive folly of his ways."[7]

SAFE IN THE FORTRESS

As we reflect on this remarkable chapter, we should note both the mercy and the warning it presents to all who set themselves against the Lord and his Savior, Jesus Christ. First, we observe God's mercy to those who observed Saul, so that the king's willful unbelief would be readily seen for the crazed folly that it was. Second, God was also showing mercy to Saul himself, placing him in circumstances that ought to have made plain to him the folly of his ways. This is how unbelievers should think about the disappointments in their lives and the failures of their character. Blaikie writes: "Oh, friends,

7. Keddie, *Dawn of a Kingdom*, 188.

if there be in you the faintest dissatisfaction with your past life, the faintest desire for a better, take advantage of the opportunity, and turn to God."[8] If you sense that God is thwarting the advancement of your sinful, selfish, or sensual ambitions, do not harden your heart but present it to God for deliverance from sin. When Balaam, the prophet hired to curse Israel, sought to go forward on his wicked errand, God sent an angel with a flaming sword to bar his way. You likewise should respond to God's opposition with words like those of Balaam: "I have sinned, for I did not know that you stood in the road against me. Now therefore, if it is evil in your sight, I will turn back" (Num. 22:26–34). Turn back from your sin and turn to God for forgiveness through the blood of his Son, Jesus Christ.

If you are determined to set your face against God, however, and to persist in your sinful resolutions, especially as you may seek to oppose God's Anointed Savior, Jesus Christ, and his people, then Saul's plight warns you of coming doom. David sang in Psalm 59, "But you, O LORD, laugh at them; you hold all the nations in derision" (v. 8). In Psalm 2, he exulted regarding all who stand in unrighteous opposition to God and his people: "You shall break them with a rod of iron and dash them in pieces like a potter's vessel" (Ps. 2:9). How much better to repent and seek the grace that may be found by anyone in Jesus Christ. Psalm 2 thus concludes:

Now therefore, O kings, be wise;
　be warned, O rulers of the earth.
Serve the LORD with fear,
　and rejoice with trembling.
Kiss the Son,
　lest he be angry, and you perish in the way,
　for his wrath is quickly kindled.
Blessed are all who take refuge in him. (2:10–12)

The promise of refuge provides comfort for God's people. David sang in Psalm 59, "O my Strength, I will watch for you, for you, O God, are my fortress. My God in his steadfast love will meet me; God will let me look in triumph on my enemies" (vv. 9–10). With God's providential hand guiding us through dangers, and God's Spirit empowering us against the spiritual

8. Blaikie, *First Samuel*, 316.

powers of darkness, believers are free to find all our safety in the Word of God and through prayer. "If God is for us," Paul reasoned, "who can be against us?" (Rom. 8:31).

The royal castle of the Scottish kings at Stirling stands on a rock, towering over the fertile lowlands of the Forth valley. Behind its high battlements, it withstood numerous sieges over eight hundred years, and in 1314 it witnessed the victory of Bannockburn, when Scotland's kingdom was recovered from English usurpation. Within the castle walls rests the palace of James V, a serene and peaceful home with lovely gardens both within and without. Within this palace, safe behind the mighty walls, the king and queen could live in peace with the joy of God's blessing on their hearts.[9]

So it is for the Christian, as David revealed through his experience of refuge with the prophets at Ramah. We are safe within the walls of God's mighty protective Spirit, freed not only to rejoice in his goodness to us but also to live in peace and blessing toward those who hate us. In such bliss, we are called by God to do as Samuel and the prophets did: to speak forth the Word of God with great joy, in the power of the Spirit through our faith. We are freed to pray even for those who hate us, that by the Spirit's power in the gospel they may be made our friends and allies. For it was while the prophets of Ramah were worshiping and exulting in God's Word that the Spirit seized their foes. May God likewise reveal his glory in our presence and his power through our witness of Christ and his gospel, that by the divine weapon of the Spirit-inspired Word we may "destroy arguments and every lofty opinion raised against the knowledge of God, and take every thought captive to obey Christ" (2 Cor. 10:4–5).

9. Keddie, *Dawn of a Kingdom*, 189.

30

ARROWS BEYOND YOU

1 Samuel 20:1–42

Jonathan said to David, "Go in peace, because we have sworn both of us in the name of the LORD, saying, 'The LORD shall be between me and you, and between my offspring and your offspring, forever.'" (1 Sam. 20:42)

t is sad to say, but from the moment that David came to fame by his victory over the giant Goliath, his days of peace in Israel were numbered. The reason was the insane jealousy of King Saul, who saw David only as a threat, despite the young man's continual record of humble and faithful service. In the chapters that follow David's victory, we are inching toward his exile, with each chapter presenting a different character study during this time of crisis and trial. In chapter 18, the key actor is David in his response to Saul's sudden attempts to take his life. Chapter 19 focuses on Saul, whose evil spirit drives him from one failed attempt against David to another. Chapter 20 returns our focus to Jonathan, Saul's son and David's covenant friend. Jonathan finds himself trapped in what many people would consider a terrible vise, with his faith and godliness competing against ambition and personal gain. Jonathan shows us how a man of God approaches a situation apparently governed by lust, fear, and hatred, but in fact governed by his faith and by the bonds of covenant fidelity.

DAVID'S PANICKED APPEAL

Seeing David at the beginning of this chapter, it is hard to remember that this is the young champion who boldly faced Goliath in the name of the Lord. Different threats take differing tolls on people, and while David could fearlessly face an uncircumcised warrior such as Goliath, he was unnerved by the open hostility of the king of God's own covenant people. Therefore, when Saul came to Ramah, David fled back in panic to Gibeah. Seeking out his friend Jonathan, he asked why he deserved such ill-treatment: "What have I done? What is my guilt? And what is my sin before your father, that he seeks my life?" (1 Sam. 20:1).

Some commentators see David's flight from Samuel and the prophets at Naioth as an indication that he was seeking worldly rather than divine aid. It is certainly true that David's panicked attitude is explained at least in part by the absence of prayer in this chapter. We get a sense that David had allowed his thoughts to dwell on the injustice of his situation and the temporal threat posed by King Saul, forgetting the reality of sin in the world as a sufficient explanation for injustice and not remembering God's sovereign care over his life. On another occasion, David would pray, "The LORD is my light and my salvation; whom shall I fear?" (Ps. 27:1), yet here we see no evidence of that light in David's life, but only the darkness of fear and alarm.

Jonathan responded to David's appeal with dismay: "Far from it! You shall not die," he answered (1 Sam. 20:2). He reminded David that he was present for Saul's councils and would know of any plot against his friend. This attitude seems incredible, since Saul had already made several direct attempts on David's life and Jonathan had recently rebuked his father's stated intent to have David killed (19:1–5). No doubt Jonathan was not merely being naive or overly charitable in denying Saul's intention: more likely, he was still coming to grips with the terrible situation and his mind had not yet accustomed itself to the evidence about his father. Matthew Henry explains, "Jonathan, from a principle of filial respect to his father, was very loth to believe that he designed or would ever do so wicked a thing."[1]

David was not persuaded by Jonathan's rosy assessment, and he answered insightfully: "Your father knows well that I have found favor in your eyes, and he thinks, 'Do not let Jonathan know this, lest he be grieved.' But truly, as the LORD lives and as your soul lives, there is but a step between me and death" (1 Sam. 20:3). David's oath signals his loss of nerve before the prospect of Saul's violence. Seeing David's distress, Jonathan asked what he could do to help. David answered by reminding him that Saul's court would celebrate a monthly ritual meal, at which David was expected to attend. "But let me go," he said, "that I may hide myself in the field till the third day at evening." Jonathan was to cover for David's absence with a falsehood, claiming that David's family had required him to return home briefly for a sacrifice. "If he says, 'Good!' it will be well with your servant," David concluded, "but if he is angry, then know that harm is determined by him" (20:5–7).

Commentators vary in their assessment of David's subterfuge, some excusing it as an understandable deception and others condemning it as a simple violation of God's command not to lie (Ex. 20:16). I think it is possible to justify this deception biblically, given God's holy war against Saul, yet it is also clear that David was acting out of fear rather than faith. This was not the kind of action that David would later be proud of, and we are reminded by the apostle Paul that "whatever does not proceed from faith is sin" (Rom. 14:23).

There is one matter, however, in which David set a good example. In his distress, he sought safety in covenant promises that had been given to him. Jonathan had covenanted his faithfulness to David, so David sought Jonathan out for help. Dale Ralph Davis comments: "In confusion and trouble, you take yourself to the one person who has made a covenant with you. In David's disintegrating world there was yet one space of sanity, one refuge still intact—Jonathan. There was covenant; there David could expect *faithfulness*."[2]

1. Matthew Henry, *Commentary on the Whole Bible*, 6 vols. (Peabody, MA: Hendrickson, 1992), 2:304.

2. Dale Ralph Davis, *1 Samuel: Looking on the Heart* (Fearn, Ross-shire, UK: Christian Focus, 2000), 168.

It was, in fact, Jonathan's covenant faithfulness to which David appealed in his despair. "Therefore deal kindly with your servant," he pleaded, "for you have brought your servant into a covenant of the LORD with you" (1 Sam. 20:8). This is an excellent way for believers to pray to our covenant God. David urges Jonathan not to hand him over to his father, and if David had committed a sin worthy of death and must be brought to justice, Jonathan should be the one to slay him: "If there is guilt in me, kill me yourself" (20:8). David knew that he would find justice in a covenant friend, just as believers who have appealed to the blood of the new covenant in Christ may confidently seek justification in the presence of God. God's covenant makes the promise, "I will be merciful toward their iniquities, and I will remember their sins no more" (Heb. 8:12, quoting Jer. 31:34), so those who have entered into covenant with God through faith in Christ may come to him to be vindicated and find protection for their souls.

JONATHAN'S OATH AND COVENANT

When Jonathan promised his goodwill and support, David asked how Jonathan would convey news of Saul's conduct. At this, Jonathan took David out into a field—apparently one familiar to them both—and made his arrangements. He spoke in the formal language of a covenant oath: "The LORD, the God of Israel, be witness! When I have sounded out my father, about this time tomorrow, or the third day, behold, if he is well disposed toward David, shall I not then send and disclose it to you? But should it please my father to do you harm, the LORD do so to Jonathan and more also if I do not disclose it to you and send you away, that you may go in safety" (1 Sam. 20:12–13).

Notice how Jonathan responds to this dreadful dilemma. He is not able to manage all the variables, nor even to reconcile his own loyalties. He is Saul's son and is duty-bound to his father, but also David's covenant friend. Moreover, he himself stands to lose much if things go the wrong way. Many people have been completely overthrown by the kind of dilemma Jonathan was in. Yet at the end of this chapter—indeed, at the end of his life—Jonathan escapes without any reproach and succeeds in upholding his conscience. What enabled him to accomplish this? The answer is *faithfulness*. Jonathan's duty was to be faithful in all his relationships and to the covenant into which he had entered. He relied on God to save him, however the Lord might ordain the events of his life. For his own part, he sought his duty and resolved to live faithfully.

First, Jonathan's duty called him to be faithful to his covenant promise to David. He thus made his arrangements to inform David of Saul's mood:

> Tomorrow is the new moon, and you will be missed, because your seat will be empty. On the third day go down quickly to the place where you hid yourself when the matter was in hand, and remain beside the stone heap. And I will shoot three arrows to the side of it, as though I shot at a mark. And behold, I will send the young man, saying, "Go, find the arrows." If I say to the young man, "Look, the arrows are on this side of you, take them," then you are to come, for as the LORD lives, it is safe for you and there is no danger. But if I say to the youth, "Look, the arrows are beyond you," then go, for the LORD has sent you away. (1 Sam. 20:18–22)

Next, Jonathan took counsel of God's revealed Word so far as he knew it. We are never told how Jonathan learned that God had appointed David to succeed Saul as king, but it is clear that Jonathan was aware of God's arrangement. This, of course, meant that Jonathan would not follow his father to the throne. Instead of resisting God's will, Jonathan put God's glory before his own and determined to serve on the side of the Lord. Knowing God's will for David's kingdom, he dutifully served that cause, accepting that his higher duty to God overrode any lesser obligation to obey his father. We should likewise make it our business to serve the cause of God's gospel regardless of the apparent cost to ourselves, in all cases obeying God's Word even if we must refuse the commands of men.

Third, having accepted God's Word, Jonathan sought his own refuge through covenant promises. For this, having bound himself to faithfulness toward David, he now bound David in covenant faithfulness to him, knowing through faith in God's Word that the royal destiny lay with David, despite his father's threats on David's life. "May the LORD be with you," he said, "as he has been with my father. If I am still alive, show me the steadfast love of the LORD, that I may not die; and do not cut off your steadfast love from my house forever, when the LORD cuts off every one of the enemies of David from the face of the earth" (1 Sam. 20:13–15).

When there was a change of dynasty in the ancient world, the universal practice called for the complete slaughter of the prior ruler's household. Jonathan thus appealed to David to spare his life and that of his children when God cleared the way for David's kingship. Jonathan was acting out of his covenant responsibility to his children and their children. To provide for them after the fall of his father's house, "Jonathan made David swear again by his love for him, for he loved him as he loved his own soul" (1 Sam. 20:17). "There has seldom, if ever, been exhibited a finer instance of triumphant faith," writes William Blaikie, "than when the prince, with all the resources of his kingdom at his beck, made this request of the helpless outlaw."[3] In this way alone, by faith in God's Word as it spoke to his situation, Jonathan secured a future for his descendants, as David later fulfilled his part of this covenant by bringing Jonathan's lame son, Mephibosheth, into his own household.

Like Jonathan, believers today are to guide our way through life's challenges by the compass of faithfulness to our covenant duties. Few of us face royal dynastic controversies, but we do confront various difficult challenges in life. Davis recalls an example of such faithfulness in the selfless ministry of his mother toward his dying father after his mind began to slip. She had promised faithfulness "in sickness and in health" and her duty to him was neither glamorous nor dramatic, but only covenantal. Davis recalls, "Nine months after my father died my mother died, perhaps because she felt she could. She had accomplished her mission: taking care of her husband."[4] The examples could be multiplied: husbands remaining faithful to difficult wives, Christians keeping an unprofitable business going to provide jobs to long-serving employees, church members pulling together during a pastoral transition, or in other cases Christians taking a costly stand for God's Word despite the scorn of church leaders and friends.

Even more importantly, believers today, like Jonathan, may find their salvation by entering into the covenant of love offered by the anointed king over God's people. Jesus calls us into his covenant embrace, promising to give us rest (Matt. 11:28), relieve our thirsty souls (John 7:37), and grant us light in the darkness (8:12), and offering us forgiveness (3:36) and resurrec-

---

3. William G. Blaikie, *Expository Lectures on the Book of First Samuel* (1887; repr., Birmingham, AL: Solid Ground, 2005), 321.

4. Davis, *1 Samuel*, 170.

tion into everlasting life (11:25–26). Jesus covenants with all who will come: "Whoever hears my word and believes him who sent me has eternal life. He does not come into judgment, but has passed from death to life" (5:24).

At Table with King Saul

Jonathan's duty to David required him to go back to the presence of his father: "When the new moon came, the king sat down to eat food. The king sat on his seat, as at other times, on the seat by the wall. Jonathan sat opposite, and Abner sat by Saul's side, but David's place was empty" (1 Sam. 20:24–25). Saul, of course, noticed David's absence, but since it was a ritual feast he supposed that David must have suffered some defilement, which one could experience by any number of means. It speaks well for David's character that Saul's natural explanation was one that represented David's careful observance of God's law. But on the second day, which was not a ritual meal, there could be no such excuse. So when Saul asked Jonathan for an explanation, his son replied with the prearranged falsehood: "Jonathan answered Saul, 'David earnestly asked leave of me to go to Bethlehem,'" since his clan was holding a sacrifice and his brother commanded his presence. "For this reason he has not come to the king's table" (20:28–29).

Whatever we think of David and Jonathan's deception, it clearly did not accomplish anything positive. Jonathan was undoubtedly a very poor liar, and a savvy person such as Saul was able to see right through his falsehood. The king's explosive response was stunning to his son: "Saul's anger was kindled against Jonathan, and he said to him, 'You son of a perverse, rebellious woman, do I not know that you have chosen the son of Jesse to your own shame, and to the shame of your mother's nakedness?'" (1 Sam. 20:30). It is a sign of grace when a believer learns to curb his or her tongue in anger, and Saul's outburst signifies the opposite. Saul vented his abuse, insulting his son by cursing Jonathan's mother, Saul's own wife. His hatred for David is seen in his referring to him as the "son of Jesse" (just as we show contempt today by referring to someone only by last name). To Saul, unrestrained in his abusive rage, Jonathan's opposition to his will in any cause—even a righteous one—earned the forfeit of his status as son. Since Jonathan refuses to curry his father's favor, even his mother is now cursed for whelping so insolent a son.

To the extent that it is worthwhile reflecting on Saul's angry invective, we can note three powerful motivators that poured out of the king's heart. The first is *shame*: so determined was Saul to master all wills that his son's righteous disobedience was a source of shame to the king. It speaks volumes about Saul's descent into depravity that he sees Jonathan's godliness as "the shame of your mother's nakedness," by which he refers to the act of a woman giving birth. Second, Saul seeks to manipulate by means of *guilt*, naming Jonathan the "son of a perverse, rebellious woman," by his failure to obey Saul's murderous will (1 Sam. 20:30). Finally, Saul appeals to *greed*: "For as long as the son of Jesse lives on the earth, neither you nor your kingdom shall be established" (20:31). Saul thus depicts a soul depraved by its rebellion against God: he sees shame in righteous conduct, he applies false guilt to motivate others to sin, and his vision is bounded by the greed of what he and his family might possess.

With these poisoned barbs planted in Jonathan's heart, Saul issues his demand: he must bring David to be killed. Unless we have experienced this kind of parental manipulation or known loved ones who have thus suffered, we little imagine the potency of this venom. The movie *Braveheart* depicts a similar encounter between the young Scottish lord Robert the Bruce (1274–1329), who later becomes one of Scotland's great heroes, and his power-groping father, the Lord of Annandale. The Bruce is pulled by the call of duty to his nation, but cowed by his father's scorn and tempted by his own lust for power. Overwhelmed by his father, the Bruce betrays Scotland by riding to battle against his countrymen in the company of its chief enemy, William I of England. The weakness the Bruce showed under the influence of his wicked father is matched only by the shame on his face when he is recognized by William Wallace, leader of the Scottish resistance. The learning experience through his failure ends up shaping the Bruce so that he will never betray his people again.

Saul's son Jonathan needed no such shameful experience to know where his covenant duty lay. He defended David to his father: "Why should he be put to death? What has he done?" (1 Sam. 20:32). At this, Saul took up his ever-present spear and hurled it to strike down his own son.

Let us reflect on the horror of Saul's moral degeneracy. How little he dreamed of this crazed and despicable conduct when he first hardened his heart against the Lord. Saul had justified making himself a servant of self-will and sin because he resented God's chastisement, and was unwilling to humble himself before the rebukes of God's Word through the prophet Samuel. I wonder whether Saul would have followed that path then if he could have seen the man that sin would make him to be. How little he reckoned on the perverting power of sin once it is embraced or the curse of God's judgment when the Lord should decide to deliver him over to iniquity! It is not without reason that Hebrews 3:12–13 urges Christians: "Take care, brothers, lest there be in any of you an evil, unbelieving heart, leading you to fall away from the living God. But exhort one another every day, as long as it is called 'today,' that none of you may be hardened by the deceitfulness of sin."

Saul's mad rage had two effects on Jonathan. First, it tore away any last hope of reason or godliness in his father. "So Jonathan knew that his father was determined to put David to death" (1 Sam. 20:33). The second effect was a bitter grief over the conduct of his father. "Jonathan rose from the table in fierce anger and ate no food the second day of the month, for he was grieved for David, because his father had disgraced him" (20:34).

Jonathan had liberated himself from the depravity of his father by choosing covenant faithfulness to God over a self-centered grasping after personal ambition. He had come to a living embrace of one of the maxims of Jesus: "Seek first the kingdom of God and his righteousness, and all these things will be added to you" (Matt. 6:33). But the grief of his father's malice burned in his heart. Saul could not accept Jonathan for the very reason that God's Word praises him. Saul thought his son a shameful fool for suffering the loss of a kingdom in order to be faithful to the covenant of love. To suffer this misunderstanding and contempt has been the lot of many who walk with the Lord. Jesus declared that his followers must all be willing to suffer this very kind of abuse: "If anyone comes to me and does not hate his own father and mother and wife and children and brothers and sisters, yes, and even his own life, he cannot be my disciple. Whoever does not bear his own cross and come after me cannot be my disciple" (Luke 14:26–27).

FAREWELL TEARS

Jonathan's bitter education at Saul's table left him with only one course of action to follow. "In the morning Jonathan went out into the field to the appointment with David, and with him a little boy" (1 Sam. 20:35). Realizing now the cunning madness of his father, and suspecting that he might be followed, Jonathan was discreet and careful. "He said to his boy, 'Run and find the arrows that I shoot.' As the boy ran, he shot an arrow beyond him. And when the boy came to the place of the arrow that Jonathan had shot, Jonathan called after the boy and said, 'Is not the arrow beyond you?' " (20:36–37). This was, of course, the prearranged signal for David to flee. Conveying his newly gained urgency and throwing away restraint, Jonathan added, "Hurry! Be quick! Do not stay!" (20:38). After sending the boy back to the city with his weapons, Jonathan went forward and David emerged from his hiding place. David acknowledged his debt to Jonathan by bowing before him three times. Then "they kissed one another and wept with one another, David weeping the most. Then Jonathan said to David, 'Go in peace, because we have sworn both of us in the name of the LORD, saying, "The LORD shall be between me and you, and between my offspring and your offspring, forever" ' " (20:41–42).

Anyone who is put off by this show of affection between godly men knows nothing of the close bond of wartime comrades, childhood friends, or covenant brothers in the Lord. Nor do we appreciate the gravity of their lamentable situation if we think their tears an unmanly display. On the eve of the American Civil War, Lewis Armistead and Winfield Scott Hancock spent a night weeping together as they departed for the war, one to assume command in the Southern army and the other in the North. Both would bitterly lament their parting, especially on the day when, as Armistead died and Hancock lay bleeding, their respective commands clashed in the climactic assault of the Battle of Gettysburg. Men of great feeling will exhibit emotion not only over their victories and losses, but also over lost and parted comrades.

David and Jonathan likewise parted for their duties on opposite sides of the conflict about to begin. The chapter ends with the statement that David "rose and departed, and Jonathan went into the city" (1 Sam. 20:42). Only once more, briefly in a desperate and dangerous setting, would the two men meet again in life. But despite the travail of the occasion, their parting was unsullied by infidelity and their consciences were clean because of their obedience to the clear call of duty. Though physically separated and pulled apart by differing obligations, "they would remain inseparably joined by the oath they swore in the Lord's name."[5]

This friendship provides an eternal example to the uplifting and purifying effect of godly brotherhood. Jonathan's covenant faithfulness may be excelled only by that of God's Son, Jesus Christ. Blaikie writes: "In the case of Jesus Christ, we have all the noble qualities of Jonathan in far higher excellence than his, and we have this further consideration, that for us He has laid down His life, and that none who receive His friendship can ever be separated from His love."[6]

"GO IN PEACE"

The final words in this bitter chapter are spoken by Jonathan: "Go in peace." What a ludicrous statement, outwardly speaking! They were departing for war and conflict. David was about to flee in panic and would live for years as a fugitive, and Jonathan was returning to what was probably the more distressing fate of continuing in service to his wicked and deranged father. How could Jonathan speak of their going in peace? His answer was the covenant they had made, which established peace between them: "Go in peace, because we have sworn both of us in the name of the LORD, saying, 'The LORD shall be between me and you, and between my offspring and your offspring, forever'" (1 Sam. 20:42). Through all the troubles to come, both men would be faithful to their covenant to the end of their days, so in the midst of such great conflict they departed in peace and lived in peace. If we will likewise commit to a life of faithfulness in covenant with others, we too will enjoy peace even in a world of woe.

More important still was the peace they received through their covenant with the Lord. Their peace rested on God's covenant promises and the faithfulness of God to keep his oath. This is where our souls find peace as well: "His oath, his covenant, his blood / support me in the whelming flood."[7] We gain peace with God through the covenant of grace, which says, "Believe in the Lord Jesus, and you will be saved, you and your household"

5. Robert D. Bergen, *1, 2 Samuel*, New American Commentary (Nashville: Broadman & Holman, 1996), 219.
6. Blaikie, *First Samuel*, 328.
7. Edward Mote, "My Hope Is Built on Nothing Less" (1834).

(Acts 16:31). Through faith in Christ's blood, we are forgiven our sins and justified with God. His covenant promise then secures peace: "Therefore, since we have been justified by faith, we have peace with God through our Lord Jesus Christ" (Rom. 5:1). Though all the world should assail us, God's covenant faithfulness and the certain hope of his blessing will calm our souls: "When all around my soul gives way, / he then is all my hope and stay."[8] Like Jonathan, we do not have the power to control the affairs of our times or restrain the sins of those around us. Nonetheless, like him, we may live in troubled times with the blessing of God's peace. Isaiah spoke of those like Jonathan when he said to the Lord, "You keep him in perfect peace whose mind is stayed on you, because he trusts in you" (Isa. 26:3).

Finally, just as Jonathan responded to the evils of his day by calling David into covenant with himself, God calls us into covenant through faith in his Son, Jesus. Christ calls us to a life of covenant faithfulness, and for this he strengthens us with the divine blessing of peace (Luke 2:14). Just as Jonathan and David separated in peace, having rested their hearts in a bond of covenant love, we rest our souls in the promised grace of our sovereign Savior and Lord. He promises to his covenant people: "Peace I leave with you; my peace I give to you. Not as the world gives do I give to you. Let not your hearts be troubled, neither let them be afraid" (John 14:27).

---

8. Ibid.

31

Unholy Flight

1 Samuel 21:1–15

David said to Ahimelech the priest, "The king has charged me with a matter and said to me, 'Let no one know anything of the matter about which I send you, and with which I have charged you.'" (1 Sam. 21:2)

Occasionally, you will hear the name of a place that seems strangely familiar. Though you cannot quite place it, it seems that you have been there before. Most Christians should respond this way to a reading of 1 Samuel 21. We hear the name "Nob," and ask, "Haven't I been there?" We read of "Gath," and ponder, "Isn't that a place I have visited?"

I say this not because most Christians have physically visited Palestine, where these ancient sites were located. Instead, we have frequented the spiritual reality that they represent. Nob is the place of David's unholy flight of fear, and Gath is the city of David's mad refuge. Few who have sought to follow Jesus Christ for any length of time have avoided these travel stops; most of us can recognize from our own experience the bitterness of what they represent.

Fortunately, God also knows Nob and Gath very well, and therefore knows how to rescue his people from these places and to use them to challenge and mold our faith. As we study David's flight through Nob and refuge in Gath, we will not only consider the folly of a believer gripped by fear, but also learn, as Dale Ralph Davis writes, that "even in their most desperate moments [the Lord] does not let go of his servants, least of all David, his king-elect."[1]

David's Fearful Flight through Nob

David was now facing a different kind of challenge from the clear and obvious danger he had earlier mastered in the Philistine giant, Goliath. The new threat to David's life, this time from Israel's own King Saul, brought David to the brink of desperation. He had appealed to the friendship of Saul's son for protection, but Jonathan had been unable to stay his father's wrath. David then took refuge with Samuel and his prophets in Ramah, but Saul had tracked him there. Learning from Jonathan that Saul was utterly determined to see him dead, David fled precipitously, taking off, it seems, with little more than the shirt on his back.

David's first stop was not far away: the priestly compound at Nob, a location about two miles south of Saul's home in Gibeah. Having appealed to the king's son and then to the prophets for his safety, David now turns to the third institution of Israel: the priests. After the fall of Shiloh, the priests had evidently moved the tabernacle to Nob, although the ark of the covenant remained in Kiriath-jearim (1 Sam. 7:2; 2 Sam. 6:3). David probably never intended to hide so near to Saul at Nob, but he may have gone to inquire of the Lord and to receive whatever help the priests might provide. Although he seems overly charitable to David, given the tenor of this chapter, it is worth mentioning Matthew Henry's suggestion that David may have fled to Nob in part because of affection: "He had given an affectionate farewell to his friend Jonathan, and cannot go till he has given the like to the tabernacle."[2]

When David arrived, however, he was unnerved by the demeanor of the priest: "Ahimelech came to meet David trembling" (1 Sam. 21:1). Evidently, news of Saul's hatred for David had spread so as to make people nervous

1. Dale Ralph Davis, *1 Samuel: Looking on the Heart* (Fearn, Ross-shire, UK: Christian Focus, 2000), 174.
2. Matthew Henry, *Commentary on the Whole Bible*, 6 vols. (Peabody, MA: Hendrickson, 1992), 2:308.

about the fugitive. The priest not only met David with shaking hands and a sweaty face, but also immediately quizzed David: "Why are you alone, and no one with you?" (21:1).

We can understand why it was surprising to see a man of David's high office unattended by an official retinue. But the abrupt greeting could only have conveyed hesitancy regarding David's status, and this seems to have unnerved David. His faith and composure were already shaken (see 1 Sam. 20:3), and now he began to falter. Back in Gibeah, David had resorted to a lie (20:6), and now at Nob he again turned to falsehood. He answered, "The king has charged me with a matter and said to me, 'Let no one know anything of the matter about which I send you, and with which I have charged you.' I have made an appointment with the young men for such and such a place" (21:2). In other words, David claimed to be on a secret mission from King Saul, with his men hidden away nearby.

There is no point, as some commentators have tried, in putting a positive face on David's false speaking, for which he can have no real excuse. David's lying is in fact getting worse, since now he straight-facedly deceives a holy priest of the Lord while present in God's holy tabernacle. This is what happens when our minds are overthrown by fear. When we have forgotten God's faithfulness and love, we easily fall into patterns of sin.

Jesus' commentary on this passage in Matthew 12:3–4 suggests that David did have at least some companions, and they may indeed have been hidden nearby, but he was absolutely not on a mission from King Saul. Just as with his previous lie, told by Jonathan to Saul, this false statement accomplished nothing positive and had several harmful results. A. W. Pink writes, "Though ingenious falsehoods may seem to promote present security, yet they insure future disgrace."[3]

Moreover, if helping David was likely to bring Ahimelech into danger, the priest had a right to know. David would have done well to disclose the truth and seek the priest's prayers and advice: it is hard to imagine godly counsel and prayer resulting in the actions that David went on to take. I have learned in pastoral ministry that Christians who are walking closely with the Lord come to see their pastor seeking prayer and counsel *before* an important decision. Christians who are pulling away from the Lord usually

---

3. A. W. Pink, *A Life of David*, 2 vols. (Grand Rapids: Baker, 1981), 1:76.

conceal their plans, and afterward see their pastor seeking forgiveness for actions that they knew were wrong all along.

In chapter 22, we learn that Ahimelech did inquire of the Lord for David (vv. 10, 15), even though David had not posed an honest question. David's main interest, however, was in provision rather than counsel: "Now then, what do you have on hand? Give me five loaves of bread, or whatever is here" (1 Sam. 21:3).

David's demand posed a problem, since the only food available at the tabernacle was consecrated bread, which sat on the table of showbread in the Holy Place and which was to be eaten only by the priest and his family (see Lev. 21). Ahimelech said, "I have no common bread on hand, but there is holy bread" (1 Sam. 21:4). The priest was willing to give this bread to David, but imposed requirements that would call for a minimum of consecration on the part of David and his men, namely, that they must "have kept themselves from women" (21:4). This prohibition does not represent a biblical notion that sexual intimacy is inherently wicked, for the Bible sees God-given sex within marriage as a great blessing. Nonetheless, the Levitical holiness code considered the loss of bodily fluids a sign of uncleanness (see Lev. 15:18; cf. Ex. 19:15). Fortunately for David, he and whatever men were with him had met this qualification, and David stated that this was a standard policy for his missions: "Truly women have been kept from us as always when I go on an expedition." Referring to the holy status of their bodies, he added, "The vessels of the young men are holy even when it is an ordinary journey. How much more today"—that is, a day when they would visit the tabernacle—"will their vessels be holy?" (1 Sam. 21:5). At this, "the priest gave him the holy bread, for there was no bread there but the bread of the Presence, which is removed from before the LORD, to be replaced by hot bread on the day it is taken away" (21:6).

Jesus once made a point about the Sabbath day by referring to this episode. The Pharisees had accused Jesus and his disciples of violating the Sabbath because they picked and ate grain as they walked through a field. Jesus answered, "Have you not read what David did when he was hungry, and those who were with him: how he entered the house of God and ate the bread of the Presence, which it was not lawful for him to eat nor for those who were with him, but only for the priests?" (Matt. 12:3–4). Jesus' point was not, as some scholars assert, that the greater obligation of mercy overrode the mere observance of God's law. No such contradiction, in fact, exists. Rather, Jesus meant that the intent of the law was fulfilled by the act of mercy. Gordon Keddie explains, "The true meaning of the ceremonial law of the showbread was expressed in its being given to David as an act of compassion and mercy providing for real need; the law was fulfilled, rather than superseded."[4] In drawing on this episode, Jesus applied its lesson to the Pharisees: "If you had known what this means, 'I desire mercy, and not sacrifice,' you would have not condemned the guiltless" (Matt. 12:7, quoting Hos. 6:6). Our Lord's reference to this passage should inform our Sabbath observance today and warn us against excessive rules that make the Lord's Day a burden. For instance, it does not violate but fulfill the Sabbath to gather for Christian fellowship in a joyful spirit, to provide a meal to shut-ins, or to engage in any other spiritually wholesome form of liberality and generosity.

Two last notes are made regarding David's brief passage at Nob. The first was the presence of a menacing figure named Doeg the Edomite, a servant of Saul who had been detained at the tabernacle and witnessed David's visit. Later, David will admit that he knew that Doeg would report the visit to Saul and that the priests would be harmed for it, yet he did nothing to intervene (see 1 Sam. 22:22). The second was David's request for a weapon, saying that he had left in haste and was thus unequipped. He received the sword of Goliath, which had been deposited in the tabernacle (probably as a trophy of God's victory). Ahimelech said, "The sword of Goliath, the Philistine, whom you struck down in the Valley of Elah, behold, it is here wrapped in a cloth behind the ephod. If you will take that, take it, for there is none but that here" (21:9). It says much that the same David who refused to wear the armor of Israel's king when he was filled with the Spirit for his battle with Goliath now rejoices to wield the weapon of his former pagan enemy. No longer relying on God's strength, he exulted in the sword, saying, "There is none like that; give it to me" (21:9).

Thus was David's passage through Nob, which became for him a place where fear gave way to sin, unbelief, and worldliness. At Nob, David sought to protect himself with a lie, permitted his behavior to endanger others, and exulted in the worldly weapons he acquired. How much better it would have been if the sight of Goliath's sword had reminded David of how God

---

4. Gordon J. Keddie, *Dawn of a Kingdom: The Message of 1 Samuel* (Darlington, UK: Evangelical Press, 1988), 196.

had earlier answered his faith, and how willing God is to help those who call on his name! Christians today should remember God's sovereign grace to us in Christ and in this be fortified against temptations to lie, cheat, or manipulate others when we feel threatened or afraid.

DAVID'S MAD REFUGE IN GATH

The best commentary on David's unbelieving passage through Nob is the destination to which it led him. Like David, whenever we pass through our Nob, engaging in willful, unbelieving flight from obedient faith in God, we are likely to place ourselves in spiritually unprofitable settings. We may not be surprised that David's flight brought him to an ungodly place, but we are surprised that he would actually flee to Goliath's hometown of Gath! Yet that is where David went: "David rose and fled that day from Saul and went to Achish the king of Gath" (1 Sam. 21:10).

This account is briefer than that of David at Nob, and involves an uncomplicated outcome. David probably fled to Gath to remove himself from Saul's domain. He may have thought that being an enemy of Saul would gain him asylum among the Philistines. He had forgotten, however, that he himself was the main source of Philistine woes and the slayer of their soldiers. (If David had forgotten the two hundred Philistine foreskins, the people of Gath had not!) No sooner had David entered the city than people recognized him and complained in alarm to King Achish: "Is not this David the king of the land? Did they not sing to one another of him in dances, 'Saul has struck down his thousands, and David his ten thousands'?" (1 Sam. 21:11). David's ten thousand *Philistines*, that is! Adding insult to injury, David had the audacity to stroll into town wearing the sword of their hero, with which David had cut off Goliath of Gath's head!

David's fearful flight had brought him to a place of refuge that turned out to be even more threatening than mad King Saul! He realized this immediately: "David took these words to heart and was much afraid of Achish the king of Gath" (1 Sam. 21:12). Apparently out of other options, David resorted to a last desperate tactic: "he changed his behavior before them and pretended to be insane in their hands and made marks on the doors of the gate and let his spittle run down his beard" (21:13). In God's providence, David's willful folly was being mocked: any plan that results in one's having to let spit drool down his beard is not a plan that has gone well! David's actions are, of course, a commentary on his own state of mind: his actions had been crazy, and now it was appropriate that he acted that way. Roger Ellsworth comments: "The man who stood calmly before Goliath because he was possessed with faith now acts like a maniac because he is possessed with fear."[5] We also remember Saul's madness, and we see that by joining Saul on the path of unbelief and sin, David was starting to resemble his nemesis.

The only positive thing to say about David's desperate action was that it worked. Achish's response is comical: "Behold, you see the man is mad. Why then have you brought him to me? Do I lack madmen, that you have brought this fellow to behave as a madman in my presence? Shall this fellow come into my house?" (1 Sam. 21:14–15). Achish probably held the common ancient superstition that harming lunatics brought bad luck. Mainly, however, he had enough crazy people already and did not need one more around in David! This was hardly a compliment to a man anointed by God as Israel's future king—and it shows the shame into which sin will bring anyone—but it did allow David to escape.

Warnings from Nob and Gath

How can we explain David's unholy conduct? He was being driven by fear, but David had faced fear before. Possibly, he had drunk from the poison serum of self-pity, thus rationalizing his sin and willful folly. He had not asked to be anointed by Samuel, but he had still served Saul faithfully. What had been the result? He was being ruthlessly hounded by a mad king! David had great promises from God, but so little providence of them. No doubt the true injustice of this situation tore his heart. The psalms he later wrote about this period of his life indicate that he was brokenhearted over his treatment and "crushed in spirit" (Ps. 34:18). Instead of taking these ailments to the Lord, however, David seems to have nurtured them, to the detriment of his own heart. Panicked, bitter, and weary, David fled from the way of faith that his self-pity saw as the root of his trouble. Thus, God's Word never figures into David's schemes, and he never stops fleeing long enough to pray for God's help in composing his frayed nerves. Passing through Nob, David

5. Roger Ellsworth, *The Shepherd King: Learning from the Life of David* (Darlington, UK: Evangelical Press, 1998), 62.

permitted himself the indulgence of sin, and by his ending up in Gath, the madness of his flight was ultimately revealed.

We can profitably discover four warnings for believers in David's conduct. The first is that *our unbelieving sins have real consequences.* David's lie to Ahimelech exposed the priest to a danger that would be fully realized in the near future. Like David at Nob, we may cover our sins with successful lies, but the sin we thus protect will inevitably harm us and others. We may neglect clear duties as Christians, spouses, and parents—especially our duty to prayer and the regular study of God's Word—but in time we will join the ranks of those who regretfully survey the wreckage in our homes and lives. We may commit ourselves to worldly values and ambitions, just as David gloated over possession of Goliath's sword. But the money, prestige, and pleasure that we gain will only result in the gloom that David experienced in Gath. This is enemy territory, and no servant of God can abide there safely! Even after believers have repented and been restored to God, the consequences of Nob and Gath may remain painfully real.

Second, David's behavior warns us that *any believer can become backslidden,* by giving ear to the counsel of fear, unbelief, and self-pity. David was a very great servant of God, a man of towering spiritual qualities. Here is the man who could be called "a man after [God's] own heart" (1 Sam. 13:14). But the best of men are men at best, and David could no more safely indulge in unbelief and sin than we can. Looking at such an example, Paul counsels us, "Let anyone who thinks that he stands take heed lest he fall" (1 Cor. 10:12). With this in mind, Jesus taught us urgently to pray, "Lead us not into temptation, but deliver us from evil" (Matt. 6:13).

A third warning reminds us not only that any of us can fall, but also *how far we can fall and how fast it can happen.* Only recently, David had been faithfully serving in Saul's court and leading Israel's armies valiantly in battle. Now he is slobbering in a corner of Goliath's hometown. This is why the Bible tells us always to consider both God's grace and our duty. Hebrews 3:12 especially urges us to beware any hardness in our hearts toward God: "Take care, brothers, lest there be in any of you an evil, unbelieving heart, leading you to fall away from the living God."

Fourth, David shows us that *even very godly people will struggle with doubts, fears, resentments, and broken hearts.* This is why we need Christian friends, on whom we may rely for counsel, sympathy, and prayer. Notice that

David's struggles occur in tandem with his separation from his covenant friend Jonathan. This is also why God provides elders and pastors in the church. Ahimelech may not have handled himself perfectly when David appeared at the tabernacle, but David still could have opened his heart and sought biblical encouragement from a man set apart to minister for God. It is because of our need for similar pastoral guidance that God places Christians into congregations, under the spiritual oversight of elders, whom God has appointed to keep "watch over your souls" (Heb. 13:17).

"TASTE AND SEE"

The apostle Paul wrote that the mistakes of the Old Testament were recorded as "examples for us, that we might not desire evil as they did" (1 Cor. 10:6). Once David departed from Gath and regained his safety, he too reflected on this low period of his life, and in Psalms 34 and 56 he recorded his thoughts, which focus mainly on God. Having considered lessons about ourselves from David's flight, we can also note four truths about God's dealings with his people.

The first lesson is that *God provides for his people in all their needs*. We are shown this providence in the bread that David was given from God's table in the tabernacle. David wrote in Psalm 34:9–10, "Oh, fear the LORD, you his saints, for those who fear him have no lack! The young lions suffer want and hunger; but those who seek the LORD lack no good thing." Davis comments: "We note that in the confusion and danger and fear David received his daily bread." The loaves from God's table were "a quiet witness that [the Lord] sustains people and supplies their needs."[6]

Do you find yourself under a heavy load of worry and cares? Do you sometimes think you will crumble under the pressure? Look, then, to God's daily provision and remember that just as God did not cast off David in his folly and sin, God will remain faithful to you.

Second, David comments on how *God protects his people in danger*. This is the main point on which David dwells in these psalms. Psalm 34:6–8 recalls: "This poor man cried, and the LORD heard him and saved him out of all his troubles. The angel of the LORD encamps around those who fear

6. Davis, *1 Samuel*, 176.

him, and delivers them. Oh, taste and see that the LORD is good! Blessed is the man who takes refuge in him!"

David realized that in his lowest moments, God's unseen help was still protecting him. Psalm 56 offers the most obvious application of this realization, namely, that when David is afraid, he should remember to trust in God: "In God, whose word I praise, in God I trust; I shall not be afraid. What can flesh do to me?" (Ps. 56:4). The second application is that while trusting God, we must then obey his laws and commands: "I must perform my vows to you, O God; I will render thank offerings to you. For you have delivered my soul from death" (56:12–13). It is noteworthy that David focuses on truthfulness in speech as a fruit of faith in God's protection: "Keep your tongue from evil and your lips from speaking deceit. Turn away from evil and do good; seek peace and pursue it" (34:13–14).

God not only protected David from Saul and the king of Gath, but also protected David from his own sin. David intended to conceal his identity among the people of Gath, but, as Pink writes, "God will not allow His people to remain incognito in this world." Thus, David was quickly recognized, just as a true believer in Christ will not be able to blend in unnoticed with the world. "And mercifully is this the case, for God will not have His own to settle down among and enjoy the friendship of His enemies."[7] Whenever God refuses to grant success to our sinful schemes, we should praise him for protecting us from becoming permanently entangled in evil.

Third, we learn from David's experience about *God's pedagogy*, that is, his wise training of his children. Not only was David doing things in this chapter, but God was acting, too. If David lost his grip on God, it was in part because God seems to have withdrawn his presence temporarily as a way of testing and training David's faith. Knowing the challenges that lay ahead for David, it seems that the Lord arranged this experience to teach David his weakness and need of constant grace. The resulting wisdom is seen in Psalm 34:4, in which David reflects, "I sought the LORD, and he answered me and delivered me from all my fears." Few of us daily seek the Lord until by painful experience we have learned our peril apart from God.

Fourth, David was persuaded through these experiences, and by God's deliverance of him in Gath, of *God's pity toward those who belong to him*.

---

7. Pink, *Life of David*, 74.

He wrote in Psalm 34:17–18, "When the righteous cry for help, the Lord hears and delivers them out of all their troubles. The Lord is near to the brokenhearted and saves the crushed in spirit." David erred by not taking his distress to a believing friend or spiritual leader, but there is a more ready help than these: the pity of God for his people.

The answer to self-pity, which bears the ill-fruit of so many dark thoughts and seemingly justifies so many destructive sins, is to seek God's pity in prayer. Most touching, perhaps, is David's statement in Psalm 56, written after these events, in which David notes the loving care with which God treats each of our sorrows. "You have kept count of my tossings," David sighs. He asks, "Put my tears in your bottle. Are they not in your book?" (Ps. 56:8). The Lord who loved us so much as to send his Son to die for our sins is also tender with balm for every wound on our hearts. We should respond, therefore, in the way that Charles Wesley's hymn counsels us: "Jesus, lover of my soul, / Let me to thy bosom fly."[8]

A Greater than David

David's sufferings have the ultimate purpose of foreshadowing the greater sufferings of God's true anointed King, the Messiah. Likewise, David's psalms, which often express a spiritual keenness higher than he seems to have personally possessed, more truly reflect the faith and devotion of his greater Son, Jesus Christ. It is God's grace for us in Christ that answers our fear and need in times of trouble. "In the world you will have tribulation," Jesus said. "But take heart; I have overcome the world" (John 16:33).

David received provision from the sacred bread of the tabernacle. But Jesus is the true bread that meets our greatest need. He said: "I am the living bread that came down from heaven. If anyone eats of this bread, he will live forever. And the bread that I will give for the life of the world is my flesh" (John 6:51). Likewise, David could praise God for his protection in sparing him from death. But God's greater protection in Jesus Christ protects us even in death. David's rejoicing in Psalm 34 applies most pointedly to Christ's sin-redeeming death on the cross: "The Lord redeems the life of his servants; none of those who take refuge in him will be condemned"

8. Charles Wesley, "Jesus, Lover of My Soul" (1740).

(Ps. 34:22). Finally, God's pity for his suffering people is most perfectly manifested in the coming of Jesus into our world. The writer of Hebrews reminds us, "For we do not have a high priest who is unable to sympathize with our weaknesses, but one who in every respect has been tempted as we are, yet without sin" (Heb. 4:15). Jesus thus gives all-sufficient grace for our every need:

> Thou, O Christ, art all I want;
> More than all in thee I find:
> Raise the fallen, cheer the faint,
> Heal the sick, and lead the blind.[9]

Jesus is willing for all this and more. "Let us then with confidence draw near to the throne of grace," the pastor of Hebrews urges us, "that we may receive mercy and find grace to help in time of need" (Heb. 4:16).

9. Ibid.

32

MURDER OF THE PRIESTS

1 Samuel 22:1–23

The king said to the guard who stood about him, "Turn and kill the priests of the LORD, because their hand also is with David . . ." (1 Sam. 22:17)

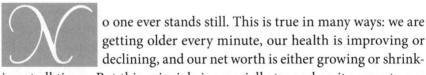o one ever stands still. This is true in many ways: we are getting older every minute, our health is improving or declining, and our net worth is either growing or shrinking at all times. But this principle is especially true when it comes to our moral character and spiritual condition. The biblical principle given by the apostle Paul applies to matters both great and small: "Whatever one sows, that will he also reap. For the one who sows to his own flesh will from the flesh reap corruption, but the one who sows to the Spirit will from the Spirit reap eternal life" (Gal. 6:7–8).

As we progress through the narrative of 1 Samuel, we find that King Saul is not standing still. He has been sowing rebellion to God's Word and mad hatred for faithful David. He has also been reaping an increasingly hardened conscience and a morally twisted character. Saul's sowing and reaping has advanced to the stage of utter apostasy. He has not succeeded in his maniacal attempts to slay David, but the now ever-present spear in his hand signifies the mortal wounds to his own spiritual condition. He has sown evil and has reaped the living hell of a warped soul.

Chapter 22 presents one of the last detailed depictions of Saul's heart, for after these events there will be little more to say about him. He has by now become wholly the servant of evil, one of Satan's chief agents in opposing God's plan of salvation. We will focus on Saul's heart condition only once more, when in chapter 28 his Satan-serving impulse leads him to seek a medium's help in speaking with the dead. All that remains for Saul after that episode is a disgraceful death and then the final judgment of God and eternal condemnation. Saul is the prototypical apostate, whose self-willed choices led day by day, decision by decision, to an eternity in hell. The apostle John, writing about the coming of the final Antichrist, noted that "many antichrists have come" (1 John 2:18). Saul became one of them, and he pictures in concentrated form the destiny awaiting those who set their hardened hearts on the path of rebellion to God. In Saul's anti-David program we see another picture of the reign of sin, as the righteous are made outcasts, sacred things are defiled, and the wicked are unleashed in a mad frenzy of violence and death.

THE RIGHTEOUS MADE OUTCASTS

Upon realizing that Saul was intent on his death, David fled in a fearful rush that took him through Nob, where the priests ministered in the tabernacle, and to the Philistine city of Gath. Finally awakening to his folly, David returned to the wilderness region of Judea, halfway between Gath and Bethlehem, taking refuge in the extensive cave system at Adullam. This respite allowed David to gather his wits, and it is apparent that he communicated with his family. Observing Saul's menacing surveillance of David's home, Jesse's household from Bethlehem fled to join David in the caves.

A person who has given himself over to sin will always fail to compartmentalize wickedness in a single portion of his or her life. Cheating will lead to lying, for instance, and lying will lead to falsely accusing, which leads to hatred and violence. Walter Chantry writes, "Injustice . . . becomes a way of life for authorities who begin to practice abusive measures."[1] We are

---

1. Walter Chantry, *David: Man of Prayer, Man of War* (Edinburgh: Banner of Truth, 2007), 70.

spared the details of the spreading viciousness of Saul's rule, but there can be no doubt that his administration began to foster widespread injustice, corruption, and abuse.

As matters worsened, a growing number of people could not tolerate Saul's regime. Becoming outlaws against the evil king, it was natural that they would seek out Saul's self-appointed rival, David: "Everyone who was in distress, and everyone who was in debt, and everyone who was bitter in soul, gathered to him. And he became captain over them. And there were with him about four hundred men" (1 Sam. 22:2). This band of four hundred formed the nucleus of what would become David's kingdom, and it is noteworthy that in the providence of God it was Saul's injustice toward David that marked the younger man out as the leader for the faithful in Israel. How often in history God has called forth leaders for his people by having them suffer persecution at the hands of the ungodly. David's skill would soon be displayed in making a disciplined and effective military force out of this band of outcasts and refugees.

There are many ways in which David typifies the coming Savior, Jesus Christ. This passage where David rallies the outcast and the unwanted of Israel is an example that is often overlooked, yet it is among the most profound. Like David at Adullam, Jesus gathered a band of followers that the world could describe only as ragtag, and that the Pharisees derided as "tax collectors and sinners" (Matt. 9:11). Fishermen such as Peter, James, and John, a tax collector such as Matthew, and nobodies such as Philip, Bartholomew, Thaddeus, and the others—not to mention the train of women, led by the once-demon-possessed Mary Magdalene (Luke 8:2)—were not the kind of followers who offered access to cultural influence or who wielded worldly power. How similar was the situation with Jesus' forerunner David and the ever-growing band of discontents that joined him in exile. Under David's influence, however, these followers formed the initial nucleus of what would become a great and glorious kingdom, the legacy of which will literally last forever. Led by God's Son, Jesus, and empowered by the Holy Spirit he sends from heaven, Christ's followers are a dynamic influence in the world, despite their lowly appearance and worldly weakness. Paul commented of the early believers: "Not many of you were wise according to worldly standards, not many were powerful, not many were of noble birth" (1 Cor. 1:26). Yet before long, the wise, powerful, and noble of the world would complain of their inability to stop the dynamic power of Christ at work in his people. "These men . . . have turned the world upside down," they cried in alarm (Acts 17:6).

Moreover, just as David was marked as a true leader by the rage of the evil king, Saul, so also was Jesus Christ commended as the Messiah by the raging hatred of the hypocritical Pharisees and cynical Roman rulers, behind whom the malicious scheming of the devil was at work. In Psalm 2, David had foretold the scenario recorded in the Gospels: "The kings of the earth set themselves, and the rulers take counsel together, against the LORD and against his Anointed" (Ps. 2:2). Jesus' ability to constantly confound his enemies, and especially his rising from the dead to overthrow even their murderous work at the cross, identifies him as the Savior foretold long years beforehand. "He who sits in the heavens laughs," David wrote; "the Lord holds them in derision" (2:4). Christ's conquest of his earthly enemies and then his triumph over the greater powers of sin and death through the resurrection mark him out as the Captain into whose care we should desire to place our futures.

Like Jesus, David was concerned not only for the great masses of God's people but also for those closest to him (see John 19:26–27). By the time of his refuge at Adullam, David's parents must have been aged, and it seems that David was concerned to remove them to a place of safety. Therefore, "David went from there to Mizpeh of Moab. And he said to the king of Moab, 'Please let my father and my mother stay with you, till I know what God will do for me'" (1 Sam. 22:3). We are not told why the king of Moab was disposed to show kindness to David. Perhaps his status as a refugee from Saul gained David favor, and perhaps his generations-old Moabite heritage, through Ruth, helped as well.

What is evident in this brief episode is that David has experienced a spiritual revival. How backslidden he was in his mad flight from Saul, through Nob and to the hometown of Goliath in Gath! But notice now that he expresses his desire to discern God's will, asking the Moabites to keep his parents "till I know what God will do for me." Two of David's psalms are attributed to his period of refuge in Adullam, and they are both significant in telling of a renewed commitment to prayer and waiting on the Lord. Psalm 57:2 says, "I cry out to God Most High, to God who fulfills his purpose for me." Psalm 142:1–2 speaks similarly: "With my voice I cry out to the LORD;

with my voice I plead for mercy to the LORD. I pour out my complaint before him; I tell my trouble before him."

The result in David's life of this renewed appeal to God in prayer and attentiveness to God's Word was the same as it would be in ours: David's faith was strengthened and he began once more to discern in a spiritual and wise manner. He thus declares his conviction: "He will send from heaven and save me; he will put to shame him who tramples on me. God will send out his steadfast love and his faithfulness!" (Ps. 57:3).

The result of David's strengthened faith is an eager willingness to obey God's Word. We see this in the appearance of a prophet named Gad, who said to David, "'Do not remain in the stronghold; depart, and go into the land of Judah.' So David departed and went into the forest of Hereth" (1 Sam. 22:5). This kind of ready obedience to God's Word is the mark of true and living faith. If we are to profess faith in David's God, then we must be willing to obey as David did when the Bible speaks clearly to our lives. In the arrival of Gad the prophet to his refuge at Adullam, David must have seen a return of God's favor for him. We likewise should treat God's Word as the surest sign of his will for our blessing, so that we prize the Scriptures and eagerly believe and obey them.

In contrast to David's renewed faith and obedience, Saul not only turned away from the Lord in hardened unbelief, but had so little tolerance for the righteous that he made them outcasts. What a warning it is when godly people no longer find your company wholesome. The path of worldliness and pride has its short-lived rewards, but the companionship of God's holy people is not one of them. If you look upon serious, committed believers in Jesus as an annoyance and if your actions make it difficult for them to be near you, then you should contemplate your danger. Realize that such believers have the blessing of God upon them, and therefore those who oppress them must dwell under the shadow of God's wrath.

THE SACRED THINGS DEFILED

News of David's movements inevitably came to the ears of malicious ruler Saul, who was holding court "at Gibeah under the tamarisk tree on the height" (1 Sam. 22:6). Never at peace in his soul, Saul grasped his ever-present spear. His servants stood about him when he began fuming at the news regarding David. Saul raved, "Hear now, people of Benjamin; will the son of Jesse give every one of you fields and vineyards, will he make you all commanders of thousands and commanders of hundreds, that all of you have conspired against me?" (22:7–8). Faithless himself, Saul never imagined that his followers could act out of simple loyalty and honest duty. His only way of appeal was to use better carrots and a bigger stick. In virtuous David, Saul saw an increasingly ominous threat. Therefore, he complained, "No one discloses to me when my son makes a covenant with the son of Jesse. None of you is sorry for me or discloses to me that my son has stirred up my servant against me, to lie in wait, as at this day" (22:8). Self-pity and fear had totally gripped Saul's heart: he could be comfortable only if those around him felt sorry for him and entered into his warped conspiracy.

Most people who find themselves in service to a ruler like Saul are frightened by this kind of wild accusation. But others see it as a golden opportunity. Such a person was Doeg the Edomite, whom we met in the previous chapter as he watched David at Nob with the priests. Doeg thus had news that would greatly interest the angry king: "Then answered Doeg the Edomite, who stood by the servants of Saul, 'I saw the son of Jesse coming to Nob, to Ahimelech the son of Ahitub, and he inquired of the LORD for him and gave him provisions and gave him the sword of Goliath the Philistine'" (1 Sam. 22:9–10).

Had Saul been in the least restrained by the commandments of God's holy law, he would have inquired as to Doeg's character and sought a second witness against the priests. The law required, "Only on the evidence of two witnesses or of three witnesses shall a charge be established" (Deut. 19:15). Saul, however, was no longer restrained by God's Word, and thus he did not hesitate to stretch out his hand to assail God's holy priests.

Saul's contempt for God is seen in his arrogant accusation of Israel's high priest, the nation's second-highest official: "Hear now, son of Ahitub," he called to Ahimelech, the form of address conveying disrespect. The high priest answered, "Here I am, my lord" (1 Sam. 22:12). Saul replied, "Why have you conspired against me, you and the son of Jesse, in that you have given him bread and a sword and have inquired of God for him, so that he has risen against me, to lie in wait, as at this day?" (22:13). Notice that Saul is angry with Ahimelech simply for performing his function as God's servant. People are likewise outraged when Christian ministers preach the commands and doctrines of God's Word, forgetting that this is the very function to which they are called by the Lord.

Ahimelech's answer reveals his innocence in ministering to David: "Who among all your servants is so faithful as David," he asked, "who is the king's son-in-law, and captain over your bodyguard, and honored in your house? Is today the first time that I have inquired of God for him? No!" (1 Sam. 22:14–15). It is possible that the priest sincerely did not realize that David was out of favor with the king, although alternatively the priest may have simply been courageously confronting Saul over his well-known injustice to David. Confronting sin is part of the job for those called to preach God's Word. Ministers of the gospel are thus to speak God's truth without fear of man. Paul stated this principle as key to his ministry: "We refuse to practice cunning or to tamper with God's word, but by the open statement of the truth we would commend ourselves to everyone's conscience in the sight of God" (2 Cor. 4:2). In this same spirit, Ahimelech called Saul to a more sane and godly way of thinking and speaking: "Let not the king impute anything to his servant or to all the house of my father, for your servant has known nothing of all this, much or little" (1 Sam. 22:15). The priests were totally uninvolved in any conspiracy against the king and did not deserve his accusations.

It was precisely because Ahimelech's reply was so noble and true that it drove Saul into a murderous rage: "You shall surely die, Ahimelech, you and all your father's house" (1 Sam. 22:16). Those who will not repent must instead attack the source of their reproach, and for having so clearly revealed Saul's unjust malice toward David, the priest and his entire household must die.

Here we see a second sign that Saul's reign had turned wholly to satanic evil: he shows no fear in defiling sacred things or assailing sacred persons. Either it did not occur to Saul or he did not care that the priests were set apart by God for holy service to himself and that violence against these men and their families would therefore give special insult to the Lord.

Those who profane the sacred things of God end up doing true injury only to themselves. We observed this principle earlier in 1 Samuel, when the ark of the covenant was placed in subjection to the idol of the Philistine god Dagon. The result was the judicial execution of the Philistine deity and the divine judgment of a deadly plague on the people. God not only preserves the holiness of his sacred truths and institutions, but sometimes uses the sacrilegious actions of such men as Saul in order to stir up many to indignation. A famous example was the revolt of the Jewish people under the leadership of Judas Maccabeus after the Seleucid king Antiochus Epiphanes displayed his arrogant contempt by profaning the Holy of Holies within the temple at Jerusalem. In similar fashion, Saul's casual defiling of no less than the high priest's entire household must have stirred up the animosity of Levitical priests throughout Israel and aroused them to sympathy for David.

God preserved a single member of the high priest's house, his son Abiathar, who took the holy emblems of the high priesthood to David's camp. William Blaikie notes:

> The very presence in his camp of Abiathar, the son of Ahimelech, who escaped the massacre, with his ephod—an official means of consulting God in all cases of difficulty—would be a visible proof to his followers and to the community at large, that God was on his side. . . . The feeling could not fail to gain strength that David's cause was the cause of God, and the cause of the country, and that, in due time, his patient sufferings and his noble services would be crowned with the due reward.[2]

Likewise, in our time, when such holy institutions as marriage are miserably defiled by both neglect and assault, Christians who uphold this divine institution in holiness and purity mark themselves as standing for God's cause in the world. The same is true for the true and uncorrupted teaching of the gospel and the faithful administration of the sacraments in the church. Those who not only desire to seek God's blessing but also wish to be known as those who stand for and rely on God's mighty grace will be all the more zealous to worship God "with reverence and awe" (Heb. 12:28) and to keep sacred those holy things that the Lord has committed to us.

THE WICKED UNLEASHED

Saul not only turned the righteous into outcasts and treated God's holy servants with contempt, but also took the final evil step of arming the wicked and unleashing their violence on the land. Despite the truthful explanation

2. William G. Blaikie, *Expository Lectures on the Book of First Samuel* (1887; repr., Birmingham, AL: Solid Ground, 2005), 348.

of no less than Israel's high priest, and despite the failure to produce more than a single witness, "the king said to the guard who stood about him, 'Turn and kill the priests of the LORD, because their hand also is with David, and they knew that he fled and did not disclose it to me'" (1 Sam. 22:17). Imagine being one of Saul's soldiers, who were mortified at the scene before them! Saul's mad hatred for David was bad enough, but this wicked assault on innocent holy men was more than they could stomach. Therefore, "the servants of the king would not put out their hand to strike the priests of the LORD" (22:17).

For Saul's guards, passive acquiescence to an evil ruler inevitably collided with orders to commit grave sins against God's law. The time had come when faithful Israelites would have to take a stand against evil or find themselves engaged in sacrilegious opposition to God. It is encouraging to learn that none of them were willing to "put out their hand to strike the priests of the LORD" (1 Sam. 22:17). This refusal to obey the king could not have failed to bring them trouble, but the words spoken later by Jesus Christ would undoubtedly have comforted them: "Do not fear those who kill the body but cannot kill the soul. Rather fear him who can destroy both soul and body in hell" (Matt. 10:28).

Perhaps Saul lacked the power to take action against his guards, but he was still able to find someone evil enough to obey his wicked demand: "Then the king said to Doeg, 'You turn and strike the priests.' And Doeg the Edomite turned and struck down the priests, and he killed on that day eighty-five persons who wore the linen ephod. And Nob, the city of the priests, he put to the sword; both man and woman, child and infant, ox, donkey and sheep, he put to the sword" (1 Sam. 22:18–19). Thus was Saul's descent into satanic darkness utterly complete. Chantry points out how far Saul had fallen: "Years earlier, Saul had not been able to bring himself to slay all the Amalekites and their cattle. Now he obliterated both priesthood and town. Not a soul was left but Abiathar who had escaped to give the account."[3]

There seems never to be a shortage of Doegs, whom Satan and evil rulers can unleash on the world at large and especially against God's people. In the time of Jesus' birth, Herod sent his guards to Bethlehem ruthlessly to slay every boy under two years of age, desperately seeking to obliterate the

3. Chantry, *David*, 74.

Redeemer. It continues today. In the week of this writing, news has spread of renewed persecution against Christians in China, with government-paid mobs descending on churches to smash property and assail worshipers, with many deaths. Meanwhile, behind the dark veil of Islam, news has come of increasing violence against Christian evangelists—even the dreadful kidnapping of Christian girls for forced marriage to abusive Muslim men.

Here in America, we should not doubt the readiness of Doegs to assail God's people, even though such coldhearted assailants are more likely to dress in the fine suits of attorneys or occupy desks in the government bureaucracy. A Christian attorney in Indiana was recently denied a license to practice law. For no other reason than his known Christian beliefs, the state government required Bryan Brown to receive a psychological assessment. After he was asked about his views regarding the final judgment, sexual morality, and biblical gender roles, Brown was declared psychologically unstable and thus unfit to practice the law.[4] Meanwhile, national legislators feverishly labor to craft legislation that will expand government funding for the clinical slaying of unborn children. In a world such as ours, Christians will often have need to turn to God with words like those of David's prayer, uttered during this time of Saul's depraved oppression: "I cry to you, O LORD; I say, 'You are my refuge, my portion in the land of the living.' . . . Deliver me from my persecutors, for they are too strong for me!" (Ps. 142:5–6).

A REFUGE FOR THE RIGHTEOUS

News of the dreadful massacre at Nob reached David through the lone escapee, Abiathar, son of the high priest: "Abiathar told David that Saul had killed the priests of the LORD" (1 Sam. 22:21). Now David's sin of speaking falsely to Ahimelech at the tabernacle was brought home with bitter clarity: "David said to Abiathar, 'I knew on that day, when Doeg the Edomite was there, that he would surely tell Saul. I have occasioned the death of all the persons of your father's house'" (22:22).

It may not have given David much comfort, but readers of 1 Samuel know that the death of these priests was the result not merely of David's sin, but

4. *Fort Wayne News-Sentinel*, December 10, 2009.

also of God's curse on the earlier sins of the negligent high priest Eli and his wicked sons, Hophni and Phinehas. God in his wrath foretold to Eli: "Behold, the days are coming when I will cut off your strength and the strength of your father's house, so that there will not be an old man in your house" (1 Sam. 2:31). God promised that only one descendant of Eli would be spared "to weep his eyes out to grieve his heart, and all the descendants of your house shall die by the sword of men" (2:33).

The fact that God had foreordained the death of the priests in his judgment on Eli's house did not lessen the extent of David's moral failure. Neither does it lessen our guilt for sin that God sovereignly overrules our affairs for his own purposes. Blaikie urges:

> What a warning this conveys to us! Are you not sometimes tempted to think that sin to you is not a very serious matter, because you will get forgiveness for it, the atoning work of the Saviour will cleanse you for its guilt? Be it so; but what if your sin has involved others, and if no atoning blood has been sprinkled on them? . . . Alas, alas! Sin is like a network, the ramifications of which go out on the right hand and on the left, and when we break God's law, we cannot tell what the consequences to others may be![5]

Now David realizes his calling as the true anointed king over Israel: no longer would his mind be absorbed only with personal fears and concerns, but with the duty for the people that had been thrust upon him. "Stay with me," he tells Abiathar; "do not be afraid, for he who seeks my life seeks your life. With me you shall be in safekeeping" (1 Sam. 22:23). How could David make such a statement, except that he now—perhaps having no other choice—laid his hands on God's promise of the kingship? Previously, Jonathan had played the role of encouraging David to believe in God's promised salvation (see 20:2). Now, the providence of God in Saul's unrestrained fury compelled David to advance into true faith in embracing his calling.

In this offer of temporal salvation, David most truly typifies the saving work of Jesus Christ. David would succeed in protecting Abiathar and many others who sought safety with him. Yet David himself knew that only the

---

5. Blaikie, *First Samuel*, 350.

Lord can be the true refuge for the righteous. That is why David prayed from his cave, with grateful thanks for the protection that only God can provide: "For your steadfast love is great to the heavens, your faithfulness to the clouds" (Ps. 57:10).

As Jesus emphasized, the refuge that we need is not primarily from the Sauls of the world, who can only kill the body, but from God's just wrath on our sin, which threatens our souls with eternal damnation. For this greatest danger, God himself has provided the refuge in sending his Son, Jesus Christ, to die in sacrifice for our sins. Jesus declared, "Whoever hears my word and believes him who sent me has eternal life. He does not come into judgment, but has passed from death to life" (John 5:24). The writer of Hebrews thus assures us that in God's covenant promise of salvation in Christ, "we who have fled for refuge . . . have strong encouragement to hold fast to the hope set before us" (Heb. 6:18).

Therefore, as the refugees of Adullam came streaming in to David—"everyone who was in distress, and everyone who was in debt, and everyone who was bitter in soul" (1 Sam. 22:2)—we must flee for refuge to Christ. There, at the refuge of his cross, the evil kingdom of Satan was cast down, the debt of sin was paid in Christ's blood, and the bitterness of the sinner's alienation from God was replaced with the sweetness of forgiving grace. Like David's band of outcasts, we flee to Christ following our dissatisfaction with the pleasures and rewards of this evil world. Since we are all born as sinners under Satan's reign, we must all experience the discontent of these refugees if we are to find safety in the grace of God in Christ, leaving all to follow Jesus. Moreover, seeking refuge with Jesus calls us to become exiles in a disapproving world. The writer of Hebrews urged: "Let us go to him outside the camp and bear the reproach he endured" (Heb. 13:13). Roger Ellsworth comments:

> It is, to be sure, a most costly decision. Those who left Saul's kingdom to join David left behind many comforts and conveniences and entered into a life that entailed sacrifice and suffering, but the peace and joy of being a follower of David far surpassed the hardships involved. So it is for all those who, by the grace of God, leave Satan's kingdom for Christ's.[6]

6. Roger Ellsworth, *The Shepherd King: Learning from the Life of David* (Darlington, UK: Evangelical Press, 1998), 73.

Jesus invites us all to flee to him for salvation, calling out to the world, "Come to me, all who labor and are heavy laden, and I will give you rest" (Matt. 11:28).

Meanwhile, we are reminded that even in the darkest hours, when Satan seems most powerfully ascendant over the world, God always preserves a remnant of faith that is precious to him. Do you still hold your citizenship in the world? If you do, you may be able to exult in its apparent success in flouting God's rule. But realize that you, like Saul, must inevitably advance in the ways of evil and the corruption of your soul. In time, the pleasures of sin will be dulled into a miserable bondage, and its wages will be death (Rom. 6:23). You can flee to Jesus Christ, the rival to the worldly despot, who has triumphed over sin through his cross. Jesus assures his beleaguered remnant of protection and provision. "In the world you will have tribulation," Jesus admitted. "But take heart," he exhorts us: "I have overcome the world" (John 16:33).

This chapter began with David's followers looking like little more than a rabble. But by the end of the chapter God had summoned David to embrace the kingship and provided him with both a priest and a prophet. These represent our great need: to be defended by a mighty King, reconciled to God's favor by an atoning Priest, and instructed into faith and salvation by a true Prophet. This is the refuge of God's people in this world: the kingly reign of God's mighty Son, the priestly ministry of Christ's sin-atoning blood, and the prophetic ministry of the Holy Scriptures. To join Jesus through faith is to unite under the banner of great David's greater Son, to whom God the Father declares: "Ask of me, and I will make the nations your heritage, and the ends of the earth your possession" (Ps. 2:8).

33

LIVING BY THE WORD

1 Samuel 23:1–14

Will the men of Keilah surrender me into his hand? Will Saul
come down as your servant has heard? O LORD, the God of
Israel, please tell your servant. (1 Sam. 23:11)

he chapters in 1 Samuel that recount the period when David
lived as an outlaw are some of the most beloved and valuable
portions of the biblical record of his life. These were the years
when David responded to great spiritual challenges with a faith that guided
him and gave him strength. Psalm 18, purportedly written after "the LORD
rescued him from the hand of all his enemies," sums up David's frame of
mind: "I love you, O LORD, my strength. The LORD is my rock and my fortress
and my deliverer, my God, my rock, in whom I take refuge" (Ps. 18:1–2).
Generations of believers have been strengthened by this and similar expressions of faith that were forged in the crucible of David's struggle.

David's spiritual struggle, though unique in some ways, was in many
ways similar to our own. David had great promises from God, but his circumstances before him did not make their fulfillment seem likely. God
had promised to raise David to the throne of Israel. How much more likely
this would have seemed in headier days, such as those after his triumph

over Goliath the giant. Back then, trust in God's promise must have been simple, just as our faith comes easily after early triumphs in the Christian life. But now, during the exile period of David's life, his faith would follow an up-and-down path—sometimes strong and vibrant, sometimes desperate and wavering. We may not have a promise of kingship over God's people, as David did, but we do have promises of blessing, help, and power from God. Just as David must have questioned God's promise to him, we also face circumstances that make God's promised salvation seem uncertain.

Chapter 23 sees David in a particularly difficult stage of his exile, though an important stage in his spiritual growth. He is challenged by the Lord to think not merely of his own survival but also of his duty to his neighbors, even as he continues to suffer the grievous plight of betrayal and hatred. God sustains David through this trial with two great resources: the revelation of his Word and the encouragement of a fellow believer.

INQUIRING OF THE LORD

The first half of the chapter focuses on David's safety in relying on God's revelation, teaching us the value of living by God's Word in all the ups and downs of life. In chapter 22, God had directed David through the prophet Gad to return to Judah. At the time, there was no explanation for this order, but the reason becomes known in chapter 23. Keilah, a walled town in the eastern farmlands of Judah, was besieged by the Philistines, who were "robbing the threshing floors" (1 Sam. 23:1). This city's economy was being ruined and its very existence threatened. News of this siege reached David's ears: "Behold, the Philistines are fighting against Keilah" (23:1). David's zeal for his country is seen in his willingness to endanger himself on behalf of this city. But first, David "inquired of the LORD, 'Shall I go and attack these Philistines?'" (23:2). Both David's zeal and his care in consulting God's Word indicate that his spiritual recovery, begun in the previous chapter, has now advanced. For this reason, the following phase of David's life will be one of his most spiritually fruitful.

God promises to bless those who turn to him for guidance. As David taught in Psalm 19, "the testimony of the LORD is sure, making wise the simple; the precepts of the LORD are right, rejoicing the heart; the commandment of the LORD is pure, enlightening the eyes" (Ps. 19:7–8). In Psalm 119:105, he declared,

"Your word is a lamp to my feet and a light to my path." In this case, God's Word guided David to rescue Keilah: "The LORD answered him, 'Arise, go down to Keilah, for I will give the Philistines into your hand'" (1 Sam. 23:4).

When David's men learned what their leader intended to do, they were understandably shaken: "Behold, we are afraid here in Judah," they objected; "how much more then if we go to Keilah against the armies of the Philistines?" (1 Sam. 23:3). It was bad enough being fugitives from Saul; they saw no need to take on the Philistine army as well. In response to their objection, "David inquired of the LORD again" (23:4).

During these events, not only was David provided with a prophet to discover God's Word, but also around this time Abiathar, son of the high priest, arrived in David's camp, having escaped the slaughter of the priests at Nob. In that slaughter, we were told that Doeg the Edomite "struck down . . . eighty-five persons who wore the linen ephod" (1 Sam. 22:18). The ephod, a sort of sacred apron, was part of the priests' uniform (see Ex. 28:6–8). One of these ephods, the high priest's, contained the Urim and Thummim, provided by God for the divining of his will (see Ex. 28:30). These lots were designed by God to give yes-or-no answers to pointed questions, or else to select a person chosen by lot.

The point we should note here is that God had now provided all the apparatus of kingship to David. Saul, the reigning king, had alienated the prophets and slaughtered the priests. David, the true and divinely anointed king, was now served by a faithful prophet and a true priest. Walter Chantry comments: "Isolated from God's servants and the means of grace, evil Saul had the company of evil spirits who manipulated his moods, his words, and his actions. Under demonic influence Saul became a man driven to kill his God-appointed successor."[1] In contrast, David, supplied by the available means of God's grace, was guided and helped in his kingly role by the prophet and the priest. David was thus equipped as a righteous servant and savior for the needy people of Israel. The true king of Israel was to rule by God's Word, in close company with the prophets and priests. We see why the Davidic kingship came to its ultimate fulfillment in Jesus Christ, who not only is King over God's people, but is himself our true Prophet and perfect High Priest as well.

1. Walter Chantry, *David: Man of Prayer, Man of War* (Edinburgh: Banner of Truth, 2007), 77–78.

Reigning through the Word

Two of the functions of God's Word are highlighted in these verses: David reigns through God's Word and David is rescued through God's Word. First, consider how David reigned over his little army by appealing to God's Word. When the people expressed their alarm at the idea of attempting to rescue Keilah, David did not resort to his own reasoning, which could easily fail, or to coercion. Instead, he agreed to inquire of God's Word once more. In this manner, David shows us the basis of effective Christian leadership even today. True spiritual leaders are not those who motivate God's people by their dynamic personality, by appeals to worldly profit, or by the coercive manipulations of guilt or abuse. Rather, true Christian leadership is based on the plain statement of God's Word.

Notice how David handled the difficult matter of persuading his men and alleviating their understandable fears. Abiathar had not yet arrived with the ephod, so David presumably inquired of the Lord through the prophet: "And the LORD answered him, 'Arise, go down to Keilah, for I will give the Philistines into your hand'" (1 Sam. 23:4). In short, God's Word gave David a clear direction for action and a promise of divine help and success. This is what Christian leaders should provide today from the written revelation of God's Word: both God's instructions and God's promises for the blessings that obedience will bring. A. W. Pink comments: "David did not storm at his men, and denounce them as cowards. . . . Nor did he argue and attempt to reason with them. Disdaining his own wisdom, feeling his utter dependency upon God, and more especially for their benefit—to set before them a godly example—he turned once more unto Jehovah."[2]

Christian leaders today do not follow David's kingly example by appealing to the latest management practices or marketing ploys, setting themselves forth as transcendent spiritual celebrities, but by bringing God's Word to the people. The kingly reign of Christ is served when, like David, believers seek direction from God's revelation, which we have in the Holy Scriptures.

Consider the leadership of a Christian father in the home. How is he to establish Christ's kingly reign? The answer is by implementing biblical standards and expectations for relationships within the family.

2. A. W. Pink, *A Life of David*, 2 vols. (Grand Rapids: Baker, 1981), 1:95–96.

The husband is to sacrificially love and lead his wife, and the wife is to help and submit to her husband (see Eph. 5:22–33). The children are to obey their parents, and the parents are to treat them with fairness and consideration (6:1–2). The basis for family relations is thus given in Holy Scripture.

Consider as well a pastor and other leaders in the church. It is popular today for churches to be organized on business principles, with boards of directors governing behind the scenes and with the congregants looked upon as customers. But Christ reigns in his church through biblical church governance—with pastors, elders, and deacons leading committed church members in accordance with the Pastoral Epistles and other New Testament instructions. Christ reigns in his church through faithful biblical teaching that centers on the cross (1 Cor. 2:2) and holds forth "the whole counsel of God" (Acts 20:27). Christ reigns in his church when leaders bring the members to God in "acceptable worship" that is regulated by God's Word, "with reverence and awe" (Heb. 12:28).

Like David, who both sought and taught God's Word, Christian leaders today—fathers and mothers in the home, pastors and elders in the church—must communicate the biblical basis for their decisions and directives. At the heart of Christian leadership is a knowledge of the Bible and an ability to convey it to followers, just as the preaching of God's Word is at the heart of the life of a church congregation.

David's obedience to God's Word was rewarded in a number of ways. The first was the unity of effort shown by his followers, who were evidently persuaded of God's will in this matter. Second, God blessed David's obedience with the fulfillment of his promise to "give the Philistines into [his] hand" (1 Sam. 23:4). As a result, "David and his men went to Keilah and fought with the Philistines and brought away their livestock and struck them with a great blow" (23:5). Here was the unexpected blessing of material provision for David's band, as the Philistine herds fell into their hands. Moreover, "David saved the inhabitants of Keilah" (23:5). Finally, it seems that in the aftermath of this success, Abiathar arrived with the high priest's ephod, including the Urim and Thummim, for even more precise revelation from God. By inquiring of God's Word, David brought unity and confidence to his followers and was attended with God's promised blessing.

Rescued by the Word

This did not mean that David was therefore free from trouble, any more than our obedience will be carefree, for there was still Saul to consider: "Now it was told Saul that David had come to Keilah. And Saul said, 'God has given him into my hand, for he has shut himself in by entering a town that has gates and bars.' And Saul summoned all the people to war, to go down to Keilah, to besiege David and his men" (1 Sam. 23:7–8).

Just as David learned this news about Saul, Abiathar arrived with the Urim and Thummim. David directly appealed to this divinely appointed means of revelation: "David knew that Saul was plotting harm against him. And he said to Abiathar the priest, 'Bring the ephod here'" (1 Sam. 23:9). We can sense David's weariness and the strain from Saul's unending malice as he calls on the Lord with such fervor, repeatedly noting God's covenant relationship to his people:

> Then said David, "O Lord, the God of Israel, your servant has surely heard that Saul seeks to come to Keilah, to destroy the city on my account. Will the men of Keilah surrender me into his hand? Will Saul come down, as your servant has heard? O Lord, the God of Israel, please tell your servant." And the Lord said, "He will come down." Then David said, "Will the men of Keilah surrender me and my men into the hand of Saul?" And the Lord said, "They will surrender you." Then David and his men, who were about six hundred, arose and departed from Keilah, and they went wherever they could go. When Saul was told that David had escaped from Keilah, he gave up the expedition. (23:10–13)

Like David, when we make a habit of carefully consulting the Lord, not only are we enabled to reign through God's Word, but we are also rescued from all manner of dangers. Consider the besetting sins of our time, such as wanton sexual indulgence and the celebration of adultery. Despite temptation and confusing moral values, Christians who diligently consult God's Word will be delivered from great sin. The Bible teaches, "Flee from sexual immorality" (1 Cor. 6:18) and "let the marriage bed be undefiled, for God will judge the sexually immoral and adulterous" (Heb. 13:4). By following this counsel, believers are spared from many woes. Young people especially, given the dissolute nature of worldly youth culture, may be tempted to adopt a sensual manner of dress or conduct, despite the lifestyle to which such an attitude often leads. God's Word rescues us from this danger. Paul reminds us of our high calling to purity and holiness: "But sexual immorality and all impurity or covetousness must not even be named among you, as is proper among saints" (Eph. 5:3).

We could make similar observations about other common sin areas. American society has suffered from a frenzy of materialism and greed, manifested in mad folly in the real estate and financial markets. Christians who have consulted God's Word will often be protected in the crashing of markets and the plummeting of real estate values, since they have been preserved from greedy folly by the Bible's teaching. Paul wrote: "Those who desire to be rich fall into temptation, into a snare, into many senseless and harmful desires that plunge people into ruin and destruction" (1 Tim. 6:9). The wisdom of God's Word protects believers from the disaster of greed, knowing that "there is great gain in godliness with contentment" (1 Tim. 6:6). Both in guiding us aright and in rescuing us from folly and sin, God's Word offers to believers the blessing of the well-known proverb: "Trust in the LORD with all your heart, and do not lean on your own understanding. In all your ways acknowledge him, and he will make straight your paths" (Prov. 3:5–6).

DISCERNING GOD'S WILL TODAY

As we apply David's example to our lives today, many will object that Christians no longer possess the prophetic resources that enabled David to gain God's answers to specific questions about his life. This objection is based on an accurate observation, for David occupied a unique role in the history of God's redeeming work and thus received special resources. How, then, do Christians today—lacking Urim and Thummim—gain God's guidance for the important decisions of our lives?

In his brief, valuable book on this topic, *Discovering God's Will*, Sinclair Ferguson guides us in the proper use of the Scriptures in discerning God's will for our important decisions.[3] Ferguson offers a number of steps that will help us in biblical decision-making today.

---

3. Sinclair B. Ferguson, *Discovering God's Will* (Edinburgh: Banner of Truth, 1982).

First, when faced with a choice, we should seek to understand *what the Bible prohibits or commands*. Christians are saved so as no longer to live in sin but to obey God's Word. Therefore, "no action which is contrary to the plain word of God can ever be legitimate for the Christian."[4]

This is one reason why it is so important for Christians to know the Ten Commandments. Any course of action that involves lying, hating another person, or seizing possessions that belong to someone else is in violation of God's law. This seems obvious, but Christians can avoid many serious mistakes if they simply place the grid of the Ten Commandments over their decision-making. The same is true when it comes to clear duties that the Bible gives. It is always God's will for us to obey his commands and never to violate his law.

Second, having ascertained which courses of action are forbidden, Christians should then consider *which options are wise and beneficial according to Bible principles*. Is the action likely to be profitable, and is it in accord with biblical priorities? If not, then even if it is not forbidden, it should still be avoided. Often this will involve occupational choices or job locations. Is this a job that will provide for my family while enabling me to be faithful as a husband, father, and Christian? Do I know of a good church where I am thinking of moving? Does this prospective husband or wife exhibit strong faith and biblical character? Is this a reasonable purchase, given my resources and my desire to support the work of the church? Will this choice strengthen my relationship with Jesus Christ or weaken my faith? Ferguson writes: "It is possible to make choices which, eventually, will tend to squeeze out our spiritual energies; to commit ourselves to things which, however legitimate in general terms, will eventually become the dominating and driving force in our lives."[5]

Third, Christians should ask *what effect a given choice or decision is likely to have on others*. How will this action affect family members, coworkers, friends, and fellow church members? It is true that the Bible teaches Christian liberty in matters of biblical permission. Yet our liberty must always be guided by responsibility and love. Paul writes that we should never allow our choices to "destroy the work of God" or "make another stumble" (Rom. 14:20). While we tend to be motivated by concerns for

4. Ibid., 66.
5. Ibid., 69.

our own personal comfort and security, God challenges us to sacrifice for the spiritual well-being of others.

Fourth, Christians should compare their proposed action *with a biblical example or illustration*. Paul wrote to the Corinthians, "Follow my example, as I follow the example of Christ" (1 Cor. 11:1 NIV). How did faithful men and women in Scripture handle this same situation? Hebrews 13:7 says that we should likewise consider the example of faithful Christian leaders: "Consider the outcome of their way of life, and imitate their faith." Most important is the example of Jesus Christ, properly understood from the Scriptures. Much that Jesus did could have been done only by him and in many cases should be done only by him. Jesus alone is Lord, and we are not to assume his prerogatives. But when it comes to his compassion for the weak and broken, his zeal for God and his ways, and his courage before worldly opposition, Jesus is indeed our great model. Notice the emphasis that Peter gave in setting forth the example of Christ, when speaking of the cross: "To this you have been called, because Christ also suffered for you, leaving you an example, so that you might follow in his steps" (1 Peter 2:21).

These principles of biblical decision-making assume two vital preconditions. The first is that we know our Bibles! We will never know God's will until we have followed Paul's command to "be transformed by the renewal of your mind, that by testing you may discern what is the will of God" (Rom. 12:2). Ferguson writes, "The chief need we have, therefore, is that of increased familiarity with and sensitivity to the wisdom of his word."[6] Accompanying a mind increasingly shaped by Scripture is a heart warmed by frequently meeting with the Lord in prayer. Notice that a priority on Scripture and prayer matches the two resources given to David: the prophetic word and priestly intercession. The Puritan John Newton appealed to these same resources in writing to a Christian friend:

> How then may the Lord's guidance be expected? . . . In general, he guides and directs his people, by affording them, in answer to prayer, the light of his Holy Spirit, which enables them to understand and to love the Scriptures. The word of God . . . is to furnish us with just principles, right apprehensions to regulate our judgements and affections, and thereby influence and direct our conduct.[7]

6. Ibid., 31.
7. Quoted in ibid., 32.

Some might consider that this kind of biblical analysis rules out what is often referred to as "God's leading" in our lives. It is true that God may lay burdens or passions on our heart and that in this way the Holy Spirit seeks to guide us, along with providential opportunities that God sets before us. Yet the Spirit's leading and God's providence never run counter to God's Word. Nothing forbidden by God is ever prompted by the Spirit, nor does God lead us in ways that are contrary to biblical principles and motives.

Sometimes Christians desire information that God simply has not promised to provide. Should a young man join the Army or the Marine Corps? There may be circumstances that lead in one way or the other, but far more important than choosing between the two is deciding to honor Christ in either service. Should a Christian man pursue marriage with Susy or Tammy? Should a Christian woman choose Bill or Bob? Assuming that both potential spouses are equally committed to Christ and show godly character, a person may feel free to marry the one to whom he or she is more naturally attracted. What really matters is that the men and women obey God's commands for how husbands and wives should love one another. The revelation that we really need from God is precisely what God has already given us in his Word: his commands and instructions for glorifying him and living in a godly, loving, and wise manner.

SIN AND SALVATION REVEALED

Not only does the Bible help us to make godly decisions, but even more importantly, God's Word informs us of the great and vital truths of life. Some of the Bible's great truths are unfolded in David's experience in this passage.

First, the Bible tells us that *we will find no hope of salvation in the ways of men*. Consider the people of Keilah. When Saul's forces drew near, David inquired of the Lord: "Then David said, 'Will the men of Keilah surrender me and my men into the hand of Saul?' And the LORD said, 'They will surrender you'" (1 Sam. 23:12). David had sacrificially endangered himself and his men in order to save the city, but as soon as a new danger came, the Keilites were all too willing to save themselves by betraying David to Saul. This is the way of the whole world, as the Bible teaches. "None is righteous, no, not one," writes the apostle Paul. "No one does good, not even one" (Rom. 3:10, 12, quoting Ps. 14:1, 3). This being true, we cannot trust our salvation into the hands of any man. This is true even of ourselves. We so seldom live up to our own highest ideals and frequently let down ourselves and others in our weakness and sin. Even when we desire to save one another, we often lack the power, as Keilah doubtless lacked the power to shield David from Saul. This is why David sang, "Put not your trust in princes, in a son of man, in whom there is no salvation" (Ps. 146:3).

Second, the Bible reveals that *we are pursued by a mighty and dreadful enemy who seeks to destroy our souls*. David had done no evil to Saul, yet Saul was bent on destroying him utterly. So we also are threatened by our evil adversary, the devil. Peter warns us, "Your adversary the devil prowls around like a roaring lion, seeking someone to devour" (1 Peter 5:8). Our enemy's hatred is not easily avoided, since he wields the power of sin, and sin is backed up with the threat of God's own law and its curse of death for sin. This is why the writer of Hebrews says that the devil subjects all mankind "through fear of death . . . to lifelong slavery" (Heb. 2:15). Paul writes, "The sting of death is sin, and the power of sin is the law" (1 Cor. 15:56). This is our great and terrible problem, that the mad enemy who hates us has gained power over us through sin and draws near to destroy us with the sword of God's holy justice. We see this terror reflected throughout David's psalms as he flees from wicked King Saul: "Strangers have risen against me; ruthless men seek my life" (Ps. 54:3). Yet behind Saul stood the greater enemy of Satan and sin, seeking David's eternal condemnation as well as our own.

Third, the Bible reveals that *we may find a refuge and safe stronghold in the grace and power of God*, whose Word speaks of a Savior who delivers us from Satan and from sin. Though the people of Keilah betrayed David and though evil King Saul still sought to take his life, the Lord saved and preserved him: "David remained in the strongholds in the wilderness, in the hill country of the wilderness of Ziph. And Saul sought him every day, but God did not give him into his hand" (1 Sam. 23:14). David therefore sang with joy, "Behold, God is my helper; the Lord is the upholder of my life" (Ps. 54:4).

God achieved our salvation by sending his own Son, Jesus Christ, into the world, to bear the punishment of our sins, to free us from the wrath of God's holy justice, and in this way to overthrow the kingdom of our great enemy the devil. David's praise to God is therefore well suited to our mouths as we trust the Lord for our own salvation: "Blessed is he whose help is the God of Jacob, whose hope is in the LORD his God" (Ps. 146:5).

34

FAITHFUL IN FRIENDSHIP

1 Samuel 23:15–29

And Jonathan, Saul's son, rose and went to David at Horesh,
and strengthened his hand in God. (1 Sam. 23:16)

wo statues in Washington, DC, together tell a remarkable story. One is the massive memorial to General Ulysses S. Grant that stands at the east end of the Reflecting Pool, literally in the morning shadow of the U.S. Capitol building. Visitors can hardly miss this majestic depiction of the famous general atop his war stallion. Grant's military leadership was decisive to the Union's victory in the Civil War, and he is considered a symbol of the force of human will, an icon of the strong man who stands against the storm when all others have shrunk back. This prominently displayed monument was erected by Grant's grateful, admiring generation as a celebration of his unique contributions.

Some two and a half miles away, in a pleasant but small and nondescript city park, stands a more commonplace memorial. The statue of this lesser-known Civil War figure, Major General John Rawlins, has had eight different locations and is hardly ever noticed by visitors. Rawlins had been a lawyer in Galena, Illinois, where Grant lived just before the war, and he became Grant's chief of staff. Rawlins knew Grant's character flaws, especially his weakness for alcohol. At the beginning of the war, Rawlins extracted a pledge from Grant to abstain from drunkenness, and when the general threatened to fall away from that promise, his friend would plead with him and support him until Grant could get back on track. In many ways, it was Rawlins who stood beside the seemingly solitary figure of Grant the great general. Rawlins's memorial is modest compared with the mounted glory afforded Grant, yet without his unheralded love and support, there were times when Grant could hardly have managed even to climb into the saddle. This is why the wise man of Ecclesiastes extolled the virtue of a friend in need: "Two are better than one, because they have a good reward for their toil. For if they fall, one will lift up his fellow. But woe to him who is alone when he falls and has not another to lift him up!" (Eccl. 4:9–10).

The Friend Who Comes

If the friendship between Grant and Rawlins is a great American story, perhaps the greatest friendship recorded in Scripture is the brotherly love between Jonathan and David. The two men met in the aftermath of David's famous victory over the Philistine giant, Goliath. First Samuel 17 tells how the entire Israelite host cowered in terror before this fearsome champion, and how the shepherd-boy David, shielded only by his faith in God and armed with only a slingshot, struck down the Philistine and led Israel to victory. Jonathan was the son and heir of Israel's King Saul, and the hero of earlier battles. In fact, Jonathan had been the darling of Israel's army before David's explosive appearance on the scene. How natural it would have been for Jonathan to resent the upstart youth. Yet exactly the opposite happened, for Jonathan presents one of the most beautiful portrayals of manly grace in all of Scripture. First Samuel 18:1 simply records that "the soul of Jonathan was knit to the soul of David, and Jonathan loved him as his own soul." Jonathan loved David because Jonathan loved the Lord and loved the faith he saw burning in young David. It is worth noting that this man who is considered among the greatest of friends was also a man of vibrant faith and purity of heart.

David's victory over Goliath must have seemed long ago, as David was brought to the brink of despair by King Saul's vicious pursuit. After his initial flight from Saul, David found refuge in the caves of Adullam, in central Judea. Having left his fortress, however, to rescue nearby Keilah from a Philistine siege, David had exposed himself to Saul's assault. Saul's rapid advance drove David and his men into the southern desert, hotly pursued by the king's superior forces. When David thus seemed on the brink of defeat, Jonathan came and provided a model of Christian friendship.

We read of David's dire situation in 1 Samuel 23:14: "David remained in the strongholds in the wilderness, in the hill country of the wilderness of Ziph. And Saul sought him every day, but God did not give him into his hand." By this time, David had been running from Saul for several years. We can imagine his extreme weariness and how slim his hold on God's promises of salvation must have been at times. No wonder this is the man who wrote: "My soul is in anguish. How long, O LORD, how long?" (Ps. 6:3 NIV).

At just this time, Jonathan returned to David. Becoming aware of David's increasingly desperate position, Jonathan acted to provide one of the classic examples of faithful friendship: "Jonathan, Saul's son, rose and went to David at Horesh, and strengthened his hand in God" (1 Sam. 23:16).

This simple statement is loaded with practical implications! For starters, Jonathan took the initiative and went to David. This was an act of sacrificial ministry. Safe at the side of his father and within the strong ranks of the pursuing army, Jonathan departed to expose himself to the danger that David was experiencing. From the comfort of the king's royal provision, he ventured out into the desert deprivation of his friend. But this is what friendship requires. A friend who is not willing, and even eager, to sacrifice time, labor, and hardship is not worthy of being called a friend at all.

Second, Jonathan was sensitive to the needs of his friend. Many of us would be willing to make sacrifices if only we understood the real needs of others. But this would require us to do what Jonathan did: to think through what David must be experiencing. Jonathan was not focused on his own hardship, the difficult situation that his friendship with David created for him, or the peril to his career aspirations. Instead, Jonathan committed his own needs to the Lord and gave his thoughts to the plight of his friend. This is the kind of attitude that Paul had in mind when he wrote to the Philippians: "Do nothing from rivalry or conceit, but in humility count others more significant than yourselves. Let each of you look not only to his own interests, but also to the interests of others" (Phil. 2:3–4).

Consider David's predicament. He was the leader of a band of weary fugitives, stranded in the desert. Paying the price of leadership, David would have turned his thoughts over to his men and their needs, while he stood alone with no peers or companions for his own comfort. While David lent his strength to others, there were none to uphold him in his weakness. Consider, today, a doctor or nurse providing care to the desperately sick: who is there to uphold and encourage the caregiver? Or consider a mother spending herself for her little children, or a rural pastor fretting alone over his flock. What friend will come alongside, seeking to understand and minister out of that understanding? Jonathan knew how great is the gift of companionship to a struggling friend.

The Bible makes it clear that God was not willing to give David up to Saul. But do you think David was consistently confident of this? Wouldn't he have found it hard to see God's protection in such a time of trial? There he was in a hostile land, with a fierce enemy hot on his heels. David could use a reminder of God's faithfulness, encouraging him to believe and continue the fight. God was about to provide that encouragement in the form of a true friend.

Jonathan went to David in his place of struggle. In the same way, our friendship today means little if we will not seek out and find our brothers and sisters in their places of need. It is good to send a note to a friend in the hospital, but better to go in person. What a difference it can make when we take a struggling friend out to lunch or stop by the office with a word of appreciation. "A friend loves at all times," says the proverb, "and a brother is born for adversity" (Prov. 17:17).

The Helping Hand

It would have meant a great deal to David just to see his faithful friend Jonathan in such a time and place of need. But Jonathan did more than show up. He did for David the single thing most needed in troubling times: "Jonathan . . . strengthened his hand in God" (1 Sam. 23:16). David's hand was trembling, in danger of slipping from the strong support that is our faith in God. Jonathan came and strengthened the grip of David's faith and hope in the Lord. William Blaikie comments: "He strengthened his hand in God. Simple but beautiful words! He put David's hand as it were into God's hand . . . , in token that the Almighty was pledged to keep and bless him, and that . . . no weapon formed against him would ever prosper."[1]

Do you ever wonder how to encourage a struggling friend? Sometimes we are tempted to encourage with words of what we will do to help or what the friend will be able to do for himself. But harsh reality will soon disclose the insufficiency of our own strength. It is a good thing to come and take another by the hand. But it is something greater to take that shaking hand and place it on the promises of God. This is exactly what Jonathan did for David: "He said to him, 'Do not fear, for the hand of Saul my father shall not find you. You shall be king over Israel, and I shall be next to you. Saul my father also knows this'" (1 Sam. 23:17). "Surely no act of friendship is so true friendship as this," says Blaikie. "To remind our Christian friends in their day of trouble of their relation to God, to encourage them to think of His interest in them and His promises to them; to drop in their ear some of His assurances . . . is surely the best of all ways to encourage the downcast."[2]

At the very moment that Jonathan said this, his father's army was bearing down on David. So on what basis did he speak this way? Jonathan spoke from his memory of the promises that God had made to David, promises that were certain to be fulfilled. We might paraphrase Jonathan's encouragement in this way: "Look, David, don't fail to put your trust in God. Remember the Lord's promise that you will be king. But in case you are doubting, let me share something with you. Even my father, Saul, knows that this is how it will all end up. So don't fear Saul, David, but trust the Lord!"

It was because Jonathan was strengthening David's grip on God's character and promises that he could say to David, "Do not fear" (1 Sam. 23:17). David was in danger of being undone by fear. Psalm 54, reportedly written on this occasion, gives honest reasons for David's terrible fear: "Strangers have risen against me; ruthless men seek my life; they do not set God before themselves" (Ps. 54:3). Since the slaughter of the priests at Nob, Saul had shown himself willing to employ desperadoes and thugs to work his violence. Such men were bearing down on David. If we have ever felt the looming threat of neighborhood bullies, of a malicious superior at work, or of corrupt and tyrannical government powers, we can put ourselves in

1. William G. Blaikie, *Expository Lectures on the Book of First Samuel* (1887; repr., Birmingham, AL: Solid Ground, 2005), 360–61.

2. Ibid., 361.

David's shoes. If David was to continue, he must have an antidote for fear, which Jonathan gave him in the promises of God.

This is what the prophet Elisha did for his servant when the two men were surrounded by enemy horsemen: "Do not be afraid," the prophet urged him, "for those who are with us are more than those who are with them." In response to the servant's doubt and unbelief, Elisha then provides an example of how our encouraging words will often need to be accompanied by prayer. Elisha prayed for precisely what his companion needed, and what we often need lest we fall prey to fear: "O LORD, please open his eyes that he may see" (2 Kings 6:16–17).

Dietrich Bonhoeffer knew the value of godly friendship in the midst of danger. A rising German Bible scholar who had been outspoken in his opposition during the early rise of Adolf Hitler, Bonhoeffer had been persuaded to go into voluntary exile, so that during the early years of Nazi domination he lived safely in America. But Bonhoeffer knew that his friends and congregation needed his presence and personal appeals to strengthen faith. Returning to Nazi Germany against the advice of many supporters, he led an underground seminary, living together with faithful Christian men preparing to minister in that difficult situation, until his opposition to Hitler ultimately led to his arrest and execution. In *Life Together*, a book recounting his experience in that secret Christian community, Bonhoeffer wrote:

> The Christian needs another Christian who speaks God's Word to him. He needs him again and again when he becomes uncertain and discouraged . . . He needs his brother man as a bearer and proclaimer of the divine word of salvation. . . . And that also clarifies the goal of all Christian community: they meet one another as bringers of the message of salvation.[3]

HELP TO PERSEVERE

Jonathan's intervention proved to be a turning point for David. Jonathan helped his friend by strengthening his hand in God so that he would not be overtaken by fear. But what was Jonathan helping David to do? The answer is that David needed help persevering in his faith. Perseverance was essential

3. Dietrich Bonhoeffer, *Life Together* (San Francisco: Harper & Row, 1954), 23.

to David's salvation: he needed not only to believe in the Lord's salvation but also to keep believing and acting on that belief.

Perseverance is utterly essential to our salvation as well. In his letter to the Colossians, Paul exulted in the believer's salvation through the blood of Christ, "if indeed you continue in the faith, stable and steadfast, not shifting from the hope of the gospel that you heard" (Col. 1:23). The Puritan Thomas Watson explained: "It is not the beginning of the Christian life that gets glory but the end of it. . . . The excellence of a building is not in having the first stone laid, but when it is finished: the glory and excellence of a Christian is when he has finished the work of faith."[4]

We will never know how close David was to giving up, perhaps abandoning his followers and fleeing Israel forever or abandoning faith to live as a true outlaw against King Saul. God's provision of Jonathan's encouragement is a sign that David was hanging by a fairly thin thread. Consider the new difficulties facing him, on top of his prior woes. First, after he had exposed his forces by rescuing the town of Keilah from the Philistines, that city responded by reporting his presence to King Saul (1 Sam. 23:12–14). Now, in the rocky Judean desert where David was trying to hide, the Ziphites were actively negotiating his betrayal to Saul (23:19). These were his own countrymen, fellow Judahites. Unlike the people of Keilah, who at least had the excuse of fear for their lives, the Ziphites operated by cold, cynical opportunism: "The Ziphites went up to Saul at Gibeah, saying, 'Is not David hiding among us in the strongholds at Horesh, on the hill of Hachilah, which is south of Jeshimon? Now come down, O king, according to all your heart's desire to come down, and our part shall be to surrender him into the king's hand'" (23:19–20). Facing no specific threat from Saul, the Ziphites contacted the king out of sheer greed, providing detailed information of David's whereabouts and offering to hand him over.

Saul, in his twisted spirituality, honored this wickedness with his imagined benediction from the Lord: "May you be blessed by the LORD, for you have had compassion on me" (1 Sam. 23:21). This attitude is typical of despots, who calculate good only in terms of their own increased power. More to the point, Saul closed the deal on David's destruction. Imagine how disheartening this news would have been to David! How especially disheartening is the

4. Thomas Watson, *A Body of Divinity* (Edinburgh: Banner of Truth, 1958), 286.

fully ripened depravity so common among the ungodly. Here, David walks in steps that his greater descendant would more perfectly tread: encircled by evil foes, betrayed by one close to him, and handed over to suffer torment and death. In Psalm 22, David prays with words of lament that Jesus would later bring to life on the cross:

> Be not far from me,
>   for trouble is near,
>   and there is none to help.
> Many bulls encompass me;
>   strong bulls of Bashan surround me;
> they open wide their mouths at me,
>   like a ravening and roaring lion. (Ps. 22:11–13)

How similar King Saul was to the ravenous enemies who gathered around Jesus as he died! Never failing to seize an opportunity to strike at David, Saul encouraged the Ziphites in their betrayal: "Go, make yet more sure," he charged them (1 Sam. 23:22). They should make certain of David's precise location:

> "Know and see the place where his foot is, and who has seen him there, for it is told me that he is very cunning. See therefore and take note of all the lurking places where he hides, and come back to me with sure information. Then I will go with you. And if he is in the land, I will search him out among all the thousands of Judah." And they arose and went to Ziph ahead of Saul. (23:22–24)

What was David to do in the face of such relentless evil? The answer is seen in the record of the early Christians, enduring centuries of violent Roman persecution and refusing to worship Caesar as "Lord," while they advanced the gospel and gave praise to God. The answer is seen in the gospel remnant that endured the tyranny and violence of decades of Communist power in Russia, Eastern Europe, and China. Faithful Christians devoted their years of unjust imprisonment to prayer, in this way unleashing gospel power upon their lands. The answer will be seen today through believers in the post-Christian West, who refuse to be absorbed into secular-humanist hedonism and falsehood, who continue the work of the church and the proclamation of the gospel of salvation in Christ's blood. What was David to do in the desert of Ziph? He was to persevere in faith, serving God and his people while awaiting the Lord's chosen time of deliverance.

David's intelligence brought news of Saul's movements: "David was told, so he went down to the rock and lived in the wilderness of Maon" (1 Sam. 23:25). The circumstances were naturally unnerving, and David's situation was deteriorating by the minute. But with his hand strengthened in the Lord by the words of Jonathan, he set his hope in God and continued on in desperate faith.

The superscription of Psalm 54 says that it was written "when the Ziphites went and told Saul, 'Is not David hiding among us?'" The psalm thus records David's prayer during this time. He began, "O God, save me by your name, and vindicate me by your might" (Ps. 54:1). This petition echoes Jonathan's reminder of God's promise, so that David prays by the Lord's name. As he presses on, David knows exactly where to place his reliance: "Behold, God is my helper; the Lord is the upholder of my life. He will return the evil to my enemies; in your faithfulness put an end to them" (54:4–5). His faith enlivening as he prays, David concludes with words of certain deliverance, not looking on his circumstances by sight but by faith in God's Word: "With a freewill offering I will sacrifice to you; I will give thanks to your name, O LORD, for it is good. For he has delivered me from every trouble, and my eye has looked in triumph on my enemies" (54:6–7). Here faith rises up as it should: like David, we most truly praise God when we thank him before he delivers us and when we give praise for the triumph that our faith has seen, though our eyes have not.

David's faith was not disappointed. Just when Saul had nearly cornered the fugitive band and it seemed that David's cause was lost, a messenger approached the king: "As Saul and his men were closing in on David and his men to capture them, a messenger came to Saul, saying, 'Hurry and come, for the Philistines have made a raid against the land.' So Saul returned from pursuing after David and went against the Philistines" (1 Sam. 23:26–28). God's deliverance was marked by the naming of the place: "Therefore that place was called the Rock of Escape" (23:28). The certainty of God's sovereign resolve to save his people is rightly compared to a great and solid rock. Blaikie comments: "If it be God's purpose to deliver you, He has thousands of unseen methods, to any one of which He may resort, when, to the eye of sense, there seems not the shadow of a hope."[5]

The Lord's faithfulness to deliver David was never in doubt, but instead David's faith was being tested for perseverance. God will likewise test our faith by trying circumstances that seem without hope, except in him. Thus, as David moved on to a new stronghold at Engedi, he departed with a renewed faith strengthened by trial. According to Jesus, this is the purpose of our whole lives, that by perseverance we not only prove our faith (see 1 Peter 1:6–7) but enter into the fullness of salvation. Notice the prominent place given to the theme of perseverance in Jesus' messages to the suffering churches of the book of Revelation:

> Be faithful unto death, and I will give you the crown of life. (Rev. 2:10)

> To the one who conquers I will give some of the hidden manna, and I will give him a white stone, with a new name written on the stone . . . (2:17)

> The one who conquers and who keeps my works until the end, to him I will give authority over the nations, . . . and I will give him the morning star. (2:26–28)

> The one who conquers, I will grant him to sit with me on my throne, as I also conquered and sat down with my Father on his throne. (3:21)

Conquering perseverance was the aim of Jonathan's brotherly encouragement. David was not called to overthrow Saul's power or keep the Ziphites from their terrible sins. David was to persevere faithfully in his own God-given calling. This meant faithful service to Israel while David awaited elevation to the throne. We today are called to persevere faithfully in the pursuit of holiness, in the work of the church, in the witness of the gospel, in the Christian parenting of our children, and in faithful performance of our duties at home, work, or school. We are not to give in when secular forces threaten to overwhelm us, when sinful fashions are made appealing, or when difficulty discourages our hearts. We are to continue, guided and inspired by Jesus' many gospel promises. "I am the light of the world," he said; "whoever follows me will not walk in darkness" (John 8:12); "Whoever

5. Blaikie, *First Samuel*, 364.

believes in me, as the Scripture has said, 'Out of his heart will flow rivers of living water'" (John 7:38, quoting Prov. 18:4). We are to persevere, offering prayers like those of David in his wilderness fatigue. In the aftermath of his escape, David prayed:

> Be merciful to me, O God, be merciful to me,
>   for in you my soul takes refuge;
> in the shadow of your wings I will take refuge,
>   till the storms of destruction pass by.
> I cry out to God Most High,
>   to God who fulfills his purpose for me.
> He will send from heaven and save me;
>   he will put to shame him who tramples on me. (Ps. 57:1–3)

Jonathan shows us that the aim of our ministry in Christian friendship is encouraging support for the perseverance that David showed. If we will but press on in faith, salvation will soon draw near. But what encouragement we sometimes need to press on in faith! The writer of Hebrews urges us: "Exhort one another every day, as long as it is called 'today,' that none of you may be hardened by the deceitfulness of sin" (Heb. 3:13).

It is touching to realize that when David and Jonathan parted in the bitter setting of the wilderness of Ziph, they were seeing each other for the last time in life. "The two of them made a covenant before the LORD. David remained at Horesh, and Jonathan went home" (1 Sam. 23:18). Apparently, Saul's son had had enough of his father's ruthless pursuing, although his duty would return him to his father's side. In his last act of friendship, he turned David's heart to rest on One who was able to do so much more than he could ever do. One of the best ways for us to serve the Lord, to reflect his glory in the world, and to fulfill God's calling on us as Christian brothers and sisters is to step off the sidelines of life, to offer our time and compassion to friends in need, and to speak words of truth and grace that lead others to (or back to) the Lord.

THE GREATER FRIEND

Scripture says that "there is a friend who sticks closer than a brother" (Prov. 18:24), and the ultimate example of that friend is the Son of God, who willingly died to free us from our sins. Like Jonathan, Jesus came from a place of safety into our world of hardship and danger. Like Jonathan, Jesus left riches and comfort to enter into our poverty. Like Jonathan, Jesus gave thought to our need and, reflecting on our misery, brought words of salvation. Indeed, if we find ourselves in need with no Jonathan at hand to strengthen our faith, we may turn to Jesus and find a ready and present friend, who is able to "sympathize with our weaknesses" and offer "grace to help in time of need" (Heb. 4:15–16).

Many heroes of the faith have found Jesus to be the best of friends. Andrew Bonar wrote in his journal of a certain wood where he would go to be strengthened through fellowship in prayer with Christ. He named it his "Wood of Ziph." He recorded, "God has often strengthened my hands, my divine Jonathan meeting me there." Jonathan Edwards on his death-bed likewise called out for "Jesus of Nazareth, my true and never-failing friend."[6] The apostle Paul said the same of his trial before Caesar: "No one came to stand by me, but all deserted me. . . . But the Lord stood by me and strengthened me" (2 Tim. 4:16–17).

Not only does Jesus strengthen our hand to believe in God, but he is the way to God's love, atoning for our sins with his own blood. Jesus says to us, "I will never leave you nor forsake you" (Heb. 13:5, quoting Josh. 1:5). Therefore, we persevere by leaning our souls upon his saving grace. And we serve Jesus well when we stand by our friends, speak to them the words that strengthen faith, and, in Christ's name, share in their troubles and sorrows. Jesus said of himself, "Greater love has no one than this, that someone lay down his life for his friends" (John 15:13). If we will be true friends to our brothers and sisters in his name, then something like that may be said of us. Christ will use our ministry to strengthen the hands and hearts of many to persevere until the day when salvation comes forever.

6. Both examples quoted in Dale Ralph Davis, *1 Samuel: Looking on the Heart* (Fearn, Ross-shire, UK: Christian Focus, 2000), 194–95.

35

A Corner of the Robe

1 Samuel 24:1–22

*See, my father, see the corner of your robe in my hand. For by
the fact that I cut off the corner of your robe and did not kill
you, you may know and see that there is no wrong or treason in
my hands. (1 Sam. 24:11)*

n the first chapter of Romans, the apostle Paul points out that
people who deny God do not do so because of a lack of evidence.
For not only were all men and women created so as to know
God, but the evidence for God bombards us in the created realm. Paul says
that "his invisible attributes, namely, his eternal power and divine nature,
have been clearly perceived, ever since the creation of the world, in the
things that have been made" (Rom. 1:20). Unbelievers therefore reject a
God whom they know, out of moral rebellion. Paul explains that "by their
unrighteousness [they] suppress the truth. . . . For although they knew God,
they did not honor him as God or give thanks to him" (1:18, 21). The result
is that "they became futile in their thinking, and their foolish hearts were
darkened" (1:21), so that they embrace and are given over by God to every
kind of perverse way of thinking and acting.

In teaching justification by faith, Paul employed a number of Old Testament examples to prove his point, including Abraham, Moses, and David. Had the apostle wanted to enlarge on the doctrine of unbelief, he could have hardly done better than the example of Israel's King Saul. Saul chose the path of his own will rather than the will of God. He is a picture of everyone today who knows the truth of God but suppresses that truth. No doubt Saul thought that as Israel's king he could stave off the consequences of rebellion against God, just as postmodern man persuades himself that he can ignore God and rewrite millennia-old rules of morality and human society, trusting in his technology, wealth, and leisure to live successfully in opposition to God's Word. Saul learned, however, that the day of reckoning can come suddenly, even at what seems to be a moment of triumph. In Romans Paul showed that unbelief always has consequences, with a price of twisted moral priorities to be paid along the way. Saul was a living illustration of this teaching.

Saul's Day of the Lord

Saul had bitter experience with the Lord's chastisement, especially during his long pursuit of David. The previous chapter saw the king bearing down on his fugitive son-in-law, only to have the Philistine army unexpectedly launch an invasion that called him away. We are not told how long it took Saul to subdue the Philistines, only that when he returned from the campaign he immediately turned his efforts back to chasing David. This shows that not all human success is a sign of God's favor. Moreover, Saul failed to reflect on these experiences, not realizing that the God who gave him victory over Israel's enemies was the same God who preserved David from his attacks. Just as Pharaoh persisted in opposition to God after ten successive plagues on Egypt, Saul persisted in his murderous efforts against David.

So it is in general with unbelievers, whose sinful and selfish plans may be checked by setbacks, sickness, or other restraints, each of which provides an opportunity to reflect on the state of their souls. Like Saul, as soon as God providentially restores him, the unbeliever plows ahead, digging his eternal grave with a renewed commitment to sin and self. So it was that when Saul returned from battle with the Philistines, he picked three thousand elite troops and set off to finish David once and for all: "Then Saul took three thousand chosen men out of all Israel and went to seek David and his men in front of the Wildgoats' Rocks" (1 Sam. 24:2).

Those who trust and serve the Lord have the blessing of knowing that God's saving help is sure to appear in time. Exactly the opposite is true of those who turn their backs on God: they can be certain that the day of God's judgment will arrive, often in a sudden and surprising way. Jesus spoke this way of the rich fool who had sought security in his earthly riches: "Fool! This night your soul is required of you" (Luke 12:20). For Saul, the day of the Lord's chastisement came equally unexpectedly, and in a way that stripped bare his royal pretense: "He came to the sheepfolds by the way, where there was a cave, and Saul went in to relieve himself" (1 Sam. 24:3). Engedi is a region of shale cliffs, with numerous caverns and a perpetual spring of fresh water, which made it a favorite place of refreshment for shepherds with their flocks. David and some of his men had fled into one of these extensive caverns, and before long Saul also entered alone. The Hebrew text says that Saul then "uncovered his feet," and most scholars are agreed that this refers to Saul's disrobing himself so as to exercise his bodily functions in privacy.

There David and his men were huddled, like little mice in the darkness of their cave, with Saul's "special forces" units down below. How secure Saul must have felt in his strength! Yet even a king must answer the call of nature, and according to the Israelite law, he was forbidden to relieve himself within the confines of the camp. Spying a harmless-looking cave, Saul ambled in to do his business.

The Bible says that "God opposes the proud but gives grace to the humble" (James 4:6, quoting Prov. 3:34), but we forget how ruthless the Lord can be in bringing low his proud opponents. What a sight for David and his men when into their hideout strode the unsuspecting king, exposing himself not only to their eyes but to their hungry blades. The men could hardly contain their delight, saying to David: "Here is the day of which the LORD said to you, 'Behold, I will give your enemy into your hand, and you shall do to him as it shall seem good to you'" (1 Sam. 24:4). Yet the Bible does not record any such prophecy, and given what would transpire here, it is likely that the men simply engaged in some creative theology. It did not take a seminary professor, they insisted, to interpret what God was doing! Dale Ralph Davis

411

imagines them as quietly breaking out in a chorus, singing: "This is the day, this is the day that the Lord hath made."[1]

To be sure, it was *a* day of the Lord for Saul, though whether or not it was *the* day of his reckoning was not yet certain. Proverbs 13:15 says, "The way of transgressors is hard" (KJV). Little did Saul imagine how humiliating his disgrace would be! Yet the God who gives over the wicked to lusts and impurity (Rom. 1:24) also gives them over to destruction at the hour of his own choosing. So long as Saul remained a mere human being, he was at the mercy of the God he had rejected, and having spurned God's mercy he could fall at any moment that the Lord chose to deliver him into the hands of his foes. Such is the lamentable plight of all who suppress the knowledge of God and spurn his merciful offer of salvation in Jesus Christ. Jesus warned that we must therefore all "be ready, for the Son of Man is coming at an hour you do not expect" (Matt. 24:44).

David's Stricken Heart

Having exposed Saul to humiliation and assault, the text turns its attention to David's side of the cave. Spurred on by the excited urging of his men, David began quietly sneaking up behind his unsuspecting enemy. Finally, he drew near, his band of followers collectively holding their breath. But David hesitated. "'*Don't hesitate, David!*' his men must have silently gasped. '*Finish him off!*' David did hesitate, before finally reaching forward to act. But it was not Saul himself for which he reached, it was only his royal robe lying on the ground."[2] This dramatic scene unfolds in the brief understatement of verse 4: "Then David arose and stealthily cut off a corner of Saul's robe."

We can imagine the outraged disappointment of David's followers as they watched David quietly return, with Saul's blood unshed. The opportunity would be lost! David returned to wage a battle of wills with his men, who could only have been frustrated by his apparent loss of nerve. But it was not a lack of nerve that stayed David's hand; indeed, as he returned to his hiding place David was grief-stricken for even the small gesture of vindictiveness

---

1. Dale Ralph Davis, *1 Samuel: Looking on the Heart* (Fearn, Ross-shire, UK: Christian Focus, 2000), 199.

2. Richard D. Phillips, *The Heart of an Executive: Leadership Lessons from the Life of King David* (New York: Doubleday, 1998), 127.

he had displayed. He said to the men: "The LORD forbid that I should do this thing to my lord, the LORD's anointed, to put out my hand against him, seeing he is the LORD's anointed" (1 Sam. 24:6).

Why was David conscience-stricken? Verse 5 says: "Afterward David's heart struck him, because he had cut off a corner of Saul's robe." David knew that the royal robe was a symbol of Saul's authority as Israel's king. We saw this in 1 Samuel 15:28, when Samuel took the tearing of Saul's robe as a symbol that the kingdom would be torn from him and given "to a neighbor of yours, who is better than you." Robert Bergen writes: "David's confiscation of a portion of the royal robe signified the transfer of power from the house of Saul to the house of David."[3]

Why was David stricken over this merciful way of sparing Saul's life? Far from congratulating himself over sparing the life of his relentless persecutor, David assailed himself with the fact that in striking out at Saul's robe, he was in effect rebelling against God. David knew that Saul did not remain on the throne by accident, but by God's sovereign will. However little respect David now had for Saul, he had a deep reverence for the office Saul held, seeing it as a manifestation of God's reign. Looking on the situation from the Godward direction, David remembered that Saul was still "the LORD's anointed" (1 Sam. 24:6), so that to strike against the king was to strike out at God. Assured of this conviction, David not only explained himself to the men but strove with them so as to prevent them from harming Saul. The New International Version most accurately renders verse 7: "With these words David rebuked his men and did not allow them to attack Saul."

Reflecting on this dramatic episode, we first ask how David reasoned through this providence. He would have agreed with the men that it was God who had placed Saul at their mercy. Yet the mere fact that God has provided an opportunity does not guarantee that he intends us to exercise it. Often, as is the case here, God tests his servants to reveal the true state of their hearts. When Jonah arrived in Joppa to find a ship bound for Tarshish already in port, God was not facilitating the prophet's rebellion but rather testing his faithfulness. God likewise tests us in the presence of opportunity to sin in order to make known to us the true condition of our hearts and to cause us to draw near to him for strength and protection. Gordon Keddie writes

---

3. Robert D. Bergen, *1, 2 Samuel*, New American Commentary (Nashville: Broadman & Holman, 1996), 239.

that "an 'open door' is not, in itself, proof of God's will. Circumstances, in God's providence, are not a substitute for the principle he has revealed in his Word, the Bible."[4]

Consider what a severe test this was for David! A. W. Pink comments:

> One stroke of his sword, and he steps into a throne. Farewell to poverty! Farewell the life of a hunted goat. Reproaches, sneers, defeat, would cease; adulations, triumphs, riches would be his. But his at the sacrifice of faith; at the sacrifice of a humbled will, ever waiting on God's time; at the sacrifice of a thousand precious experiences of God's care, God's provision, God's guidance, God's tenderness. No, even a throne at that price is too dear. Faith will wait.[5]

It would not have been hard to justify slaying Saul. The king was guilty and deserved to die for the murder of the priests at Nob, if not for the rest of his many crimes. Moreover, removing Saul might lead to a national restoration of Israel to the Lord. Finally, since David was anointed by God for the kingship, he might be acting within his rights. How many Christians today would give in to such arguments, justifying sinful or unbiblical means with the godly ends that they are pursuing, reasoning that results are all that really matter. David, however, realized that he stood at a critical turning point in his life. God had promised him the throne. Would he take it in merciless blood, slaying with his own hand the anointed of the Lord and with that same bloody hand placing the crown of God's people on his own head? Whether David would reign was never in doubt, God's having promised it. But how David would reign and what kind of kingdom his leadership would produce was at stake in the darkness of the cave at Engedi. He realized that it was vitally important for his relationship to God and for his future as God's servant that he restrain himself from convenient and self-serving sins.

David shows, in contrast to Saul, the power of God's Word to govern one's passions and restrain them from exploding into violence and sin. Saul is a man who knows but suppresses the truth of God. His reign, therefore, is one of violence and unrestrained tyranny. So powerful is his inner turmoil that

4. Gordon J. Keddie, *Dawn of a Kingdom: The Message of 1 Samuel* (Darlington, UK: Evangelical Press, 1988), 224.

5. A. W. Pink, *A Life of David*, 2 vols. (Grand Rapids: Baker, 1981), 1:114.

he literally walks around carrying a spear, with which he may impulsively strike at any time. David, by contrast, not only knows God, but makes God's Word "a lamp to [his] feet and a light to [his] path" (Ps. 119:105). The result is a self-control that is practically impossible for any other kind of man. David is beset with overwhelming pressures to act violently, urged by men who had sacrificed everything for him, and with frustration pent up over years of injustice and cruel pursuit by this tyrant who had seemingly ruined his life. Moreover, David's act would take place in the dark, giving him full opportunity to shape the record of it as he saw fit.

How many noble hearts have failed under trials less potent than David's! Scotland's Robert the Bruce faced a similar trial when he met with his rival for the throne, the traitorous John Comyn, in the Greyfriars Chapel. So bitter was the Bruce's hatred and indignation that he could not restrain his hand from plunging a knife into Comyn's breast. Bruce would spend the rest of his life seeking to undo this bloody foundation to his reign as king of Scotland.

So what force restrained David's hand under even greater pressure to slay? The answer is that the weight of God's Word upon his conscience gave David self-control so that he did not fall victim to sinful passion. David reflected that Saul was "the LORD's anointed" (1 Sam. 24:6). Perhaps he also dwelt on the sixth commandment, "You shall not murder" (Ex. 20:13), and the injunction of Exodus 22:28, forbidding Israelites to curse their ruler. William Blaikie sums up David's motivation in words that express our only hope to avoid being led to ruin by our sinful passions: "He acted in utter contempt of what was personal and selfish, and in deepest reverence for what was holy and Divine."[6] To govern the will by a reverence for God is sure proof of a heart trained by frequent consultation of God's Word.

OUTSIDE THE CAVE

David escaped a sin that would have stained his entire future, despite the approval of his supporters. A David who slew Saul would have been like Lady Macbeth in Shakespeare's classic play, forever seeking to expunge the damning stain of blood. What kind of kingdom could David have ruled if he had gained the throne by coldbloodedly slaying

6. William G. Blaikie, *Expository Lectures on the Book of First Samuel* (1887; repr., Birmingham, AL: Solid Ground, 2005), 368.

his predecessor? Christians can likewise avoid the calamities that are so commonplace among the ungodly—financial frauds, sexual infidelities, and relationship-severing fits of anger—by submitting our conduct to the rule of Scripture.

On the positive side, we also see how David was enabled to provide spiritual leadership even in the face of Saul's wicked authority. The contrast between David and Saul, so clear inside the cave—one of them cursed and the other blessed with spiritual power—is equally clear outside the cave. Starting with David, we see how faithful submission to God and his Word empowers us to exert spiritual blessing in any situation.

First, God's power enabled David to be a peacemaker, in the face of the most wicked hostility: "Afterward David also arose and went out of the cave, and called after Saul, 'My lord the king!' And when Saul looked behind him, David bowed with his face to the earth and paid homage" (1 Sam. 24:8). How could David bow to such a despot as Saul, who had done everything to ruin him? The answer is that David had committed himself into the hands of God, leaving his own care to God's sovereign will. Moreover, instructed by the Scriptures, he left vengeance to the Lord. "Beloved, never avenge yourselves," Paul wrote, "but leave it to the wrath of God, for it is written, 'Vengeance is mine, I will repay, says the Lord'" (Rom. 12:19, quoting Deut. 32:35). Imagine the astonished look on Saul's face, first to realize his narrow escape and then to see his sworn enemy bowing in obeisance. Despite his grievances against the king, David had a faith that empowered him to approach Saul not as an outlaw or enemy but as the faithful subject he had desired to be. "Rather than falling upon Saul in a murderous attack, David fell upon the ground 'and prostrated himself with his face to the ground,'"[7] approaching the king peaceably and with proper respect.

David then spoke to Saul: "Why do you listen to the words of men who say, 'Behold, David seeks your harm'?" (1 Sam. 24:9). This was a generous way of interpreting Saul's policy against David. Pink observes, "Most graciously did David throw the blame upon Saul's courtiers, rather than upon the king himself."[8] It is possible that David was aware of some truth in this claim, since Saul surrounded himself with many who would

---

7. Bergen, *1, 2 Samuel*, 240.
8. Pink, *Life of David*, 1:120.

consider David a rival. David's speech, however, was designed to subdue rather than inflame Saul's hostility. How many disputes that have escalated to sever friendships and family bonds might have been dissolved by this generous spirit of reconciliation! That even Saul responded favorably to David's peaceful entreaty proves the teaching of Proverbs 15:1, "A soft answer turns away wrath."

Second, men and women who live in subjection to God's Word are able to show their goodwill toward all others. We live in a society increasingly torn into tribes and factions, with each isolated by the hostility of others. Living in accordance with God's Word, Christians should be like David, who demonstrated to Saul that his motives and intentions were friendly. David said:

> Behold, this day your eyes have seen how the LORD gave you today into my hand in the cave. And some told me to kill you, but I spared you. I said, "I will not put out my hand against my lord, for he is the LORD's anointed." See, my father, see the corner of your robe in my hand. For by the fact that I cut off the corner of your robe and did not kill you, you may know and see that there is no wrong or treason in my hands. I have not sinned against you, though you hunt my life to take it. (1 Sam. 24:10–11)

There can be no doubt that Saul, hearing David's words, reflexively gazed down to the hem of his robe. Seeing the torn corner, Saul would experience the reality striking home with telling force. David's knife had come within easy striking distance of Saul's flesh; the man of faith had declined to do to Saul what Saul had spent years trying to do to him. David was proved to be a man of godly principles, and thus virtually the only kind of person who can be trusted not to do harm but only good. So it should be with all believers: our demonstrated record of faithfulness, self-control, and love should commend us as those few who can be trusted when integrity matters most.

This emphasis formed an important part of the early church's defense of Christianity against pagan slander. In his *First Apology*, Tertullian could plainly assert that the Christians were Caesar's most loyal, peaceable, and trustworthy citizens, so that only mad, self-destructive impulses could seek their demise. He wrote to the emperor: "In the performance of our good deeds we do not make any exception of persons; for we do them for our own sakes, and seek to obtain the [blessing] of praise or reward, not from man, but from God. . . . We are the same towards the emperors as towards our neighbors. For we are alike forbidden to wish, or do, or speak, or think, evil of anyone."[9] Can Christians make such a claim today? If we did, the sordid record of many pastors and other public Christians, falling into the very sins so common to the pagan society, would mock the Christian claim to sincere integrity and goodwill. Holding the corner of Saul's robe, David had tangible proof that testified to his goodwill and fidelity. Each Christian should ask what proof of goodwill we could display before our neighbors, coworkers, and even enemies.

Third, David shows how believers may respectfully deliver God's rebuke to sin. He declared to Saul: "May the LORD judge between me and you, may the LORD avenge me against you, but my hand shall not be against you. As the proverb of the ancients says, 'Out of the wicked comes wickedness.' But my hand shall not be against you. After whom has the king of Israel come out? After whom do you pursue? After a dead dog! After a flea!" (1 Sam. 24:12–14). David was wise to offer this reproof after he had first proved his peace and goodwill. Having previously spoken with humility to soften Saul's heart, he had earned Saul's consideration as he now expressed a godly reproof.

Finally, David concluded his remarkable embassy by appealing to the Lord for his safety and success: "May the LORD therefore be judge and give sentence between me and you, and see to it and plead my cause and deliver me from your hand" (1 Sam. 24:15). This appeal to God gave force to David's prior assurance, "I will not put out my hand against my lord, for he is the LORD's anointed" (24:10). In this way, David advanced his appeal for Saul to rethink his violent pursuit, for those who appeal to God's justice may be counted on to obey God's Word in living peaceably with all men (see Rom. 12:18). When believers today find ourselves in disputes or disagreements, we should remember that our appeal to God's justice obliges us to act carefully in obedience to the Lord's Word. Paul advised, "In your anger do not sin" (Eph. 4:26 NIV, quoting Ps. 4:4). This is a principle that Christians should apply to every situation, so that our integrity may both glorify God and promote reconciliation with our opponents.

9. Tertullian, *First Apology*, 36.

Saul's Tearful Self-Refutation

The success of David's godly appeal is seen not in any lasting change on Saul's part, but in the further contrast between their consciences. His spirit bound in submission to God's Word, David spoke peaceably in a way that matched the evidence of his life. Saul, on the other hand, could express his conscience only in a manner that condemned the chief priorities of his own life. How often this is the case for the testimony of unbelief!

Three features of Saul's reply stand out, beginning with the tearful blessing he utters for David: "As soon as David had finished speaking these words to Saul, Saul said, 'Is this your voice, my son David?' And Saul lifted up his voice and wept" (1 Sam. 24:16). Whatever little capacity for love was left in Saul's blackened heart, David's humble entreaty succeeded in drawing it out. But David could not bring about true repentance in Saul, since only the regenerating work of the Holy Spirit can truly change the heart. The king showed his true colors, admitting, "You are more righteous than I, for you have repaid me good, whereas I have repaid you evil" (24:17). This is typical of unbelieving piety, which always seeks to reserve some self-justification: not that Saul is wholly unrighteous, but simply that David is more righteous than Saul. Contrast Saul's plea with the humble repentance of the tax collector in Jesus' parable, whose true repentance implored, "God, be merciful to me, a sinner!" (Luke 18:13). Those who truly repent have nothing to say for their own righteousness, but are filled with conviction over their many sins. Still, Saul at least admitted David's righteous conduct in sparing his life as the proof of his goodwill: "For if a man finds his enemy, will he let him go away safe? So may the LORD reward you with good for what you have done to me this day" (1 Sam. 24:19). With these words, Saul implicitly called down God's judgment on his unrepentant persecution of innocent David.

Second, Saul made a stunning revelation that publicly announced the futility of his ungodly life: "And now, behold, I know that you shall surely be king, and that the kingdom of Israel shall be established in your hand" (1 Sam. 24:20). In similar fashion, unbelievers today frequently complain about the vanity of pursuing fame and fortune, despite their inability to stop pursuing these very things. Knowing that he was wrong did not keep Saul from pursuing David's life, just as unbelievers who admit the purposelessness of their existence are not able to change their lives without the gracious intervention of God through his gospel.

Third, Saul pitifully pleaded with David to spare his household in the inevitable event of David's ascent to the throne: "Swear to me therefore by the LORD that you will not cut off my offspring after me, and that you will not destroy my name out of my father's house" (1 Sam. 24:21). The same David who had cut off the corner of his robe had power to cut off Saul's entire line and name, and Saul sought his mercy, without any word of mercy to David in return.

Note that David did not even bother to ask Saul's pledge in sparing his life. He had committed himself to the Lord, and while forgiving Saul on God's behalf, David knew better than to trust a word that fell from Saul's unregenerate lips. In relying on David's mercy, Saul bore eloquent testimony of the surpassing blessing that comes to those who trust the very God whom Saul had rejected. Saul could not face the reality of the situation before him without condemning his unbelief, bearing testimony in his appeal to David that God can and does create men and women after his own heart (1 Sam. 13:14), believers who can be trusted to live on a plane higher than that to which Saul would even bother to aspire.

THE CROWN AND THE CROSS

In the cave of Engedi, we observe David at one of the highest spiritual pinnacles of his entire life. What a difference it made to his future that he honored the Lord during this time of trial! And how important it is for us that we pass the tests of faith that God sets before us, for in many cases our future usefulness to the Lord may be on the line.

Thinking of David in his merciful restraint toward King Saul, we are reminded of the greater and more significant example of his descendant Jesus Christ. Indeed, the biblical account of David is meant to portray the character and achievement of Jesus in saving us from our sins. How vital it was for our salvation that Jesus did not reach out to seize his throne in a manner contrary to God's plan. The devil sought this as perhaps the best chance to turn the Messiah from his saving course. Satan laid before Jesus "all the kingdoms of the world and their glory. And he said to him, 'All these I will give you, if you will fall down and worship me'" (Matt. 4:8–9). Why should Jesus take his kingdom at the feet of Satan? Because Satan offered the crown without the cross. This is always Satan's false appeal to God's people. Satan promised Jesus nothing less than what God had ordained. What difference would the means employed make? he would have argued! The difference lay in our salvation, and Jesus knew that the very nature of his kingdom lay in the balance: only by doing God's work in God's way would Jesus truly receive God's reward for himself and his people.

Are you tempted to seek the crown of salvation without the cross of a life governed by obedience to God's Word? Are you tempted to justify sinful or worldly means because the outward results will come more easily? May God grant us the power, along with David, looking at the crucified and resurrected Jesus, never to lay our hands on the blessings that God has promised in a manner contrary to the will of God in his Word. Let us instead commit to receive whatever blessings God has for us from God's own hand or not at all. In any other way the blessings are lost, the harvest is polluted, and the cup of salvation is spoiled with the taint of sin and worldly compromise. "Wait for the LORD and keep his way," David counsels us, "and he will exalt you to inherit the land; you will look on when the wicked are cut off" (Ps. 37:34).

36

INSULT AND INJURY

1 Samuel 25:1–31

*Please forgive the trespass of your servant. For the LORD will
certainly make my lord a sure house, because my lord is fighting
the battles of the LORD, and evil shall not be found in you so
long as you live. (1 Sam. 25:28)*

Some news is so momentous that it can be reported only in stark
facts. Thus on April 13, 1912, the *Boston Daily Globe* headline
read, "Titanic Sinks, 1500 Die." Thirty-three years later on that
date, the *San Francisco Chronicle* announced, "FDR Dies!" On September 12,
2001, the *New York Times* headline read, "America Attacked." In this same
spirit of emphatic brevity, 1 Samuel 25:1 announces, "Now Samuel died."
Thus was reported a watershed in the history of God's ancient people Israel
as significant as the death of Moses so many years beforehand. Not only
was Samuel the greatest of Israel's leaders since at least Joshua, Moses' successor, but his departure also sealed a decisive transition in Israel's divinely
appointed governance, from Spirit-empowered judges to royal dynasties.

Samuel was the last of the judges and the founder of the school of the
prophets, a line that would culminate in the life and work of Jesus Christ.
Moreover, the Lord gave Samuel the task of anointing, protecting, and pre-

paring the great romantic champion of the Old Testament, King David, whose throne was erected for the eternal reign of Jesus, God's and David's Son. Thus, though Samuel had abdicated day-to-day leadership of Israel with the coronation of King Saul, the old prophet-judge did not lay down his life until Saul had publicly acknowledged David's right to rule in his place. First Samuel 24 concludes with Saul's admission to David, "I know that you shall surely be king, and that the kingdom of Israel shall be established in your hand" (v. 20). Only then are we permitted to learn, "Now Samuel died" (1 Sam. 25:1).

When great and godly men die, even their detractors are forced to mourn their passing. Therefore, "all Israel assembled and mourned for him, and they buried him in his house at Ramah" (1 Sam. 25:1). This raises the question: Was David present for Samuel's burial? The answer seems to be "No." Saul's relentless pursuit had driven David into the southern desert regions, and it is doubtful that David would have come back north to Israel's heartland for Samuel's burial, especially since our text places him still farther south, deep into the desert of the Sinai Peninsula, "down to the wilderness of Paran" (25:1). Did David feel even more vulnerable with Samuel's departure, so that he put distance between himself and Saul? Sensing a final and decisive period in his life, did David retreat into the desert to be closer to God, prefiguring Jesus' sojourn into the wilderness after his baptism? Given David's conduct in this chapter, it seems likely that his retreat was based more on fear than on faith. Still, David must have realized that a time of testing was before him that would determine his worthiness to rule as Israel's king.

DAVID'S HUMBLE APPEAL

After David's personal retreat into the same desert where Israel had sojourned in the exodus, he returned to his small army and its many problems. Most immediate was the problem of logistics, as David relied on the surrounding populace to support his sizable force of six hundred fighters, along with families and camp followers. Not far from Ziph, to which he had fled earlier, were the towns of Maon and Carmel. There David encountered the servants of a man named Nabal. This man "was very rich; he had three thousand sheep and a thousand goats" (1 Sam. 25:2). David knew that he was obligated to ensure his army's good behavior, and there is every evidence

423

that he did his best to live in peace with the surrounding populace. Later we hear from Nabal's workers that David's "men were very good to us, and we suffered no harm, and we did not miss anything when we were in the fields, as long as we went with them. They were a wall to us both by night and by day, all the while we were with them keeping the sheep" (25:15–16).

In short, David was a good neighbor. Instead of allowing his men to take liberties with the available livestock or to use their superior armed strength to intimidate and exploit the nearby people, David's men protected the innocent who were around them. They respected property. They lived out Paul's teaching to the churches in Galatia: "As we have opportunity, let us do good to everyone, and especially to those who are of the household of faith" (Gal. 6:10). Far from the natural expectation that a certain amount of loss was inevitable from having a large roving band in the region, Nabal's property was unusually preserved so that his gain was increased. David's example also shows the difference that Christian leadership should make. How different was the conduct of the Confederate Army of Northern Virginia in its invasion of Pennsylvania than the Union Army of Tennessee in its famous "March to the Sea." The Southern Army led by the Christian general Robert E. Lee respected property and paid for all the provisions it used, whereas the Union Army led by William Tecumseh Sherman wreaked such violence and destruction that its passage was still resented by Southerners a hundred years later. David not only restrained the violence of his army, but made their presence a source of help to those nearby. This is the difference that Christians should make in our communities, neighborhoods, and families: our presence should be an unusual source of benefit and blessing to those around us. As David's men were "very good" to Nabal's household, people who know us at work, around the block, or at play should say, "It is so good to know them!"

It was important for David to have a good reputation with his neighbors. As one called to rule as king over Israel, he had to uphold not only the letter but also the spirit of the law, including its requirements for justice and mercy. Here David proved himself to be a good shepherd not only over his own flock but over the flocks of those nearby, demonstrating his fitness to lead God's people. Since Nabal's men stated that David's force was "a wall to us both by night and by day," we see that David embraced God's requirement that we be our neighbor's keeper (Gen. 4:9).

All this while, however, David himself was in considerable need. His service to the Lord required support from God's people, and with hundreds of mouths to feed every day, David needed generous supply and aid. Knowing that it was the time for the shearing of Nabal's vast flocks, David sent ten delegates to seek provision from the wealthy landowner.

Just as David's neighborliness provides a model for us, so also does David's gracious approach to Nabal in seeking aid. "Go to Nabal and greet him in my name," David ordered. "And thus you shall greet him: 'Peace be to you, and peace be to your house, and peace be to all that you have'" (1 Sam. 25:5–6). William Blaikie comments, "No envying of his prosperity—no grudging to him his abundance; but only the Christian wish that he might have God's blessing with it, and that it might all turn to good."[1] David's men were to point out that Nabal's shepherds had been protected from harm, losing none of their flocks while David's band was around. As the recent experience of Keilah had shown, the nearby Philistines posed a real threat to large herds (1 Sam. 23:5), a threat that David had averted for Nabal. Nabal could learn of this from his own people. "Therefore," they were to ask, "let my young men find favor in your eyes, for we come on a feast day. Please give whatever you have at hand to your servants and to your son David" (25:8).

David's request was humble—he named himself as "your son David"— and it was reasonable, asking for logistical support at a time when Nabal enjoyed abundance. With all this in mind, David must have sent his men with the expectations of a friendly and generous response. After all, he was not treating with Canaanites but fellow Israelites, even fellow Judahites. Nabal hailed from the noble clan of Caleb, noted in Israel's history for godliness and faith. Given his treatment of Nabal's shepherds, the respectfulness of his manner, and the timing of his appeal, David had every expectation of a kind and generous response, a properly neighborly return for the good that David had performed for rich Nabal.

Nabal's Hard-Hearted Reply

The biblical account of David is a study in contrasts. On this occasion, we meet another man who contrasts sharply with David. Nabal had assets—

1. William G. Blaikie, *Expository Lectures on the Book of First Samuel* (1887; repr., Birmingham, AL: Solid Ground, 2005), 383.

namely, his riches and the good name of his Calebite family—but he lacked character. He "was harsh and badly behaved" (1 Sam. 25:3). Nabal was to money what Saul was to power: he was corrupted to such an extent that his very name meant "fool." This does not signify silly playfulness, but "implies viciousness, atheism, and materialism."[2] Walter Brueggemann comments: "His life is determined by his property. Nabal lives to defend his property, and he dies in an orgy, enjoying his property. Only after being told of his riches are we told his name."[3] We may wonder whether David had Nabal in mind when he penned Psalm 14:1: "The fool says in his heart, 'There is no God.' They are corrupt, they do abominable deeds, there is none who does good." In the Hebrew, this reads, "Nabal says in his heart, 'There is no God.'"

Psalm 14 perfectly describes Nabal in his hard-hearted reply to David's plea for help. He not only refused to share out of his abundance, but also added insult to injury. He answered David's servants, "Who is David? Who is the son of Jesse? There are many servants these days who are breaking away from their masters" (1 Sam. 25:10). It is obvious that Nabal knew very well who David was, since he named David's father, even as he pretended to view him as a no-account. Indeed, it is not realistically possible that David's fame had not preceded him to Maon and Carmel. Nabal went further and scorned David as a mere renegade who was beneath his charity: "Shall I take my bread and my water and my meat . . . and give it to men who come from I do not know where?" (25:11).

Nabal provides a model for a wrong attitude toward wealth and possessions. How little he considered God's generosity toward himself in his response to David's humble request. Blaikie writes: "It was the time of sheep-shearing, when the flocks were probably counted and the increase over last year ascertained; and by a fine old custom it was commonly the season of liberality and kindness. A time of increase should always be so; it is the time for helping poor relations . . . , for acknowledging ancient kindnesses, for relieving distress, and for devising liberal things for the Church of Christ."[4]

What led Nabal to be so miserly with his money? The answer is found in verse 11, where the words *I* and *my* occur so frequently: "Shall I take my bread

2. Daniel M. Doriani, *David the Anointed* (Philadelphia: Great Commission Publications, 1984), 63.
3. Walter Brueggemann, *First and Second Samuel*, Interpretation (Louisville: John Knox, 1990), 175.
4. Blaikie, *First Samuel*, 383.

and my water and my meat that I have killed for my shearers and give it to men who come from I do not know where?" We are reminded of the rich fool in Jesus' parable, who spoke so constantly in the first person that he had only himself to talk to: "I will do this: I will tear down my barns and build larger ones, and there I will store all my grain and my goods. And I will say to my soul, Soul, you have ample goods laid up for many years; relax, eat, drink, be merry" (Luke 12:18–19). The problem was, as Jesus points out, that his own life did not even belong to himself, much less his possessions: "God said to him, 'Fool! This night your soul is required of you, and the things you have prepared, whose will they be?'" (12:20). "So is the one," Jesus concludes, "who lays up treasure for himself and is not rich toward God" (12:21).

Nabal heaped false charges upon David—denouncing him as a no-account scoundrel—because he did not want to admit that he loved money more than his fellow man. In the same way, the greedy man today does not merely refuse to give to the needs of the poor, but adds abusive comments about their laziness; he holds his wallet tight when funds are requested for the work of the gospel, complaining that the church cares only about money. In fact, the true reason for greed is idolatry (Col. 3:5): not merely the idolatry of worshiping money, but the idolatry of worshiping self. In contrast to Nabal and the rich fool of Jesus' parable, while we will want to be prudent in the use of money, we should rejoice at contributing to those in need and especially at an opportunity to befriend and assist the servants of God in the cause of world missions, church planting, and evangelism.

Put yourself in David's shoes as the report came back from Nabal's feast. For years now, David had been hunted by Saul. Why? Because God had anointed David as the true king over the people. Meanwhile, David was burdened with the anxiety of feeding his large band of followers, and their need must have been pressing. David had labored to restrain his men and respect the local landowners. Now, having patiently endured threats from the great of the world, such as King Saul, he was forced to endure insults from the low of the world—Nabal. In the previous chapter, when Saul stumbled into the cave and placed himself at David's mercy, the young hero had responded with grace and faith, even bowing to Saul and pleading his cause once the king had departed from the cave. How will David handle this new and different challenge, not from the Lord's anointed but from a man who was so lowly as even to be named *Fool*?

The answer is that David did not respond to this frustration very well at all: "David said to his men, 'Every man strap on his sword!' And every man of them strapped on his sword. David also strapped on his sword. And about four hundred men went up after David, while two hundred remained with the baggage" (1 Sam. 25:13).

David's violent reaction offers us a number of significant lessons. First, David fell so easily into sin because he was not on his guard against it. Surely this explains much of the difference between his self-control in the presence of Saul versus his furious passion at the insult from foolish Nabal. We are likewise easily led into sin when we are not expecting a challenge to our character and grace. Peter provided an example of this on the night of Jesus' arrest. Expecting trouble when Judas arrived with soldiers, Peter was bold in his faithful stand for Jesus. But later that evening, after he had followed Jesus to the high priest's house, Peter's guard was down and his faith was easily felled by a question from a serving woman (John 18:10, 17).

Moreover, it is worth noting that David's ungodly response to Nabal came on the heels of his notable success in sparing King Saul. We tend to respond to spiritual success by relying on ourselves and loosening our dependence on God's grace through prayer and God's Word. Once his flesh was unrestrained by reliance on God, David was transformed into just another Saul. Saul reacted to a perceived affront by ordering the death of all the priests at Nob; now David intends to answer Nabal's insult by slaying all the men of that household (1 Sam. 25:22). A. W. Pink comments:

> No man stands a moment longer than divine grace upholds him. The strongest are weak as water immediately the power of the Spirit is withdrawn; the most mature and experienced Christian acts foolishly the moment he be left to himself; none of us has any reserve strength or wisdom in himself to draw from: our source of sufficiency is all treasured up for us in Christ, as soon as communion with Him be broken, as soon as we cease looking alone to Him, we are helpless.[5]

Finally, David's reaction makes it clear that he had grown to expect a certain amount of respect to be paid to his person and name. It is especially easy for God's choice servants to develop a prideful concern for their

5. A. W. Pink, *A Life of David*, 2 vols. (Grand Rapids: Baker, 1981), 1:134.

reputation, so that they are easily vexed by the kind of insult that Nabal cast against David. How different was the attitude of Jesus, having humbled himself to the obedience of the cross, when he was mocked by the Jewish leaders and Roman soldiers. Peter writes to believers: "Christ also suffered for you, leaving you an example, so that you might follow in his steps. . . . When he was reviled, he did not revile in return; when he suffered, he did not threaten, but continued entrusting himself to him who judges justly" (1 Peter 2:21–23). With this in mind, a good test of our Christlikeness is our response to those who speak ill of us or misrepresent our actions. If we have humbled ourselves at the cross, we will realize that the worst that others can say of us hardly compares to the true depth of our sin. Especially when we are reviled for our Christian confession, the Bible urges us to embrace the privilege of suffering verbal abuse together with Christ.

Abigail's Judicious Embassy

So far, Samuel's legacy has not been honored very well, either by David or by Nabal. This explosive situation brings forth a woman, however, who embodies the very opposite of what her husband exhibits. Abigail was introduced in verse 3 as the wife of Nabal, a woman both "discerning and beautiful." This godly woman's wisdom and shining character were sorely tried by what had transpired. News was brought to her by one of the servants:

> Behold, David sent messengers out of the wilderness to greet our master, and he railed at them. Yet the men were very good to us, and we suffered no harm, and we did not miss anything when we were in the fields, as long as we went with them. They were a wall to us both by night and by day, all the while we were with them keeping the sheep. Now therefore know this and consider what you should do, for harm is determined against our master and against all his house, and he is such a worthless man that one cannot speak to him. (1 Sam. 25:14–17)

It tells us much about the affairs in this house that the servant came to Nabal's wife when a life-and-death matter arose. Whereas the master was so vile that his men could not reason with him, Abigail was approachable and reliable. Gordon Keddie writes: "Abigail looks like the competent wife who had been called upon before to rectify some of her husband's

429

pig-headedness. Men like that rarely know how much they owe to the faithfulness of their wives."[6]

Abigail wasted no time in acting to save her husband and family. Some might question her submissiveness, given that she treated with David behind Nabal's back. But this concern fails to reckon with the dire threat to their mere survival. Keddie comments: "Wifely submissiveness does not extend to initiating fruitless arguments, still less to potentially suicidal delay."[7]

Immediately, she directed that supplies be gathered for an offering to David: "Abigail made haste and took two hundred loaves and two skins of wine and five sheep already prepared and five seahs of parched grain and a hundred clusters of raisins and two hundred cakes of figs, and laid them on donkeys. And she said to her young men, 'Go on before me; behold, I come after you'" (1 Sam. 25:18–19). This offering, sent straight to David, would have alleviated neither his material need nor the offense to his pride. It would, however, signal the good intentions and respect of the one who sent it.

As Abigail drew near to David's advancing party, the terrain permitted her to hear what David was saying before she was seen. What she heard revealed that things were as bad as they could be, since in his violent passion David now went so far as to vow destruction on Nabal's house: "God do so to the enemies of David and more also, if by morning I leave so much as one male of all who belong to him" (1 Sam. 25:22). These were fearful words for Abigail to hear from a man of David's military reputation, backed by so formidable an armed force. Abigail wasted no time in hastening to David with an embassy of peace, her actions and speech displaying the full depth of her discernment and inner beauty.

We can track Abigail's appeal to David for restraint in five steps that should be followed by Christians when seeking to turn an aggrieved fellow believer from anger. First, Abigail *humbled herself* in David's presence: "When Abigail saw David, she hurried and got down from the donkey and fell before David on her face and bowed to the ground" (1 Sam. 25:23). Our culture despises one who will abase himself or herself before a foe, but in God's kingdom this is a mark of special grace. Pink comments on Abigail's

---

6. Gordon J. Keddie, *Dawn of a Kingdom: The Message of 1 Samuel* (Darlington, UK: Evangelical Press, 1988), 235.
7. Ibid.

humility: "Nabal had insulted [David] as a runaway slave, but his wife owns him as a superior, as her king in the purpose of God."[8]

Second, Abigail *confessed the guilt* of her sin: "She fell at his feet and said, 'On me alone, my lord, be the guilt'" (1 Sam. 25:24). We might object that it was Nabal, not Abigail, who had wronged David. But as his wife, she owned the sin of her husband and acknowledged it before David. This was not the kind of halfhearted confession so commonly heard today: "I am sorry that you feel the way you do," and so forth. Abigail was sorry not that David was angered but that her husband had offended. Here we see her sterling wisdom, for in this stroke she confronted David not with the guilt of her worthless husband, but with the penitence of a beautiful and servant-hearted woman. Nabal had sinned against David in withholding what his services had earned (Deut. 24:15), and reconciliation with David required confession of this sin. So also must we confess sins that stand between us and others if we wish to honor the Lord in godly reconciliation.

Third, Abigail *offered restitution* for the wrong done to David. David had been denied rightful provision, so Abigail brought the food supplies to give him. "Now let this present that your servant has brought to my lord be given to the young men who follow my lord," she said (1 Sam. 25:27). Equally important, whereas David had been publicly reviled by Nabal, Abigail made amends by publicly praising his greatness: "Please forgive the trespass of your servant. For the LORD will certainly make my lord a sure house, because my lord is fighting the battles of the LORD, and evil shall not be found in you so long as you live" (25:28). The New Testament makes it clear that confession of sin is to be accompanied by sincere attempts to redress wrongs. It did not occur to Zacchaeus, for instance, to confess his sins and proclaim his faith in Jesus without adding, "If I have defrauded anyone of anything, I restore it fourfold" (Luke 19:8). Here, Abigail restores David's honor by making the first pronouncement, apparently as led by the Holy Spirit, of David's eternal dynasty.

Fourth, Abigail *pleaded for forgiveness* on David's part: "Please forgive the trespass of your servant" (1 Sam. 25:28). It was only after she had humbly approached David, confessed the sin of her house, made a sincere effort to

8. Pink, *Life of David*, 1:146.

redress the sin, and pleaded for forgiveness that Abigail, fifth, *appealed to David's sense of godliness.* When we have wronged others, we should appeal to them to respond in godly ways, but only after we have confessed any sins committed and have acted to make up for harm we have done. Abigail's appeal to David was forceful not only by her actions, but also by the persuasive power of her words.

Abigail first appealed to David not to respond in kind to the foolish behavior of Nabal: "Let not my lord regard this worthless fellow, Nabal, for as his name is, so is he. Nabal is his name, and folly is with him. But I your servant did not see the young men of my lord, whom you sent. Now then, my lord, as the LORD lives, and as your soul lives, because the LORD has restrained you from bloodguilt and from saving with your own hand, now then let your enemies and those who seek to do evil to my lord be as Nabal" (1 Sam. 25:25–26). In effect, she was warning David not to respond to Nabal by becoming like him, but rather to be grateful for her own restraining ministry, through which the Lord himself had kept David from evil.

Her second appeal picks up on this theme. Instead of acting like godless Nabal, David should act like the servant of the Lord that he was, and especially to exhibit the gracious characteristics of one marked and favored by the Lord: "If men rise up to pursue you and to seek your life, the life of my lord shall be bound in the bundle of the living in the care of the LORD your God. And the lives of your enemies he shall sling out as from the hollow of a sling" (1 Sam. 25:29). Was Abigail so skillful as to mention a sling to remind David of his victory through faith over Goliath? She probably was. Furthermore, she continues, David will be grateful in years to come that he took Abigail's advice and forswore his bloody vengeance: "And when the LORD has done to my lord according to all the good that he has spoken concerning you and has appointed you prince over Israel, my lord shall have no cause of grief or pangs of conscience for having shed blood without cause or for my lord taking vengeance himself" (25:30–31). Pink summarizes: "She pleaded with David that he would let his coming glory regulate his present actions, so that in that day, his conscience would not reproach him for previous follies." Pink applies this truth to us: "If we kept more before us the judgment-seat of Christ, surely our conduct would be more regulated thereby."[9]

With these skillful words, Abigail turned David's heart from his murderous rage, so that he accepted her gift and replied with words of peace. God's grace was with David to make him willing not only to grant forgiveness but also to repent of his own foolish and unbelieving plans. God shows us that ungodly vows should be humbly repented of rather than stubbornly kept. "Herein are the children of God made manifest; they are tractable, open to conviction, willing to be shown their faults; but the children of the devil are like Nabal—churlish, stubborn, proud, unbending."[10] If we, like David, are willing to receive godly appeals from wise and faithful voices like Abigail's, we will avoid the ill effects of much folly and will be spared many regrets that would plague us in later life.

THE GOSPEL ACCORDING TO ABIGAIL

Abigail's wise approach to David not only averted disaster. Her actions also remind us of the gospel of salvation that comes to us upon the path of unbelief, sin, and destruction. Abigail is not formally a type of Christ in the same manner as David was. Yet her gracious ministry to David presents strong analogies to the grace by which Jesus meets us and brings us to salvation.

Like Abigail, Jesus came into our midst in a humble manner. Paul writes that he "made himself nothing, taking the form of a servant, being born in the likeness of men" (Phil. 2:7). Then, like innocent Abigail taking the guilt of Nabal's sin onto herself, Jesus took up our sins to bear them before God. "All we like sheep have gone astray," Isaiah foretold, "and the LORD has laid on him the iniquity of us all" (Isa. 53:6). Not only this, but Jesus also offered to God what was due to him from us, namely, a perfect life of obedience to the law. Jesus fulfilled all righteousness on our behalf, and presents his righteousness to God as the obedience owed by us; by way of analogy, Abigail presented David with the provisions owed to him by Nabal, satisfying the demands of justice so as to avert his wrath. Finally, as Abigail appealed for forgiveness and directed David

9. Ibid., 1:147.
10. Ibid.

to a godly response, Jesus speaks to us of the cleansing of our sins and then calls us to a sanctified life. As he said to one sinner brought to him, Jesus declares to all his people: "[I do not] condemn you; go, and from now on sin no more" (John 8:11).

As Abigail saved Nabal from the sinful wrath of David's anger, Jesus Christ has saved us from the just wrath of the holy God. Let us profit from her gracious example, as David did, but also see in her example a gracious appeal to salvation through faith in Jesus Christ.

37

THE LORD WILL REPAY

1 Samuel 25:32—44

*When David heard that Nabal was dead, he said, "Blessed be
the LORD who has avenged the insult I received at the hand
of Nabal, and has kept back his servant from wrongdoing.
The LORD has returned the evil of Nabal on his own head."
Then David sent and spoke to Abigail, to take her as his wife.*
(1 Sam. 25:39)

rominent among the Bible's doctrines in dispute today is the
idea of God's retributive justice. This concept of divine judgment was summarized by the apostle Paul when he asserted,
"Vengeance is mine, I will repay, says the Lord" (Rom. 12:19, quoting Deut.
32:35). A number of scholars today object to this doctrine, denying that God
"gets even" with sinners through judicial retaliation. Stephen Travis, for
instance, has written that "the judgment of God is to be seen not primarily
in terms of retribution, whereby people are 'paid back' according to their
deeds."[1] He and other opponents of this doctrine object that divine retribution encourages violence.

Against this denial stands the witness of both Testaments, where God's
justice is clearly retributive. When Achan disobeyed God by stealing from

---

1. Stephen H. Travis, preface to *Christ and the Judgment of God: Divine Retribution in the New
Testament* (Basingstoke, UK: Marshall Pickering, 1986).

the sack of Jericho, his punishment was to be stoned to death along with his family and possessions and have their remains burned (Josh. 7:24–26). Why? Joshua explained in the clear language of retribution: "Why did you bring trouble on us? The Lord brings trouble on you today" (7:25). The same kind of judgment is observed in the New Testament. Consider the fate of Ananias and Sapphira, who lied to the Holy Spirit about the money they had given to the church and were slain at the word of the apostle Peter (Acts 5:1–10). Moreover, the Bible's depiction of the final judgment is pure retribution for the wicked: "the dead were judged by what was written in the books, according to what they had done" (Rev. 20:12).

Not only does the Bible prove God's unyielding punishment on all sin, but acceptance of this truth is essential to both biblical faith and practice. Few chapters of the Bible demonstrate this principle in such living color as 1 Samuel 25, where the outcome of events rests on the great truth that the Lord will always repay.

Leaving Vengeance to God

Despite claims that belief in divine retribution promotes violence in human society, the biblical record shows that the opposite is true. An example is seen when David advanced with bloody intent on the home of Nabal, the rich fool who had denied him provisions and heaped abuse on his name. Whereas David's faith in God's justice had previously enabled him to avoid sinning against King Saul, his failure to remember contributed to his violent attitude toward Nabal. On the way, however, David was met by Nabal's beautiful and discerning wife, Abigail. She not only brought the supplies that David had asked for, but also brought words of warning regarding God's justice that David needed to hear. Abigail explained that she had come to restrain David "from bloodguilt," by taking vengeance "with your own hand" (1 Sam. 25:26). She further argued that in later times, when God's promise to make David king had been fulfilled, he would be glad for not "having shed blood without cause or for my lord taking vengeance himself" (25:31). In Abigail's biblical reasoning, David must refrain from taking vengeance precisely because God would *not* so refrain.

Abigail was repeating a principle expressed clearly in the Holy Scriptures: when humans are sinned against, they are not to take vengeance into their own hands but to leave vengeance to the Lord. Abigail was possibly referring to Deuteronomy 32:35, where God declared: "Vengeance is mine, and recompense, for the time when their foot shall slip; for the day of their calamity is at hand, and their doom comes swiftly."

These words form part of the Song of Moses, in which the great redeemer concluded his ministry with a song of praise for all that God had done in the exodus. In this song, Moses condemned not only the opposition of pagan nations but also the hardened unbelief of Israel. The latter had been Moses' greater problem, as Israel frequently rebelled against his authority and complained against the Lord. For instance, when Korah, Dathan, and Abiram led a rebellion against Moses in the wilderness, God answered by opening the ground to swallow up these rebels, along with their families (Num. 16:31–33). Afterward, the entire congregation of the Israelites rose against Moses and Aaron, advancing against the tent of meeting where God's servants dwelt. God responded by sending a plague upon the Israelites that slew almost fifteen thousand people (16:41–50). God thus vindicated the righteousness of his vengeance against Korah's rebellion by sending further retribution against the enemies of Moses. In remembrance of these and similar events, Moses sang of God's vengeance: "For the LORD will vindicate his people and have compassion on his servants" (Deut. 32:36). God's vengeance on his enemies will show him to be the true God, even as he exposes the idols of those who rebel against his rule.

We sometimes hear it stated as a rule that God's people must always do what God does, yet here is an example of exactly the opposite. God's people are *not* to take vengeance precisely because we know that God *will*. Moses did not pray to a God who was indifferent toward evil, but to One whose wrath burned against sin and rebellion. Retribution belongs to the Lord, who is just and perfect in his judgment. Some men and women, serving in public office, do have the duty of prayerfully distributing civil justice (Rom. 13:4). But apart from such notable exceptions, we fallible men and women should leave vengeance to the God whose justice never fails and never errs.

David had therefore been on the brink of committing gross sins in his anger against Nabal. Just before the arrival of Nabal's wife, he had boasted to his men that by the morning he would not have left a single male alive in all of Nabal's house. Now remembering the Lord, David praised both God and Abigail for delivering him from his violent passion: "Blessed be the

LORD, the God of Israel, who sent you this day to meet me! Blessed be your discretion, and blessed be you, who have kept me this day from bloodguilt and from avenging myself with my own hand!" (1 Sam. 25:32–33). How relieved David was to be turned from his sinful path: "For as surely as the LORD the God of Israel lives, who has restrained me from hurting you, unless you had hurried and come to meet me, truly by morning there had not been left to Nabal so much as one male" (25:34).

Abigail's embassy reminds us that the best counsel is that which turns us to the Lord and declares his commands. Likewise, David's response shows that the best decision is always the one that yields to Holy Scripture. People do not always take biblical reproof for the blessing that it is. "But David knew how much courage and discernment it took for Abigail to act as she did. . . . She had both saved lives and kept him from a tragic sin, that of avenging himself with his own hand."[2] David realized what John Murray would later summarize: "The essence of ungodliness is that we presume to take the place of God, to take everything into our own hands. It is faith to commit ourselves to God, to cast all our care on him and to vest all our interests in him."[3] David's responsive heart to biblical correction was one of the chief factors that account for his greatness as a man of God. Such humility before God's Word is a recurrent feature among the exemplary figures of the Bible.

David concluded his meeting by restoring his peaceful demeanor toward Nabal's wife and thus toward Nabal himself: "Then David received from her hand what she had brought him. And he said to her, 'Go up in peace to your house. See, I have obeyed your voice, and I have granted your petition'" (1 Sam. 25:35). Had Nabal crossed his path, David's biblical duty would have been to extend the same peace and blessing to him as to his wife. Paul applies the lesson by explaining how Christians, knowing that God will repay, should respond to those who have harmed us: "'If your enemy is hungry, feed him; if he is thirsty, give him something to drink; for by so doing you will heap burning coals on his head.' Do not be overcome by evil, but overcome evil with good" (Rom. 12:20–21, quoting Prov. 25:21–22). According to the Bible, while only God is competent to execute vengeance, we are all empowered and authorized to extend mercy. According to Charles Hodge,

2. Gordon J. Keddie, *Dawn of a Kingdom: The Message of 1 Samuel* (Darlington, UK: Evangelical Press, 1988), 239.

3. John Murray, *The Epistle to the Romans* (Grand Rapids: Eerdmans, 1968), 141.

"To heap coals of fire on anyone is a punishment which no one can bear; he must yield to it. Kindness is no less effectual; the most malignant enemy cannot always withstand it. The true and Christian method, therefore, to subdue an enemy is to 'overcome evil with good.'"[4]

WICKEDNESS REPAID WITH DISMAY AND DEATH

The best proof that David was right in leaving vengeance to the Lord is what subsequently happened to foolish Nabal. When last we saw him, this miserly rich man was denying needed provision to David and his patriotic band. When it came to himself, however, Nabal was willing enough to spend lavishly. He was not only drunk with greed, but literally drunk in enjoying his riches: "Abigail came to Nabal, and behold, he was holding a feast in his house, like the feast of a king" (1 Sam. 25:36). Not only did Nabal think of himself as a king, but he reminds us of a particular king: King Saul! The contrast with David is clear: at the very moment that David was blessing Abigail for helping him to remain in the right with God, Nabal was indulging himself in sinful pleasures, in violation of God's law.

Nabal reminds us of the rich man in Jesus' parable, who "feasted sumptuously every day," while refusing to provide even his table scrapings for poor Lazarus, who begged at his gate (Luke 16:19–21). Moreover, Nabal embodies the false security of sinners who plunge lustily into sin, having so far escaped divine judgment that they imagine themselves beyond God's reach (see Eccl. 8:11). A. W. Pink writes, "The fool Nabal vividly portrays the case of multitudes all around us. The curse of God's broken law hanging over them, yet 'feasting' as though all is well with their souls for eternity."[5]

Nabal's depravity is seen not only in his drunkenness and greed but also in his relationships. Earlier in the chapter, we saw that his faithful servants considered him "such a worthless man that one cannot speak to him" (1 Sam. 25:17). In her embassy to David, his wife had similarly been forced to call him a "worthless fellow" (25:25); this cannot have been a pleasant admission for a woman of such virtue. Given that the occasion for this drunken bout was the shearing feast, Cyril Barber suggests that Nabal's guests were "the migrant shearers . . . with whom he seems to have a great

---

4. Charles Hodge, *A Commentary on Romans* (Edinburgh: Banner of Truth, 1972), 402.

5. A. W. Pink, *A Life of David*, 2 vols. (Grand Rapids: Baker, 1981), 1:152.

deal in common. . . . If people are to be judged by the company they keep, it is significant that Nabal had established rapport with the least desirable members of Hebrew society."[6] For many sinners, the contempt of the discerning and the company of the depraved is a foretaste of the final judgment that awaits them in hell.

In the eyes of the world, a rich man such as Nabal was in an enviable situation. But through the lens of Scripture we see him as ripe for God's judgment. Abigail had assured David that "the lives of your enemies [God] shall sling out as from the hollow of a sling" (1 Sam. 25:29), and Nabal had placed himself in precisely such a vulnerable place for judgment. But before his deadly punishment would come the dismay that confronts all who realize too late the error of their sinful ways. For Nabal, this dismay arrived the next morning, when his wife could finally address him. "In the morning, when the wine had gone out of Nabal, his wife told him these things, and his heart died within him, and he became as a stone" (25:37). For all her discretion in speaking to David, we have no idea how mildly Abigail broke the news to her husband of his narrow escape from death by David's sword. Perhaps, in her disgust, Abigail was not discreet at all. In any case, the shock of the news brought such dismay to Nabal that "his heart died within him," which perhaps signifies a heart attack or stroke. Finally, "about ten days later the Lord struck Nabal, and he died" (25:38). Many sinners today delude themselves with the idea that when the reality of judgment is brought to their minds, they will have time and opportunity to repent and be saved. Nabal shows the folly of this thinking, for the dismay of judgment was itself a kind of death from which he could not recover.

Notice that Nabal did not simply die from "natural causes" as a result of his earlier convulsion. It was the Lord who struck Nabal. God had taken vengeance for Nabal's sin against God's anointed king, David, just as he is sure to do in the final judgment against all who despise Jesus Christ, of which David's kingdom was a type. Nabal's sin had been against God personally, and his judgment had been administered personally by God against him. Nabal's demise was not the natural outworking of impersonal rules of divine providence: God himself had struck Nabal down as retribution

---

6. Cyril J. Barber, *The Books of Samuel*, 2 vols. (Neptune, NJ: Loizeaux, 1994), 1:269.

for his sin. Nabal's wickedness had been repaid in God's timing, a timing that was and is far swifter than sinners like Nabal might foolishly hope.

Not only was Nabal's sin repaid, but his judgment was also celebrated. Here is a man for whom no one seems to have mourned. David, hearing the news, openly rejoiced: "He said, 'Blessed be the LORD who has avenged the insult I received at the hand of Nabal, and has kept back his servant from wrongdoing. The LORD has returned the evil of Nabal on his own head'" (1 Sam. 25:39).

David might have rejoiced for any of several reasons, none of which would have implicated him in unholy glee over the demise of his enemy. First, he may have rejoiced in the display of God's glory that the Lord's judgment always involves. In Psalm 58:10–11, he writes in just this way: "The righteous will rejoice when he sees the vengeance; he will bathe his feet in the blood of the wicked. Mankind will say, 'Surely there is a reward for the righteous; surely there is a God who judges on earth.'" The key to this statement is the glory of God's righteousness that is displayed before the eyes of men. Pink explains:

> It was not the exercise of a spirit of malice, which took delight in seeing the destruction of their foes: no indeed, for in the Old Testament the divine command was, "Rejoice not when thine enemy falleth" (Prov. 24:17). Instead, it was the heart bowing in worship before the governmental dealings of God, adoring that Justice which gave unto the wicked their due.[7]

If we are tempted to think that such an attitude of glory in God's judgment is inappropriate to the New Testament age of grace, then we should consider the heavenly praise revealed in the last book of the Bible. For in the fall of Babylon the Great, the voices in heaven sing with delight: "Rejoice over her, O heaven, and you saints and apostles and prophets, for God has given judgment for you against her!" (Rev. 18:20). Indeed, in heaven souls set free from the motivations of sin, perfected in holiness, sing hallelujahs for the glory and power displayed in God's judgment: "For his judgments are true and just; for he has judged the great prostitute who corrupted the earth with her immorality, and has avenged on her the blood of his servants. . . . Hallelujah! The smoke from her goes up forever and ever" (19:1–3).

7. Pink, *Life of David*, 1:154.

In David's case, we can conceive of at least two other worthy motives for his rejoicing in Nabal's demise. First, David must have seen in this affirmation of God's justice the future vindication of his own cause versus wicked King Saul. Remember that David was still a hunted fugitive, restraining himself from violence while Saul's hatred continued to run free against him. In this way, God's judgment of Nabal may have inspired resolutions like the one we read from David in Psalm 37:7: "Be still before the LORD and wait patiently for him; fret not yourself over the one who prospers in his way, over the man who carries out evil devices!" God's justice is always equally sure, but in his sovereign wisdom his justice is not equally swift. While waiting for the Lord to vindicate David from Saul's hateful accusations, he must have been encouraged to note how the Lord acted in the case of Nabal.

Added to this comfort for his faith, God's judgment must have relieved David in that his enemy had not fallen by his own sinful vengeance, as David had previously intended. Psalm 37 continues by urging us to keep both hand and heart free from malice:

> Refrain from anger, and forsake wrath!
>   Fret not yourself; it tends only to evil.
> For the evildoers shall be cut off,
>   but those who wait for the LORD shall inherit the land.
> In just a little while, the wicked will be no more;
>   though you look carefully at his place, he will not be there.
> But the meek shall inherit the land
>   and delight themselves in abundant peace. (Ps. 37:8–11)

FAITH REPAID WITH LIFE AND LOVE

In contrast to her husband's depraved folly, Abigail is an image of feminine virtue. What a calamity it was for such a woman to be married to so worthless a man as Nabal. One suspects that Nabal's material wealth explains this union, perhaps through an injudicious arrangement on the part of Abigail's father (thus belying her name, which means "my father's joy" or "my father is strength"). How lamentable it is today when young Christian women give their hearts to ungodly men, simply because of their worldly attractions, facing as a result a lifetime of spiritual disunity and marital strife. Paul speaks on this vital matter with forceful language: "Do not be unequally yoked with unbelievers. For what partnership has righteousness with lawlessness? Or what fellowship has light with darkness?" (2 Cor. 6:14). Still, through faith in the Lord, Abigail's virtue had not been destroyed even in such a marriage. William Blaikie comments that "luxury had not impaired the energy of her spirit, and wealth had not destroyed the regularity of her habits."[8]

Abigail's character also provides something of an ideal for Christian men who seek for a bride. Not only is Abigail cited for beauty, but more importantly she is noted for discretion and wisdom, generosity of spirit, humble servanthood, and biblical devotion. As Proverbs 31:10 exclaims of such a woman, "An excellent wife who can find? She is far more precious than jewels." Young women would likewise do well to seek in Abigail a model for their own godly character. For all her outward beauty, it is mainly the beauty of her holiness that shines forth. "Charm is deceitful, and beauty is vain," concludes Proverbs 31, "but a woman who fears the LORD is to be praised" (31:30).

Indeed, Abigail reveals the positive side of God's certain recompense. Just as Nabal was repaid for his wickedness with dismay and death, Abigail was blessed through her godly treatment of David. Consider how many times such a woman must have grieved the misery of her marriage! Abigail's life with Nabal must have often seemed like a dreary prison. But humble faith and servantlike humility had gained their reward in a new life that would be filled with love. For David knew a treasure when he saw one, and he wasted no time following up on Nabal's death with a proposal to the now-widowed Abigail: "David sent and spoke to Abigail, to take her as his wife" (1 Sam. 25:39). His servants approached her and said, "David has sent us to you to take you to him as his wife" (25:40). This form of proposal may not have measured up to today's romantic standards, but since it came from so great and good a man as David, who for all his own sins was "a man after [God's] own heart" (13:14), Abigail could only have been thrilled at God's blessing.

In responding to David's proposal, Abigail retained her humility and servantlike demeanor: "She rose and bowed with her face to the ground and said, 'Behold, your handmaid is a servant to wash the feet of the servants of my lord'" (1 Sam. 25:41). Abigail not only would accept David's proposal, but also would be a true wife for him in keeping with the servant-calling of

8. William G. Blaikie, *Expository Lectures on the Book of First Samuel* (1887; repr., Birmingham, AL: Solid Ground, 2005), 385.

a believer in the Lord. Mounting a donkey and taking her serving women with her, Abigail obeyed her new husband's first command and followed David's messengers in order to become his wife.

The chapter concludes with a statement that seems to sully the purity and joy of the occasion. On the one hand, we find that "Saul had given Michal his daughter, David's wife, to Palti the son of Laish, who was of Gallim" (1 Sam. 25:44). Always vigilant to wound David in any way possible, Saul sought not only to afflict David's heart with the painful thought of his wife's being given to another man, but probably also to secure political arrangements advantageous to himself and injurious to David. On the other hand, "David also took Ahinoam of Jezreel" to be his wife along with Abigail (25:43). However distressing it may have been for Abigail to find that she was one of two wives that David would take, this was not an unaccustomed practice for a man of David's public stature in that time. Still, we should observe that David's polygamy failed to uphold God's design for marriage and would in the end lead to great harm to both David and his household.

The point that seems to be intended, however, is that not only had God repaid Abigail for her faith, but God had provided for David's need as his servant continued to trust in him. David was thus compensated for the wrongful taking of his idolatrous first wife, Saul's daughter Michal, by receiving a woman of such beauty and discretion as Abigail. Moreover, through her ties to the surrounding community, God provided David with resources of wealth and connections that would aid his rise among the people of Judah. An episode that began with frustration and shame, so that David very nearly fell into gross sin against the Lord, ended up by God's grace with a source of refreshment, support, and discernment to sustain David in many a trial yet to come. God's grace reveals a truth that David relayed in Psalm 37:4, "Delight yourself in the LORD, and he will give you the desires of your heart."

NEW LIFE AS DAVID'S BRIDE

As we consider Abigail, riding forth on her donkey to enter into David's marital love, we see a beautiful picture of the blessing that awaits all who look in faith to Jesus Christ, David's greater descendant. Abigail's earlier speech to David made it clear that she believed God's promises about his glory and kingdom, referring to "all the good that he has spoken concerning you" and the fact that God "has appointed you prince over Israel" (1 Sam. 25:30). Faith in Jesus is likewise belief in God's promises concerning his true Son and divine King. "Your throne, O God, is forever and ever," the Scripture says of him; "the scepter of uprightness is the scepter of your kingdom" (Heb. 1:8, quoting Ps. 45:6). Abigail came to David, knowing that as his bride she would reign with him in the day of God's fulfillment; we likewise look to Jesus, knowing that we will reign with him as heirs of God's heavenly glory (Rom. 8:17). Thus, Matthew Henry remarks, "those who join themselves to Christ must be willing now to suffer with him, believing that hereafter they shall reign with him."[9]

Abigail left behind her former life—a life made sordid by association with corruption and sin—to begin a new life with God's anointed servant. In turning to Jesus Christ, we likewise turn our backs on the old life of sin, glad to suffer the loss of all things in this life for his sake, in order that we may bear his name in both present disgrace and eternal glory, sure that in his love we will be repaid with eternal life.

There is one more point of contact between Abigail's marriage to David and our salvation in Jesus Christ. How was it, after all, that Abigail decided to give her love to noble David? Because he had sent his servants with an invitation. You, too, have a personal invitation to enter into a relationship of love and salvation with Jesus Christ. His offer is contained in the gospel message, presented to you by Christ's servants the prophets and apostles in the Holy Scriptures. He says, "Come to me, all who labor and are heavy laden, and I will give you rest" (Matt. 11:28). "Come," Jesus says again. "Whoever is thirsty, let him come; and whoever wishes, let him take the free gift of the water of life" (Rev. 22:17 NIV). What a blessed occasion for Abigail when she learned of David's marriage proposal! How blessed, as well, for every sinner to receive and accept the saving message of Christ. Jesus says to us: "Whoever hears my word and believes him who sent me has eternal life. He does not come into judgment, but has passed from death to life" (John 5:24).

9. Matthew Henry, *Commentary on the Whole Bible*, 6 vols. (Peabody, MA: Hendrickson, 1992), 2:329.

38

THE RIGHTEOUS KING

1 Samuel 26:1—25

The LORD rewards every man for his righteousness and his
faithfulness, for the LORD gave you into my hand today, and
I would not put out my hand against the LORD's anointed.
(1 Sam. 26:23)

On May 11, 1685, eighteen-year-old Margaret Wilson was condemned for refusing to swear the Oath of Abjuration, that notorious statement of allegiance to King James VII not only as sovereign ruler over Scotland but also as sovereign over the church of Jesus Christ. Margaret was most willing to acknowledge the king as her secular sovereign, but as a Christian, she could not swear the rule over her soul to anyone but Christ. Jesus, she insisted, was sole sovereign over his kingdom, and into his hands alone she committed her eternal destiny.

For this "crime," Margaret was tied to a stake in the Solway River, awaiting the inrushing tide. Tied farther out into the water was her older companion, Margaret Lachlison, so that the younger Margaret could witness her drowning and reconsider her obstinate refusal to swear allegiance to James VII. Young Margaret was undaunted by the spectacle, however, declaring that Christ was himself suffering in her friend. Then, as the waters swirled toward her own post, Margaret recited aloud the eighth chapter of Romans, concluding with Paul's great promise that not even death can separate believers from the love of God in Christ Jesus.

On came the waters, and after she had suffered for a while, Margaret's persecutors removed her from her post. Splaying her onto the beach, where she gasped for air, they asked if she would pray for King James. She would pray for his salvation, she assured them, since "I wish the salvation of all men." But would she swear the oath of spiritual allegiance to Scotland's king? "I will not," she said. At this, a soldier pushed her weakened body back into the waters and held her underneath until she died.[1]

We live now in a time in which professed Christians in the West are scarcely bold enough to withstand even the fads and fashions of a culture in rebellion to Christ's rule. Margaret Wilson would surely reprove us, as Jesus taught, not to "fear those who kill the body but cannot kill the soul," rather fearing "him who can destroy both soul and body in hell" (Matt. 10:28). Moreover, her more advanced experience with worldly powers would direct us to ponder the words recorded in the Psalms: "It is better to take refuge in the LORD than to trust in man. It is better to take refuge in the LORD than to trust in princes" (Ps. 118:8–9).

SAUL'S ADVANCED DEPRAVITY

If believers need instruction in not trusting worldly powers, Israel's King Saul provides a convincing lesson. First Samuel chapter 26 presents Saul's depravity once more, on a second occasion when David graciously spared an enemy who was at his mercy. Because of the similarity between chapters 24 and 26, in which David forbears to slay King Saul, critical scholars are united in denying the historical accuracy of the accounts, assuring us that two such similar events cannot be accepted as being possible. Yet just as with other so-called discrepancies in the Bible, only an independent knowledge of the events in question could prove error in the Scriptures. Lacking these, and believing the Bible's testimony to be the inspired Word of God, we have good reason to accept the events of 1 Samuel 26 as not only genuine but also instructive for our faith.

1. Alexander Smellie, *Men of the Covenant* (Edinburgh: Banner of Truth, 1960), 416–20.

Admittedly, not much had changed in Saul since his last appearance. In this, he well represents the wicked corruption that afflicts all earthly powers apart from the saving grace of God. Notice, for instance, how ready Saul was to commit evil. The chapter begins with David's taking refuge once more in the wilderness of Ziph. Critical scholars doubt that David would return to this place of prior betrayal (see 1 Sam. 23:19–20), but there cannot have been too many suitable hideouts for David and his band of six hundred. History did, in fact, repeat itself: "the Ziphites came to Saul at Gibeah, saying, 'Is not David hiding himself on the hill of Hachilah, which is on the east of Jeshimon?'" (26:1).

Given Saul's words at the end of his prior meeting with David, outside the cave of Engedi where his life had been spared, we might expect the king to ignore this intelligence. Saul had, after all, vindicated David of treason (1 Sam. 24:20). We might expect Saul, therefore, to send the Ziphites away with an admonition to leave David alone. Yet exactly the opposite happened: "Saul arose and went down to the wilderness of Ziph with three thousand chosen men of Israel to seek David in the wilderness of Ziph" (1 Sam. 26:2).

What explains this about-face? The answer is that man in sin is ever ready to commit evil. This reality is all the more true of men and women who exercise great power, and whose graceless hearts carry the weight of privilege and authority. Consider the never-ceasing news of political leaders today, who one after another fall prey to sexual sins, dishonesty, fraud, and cover-ups, despite the proven likelihood of their being caught. Why do they leap at opportunities to sin? Because, having inflamed themselves with the hot passions of power and pride, their depraved natures draw them into self-destroying sin.

Had Saul not figured out by now that God was not going to permit him to take David's life, as he had himself admitted after their last meeting? Yet how irrational sin is in the mighty! How could Scotland's king think that publicly drowning a teenage girl would enhance his spiritual authority? How can Communist despots in China today fail to notice that their persecution of house churches only causes them to grow? The problem is the corruption of man's depraved nature: it is ever ready to commit sin and forget God's punishment for those who do evil. This is a problem not confined to the high and mighty. Do you, having seized the sovereign reins of your own life and choices, not realize the peril of sinful desires?

It is sin, not faith, that is blind, and ever ready to follow one disaster with a renewed zeal for another.

Aware of this tendency, David had not entrusted himself to Saul after the king's superficial penitence at Engedi. David's wise answer reminds us of Jesus' response to the superficial praise he received in the early months of his ministry: "Jesus on his part did not entrust himself to them, because he knew all people . . . , for he himself knew what was in man" (John 2:24–25). Christians who gain in wisdom regarding the world, learning the truth about its depravity from God's Word, will understand what Margaret Wilson came to know early in life, when she entrusted her soul only to Jesus, even at the cost of an early exit from the realm of wicked and worldly kings in this life.

DAVID'S GROWTH IN GRACE

As noted, there is no compelling reason to see chapter 26 as merely another version of the events in chapter 24. Anyone who has been in an abusive relationship like David's with Saul can tell you that the same scenes tend to be replayed over and over, contrary to liberal claims that these chapters are too similar for both to be true. Most importantly, however, by reflecting on the material found in chapters 24–26, we discern an important advance in David's spiritual understanding and maturity. Whereas Saul returns unchanged by his experience, David's experience under God's tutelage has brought a notable growth in grace. We see this in the unfolding of events at Saul's military camp.

Learning of Saul's advance from his scouts, David went forward to see the enemy host for himself. Saul was encamped on a hill "beside the road on the east of Jeshimon" (1 Sam. 26:3). There, David spied Saul's entire host asleep on the ground. Seeing Saul himself at the center, with his general Abner nearby, David proposed to go down to the king in his camp. He asked, "Who will go down with me into the camp to Saul?" (26:6). His nephew Abishai, the son of Zeruiah, David's sister, agreed. "So David and Abishai went to the army by night. And there lay Saul sleeping within the encampment, with his spear stuck in the ground at his head, and Abner and the army lay around him" (26:7). Just as his followers had urged David in the cave of Engedi, Abishai asked David for permission to "pin [Saul] to the earth with one stroke of the spear" (26:8). David refused: "Do not destroy him, for who

449

can put out his hand against the LORD's anointed and be guiltless?" (26:9). Instead, David decided to take Saul's spear—so well known as the symbol of Saul's hatred against him—and the water jar near the king's head. With these possessions, David and his companion stole away into the night with no one waking, since "a deep sleep from the LORD had fallen upon them" (26:12).

David gave Abishai two reasons for not slaying Saul. The first was that God's people must never seek their own benefit by violating God's Word. Saul had been appointed king by God and must therefore be shown reverence and respect (see Ex. 22:28). We see this principle affirmed in the New Testament when Paul commands Christians to "be subject to the governing authorities" (Rom. 13:1). Gordon Keddie writes: "We are to fear God and honour the king. We are to pray for princes and those in authority. We are to recognize that God has instituted civil government and it is to be obeyed."[2] This does not involve rendering to Caesar what belongs to God, as Scotland's King James required when his soldiers drowned Margaret Wilson, nor does it justify violating God's law in order to keep the commands of men. It does, however, require respectful conduct toward the person and office of civil rulers. David's example urges that this respectfulness is called for especially when God's people may be in opposition to government policies. In a democratic nation such as America, where citizens have the right to contest the policies of its leaders, Christians must be careful to treat national, state, and local officials with the personal respect due to those who have been established in office by God.

David also realized that it would be sinful to take personal revenge against Saul, a lesson that had been magnified in the previous chapter. Abishai's lusty offer to pin Saul to the earth with his spear shows all the marks of vengeance for Saul's earlier attempts to pin David to the palace wall with the very same weapon. Alexander Maclaren comments, "Abishai represents the natural impulse of us all—to strike at our enemies when we can, to meet hate with hate, and do to another the evil that he would do to us."[3] Yet to do this is to sin, as David knew well. In the recent episode with Nabal, Abigail had reminded him that taking vengeance incurs bloodguilt before the Lord. Later, during the civil war that followed Saul's death, David would

---

2. Gordon J. Keddie, *Dawn of a Kingdom: The Message of 1 Samuel* (Darlington, UK: Evangelical Press, 1988), 244.

3. Alexander Maclaren, *Expositions of Holy Scripture*, 17 vols. (Grand Rapids: Baker, 1982), 2:369.

be glad that he had not endorsed the bloodthirsty methods of Abishai and his brothers, at one point complaining that "these men, the sons of Zeruiah, are too harsh for me" (2 Sam. 3:39 NKJV).

On this occasion, David did not struggle with temptation to strike Saul in personal vengeance. We can see the reason why by looking closely at his answer to Abishai in verses 9–11, in which David cites the name of the Lord no less than five times. This shows that the way to restrain our sinful passions is to keep God constantly in mind, remembering his Word, submitting to his will, and honoring his name.

David's second reason for sparing Saul was that God's people should not force God's providence. Here was the lesson that David had learned in chapter 25 in his dealings with foolish and greedy Nabal. In his wrath over Nabal's insults, David had been on the brink of committing mass murder, until Nabal's gracious wife Abigail intervened. In the aftermath, God had taken care of Nabal in a better way than David could have ever devised. David learned from this episode to wait upon the Lord in the confident hope that he would work things out justly and wisely. David exercises his sanctified imagination in verse 10, telling Abishai, "As the Lord lives, the Lord will strike him, or his day will come to die, or he will go down into battle and perish."

David's growth in grace involved his awareness of God's sovereignty in the affairs of men, combined with God's goodness, justice, and wisdom. Knowing that he served an omnipotent, sovereign, faithful God who had promised his salvation, David preferred to await God's solution to the problem of Saul rather than to force his own. How much better it was in years to come that David waited for God's timing and God's solution in dealing with Saul. The moral and spiritual authority so necessary to David's kingdom would have been impossible with Saul's blood on his hands. David reasoned that if God intended for him to be king, and if Saul's wickedness stood in the way of his reign, then God would take action against Saul. William Blaikie laments, "Alas! Into how many sins, and even crimes, have men been betrayed through unwillingness to wait for God's time!"[4] Rather than taking matters into our own hands when confronted with a hostile employer, abusive parents, or even a persecuting government, God's people are to wait upon the Lord

---

4. William G. Blaikie, *Expository Lectures on the Book of First Samuel* (1887; repr., Birmingham, AL: Solid Ground, 2005), 376.

in prayerful humility, refraining from anger and violent retribution. To be sure, David defied Saul so far as his duty to God required, just as Margaret Wilson steadfastly refused to vow King James as sovereign over her soul. But both believers were blessed by humbly obeying God's Word as they patiently awaited God's timing for their deliverance.

One way to encourage our faith while we wait upon the Lord is to take note of the many helps that God provides. Consider the mysterious slumber that placed Saul's army at David's mercy. David may not have known it, but "a deep sleep from the LORD had fallen upon them" (1 Sam. 26:12). Whether or not we can see how it is happening, believers can be assured of God's constant aid and protection, even in trials. David wrote in Psalm 34:7–8: "The angel of the LORD encamps around those who fear him, and delivers them. . . . Blessed is the man who takes refuge in him!"

The result of David's growth in grace was a corresponding increase in his spiritual authority among the people. In previous chapters, while David was learning these lessons, the events related mainly to David himself. But now, armed with a gracious obedience in God's Word, David is placed in a position of great spiritual usefulness to others. Having grown in grace, he is equipped to lead God's people.

Notice, for instance, the significance of his removal of Saul's spear. This weapon had become the symbol of Saul's regime, an ever-present emblem of his royal militancy (see 1 Sam. 22:6). There it stood, impaled in the ground by the slumbering king, and David realized the significance of its removal. Perhaps this symbolized the ends that David's leadership served: the removal of sin from the realm and a commitment to peace among God's people.

Notice, as well, David's boldness in reproving the failure of Saul's army. This is the first time that David not only addresses Saul but also speaks with authority to those who served the king. He upbraids them for falling asleep on their watch, a capital offense in practically every army throughout history. Having moved to a safe location, David directs his rebuke at Abner, Saul's general: "Why then have you not kept watch over your lord the king? For one of the people came in to destroy the king your lord. This thing that you have done is not good. As the LORD lives, you deserve to die, because you have not kept watch over your lord, the LORD's anointed. And now see where the king's spear is and the jar of water that was at his head" (1 Sam. 26:15–16). What has given David the spiritual authority to assume this leadership role? One answer is God's calling on his life to sacred office, but inseparable from this calling is his example of personal godliness in obedience to God's Word. David's unwillingness to strike sinfully at Saul had given him a platform from which to exhort others. The daily, practical godliness of any believer, and especially of a Christian leader, will grant him or her a credible platform to speak out against sin and corruption in the world around us. But when Christian leaders fall into the same kinds of sin so rampant in the world, the moral authority of the entire church is compromised.

DAVID'S LAST WORDS WITH SAUL

Throughout 1 Samuel, we have seen David contrasted to King Saul. From the start, David was intended as God's replacement for the apostate leader (see 1 Sam. 13:14). In this chapter, we see them together for the last time— Saul advanced in his depravity and David growing in God's grace. On these respective courses, time has served only to widen the gap between the two. Imagine how great the gulf is when advanced into eternity! The real difference, of course, was their respective relationship with God, which set them on their different trajectories. Our standing with the Lord is what matters most about each of us. A relatively moral person who is a stranger to God's grace is bound to move in a godless direction, if only in his or her heart. A relatively immoral person who comes to faith in Christ, however, is bound to become more and more holy over time. The same principle holds true for our response to the ministry of God's Word. Those, like David, who trust God's Word in humble faith will find themselves growing in grace, starting right where they are. Those, like Saul, who harden their hearts against God's Word set their feet on a darkened path downward into depravity, a path on which even present virtues are sure to be corrupted and destroyed.

Although we will see Saul again in this book, this nighttime meeting at the camp would be the last time that David would see Saul. David had reproved Abner, when Saul awoke and recognized the voice: "Is this your voice, my son David?" David answered, "It is my voice, my lord, O king" (1 Sam. 26:17). This final interview contains three emphases that continue to exhibit David's growth in grace. David was a realist about Saul and did not sentimentalize this opportunity to speak. Instead, David took the opportunity to seek the greatest good for Saul's soul, beginning with *a sincere call for his tormentor to repent.*

David's call for repentance took the form of questions: "Why does my lord pursue after his servant? For what have I done? What evil is on my hands?" (1 Sam. 26:18). As in their prior meeting at Engedi, David pleaded his innocence while presenting proof of his goodwill—the spear and water jug that evidenced his sparing of Saul's life. Despite this goodwill, so amply demonstrated, Saul's servants had made David a virtual exile from the land of promise. The persecution was tantamount to removing David's "share in the heritage of the LORD, saying, 'Go, serve other gods'" (26:19). This statement reflects the theology of geography at work in the Old Testament, since one needed to worship God at his tabernacle to benefit from the atoning sacrifices made there. Saul was driving David into the cursed condition of paganism by depriving him of God's sacred ordinances. For what reason has Saul allowed his government to be dominated by the mad pursuit of one mere servant—and a loyal one at that? "The king of Israel has come out to seek a single flea like one who hunts a partridge in the mountains" (26:20). With these words, David confronted Saul with his mad folly, calling him to repentance.

Many Christians will find themselves driven out from families, career fields, or other blessings as the result of sinful resentments and hatred. Like David, believers should take prudent steps to protect themselves and should refrain from sin while waiting on God's deliverance. But as they have opportunity, they should calmly reason in an attempt to bring repentance. This same model applies to political action in a secular state. Christians should boldly speak truth regarding matters of sin, calling the government to repentance, but we must be able to do so with evidence of our own godliness and goodwill.

David realized, of course, that a mere call to repentance was not likely to strike home in a hardened heart such as Saul's. Therefore, he added a second message, *a call to true religion*: "Now therefore let my lord the king hear the words of his servant. If it is the LORD who has stirred you up against me, may he accept an offering, but if it is men, may they be cursed before the LORD" (1 Sam. 26:19).

As David understood the situation, there were two likely sources for Saul's mad wickedness. The first was God's wrathful chastisement. Saul should consider that his impaired reasoning may have resulted from God's judgment on his sins. This is not a message that people today, any more than Saul, are likely to receive happily. But David continued by reminding Saul that God has provided a way of cleansing and restoration to his favor, namely, the blood sacrifices of atonement. David knew that in these offerings, God promised forgiveness and peace—and in this way he looked forward to the coming of the true and great sacrifice, God's own Son, Jesus Christ. John the Baptist identified Jesus in just these terms, crying out, "Behold, the Lamb of God, who takes away the sin of the world!" (John 1:29).

In effect, David was offering to go with Saul to the Lord for their mutual appeal to the sacrificial blood for forgiveness and renewal. This appeal sets an example for us in our dealings with hostile individuals in a hostile culture. When faced with intractable hostility, we should invite those who oppose us to meet us at the level ground beneath Christ's cross, taking the place of sinners who appeal to God's grace in Christ's blood. Here, for instance, is where marital harmony is gained and where marital strife is reconciled: by mutual confession of sin and mutual appeal to forgiving grace. Likewise, in the Christian witness before the world, we must not merely denounce sin under God's judgment, but also show forth the cleansing grace of God in the blood of Christ, by which even our fiercest opponents might be forgiven and restored to God.

David couples with this appeal *a warning about the danger of evil company*: "If it is men, may they be cursed before the LORD" (1 Sam. 26:19). Once we are reconciled to God through Christ's blood, we must shun the counsel of the wicked if we are to remain in the blessing of God's peace.

As had happened in their prior meeting, Saul responded to David's pleas with a superficial repentance: "I have sinned," he confessed. "Return, my son David, for I will no more do you harm, because my life was precious in your eyes this day. Behold, I have acted foolishly, and have made a great mistake" (1 Sam. 26:21). Some would have us believe that Christians must not only forgive but also immediately renew our trust on the basis of an assurance like this. David knew better. What was missing from Saul's confession? There was no turning to God and therefore none of the deep work in Saul's life that alone could arrest the progress of sin's corruption. Saul was happy now, realizing that David could have taken his life, but this goodwill lacked the resources to prevail. He is the portrait of those today who grieve the consequences of their sins but not their sinful condition itself, those who insist that they are sorry but resist dealing with their underlying evil by turning to God in true faith. True repentance on Saul's part would have been expressed in a resolve to depart for the altar of the Lord, there to deal with his great sin before God, and only afterward to offer protestations of good faith to his injured servant.

David realized the superficiality of Saul's words, and this is probably indicated by his immediate reference to the notorious weapon in his hand: "Here is the spear, O king! Let one of the young men come over and take it" (1 Sam. 26:22). A repentant Saul would have begged David to keep it, if not destroy it, as an emblem of his wicked corruption. David can only conclude by placing the matter into God's hands, reminding Saul that he will reap what he sows: "The LORD rewards every man for his righteousness and his faithfulness, for the LORD gave you into my hand today, and I would not put out my hand against the LORD's anointed" (26:23). David's reward for his good faith and obedience to God's Word was not relief from Saul's malicious pursuit, but rather a clean conscience before God and a resolved faith in God's vindication. As Christians, we should all have the same as our goal in every arena of strife—personal and public—acquitting ourselves peaceably and refusing the false peace of insincere repentance, while continuing to wait upon the God of both justice and grace.

As we continue our studies in 1 Samuel, we will soon see how God's justice pursues and overtakes reprobate Saul. What a sad blessing it would be for David on that day to recall that in response to his just and gracious dealings, the last words he ever heard from Saul's mouth were those of vindication of his own cause: "Then Saul said to David, 'Blessed be you, my son David! You will do many things and will succeed in them.' So David went his way, and Saul returned to his place" (1 Sam. 26:25).

THE RIGHTEOUS KING

On the same day that Margaret Wilson perished beneath the Solway waters—May 11, 1685—seventeen-year-old Andrew Hislop stood before a royal firing squad. His crime had been assisting his mother in offering shelter to a religious dissenter and refusing to swear the worldly king as sovereign over his soul. When the guns were loaded, Andrew was told to cover his face. With the same assurance in God that David showed before Saul, the young believer declined. "I can look you in the face," he answered; "I have done nothing of which I need to be ashamed. But how will you look in that day when you shall be judged by what is written in this Book?" The muskets fired and the bullets tossed Andrew's body to the ground, his hands still holding forth the Word of God to his murderers.[5]

David had come to realize that if he were to serve as a true king in service to the Lord, then he must commit himself to being a righteous king, trusting the Lord, waiting on God's timing, and submitting himself in obedience to God's Word. In years to come, David would exhibit a mixed record of success, although Israel would prosper under his generally righteous rule. More importantly, David typified the greater and truly righteous King who won the dying allegiance of both Margaret Wilson and Andrew Hislop, an allegiance they would not surrender even upon pain of death. Both refused the allegiance of a sin-maddened world in order to find salvation in the realm of the true and righteous King of heaven. Both, in their own way, reminded their persecutors of the righteous judgment before which every sinner must someday stand.

The writer of Hebrews, ministering to yet another body of afflicted believers, made a similar appeal. He wrote to remind a group of persecuted Jewish Christians that there is a true and righteous King in whose hands we may safely rest our souls. In Jesus, we see a King who himself has secured the righteousness in which we may stand before the judgment throne of God. Hebrews 1:8–9 declares to him, "Your throne, O God, is forever and ever, the scepter of uprightness is the scepter of your kingdom. You have loved righteousness and hated wickedness; therefore God, your God, has anointed you with the oil of gladness beyond your companions" (quoting Ps. 45:6–7). While the evil powers of this world may have their day, Hebrews 1:11–12 continues, "they will perish, but you remain; they will all wear out like a garment, like a robe you will roll them up, like a garment they will be changed. But you are the same, and your years will have no end" (quoting Ps. 102:26–27).

5. Smellie, *Men of the Covenant*, 386–87.

457

It was in the robe of Christ's righteousness that David, together with the Scottish martyrs, desired to stand before the affront of the earth's wicked rulers. It was for that righteous kingdom that he desired to offer his life, as should we today. He would learn, as all the martyrs have surely discovered in glory, the truth of what he wrote in Psalm 37:16–18:

> Better is the little that the righteous has
>   than the abundance of many wicked.
> For the arms of the wicked shall be broken,
>   but the LORD upholds the righteous.
> The LORD knows the days of the blameless,
>   and their heritage will remain forever.

39

CROSSING THE LINE

1 Samuel 27:1—28:2

*Then David said in his heart, "Now I shall perish one day by the
hand of Saul. There is nothing better for me than that I should
escape to the land of the Philistines. Then Saul will despair of
seeking me any longer within the borders of Israel, and I shall
escape out of his hand." (1 Sam. 27:1)*

A number of years ago, a society for the spread of atheism published a tract exposing the depravity of various Bible heroes. Under the face of Abraham an inscription read that here was a coward who was willing to sacrifice the honor of his wife to save his own skin. It listed the places where the Bible admits this and then where the Bible calls him "the friend of God." "What kind of God," it asks, "would befriend so dishonorable a man?" Under Jacob's picture was the Bible's description of him as a liar and a cheat, and also where God makes him the prince of his people. What does this say about the character of a deity who would call himself "the God of Jacob"? Next came the reminder that Moses was a murderer, yet God picked Moses to bring his law into the world. David was the worst of all. He seduced Bathsheba and then had her husband killed to cover it up. Yet this is "the man after God's own heart," the leaflet reminded.

What kind of God could find so much to praise in such a man, and why would anyone serve him?

How do we, as Christians and followers of the Bible's God, answer this exposé? The first thing to say is that everything the atheist tract says is true. It is true—no, it is a glorious truth—that the heroes of the Bible, excepting Jesus Christ, are all scoundrels and criminals, breakers of God's law and sinners to the core. This shows the Bible's honesty; no other religious tome dares to display the human weakness and sins of its heroes the way the Bible does, because the Bible is not trusting in man but in God.

Furthermore, it is true that God saves such people, making them his own friends and children and servants. God "justifies the ungodly," Paul writes (Rom. 4:5). On this, at least, we agree with the atheists. The difference is that we see this as God's glory and not his shame. Since we are sinners like the people in the Bible, the fact that God saves sinners commends him for our affection instead of subjecting him to our disdain.

OUT OF ISRAEL

In the Bible's long account of the life and reign of David, there are numerous incidents that show his need of God's forgiving mercy and grace. Probably foremost among them is the account of his sin with Bathsheba (2 Sam. 11). But another prominent chapter displaying the weakness of David's flesh is 1 Samuel 27. David's sin with Bathsheba shows David's weakness in his time of strength and power, whereas this chapter shows his weakness in a time of anxiety and affliction. The commentators are virtually unanimous in their harsh denunciation of David's decision to flee King Saul by taking refuge among Israel's enemies, the Philistines.

The argument against David's actions centers on his sudden failure to believe the promises of God. We see this both in the fact of David's flight from Israel and in the location to which he fled. As is typical for David when he is not acting by faith, the account of his actions is sudden and brief: "Then David said in his heart, 'Now I shall perish one day by the hand of Saul. There is nothing better for me than that I should escape to the land of the Philistines. Then Saul will despair of seeking me any longer within the borders of Israel, and I shall escape out of his hand.' So David arose and went over, he and the six hundred men who were with him, to Achish the son of Maoch, king of Gath" (1 Sam. 27:1–2).

David flees from Israel because he has persuaded himself that "the hand of Saul" is about to prevail in taking his life. This is a remarkable assessment, given the abundance of evidence in his recent experience that the hand of Saul was impotent against God's protective care. In chapter 23, Saul was about to stretch out his hand and seize David when a sudden assault of the Philistines diverted his forces (1 Sam. 23:27–28). In chapter 24, when Saul came hunting for David, the Lord placed Saul at David's mercy in the cave of Engedi. More recently, God placed a deep sleep on Saul's entire army so that David could enter the camp and remove Saul's spear. All of this was strong evidence of Saul's impotence against God's promise to raise David to the throne. When Abigail intervened to deflect David from his violent plans against her husband, Nabal, she spoke of these things as common knowledge: "If men rise up to pursue you and to seek your life, the life of my lord shall be bound in the bundle of the living in the care of the LORD your God" (25:29). How, then, does David now conclude, "Now I shall perish one day by the hand of Saul" (27:1)? The chapter begins by saying that "David said in his heart." David counseled his heart with unbelieving words, so it is no wonder that his heart responded not in faith but in folly and unbelief.

David's unbelief was seen in his flight from Israel, but his folly lay in his return to the enemy city of Gath. David had fled there before, at the beginning of Saul's persecution, and the result had been nearly disastrous (1 Sam. 21:10–15). On that occasion, David saved himself from the Philistines' malice only by pretending to be insane. How could David now think to find safety in such an ungodly place? A. W. Pink ascribes David's folly to a tendency to unbelief that every believer experiences: "Alas, when unbelief dominates us, God is forgotten, and deliverance, our own ease, obsess the mind; and hence it is that—unless divine grace interpose—we seek relief in the wrong quarter and by unspiritual means. Thus it was here with David: he and his men passed over unto Achish, the king of Gath."[1]

This assessment of David's actions is indisputable. Yet we should still listen to David's explanation. One thing David meant when he spoke of perishing at Saul's hand was that in his assessment, Saul would never

---

1. A. W. Pink, *A Life of David*, 2 vols. (Grand Rapids: Baker, 1981), 1:183.

leave him in peace, despite the king's occasional expressions of repentance and promises of restraint. This assessment was completely accurate. As a result, there was no place in Israel where David could safely rest. His recent return to Ziph—a place where the people had betrayed him once before, as they immediately did again—indicates that there were not many suitable sources of refuge in Israel for a band as large as David's. David's stressful encounter with Nabal in chapter 25 shows that David faced logistical requirements that could not be easily met while he and his followers were fugitives in the land. Verse 3 indicates that the care of his wives, Ahinoam and Abigail, was on David's mind, in addition to the well-being of the wives and children of his men, so that the total community under David's care may have numbered around two thousand. How could David continue to subject his own wives, along with the families of his soldiers, to such deprivation and danger? On top of this was the wear and tear of all this stress on David's own nerves. Dale Ralph Davis comments: "Hunted, tracked, and attacked by Saul; treacherously exposed; making thrilling escapes (e.g., 23:24–29) and executing daring escapades (e.g., chapters 24, 26)—nine chapters full of high-blood-pressure narrative. It's the stuff that makes great movies but takes its toll on real people."[2]

We have an example here, I believe, of how easy it is for us to be piously critical of others without considering their very real difficulties. When considering biblical figures, we can easily offer a simplistic answer to their problems. If David trusted God, we might say here, he would simply ignore Saul's threats in light of God's promised care. We apply this same approach to situations today. When considering a pastor who faces opposition and criticism from his unspiritual and worldly congregation, we say, "He just needs to continue doing what the Bible teaches." This is true, yet we little consider the social rejection that his wife and children endure and the wearying effects of his daily diet of conflict, slander, and criticism. To give another example, we consider a Christian wife who faces emotional harassment, biting criticism, and harsh treatment from her husband on a daily basis. We rightly say that she needs to put her trust in God and honor her marital vows, yet we should also consider what wounds this emotional environment

2. Dale Ralph Davis, *1 Samuel: Looking on the Heart* (Fearn, Ross-shire, UK: Christian Focus, 2000), 224–25.

is inflicting on her heart. How different things look from the inside, and how much more charitably we assess our own compromises and failures when under trial than those of others.

One answer that David would surely give to his critics is that prudence is not opposed to faith. The same God who promised him salvation also entrusted him with the care of a great many lives. David's duty required him to take prudent steps to avoid danger. Trusting in God did not require David to trust in Saul and place himself at the king's nonexistent mercy. Neither did trusting God's promise relieve David of the duty of finding a suitable base for his band. Jesus himself modeled prudence in his response to the threat of the Pharisees, showing that faith does not require a suicidal zealotry. In John 7, Jesus delayed going to Jerusalem for the Feast of Tabernacles "because the Jews were seeking to kill him" (John 7:1). None will accuse Jesus of unbelief for failing to walk into an open trap, even though Jesus was aware of God's care and protection. Even while trusting God's promise, David had to reckon with Saul's unceasing malice, and his duty to God required him to seek a place of safety for his followers.

David's example warns Christians against engaging in sentimental acts of folly. A Christian mother may be required to take prudent steps to protect her children from a violent husband. Missionary leaders will find it wise to consider the danger in certain parts of the world. Church leaders are wise to carefully examine the doctrinal standards of other churches or ministries that desire to enter into a partnership. While faith in Christ inspires his servants with a fearless spirit in the face of earthly threats, the duty of Christians who are entrusted with the lives of others and with the resources of a ministry requires us to give proper attention to matters of care and protection.

A BOUNDARY CROSSED

So which stance toward David is right: criticism or sympathy? Both are right, up to a point. Yet in the end, in joining up with the ungodly Philistines, Israel's enemy, David crossed a line that should never have been crossed. The language of verse 2 seems to acknowledge this point: "David arose and went over" (1 Sam. 27:2). John Woodhouse notes: "David crossed a boundary that day, and not just a geographical one. He 'went over' to the other side."[3] We can understand his need to find a safe refuge for his people, and his desire for a good night's sleep away from danger. We can imagine how difficult it was to find such a place in Israel with Saul as king. Yet there were places where David could not go without breaking faith, and one of these was Philistia.

One searches the Bible in vain for an example of Israelites' seeking salvation outside the land of promise, appealing to the care of the ungodly, that did not entangle them in sin and the curses of unbelief. When Abraham sought refuge in Egypt, he quickly fell into sin and danger (Gen. 12:10–20). Lot destroyed his family by taking them to Sodom (Gen. 13:10–13), as did the husband of Naomi when he took his family to Moab in time of famine (Ruth 1:2–3). The sons of Jacob were blessed with food from the royal granaries of Egypt established by their brother Joseph, but their sojourn in Egypt soon devolved into slavery (Ex. 1:8–14). Given these biblical examples, we cannot expect blessing to result from David's flight out of Israel and into Philistia.[4]

The same is true for the beleaguered pastor I mentioned earlier: for all our sympathy, there are compromises with his congregation that he cannot faithfully make, especially those involving the integrity of his Bible teaching. The same is true for an emotionally tormented wife or disappointed husband. To take steps of prudence in improving or managing a painful relationship is one thing, but to seek solace in the love of another man or woman or to pursue an unbiblical divorce is crossing the line into disobedience of God's Word. David crossed the line of disloyalty when he departed Israel for Gath, and he could not avoid harmful consequences from his action. We cross the line between prudence and the folly of sin, so that we are no longer trusting the Lord, when we violate our sacred vows or transgress the clear commandments of God's Word.

If we marvel at David's unbelieving actions, we realize that this episode fits a pattern seen on previous occasions. We read of no prayers to God for wisdom, no consultation of God's Word, and no appeal to the counsel of godly friends. The dynamics of godliness versus sin are usually straightforward and consistent. God has established means of grace to strengthen the faith of his people. When we neglect these means of grace—the Word,

---

3. John Woodhouse, *1 Samuel: Looking for a Leader* (Wheaton, IL: Crossway, 2008), 500.

4. When Jesus' parents fled to Egypt at God's command, they went to the Jewish exiles there, not to the pagan rulers (Matt. 2:13–15).

prayer, and gathered worship—our faith wanes and our tendency to sin and folly grows. This poor example from such a spiritual giant as David proves to us that especially when we are suffering under trials, Christians must hold fast to their Bibles, draw near to God in fervent prayer, and be especially devoted to the worship of God among his people. Isaiah said that "they who wait for the Lord shall renew their strength; they shall mount up with wings like eagles" (Isa. 40:31). In his panic, David had ceased waiting on the Lord's timing for his deliverance, casting himself along a path of unbelief that could lead only to trouble.

David in Ziklag

If it is true that David's last visit to Gath resulted in near disaster, it is also true that much had been altered since then. Previously, David had been known to the Philistines as the slayer of their people (1 Sam. 21:11), but now he was famous as the fugitive from Israel's King Saul. Moreover, David now appeared with a formidable fighting force to add to the strength of Achish. Probably for these reasons, David was welcomed at Gath, and his settlement in Goliath's former hometown had the immediately desired result: "When it was told Saul that David had fled to Gath, he no longer sought him" (27:4). David had succeeded in finally shaking off Saul's pursuit—but at what cost?

David immediately requested that his band be given their own town, rather than remain in the city of Gath. This arrangement seems to have been mutually agreeable. Achish can hardly have desired to have so large a force on his front porch, nor would he welcome the obligation to supply so many mouths. David would be better able to pursue his own agenda farther away from official notice. The town of Ziklag was provided to David, probably near the southern Judean desert, and here David could operate independently of Achish and safe from Saul's reach. Ziklag, it turns out, was a town allotted to the tribe of Judah during the distribution under Joshua (Josh. 15:31), but had never been captured. Through his cunning, David secured this rightful possession of Israel, and verse 6 says, "Therefore Ziklag has belonged to the kings of Judah to this day."

Three themes arise from the sixteen months that David and his band lived at Ziklag in Philistia. The first is David's cleverness in managing a most delicate situation. By seemingly crossing over to the Philistines, he risked the ruin of his reputation in Israel. In fact, this is exactly what Achish thought was happening. First Samuel 27:12 states that "Achish trusted David, thinking, 'He has made himself an utter stench to his people Israel; therefore he shall always be my servant.'" This is precisely what David wanted Achish to think. David was not, however, conducting raids against Israel, as he told Achish he was doing (1 Sam. 27:10). Instead, David was conducting warfare against Israel's perennial enemies nearby: "against the Geshurites, the Girzites, and the Amalekites, for these were the inhabitants of the land from of old, as far as Shur, to the land of Egypt" (27:8). If we wonder how David was able to pull off so large a subterfuge for so long, the answer is given in verse 9: "And David would strike the land and would leave neither man nor woman alive, but would take away the sheep, the oxen, the donkeys, the camels, and the garments, and come back to Achish."

Raiding warfare was David's expertise, and he was utterly effective in both wiping out his enemies and covering up his trail. David's motto in Ziklag was straight out of an old Western movie: "Dead men tell no tales." By means of systematic genocide he cleverly succeeded in prospering his people, winning the approval of Achish, and avoiding a formal betrayal of his native country. On the surface, David's cunning was winning the day. But the price he was paying was not hidden as easily as the identity of his victims. Gordon Keddie writes: "David was brilliant and successful, but he slaughtered whole communities and lied through his teeth to Achish in the process. He had left his principles in the mountains of Judah and boxed himself into a corner where deceit and ruthlessness were the staples that kept him alive."[5]

More positively, we should give David credit for devoting himself to the cause of his people and God's long-standing calling for Israel to complete the conquest of the Promised Land. David could rightly defend his actions, pointing out that while he had been unjustly driven into exile, he nonetheless did what he could to pursue the work of God and the well-being of Israel. Moreover, if we are repulsed by David's bloodthirsty tactics, he might point out that this wholesale slaughter was part and parcel of ancient warfare. Furthermore, these were all wicked nations under the ban of God's judgment. David was in fact fulfilling the holy-war mandate that Saul had been

5. Gordon J. Keddie, *Dawn of a Kingdom: The Message of 1 Samuel* (Darlington, UK: Evangelical Press, 1988), 251–52.

punished for failing to carry out. "Go and strike Amalek and devote to destruction all that they have," the Lord had commanded Saul. "Do not spare them, but kill both man and woman, child and infant, ox and sheep, camel and donkey" (1 Sam. 15:2–3). For this reason, Robert Bergen sees reason only to praise David for his actions during this period: "David redeemed his time in exile, using it to resume Israel's conquest of Canaan. . . . Thus, David's obedience to the Torah warfare regulations caused him to prosper."[6]

For all the truth there may be in that assessment, it also remains true that David was becoming practiced at deceit, and thus at violating God's law. Though Achish was a Philistine pagan, David had accepted his lordship and therefore owed him integrity. Moreover, while David was in fact executing God's holy-war judgment on the banned peoples among whom he raided, the text states that his slaughter was performed not for the glory and service of God but to ensure that no one lived who could expose his lies to the Philistine leaders (1 Sam. 27:11).

A balanced reading of these events shows a mixture of faith and ungodly compromise on David's part. The only real vindication for his actions is to argue that the ends justify the means. That is not, however, the ethic propounded in David's psalms. After his earlier visit to Gath, David wrote: "Keep your tongue from evil and your lips from speaking deceit. Turn away from evil and do good; seek peace and pursue it" (Ps. 34:13–14). This was hardly the motto of David's sojourn in Ziklag! David reminds us what a difference there is in seeking the Lord's deliverance as opposed to achieving one's own salvation by cunning and craft. It is no surprise that during the entire period of David's time in Philistia we read nothing of prayer, worship, the ministry of priests, or God's Word. In scrambling to work out his own salvation, David was compromising the values he had so carefully protected in earlier days, setting an example that could not possibly serve his people well after he finally came into his kingship.

The third theme of David's time in Ziklag fits this picture. For all his cunning, David was not able to manage the unforeseen consequences of his deceitful actions. Chapter 27 ends with Achish thoroughly taken in by David's deception. Chapter 28 begins, however, with an alarming result that David had never foreseen: "In those days the Philistines gathered their forces

6. Robert D. Bergen, *1, 2 Samuel*, New American Commentary (Nashville: Broadman & Holman, 1996), 261–62.

for war, to fight against Israel. And Achish said to David, 'Understand that you and your men are to go out with me in the army'" (1 Sam. 28:1). We can imagine David scrambling for something to say. He replied with as much ambiguity as he could muster: "Very well, you shall know what your servant can do." Achish answered, "Very well, I will make you my bodyguard for life" (28:2). This placed David in an even more difficult position than when he was fleeing from King Saul. He had been so successful in persuading the Philistines of his loyalty that their king was willing to trust David to join the attack against Israel, the very people David was determined never to harm. The only suitable response to David is the saying designed to warn children against lying: "Oh what a tangled web we weave, when first we practice to deceive!"

Speaking to Your Heart

Out of the folly of David's unbelief in crossing the line into Philistia, and the tangled weaving of deceit and compromise that resulted, there are at least three important lessons for us today. The first can be approached through the opening words of chapter 27: "Then David said in his heart." Our daily attitude of faith or unbelief depends in large part on what thoughts we cultivate and what sermons we preach to our own hearts. In this respect, we can trace David's downfall in chapter 27 to words that he spoke to Saul in the previous chapter, words that indicate the thoughts that were racing through David's mind. "They have driven me out this day," David complained, "that I should have no share in the heritage of the Lord, saying, 'Go, serve other gods'" (1 Sam. 26:19). David had been feeling sorry for himself, nurturing resentment over the injustice of his situation in Israel, and thus playing in his mind thoughts that soon would take form in his actions.

This reminds us not only of the necessity of daily appeal to the Bible but also of the purpose of our devotion to Scripture and prayer, namely, to form our thoughts on the basis of things that are true and edifying, and that guard us from sin and error. David's psalms model this ministry of preaching to one's own heart, as can be seen in Psalm 42:5: "Why are you cast down, O my soul, and why are you in turmoil within me? Hope in God; for I shall again praise him, my salvation." In Psalm 73, Asaph tells a similar tale. He had become bitter over the unjust prosperity and happiness of wicked, unbelieving people, and his heart was becoming hard. But then, he said, "I went into the sanctuary of God; then I discerned their end. Truly you set them in slippery places; you make them fall to ruin" (Ps. 73:17–18). In other words, once he returned to God's house and placed himself under the ministry of the Word, Asaph began thinking clearly about the judgment of the wicked and the salvation of those who trust in God. The result of this mind- and heart-control was a renewed faith that walked with uprightness before the Lord. Like David in Psalm 42, we must be sure to preach gospel truth to ourselves—remembering that God has loved us by sending his Son, Jesus, to die for our sins and grant us eternal life. Moreover, like Asaph in Psalm 73, we must be regular in attending the worship of the church, lest the dark strands of unbelief, fear, and resentment weave a tangle in our minds.

Second, David's plan in fleeing to Philistia may be assessed by appeal to Proverbs 14:12: "There is a way that seems right to a man, but its end is the way to death." We sympathize with David for the strain and fatigue that must have contributed to his actions, along with the burden of responsibility for so many men and their families. We can easily see how his cunning strategy would have appealed to him, especially given its early success in ridding him of Saul's pursuit. But in so doing, according to his own spur-of-the-moment cleverness, David crossed a line that placed his entire future in grave jeopardy. Despite months of success in duping Achish, David ends the episode by becoming attached to the Philistine vanguard for an invasion of Israel.

The lesson is that true wisdom is always achieved by submission to the precepts and commands of God's Word. David would have done better by emulating a different proverb: "Trust in the LORD with all your heart, and do not lean on your own understanding. In all your ways acknowledge him, and he will make straight your paths" (Prov. 3:5–6). In the end, it is not our job to save ourselves; as Jonah learned from within the great fish, "Salvation belongs to the LORD!" (Jonah 2:9). Proverbs does not tell us to abandon our own understanding, but it does tell us not to lean on that understanding. It is always God on whom we must lean, and if we are relying on the Lord to be our salvation, we will find it easier to retain the wisdom of walking in the straight paths of his Word.

Finally, David was foolish in fleeing from Israel because of the geography of salvation that is taught in the Old Testament. Once God had placed his people in the Promised Land, salvation was always, and only, to be found there. In years to come, David would capture Jerusalem to be Israel's capital and then his son Solomon would build the holy temple of the Lord there on Mount Zion. Salvation would come only through those who came to the Lord in his holy place. All of this prefigured the coming of Jesus Christ, in whom God dwells among his people. There is now no salvation outside of Jesus Christ (Acts 4:12). To flee to some other salvation when trouble looms, to quarrel with the obligation to obey Christ's Word so as to chart our own way, or to wander from the fold of Christ's church is to risk an eternal separation that far outstrips the danger that David courted in fleeing to Gath. Whatever else happens to us in life, whatever persecution we suffer or hardships we endure, whatever injustice we experience or crosses we must bear, we must remain in Jesus Christ, trusting in the only Savior for the forgiveness of our sins and obediently submitting to his will. Ours is not to sort out our own salvation in life, but rather to flee to the salvation offered by God in Christ, holding fast to him in all things.

If only we remain in Christ, we can be certain that God will save us in the end, even as he will protect us according to his will along the way. An unhealthy marriage, career disappointments, or ungodly changes in our culture, to name a few typical threats to our happiness, may cause us anxiety and distress. But by remaining in Christ through a persevering faith, as David should have remained in Israel, we can be certain of being present for the great day when all of God's people will enter the full glory of salvation. With our eyes fixed on the inheritance of glory that we will share with Christ, we therefore sing:

> O sweet and blessed country, the home of God's elect!
> O sweet and blessed country that eager hearts expect!
> Jesus, in mercy bring us to that dear land of rest;
> Who are, with God the Father and Spirit, ever blest.[7]

---

7. Bernard of Cluny, "Jerusalem the Golden" (12th c.).

40

DARK NIGHT OF THE SOUL

1 Samuel 28:3—25

Samuel said, "Why then do you ask me, since the LORD has
turned from you and become your enemy? The LORD has done
to you as he spoke by me, for the LORD has torn the kingdom
out of your hand and given it to your neighbor, David."
(1 Sam. 28:16–17)

*I*n some mystical strands of Christianity, there is a phenomenon
known as "the dark night of the soul." This term was coined
by the sixteenth-century Roman Catholic mystic Saint John of
the Cross, who wrote a famous poem and treatise on this theme. "The dark
night of the soul" describes the experience of a person who endures a night
or longer period of spiritual torment, which is usually followed by an experience of God's blessing and peace. Shortly after the death of Mother Teresa,
famous for her decades of service to the orphans of Calcutta, her memoirs
revealed a dark night of spiritual struggle that lasted from 1950 until her
death in 1997. "The silence and the emptiness is so great," she stated, "that
I look and do not see,—Listen and do not hear."[1] Mother Teresa recorded

1. Quoted in David van Biema, "Mother Teresa's Crisis of Faith," *Time*, Aug. 23, 2007, http://www
.time.com/time/world/article/0,8599,1655415,00.html.

471

how her unrelieved spiritual struggles fueled her drive for achievement and good works.

First Samuel 28 discloses Israel's King Saul in a briefer but more deadly night of darkness, one in which he found no redemption and from which his hardened soul produced no good deeds. Saul's dark night of the soul was a prelude to the longer, endless darkness that would come to him in death because of his hardened unbelief and unforgiven sin.

WITHOUT A WORD

In preparing to tell us about Saul's night of darkness, chapter 28 first informs us of the prophet Samuel's death: "Now Samuel had died, and all Israel had mourned for him and buried him in Ramah, his own city" (v. 3). It had been Samuel who anointed Saul as Israel's king and brought him messages from the Lord. These messages had ceased before Samuel died, yet the great judge and prophet's death gave a sense of finality to Saul's alienation from God.

Second, we are told that Saul had previously removed "the mediums and necromancers out of the land" (1 Sam. 28:3). This was in accordance with God's Word, which declared, "There shall not be found among you anyone who . . . practices divination or tells fortunes or interprets omens, or a sorcerer or a charmer or a medium or a necromancer or one who inquires of the dead" (Deut. 18:10–11). It was for these occult "abominations" that God was judging the Canaanites (18:12).

The significance of these two facts is found in Saul's suddenly pressing need for divine help, as the Philistines assembled to launch a massive invasion of Israel. Mobilizing his forces at Gilboa to meet the threat, Saul "was afraid, and his heart trembled greatly" (1 Sam. 28:5). This statement is a commentary on the general state of Saul's soul. There is little doubt that he was faced with an overwhelming Philistine host. Yet he possessed no faith with which to take courage. The Philistines had approached Saul in a region where some of Israel's greatest victories had taken place by God's intervening power. Nearby, Barak and his hastily gathered militia had overthrown the host of the Canaanites (Judg. 4), and Gideon's tiny band had years before overthrown the Midianite host (Judg. 7). Nonetheless, Saul was gripped by the unbelief of his spiritual and moral darkness. Suddenly, he became aware, as seems not to have happened for years, of his need for a word of hope from the Lord.

If Saul's first problem was the Philistine invasion, his second problem was that God refused to answer him when he called: "When Saul inquired of the Lord, the Lord did not answer him, either by dreams, or by Urim, or by prophets" (1 Sam. 28:6). These were the three means by which God typically communicated with his servants in those days, and none was available to Saul. Most noteworthy is the reference to the Urim, the lot held within the high priest's ephod by which divination could be received from God. The problem was that Saul had slain all the priests, except Abiathar, who had taken the ephod to David. (Around this same time, David would successfully appeal to God by means of the Urim, receiving vitally important direction from the Lord; see 1 Sam. 30:7–8.) It is possible that Saul had appointed his own high priest and had another Urim made, but God refused to honor Saul's self-serving religion. Having earlier been repudiated by Samuel for disobedience, and then having wickedly slain the Lord's holy priests, Saul must have found the silence of God's refusal to speak deafening.

God's refusal to answer Saul presents an interesting question in light of the Bible's frequent promise that God will answer those who call on his name. Did not the prophet Joel declare, echoed by the apostle Paul, that "everyone who calls on the name of the Lord shall be saved" (Joel 2:32; Rom. 10:13)? The evident explanation is that while Saul went through the mechanics of an appeal to the Lord, his heart never opened even one inch toward repentance and true faith. In years to come, some of Israel's most wicked kings, Ahab and Manasseh, would find God's mercy through even a small expression of true contrition (1 Kings 21:29; 2 Chron. 33:12–13). So why not Saul? The answer is given in 1 Chronicles 10:14, which explains that Saul "did not seek guidance from the Lord. Therefore the Lord put him to death." Saul sought comfort but not guidance, and his unyielded heart was met by God's unyielding rejection.

Thus, Saul is a dreadful reminder of the danger of apostasy. An apostate is not a true believer in Christ who later falls away. Instead, an apostate is a professed believer, an outward member of the believing community, who instead of engaging the Lord in true faith hardens his heart in sin. The ultimate result is not merely unbelief but a seared conscience and a heart hardened to a point of no return (see Heb. 6:4–6). William Blaikie explains Saul's plight in this condition:

> Saul was incapable of that exercise of soul which would have saved him and his people. Most terrible effect of cherished sin! It dries up the fountains of contrition and they will not flow. It stiffens the knees and they will not bend. It paralyses the voice and it will not cry. It blinds the eyes and they see not the Savior.[2]

Saul was willing, in his dark night of the soul, to engage in outward motions intended to manipulate aid from God. But the Lord's ear is open only to those of a broken heart and contrite spirit. What a dreadful thing it is to harden the heart against the Lord and his Word! Ultimately, time runs out for the apostate, and even the opportunity for repentance is gone. So it was for Saul, as later it would be for all Israel, when God would say, "I will not listen when they call to me in the time of their trouble" (Jer. 11:14). Blaikie comments: "How infinitely precious would one tear of genuine repentance have been in that dark hour! It would have saved thousands of the Israelites from a bloody death; it would have saved the nation from defeat and humiliation."[3]

Saul's hardened obstinacy is made clear in his response to God's silence: "Saul said to his servants, 'Seek out for me a woman who is a medium, that I may go to her and inquire of her.' And his servants said to him, 'Behold, there is a medium at En-dor'" (1 Sam. 28:7). Earlier, Saul had rightly prohibited mediums and necromancers—those who sought divination from the dead—although his prohibition's evident failure seems to testify to Saul's lack of spiritual authority in the land. Now his lack of spiritual vitality is proved as he turns to these occult diviners, seeking to replace from the dead the voice of the living God.

Perhaps because the mediums had come to fear him, or perhaps because of his guilty conscience in fear of God, Saul put on a disguise for his journey to En-dor, where a woman was known to speak with the dead. Upon arriving, Saul asked her, "Divine for me by a spirit and bring up for me

---

2. William G. Blaikie, *Expository Lectures on the Book of First Samuel* (1887; repr., Birmingham, AL: Solid Ground, 2005), 406.

3. Ibid., 407.

whomever I shall name to you" (1 Sam. 28:8). The "Witch of En-dor," as she has been known, replied in fear: "Surely you know what Saul has done, how he has cut off the mediums and the necromancers from the land. Why then are you laying a trap for my life to bring about my death?" (28:9). How remarkable it is that Saul comforted the woman by swearing in the name of the Lord—Israel's God—"As the LORD lives, no punishment shall come upon you for this thing" (28:10). Here is yet another sign of Saul's hardened spiritual condition: in order to violate God's law and ensure protection to an occultist under God's condemnation, Saul vows in the Lord's name!

Granted this assurance, the woman asked Saul, "Whom shall I bring up for you?" Saul answered, "Bring up Samuel for me" (1 Sam. 28:11). Here is yet another twist in the contorted plot. Though Saul breaks both God's law and his own prohibition, it is yet God's servant that he seeks. Saul knows and believes the truth that salvation can come only from God—the God against whom he has hardened his heart—so if God will not speak to Saul, Saul will seek to raise the spirit of one to whom God does speak, Samuel. What a dreadful state to recognize the need for truth from God while being too hardened to come to God himself! We see this spiritual desperation today in people who do not and cannot pray to God but who seek out the prayers of believers. What should such a person do to gain direct access to the mercy of God? The answer is to heed the call of Jesus Christ by bringing the burden of your sin to his cross, and there gaining confidence to "draw near to the throne of grace," and thus "receive mercy and find grace to help in time of need" (Heb. 4:16).

God's Prophet Raised?

After Saul had identified Samuel as the spirit to be summoned, the text says that "the woman saw Samuel," and then "cried out with a loud voice." At this point, she realized that her client must be none other than King Saul: "Why have you deceived me? You are Saul." The king asked her what she saw, and she answered, "I see a god coming up out of the earth." "What is his appearance?" Saul urgently inquired. "She said, 'An old man is coming up, and he is wrapped in a robe'" (1 Sam. 28:12–14).

This raises a question on which expositors of Scripture have differed: did the witch really summon the spirit of Samuel from the grave? Most commentators in the course of church history have denied that Samuel truly was summoned. A popular view of the early church was that the evil woman had summoned Satan to appear in the guise of the prophet Samuel. Tertullian wrote, "God forbid we should believe that any soul, much less a prophet, could be called forth by a demon."[4] In the time of the Reformation, Martin Luther argued, "Who could believe that the souls of believers, who are in the hand of God and in the bosom of Abraham, were under the power of the devil . . . ?"[5] John Calvin added that "God would never have allowed His prophets to be subjected to such diabolical conjuring . . . , as if the devil had power over the bodies and souls of the saints which are in His keeping."[6] On these grounds, Luther asserted that the supposed appearance was a deception of Satan, whereas Calvin suspected a delusion in the minds of Saul and the abominable woman.

The problem with this denial is that there are elements in the text that cannot be so easily dismissed. First, not only did Saul and the woman describe the spirit as Samuel, but the inspired writer agrees. Verse 15 states, "Samuel said to Saul." Moreover, the summoned spirit replied to Saul with the very message that Samuel had given him in life: "The LORD has done to you as he spoke by me, for the LORD has torn the kingdom out of your hand and given it to your neighbor, David" (1 Sam. 28:17). A deluded Saul seeking comfort would not likely have conjured these words, and if Satan had appeared to deceive Saul, it is not obvious why he would have spoken such truth. Moreover, the spirit uttered a prophecy that came true: "Tomorrow you and your sons shall be with me. The LORD will give the army of Israel also into the hand of the Philistines" (28:19). Speaking from the realm of the dead, the spirit expected to see Saul and his sons in the same realm on the very next day.

Does this mean that a servant of Satan actually succeeded in raising the soul of a prophet, one who had entered death in God's saving care? The answer of most commentators today is that the Bible does seem to state that Samuel was summoned, yet it could not have been by the demonic power of the medium that this happened. Therefore, it is most likely that Samuel came

4. John R. Franke, ed., *Joshua, Judges, Ruth, 1–2 Samuel*, Ancient Christian Commentary on Scripture, Old Testament vol. 4 (Downers Grove, IL: InterVarsity Press, 2005), 321.

5. Quoted in Carl Friedrich Keil and Franz Delitzsch, *Commentary on the Old Testament*, 10 vols. (Peabody, MA: Hendrickson, 1996), 2:544n1.

6. Ibid., 2:544–45n1.

not at the command of the witch but at the unexpected will of God. This would explain why the woman cried out in shock when she saw the spirit, whom she initially identified as a "god": "When the woman saw Samuel, she cried out with a loud voice" (1 Sam. 28:12). This suggests that her regular occult activities were fraudulent and that she was just as shocked as Saul when an actual spirit from the dead appeared. Matthew Henry comments: "God permitted, on this one occasion, the soul of a departed prophet to come as a witness from heaven, thus sending him to confirm the word he had spoken on earth."[7] Carl Keil and Franz Delitzsch add that Samuel's appearance "was of such a character, that it could not fail to show to the witch and the king, that God does not allow His prohibitions to be infringed with impunity."[8]

We should remember that Samuel was not the last of God's dead servants to appear on earth in spirit form. The Gospels record that the spirits of Moses and Elijah appeared with Jesus on the Mount of Transfiguration (Matt. 17:3). This reminds us that souls of those who die in Christ yet live in glory. Whereas the two Old Testament greats, Moses and Elijah, appeared in order to rejoice with Jesus in the gospel, when Samuel appeared to apostate Saul before the coming of Christ, he came with only the grim condemnation of the law.

MESSAGE FROM THE DEAD

I noted earlier the wretched state of a hardened and apostate heart in Saul's inability to commune with God. This lamentable reality was only amplified when Saul heard the message that Samuel came to deliver. Saul greeted the spirit of Samuel with reverence: "He bowed with his face to the ground and paid homage" (1 Sam. 28:14). Henry suggests that Saul acted this way at the witch's direction, pointing out the irony that the very king who would not submit to the Word of God was all too ready to obey the word of the witch.[9] This reminds us that those who refuse to serve the Lord in faith cannot avoid the bondage of cruel obedience to Satan.

7. Quoted in Gordon J. Keddie, *Dawn of a Kingdom: The Message of 1 Samuel* (Darlington, UK: Evangelical Press, 1988), 272.

8. Keil and Delitzsch, *Commentary on the Old Testament*, 2:546.

9. Matthew Henry, *Commentary on the Whole Bible*, 6 vols. (Peabody, MA: Hendrickson, 1992), 2:337.

Samuel spoke to Saul, demanding, "Why have you disturbed me by bringing me up?" Saul answered, "I am in great distress, for the Philistines are warring against me, and God has turned away from me and answers me no more, either by prophets or by dreams. Therefore I have summoned you to tell me what I shall do" (1 Sam. 28:15). Samuel responded with surprise: how could Saul expect a word of God through Samuel when the king was forsaken of the Lord? The prophet said, "Why then do you ask me, since the LORD has turned from you and become your enemy?" (28:16). Samuel was, after all, a servant of the Lord, and thus would have no aid to report for an enemy of God.

Saul pictures here every man who forsakes God's repeated appeals, who first declines to embrace the gospel and then hardens his heart against the whole of God's Word, only to arrive at the day when a wrathful God is no longer willing to speak with words of grace. In life, such a person finds the idea of serving God annoying, desiring nothing more than to be rid of God and his Word. Yet he little considers that the worst thing that could happen would be for God to fulfill his wish. If you are such a person, what would happen to you if God were to remove all his influence from your life, forsaking you as you have forsaken him in your pride and sinful desire? Blaikie warns: "O sinner, if ever thy wish should be fulfilled, how wilt thou curse the day in which thou didst utter it! When vile lusts rise to uncontrollable authority—when those whom you love turn hopelessly wicked, when you find yourselves joyless, helpless, hopeless, when you try to repent and cannot repent, when you try to pray and cannot pray, when you try to be pure and cannot be pure—what a terrible calamity you will then feel it that God is departed from you!" He concludes from reflection: "Trifle not, O man, with thy relation to God."[10]

Saul learned further that the God who refused him blessing was also working toward his overthrow. Samuel continued by informing Saul that it was actually the Lord who had brought the Philistine host to his doorstep: "The LORD has done to you as he spoke by me, for the LORD has torn the kingdom out of your hand and given it to your neighbor, David. Because you did not obey the voice of the LORD and did not carry out his fierce wrath against Amalek, therefore the LORD has done this thing to you this

10. Blaikie, *First Samuel*, 411–12.

day" (1 Sam. 28:17–18). This refers to Saul's disobedience to God's Word in chapter 15, when the Lord instructed the king to annihilate his enemies the Amalekites. Saul had treated God's commands lightly, but God treated them as matters of the greatest significance. Saul thought his sin to be a matter easily brushed aside, but God thought it deadly rebellion to his sovereign rule. Saul would not listen to God, and now God would not speak to Saul, except to announce the arrival of his long-awaited judgment. The Saul who would not heed the Word of the Lord would face the shouts of the Philistine offensive.

In his riveting account of the fall of Berlin in the last weeks of World War II, Cornelius Ryan recounts a telephone call placed to Adolf Hitler from his minister of propaganda, Joseph Goebbels. To the west, the American Army had crossed the Rhine River and was racing for Berlin, while in the East the Soviet Red Army was crashing against the paper-thin German defenses. Nonetheless, Goebbels called the führer with jubilant news. He had recently informed Hitler of astrological predictions that foretold hard blows for Germany in early April but an overwhelming victory in the second half of the month. News had just arrived confirming the message in the stars, for the American president, Franklin D. Roosevelt, had just died. Yet how wrong Goebbels's divination was! Little did Hitler and Goebbels realize the complete destruction that must result from the wicked folly of their sins. By the end of the month, the triumph foretold by Goebbels's horoscopes had not appeared, and on April 30 Hitler committed suicide, followed on the next day by Goebbels himself.[11] Whatever the stars or other idolatrous deceptions may suggest, the inevitable result of sin is the judgment of a holy God.

Not only did Samuel remind Saul, first, that God had forsaken him in silence, and second, that God was visiting Saul with judgment, but he concluded with a third message: that God was consigning Saul to the condemnation of death. Samuel concluded: "Moreover, the LORD will give Israel also with you into the hand of the Philistines, and tomorrow you and your sons shall be with me. The LORD will give the army of Israel also into the hand of the Philistines" (1 Sam. 28:19).

Here is the final calamity of divine abandonment. When man abandons God, he desires only that God leave him to his own devices. But when God

11. Cornelius Ryan, *The Last Battle*, cited in Dale Ralph Davis, *1 Samuel: Looking on the Heart* (Fearn, Ross-shire, UK: Christian Focus, 2000), 232–33.

abandons man, he assigns for him the judgment of death (Rom. 6:23). Sinful man has violated God's law and rebelled against God's sovereign rule. The only result possible if God is to retain his justice, honor, and sovereign rights is the result foretold by Jesus in his parable of the ten minas. At the time of his coming, the sovereign Lord must issue his decree of judgment and death: "As for these enemies of mine, who did not want me to reign over them, bring them here and slaughter them before me" (Luke 19:27).

If we think this is a dreadful picture of God's justice and wrath, let us not forget his spurned offer of grace in the sacrificial blood of his own Son. If you have heard but refused the gospel offer of forgiveness through the atoning blood of Christ, your judgment will be not only for rebellion against divine authority but also for contempt of saving grace. The application from Saul's plight is both urgent and insistent: "Seek the LORD while he may be found; call upon him while he is near; let the wicked forsake his way, and the unrighteous man his thoughts; let him return to the LORD, that he may have compassion on him, and to our God, for he will abundantly pardon" (Isa. 55:6–7).

FEAR AND LOATHING

No longer possessing even the possibility of repentance, Saul was left to fear and loathing in this last dark night of his soul. He "fell at once full length on the ground, filled with fear because of the words of Samuel" (1 Sam. 28:20). It had been a wretched day for the king, in which he had not eaten all day and night. Seeing him in this shape, the woman came to Saul and spoke to him with kindness. Since she had obeyed Saul, he should now obey her: "'Let me set a morsel of bread before you; and eat, that you may have strength when you go on your way.' He refused and said, 'I will not eat.' But his servants, together with the woman, urged him, and he listened to their words. So he arose from the earth and sat on the bed" (28:22–23). How much worse were things for Saul now that he had consulted the medium and heard from the spirit of dead Samuel. For not only was he faced with the predicament of the Philistine onslaught, but even worse was the dark specter of abandonment from God for judgment and death.

At this point, we remember David and his many trials. David had been harried by Saul for years and now had fled Israel for refuge among the Philistines. Yet David retained by faith his access to God and his grace. The true Urim of divine revelation had been sent away from Saul to David, so David could restore himself from folly by seeking light from the Lord, just as we who possess our Bibles may restore ourselves by appeal to God's Word.

In light of Saul's sin-darkened plight, Dale Ralph Davis urges Christians to reflect on their situation in this context:

> You may be exhausted from work. In fact, your employer may be giving you a raw deal . . . You have lost your health or family troubles are now cropping up. The text says there is something far worse. Do you realize what a solace it is in the face of all your failure to have access to the throne of grace and the smiling face of God in prayer? Do you realize that all that you have suffered is not nearly so tragic as someone moaning, "*God* has turned away from me"?[12]

Just as there is no greater misery than to realize yourself abandoned by God in the hour of need, there is no greater solace than to remember God's gracious help for those who call on him in faith. Let us call on Jesus, believing his promise for all who belong to him through simple faith: " 'I will never leave you nor forsake you.' So we can confidently say, 'The Lord is my helper; I will not fear; what can man do to me?' " (Heb. 13:5–6, quoting Josh. 1:5; Ps. 118:6).

Lacking any comfort from the Lord, Saul contented himself with such diversions as he could find. Perhaps understanding the import of Samuel's words of woe, the witch prepared a final meal fit for a king: "Now the woman had a fattened calf in the house, and she quickly killed it, and she took flour and kneaded it and baked unleavened bread of it, and she put it before Saul and his servants, and they ate. Then they rose and went away that night" (1 Sam. 28:24–25). Perhaps Saul was able to forget what awaited him in the morning, and the eternity that would follow his death, just as unbelievers often seek to shrug off the ill-ease of their souls. This was Saul's last supper, in the darkness of his soul's last night on earth, with the company of only his servants and a condemned witch!

OUT OF DARKNESS

Reflecting on Saul, we remember another Last Supper, when Jesus Christ gathered in the upper room with his disciples on the night of his arrest. Saul

12. Davis, *1 Samuel*, 239.

481

brings to mind one of the disciples, who for all his privileges as one close to the Savior had nonetheless forsaken Jesus in his heart. John says of Judas Iscariot that "after receiving the morsel of bread, he immediately went out. And it was night" (John 13:30). The apostle was noting not merely the time, but also the state of Judas's soul and the destiny to which he was turning in unbelief. Like Saul, Judas had a heart of darkness. Jesus' words about Judas are true of all those who turn from his light to the darkness of sin and Saul-like self-rule: "It would have been better for that man if he had not been born" (Matt. 26:24).

After the meal, Jesus himself would head into darkness. Like Saul, Jesus bore the curse of a prophesied death upon his head. The only completely righteous man, the One who had perfectly obeyed the will of God every moment of his life, the Son of David who was far more unlike Saul than even David, would be nailed to a cross to die for sin. Mark records: "When the sixth hour had come, there was darkness over the whole land until the ninth hour. And at the ninth hour Jesus cried with a loud voice, . . . 'My God, my God, why have you forsaken me?'" (Mark 15:33–34). As God's Son prepared to die in the sin-cursed darkness, the words spoken by Saul to Samuel could equally be said by him: "God has turned away from me and answers me no more" (1 Sam. 28:15).

Yet how great—how infinitely great—was the difference between Saul in the darkness of his own sin and Jesus in the darkness of sins he did not commit. Saul, with his hardened heart and in his rebellion against God, had entered a darkness that would last forever in hell. But the Savior, Jesus Christ, in obedience to the saving will of the Father and in compliance with God's covenant for our salvation, entered the darkness of condemnation in order that he might take its curse away forever from the people who belong to him in faith. Jesus entered the darkness of the cross that we might enter the life and light of his resurrection glory. Saul's account ends with the words "they rose and went away that night," with only the darkness of divine abandonment before him (1 Sam. 28:25). Jesus also entered the darkness, but on the third day he rose in the light of the open tomb, and all those who place their sins on his cross may know the joy of eternal life in his grace. Of them the gospel declares that "neither death nor life, nor angels nor rulers, nor things present nor things to come, nor powers, nor height nor depth, nor anything else in all creation, will be able to separate us from the love of God in Christ Jesus our Lord" (Rom. 8:38–39).

41

MARCHING WITH THE ENEMY

1 Samuel 29:1—11

David said to Achish, "But what have I done? What have you found in your servant from the day I entered your service until now, that I may not go and fight against the enemies of my lord the king?" (1 Sam. 29:8)

The historical books of the Bible are not bare records of past events, but theologically and pastorally shaped narratives. To this end, they are written with remarkable skill, employing careful construction for the sake of suspense and meaning. One example is the narrative flow of 1 Samuel chapters 24 to 26, which present David as growing in grace while Saul declines in depravity. An even better example is chapters 27 to 31, where the sacred historian shapes the timeline to make his point with subtlety.

To see this narrative craftsmanship, we should line up the action in the final chapters of 1 Samuel. In chapter 27, David seeks salvation from Saul's malice by turning to the Philistines. In chapter 28, Saul seeks salvation from God's rejection by turning to an occult medium. In chapter 29, David is saved from the Philistines; in chapter 31, Saul is destroyed by the Philistines. The point of this arrangement is not that David is wiser or more virtuous than Saul (though undoubtedly he is). The point, rather, is that David's relationship with the God of grace makes the vital difference. David is saved from his error, while Saul, having turned his heart away from the Lord, is destroyed in his folly. The lesson of these chapters is summarized by David in Psalm 118: "The LORD is my strength and my song; he has become my salvation. . . . The LORD has disciplined me severely, but he has not given me over to death" (Ps. 118:14, 18).

UNDER THE PHILISTINE BANNER

We can see how the inspired author has rearranged events by noting the geography in the progression of these chapters. First Samuel 28:4 shows the Philistines and Saul facing off at Shunem and Gilboa, in the rich northern region of Galilee, which the Philistines had invaded. In chapter 29, however, David is back with the Philistines at Aphek in the Plain of Sharon over thirty miles to the south. This means that chapter 29 not only shifts the action from Saul to David, but takes us back several days to the Philistine mobilization. When last we saw David, he had unexpectedly been promoted to the position of bodyguard of the Philistine lord, Achish. The writer left us hanging, wondering how David would ever get out of this predicament. Having heightened our suspense by shifting the action to Saul's night of spiritual darkness, the author now returns to resolve David's dilemma. The writer clearly intends for the suspense to heighten our awareness of the magnitude of the problem that David had arranged for himself.

The mention of Aphek is ominous, since this was the location of the Philistine camp in the battle when Israel was swept away, when the ark of the covenant was captured, and after which Eli the high priest died (1 Sam. 4:1). This disaster had precipitated the appointment of Saul as the king demanded by the people to lead them against the Philistines. Although David does not know it, we know that Saul's death in the coming battle is preordained. John Woodhouse writes: "What happened once at Aphek before Saul became king was about to happen again and bring his reign to an end. In the end the king 'like all the nations,' who would 'go out before us and fight our battles' (1 Sam. 8:20), had failed."[1] Whether or not David

---

1. John Woodhouse, *1 Samuel: Looking for a Leader* (Wheaton, IL: Crossway, 2008), 521.

was aware of it, the reader is meant to note the distressing irony of David's joining the Philistine assembly at such a time and place. Taking matters into his own hands instead of waiting for the Lord had not worked out so well for David.

We might summarize David's problem this way: having foolishly sought salvation through the Philistines, he now needed to be saved from his friendship with the Philistines. Previously, David's problem had been the hatred of Israel's apostate King Saul. How great a problem that seemed at the time! But now David had a problem that threatened more than just his life: he must be saved from his alliance with the enemies of God. For sixteen months, David had cunningly navigated his precarious situation, making the Philistines think that he was helping them against Israel while making sure that he did no actual harm to God's people. As generally happens, David's cunning was unable to control the variables, and his intrigue was revealed as a falling house of cards. The worst of all scenarios had occurred: his new Philistine lord had gone to war against Israel.

With the Philistine army, including David, mobilizing against God's covenant people, David was hemmed in to a decisive choice that would determine his fate. If David showed loyalty to Achish, his new lord, he must now be wholly opposed to his own people, Israel. David would be an apostate, in the lamentable condition later described by the apostle Paul: "separated from Christ, alienated from the commonwealth of Israel and strangers to the covenants of promise, having no hope and without God in the world" (Eph. 2:12). But how could David extricate himself from his obligations to the Philistines? As so often happens when God's people dabble in sin and worldliness, David was now further in than he imagined possible, perhaps so far in that he would never get out.

Leading a Double Life

We should reflect on how David's story speaks to God's saving plan that would culminate in the coming of Christ, and how David's life sheds light on our faith today. We have often treated David as a type who foreshadows the person and work of Jesus Christ. This was classically the case in David's victory over the Philistine giant, Goliath. But having crossed over to the Philistines, David no longer functions as a forerunner of Jesus. How, then, does David's experience here point forward to the new covenant and inform the lives of Christians today?

The answer is that, having stepped out of his typecast role as a forerunner of Christ, David is now a typically wayward servant of God. He has made a classic mistake to which we are also prone: attempting to lead a double life with respect to Christ and the world. David had sought a temporal salvation from the Philistines while he sought his eternal salvation with God. David was like a person today who wants to go to heaven and so professes faith in Jesus. But he also wants financial security, so he hoards his money and follows the stock market with religious devotion. He wants a satisfying career, so he compromises his integrity in the workplace. He wants pleasure and approval, so he drinks from the trough of sensual worldly entertainment. And desiring an eternity in heaven, on Sundays he goes back and pays his respects to Jesus Christ at church.

What is the problem with this approach to life, with David's quest for earthly security among the Philistines and eternal security with God? The problem is that the two are at war! The situation is well described by Paul's inquiry: "what partnership has righteousness with lawlessness? Or what fellowship has light with darkness? What accord has Christ with Belial?" (2 Cor. 6:14–15). In the end, David could not maintain his allegiance to the Philistines—together with their approval and protection—without abandoning his loyalty to God, and vice versa. So it is for the professing Christian. In order to gain an earthly salvation from the world, we will not be able to live the life of faith that is required of those who hope for heaven through Jesus Christ.

Reflecting this way on David, we realize that not only is he similar to many professing Christians today, but he has especially become like his nemesis, Saul. How distressing a realization this is, since we know that Saul's judgment of death is right around the corner! The people of Israel had demanded Saul because they wanted a king "like all the nations" (1 Sam. 8:20), and Saul was taller, more handsome, and more resourceful than his peers. David, in turning from his reliance on the Lord, had cast his future on his own possession of similar qualities. Just as Saul's unbelieving pragmatism was leading him to ruin, so also had David's unbelieving pragmatism put him between a rock and a hard place.

There was, however, one decisive difference between David and Saul. The difference was David's relationship with the Lord. Saul, having hardened himself to the Lord, had ultimately been repudiated by God. David, however, had not yet lost his faith. Ultimately, the difference between the two men—the reason why one was an apostate to be judged and the other a backslider to be lovingly disciplined—is the sovereign grace of God. God's preserving grace is undoubtedly the reason why David's faith prevailed. This is the point made by the writer as he arranges the scenes at the end of 1 Samuel. Whereas the decisive factor in Saul's failed kingship was his reliance on strength, skill, and cunning, David's kingship would rest on a different foundation altogether. David was to learn that for all his prodigious ability, his self-reliant plans had led him to the brink of eternal ruin, so that his true and only hope lay in the grace of his saving God.

SEND HIM BACK!

This venture into Philistia represents the most spiritually dangerous period of David's life. David had crossed the line, violating his faith in God, when he passed over from Israel into the sanctuary of Philistia. Yet while his faith had failed, it had not died. We see this in David's sixteen-month campaign against Israel's enemies, during which he refused to act as an enemy of God's people even though he had sought succor in the refuge of Israel's enemies. David had not apostatized. He had not forsaken trust in the Lord. But David had failed nonetheless. Saul's persecution had overthrown him, so that if David's flight to Philistia had not disqualified him for Israel's kingship, it had brought him to within a razor's edge of doing so. All David had left was the grace of God to deliver him. The events of this chapter and those to come show that God's grace is enough. The grace of God, if that is all we have, is enough to deliver us from evil—the world's evil and our own—and lead us into salvation.

Ironically, when God was pleased to deliver his wayward servant from the vise into which he had stuck his head, it was the Philistines whom the Lord used as the instrument for saving David from the Philistines. To see this, we return to the muster at Aphek: "As the lords of the Philistines were passing on by hundreds and by thousands, and David and his men were passing on in the rear with Achish, the commanders of the Philistines said, 'What are these Hebrews doing here?'" (1 Sam. 29:2–3).

The Philistine nation was ruled by the lords of its five chief cities, of whom Achish was one. As the various lords with their forces arrived at the muster, they were aghast to see Israelite troops present. Achish thought he could explain this easily enough, but his answer proved more troubling yet: "Is this not David, the servant of Saul, king of Israel, who has been with me now for days and years, and since he deserted to me I have found no fault in him to this day" (1 Sam. 29:3). These Israelites were mercenaries, he explained, and they had proved to be reliable in his service. We see here that David's duplicity had been wholly successful in duping Achish, who believed that David had betrayed his people and left himself no choice but to throw in his lot with the Philistines.

The other Philistines were not so easily persuaded, however, and they pressed their argument with anger at Achish. Their first argument consisted of an appeal to prudence: "Send that man back, that he may return to the place to which you have assigned him. He shall not go down with us to battle, lest in the battle he become an adversary to us. For how could this fellow reconcile himself to his lord? Would it not be with the heads of the men here?" (1 Sam. 29:4). A number of commentators suggest that, based on the evidence, the Philistine lords had correctly divined David's intent. The last thing they wanted as they launched into battle with Israel was an armed band of Israelites to their rear.

In addition to the argument from prudence, the Philistine leaders argued from history: "Is not this David, of whom they sing to one another in dances, 'Saul has struck down his thousands, and David his ten thousands'?" (1 Sam. 29:5). This persistent theme song to David's military glory, struck up in earlier days by the adoring women of Israel, had caused David more trouble than it was worth. It was Saul's hearing these lyrics that had first turned his heart in envy against his faithful servant. The Philistine commanders were irate that Achish could possibly be so naive as to think it safe to include David—*the* David—in the order of battle for their invasion of Israel.

The Philistine lords correctly assessed the situation with regard to David. If they had had Bibles, they could have provided numerous proof texts for their arguments, starting in Genesis chapter 3. Why is there always an incompatibility between God's people and the world? The main reason is that God has willed it to be so. When Adam and Eve cast our race into the fall by their disobedience to God's command, the Lord responded with a series of curses on all the participants: the serpent, the woman, and the man. The purposes of these curses were both penal and redemptive. In particular, God cursed the serpent, behind which stood Satan, with these words: "I will put enmity between you and the woman, and between your offspring and her offspring; he shall bruise your head, and you shall bruise his heel" (Gen. 3:15).

This foundational promise of our salvation, known by theologians as the *protoevangelion*, or "first gospel," establishes two priorities. The first is hostility between the woman and her offspring and Satan and his offspring. This refers to the line of believing children who would come from Adam and Eve and the line of the unbelieving, worldly people who would follow in the sinful ways of the devil. These two lines appear in the very next chapter, Genesis 4, when unbelieving Cain so resented God's favor for his believing brother, Abel, that he slew him in anger. The second gospel priority was that a particular offspring of Eve would be born to overthrow the reign of Satan and sin. "He shall bruise your head," God promised the serpent, "and you shall bruise his heel" (Gen. 3:15). Satan struck his blow against Jesus Christ when he arranged his torturous death on the cross. In the process, however, Jesus crushed the head of Satan, casting down his rule over Christ's people by paying the penalty for their sins in his own blood.

What the Philistine lords sensed, and what David should have known from his Bible, is that these two priorities necessarily go together. Those who belong to the Savior so as to be forgiven and justified with God are also people who experience the hostility of the unbelieving world and who thus cannot successfully collaborate with the ungodly. Jesus told his disciples: "If you were of the world, the world would love you as its own; but because you are not of the world, but I chose you out of the world, therefore the world hates you" (John 15:19). A David cannot ultimately march in the ranks of the Philistines because of a God-established enmity between the two.

David's example in this chapter shows that this enmity between God's people and the world is established partly for the protection of believers. The world's pleasures and treasures are tangible to our senses, whereas the blessings of heaven are invisible apart from faith (2 Cor. 5:7). Therefore, lest God's people be so foolish as to cultivate collaboration with worldly powers, God has placed an enmity in the hearts of the world toward his people. While David could comfortably endure his alliance with the Philistines, the Philistine commanders looked upon a servant of the Lord with a God-ordained hostility, so that they objected, "What are these Hebrews doing here?" (1 Sam. 29:3). Christians who realize this biblical priority, along with the Bible's command for a moral and spiritual separation, if not always a physical separation (see Ex. 33:16), will be neither surprised nor dismayed by the hostility of the world but will recognize God's protective care over our eternal souls.

PRAISE OF THE UNGODLY

If the Philistine lords were hostile to David's presence, Achish could not say enough in David's defense. One of the ironies of this chapter is that almost half its content involves Achish defending David's loyalty, when in fact David has not been loyal to him at all!

After receiving the angry demands of his fellow rulers, "Achish called David and said to him, 'As the LORD lives, you have been honest, and to me it seems right that you should march out and in with me in the campaign. For I have found nothing wrong in you from the day of your coming to me to this day. Nevertheless, the lords do not approve of you. So go back now; and go peaceably, that you may not displease the lords of the Philistines'" (1 Sam. 29:6–7). We would think that these words represented to David his deliverance from a dire situation, namely, marching with the Philistine army in battle against Israel. How surprising it is, then, to hear David's indignant objection: "But what have I done? What have you found in your servant from the day I entered your service until now, that I may not go and fight against the enemies of my lord the king?" (29:8). Apologetically, Achish answered David, "I know that you are as blameless in my sight as an angel of God. Nevertheless, the commanders of the Philistines have said, 'He shall not go up with us to the battle.' Now then rise early in the morning with the servants of your lord who came with you, and start early in the morning, and depart as soon as you have light" (29:9–10). Achish was sorry that David was so unfairly denied the opportunity to march against his own people, agreeing that David had earned the privilege. Nonetheless, the Philistine lords had spoken, and there was nothing else to be done. The chapter thus concludes: "So David set out with his men early in the morning to return to the land of the Philistines. But the Philistines went up to Jezreel" (29:11).

What was David doing? There are two schools of thought. One is that David was merely carrying forward his false loyalty to its necessary end, lest his duplicity be suspected. Matthew Henry expresses this view, writing, "He seemed anxious to serve him when he was at this juncture really anxious to leave him, but he was not willing that Achish should know that he was."[2]

The other view of David's objection is that the Philistine lords had accurately perceived David's true intent, namely, to turn on them in the heat of battle so as to strike a decisive blow for Israel. Clues of this intention may be gleaned from David's conversation. Notice how taken in Achish was by David, swearing by David's God (1 Sam. 29:6) and declaring David as "blameless in my sight as an angel of God" (29:9). David had apparently been emboldened by Achish's naiveté so that he spoke in language that was capable of multiple meanings. He expressed his zeal to "go and fight against the enemies of my lord the king" (29:8). Achish assumed that David was referring to him as the king and Israel as his enemies, whereas David may well have been speaking in deceptive language designed to justify himself in all events. The language "my lord the king" was David's habitual designation for King Saul (see 24:8; 26:19), and the title that would be used of David himself on countless occasions after he assumed the throne of Israel. This interpretation of David's words is certainly consistent with the brazenness with which David had lied to and deceived Achish from virtually the moment he arrived. If this understanding is correct, then David was sincerely trying to overturn the order of the Philistine lords, so that he might put into action his desperate plan to redeem himself and rescue Israel by means of a sneak attack from within the Philistine ranks.

How may we assess this concluding section of the chapter? First, we should note that praise from unbelievers is often commendable. The conduct of God's people should be such as to earn the honest approval of even worldly leaders, neighbors, and coworkers. Henry writes: "God's people should behave themselves always so inoffensively as is possible to get the good word of all they have dealings with; and it is a debt we owe to those who have acquitted themselves well to give them the praise of it."[3]

2. Matthew Henry, *Commentary on the Whole Bible*, 6 vols. (Peabody, MA: Hendrickson, 1992), 2:341.
3. Ibid.

The problem in this case is that Achish praised David not because of services well rendered and honestly presented but because of David's success in deceiving his Philistine lord as to his actual behavior! David was like an employee who gained promotion not through honest work and achievement but through the falsification of reports and the stealing of credit from others. In this respect, Achish's praise merely shows how deeply David had compromised himself by seeking a salvation according to his own wit and wisdom. The Bible commands God's people to embody candor and honesty, especially when dealing with people who have a right to expect integrity from us: "Let your 'yes' be yes and your 'no' be no," says James 5:12. The only reason Achish praised David was that the Philistine thought David had betrayed his own people, that he was wickedly serving as a piratical traitor in raiding the people of Israel, and that he therefore could never go home and was stuck in his service to the king of Gath. In other words, David's praise from Achish resulted from his dishonest manipulations and from Achish's approval of the wickedness that he thought David was performing. Praise like this is not the commendation that gains approval from God.

Sadly, David's approach to gaining the praise of the world is one that many professing believers adopt today. They try to become as much like the world as possible without ultimately renouncing their faith in Jesus Christ. In this respect, we see that the hostile Philistine lords show better judgment than Achish, who comes across as a weakling and a fool. The other Philistine lords looked on David and his followers and objected, "What are these Hebrews doing here?" (1 Sam. 29:3). They did not esteem a believer like David merely because he wore Philistine colors, and they did not trust a man who pretended to be a Philistine though in heart still an Israelite. Alexander Maclaren writes of this kind of compromised follower of Christ: "Do you think that the world respects that type of Christian, or regards his religion as the kind of thing to be admired? No; the question that they fling at such people is the question which David was humiliated by having pitched at his head—'What do these Hebrews here?' 'Let them go back to their mountains. This is no place for *them*.' The world respects an out-and-out Christian; but neither God nor the world respects an inconsistent one."[4]

4. Alexander Maclaren, *Expositions of Holy Scripture*, 17 vols. (Grand Rapids: Baker, 1982), 2:382–83.

Second, we note that, once again, David is saved by the intervening grace of God. We can imagine him frustrated as he departs from Aphek, taking his armed band away from the decisive battle of that generation. How difficult it is for believers to leave behind their worldly-wise cunning in order to wait on the Lord in obedience to his Word! This is a lesson that virtually all believers find difficult to learn, but that God is determined to teach us through many trials and gracious deliverances.

What would have happened, we wonder, if the Lord had permitted David to pursue what seems to have been his plan on this occasion? Would David have succeeded, marching in the Philistine ranks to the battle lines opposed to Saul? How would he and his men have reacted when they looked across the plain and saw their neighbors, their cousins, and the banners of Israel waving in the "enemy" host? It is possible, especially for a man as gifted and charismatic as David, that he could have pulled the strategy off, striking into the Philistines' backs at the decisive moment of the battle and saving the day for themselves and for God's people. But how great the risks were and how serious the repercussions even in success! What foreign king would ever trust such a David, when he became king, and how could his followers ever be sure what their leader really meant when he spoke with such multishaded words and displayed such practiced deceit? Moreover, what excesses might David turn to next if he were to succeed in so reckless and precarious a plan as the one he hatched in Philistia? The Lord's opinion of David's stratagem may be gleaned by the divine veto of providence: God saved David not only from the Philistines but also from himself by means of the suspicious Philistine lords. It will be interesting, when we view our own lives from the perspective of heaven, to discover how many of the Lord's interventions we will have to thank him for—interventions that frustrate us now but are actually saving us from our folly and unbelief. David may have appeared as blameless as an angel to Achish, but his conduct did not stand up well in the actual presence of the angels of God.

In his grace, God delivered David from his folly and his enemies. One result of David's venture into worldliness, however, is that he was absent from the great battle of his people in that generation. To be sure, the blame for this absence largely rests on King Saul for driving David out of Israel. Yet David, by consulting his own counsel instead of God's Word and by stirring up his own cunning instead of appealing to God in prayer, pursued a course of action that rendered him useless in the day of his people's need.

The same is true today of many Christians who have adopted the ways of worldliness rather than pursuing the path of godliness set forth in Scripture, who live as close as possible to the world instead of as close as possible to God. Many such people will be saved in the end, through a weak yet nonetheless saving faith in Jesus Christ. But in the battle for truth and godliness in our generation, in the work of the gospel for the saving of souls, they will have contributed virtually nothing. Paul writes that in the day of Christ's coming, "each one's work will become manifest, for the Day will disclose it." He who builds his life on the rock of God's Word and has pursued a life of faithful, godly ministry will find his work to have survived, and "he will receive a reward" (1 Cor. 3:13–14). But others, who lived in constant compromise with the world, will find their life's contribution burned up as dross, however impressive it may have seemed to worldly eyes. Of such a person, Paul writes, "he himself will be saved, but only as one escaping through the flames" (1 Cor. 3:15 NIV). So it was for David as his band marched away from the battle back to his base at Ziklag.

No Guilt in Him

I have said that in Philistia David's actions do not typify the person and work of Jesus Christ. Yet in the words of Achish to David, we hear an advance echo of words that would be said to Jesus in the trial before his crucifixion. Achish said to David, "I have found nothing wrong in you from the day of your coming to me to this day" (1 Sam. 29:6). In the light of God's revelation, those words regarding David are proved to be false. If the world should say the same of us, the light of truth will reveal them to be false as well. But in his trial before Pontius Pilate, nearly the identical words were said of Jesus Christ. Pilate declared of Jesus: "Behold, I did not find this man guilty of any of your charges against him" (Luke 23:14). Having examined Jesus thoroughly, Pilate rendered a verdict that stands up in the courts of angels and of God: "I find no guilt in him" (John 18:38).

It is only because these words, falsely spoken to David, were true of Jesus Christ, and because Jesus did not save himself from the penalty of death that our sins deserve, that we like David have a Savior to deliver us from evil.

The great difference between David and Saul, and the difference between Christians today and the unbelieving world, is not that we are found worthy of praise, with no guilt or folly on our record. The difference is that we have embraced by faith the Savior who alone is worthy of this praise, and who by his sacrificial death has freed us not only from the condemnation of men but also from the condemnation of God, so that we may serve him in the battle for this age and afterward enter into eternal life. Jesus said, "Whoever hears my word and believes him who sent me has eternal life. He does not come into judgment, but has passed from death to life" (John 5:24).

42

STRENGTHENED IN THE LORD

1 Samuel 30:1–31

David was greatly distressed, for the people spoke of stoning him, because all the people were bitter in soul, each for his sons and daughters. But David strengthened himself in the LORD his God. (1 Sam. 30:6)

Jacob DeShazer was born into a Christian family but grew up as a rebel to his parents' faith. In 1942, having enlisted in the Air Force, Jacob was on board the USS *Hornet* in the Pacific Ocean preparing for what history would remember as the famous Doolittle Raid. Named for its commander, Lieutenant Colonel James Doolittle, this raid would be America's first reprisal for the Japanese attack on Pearl Harbor. The Easter service held on the aircraft carrier's deck was packed with airmen, but DeShazer had no interest. Two weeks later, Jacob took off with his squadron and as bombardier made sure that his plane's bombs hit their targets in the city of Nagoya, Japan.

The Doolittle raid was a one-way trip, with the plan calling for the crews to bail out of their planes over neutral China. Two of the bombers strayed over Japanese-held territory, however, including DeShazer's, and Jacob was taken into custody as a prisoner of war.

The next three years would be hellish for DeShazer and his friends. They were tortured into making confessions and held for months in solitary confinement. Several were publicly executed and the rest held as war criminals. Jacob kept himself going by cultivating an intense hatred of his Japanese captors. In time, the few surviving airmen were transferred to a military prison in China and provided with basic amenities, including a single Bible to read. When it came Jacob's turn to possess the Bible, he read it straight through, starting in Genesis, seeing the Old Testament prophecies confirmed in the New Testament portrait of Jesus. In his reading of Romans 10:9, he received grace from God to believe, confessed his sins, and knew the joy of God's forgiveness. As Paul had written, DeShazer called upon the name of the Lord and was saved. He later wrote: "How my heart rejoiced in my newness of spiritual life, even though my body was suffering so terribly from the physical beatings and lack of food."[1] In the lowest depth of agony, God had given life to Jacob DeShazer's soul.

Disaster at Ziklag

Jacob DeShazer was not the first person who needed to be brought low before his heart was opened to call on the Lord for salvation. A more famous example is the Old Testament's great hero, David. David had fled from the persecution of Israel's King Saul to seek refuge among the Philistines, an action that the Bible regards as going over to the ungodly (1 Sam. 27:2). To fit in among the wicked, David adopted a life of deceit as he secretly made war on Israel's enemies. His cunning came to an end when the Philistines gathered to invade Israel, forcing David to side openly with Israel's enemies or turn traitor against his new friends. Just when David seemed trapped, God delivered him by means of the suspicious Philistine lords, who objected to having an Israelite contingent in their army. Chapter 29 concludes with David still plotting his designs, reluctantly marching away from the scene of action to his base in the southern desert.

Chapter 30 picks up at the end of David's and his men's sixty-mile march to Ziklag. During the three-day journey their hearts must have been lifted at the thought of relaxation after so much stress, as well as joyful reunions with wives

1. Quoted in Don Stephens, *War and Grace: Short Biographies from the World Wars* (Darlington, UK: Evangelical Press, 2005), 135–44.

and children. As the band drew near, however, they may have been alarmed at the sight of smoke on the horizon; we can easily imagine the ranks breaking and men racing forward to their homes. The sight that greeted them was the stuff of nightmares: "The Amalekites had made a raid against the Negeb and against Ziklag. They had overcome Ziklag and burned it with fire and taken captive the women and all who were in it, both small and great. . . . And when David and his men came to the city, they found it burned with fire, and their wives and sons and daughters taken captive" (1 Sam. 30:1–3). After all the deprivations of so many years—month after month of harassment, flight, and danger—David had now reached the end of his rope. The entire city was empty, Amalekite raiders' having seized the Israelites' wives and children, no doubt to be sold into slavery under the most desperate conditions. Among the missing were David's two wives, Ahinoam and Abigail (30:5). It was just too much to face, and "David and the people who were with him raised their voices and wept until they had no more strength to weep" (30:4).

This blow not only was too much for David to bear, but was also the last straw for his weary men. They had joined David because of their own troubles with Saul, but also because of the promise of blessing attached to the young hero. There had been high moments, but their hearts could no longer bear the bitterness of affliction to which David had led them. Enough was enough, and the men now vented their anger at their leader: "David was greatly distressed, for the people spoke of stoning him, because all the people were bitter in soul, each for his sons and daughters" (1 Sam. 30:6).

This was rock-bottom for David. He was separated from the people of Israel and the ordinances of saving religion. His desperate plans to buy time had bought disaster instead. The wives in which he had taken comfort were suffering unknown horrors because of David's failure, and his men, having lost children as well as wives, were done with following him. David largely deserved their scorn, having incredibly left his base completely unguarded while he marched off with the Philistines, leaving the Amalekite raiders he had provoked for sixteen months free to strike and pillage. Dale Ralph Davis comments:

> Here is a sobering and disturbing picture for God's people. Are there not times when you think it cannot get any worse? And 1 Samuel 30 says, Yes, it can. There are times when you conclude that your present trouble is the last

straw; you simply cannot take any more. Then comes Ziklag, the last straw after the last straw.[2]

We can think of at least two reasons why David suffered so greatly at Ziklag. The first was that he was backslidden with respect to his faith, so that all his woes were ultimately of his own making. Second, however, we know that God was preparing David for a singularly important leadership role, and thus was determined to gain David's attention and draw his heart back to trusting obedience.

What was David to do in this shocking situation, with his men literally gathering stones to put an end to his life and rule? From a leadership perspective, the best thing that a doubted leader can do is simply to lead. When I was a lieutenant in the army, a story was told of a tank company that mutinied during the Vietnam war because of fatigue and despair. Their colonel arrived, relieving the captain of his command and ordering the soldiers to follow him in an attack on the enemy. The angry soldiers asked why the colonel thought they would follow him. He answered, "Because I'm the colonel, and the food, ammunition, and artillery support go where I go!" One by one, the tanks began following the colonel and obedience was restored. David did something similar when he summoned the high priest, Abiathar, and asked him to inquire of the Lord. If the men of David's band wanted to get their wives and children back, they needed God's help, and God revealed himself only to his anointed servant, David.

Before mastering his men, however, David had to master himself. His long bout of self-reliance had led him to the brink of death, so it was time to abandon his program of self-salvation. At this moment of utter desperation, David did the one thing most needed: "David strengthened himself in the LORD his God" (1 Sam. 30:6). If David had previously appealed to his own resources, with virtually no prayer and no recourse to God's Word, he now turned from his own strength and applied himself to the Lord. When we read that David "strengthened himself in the LORD his God," this does not mean that he performed some ritual that would supposedly provide him with divine aid, nor that the emotional intensity of

2. Dale Ralph Davis, *1 Samuel: Looking on the Heart* (Fearn, Ross-shire, UK: Christian Focus, 2000), 250–51.

the situation placed him on a higher spiritual plane, but rather that by faith alone he laid hold of the Lord and his salvation promises.

What does it mean to "strengthen yourself" in God? We get a clue from the occasion earlier in 1 Samuel when Jonathan came to David in his distress and "strengthened his hand in God" (1 Sam. 23:16). Jonathan did this by reminding David of God's promise to elevate him to the throne, so that even Saul knew he could not succeed against David (23:17). This incident suggests that now at Ziklag, lacking Jonathan's help, David reminded himself of God's promises. No doubt he also recalled the Lord's prior help in saving him and reflected on God's nature, including his omnipotence, faithfulness, and sovereignty. Adding all these attributes together, David recovered from his fear and distress by thinking about God and personally appealing to God for salvation. Whereas Saul in his distress had sought comfort from an occult witch, receiving God's judgment of death (1 Sam. 28), David turned for strength to the Lord and received new life.

Another example of a believer's turning to God for strength is the Scottish pastor Andrew Bonar, who noted in his diary entry for October 15, 1864 that he had been meditating on Nahum 1:7, "The LORD is good, a stronghold in the day of trouble; he knows those who take refuge in him" (RSV). Later in the day, Bonar suffered the death of his dearly beloved wife, Isabella, and he remembered the Bible verse he had studied. He commented, "Little did I think how I would need it half an hour after." For years afterward, Bonar would record Nahum 1:7 in his diary record for October 15. Why? Because in his grief for the loss of his wife, he was strengthening himself in the Lord with the Word of God.[3]

A further example of turning to God for strength comes from the pioneering missionary to Africa, David Livingstone. On occasions when Livingstone felt himself giving in to fear, he would remember Jesus' words, "Go ye therefore, and teach all nations, baptizing them in the name of the Father, and of the Son, and of the Holy Ghost: teaching them to observe all things whatsoever I have commanded you: and, lo, I am with you alway, even unto the end of the world" (Matt. 28:19–20 KJV). Remembering that Christ had sent him with the gospel, Livingstone strengthened his heart in the knowledge that Christ would protect him.[4]

3. Ibid., 254.
4. William G. Blaikie, *Expository Lectures on the Book of First Samuel* (1887; repr., Birmingham, AL: Solid Ground, 2005), 421–22.

How are we to follow these examples, strengthening ourselves in the Lord in times of need? Roger Ellsworth comments:

> To strengthen ourselves in God means we remind ourselves of what Scripture says about God and his promises, and we bring those truths to bear on the situation. Every trial causes opposing voices to ring in the ears of the child of God. One is the voice of our circumstances, telling us that our situation is hopeless. The other is the voice of faith, telling us that our God is sufficient for the trial.[5]

Following God's Word

From the moment of his return to faith in the Lord, David was a changed man. In the rest of the chapter, David shows us what to do when we have turned our hearts to God, whether for the first or the hundred-and-first time. Having renewed his faith in the Lord and received the strength that comes from God, David immediately consulted God's Word for guidance: "David inquired of the Lord, 'Shall I pursue after this band? Shall I overtake them?' He answered him, 'Pursue, for you shall surely overtake and shall surely rescue'" (1 Sam. 30:8). David received this revelation through the Urim kept in the high priest's ephod, a special provision that God had made for Israel's leaders. It is the first time we read of David's seeking God's Word since he entered Philistia, and it marks the turning point in this phase of his life. No longer charting his own weaving course, David can once again plot the straight line of God's revealed will.

There was no way to know where the raiding Amalekites had gone, since they were a nomadic people. So God told David to go forward as best he could, in the same way that God will often call believers today to obey him without a clear end in sight. David vigorously applied himself to obedience: "So David set out, and the six hundred men who were with him, and they came to the brook Besor, where those who were left behind stayed. But David pursued, he and four hundred men" (1 Sam. 30:9–10). Here David sets an example for new believers as well as those repenting from backsliding. A critic might say that David was heading into a trackless desert with remarkably

5. Roger Ellsworth, *The Shepherd King: Learning from the Life of David* (Darlington, UK: Evangelical Press, 1998), 119.

poor odds of ever finding the Amalekites. David would reply that obeying God's clear commands was both his duty and his hope.

There are at least two reasons why obeying God's Word works out well in our lives. The first is that God's commands are good, so that by obeying the Scriptures we will be acting in ways that benefit ourselves and others. The second reason why obeying God's commands turns out well is that God sovereignly blesses the obedience of his people. Not only does the Bible itself "work," but God makes it work and adds his special blessing to those who trust him and obey his Word. This will be true for believers today, just as it was true for David: God provides all that is needed to preserve and sustain his faithful people.

In David's case, God's providential blessing came in the form of an Egyptian servant who had been abandoned in the desert by his Amalekite master. David's men found him and refreshed the Egyptian with food and drink (1 Sam. 30:11–12). When they questioned the man, they learned that the Amalekites had been raiding into Judah and the "Negeb of Caleb," and they had also "burned Ziklag with fire" (30:14). David asked whether the man would lead him to the Amalekites and he agreed, provided that David did not harm or betray him (30:15). Armed with this ideal reconnaissance, David was able to surprise his enemies, who were so secure in their false confidence that they were "eating and drinking and dancing," without having set a watch (30:16):

> David struck them down from twilight until the evening of the next day, and not a man of them escaped, except four hundred young men, who mounted camels and fled. David recovered all that the Amalekites had taken, and David rescued his two wives. Nothing was missing, whether small or great, sons or daughters, spoil or anything that had been taken. David brought back all. (30:17–19)

It is evident that David could never have found his enemies if God had not provided the Egyptian servant to lead him. Likewise, by trusting in God's Word, we will learn the truth of Paul's promise: "My God will supply every need of yours according to his riches in glory in Christ Jesus" (Phil. 4:19). The same God who had brought David low in order to restore his heart was fully capable of restoring to David all he had lost.

Like David, when we have turned our hearts to the Lord, we should study his Word and aggressively put into practice all that God commands. Jacob

DeShazer discovered this truth immediately after trusting Christ as his Savior. Up to this time, DeShazer had been the most recalcitrant prisoner, burning with a hatred for the Japanese. But he learned in the Bible that Jesus wanted him to forgive as he had been forgiven. That very day, a prison guard whom DeShazer often antagonized trapped his foot in a doorway and physically abused him. Instead of responding with his typical venom, Jacob remembered Christ's Word and did not revile his tormentor. On subsequent days he greeted the guard with kindness, which led to conversations and ultimately to a kind of friendship. In coming months, the once-brutal guard went so far as to sneak food to the malnourished DeShazer, possibly saving his life. The prisoner concluded that God not only was testing him for obedience but was also showing him how unexpected blessings arise from obedience to God's revealed Word.[6]

Grace Recovered

The events that followed David's victory showed that by turning back to the Lord, he recovered not only his obedience but also his wisdom and grace. On the way out to pursue the Amalekites, a third of David's force, two hundred men, had been unable to continue in the harsh desert climate. These two hundred stayed behind to guard David's supplies along the river Besor (1 Sam. 30:10). After the victory, some of the four hundred who had continued to the end objected to the two hundred's sharing in the spoils: "Then all the wicked and worthless fellows among the men who had gone with David said, 'Because they did not go with us, we will not give them any of the spoil that we have recovered, except that each man may lead away his wife and children, and depart'" (30:22). David disagreed, saying: "'You shall not do so, my brothers, with what the Lord has given us. He has preserved us and given into our hand the band that came against us. Who would listen to you in this matter? For as his share is who goes down into the battle, so shall his share be who stays by the baggage. They shall share alike'" (30:23–24).

David's opposition to the scoundrels' plan was based on two points. The first was the solidarity that is fundamental to believers as God's covenant

6. Stephens, *War and Grace*, 144–45.

people. Not all had run the same risks or performed the same tasks, but all had contributed in their own way and therefore ought to share: "For as his share is who goes down into the battle, so shall his share be who stays by the baggage." This emphasis echoes the apostle Paul's teaching on the unity of Christians as the body of Christ: "The eye cannot say to the hand, 'I have no need of you,' nor again the head to the feet, 'I have no need of you.' On the contrary, the parts of the body that seem to be weaker are indispensable . . . If one member suffers, all suffer together; if one member is honored, all rejoice together" (1 Cor. 12:21–26). Realizing this, churches today should regard those who pray for missions just as highly as those who go out on the mission field. Instead of merely relying on the gifts of effective preachers, Christians should commit themselves to praying for the ministry of the Word and should be zealous in inviting nonbelievers to come and hear the gospel that is proclaimed.

Second, and even more significantly, David's attitude toward the victory and the spoils was marked by his gratitude for God's grace. David's key statement is seen in verse 23: "You shall not do so, my brothers, with what the Lord has given us. He has preserved us and given into our hand that band that came against us." Their recovered spoils, along with the Amalekite property, did not come to David's band by his or anyone else's clever scheming. The key reality is seen in David's words: "what the Lord has given us." "All was of grace as far as David was concerned. The victory was not what he and his men had achieved, but what God had given. Because they had been the recipients of God's grace in battle, they must now demonstrate that grace to those who stayed behind."[7]

Not only has grace infected David's reasoning—a sure sign that one has turned to the Lord in true faith—but also his conduct as a leader is now marked by grace. A leader inspires confidence when his judgments reflect the precepts and principles of God's Word. Notice as well the mildness with which David addressed the men described in Scripture as "wicked and worthless" (1 Sam. 30:22). He did not berate or insult them, but graciously addressed them as "my brothers" (30:23), thus appealing to their best nature. An example of how the New Testament commends David's example to Christian leaders today is seen in Paul's advice to young pastors: "Do not

7. Ellsworth, *The Shepherd King*, 121.

rebuke an older man but encourage him as you would a father, younger men as brothers, older women as mothers, younger women as sisters, in all purity" (1 Tim. 5:1–2).

How different David was, once restored to faith in God, from both the pagan Philistines and tyrannical King Saul. John Woodhouse comments: "David was a peacemaker among his people. The authority that David was beginning to assume was not that of a tyrant. This people, even these troublesome ones, were his 'brothers.'"[8] So agreeable was David's policy that in later years it formed the basis of a standing rule under his reign (1 Sam. 30:25). Matthew Henry suggests David's gracious conduct as a fixed rule for all Christian leaders: "Superiors often lose their authority by haughtiness, but seldom by courtesy and condescension."[9]

Generous Giving

The chapter concludes with a depiction of one additional result of David's return to the Lord in faith: his generosity in giving gifts to those in need: "When David came to Ziklag, he sent part of the spoil to his friends, the elders of Judah, saying, 'Here is a present for you from the spoil of the enemies of the Lord'" (1 Sam. 30:26).

While each of David's men recovered his family members and property, it seems that David reserved for himself most if not all of the Amalekite goods seized in the attack (see 1 Sam. 30:20). With these flocks and herds David made gifts to his fellow Jews. After sixteen months of self-imposed exile, in which David fended mainly for himself, his restoration to God has resulted in a restoration of his compassion and love for the people of God. The evidence of God's grace in our lives similarly ought to move us to consider what we can do for the church and for other people.

David's gifts went to "his friends, the elders of Judah, saying, 'Here is a present for you from the spoil of the enemies of the Lord'" (1 Sam. 30:26). Some commentators see this gift as a crass political maneuver to strip support from Saul or an example of cronyism, since the Bible cites David's friends as the recipients. Undoubtedly, David was remembering God's

---

8. John Woodhouse, *1 Samuel: Looking for a Leader* (Wheaton, IL: Crossway, 2008), 539.
9. Matthew Henry, *Commentary on the Whole Bible*, 6 vols. (Peabody, MA: Hendrickson, 1992), 2:345.

anointing of him as Israel's true king and was acting in response to that calling. It is most likely that David did not name the elders because they were his friends, but to the contrary David named them friends because they were the elders of God's people. Robert Bergen comments: "As would be expected of the Lord's anointed, David had fought the Lord's enemies. As would be expected of the Lord's anointed, he was now bringing blessing to the Lord's people."[10]

David had thus been liberated not only from his sin and the danger of his circumstances, but also from the soul-poisoning effects of living only for himself, instead putting his mind on the needs of God's people and kingdom. Since the cities cited as receiving gifts from David are all located in the southern region of Judah, where David had so long sought refuge from Saul (1 Sam. 30:27–31), David had probably been helped by them in his need, so that he thinks of their needs in his time of plenty. This is precisely how those who have come to God in faith should act toward one another.

Notice that, having lost everything through willful unbelief, David now has all that and more restored to him once he walks with God in faith. David's experience is mirrored in the lives of God's people in all times. Like David, whenever we turn away from the Lord, neglecting worship and God's Word, giving free rein to our sinful passions, our descent into misery and despair can be far swifter and steeper than we ever imagined. How far David had fallen while in Philistia, ending with the disaster at Ziklag! How far and how fast any Christian may fall if we harden our hearts to the Lord! But also like David, when we lay hold of the Lord in new or renewed faith, seeking and obeying God's Word, our progress in godliness and blessing can be surprisingly rapid. Many people, having turned to God in a living faith and attending diligently to faithful preaching and engaging in private devotion to God's Word and prayer, have seen their faith and godliness grow dramatically in a mere span of months, all by God's power. Turning to God in obedient faith, David not only gained many blessings for himself but was also made by God into a blessing for many other people.

10. Robert D. Bergen, *1, 2 Samuel*, New American Commentary (Nashville: Broadman & Holman, 1996), 280.

Gifts from the King

David in this passage points us toward Jesus Christ in a number of ways. As David strengthened himself in God, so also Jesus fortified himself in prayer as he prepared to take up the cross (John 17:1–5). Like David in his sweeping victory over the Amalekites, setting free the women and children of his people, so also Jesus has overthrown our strong captor and set us free from the domain of sin and judgment. In this battle, we have done even less to conquer than the men who stayed behind to guard David's baggage, yet Christ has graciously admitted us into his victory. Finally, as David took from his own share and gave to the needy in Judea, so also Jesus gave gifts to his church after his resurrection and ascension. Paul wrote: "When he ascended on high he led a host of captives, and he gave gifts to men" (Eph. 4:8, quoting Ps. 68:18). In that context, Paul cites Christ's gift of faithful spiritual leaders for God's people (Eph. 4:11–12). But Christ's greatest gift is eternal life, granted through faith by the power of the Holy Spirit, whom Christ has sent from heaven (cf. Gal. 3:14). In both the ancient world and today, kings give gifts to their people when they are crowned, and Jesus' most precious gift is the salvation he purchased with his own precious blood (1 Peter 1:18–19), a salvation that any sinner can receive through simple faith.

This is what Jacob DeShazer discovered when he surrendered his life to Jesus in his prison cell. He learned that Christ wanted him to give gifts to those he had formerly hated. The first was the gift of his prayers, as he spent much of his time in his cell praying for the salvation of his guards and for the Japanese people as a whole. Then, when the war ended, Jacob enrolled in a Bible college to prepare himself to return to Japan as a missionary, enabling him to give the best of all gifts: a witness to the gospel of Jesus Christ, so that others could receive God's gift of eternal life through faith in him. In the years to come, DeShazer would start a church in Nagoya, the city he had bombed just a few years earlier, and he wrote a tract describing his conversion that was greatly used to lead Japanese people to faith in Christ. One man who picked up the tract and believed in Jesus was Mitsuo Fuchida, the Japanese air commander who had led the air raid against Pearl Harbor, and who had fallen into despair after his nation's defeat. DeShazer and Fuchida went on to hold evangelistic meetings together, taking the blessings that

God had graciously given to them in Christ and giving the gospel message of salvation to many others who believed and were saved.[11]

In giving gifts to his people out of the treasure of his own spoils, David foreshadows Christ's graciousness as our true King. Like David with his followers, Jesus calls us his "friends" (John 15:15) and pledges to meet all our needs, especially our need of forgiveness and eternal life. "The good shepherd lays down his life for the sheep," Jesus said (10:11). Most marvelously, Christ's gospel gift is such that when we give it to others, we do not lose it but possess it more strongly and richly for ourselves. What an incentive for us all to strengthen ourselves in the Lord and start following his Word in renewed faith. Who can tell what God will do in and through any of us if we yield ourselves unreservedly to Jesus?

11. Stephens, *War and Grace*, 135–44.

43

Saul's Tragic End

1 Samuel 31:1–13

*Now the Philistines fought against Israel, and the men of Israel
fled before the Philistines and fell slain on Mount Gilboa. And
the Philistines overtook Saul and his sons, and the Philistines
struck down Jonathan and Abinadab and Malchi-shua, the sons
of Saul. (1 Sam. 31:1–2)*

In every life a primary theme can be discerned. The life of my
father, a thirty-year career army officer, was dominated by his
commitment to duty. There were, of course, many other things
that could be said of him, but the primary factor in his decisions was always
his sense of duty. For other men, the dominant theme is personal ambition,
so that the deciding factor in their actions is what will best advance their
own interests. In the lives of many corporate titans, it seems that a hunger
for wealth, power, or achievement dominate; and according to the tabloid
covers, the main theme in the lives of movie stars and singers is a craving
for attention and pleasure.

Christians will also have a dominant theme to their lives. The Bible provides appropriate virtues as righteousness, peace, and joy in the Holy Spirit
(Rom. 14:17), or faith, hope, and love (1 Cor. 13:13). If we were to summarize

David's life, we might say that his dominant theme was faith, just as Paul's was gospel passion and Peter's was love for Jesus Christ.

As we come to the end of the Bible's account of Israel's King Saul, and to the end of Saul's life, it is not hard to see that the dominant theme of his life was his hard-hearted impenitence. The prophet Isaiah lists repentance coupled with faith as the key to receiving God's blessing: "Let the wicked forsake his way, and the unrighteous man his thoughts; let him return to the LORD, that he may have compassion on him, and to our God, for he will abundantly pardon" (Isa. 55:7). Sadly, Saul's life was a bitter record of God's way forsaken and God's pardon forfeited by his refusal to repent. Alexander Maclaren summarizes: "There is no sign that he ever sought to cultivate his moral character . . . , and a long course of indulgence in self-will developed cruelty, gloomy suspicion, and passionate anger, and left him the victim and slave of his own causeless hate."[1] There could be only one end for such a life as Saul's, an end as tragic as it is unnecessary for those who have witnessed the grace and power of God.

The Bitter End of King Saul

The writer of 1 Samuel has been working himself up to tell the story of Saul's final defeat since chapter 28. However expected it may be, the rout of Israel's army at Mount Gilboa was a national disaster of monumental proportions, rivaling (and largely mirroring) the terrible loss in the battle of Ebenezer two generations earlier (1 Sam. 4). Israel's armed might was broken, her leadership was slain, her land occupied, and her religion disgraced. Having told us of the Philistine invasion, along with God's promised judgment on Saul in this battle, the writer of 1 Samuel reverts to the story of David in chapters 29 and 30 before returning to Saul's tragic end in chapter 31. David's victory over the Amalekites in the south and Saul's defeat by the Philistines in the north took place virtually simultaneously, and we are intended to note the contrasts between them.

Once the writer focuses back on Saul's defeat, there is little for him to tell. Maneuvering north from their base at Aphek, the Philistines advanced southeast along the plain of the Valley of Jezreel, their chariots ranging

1. Alexander Maclaren, *Expositions of Holy Scripture*, 17 vols. (Grand Rapids: Baker, 1982), 2:403.

freely on the level ground of this traditional invasion route. According to verse 1, the Israelites "fled before the Philistines," and then sought to make a stand on the slopes of Mount Gilboa. There, the Philistine archers entered the fray, and many of the Israelites "fell slain" (1 Sam. 31:1). As the Israelites fell back, the retreat became a rout and their army was broken.

Once God had removed his aid from Saul, this was the inevitable end, given the decay of his regime and the might of the Philistines. This was the end that would have come to Saul many times in the past if God had not intervened. Now that God had decreed the time for Saul's judgment, spoken the previous night by the disturbed soul of the prophet Samuel (1 Sam. 28:19), and since his anointed successor David was far removed from the battlefield, there was nothing to stop the Philistines from sweeping over Saul's army. It was time for "Ichabod" to be pronounced over Saul's reign, since the glory of the Lord had long since departed (see 4:21–22).

Most tragic is the fact that Saul did not die alone in this battle, for "the Philistines overtook Saul and his sons, and the Philistines struck down Jonathan and Abinadab and Malchi-shua, the sons of Saul" (1 Sam. 31:2). This proves that the Israelite leaders did not shrink from the fight. We can especially imagine Jonathan, the God-honoring hero of so many battles, rallying Saul's troops and holding the line until he was finally felled by a Philistine arrow or sword. Jonathan's eulogy will be sung by David in 2 Samuel 1, but Dale Ralph Davis offers a brief obituary: "He remained a true friend to David and a faithful son of Saul. He surrendered his kingship to David (18:1–4); he sacrificed his life for Saul. In this hopeless fiasco Jonathan was nowhere else but in the place Yahweh had assigned to him—at the side of his father."[2]

The theme of Jonathan's life was faithfulness, and he shows us that a worthy life does not depend on circumstances. He lived in most dangerous times and suffered from a most thankless obligation to his mad father. Through it all, Jonathan's faithfulness to God, to his friends, and to his father allowed him to persevere with integrity, and to smell the roses of his life despite the many thorns. We tend to think that his death, along with the deaths of his lesser-known brothers, was the great tragedy of this battle, but Davis objects. "What is tragic," he asks, "about remaining faithfully in the calling

---

2. Dale Ralph Davis, *1 Samuel: Looking on the Heart* (Fearn, Ross-shire, UK: Christian Focus, 2000), 262.

God has assigned us?"[3] In the light of eternity, Jonathan's death was not so much tragic as glorious; through his faith in the Lord, Jonathan escaped from tragedy to enter into glory forever. Jonathan died while fulfilling his duty; he died a warrior's death and received a faithful servant's reward.

Not only does the account of Israel's defeat involve an inevitable and a tragic end, it climaxes with the bitter end for Saul: "The battle pressed hard against Saul, and the archers found him, and he was badly wounded by the archers" (1 Sam. 31:3). At this point, Saul realized that the end had indeed come. His sons were fallen and his army scattered. Saul was wounded as the Philistines drew near. He therefore turned to his armor-bearer and gave a final royal command: "Draw your sword, and thrust me through with it, lest these uncircumcised come and thrust me through, and mistreat me" (31:4). Saul's concern about a drawn-out, torturous, and disgraceful death was well founded, since this was a common practice among victorious pagans such as the Philistines. His armor-bearer, however, refused to slay the king, "for he feared greatly"; that is, like David he feared God and refused to slay the Lord's anointed. "Therefore Saul took his own sword and fell upon it," after which his armor-bearer fell on his sword "and died with him" (31:4–5).

Saul's suicide raises some questions. Most commentators consider it a simple act of self-murder. Herman Hoeksema states that "the suicide is not a brave man, but a wicked coward," who removes himself from this life "to open his eyes in hell."[4] We must soften this stance in the case of the mentally ill or those so seriously depressed that their reasoning is impaired, in which case something other than true suicide may have occurred. There are examples of believing Christians who struggled with depression and wrestled with urges to take their own lives, such as the great hymnist William Cowper, who was kept from this dreadful end by the ministry of his close friend John Newton.

Saul's suicide was not the result of an irrational impulse, however, but a calculated decision. From a worldly perspective, it was an understandable choice: humanly speaking, Saul had no chance of survival and the prospect of torture was real. This assumes that Saul had no other perspective; thus, his suicide is the last nail in the coffin of the faith he once professed.

3. Ibid.
4. Quoted in Gordon J. Keddie, *Dawn of a Kingdom: The Message of 1 Samuel* (Darlington, UK: Evangelical Press, 1988), 273.

Maclaren comments, "If Saul had had any faith in God, any submission, any repentance, he could not have finished a life of rebellion by a self-inflicted death, which was itself the very desperation of rebellion."[5]

Perhaps more troubling than what Saul *did* in that hour of despair is what Saul *did not do*. There is no cry to God for help. There is no appeal to heaven for mercy. We read nothing along the lines of the pleas that virtually fill David's psalms. Years earlier, on the night when Saul had sent ruffians to slay David in his house, David prayed, "Deliver me from my enemies, O my God; protect me from those who rise up against me; deliver me from those who work evil, and save me from bloodthirsty men" (Ps. 59:1–2). Now, with the Philistines circling in, Saul has no such prayers in his quiver. Thus, he dies as he had lived, in hardened self-will and without faith in God's salvation, not even crying out to the Lord with his dying breath. "All through his reign no hand had injured him but his own; and, as he lived, so he died, his own undoer and his own murderer."[6]

TRAGIC THEMES CONCLUDED

As we observe the tragic end of Saul, we can also note the calamitous end of the main themes that governed his life and times. Saul's kingship arose from Israel's demand to have "a king over us, that we also may be like all the nations" (1 Sam. 8:19–20). What the Israelites saw as a practical solution to their military predicament was denounced by God as idolatry. Israel had been created to be unique among the nations in that God was its sovereign. Yet the people wanted to be led into battle by a visibly impressive king, who would "go out before us and fight our battles" (8:20). The end result of this idolatry was the death of both the king they had desired and the army he led.

Israel's experience shows us what is always the end of idolatry. The greatest example is the destruction of Jerusalem in 587 b.c. and the Babylonian exile that followed. The prophet Jeremiah made it clear that this calamity resulted from the people's persistent chasing after idols (see Jer. 2:1–13). The end was the people's subjection into the hands of idol-worshipers. Since Israel was determined to serve idols, the Lord gave them over to live as slaves in a land of idols.

5. Maclaren, *Expositions of Holy Scripture*, 2:402.
6. Ibid.

So it was after Saul's death: "when the men of Israel who were on the other side of the valley and those beyond the Jordan saw that the men of Israel had fled and that Saul and his sons were dead, they abandoned their cities and fled. And the Philistines came and lived in them" (1 Sam. 31:7). So great was the disaster of this battle that the Israelites living in the fertile region behind Mount Gilboa, including the cities along the Jordan River and even on the eastern side, abandoned their land and fled. Therefore, the end of idolatry was the domination of their land and cities by the servants of idols.

A by-product of this disaster shows another tragic result of idolatry among God's people: the public disgrace of the Lord's name. The gospel of the Philistines would now be preached far and wide, declaring Dagon's supremacy over Yahweh. Here was the greater calamity of Israel's idolatry: the Lord's disgrace in the lives of his people. The head and armor of the Israelite king became the emblems of the Philistines' boasting, carrying them as "good news to the house of their idols and to the people" (1 Sam. 31:9).

This example supplies two reasons why Christians should refuse to worship and serve the idols of our day—false gods such as money, power, pride, and pleasure. The first reason is that our service to idols will conclude with the idols' power over our lives. Those who give themselves to sin in support of their idols find that they become unable to cease the sins, their hearts having been captured and ruled by the idols they foolishly serve.

Consider the case of young Aaron Burr, the grandson of Jonathan Edwards, in whose birth eight lines of gospel preachers converged. Gifted with a brilliant mind, Burr became proud in his thoughts and was consumed by an idolatrous desire for praise. During a revival meeting at Yale College, Burr felt moved by the Holy Spirit as the gospel was preached. After the sermon an invitation was given for those interested in professing their faith in Christ to meet in an adjoining room. Along with a great many other students, Burr got up from his pew and headed toward the room. But at that moment someone noticed him and cried out, "Look at Aaron Burr going into the inquiry room!" Blushing, Burr turned back and covered his embarrassment. "I was only fooling," he jested.[7] Ashamed to be seen humbly turning to Christ for salvation, Aaron Burr never did bend his knee to Jesus.

7. Basil Miller, *The Preacher's Magazine* 17, 10 (1942): 253.

Ultimately, the pride in his heart would lead him to commit treason against his country and cause his name to go down in infamy.

What is particularly sad about the case of Aaron Burr is the outstanding Christian example set for him by his parents. Unfortunately for Burr, his father, a winsome gospel preacher, died before his son could grow up under his influence. But the godliness of his mother, Jonathan Edwards's daughter Esther Edwards Burr, showed an attitude that her son would have done well to adopt, as would we. In her grief and anxiety over her husband's death, she wrote: "O, I am afraid I shall conduct myself so as to bring dishonour on my God and the religion I profess! No, rather let me die this moment, than be left to bring dishonour on God's holy name."[8] Like Esther's wayward son Aaron Burr, King Saul little considered how his life and death would dishonor the Lord and give aid to the enemies of his people.

Saul's death shows the end that awaits every impenitent life. The king began with great privileges and blessings but engaged in a self-willed disobedience to God. When reproved, Saul hardened his heart and launched himself on a downward trajectory of pride, hatred, and despair. His last years were marked by his mad hatred of faithful David, his murder of God's holy priests (1 Sam. 22:18–19), and the quest for aid from a servant of the devil (28:7–8). It is hardly surprising that this impenitent life ended by thrusting his body upon a sword. Saul had been slaying his soul every time he turned away from God's proffered mercy, so it was only fitting that his last unrepentant act was to murder himself.

Saul's example is not an isolated one. The same end is in store for all who turn from the Lord and refuse to repent. Consider the man who abandons his wife and children for a life of sensual pleasure. Or consider a child who abandons the faith of his or her parents in pursuit of worldly approval or sin. Pastors and spiritually minded friends plead the folly of this self-defeating course, but their flesh has been raised up with pride, rebellion, and desire. They will not listen and will not turn. The end of their course, if they refuse to repent, can only be the same as Saul's: death and damnation.

If Saul had ever truly repented, we can be sure of his acceptance and blessing by God. The example of even more wicked kings who did call on the Lord and were saved proves this. Probably the most notoriously evil of

8. Quoted in Davis, *1 Samuel*, 264.

Israel's kings was Manasseh, the son of godly King Hezekiah. Here was the man who promoted child sacrifice in the Valley of Gehenna and is traditionally reputed to have ordered the murder of the prophet Isaiah. Yet when God gave Manasseh into the hands of his enemies, the wicked king repented of his sins and called on the Lord to save him (2 Chron. 33:12–13). Perhaps Manasseh had heard the good news that Isaiah had preached: "Turn to me and be saved, all the ends of the earth!" declares the Lord (Isa. 45:22). Saul had been blessed to receive the ministry of the great prophet Samuel, yet the hard-hearted king would not turn to seek the Lord. Thus, writes Maclaren, "he who rebels against God mars his own character," a precept proved in Saul's life and death:

> The miserable years of Saul, haunted and hunted as by a demon by his own indulged and swollen rebellion and unsleeping suspicion, are an example of the sorrows that ever dog sin; and, as he lies there on Gilboa, the terrible saying recurs to our memory: "He that being often reproved hardeneth his neck, shall suddenly be destroyed, and that without remedy."[9]

God's Judgment on the Hard-Hearted

If the theme of Israel was idolatry and the theme of Saul's life was his refusal to repent, then the theme governing God's response was that of judgment. God had long threatened Saul with judgment, starting with his reproofs in 1 Samuel 15:23–28. Had he known Hannah's Song, Saul would have taken its threats seriously. Sketching out the themes of this era of history, Hannah concluded: "The adversaries of the Lord shall be broken to pieces . . . The Lord will judge the ends of the earth" (1 Sam. 2:10). Saul should also have profited from the poor example of Eli and his sons, whose promised death arrived exactly on God's schedule (2:27–34; 4:12–22). But Saul did not profit from the experiences of others, and thus the judgment threatened on the night before this battle (28:19–20) came to him with terrible efficiency.

A great judgment awaits everyone. The Bible warns that "it is appointed for man to die once, and after that comes judgment" (Heb. 9:27). Paul writes that "we must all appear before the judgment seat of Christ, so that each one

---

9. Maclaren, *Expositions of Holy Scripture*, 403.

may receive what is due for what he has done in the body, whether good or evil" (2 Cor. 5:10). God's judgment is promised on all unrepentant sinners, and its end is coming swiftly.

Fortunately, the fulfillment of God's Word regarding Saul's judgment reminds us of the confidence we may have in the whole message of the Bible. If God's promise of judgment on Saul was true, then God's gospel promises of eternal life to those who believe are equally true. "Israel may fall on Gilboa, Saul may fall on his sword, but the word of Yahweh will not fall."[10] Jesus insisted, "Heaven and earth will pass away, but my words will not pass away" (Matt. 24:35). Since there is a certainty of judgment on those who will not turn, and also an assurance of salvation for all who repent and believe, the great issue in every life is therefore how we stand toward the salvation offered to sinners in Jesus Christ. Jesus said, "Truly, truly, I say to you, whoever hears my word and believes him who sent me has eternal life. He does not come into judgment, but has passed from death to life" (John 5:24).

For all of Saul's outward adherence to Israel and his belief in the existence of God, he had never repented and turned to the Lord in a true and living faith. On Mount Gilboa, Israel's idolatry, Saul's impenitence, and God's judgment all came together in a disastrous end that could have been averted if only Saul had humbled himself before the Lord, called to the Lord for salvation, and sought the grace of the Lord to turn from his rebellion and sins. Because of this single difference, Saul died while David lived, just as Saul will spend eternity in the condemnation of hell while David dwells above in the glory of heaven. This is the decisive issue in every life: will we repent and be saved, or will we harden our hearts against God and perish?

Tragedy Countered by Grace

The final chapter of 1 Samuel really does not mark the end of a book in the Bible, since 1 and 2 Samuel join together as a single, whole book. Yet the end of 1 Samuel does mark an important divide in the life of David and Israel. The record of Saul's death marks an appropriate end in God's judgment, yet the book concludes with the heroic raid of the men

10. Davis, *1 Samuel*, 262–63.

of Jabesh-gilead, providing a stirring reminder of the grace that provides the hope for Israel's future.

Having won the battle, the Philistines gleefully entered the nearby cities abandoned by the fleeing Israelites. So complete was their victory that the next day the bodies of the Israelite leaders still lay untended on the battle-field. Therefore, "when the Philistines came to strip the slain, they found Saul and his three sons fallen on Mount Gilboa" (1 Sam. 31:8). Saul may have escaped torment alive, but he could not avoid the abuse of his remains in death: "They cut off his head and stripped off his armor and sent messengers throughout the land of the Philistines, to carry the good news to the house of their idols and to the people" (31:9).

After Saul's head had been removed, his body, together with his sons' remains, was "fastened . . . to the wall of Beth-shan," and his armor was housed as a trophy "in the temple of Ashtaroth" (1 Sam. 31:10). Beth-shan was an important walled city at the junction of the Jezreel Valley and the valley of the Jordan River. It was the easternmost of the old Canaanite cities that Israel had failed to capture. Excavations at Beth-shan have discovered the intact remains of a temple that was probably used for the worship of Philistine gods such as Dagon and Ashtaroth, and in which Saul's head and armor were possibly housed to boast of their victory over the God of Israel.[11] The battle was over, the victory was won, and now all that remained was for the wicked to enjoy the spoils of the triumph of their gods.

Yet in the morning of the next day, or one of the next days, the Philistines awoke to discover that there was yet hope among the beleaguered people of God. The people of Jabesh-gilead, a remaining Israelite fortress ten miles away across the Jordan, "heard what the Philistines had done to Saul," and "all the valiant men arose and went all night and took the body of Saul and the bodies of his sons from the wall of Beth-shan, and they came to Jabesh and burned them there. And they took their bones and buried them under the tamarisk tree in Jabesh and fasted seven days" (1 Sam. 31:11–13).

Remember Jabesh-gilead? It was the city to which Saul had boldly sent relief at the beginning of his reign, when Nahash the Ammonite had besieged the city and threatened to remove the right eye from all the men (1 Sam.

---

11. Joyce G. Baldwin, *1 & 2 Samuel*, Tyndale Old Testament Commentaries (Downers Grove, IL: InterVarsity Press, 1988), 171.

11:1–11). That was forty years past, and perhaps the finest act in all of Saul's reign. For forty years, the people of Jabesh-gilead had kept alive the memory of their debt to King Saul. The disgrace of Saul's remains at Beth-shan was too much for their hearts to bear, so they despised the dangers and put their gratitude and love into action. While the Philistines slept, they gathered the remains of Saul and his sons and brought them to Israelite soil for a decent burial.

After all of Saul's hard-hearted sin, despite his descent into murderous tyranny and even occult satanism, God nonetheless concludes his account with a remembrance of Saul's one godly and obedient act. Likewise, selfless acts of goodness and mercy will form our own legacy, sowing seeds of gratitude and love to flourish when we have gone, just as it is our witness to the kingdom of Christ that will provide hope when all else has failed.

The fact that 1 Samuel ends with a courageous act of gratitude toward Saul says more about God than it does about Saul. It reminds us that even the worst of lives has borne the image of God and has shared at least sparks of God's goodness and love. This concluding note also shows how eager God is to bless and reward the least acts of faith and obedience. Even the death of a hardened rebel such as King Saul provides us with an incentive to repent of our sins, turn to the Lord in true faith, and serve the Lord wholeheartedly in this dark and dangerous world.

Faith amid Darkness

At the end of Alan Jay Lerner's musical *Camelot* is a heartwarming scene in which King Arthur, unable to sleep before the battle with Lancelot that marks the end of his reign, is seen warming himself beside a dying fire. A sound is heard in the bushes, and Arthur calls out to know who is there. Out steps a young boy into the faint glow. "Who are you?" asks the king. "Tom, sir," he replies. "And why have you come here?" asks Arthur. "To see the fight, sir." Arthur realizes that here, amid the dying embers of his reign, this youth has come with an innocent faith in his cause. The king's reign had been shattered by sin, betrayal, and senseless passion, but here is a child who believes. So Arthur sends young Tom away from the battle to safety and commissions him with a royal duty, to tell the story of his reign:

"Don't let it be forgot / That there once was a spot / For one brief shining moment / Called Camelot."[12]

The valiant men of Jabesh-gilead arrive at the end of 1 Samuel in the role of true belief in the midst of disaster, very much like the boy Tom in Lerner's *Camelot*. There is a reason why the exploits of the valiant men of Jabesh-gilead are still read and celebrated by the people of God, three thousand years after their nighttime raid. The reason is not merely that someone wrote it down to preserve the memory. The greater reason is that their side won. The kingdom in which they had believed recovered from defeat. Indeed, within a short time these true and valiant believers would see a newly anointed king, a man after God's own heart, burst forth in conquering might. While Saul was dying, David was gaining a victory by God's power. Before long, what may have seemed a vain gesture of faith would be praised by messengers arriving with David's royal blessings and pledges of reward (2 Sam. 2:4–7).

The heroic men of Jabesh-gilead prove that in dark times, when ungodliness seems to have prevailed in society and the church seems to have succumbed to pagan assaults, the best thing that a valiant Christian man or woman can do is to simply take a stand for godliness, truth, and holy love. For wherever Jesus Christ is served in true faith and obedience to his Word, there is a new beginning in which the grace of his kingdom may grow.

The men of Jabesh-gilead remind us of the women who came to the tomb where Jesus' body had been laid to rest. Jesus was even more unlike Saul than David was: Saul was in fact the very antithesis of the holy person of Jesus Christ. Yet like Saul, Jesus had been beset by pagan soldiers, and just as Saul's remains were left in boastful contempt on the walls of Beth-shan, Jesus' body was strung up in derision on a cross. Like the Jabesh-gileadites who came to take Saul's remains, two men, Joseph of Arimathea and Nicodemus the Pharisee, lovingly removed Christ's lifeless body from the cross and gave it a burial more fitting to his beloved memory. Three days later, the heroic women, two Marys and Joanna, appeared at Jesus' tomb with spices to anoint his body. They came because for all the proof of defeat, despite the unavoidable reality that Jesus was dead, their hearts still treasured what Jesus had taught and lived. Like the men of Jabesh-gilead, whose faithful love foretold a new beginning even at Saul's end, the devotion of these women

12. Quoted in Cyril J. Barber, *The Books of Samuel*, 2 vols. (Neptune, NJ: Loizeaux, 1994), 1:317–18.

spoke of faith unconquered and hearts unbowed by the reality of sin in the world. Just as the faithful of Jabesh-gilead were the first to be praised by the newly anointed King David (2 Sam. 2:5), the faithful women were rewarded with the first news of Jesus' resurrection, the angels proclaiming, "He is not here, for he has risen" (Matt. 28:6).

Do we not also have reasons to stand up for the kingdom of Christ? Can we not look into our own history and see the claims of God's love upon our hearts, along with his gospel promises in the Bible? If so, let us be the ones who, like fictional King Arthur's young Tom, keep faith alive and keep telling the story. Let us, like the bold men of Jabesh-gilead, be disciples who prize the honor of Christ's kingdom and will not shrink back in times of danger. For we serve more than the honored memory of a dead king. We serve a resurrected, living Lord who reigns on heaven's throne, who has promised to return in glory and power to save his people. If David noticed the fidelity of the men of Jabesh-gilead, then surely Christ will not fail to honor those who stand for him now. "Well done, good and faithful servant," he has promised to say (Matt. 25:23)—and such valiant believers will enter into the joy of their triumphant King forever.

Index of Scripture

525

Index of Subjects and Names